11th Edition

UNDERSTANDING COMPUTERS:

TODAY AND TOMORROW

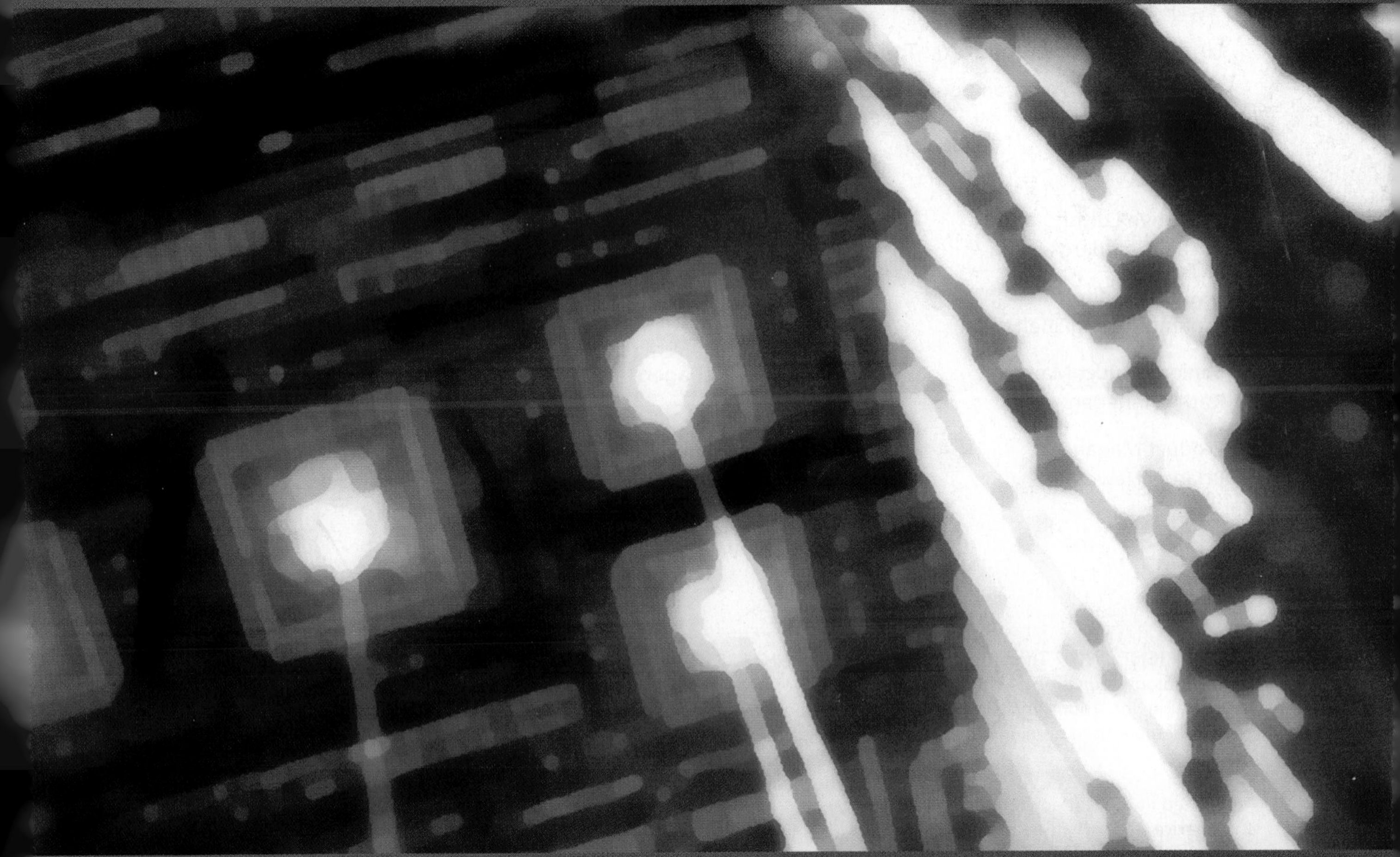

INTRODUCTORY

DEBORAH MORLEY
CHARLES S. PARKER

THOMSON
COURSE TECHNOLOGY

Australia • Canada • Mexico • Singapore • Spain • United Kingdom • United States

Understanding Computers: Today and Tomorrow, 11th Edition
is published by Thomson Course Technology

Executive Editor:
Rachel Goldberg

Associate Editor:
Amanda Young Shelton

Senior Product Manager:
Kathy Finnegan

Product Manager:
Brianna Hawes

Associate Product Manager:
Shana Rosenthal

Editorial Assistant:
Janine Tangney

Marketing Manager:
Joy Stark

Marketing Coordinator:
Melissa Marcoux

Developmental Editor:
Pam Conrad

Production Editor:
Jennifer Goguen McGrail

Composition:
GEX Publishing Services

Text and Cover Designer:
Joel Sadagursky

Printed in the United States of America

2 3 4 5 6 7 8 9 BM 10 09 08 07 06

For more information, contact Thomson Course Technology, 25 Thomson Place, Boston, Massachusetts, 02210.

Or find us on the World Wide Web at: www.course.com

ISBN-13: 978-1-4188-6054-7
ISBN-10: 1-4188-6054-9

PREFACE

In today's computer-oriented society, computers and technology impact virtually everyone's life. *Understanding Computers: Today and Tomorrow, 11th Edition* will ensure that students are current and informed in order to thrive in our technologically oriented, global society. With this new edition, students not only learn about relevant cutting-edge technology trends, but also gain a better understanding of technology in general and the important issues surrounding technology today. This information will give students the understanding they need to succeed in today's world.

This nontechnical, introductory text explains in straightforward terms the importance of learning about computers, the various types of computer systems and their components, the principles by which computer systems work, the practical applications of computers and related technologies, and the ways in which the world is being changed by these technologies. The goal of this text is to provide the reader with a solid knowledge of computer fundamentals, an understanding of the impact of our computer-oriented society, and a framework for using this knowledge effectively in their lives.

KEY FEATURES

Based on the fundamental chapters of the 16-chapter Comprehensive version of *Understanding Computers: Today and Tomorrow, 11th Edition* text, this 9-chapter Introductory version is current and comprehensive. Flexible organization and an engaging presentation combined with learning tools in each chapter help the student master important concepts. Numerous marginal notations lead students to the Understanding Computers Web site where they can access numerous **Interactive Activities**, **Testing Activities**, and **Study Tools/Additional Resources**.

Currency and Accuracy

The state-of-the-art content of this book and its Web site reflect the latest technologies, trends, and classroom needs. Throughout the writing and production stages, enhancements were continually made to ensure that the final product is as current and accurate as possible.

Comprehensiveness and Depth

Accommodating a wide range of teaching preferences, *Understanding Computers: Today and Tomorrow, 11th Edition* provides comprehensive coverage of traditional topics while also covering relevant, up-to-the minute new technologies and important societal issues, such as dual-core CPUs, nanotechnology, blue laser and hybrid CD/DVD discs, holographic storage, OLED displays, 3D displays, and other new and emerging types of hardware; biometric access systems, e-tokens, and other access technologies; new software, such as Windows Vista, as well as Linux and other open source software programs that are growing in importance; new communications technologies, such as RFID, mesh networks, broadband over power lines (BPL), WiMAX, Mobile-Fi, Voice over IP (VoIP) and Voice over W-Fi; new and growing Internet applications, such as digital data distribution, place-shifting, blogs, podcasting, online music, mobile TV, video-on-demand (VOD), and legal P2P file sharing; security and privacy issues, such as war driving, spyware, identity theft, phishing, and pharming. The Comprehensive 16-chapter version of *Understanding Computers: Today and Tomorrow, 11th Edition* includes additional coverage of multimedia, e-commerce, systems, programming, databases, and important societal issues surrounding the use of computers, such as computer security, privacy, intellectual property rights, ethics, health, access, and the environment.

Readability

We remember more about a subject if it is presented in a straightforward way and made interesting and exciting. This book is written in a conversational, down-to-earth style—one designed to be accurate without being intimidating. Concepts are explained clearly and simply, without the use of overly technical terminology. Where complex points are presented, they are explained in an understandable manner and with realistic examples from everyday life.

Chapter Learning Tools

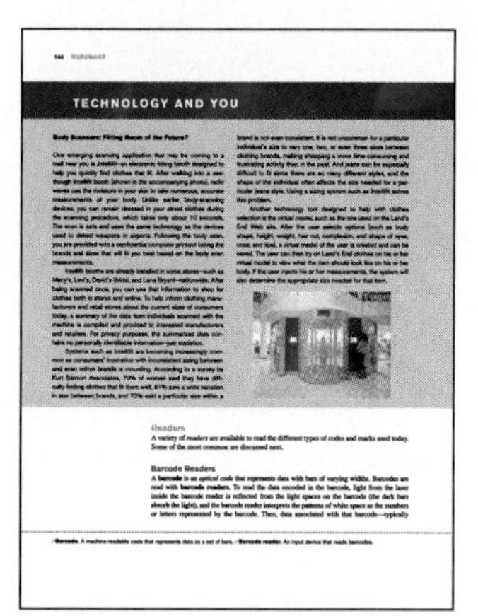
TECHNOLOGY AND YOU

Readers

Barcode Readers

1. **Outline, Learning Objectives, and Overview:** For each chapter, an **Outline** of the major topics covered, a list of student **Learning Objectives**, and a **Chapter Overview** help instructors put the subject matter of the chapter in perspective and let students know what they will be reading about.

2. **Boldfaced Key Terms and Running Glossary:** Important terms appear in boldface type as they are introduced in the chapter. These terms are defined at the bottom of the page on which they appear and in the end-of-text glossary.

3. **Chapter Boxes:** In each chapter, a **Trend** box provides students with a look at current and upcoming developments in the world of computers; an **Inside the Industry** box provides insight into some of the practices that have made the computer industry unique and fascinating; a **How it Works** box explains in more detail how a technology or product works; and a **Technology and You** box takes a look at how computers and technology are used in your everyday life.

TIP

There are numerous online blog search engines and directories—such as BlogStreet.com—to help you find blogs that meet your interests.

4. **Marginal Tips: TIP** marginal elements feature time-saving tips or ways to avoid a common problem or terminology mistake, or present students with interesting additional information related to the chapter content.

5. **Illustrations and Photographs:** Instructive, current full-color illustrations and photographs appear throughout the book to help illustrate important concepts. Figures and screenshots feature the latest hardware and software products and are carefully annotated to convey important information.

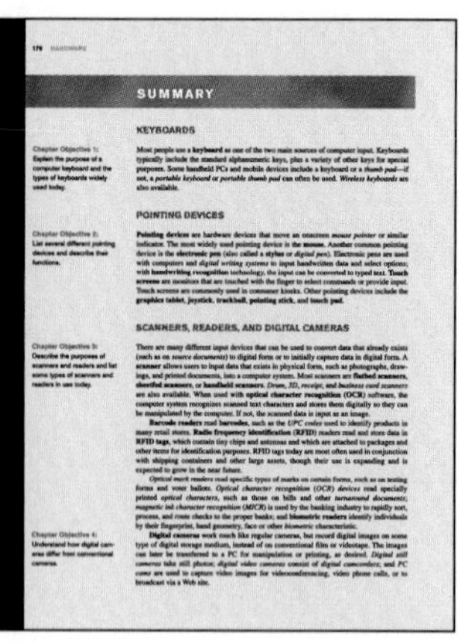
SUMMARY

KEYBOARDS

POINTING DEVICES

SCANNERS, READERS, AND DIGITAL CAMERAS

6. **Summary and Key Terms:** The end-of-chapter material includes a concise, section-by-section **Summary** of the main points in the chapter. The chapter's Learning Objectives appear in the margin next to the relevant section of the summary so that students are better able to relate the Learning Objectives to the chapter material. Every boldfaced key term in the chapter also appears in boldface type in the summary.

7. **Review Activities and Projects:** End-of-chapter activities allow students to test themselves on what they have just read. A matching exercise of selected **Key Terms** helps students test their retention of the chapter material. A **Self-Quiz** (with the answers listed at the end of the book) consists of ten true-false and completion questions. Five additional easily graded matching and short-answer **Exercises** are included for instructors who would like to assign graded homework. A **Discussion Question** for each chapter provides a jumping off point to get classroom discussion started. End-of-chapter **Projects** require students to extend their knowledge by doing research and activities beyond merely reading the book. Organized into six

types of projects (Hot Topics, Short Answer/Research, Hands On, Writing About Computers, Presentation/Demonstration, and Group Discussion), the projects feature explicit instructions so that students can work through them without additional directions from instructors. Special marginal icons denote projects that require Internet access.

8. **Understanding Computers Web Site:** Throughout each chapter, **Further Exploration** marginal elements direct students to the Understanding Computers Web site where they can access collections of links to Web sites containing more in-depth information on a given topic from the text. At the end of every chapter, students are directed to the Understanding Computers Web site to access a variety of **Interactive Activities**, **Testing Activities,** and **Study Tools/Additional Resources**.

FURTHER EXPLORATION

For links to further information about CPUs, go to www.course.com/uc11/ch02

References and Resources Guide

A **References and Resources Guide** at the end of the book brings together in one convenient location a collection of computer-related references and resources, including a Computer History Timeline, Coding Charts, and a Guide for Buying a PC.

NEW TO THE 11TH EDITION

Streamlined Introduction Chapter

To help get students up and running even faster, this edition features a single consolidated introductory chapter containing the key topics previously contained in Chapters 1 and 2.

New "Network and Internet Security" Chapter

To better cover the vast number of important issues related to network and Internet security today, these topics are now in their own chapter—**Chapter 9, "Network and Internet Security,"** which is located at the end of the **Networks and the Internet** module. Additional security topics related to computers are still discussed, along with privacy, intellectual property rights, ethics, health, access, and the environment, in the **Computers and Society** module in the Comprehensive 16-chapter version of this textbook.

Expert Insight

In this exciting new feature located at the end of each module, industry experts provide students with personal insights on topics presented in the book, including their personal experiences with technology, key points to remember, and advice for the future. The experts, professionals from these major companies—**Nokia, Hewlett Packard, Novell,** and **The Hanover Insurance Group**—provide a unique perspective on the module content and how the topics discussed in the module impact their lives, their industry, what it means for the future, and more!

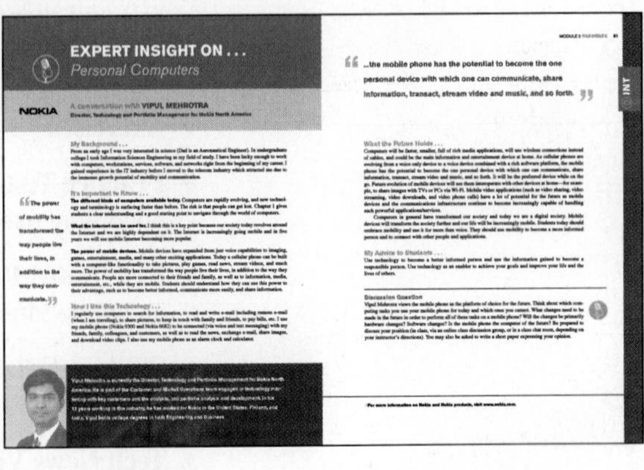

Expanded Web Site Content

The **Understanding Computers Web site** includes a wealth of information at your fingertips to help enhance the classroom experience and to help students master the material covered in the book. Some of the content featured on the site includes new and updated **Self-Quizzes, Exercises, and Practice Tests**. The site also features interactive activities, such as **Student Edition Labs** and **Tech News Video Projects**. In addition, many other resources, including **Online Study Guides, Online Glossary, Online Crossword Puzzles, Further Exploration** links, and **Online References and Resources Guide** content, are available for use.

Student and Instructor Support Materials

Understanding Computers: Today and Tomorrow, 11th Edition is available with a complete package of support materials for instructors and students. Included in the package are the Understanding Computers Web site, Instructor Resources (available on CD and online), and SAM Computer Concepts.

The Understanding Computers Web Site

The Understanding Computers Web site is located at **www.course.com/uc11** and provides media-rich support for each chapter of the book.

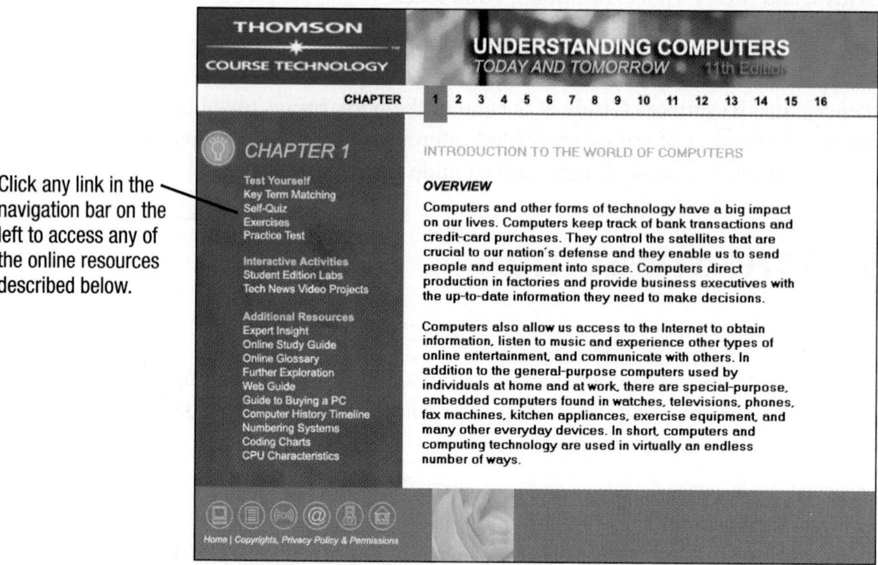

The Web site includes the following:

- **Key Terms Matching**—this feature allows students to test their knowledge of selected chapter key terms by matching the terms with their definitions.
- **Self-Quiz**—this feature allows students to test their retention of chapter concepts.
- **Exercises**—this feature reviews the concepts and terms covered in the chapter.
- **Practice Test**—this feature allows students to test how ready they are for upcoming exams.
- **Crossword Puzzles**—this feature incorporates the key terms from each chapter into an online interactive crossword puzzle.
- **Student Edition Lab**—this feature reinforces and expands the concepts covered in the chapters.
- **Tech News Video Project**—this feature includes the complete **Tech News Video Project** associated with the chapter, as well as a link to watch the appropriate video.
- **Additional Resources**—this feature includes a wide range of additional resources, such as an **Online Study Guide** and **Online Glossary** for each chapter; **Further Exploration** links, a **Web Guide**, a **Guide to Buying a PC**, and a **Computer History Timeline**; more information about **Numbering Systems**, **Coding Charts**, and **CPU Characteristics**; and much, much more!

Instructor Resources

Course Technology instructional resources and technology tools provide instructors with a wide range of tools that enhance teaching and learning. These tools can be accessed from the Instructor Resources CD or at www.course.com.

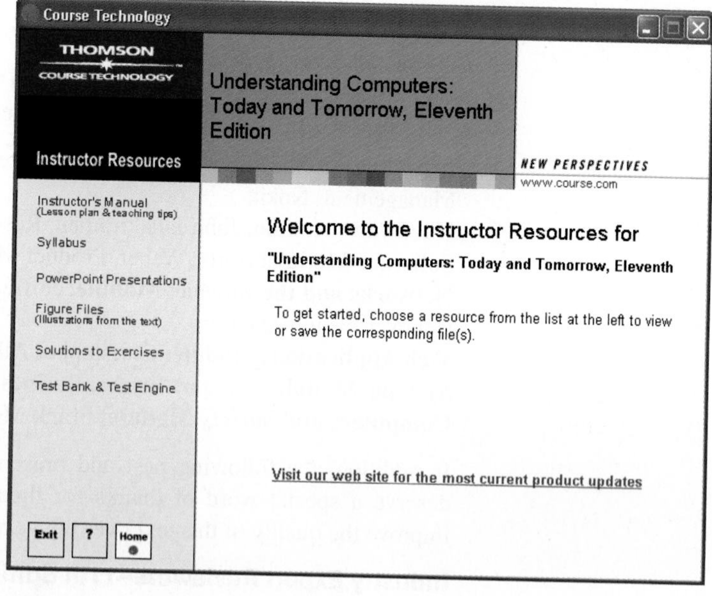

Electronic Instructor's Manual

The Instructor's Manual is written to provide instructors with practical suggestions for enhancing classroom presentations. For each of the 16 chapters in the text, the Instructor's Manual provides: **Instructor Notes, Troubleshooting Tips, Quick Quizzes, Classroom Activities, Discussion Questions, Key Terms,** a **Chapter Quiz**, and more!

ExamView Test Bank

This textbook is accompanied by ExamView, a powerful testing software package that allows instructors to create and administer printed, computer (LAN-based), and Internet exams. ExamView includes over 2,400 questions that correspond to the topics covered in this text, enabling instructors to create exams mapping exactly to the content they cover. The computer-based and Internet testing components allow instructors to administer exams over the computer and also save by grading each exam automatically.

PowerPoint Presentations

This book comes with **Microsoft PowerPoint slides** for each chapter. These are included as a teaching aid for classroom presentation, to make available to students on the network for chapter review, or to be printed for classroom distribution. Instructors can customize these presentations to cover any additional topics they introduce to the class. **Figure Files** for all figures in the textbook are also available for instructor use.

Blackboard and WebCT content

We offer a full range of content for use with Blackboard and WebCT to simplify the use of Understanding Computers in distance education settings. Contact your sales representative for more details.

SAM Computer Concepts

Instructors who have chosen to use SAM Computer Concepts (assessment and training software) in their courses have access to hands-on assessment and interactive training simulations that reinforce lessons presented in this text.

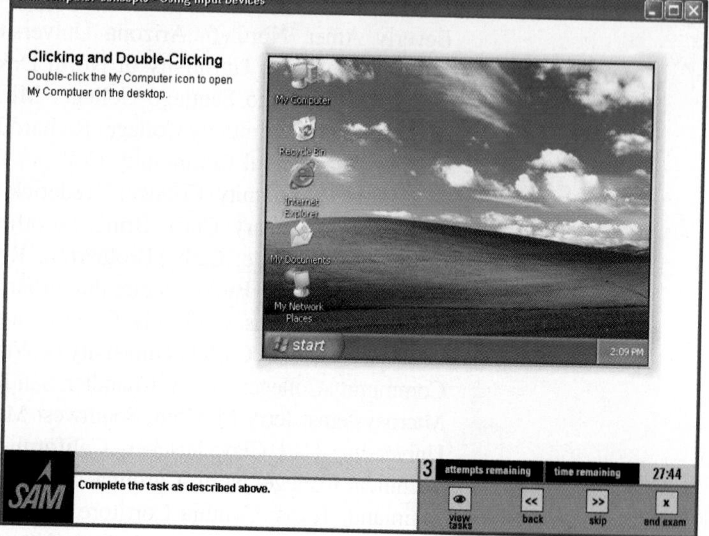

ACKNOWLEDGEMENTS

We would like to extend a special thank you to all of industry professionals who reviewed module content and who provided their expertise for the new **Expert Insight** feature:

Introduction Module: Vipul Mehrotra, Director, Technology and Portfolio Management, Nokia
Hardware Module: John Janakiraman, Research Manager for Data Center Architecture, HP Labs
Software Module: Aaron Weber, Product Marketing Manager, Novell
Networks and the Internet Module: Jeffrey Bardin, Chief Information Security Officer, The Hanover Insurance Group.
Web Applications Module: Christopher Allen, Head of Product Strategy, Yahoo! Music
Systems Module: Anthony Briggs, Business Information Officer, Best Buy
Computers and Society Module: Frank Molsberry, Technologist, Dell Inc.

In addition, the following past and present industry expert and educational reviewers of this text deserve a special word of thanks for their thoughtful suggestions that have helped to define and improve the quality of this text over the years.

Industry Expert Reviewers–11th Edition

Janice K. Mahon, Vice President of Technology Commercialization, Universal Display Corporation
Dr. Nhon Quach, Next Generation Processor Architect, AMD
Jos van Haaren, Department Head Storage Physics, Philips Research Laboratories
Terry O'Kelly, Technical Communications Manager, Memorex
Randy Culpepper, Texas Instruments RFID Systems
Aaron Newman, CTO and Co-Founder, Application Security Inc.
John Nash, Vice President of Marketing, Visible Systems
Dr. Maressa Hecht Orzack, Director, Computer Addiction Study Center

Industry Expert Reviewers–Previous Editions

Alan Charlesworth, Staff Engineer, Sun Microsystems; Khaled A. Elamrawi, Senior Marketing Engineer, Intel Corporation; Timothy D. O'Brien, Senior Systems Engineer, Fujitsu Software; John Paulson, Manager, Product Communications, Seagate Technology; Omid Rahmat, Editor in Chief, Tom's Hardware Guide; Jeremy Bates, Multimedia Developer, R & L Multimedia Developers; Charles Hayes, Product Marketing Manager, SimpleTech, Inc.; Rick McGowan, Vice President & Senior Software Engineer, Unicode, Inc.; Russell Reynolds, Chief Operating Officer & Web Designer, R & L Multimedia Developers; Rob Stephens, Director, Technology Strategies, SAS; Dave Stow, Database Specialist, OSE Systems, Inc.

Educational Reviewers

Beverly Amer, Northern Arizona University; James Ambroise Jr., Southern University, Louisiana; Virginia Anderson, University of North Dakota; Robert Andree, Indiana University Northwest; Linda Armbruster, Rancho Santiago College; Michael Atherton, Mankato State University; Gary E. Baker, Marshalltown Community College; Richard Batt, Saint Louis Community College at Meremec; Luverne Bierle, Iowa Central Community College; Fariba Bolandhemat, Santa Monica College; Jerry Booher, Scottsdale Community College; Frederick W. Bounds, Georgia Perimeter College; James Bradley, University of Calgary; Curtis Bring, Moorhead State University; Brenda K. Britt, Fayetteville Technical Community College; Cathy Brotherton, Riverside Community College; Chris Brown, Bemidji State University; Janice Burke, South Suburban College; James Buxton, Tidewater Community College, Virginia; Gena Casas, Florida Community College, Jacksonville; Thomas Case, Georgia Southern University; John E. Castek, University of Wisconsin-La Crosse; Mario E. Cecchetti, Westmoreland County Community College; Jack W. Chandler, San Joaquin Delta College; Alan Charlesworth, Staff Engineer, Sun Microsystems; Jerry M. Chin, Southwest Missouri State University; Edward W. Christensen, Monmouth University; Carl Clavadetscher, California State Polytechnic University; Vernon Clodfelter, Rowan Technical College, North Carolina; Joann C. Cook, College of DuPage; Laura Cooper, College of the Mainland, Texas; Cynthia Corritore, University of Nebraska at Omaha; Sandra Cunningham, Ranger College; Marvin Daugherty, Indiana Vocational Technical College; Donald L. Davis, University of

Mississippi; Garrace De Groot, University of Wyoming; Jackie Dennis, Prairie State College; Robert H. Dependahl Jr., Santa Barbara College, California; Donald Dershem, Mountain View College; John DiElsi, Marcy College, New York; Mark Dishaw, Boston University; Eugene T. Dolan, University of the District of Columbia; Bennie Allen Dooley, Pasadena City College; Robert H. Dependahl Jr.; Santa Barbara City College; William Dorin, Indiana University Northwest; Mike Doroshow, Eastfield College; Jackie O. Duncan, Hopkinsville Community College; John Dunn, Palo Alto College; John W. Durham, Fort Hays State University; Khaled A Elamrawi, Senior Marketing Engineer, Intel Corporation; Hyun B. Eom, Middle Tennessee State University; Michael Feiler, Merritt College; Terry Felke, WR Harper College; J. Patrick Fenton, West Valley Community College; James H. Finger, University of South Carolina at Columbia; William C. Fink, Lewis and Clark Community College, Illinois; Ronald W. Fordonski, College of Du Page; Connie Morris Fox, West Virginia Institute of Technology; Paula S. Funkhouser, Truckee Meadows Community College; Janos T. Fustos, Metropolitan State; Gene Garza, University of Montevallo; Timothy Gottleber, North Lake College; Dwight Graham, Prairie State College; Wade Graves, Grayson County College; Kay H. Gray, Jacksonville State University; David W. Green, Nashville State Technical Institute, Tennessee; George P. Grill, University of North Carolina, Greensboro; John Groh, San Joaquin Delta College; Rosemary C. Gross, Creighton University; Dennis Guster, Saint Louis Community College at Meremec; Joe Hagarty, Raritan Valley Community College; Donald Hall, Manatee Community College; Jim Hanson, Austin Community College; Sallyann Z. Hanson, Mercer County Community College; L. D. Harber, Volunteer State Community College, Tennessee; Hank Hartman, Iowa State University; Richard Hatch, San Diego State University; Mary Lou Hawkins, Del Mar College; Ricci L. Heishman, Northern Virginia Community College; William Hightower, Elon College, North Carolina; Sharon A. Hill, Prince George's Community College, Maryland; Alyse Hollingsworth, Brevard College; Fred C. Homeyer, Angelo State University; Stanley P. Honacki, Moraine Valley Community College; L. Wayne Horn, Pensacola Junior College; J. William Howorth, Seneca College, Ontario, Canada; Mark W. Huber, East Carolina University; Peter L. Irwin, Richland College, Texas; John Jasma, Palo Alto College; Nicholas JohnRobak, Saint Joseph's University; Elizabeth Swoope Johnson, Louisiana State University; Jim Johnson, Valencia Community College; Mary T. Johnson, Mt. San Antonio College; Susan M. Jones, Southwest State University; Amardeep K. Kahlon, Austin Community College; Robert T. Keim, Arizona State University; Mary Louise Kelly, Palm Beach Community College; William R. Kenney, San Diego Mesa College; Richard Kerns, East Carolina University, North Carolina; Glenn Kersnick, Sinclair Community College, Ohio; Richard Kiger, Dallas Baptist University; Gordon C. Kimbell, Everett Community College, Washington; Mary Veronica Kolesar, Utah State University; Robert Kirklin, Los Angeles Harbor Community College; Judith A. Knapp, Indiana University Northwest; James G. Kriz, Cuyahoga Community College, Ohio; Joan Krone, Denison University; Fran Kubicek, Kalamazoo Valley Community College; Rose M. Laird, Northern Virginia Community College; Robert Landrum, Jones Junior College; Shelly Langman, Bellevue Community College; James F. LaSalle, The University of Arizona; Linda J. Lindaman, Black Hawk College; Chang-Yang Lin, Eastern Kentucky University; Alden Lorents, Northern Arizona University; Paul M. Lou, Diablo Valley College; Deborah R. Ludford, Glendale Community College; Kent Lundin, Brigham Young University-Idaho; Barbara J. Maccarone, North Shore Community College; Donna Madsen, Kirkwood Community College; Wayne Madison, Clemson University, South Carolina; Donna L. Madsen, Kirkwood Community College; Randy Marak, Hill College; Gary Marks, Austin Community College, Texas; Kathryn A. Marold, Ph.D., Metropolitan State College of Denver; Cesar Marron, University of Wyoming; Ed Martin, Kingsborough Community College; Vickie McCullough, Palomar College; James W. McGuffee, Austin Community College; James McMahon, Community College of Rhode Island; William A. McMillan, Madonna University; Don B. Medley, California State Polytechnic University; John Melrose, University of Wisconsin—Eau Claire; Dixie Mercer, Kirkwood Community College; Mary Meredith, University of Southwestern Louisiana; Marilyn Meyer, Fresno City College; Carolyn H. Monroe, Baylor University; William J. Moon, Palm Beach Community College; Marilyn Moore, Purdue University; Marty Murray, Portland Community College; Don Nielsen, Golden West College; George Novotny, Ferris State University; Timothy D. O'Brien, Senior Systems Engineer, Fujitsu Software; Richard Okezie, Mesa Community College; Joseph D. Oldham, University of Kentucky; Dennis J. Olsen, Pikes Peak Community College; Bob Palank, Florissant Community College; John Paulson, Manager, Product Communications, Seagate Technology; James Payne, Kellogg Community College; Lisa B. Perez, San Joaquin Delta College; Savitha Pinnepalli, Louisiana State University; Delores Pusins,

Hillsborough CC; Mike Rabaut, Hillsborough CC; Omid Rahmat, Editor in Chief, Tom's Hardware Guide www.tomshardware.com; Robert Ralph, Fayetteville Technical Institute, North Carolina; Herbert F. Rebhun, University of Houston-Downtown; Arthur E. Rowland, Shasta College; Kenneth R. Ruhrup, St. Petersburg Junior College; John F. Sanford, Philadelphia College of Textiles and Science; Kammy Sanghera, George Mason University; Carol A. Schwab, Webster University; Larry Schwartzman, Trident Technical College; Benito R. Serenil, South Seattle Community College; Allanagh Sewell, Southeastern Louisiana University; Tom Seymour, Minot State University; John J. Shuler, San Antonio College, Texas; Gayla Jo Slauson, Mesa State College; Harold Smith, Brigham Young University; Willard A. Smith, Tennessee State University; David Spaisman, Katherine Gibbs; Elizabeth Spooner, Holmes Community College; Timothy M. Stanford, City University; Alfred C. St. Onge, Springfield Technical Community College, Massachusetts; Michael L. Stratford, Charles County Community College, Maryland; Karen Studniarz, Kishwaukee College; Sandra Swanson, Lewis &Clark Community College; Tim Sylvester, Glendale Community College; Semih Tahaoglu, Southeastern Louisiana University; William H. Trueheart, New Hampshire College; Jane J. Thompson, Solano Community College; Sue Traynor, Clarion University of Pennsylvania; James D. Van Tassel, Mission College; James R. Walters, Pikes Peak Community College; Joyce V. Walton, Seneca College, Ontario, Canada; Diane B.Walz, University of Texas at San Antonio; Joseph Waters, Santa Rosa Junior College, California; Liang Chee Wee, University of Arizona; Merrill Wells, Red Rocks Community College; Fred J. Wilke, Saint Louis Community College; Charles M. Williams, Georgia State University; Roseanne Witkowski, Orange County Community College; David Womack, University of Texas, San Antonio; George Woodbury, College of the Sequoias; Nan Woodsome, Araphoe Community College; James D. Woolever, Cerritos College; Patricia Joann Wykoff, Western Michigan University; A. James Wynne, Virginia Commonwealth University; Robert D. Yearout, University of North Carolina at Asheville; Israel Yost, University of New Hampshire; and Vic Zamora, Mt. San Antonio College.

We would also like to thank the people on the Course team—their professionalism, attention to detail, and enormous enthusiasm makes working with them a pleasure. In particular, we'd like to thank Rachel Goldberg, Amanda Young Shelton, Brianna Hawes, Pam Conrad, and Jennifer Goguen McGrail for all their ideas, support, and tireless efforts during the design, writing, rewriting, and production of this book. Thanks to Joseph Gorzynski and Tim Reczek for managing the development of the Understanding Computers Web site, Shana Rosenthal for managing the Instructor's Resource package, Janine Tangney for all her assistance, and Joy Stark for her efforts on marketing this text. We would also like to thank Joel Sadagursky for working on the new interior and cover design. Thanks also to Kristen Duerr and Nicole Pinard.

We are also very appreciative of the numerous individuals and organizations that were kind enough to supply information and photographs for this text.

We sincerely hope you find this book interesting, informative, and enjoyable to read. If you have any suggestions for improvement, or corrections that you'd like to be considered for future editions, please send them to deborah.morley@thomson.com.

Deborah Morley
Charles S. Parker

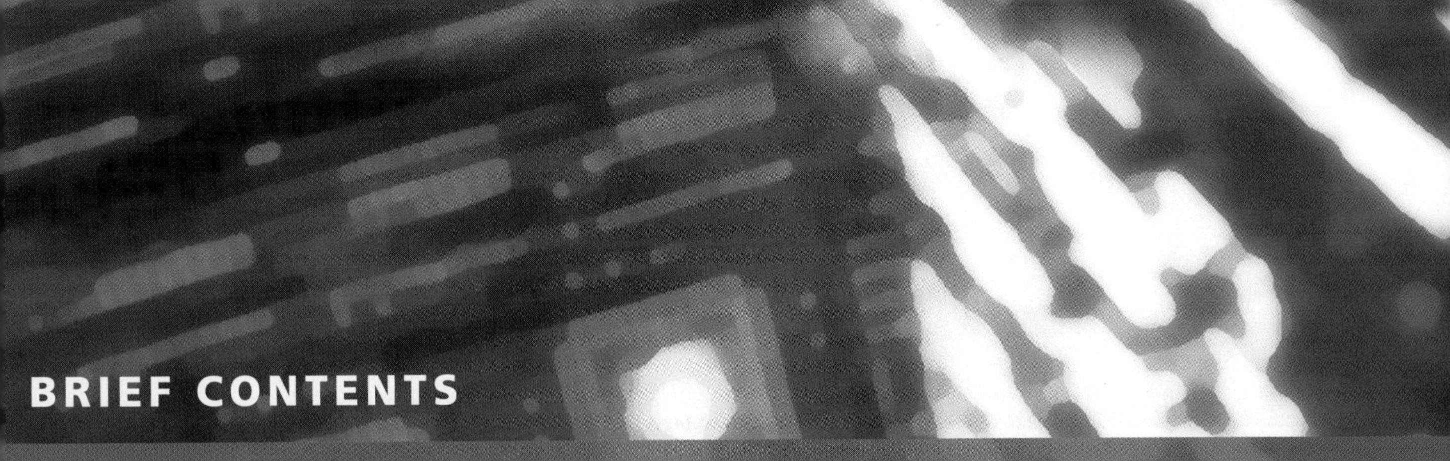

BRIEF CONTENTS

CONTENTS

11th Edition

UNDERSTANDING COMPUTERS:

TODAY AND TOMORROW

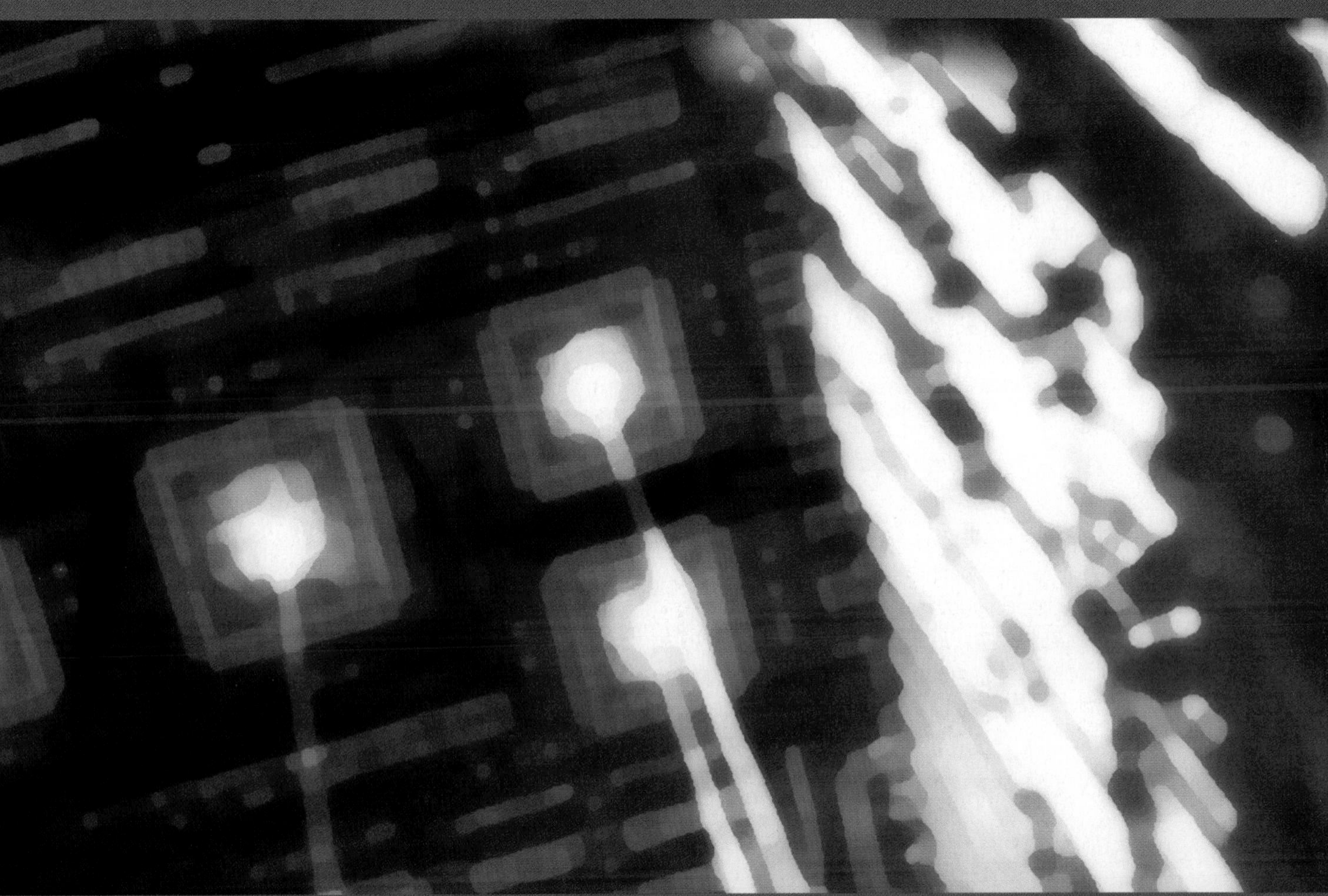

MODULE
INTRODUCTION

We live in an age of computers. People today use computers to pay bills, shop, manage investments, communicate with others, prepare taxes, play games, research products, download and listen to music, make travel arrangements, check current news and weather, look up phone numbers, map locations, modify and print digital photos, and perform other important daily tasks. Businesses, government agencies, and other organizations use computers and related technologies to facilitate day-to-day transactions, provide better services to customers, and assist managers in making good decisions. Because they are so embedded in our society today, it is essential to know something about computers and what they can do.

This module introduces you to computers and some of their uses. Chapter 1 helps you to understand what computers are, how they work, and how people use them. In addition, Chapter 1 presents important terms and concepts that you will encounter throughout this text and in discussions about computers with others. It also includes a brief look at how to use a computer to perform basic tasks and to access resources on the Internet and the World Wide Web.

“. . . today we are a digital society. Mobile devices will transform the society further and our life will be increasingly mobile. Students today should embrace mobility . . .”

For more comments from Guest Expert Vipul Mehrotra of Nokia North America, see the Expert Insight on . . . Personal Computers feature at the end of the module.

N THIS MODULE

1 CHAPTER Introduction to the World of Computers

OUTLINE

Overview
Computers in Your Life
- Why Learn About Computers?
- Computers in the Home
- Computers in Education
- Computers in the Workplace
- Computers on the Go

What Is a Computer and What Does It Do?
- Data vs. Information
- Computers Then and Now
- Hardware
- Software
- Computer Users and Professionals

Computers to Fit Every Need
- Mobile Devices
- Personal Computers
- Midrange Servers
- Mainframe Computers
- Supercomputers

Computer Networks and the Internet
- What Are the Internet and the World Wide Web?
- Accessing a Network or the Internet
- Surfing the Web
- Searching the Web
- E-Mail

Computers and Society
- Benefits of a Computer-Oriented Society
- Risks of a Computer-Oriented Society
- Differences in Online Communications
- The Anonymity Factor
- Information Integrity

LEARNING OBJECTIVES

After completing this chapter, you will be able to:

1. Explain why it is essential to learn about computers toda and discuss several ways computers are integrated into our business and personal lives.
2. Define a computer and describe its primary operations.
3. List some important milestones in computer evolution.
4. Identify the major parts of a personal computer, including input, processing, output, storage, and communications hardware.
5. Define software and understand how it is used to instruc the computer what to do.
6. List the five basic types of computers, giving at least one example of each type of computer and stating what that computer might be used for.
7. Explain what a network, the Internet, and the World Wide Web are, as well as how computers, people, and Web pages are identified on the Internet.
8. Describe how to access a Web page.
9. Discuss the societal impact of computers, including some benefits and risks related to their prominence in our socie

OVERVIEW

Computers and other forms of technology impact our lives daily. We encounter computers in stores, restaurants, and other retail establishments. We use computers and the Internet regularly to obtain information, listen to music and experience other types of online entertainment, buy products and services, and communicate with others. Many of us carry a computer, cell phone, or other electronic device with us at all times so we can remain in touch with others on a continual basis and access Internet information as we need it. It is even becoming more common to use these portable devices to pay for purchases, play online games with others, watch TV and movies, and much, much more. Businesses use computers to keep track of bank transactions, inventories, sales, and credit card purchases; control robots and other machines in factories; and provide business executives with the up-to-date information they need to make decisions. The government uses computers to control the satellites that are crucial to our nation's defense and that are used to send people and equipment into space. In addition to the *general-purpose computers* used by individuals, there are special-purpose, *embedded computers* found in watches, televisions, telephones, game set-top boxes, kitchen appliances, exercise equipment, cars, and scores of other everyday devices. In short, computers and computing technology are used in an endless number of ways.

Fifty years ago, computers were used primarily by researchers and scientists. Today, computers are an integral part of our lives. Experts call this trend *pervasive computing*, in which few aspects of daily life remain untouched by computers and computing technology. With pervasive computing–also referred to as *ubiquitous computing*–computers are found virtually everywhere. Embedded computing technology is integrated into scores of devices to give those devices additional functions or to enable them to communicate with other devices on an on-going basis. Because of the prominence of computers in our society, it is important to understand what a computer is, a little about how a computer works, and the implications of living in a computer-oriented society.

Understanding Computers: Today and Tomorrow is a guide to computers and related technology. It will provide you with a comprehensive introduction to computer concepts and terminology and give you a solid foundation for future study. It will also provide you with the basic knowledge you need to understand and use computers in school, on the job, and in your personal life.

Chapter 1 is designed to help you understand what computers are, how they work, and how people use them. It introduces the important terms and concepts that you will encounter throughout this text and in discussions about computers with others, as well as provides an overview of the history of computers. It gives an explanation of the various categories of computers that today's users may encounter, as well as takes a brief look at how to use a computer to perform basic tasks and to access resources on the Internet and the World Wide Web. The chapter closes with a look at the societal impact of computers. Most of the computer concepts introduced in this chapter are discussed in more detail in subsequent chapters of this text, but Chapter 1 is intended to give you an overall understanding of what a computer is and the knowledge, skills, and tools necessary to use a computer and the World Wide Web to complete the projects and online activities that accompany this textbook. ■

COMPUTERS IN YOUR LIFE

Why Learn About Computers?

Prior to about 1980, computers were large and expensive, and few people had access to them. Most computers used in organizations were equipped to do little more than carry out high-volume paperwork processing, such as issuing bills and keeping track of product inventories. The average person did not need to know how to use a computer for his or her job, and it was uncommon to have a computer at home. Furthermore, the use of computers generally required a lot of technical knowledge. Because there were so few good reasons or opportunities for learning how to use computers, the average working person was unfamiliar with them.

Suddenly, in the early 1980s, things began to change. *Microcomputers*—inexpensive personal computers that you will read about later in this chapter—were invented and computer use increased dramatically. Today, more than 60% of all U.S. households include a personal computer, and most individuals use a computer of some sort or another on the job. Whether you become a teacher, attorney, doctor, salesperson, professional athlete, musician, artist, manager, executive, or skilled tradesperson, you will likely use a computer to obtain and evaluate information and to communicate with others. Today's computers, with their almost dizzying speeds and high levels of accuracy and reliability, are very useful tools for these purposes; they are also continually taking on new roles in our society, such as providing a means of entertainment and facilitating the tasks we need to accomplish in day-to-day life. In fact, computers and traditional devices we use everyday—such as the telephone, television, stereo, and music player—have begun to *converge* into single units with multiple capabilities. As a result of this *convergence* trend, the computer has moved beyond being primarily a productivity tool into a personal entertainment and communications hub that can be used to help individuals obtain information from the Internet, organize and access multimedia content, communicate with others, and more (see Figure 1-1).

FIGURE 1-1
Convergence.
Today's computers typically take on the role of multiple devices.

HANDHELD DEVICES
Typically include the functions of a telephone, organizer, music player, gaming device, Web browser, and digital camera.

HOME COMPUTERS
Can often be used as a telephone, television, and stereo system, in addition to their regular computing functions.

Just as you can learn to drive a car without knowing much about car engines, you can learn to use a computer without understanding the technical details of how a computer works. However, a little knowledge gives you a big advantage. Knowing something about cars can help you to make wise purchases and save money on repairs. Likewise, knowing something about computers can help you buy the right one for your needs, get the most efficient use out of it, and have a much higher level of comfort and confidence along the way. Therefore, basic **computer literacy**—knowing about and understanding computers and their uses—is an essential skill today for everyone. The next few sections illustrate how computers are currently used in the home, at school, in the workplace, and while you are on the go.

>**Computer literacy.** The knowledge and understanding of basic computer fundamentals.

Computers in the Home

Home computing has increased dramatically over the last few years as computers and Internet access have become less expensive and an increasing number of computer-related consumer activities have become available. Use of the Internet at home to look up information, exchange *e-mail* (electronic messages), shop, download music and movies, research products, pay bills and manage bank accounts, check news and weather, store and organize digital photos, play games, plan vacations, and so forth has grown at an astounding pace. Home computing for work purposes is also increasing rapidly. Checking office e-mail from home or otherwise working at home in the evening is normal for many jobs. Working entirely from home, such as *telecommuting* for a company or working from home as a consultant or other self-employed individual, is more acceptable today as a result of fast Internet access and the wide use of e-mail, telephone calls, teleconferencing, and videoconferencing for business communications. Wireless networking connections have added to the convenience of home computing, allowing the use of computers in places other than traditional locations, such as a home office. For instance, e-mail can be answered from the backyard or living room, recipes can be looked up in the kitchen, games can be played on the patio, and so forth (see Figure 1-2).

Computing technologies also make it possible to have *smart appliances*—traditional appliances with some type of built-in computer or communications technology. For instance, the smart oven shown in Figure 1-2 both refrigerates and cooks and can be controlled by the user via a telephone or the Internet. *Smart homes*—in which household tasks (such as watering the lawn, turning the air conditioning on or off, making coffee, monitoring the security of the home and grounds, and managing Internet access and home entertainment devices) are controlled by a main computer in the home—are also becoming closer to reality.

REFERENCE, EDUCATION, AND COMMUNICATIONS
Many individuals today have access to the Internet at home; retrieving information, playing online games, and exchanging e-mail are popular home computer activities.

ENTERTAINMENT AND SHOPPING
Computers and the Internet offer a host of entertainment and online shopping activities.

DIGITAL MEDIA DELIVERY
Computers are becoming a central hub for delivering digital media (such as digital photos, downloaded music, and recorded TV shows) to home entertainment systems.

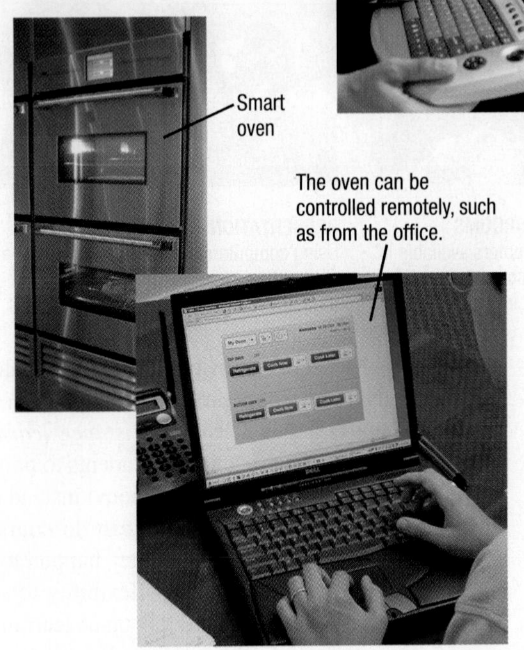

Smart oven
The oven can be controlled remotely, such as from the office.

SMART APPLIANCES
Smart appliances (such as the smart oven shown here that is controlled via a telephone or the Internet) are regular appliances with some type of built-in computer technology.

FIGURE 1-2
Computer use at home.

Computers in Education

Today's youths could definitely be called the *computing generation*. Baby boomers may have been introduced to computers at college or on the job, and older Americans may never have used a computer until after retirement, if at all, but many of today's young people have been brought up with computing technology. From video games to computers at school and home, most children and teens today have been exposed to computers and related technology all their lives. Although the amount of computer use varies from school to school, students in elementary and secondary schools typically have access to computers either in the classroom or in a computer lab, and virtually all colleges have some sort of computing facility available for student use.

With the increased availability of computers and Internet access, the emphasis on computer use in K–12 schools has evolved from straight drill-and-practice programs to using the computer as an overall student-based learning tool. Today, students use multimedia programs to enhance learning; productivity software—such as *word processors* and *presentation software*—for creating papers and electronic presentations; and the Internet for research. K–12 teachers also typically use computers for a variety of tasks, such as creating lesson plans, researching topics, and submitting daily attendance reports and other required school information.

At colleges and universities, computer use is typically much more integrated into daily classroom life than in K–12 schools. Computers are commonly found in classrooms (see Figure 1-3), computer labs, dorms, and libraries. A growing number of college campuses have *wireless hotspots* on campus that allow students to use their PCs to connect wirelessly to the college network and the Internet from anywhere on campus. College students today are typically expected to use the Internet for research, as well as to use computers to prepare papers and classroom presentations and to access online course materials. In fact, some institutions require a computer for enrollment. For a look at how handheld computers are being used by medical school students, see the Technology and You box.

FIGURE 1-3
Computer use in education.

COMPUTER LABS AND CLASSROOMS
Many schools today have computers available in a lab or the library, as well as computers or Internet connections in classrooms for student use.

PRESENTATIONS
Using computers and projection equipment, both students and teachers can deliver effective classroom presentations.

DISTANCE LEARNING
With distance learning, students—such as this U.S. Marine—can take classes from home or wherever they happen to be at the moment.

Most college instructors use computers to prepare handouts and exams, to prepare and deliver classroom presentations and lectures, and to create and maintain course Web pages. Many colleges also offer *distance learning*—a common alternative to traditional classroom learning that allows students to participate from their current location (via their computers and Internet connections) instead of physically going to the educational institution. Distance learning students can do coursework and participate in class discussions from home, work, or wherever they happen to be at the moment. Consequently, distance learning gives students greater flexibility to schedule class time around their personal, family, and work commitments. Distance learning also allows students, such as individuals located in very rural areas or stationed at military posts overseas, to take courses when they are not able to physically attend classes.

Computers in the Workplace

Although computers have been used in the workplace for years, their role is continually evolving. Originally used as a research tool for computer experts and scientists, and then as a productivity tool for office workers, the computer is used today by all types of employees

TECHNOLOGY AND YOU

Wired Med Students

From Stanford University to the University of Florida to the University of Cambridge, medical students are going high-tech. Although some medical schools strongly recommend that their med students acquire a handheld PC, many now require their use–particularly for third- and fourth-year students. Handheld PCs are also beginning to be required for students in dental, nursing, and pharmacological programs.

Medical students today commonly use handheld PCs to access class-specific materials, medical dictionaries, and drug databases; view high-resolution digital images, such as X-rays and microscope images; and communicate with classmates and instructors. If the hospital system supports it, medical residents can also view and update patient files, and physicians can access any patient's record at any time–a convenience, as well as an immense time-saver. For example, one family practice center in Oregon that supplied handheld PCs to its physicians and residents for patient data access found that the time required for reviewing charts, lab results, and other data dropped from 6.3 hours per week to 2.7 hours per week per physician–less than half the time it took before.

Although a little slow to embrace handheld PCs in the past, the medical community is quickly catching up. New useful medical applications designed for handheld PCs–such as those that perform medical calculations or allow physicians to quickly look up drug dosages and possible interactions–are rapidly changing the practice of medicine. When doing rounds in the hospital, chart information can be entered into the handheld PC and, assuming the handheld PC is connected to a wireless network, this information can be transferred automatically to the main computer systems for the hospital and the physician's office. Handheld PCs can also be used to send prescriptions electronically to the appropriate pharmacy. In addition to reducing errors–a Harvard study found that using electronic prescriptions reduced errors by 55 percent–electronic prescriptions also allow the patient records to be checked automatically for drug allergies, potential problems with other medicine the patient is currently taking, and other important concerns. For closer monitoring of critical hospital patients, some hospitals use electronic monitors to transmit clinical data–such as heart rate, respiration, blood pressure, and even photographs of the patient–to the attending physician via his or her handheld PC on a continual basis. For example, Miami Children's Hospital uses Palm PCs and a continuous monitoring system to allow physicians to check on children before and after surgery at any time of the day or night. PDAs are also being used to fulfill the continuing education required of all physicians, allowing them to take online courses via their handheld PCs.

Despite the late start, handheld use in the medical community has now passed that of the general population. According to Forrester Research and the American Medical Association, well over half of all physicians own handheld PCs. While some physicians and hospitals use tablet PCs instead, the ability to carry a handheld PC in a lab coat pocket is a big advantage. This portability factor, along with the trend of medical schools and hospitals requiring handheld PC use, points to increased growth in this area. Thanks to handheld PCs and prescription software, even one of the oldest standing doctor jokes–illegible handwriting–may soon become irrelevant.

in all types of businesses—from the CEO of a multinational corporation, to the check-out clerk at the grocery store, to the traveling sales professional, to the police officer on patrol, to the insurance adjuster in the field, to the doctors and nurses at the local hospital, to the auto mechanic at the local garage. In essence, the computer has become a universal tool for on-the-job decision making, productivity, and communications (see Figure 1-4).

One of the fastest growing new uses for workplace computing is in the service industry, in which service professionals—such as food servers, repair technicians, and delivery people—use portable computers to record and process customer orders (a technique referred to as *linebusting*), as well as to capture customer signatures for purchases, deliveries, and other provided services. Some computers are even small enough to be embedded in clothing or worn on the body. For instance, *wearable PCs* available today

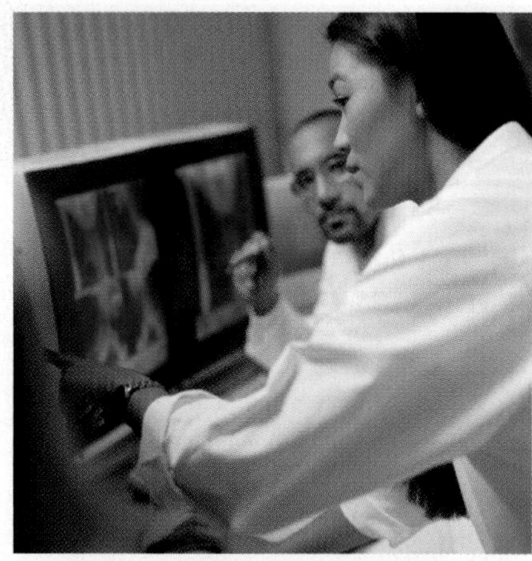

PRODUCTIVITY AND DECISION MAKING
Many individuals today use a computer at work to perform on-the-job tasks efficiently and accurately, as well as to help them evaluate alternatives and make decisions.

CUSTOMER SERVICE
Service professionals frequently use computers to process orders and store customer signature authorizations.

COMMUNICATIONS
Handheld or wearable computers are used by employees who need to record data or access remote data when they are out of the office.

FIGURE 1-4
Computer use in the workplace.

FURTHER EXPLORATION

For links to information about computer certification programs, go to www.course.com/uc11/ch01

are small enough to be worn on a belt (see the rightmost photo in Figure 1-4) and can use a *microdisplay*—a tiny display screen often fitted into glasses or goggles—to display images close to the eye to simulate viewing images on a large monitor. Wearable PCs are currently used by employees in a variety of industries, such as warehouse and construction workers, police and fire personnel, delivery and other types of service workers, doctors and nurses, and telephone repair personnel.

Computers are also used extensively by military personnel for communications and navigational purposes, as well as to control missiles and other weapons, identify terrorists and other potential enemies, and perform other necessary tasks. To update their computer skills, when needed, employees in all lines of work today may take computer training classes or enroll in computer certification programs.

Computers on the Go

In addition to using computers in the home, at school, and in the workplace, most people encounter and use all types of computers in other aspects of day-to-day life—from depositing or withdrawing money at an ATM machine, to using an ID card to gain access to a local gym, to using a *smart card* or other device to pay for gas or parking, to using a portable *global positioning system* (*GPS*) for navigation while traveling or hiking. As they become more integrated into our society, computers are becoming easier to use. For example, electronic *kiosks*—small self-service computer-based stations providing information or other services to the public—usually include a screen that is touched with the finger to select options and request information. Kiosks are commonly placed in hotels, conference centers, retail stores, and other public locations to allow consumers to look up information or purchase products. Some kiosks allow individuals to copy color photographs or print photos taken with a *digital camera*; others enable individuals to check themselves out at a retail store, or print a ticket or boarding pass at the airport (see Figure 1-5).

For Internet access while on the go, computers and *Wi-Fi hotspots* (Internet access points that enable consumers to connect wirelessly to the Internet using their portable computers) are being installed increasingly in a wide variety of public locations, such as libraries, airports, health clubs, coffeehouses, hotels, taxis, parks, restaurants, and *Internet cafés*. Some of these locations charge for access; others offer free access as a courtesy to customers, such as the unlimited access some hotels offer guests or the free access some McDonald's locations offer customers making a minimum purchase. It is also becoming increasingly common for individuals to carry Web-enabled cell phones, handheld computers, or similar portable devices to remain electronically in touch with others and to obtain stock quotes, driving directions, airline flight updates, movie times, and other needed information while on the go via their cellular providers.

WHAT IS A COMPUTER AND WHAT DOES IT DO?

A **computer** can be defined as a programmable, electronic device that accepts data, performs operations on that data, presents the results, and can store the data or results as needed. Being *programmable*, a computer will do whatever the instructions—called the *program*—tell it to do. The programs being used with a computer determine the tasks the computer is able to perform.

The four operations described in this definition are more technically referred to as *input*, *processing*, *output*, and *storage*. These four primary operations of a computer can be defined as follows:

- **Input**—entering data into the computer.
- **Processing**—performing operations on the data.
- **Output**—presenting the results.
- **Storage**—saving data, programs, or output for future use.

PORTABLE COMPUTERS
Many people today carry a portable PC with them at all times or when they travel in order to remain in touch with others and Internet resources.

SELF-SERVICE KIOSKS
Electronic kiosks are widely available to view conference or gift registry information, print photographs, order products or services, facilitate self check-in and check-out, and more.

GPS APPLICATIONS
Computers and handheld devices with built-in GPS capabilities can be used for navigational purposes, such as to show users their exact geographical location or to plan the most efficient route to a destination.

HOTELS AND COFFEEHOUSES
Many hotels and restaurants offer free or fee-based Internet access to their customers, either via installed computers or wireless access (as in the Athens location shown here).

FIGURE 1-5
Computer use while on the go.

For example, let's assume that we have a computer that has been programmed to add two numbers. As shown in Figure 1-6, *input* occurs when data (in this example, the numbers 2 and 5) is entered into the computer; *processing* takes place when the computer program adds those two numbers; and *output* happens when the sum of 7 is displayed on the monitor. The *storage* operation occurs any time the data, program, or output is saved for future use.

For an additional example, let's look at a supermarket barcode reader to see how it fits this definition of a computer. First, the grocery item being purchased is passed over the barcode reader—*input*. Next, the description and price of the item are looked up—*processing*. Finally, the item description and price are displayed on the cash register and printed on the receipt—*output*—and the inventory, ordering, and sales records are updated—*storage*.

This progression of input, processing, output, and storage is sometimes referred to as the *IPOS cycle* or the *information processing cycle*. In addition to these four primary computer operations, today's computers typically also perform *communications* functions,

>**Computer.** A programmable, electronic device that accepts data input, performs processing operations on that data, and outputs and stores the results. >**Input.** The process of entering data into a computer; can also refer to the data itself. >**Processing.** Performing operations on data that has been input into a computer to convert that input to output. >**Output.** The process of presenting the results of processing; can also refer to the results themselves. >**Storage.** The operation of saving data, programs, or output for future use.

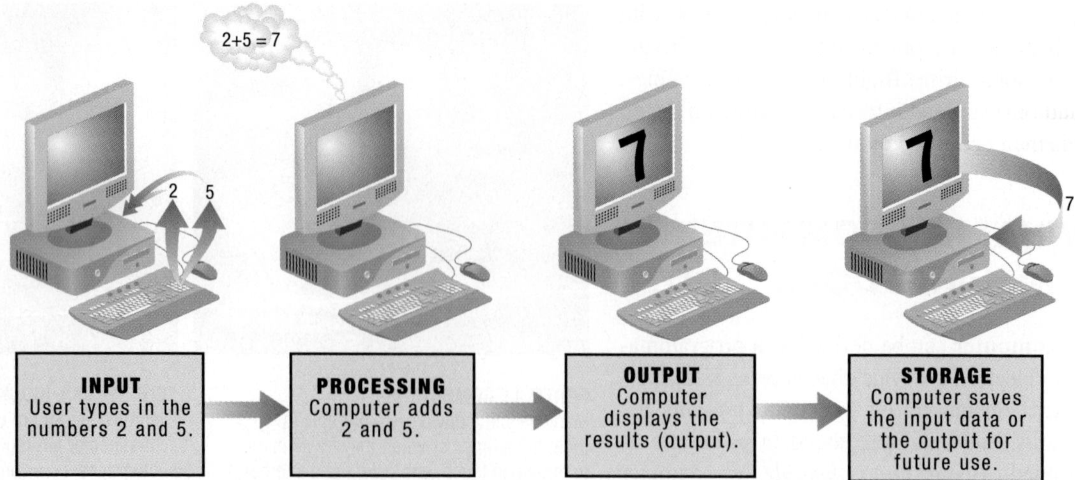
2+5 = 7
2
5
7
7
7
INPUT
User types in the numbers 2 and 5.
PROCESSING
Computer adds 2 and 5.
OUTPUT
Computer displays the results (output).
STORAGE
Computer saves the input data or the output for future use.

FIGURE 1-6
The information processing cycle.

such as retrieving data via the Internet, updating information located in a shared company database, or exchanging e-mail messages. Therefore, **communications**—technically an input or output operation, depending on which direction the information is going—is increasingly considered the fifth primary computer operation.

Data vs. Information

As just discussed, a user inputs **data** into a computer, and then the computer processes it. Almost any kind of fact or set of facts can become computer data—the words in a letter to a friend, the text and pictures in a book, the numbers in a monthly budget, a photograph, a song, or the facts stored in a set of employee records. Consequently, data can exist in many forms, such as to represent *text* (words consisting of standard alphabetic, numeric, and special characters), *graphics* (illustrations or photographs), *audio* (sound, such as music or voice), or *video* (live video or video clips). When data is processed into a meaningful form, it becomes **information**.

Information is frequently generated to answer some type of question. An individual might want to know, for example, how many of a firm's employees earn more than $100,000, how many seats are available on a particular flight from Los Angeles to San Francisco, or what Babe Ruth's home run total was during a particular baseball season. Of course, you don't need a computer system to process data into information. Anyone can go through an employee file and make a list of people earning a certain salary. By hand, however, this work would take a lot of time, especially for a company with thousands of employees. Computers, however, can perform such tasks almost instantly with accurate results.

Information processing (the conversion of data into information) is a vital activity today because the success of many businesses depends heavily on the wise use of information. Because better information often improves employee decisions and customer service, many companies today regard information as one of their most important assets and consider the creative use of information a key competitive strategy.

Computers Then and Now

The basic ideas of computing and calculating are very old, going back thousands of years. However, the computer in the form in which it is recognized today is a fairly recent invention.

>**Communications.** The transmission of data from one device to another. >**Data.** Raw, unorganized facts. >**Information.** Data that has been processed into a meaningful form.

In fact, personal computers have only been around since the late 1970s. The history of computers is often referred to in terms of *generations*, with each new generation characterized by a major technological development. The next sections summarize some early calculating devices and the different computer generations.

Precomputers and Early Computers (before approximately 1945)

Based on archeological finds, such as notched bones, knotted twine, and hieroglyphics, experts have concluded that ancient civilizations had the desire to count and compute. The *abacus* is considered by many to be the earliest recorded calculating device. Believed to have been invented by the Babylonians sometime between 500 B.C. and 100 B.C., the abacus and similar types of counting boards were used primarily as an aid for basic arithmetic calculations.

Other early computing devices include the *slide rule*, the *mechanical calculator*, and Dr. Herman Hollerith's *Punch Card Tabulating Machine and Sorter*. This device (see Figure 1-7) was the first electromechanical machine that could read *punched cards*—special cards with holes punched in them to represent data. In the first successful case of an information processing system replacing a paper-and-pen-based system, Hollerith's machine was used to process the 1890 U.S. Census data and was able to complete the task in two and a half years, instead of the decade it usually took to process the data by hand. Hollerith's company eventually became *International Business Machines (IBM)*.

FIGURE 1-7
A brief look at computer generations.

PRECOMPUTERS AND EARLY COMPUTERS
Dr. Herman Hollerith's Punch Card Tabulating Machine and Sorter is an example of an early computing device. It was used to process the 1890 U.S. Census in about one-quarter of the time usually required to tally the results by hand.

FIRST-GENERATION COMPUTERS
First-generation computers, such as ENIAC shown here, were large, bulky, used vacuum tubes, and had to be physically wired and reset to run programs.

SECOND-GENERATION COMPUTERS
Second-generation computers, such as the IBM 1401 mainframe shown here, used transistors instead of vacuum tubes so they were physically smaller, faster, and more reliable than earlier first-generation computers.

THIRD-GENERATION COMPUTERS
The integrated circuit marked the beginning of the third generation of computers. These chips allowed the introduction of smaller computers, such as the DEC PDP-8 shown here, which was the first commercially successful minicomputer.

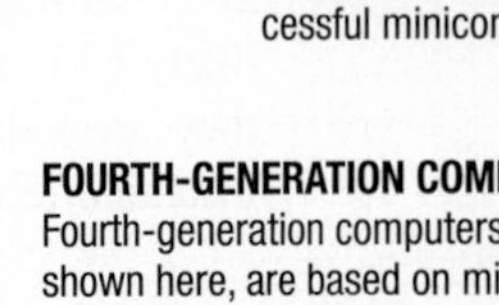

FOURTH-GENERATION COMPUTERS
Fourth-generation computers, such as the original IBM PC shown here, are based on microprocessors. Most of today's computers fall into this category.

First-Generation Computers (approximately 1946–1957)

The first computers were enormous, often taking up entire rooms. They were powered by thousands of *vacuum tubes*—glass tubes that look similar to large, cylindrical light bulbs—that needed replacing constantly, required a great deal of electricity, and generated a lot of heat. *First-generation computers* could solve only one problem at a time since they needed to be physically rewired with cables to be reprogrammed (see Figure 1-7), which typically took several days (sometimes even weeks) to complete and several more days to check before the computer could be used. Usually paper punched cards and paper tape were used for input, and output was printed on paper.

Two of the most significant examples of first-generation computers were *ENIAC* and *UNIVAC*. ENIAC, shown in Figure 1-7, was the world's first large-scale, general-purpose computer. Although it was not completed until

1946, ENIAC was developed during World War II to compute artillery-firing tables (the settings to be used when firing different weapons under various conditions) for the U.S. Army. Instead of the 40 hours required for a person to compute the optimal settings for a single set of conditions and a single gun using hand calculations, ENIAC could complete the same calculations in less than two minutes. UNIVAC, released in 1951, was initially built for the U.S. Census Bureau and was used to analyze votes in the 1952 U.S. presidential election. Interestingly, its correct prediction of an Eisenhower victory only 45 minutes after the polls closed was not publicly aired because the results were not trusted. Despite this initial mistrust of its capabilities, UNIVAC did go on to become the first computer to be mass produced for general commercial use.

TIP

For a more detailed timeline regarding the development of computers, see the "Computer History Timeline" located in the References and Resources Guide at the end of this book.

Second-Generation Computers (approximately 1958–1963)

The second generation of computers began when the *transistor*—a small device made of semiconductor material that acts like a switch to open or close electronic circuits—started to replace the vacuum tube. Transistors allowed *second-generation computers* to be physically smaller, more powerful, cheaper, more energy-efficient, and more reliable than first-generation computers. Typically, programs and data were input on punched cards and magnetic tape, output was on punched cards and paper printouts, and magnetic tape and disks were used for storage (see Figure 1-7). *Programming languages* (such as *FORTRAN* and *COBOL*) were also developed and implemented during this generation.

Third-Generation Computers (approximately 1964–1970)

The replacement of the transistor with *integrated circuits* (*ICs*) marked the beginning of the third generation of computers. Integrated circuits incorporate many transistors and electronic circuits on a single tiny silicon *chip*, allowing *third-generation computers* to be even smaller and more reliable than computers in the earlier computer generations. Instead of punched cards and paper printouts, keyboards and monitors were introduced for input and output; magnetic disks were typically used for storage. An example of a third-generation computer is shown in Figure 1-7.

Fourth-Generation Computers (approximately 1971–present)

A technological breakthrough in the early 1970s made it possible to place an increasing number of transistors on a single chip. This led to the invention of the *microprocessor* in 1971, which ushered in the fourth generation of computers. In essence, a microprocessor contains the core processing capabilities of an entire computer on one single chip. The original IBM PC (see Figure 1-7) and Apple Macintosh, and most of today's modern computers, fall into this category. *Fourth-generation computers* typically use a keyboard and mouse for input, a monitor and printer for output, and magnetic disks and optical discs for storage. This generation also witnessed the development of *computer networks*, *wireless technologies*, and the *Internet*.

FURTHER EXPLORATION

For links to further information about the history of computers, go to www.course.com/uc11/ch01

Fifth-Generation Computers (now and the future)

Although some people believe that the fifth generation of computers has not yet begun, most think it is in its infancy stage. *Fifth-generation computers* have no precise classification, since experts tend to disagree about the definition for this generation of computers. However, one common opinion is that fifth-generation computers will be based on *artificial intelligence*, allowing them to think, reason, and learn. Voice recognition will likely be a primary means of input, and computers may be constructed differently than they are today, such as in the form of *optical computers* that process data using light instead of electrons.

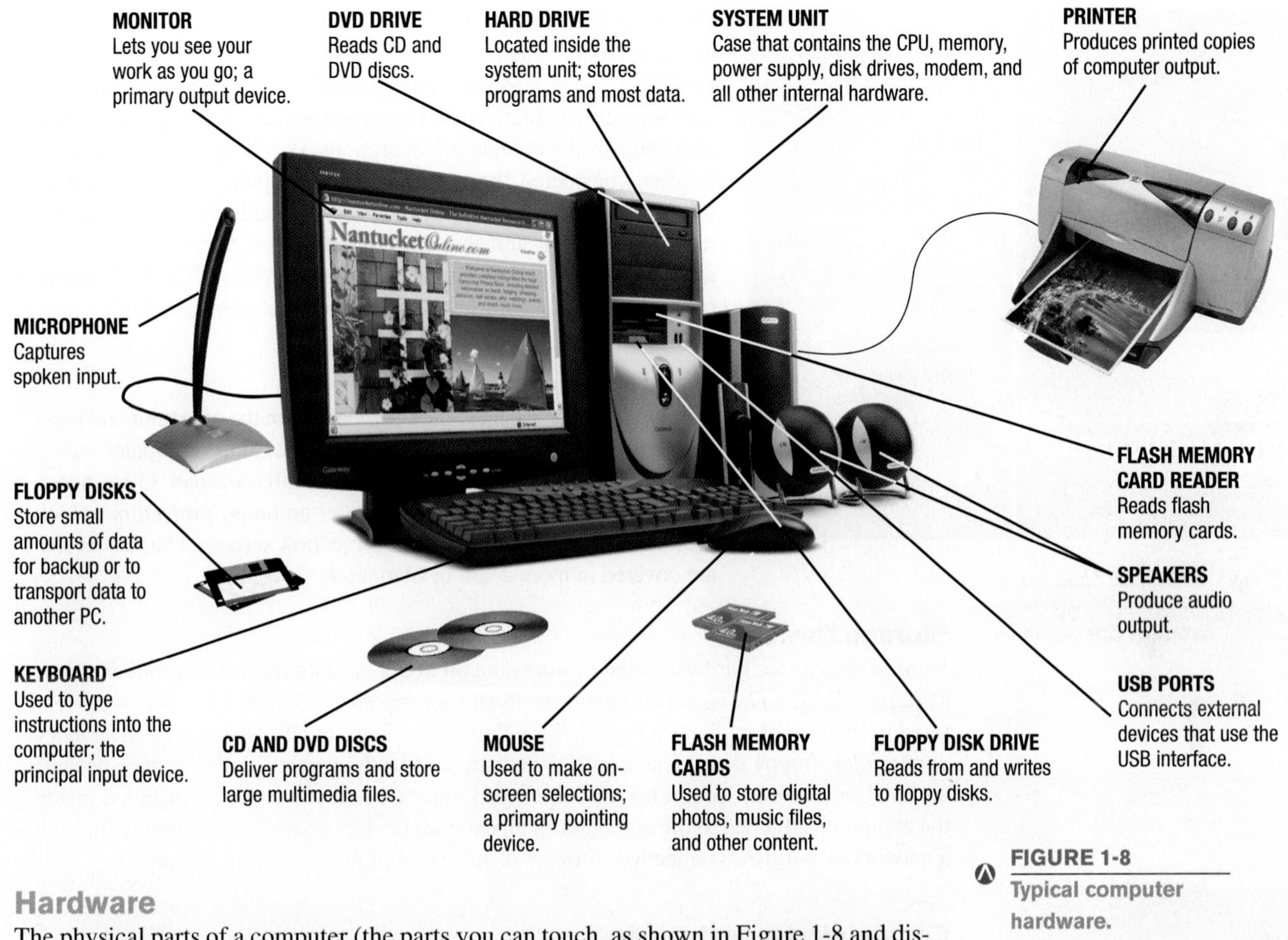
MONITOR
Lets you see your work as you go; a primary output device.
DVD DRIVE
Reads CD and DVD discs.
HARD DRIVE
Located inside the system unit; stores programs and most data.
SYSTEM UNIT
Case that contains the CPU, memory, power supply, disk drives, modem, and all other internal hardware.
PRINTER
Produces printed copies of computer output.
MICROPHONE
Captures spoken input.
FLOPPY DISKS
Store small amounts of data for backup or to transport data to another PC.
KEYBOARD
Used to type instructions into the computer; the principal input device.
CD AND DVD DISCS
Deliver programs and store large multimedia files.
MOUSE
Used to make on-screen selections; a primary pointing device.
FLASH MEMORY CARDS
Used to store digital photos, music files, and other content.
FLOPPY DISK DRIVE
Reads from and writes to floppy disks.
FLASH MEMORY CARD READER
Reads flash memory cards.
SPEAKERS
Produce audio output.
USB PORTS
Connects external devices that use the USB interface.

FIGURE 1-8
Typical computer hardware.

Hardware

The physical parts of a computer (the parts you can touch, as shown in Figure 1-8 and discussed next) are collectively referred to as **hardware**. The instructions or programs used with a computer—called *software*—are discussed in a later section.

Hardware components can be *internal* (located inside the main box or *system unit* of the computer) or *external* (located outside of the system unit). External hardware components typically plug into connectors called *ports* located on the exterior of the system unit. There are hardware devices associated with each of the five computer operations previously discussed (input, processing, output, storage, and communications), as summarized in Figure 1-9.

Input Devices

An *input device* is any piece of equipment that is used to input data into the computer. The most common input devices today are the *keyboard* and *mouse* (shown in Figure 1-8). Other possibilities include *scanners*, *touch screens*, *digital cameras*, *electronic pens*, *touch pads*, *fingerprint readers*, *joysticks*, and *microphones*. Input devices are discussed in more detail in Chapter 4.

>**Hardware.** The physical parts of a computer system, such as the keyboard, monitor, printer, and so forth.

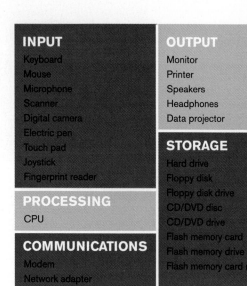

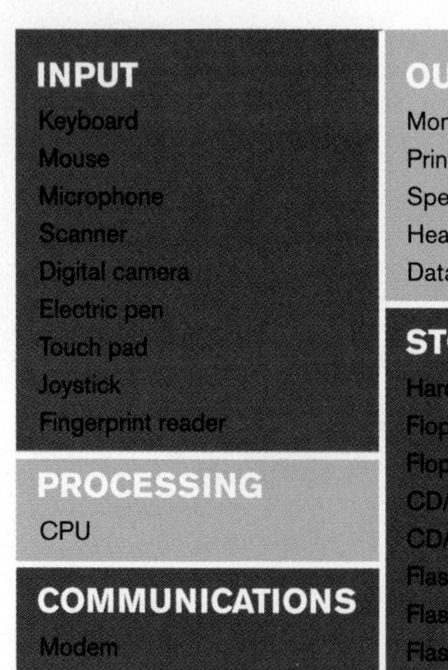

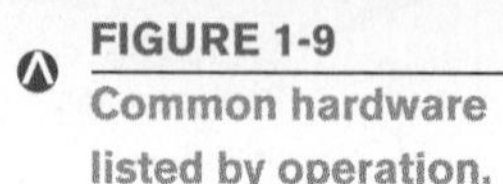

FIGURE 1-9
Common hardware listed by operation.

Processing Devices

The main *processing device* for a computer is the *central processing unit* (*CPU*). The CPU is a chip located inside the system unit that performs the calculations and comparisons needed for processing; it also controls the computer's operations. For these reasons, the CPU is often considered the "brain" of the computer. Also involved in processing are various types of *memory*—additional chips located inside the system unit that the computer uses to temporarily store data and instructions while it is working with them. The CPU, memory, and processing are discussed in more detail in Chapter 2.

Output Devices

An *output device* accepts processed data from the computer and presents the results to the user, most of the time on the computer screen (*monitor*), on paper (via a *printer*), or though a *speaker*. Other possible output devices include *headphones* and *data projectors* (which project computer images onto a projection screen). Output devices are covered in more detail in Chapter 4.

Storage Devices

Storage devices are hardware used to store data on or access data from *storage media*, such as *floppy disks*, *CD discs*, *DVD discs*, or *flash memory cards*. The storage hardware featured in Figure 1-8 includes a *hard drive*, a *floppy disk drive*, a *DVD drive*, a *flash memory card reader*, floppy disks, CD discs, DVD discs, and flash memory cards. Storage devices are used to save data, programs, or output for future use and can either be installed inside the computer, attached to the computer as an external device, or accessed remotely through a network or wireless connection. Storage is discussed in more detail in Chapter 3.

Communications Devices

Communications devices allow users to communicate electronically with others and to access remote information via the Internet or a home, school, or company network. The two most common types of communications hardware are *modems* (used to connect a computer to the Internet) and *network adapters* (used to connect a computer to a computer network). A variety of modems and network adapters are available because there are different ways to connect to the Internet and computer networks, such as via telephone lines or a *cable*, *satellite*, *cellular network*, or *Wi-Fi* connection. Communications hardware and computer networks are discussed in more detail in Chapter 7.

Software

The term **software** refers to the programs or instructions used to tell the computer hardware what to do. Software is generally purchased on a CD or DVD or downloaded from the Internet. In either case, once the program has been obtained, it usually needs to be *installed* on a computer before it can be used. An alternative is running programs directly from the Internet without installing them on your computer. Instead, the programs are accessed via Web pages. Installing and using software programs is discussed in Chapters 5 and 6.

Computers use two basic types of software: *system software* and *application software*. The differences between these types of software are discussed next.

>**Software.** The instructions, also called computer programs, that are used to tell a computer what it should do.

System Software

The programs that allow a computer to operate are collectively referred to as *system software*. The main system software program is the **operating system**, which starts up the computer and controls its operation. Common operating system tasks include setting up new hardware, allowing users to run other types of software, and allowing users to manage the documents stored on their computers. Without an operating system, a computer cannot function at all. Common operating systems are *Windows*, *Mac OS*, and *Linux*, which are all discussed in more detail in Chapter 5.

To begin to use a computer (assuming that the computer is already out of the box and the cables are correctly connected), the user first turns on the power by pressing the power button, and then the computer begins to **boot**. During the *boot process*, part of the computer's operating system is loaded into memory, the computer does a quick diagnostic on the computer, and then it launches any programs—such as an *antivirus* or *instant messaging* (*IM*) program—designated to run each time the PC starts up.

Once a computer has finished the boot process, it is ready to be used and waits for input from the user. The manner in which an operating system or any other type of program interacts with its users is known as its *user interface*. Older software programs used a text-based *command line interface*, which required the user to type precise instructions indicating exactly what the computers should do. Most programs today use a *graphical user interface* or *GUI* (pronounced "goo-ey"), which uses graphical objects (such as *icons* and *buttons*) that are selected with the mouse to tell the computer what to. For instance, the Windows **desktop** (the user's basic workspace—the place where documents, folders, programs, and other objects are displayed when they are being used) shown in Figure 1-10 contains the following objects.

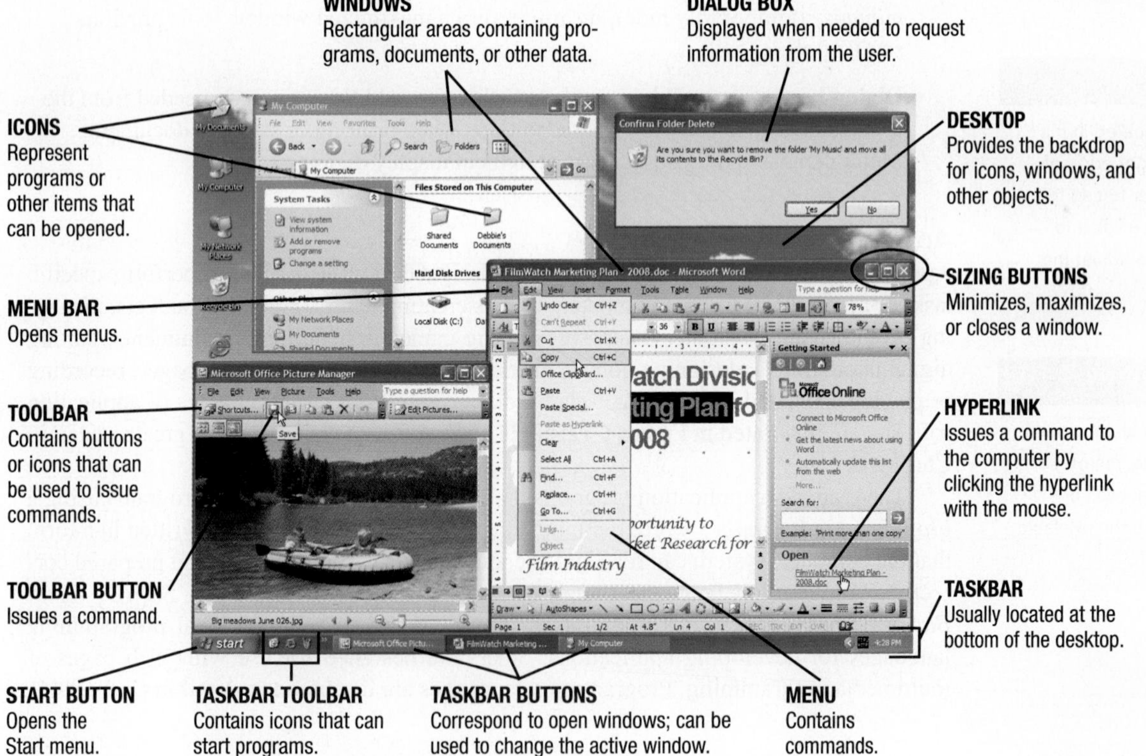
WINDOWS
Rectangular areas containing programs, documents, or other data.
DIALOG BOX
Displayed when needed to request information from the user.
ICONS
Represent programs or other items that can be opened.
DESKTOP
Provides the backdrop for icons, windows, and other objects.
MENU BAR
Opens menus.
SIZING BUTTONS
Minimizes, maximizes, or closes a window.
TOOLBAR
Contains buttons or icons that can be used to issue commands.
HYPERLINK
Issues a command to the computer by clicking the hyperlink with the mouse.
TOOLBAR BUTTON
Issues a command.
TASKBAR
Usually located at the bottom of the desktop.
START BUTTON
Opens the Start menu.
TASKBAR TOOLBAR
Contains icons that can start programs.
TASKBAR BUTTONS
Correspond to open windows; can be used to change the active window.
MENU
Contains commands.

FIGURE 1-10
The Windows desktop. Icons, buttons, menus, and other objects can be used to issue commands to the computer.

>**Operating system.** A type of system software that enables a computer to operate and manage its resources and activities. >**Boot.** To start up a computer. >**Desktop.** The background work area displayed on the screen in Microsoft Windows.

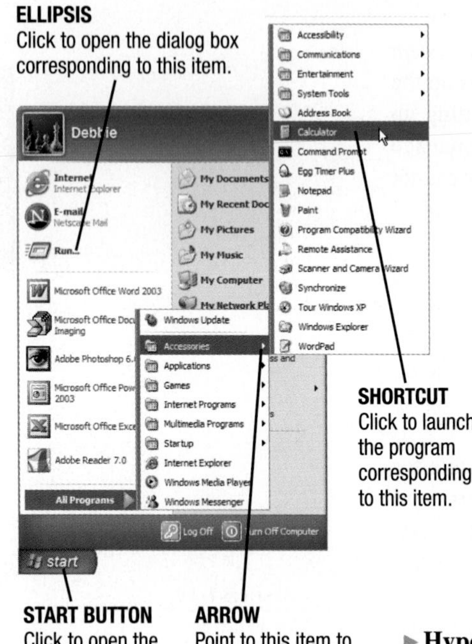

ELLIPSIS
Click to open the dialog box corresponding to this item.
SHORTCUT
Click to launch the program corresponding to this item.
START BUTTON
Click to open the Start menu.
ARROW
Point to this item to open a submenu.

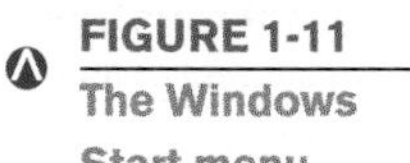
FIGURE 1-11
The Windows Start menu.

- **Windows**—rectangular areas in which programs, documents, and other content is displayed on the desktop.
- **Icons**—small pictures located on the desktop, a toolbar, or in a window that represent programs, documents, or other elements that can be opened.
- **Menus**—text-based lists that appear at the top of many windows and can be used to issue commands to that program. Items contained on a menu either display another, more specific, menu; open a dialog box to prompt the user for more information; turn a feature on or off; or execute a command.
- **Toolbars**—sets of icons or buttons, called *toolbar buttons*, that can be clicked with the mouse to issue commands, such as printing or saving a document.
- **Taskbar**—a bar located along the bottom of the desktop which houses the *Start button* at the left edge (used to open the *Start menu*—shown in Figure 1-11—which is used to launch programs), *taskbar toolbar* and *taskbar buttons* in the center (used to launch programs and switch between open windows), and a clock and other indicators in the *system tray* at the far right edge.
- **Hyperlinks**—text or images (located on the desktop, a Web page, or a program option) that are clicked to display more information; hyperlinks found on Web pages are discussed in more detail later in this chapter.
- **Sizing buttons**—small buttons located at the top-right corner of each window that are used to resize the window, such as to *maximize* (enlarge as big as possible), *minimize* (temporarily hide), *restore* (return a maximized window to its previous size), or *close* (exit) it.
- **Dialog boxes**—a small box displayed whenever additional input is needed from the user, such as to specify the desired options when printing or saving a document. Menu items with ellipses (. . .) next to them display dialog boxes.

TIP

Point to the clock located in the system tray at the right edge of the Windows taskbar to see the current date; double-click it to view a calendar or to adjust the date or time.

TIP

Taskbar buttons can also be used to minimize, maximize, restore, or close windows. Right-click a taskbar button to see the available options.

Application Software

Application software consists of programs designed to allow people to perform specific tasks or applications using a computer, such as creating letters, preparing budgets, managing inventory and customer databases, playing games, scheduling appointments, editing digital photographs, designing homes, making travel plans, viewing Web pages, recording or playing CDs, and exchanging e-mail. Some examples of common types of application software are illustrated in Figure 1-12; application software is discussed in greater detail in Chapter 6.

There are also application programs that help users write their own programs using a *programming language*. A programming language is a set of commands written in a form that the computer system can read and use, once the program is written and prepared correctly. Programming languages come in many varieties—for example, *BASIC*, *Visual Basic*, *Pascal*, *COBOL*, *C++*, and *Java*. Some languages are traditional programming languages for developing applications; others are designed for use with Web pages or multimedia programming. Programming languages are discussed in detail in Chapter 13.

>**Window.** A rectangular area in which programs, documents, and other content are displayed. >**Icon.** A small graphical image that invokes some action when selected. >**Menu.** A set of options (usually text-based) used to issue commands to the computer. >**Toolbar.** A set of icons used to issue commands to the computer. >**Taskbar.** The bar located at the bottom of the Windows desktop that contains the Start button, task buttons, and the system tray. >**Hyperlink.** Text or an image that is linked to a Web page or other type of document. >**Sizing button.** Small buttons located at the top-right corner of a window used to resize the window. >**Dialog box.** A window that requires the user to supply additional information. >**Application software.** Programs that enable users to perform specific tasks on a computer, such as writing a letter or playing a game.

WORD PROCESSING PROGRAMS
Allow users to create written documents, such as reports, letters, and memos.
SPREADSHEET PROGRAMS
Allow users to create documents containing numbers and computations, such as budgets, expense reports, and financial statements.
GAMES
Allow both kids and adults to perform educational and/or entertainment activities.
MULTIMEDIA PROGRAMS
Allow users to perform tasks, such as playing music or video clips stored on a computer, CD, or Web page; listening to Internet radio stations; creating audio CDs; and transferring home movies to DVD discs.
WEB BROWSERS
Allow users to view Web pages and other information located on the Internet.
E-MAIL PROGRAMS
Allows users to compose, send, receive, and manage electronic messages sent over the Internet or a private network.

FIGURE 1-12

Application software. Application software can help individuals work more productively at their jobs, as well as provide entertainment.

Computer Users and Professionals

In addition to hardware, software, data, and *procedures* (the predetermined steps to be carried out in particular situations), a computer system includes people. The people involved in a computer system include both the people who make the computers work and those who use them.

Computer users, or *end users*, are the people who use a computer to obtain information. Anyone who uses a computer is a computer user, including an accountant electronically preparing a client's taxes, an office worker using a word processing program to create a letter, a shop-floor supervisor using a computer to check and see whether workers have met the

>**Computer user.** A person who uses a computer.

day's quotas, a college student analyzing science lab data, a child playing a computer game, and a person bidding at an *online auction* over the Internet.

Programmers, on the other hand, are computer professionals whose primary job responsibility is to write the programs that computers use. Although some computer users may do small amounts of programming to customize the software on their desktop computers, the distinction between a computer user and a programmer is based on the work that the person has been hired to do. In addition to programmers, organizations may employ other *computer professionals*. For instance, *systems analysts* design computer systems to be used within their companies. *Computer operations personnel*, in contrast, are responsible for the day-to-day operations of large computer systems. Computer operations personnel are also often employed to help train users or assist them with their desktop computers and to troubleshoot user-related problems. Computer professionals and computer careers are discussed in more detail in Chapter 12.

COMPUTERS TO FIT EVERY NEED

The types of computers available today vary widely from the pocket-sized computers that do a limited number of computing tasks, to the powerful and versatile *desktop computers* and *portable PCs* found in homes and businesses, to the superpowerful computers used to control the country's defense systems. Computers are generally classified in one of five categories, based on size, capability, and price.

- *Mobile devices*—cellular phones and other communications devices with computer or Internet capabilities.
- *Personal computers*—conventional *desktop*, *notebook*, *tablet*, and *handheld computers*.
- *Midrange servers*—computers that host data and programs available to a small group of users.
- *Mainframe computers*—powerful computers used to host a large amount of data and programs available to a wide group of users.
- *Supercomputers*—extremely powerful computers used for complex computations and processing.

FIGURE 1-13
Mobile devices.

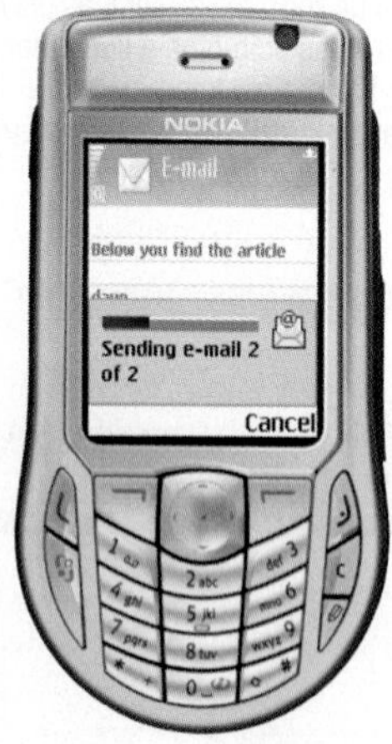

SMART PHONE

SMART WATCH

In practice, classifying a computer into one of these five categories is not always easy or straightforward. For example, some high-end personal computers are as powerful as midrange servers, and some personal computers today are nearly as small as a Web-enabled cell phone or other mobile device. In addition, technology changes too fast to have precisely defined categories. Nevertheless, these five categories are commonly used to refer to groups of computers designed for similar purposes.

Mobile Devices

A **mobile device** (see Figure 1-13) is loosely defined as a very small device that has some built-in computing or Internet capability. Mobile devices today are typically based on cellular phones; these devices are often referred to as *smart phones*. Smart phones can be used to access the Web and e-mail wirelessly, take digital photos, play games, and access calendars, address books, and other personal productivity features, in addition to performing their regular telephone functions. Mobile devices based on wristwatches are called *smart*

>**Programmer.** A person whose primary job responsibility is to write, maintain, and test computer programs. >**Mobile device.** A very small device, usually based on a wireless phone, that has some type of built-in computing or Internet capability.

watches. Smart watches can download weather, sports scores, news headlines, and other content wirelessly from the Internet; some can be used to transfer personal files, store and play music files, or store voice recordings.

Because of their typically small screen size and tiny, crowded keyboards, today's mobile devices are most appropriate for individuals wanting constant e-mail and messaging ability—as well as occasional updates on stock prices, weather, directions, and other timely information—rather than general Web browsing and computing. This is expected to change in the future, however, as cell phones, mobile devices, and portable computers continue to converge and wireless capabilities continue to improve. In some countries, this has already happened more than in the United States. For instance, smart phones currently available in Japan can be used for videoconferencing, storing gym IDs and concert tickets in digital form, purchasing products (via a built-in *digital wallet* into which users can transfer cash values), and even unlocking apartment doors. For a look at an emerging mobile device application available in the United States—*mobile TV*—see the Trend box.

Personal Computers

A **personal computer** (**PC**) or **microcomputer** is a small computer system designed to be used by one person at a time. PCs are small enough to fit on a desktop, inside a briefcase, or even inside a shirt pocket and are widely used in homes, small businesses, and large businesses alike. For instance, an individual might use a PC at home to play games, pay bills, prepare his or her taxes, exchange e-mail, and access Web pages. A small business might use its PCs for a variety of computing tasks, including tracking merchandise, preparing correspondence, creating marketing material, billing customers, responding to customer e-mails, updating the company Web site, and completing routine accounting chores. A large business might use PCs as productivity tools for office personnel and as analysis tools for decision makers, to name just two important applications. Office PCs are also commonly connected to a company *computer network* to provide access to company files, as well as to the company's Internet connection. Personal computers are available in a variety of configurations, as discussed next.

Desktop PCs

Conventional PCs are often referred to as **desktop PCs** because the complete computer system (system unit, monitor, keyboard, mouse, and so forth) fits on or next to a desk. The most common style of desktop PC today is with a *tower case*; that is, with a system unit that is designed to sit vertically, typically on the floor (see Figure 1-14). Desktop PCs can also have a *desktop case* that is designed to be placed horizontally on a desk's surface, usually with the monitor sitting on top of the system unit, as shown in Figure 1-14, although it is more common today for desktop cases to be used with *mini PCs*—very tiny desktop PCs that sit on the desk next to the monitor. A third possibility is the *all-in-one* desktop PC case, which incorporates the monitor and system unit into a single piece of hardware. While the conventional appearance of a desktop PC is a fairly large white or black box, desktop PCs are getting smaller and are now available in a variety of colors and designs. For a look at an emerging industry trend regarding PC appearance—*PC modding*—see the Inside the Industry box.

Desktop PCs typically cost between $500 and $2,500 and usually conform to one of two standards: *PC-compatible* or *Macintosh*. PC-compatibles (sometimes referred to as *Windows PCs* or *IBM-compatible PCs*) evolved from the original IBM PC—the first personal computer widely accepted for business use—and are the most common type of

TIP

For more tips on buying a PC, see the "Guide to Buying a PC" in the References and Resources Guide located at the end of this book.

>**Microcomputer.** A type of computer based on a microprocessor and designed to be used by one person at a time; also called a **personal computer** or **PC**. >**Desktop PC.** A PC designed to fit on or next to a desk.

TREND

Mobile TV

The entertainment factor of mobile phones just went up a big notch. In addition to the games and Web access that smart phones already provide, a hot new application is *mobile TV* (see the accompanying figure). Live television programming delivered via cell phones is now available in a number of countries, including the United States. One of the leaders is this area is *MobiTV*, which offers over 20 channels of news, music videos, comedies, and cartoons, including content from MSNBC, ABC News, FOX Sports, ToonWorld TV Classics, C-SPAN, and The Discovery Channel. The service costs less than $10 per month and is available through a number of wireless providers, including Sprint, Verizon, and Cingular. Content is even being developed specifically for mobile TV. For example, Twentieth Century Fox has created a new series of one-minute dramas based on its hit show *24*. The episodes–called *mobisodes*, short for "mobile episodes"–are based on the characters and actors in the TV show and became available in 2005.

A related alternative to live mobile TV is *mobile video-on-demand*–video clips that are delivered to a cell phone on demand, whenever the user requests it. Mobile video-on-demand typically includes short news clips, music videos, TV show updates, and more. Content is available 24/7 and the video clips are updated throughout the day in order to offer breaking news stories and up-to-date sports scores as they happen. Two examples of mobile video-on-demand providers are *GoTV* and Verizon's *Vcast* service.

Mobile TV is just beginning, but is expected to soon develop into a major market. For example, the ARC Group research company projects that, by 2008, 250 million consumers worldwide will be watching some form of mobile TV or video, generating more than $5 billion in annual revenues.

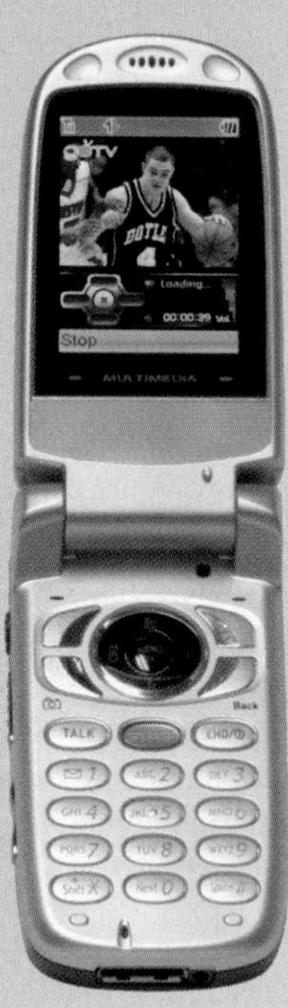

FIGURE 1-14
Typical styles for desktop PCs.

TOWER CASE

DESKTOP CASE

ALL-IN-ONE CASE

personal computer used today. In general, PC-compatible hardware and software are compatible with all brands of PC-compatible computers—such as those made by Dell, Hewlett-Packard, NEC, Acer, Fujitsu, and Gateway—and these computers typically run the Microsoft Windows operating system. Macintosh computers are made by Apple, use the Mac OS operating system, and often use different hardware and software than PC-compatible computers. Although PC-compatible computers are by far the most widely used, the Mac is traditionally the computer of choice for artists, designers, and others who require advanced graphics capabilities. But because there are virtually no Macintosh-compatible computers on the market to help drive down the price, Macs tend to cost more than PC-compatible computers with comparable hardware. A user who is deciding between these two *platforms* must consider what the computer will be used for and if it needs to be compatible with any other PCs, such as a school or office computer. For a brief introduction to the steps involved in setting up a new desktop PC, see the How it Works box on page 27.

Portable PCs

Portable PCs are computers that are designed to be easily carried around, such as in a carrying case, briefcase, purse, or pocket, depending on their size. Portable computers are essential for many workers, such as salespeople who need to make presentations or take orders from clients off-site, agents who need to collect data at remote locations, and managers who need computing and communications resources as they travel. For workers who need computer access on the go but do not have their hands free, wearable computers can be used. Portable PCs today usually come with built-in communications capabilities, so the PCs can be easily connected to an office network or the Internet. Increasingly, individuals are buying portable PCs as their primary computer; in fact, monthly sales of portable *notebook PCs* (a type of portable PC discussed next) surpassed monthly sales of desktop PCs for the first time in May 2005, according to the research firm Current Analysis.

Two types of portable PCs that are about the size of a standard paper notebook or ruled tablet are *notebook computers* and *tablet PCs* (see Figure 1-15). Both are designed for users who need a fully functioning computer that they can easily take with them wherever they go, but have different physical characteristics.

FIGURE 1-15
Notebook and tablet PCs.

>**Portable PC.** A small personal computer, such as a notebook, tablet, or handheld PC, designed to be carried around easily.

INSIDE THE INDUSTRY

PC Modding

Similar to hot-rodders, who create custom cars, *PC modders* modify high-performance PCs into functional works of art. Often the goal is a case design that reflects the modder's personality or interests. Sometimes the reason to modify a PC is to increase its functionality for specific power-hungry tasks, such as PC gaming.

Most PC modders build their PCs completely from the ground up, beginning with the motherboard and adding the newest and fastest components. Although most modified PCs still contain similar components to conventional PCs—such as a motherboard, hard drive, expansion cards, RAM, cabling, and fans—often the components need to be connected in an unconventional manner to fit inside the desired case design. Some interesting case components used by PC modders include furniture, BBQs, toys, old radios, coffeemakers, fishtanks, model cars (see the accompanying photos), and custom-made fiberglass and acrylic cases. Often custom cutouts in the system unit case and custom lighting add to the overall effect; custom paint jobs are the norm. Some PC modders create PCs just for their own enjoyment or to display at computer shows; others sell their creations to friends or as a business. Companies that sell PC-modding supplies (such as clear cases, glow-in-the-dark cables, fan sculptures, and water cooling systems) also sometimes sell kits for the beginning modder.

While not everyone may be ready for a PC that looks like the Starship Enterprise or a LEGO creation, with the increased amount of time people are spending with their PCs, it is becoming more common to want a computer that is fun to look at. Along this line of thought, some PC manufacturers are designing PCs with style in mind. For example, the two retail PCs in the accompanying photo are more mod than a conventional computer, but are available for sale to the general public.

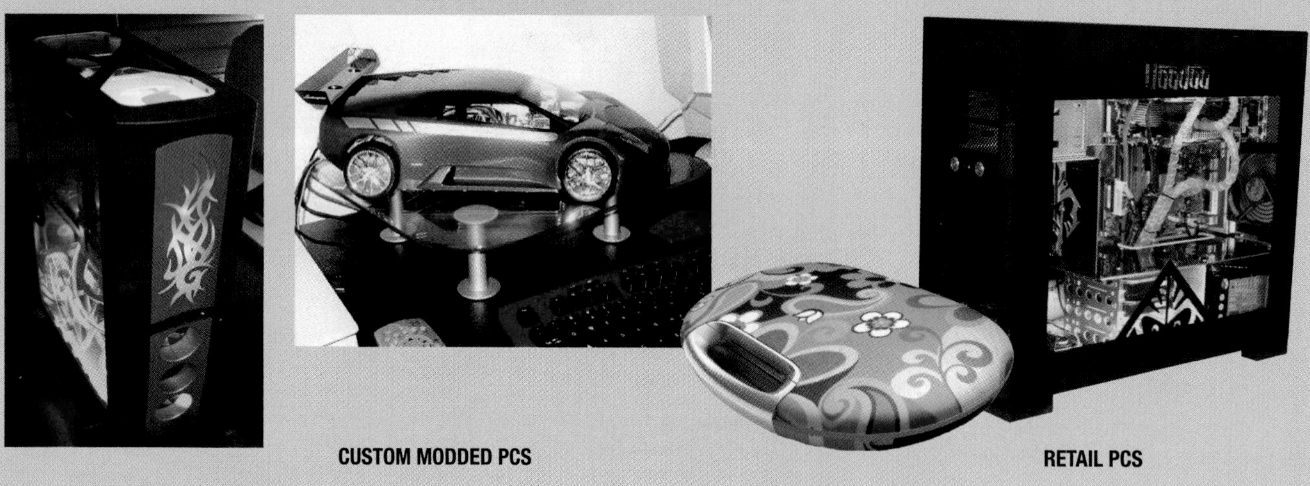

CUSTOM MODDED PCS

RETAIL PCS

TIP

PCs that allow pen input—such as tablet PCs—are convenient in crowded situations, as well as in places where the clicking of a keyboard would be annoying to others.

Notebook computers (also called *laptops*) are fully functioning computers that open to reveal a screen and keyboard. Most notebooks follow the traditional *clamshell* design in which the monitor is on the inside top half of the PC, and the keyboard and touch pad are on the inside bottom half, as shown in Figure 1-15. **Tablet PCs** can use either a *slate* or a *convertible tablet PC* design. Slate tablets include what looks like just the top half of a notebook PC. Typically slate tablets are not used with a keyboard; instead, a special pen is used to select objects and write electronically on the screen (the handwritten text can later be converted to typed text, if desired). Convertible tablet PCs are essentially a combination of a notebook computer and a slate tablet PC. In its notebook format, a convertible tablet PC is used just the same as a notebook PC; that is, with keyboard and touch pad input.

>**Notebook computer.** A fully functioning portable PC that opens to reveal a screen and keyboard. >**Tablet PC.** A portable PC about the size of a notebook that is designed to be used with an electronic pen.

When the screen is rotated and then closed with the screen facing out, the device resembles a slate tablet PC, and just pen input is used. Although similar in capabilities to their desktop cousins, notebook computers and tablet PCs tend to cost more, have smaller screens, and use denser keyboard arrangements (if a keyboard exists). Most notebook computers and tablet PCs are designed to run on rechargeable batteries, although many come with adapters that allow them to be plugged into a power outlet, as well. Both notebook computers and tablet PCs also tend to use alternative pointing devices (such as an electronic pen or a touch pad) instead of a mouse, although a mouse can be connected to the computer, if it has an available *mouse port*.

Handheld computers (sometimes called *pocket computers*) are about the size of a paperback book or pocket calculator. Handheld computers have a built-in keyboard, a *thumbpad* (such as on the BlackBerry handheld computer shown in Figure 1-16), or—like tablet PCs—the screen is touched with an electronic pen to provide input. Handheld PCs are typically battery powered and are sometimes referred to as *personal digital assistants*, or *PDAs*, since they usually provide personal organizer functions (such as a calendar, appointment book, and address book), as well as messaging, electronic mail, and other communications functions. As the capabilities of handheld PCs have improved—for instance, the tiny, fully functioning Oqo PC shown in Figure 1-16 runs Windows XP and Windows applications—they are becoming increasingly practical for day-to-day tasks. In fact, fully functioning handheld computers with telephone and Internet capabilities can conceivably replace both a desktop PC and cell phone.

For individuals who choose to use both a desktop and a portable computer, the ability to share information and synchronize data between the two computers is an important consideration. Some handheld PCs come with a cradle that attaches via a cable to the user's primary PC. After the user docks the handheld PC by inserting it into the cradle, the data on the two PCs can be updated (see Figure 1-17). Other portable PCs come with *infrared* capabilities that allow the user to "beam" data from that device to his or her primary PC. Still others can store data on flash memory cards, which can then be inserted into a desktop PC's flash memory card reader to retrieve the data. And with some types of *wireless networking* technology, it is possible for portable and desktop PCs to be in communication with each other and to synchronize data whenever they are within a specific range. Some services can even sync a handheld computer or mobile device to a desktop PC via the Internet on a continual basis, so changes made to your schedule or contact list on your primary PC are automatically reflected on your portable PC or device.

For users who prefer to use a portable PC as their primary PC but want the features of a desktop computer when working at home or in the office, *docking stations* and *notebook stands* can be used. Docking stations connect a portable PC (typically a notebook or tablet PC) to *peripheral devices*, such as a monitor, keyboard, mouse, and printer. The peripheral devices are always attached to the docking station, so as soon as the PC is connected to the docking station (via a special slot or connector), it can be used as a regular desktop PC (see Figure 1-17). Notebook stands raise a notebook PC up to an appropriate height, so the notebook's screen can be used instead of an external monitor. Some notebook stands include connectors for a keyboard and mouse; if not, those devices can be connected directly to the notebook PC.

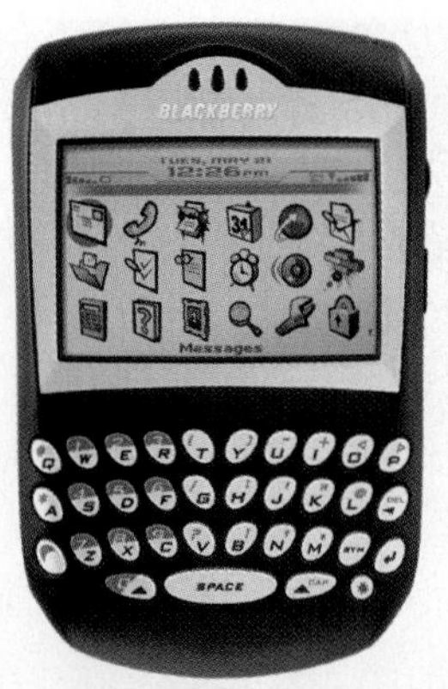

BLACKBERRY HANDHELD PC

OQO FULLY FUNCTIONING PC

FIGURE 1-16
Handheld computers. Handheld computers come in a variety of sizes and capabilities.

FURTHER EXPLORATION

For links to further information about personal computers, go to www.course.com/uc11/ch01

Thin Clients and Internet Appliances

Most personal computers today are sold as stand-alone, self-sufficient units that are equipped with all the necessary hardware and software to operate independently. In other words, they can perform input, processing, output, and storage without being connected to a network,

>**Handheld computer.** A portable PC about the size of a paperback book or pocket calculator.

CRADLES
Handheld PCs are often docked into a special cradle to synchronize the data on the handheld PC with the data on the primary PC.

DOCKING STATIONS
Once a portable PC is connected to a docking station, the monitor and other hardware connected to the docking station can be used.

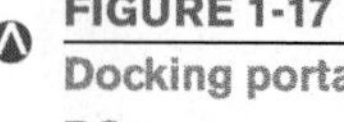

FIGURE 1-17
Docking portable PCs.

although they can be networked if desired. In contrast, a device that must be connected to a network to perform processing or storage tasks is referred to as a *dumb terminal.* Somewhere between a PC and a dumb terminal are devices that may be able to perform a limited amount of independent processing but are designed to be used with a network. Two examples of these are *thin clients* and *Internet appliances.*

A **thin client**—also called a *network computer (NC)*—is designed to be used in conjunction with a company network. Instead of using their own local disk drives for storage and their own CPUs for processing, these computers utilize a network server for those tasks. The primary advantage of thin clients is lower cost of hardware and software, as well as easier maintenance, since all software is located on the server. Disadvantages include having limited or no local storage (although this is an advantage for companies with highly secure data that need to prevent data from leaving the facility) and not being able to function as a stand-alone computer when the network is not working.

Network computers or other devices designed primarily for accessing Web pages and/or exchanging e-mail are called **Internet appliances** (sometimes also referred to as *Internet devices, information appliances,* or *Web pads*). As shown in Figure 1-18, these devices can take on a variety of configurations. Some look like a small PC but cannot run any software other than their Web browser or e-mail programs and so cannot be used as general-purpose computers. Some are designed to be located in the home and connect to the Internet via a standard telephone line; others (such as the portable Internet appliance shown in Figure 1-18) are portable and designed to access the Internet via a cell phone network. In addition to portability, some portable Internet appliances—such as the one in Figure 1-18—have a fairly large screen size, so Web pages display more like they do on conventional PCs, instead of only showing limited, modified content as is needed on many smart phones and portable PCs. Some Internet appliances—such as the MSN TV 2 device shown in Figure 1-18—take the form of a *set-top box* that connects to a TV. Increasingly, these devices facilitate the delivery

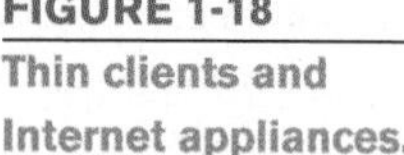

FIGURE 1-18
Thin clients and Internet appliances.
These devices are designed to be used only with company networks or the Internet.

THIN CLIENT

PORTABLE INTERNET APPLIANCE

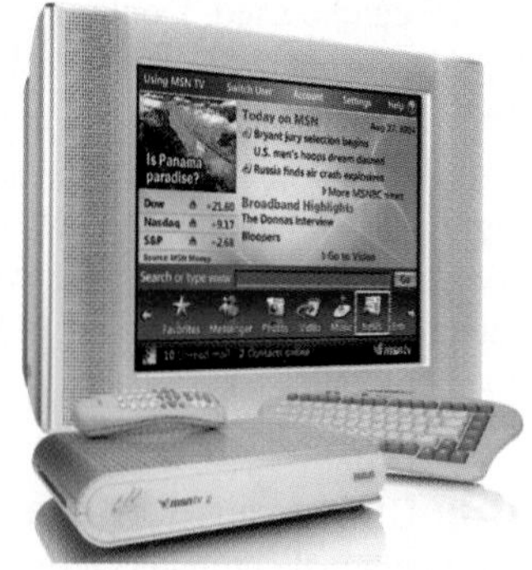

SET-TOP BOX INTERNET APPLIANCE

>**Thin client.** A PC designed to access a network for processing and data storage, instead of performing those tasks locally; also called a network computer (NC). >**Internet appliance.** A specialized network computer designed primarily for Internet access and/or e-mail exchange.

HOW IT WORKS

Setting Up a New PC

Before setting up a new PC, it is a good idea to give a little thought to its location. It should be close to a telephone jack (if one is needed), and it should have its own power outlet. In addition, the location should have enough room for ventilation, and it should not be in direct sunlight. Although set-up procedures vary from system to system, the basic steps involved in setting up a typical desktop PC are shown in the accompanying illustration. In a nutshell, you need to unpack and connect the components, install additional software, set up your initial connection, and then you are good to go.

After your system is up and running, you will need to back up your data periodically so it will not be lost if your computer fails. If you computer does malfunction, you can restore the PC to its original setup using the system backup and then restore your data from your backup medium. Some new PCs come with a *restore disc* for this purpose and some operating systems, such as Windows XP, also automatically create *restore points* to which your computer settings can be rolled back if there is ever a problem with your computer. Even though using the operating system's system restore option usually does not alter your data files, it is still good practice to back up your data on a regular basis. You will also want to back up any application software that was preinstalled on your PC but not supplied on disc, and back up any programs that you download from the Internet. Some PCs include some type of "Make discs" option to easily perform this task.

1. Unpack all components and locate the installation guide to refer to during the setup process.

2. Plug all cables (for the monitor, mouse, keyboard, printer, speakers, and so on) into the appropriate port on the system unit. For speakers, usually just one speaker is connected to the system unit; the second speaker connects directly to the first speaker.
   For conventional modems, the cord from the telephone wall jack is plugged into the appropriate port on the system unit; the second telephone port on the PC can be used for a telephone, if desired.

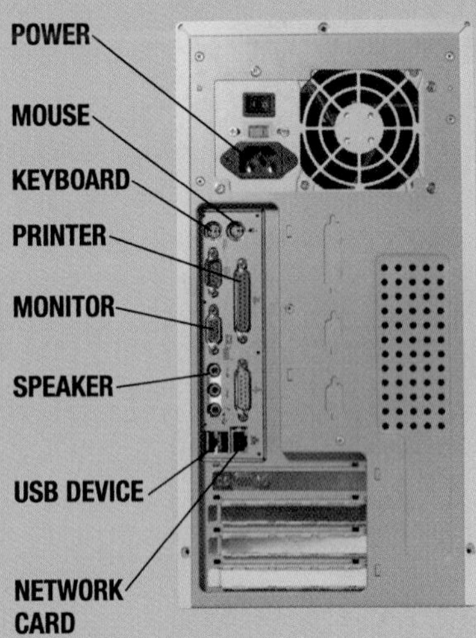

3. Plug all power cords (for the system unit, monitor, printer, scanner, powered subwoofer, and so on) into a surge suppressor power strip, then turn the power on.

4. Install any additional software you have obtained, set up your Internet or network connection, and customize the desktop display.

5. Back up your PC and any programs that were preinstalled on your PC but not supplied on disc. Store the discs in a safe place and enjoy your new PC!

of other types of digital content (such as digital photos, recorded television shows, and downloaded movies and music), in addition to Web pages and e-mail.

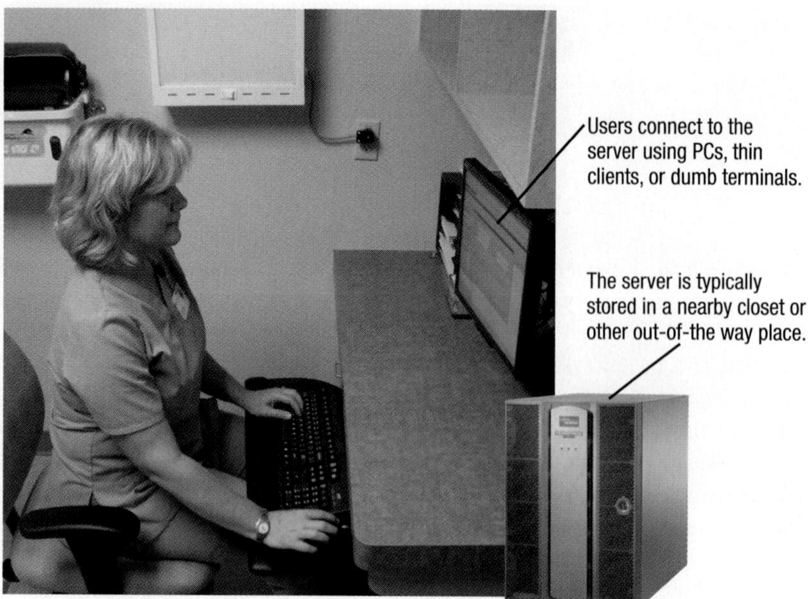

Users connect to the server using PCs, thin clients, or dumb terminals.
The server is typically stored in a nearby closet or other out-of-the way place.

FIGURE 1-19
Midrange servers.
Midrange servers are used to host data and programs on a small network, such as a school computer lab or medical office network.

Midrange Servers

A **midrange server**—also sometimes called a *minicomputer* or *midrange computer*—is a medium-sized computer used to host programs and data for a small network. Typically larger, more powerful, and more expensive than a desktop PC, a midrange server is usually located in a closet or other out-of-the way place and can serve many users at one time. Users connect to the server through a network, using their desktop computer, notebook PC, thin client, or a dumb terminal consisting of just a monitor and keyboard (see Figure 1-19). Midrange servers are often used in small- to medium-sized businesses, such as medical or dental offices, as well as in school computer labs.

Some midrange servers consist of a collection of individual *circuit boards* called *blades*; each blade contains the hardware necessary to provide the complete processing power of one PC. These servers—called *blade servers*—are much easier to expand and upgrade than traditional servers, and are more secure. With some blade servers, the processing power of the blades is shared among users. With others, each user has his or her own individual blade, which functions as that individual's PC, but the blades are locked in a secure location instead of having that hardware located on each employee's desk. In either case, the hardware designed specifically for user access to a blade server is often called a *blade PC*.

Mainframe Computers

A **mainframe computer** (see Figure 1-20) is the standard choice for large organizations—such as hospitals, universities, large businesses, banks, and government offices—that need to manage large amounts of centralized data. Larger, more expensive, and more powerful than midrange servers, mainframes usually operate 24 hours a day, serving thousands of users connected to the mainframe via PCs, thin clients, or dumb terminals, in a manner similar to the way users connect to midrange servers. During regular business hours, a mainframe runs multiple programs as needed to meet the different needs of its wide variety of users. At night, it commonly performs large processing tasks, such as payroll and billing. Today's mainframes are sometimes referred to as *high-end servers* or *enterprise-class servers* and usually cost at least several hundred thousand dollars each.

Supercomputers

Some applications require extraordinary speed, accuracy, and processing capabilities—for example, sending astronauts into space, controlling missile guidance systems and satellites, forecasting the weather, exploring for oil, and assisting with some kinds of scientific

>**Midrange server.** A medium-sized computer used to host programs and data for a small network. >**Mainframe computer.** A computer used in large organizations (such as hospitals, large businesses, and colleges) that need to manage large amounts of centralized data and run multiple programs simultaneously.

research. **Supercomputers**—the most powerful and most expensive type of computer available—were developed to fill this need. Some relatively new supercomputing applications include hosting extremely complex Web sites and decision-support systems for corporate executives, and three-dimensional applications, such as 3D medical scans, image projections, and architectural modeling. Unlike mainframe computers, which typically run multiple applications simultaneously to serve a wide variety of users, supercomputers generally run one program at a time, as fast as possible.

FIGURE 1-20
Mainframe computers.
Mainframes computers, such as the one shown here, are usually located in a climate-controlled room; users connect to the mainframe via PCs, thin clients, or dumb terminals.

Conventional supercomputers can cost several million dollars each. To reduce the cost, it has become more common to build less-expensive supercomputers by connecting hundreds of smaller computers—increasingly midrange servers running the Linux operating system—into a *supercomputing cluster* that acts as a single computer. The computers in the cluster usually contain several CPUs each and are dedicated to processing cluster applications. The resulting supercomputer is often referred to as a *massively parallel processor (MPP)* computer. For example, one of the fastest supercomputers in the world, IBM's *Blue Gene/L* (shown in Figure 1-21), contains 65,536 nodes containing two CPUs each for a combined total of 131,072 CPUs. This supercomputing cluster, built for the U.S. Department of Energy, was installed at Lawrence Livermore National Laboratories in mid-2005. It cost approximately $100 million, will perform about 360 *teraflops* (trillions of *floating point operations per second*) when fully installed and configured (only one-half the machine was installed initially), runs the Linux operating system, and is used primarily to conduct nuclear weapons simulations to help ensure the safety, security, and reliability of the nation's nuclear weapon stockpile.

A concept related to cluster computing is *grid computing*—a growing trend of utilizing the unused processing power of a large number of computers—typically PCs—connected through the Internet to work together on a single task, on demand. For instance, consumers can volunteer their PCs to be used for scientific or medical research purposes and their PCs' processing power will be tapped (via the Internet) when needed by the research organization. New grid computing services are beginning to be offered to provide companies with immense processing power on demand, similar to the way electricity is delivered as it is needed. For instance, businesses can form a grid of their employee's PCs and sell that processing power during off-hours (whenever employees are not at work) to those who need it.

BLUE GENE/L SUPERCOMPUTER
Here the supercomputer is partially installed; the racks containing the circuit boards are visible on some units.

BLUE GENE/L CIRCUIT BOARDS
Each rack holds several circuit boards; each circuit board contains four processors.

FIGURE 1-21
The Blue Gene/L supercomputer.
Supercomputers are used for specialized situations in which immense processing speed is required.

>**Supercomputer.** The fastest, most expensive, and most powerful type of computer.

COMPUTER NETWORKS AND THE INTERNET

Many computers today are connected to a *computer network*. A **computer network** is a collection of hardware and other devices that are connected together so that users can share hardware, software, and data, as well as electronically communicate with each other. As shown in Figure 1-22, many networks use a *network server* to manage the data flowing through the network devices and the resources on a network. For example, a network server might control access to shared printers and other shared hardware, as well as to shared programs and data. The other computers on a network that access network resources through the network server are called *clients*.

Computer networks exist in many sizes and types. For instance, a home network might connect two computers inside the home to share a single printer and Internet connection, as well as to exchange files. A small office network of five or six computers might be used to enable workers to access the company database, communicate with other employees, and access the Internet. A large corporate network might connect all of the offices or retail stores in the corporation, creating a network that spans several cities or states. A public wireless network—such as those available at some coffeehouses, restaurants, public libraries, and parks—might be used to provide Internet access to customers or the general public. Chapter 7 discusses networks in greater detail.

FIGURE 1-22
Example of a computer network.

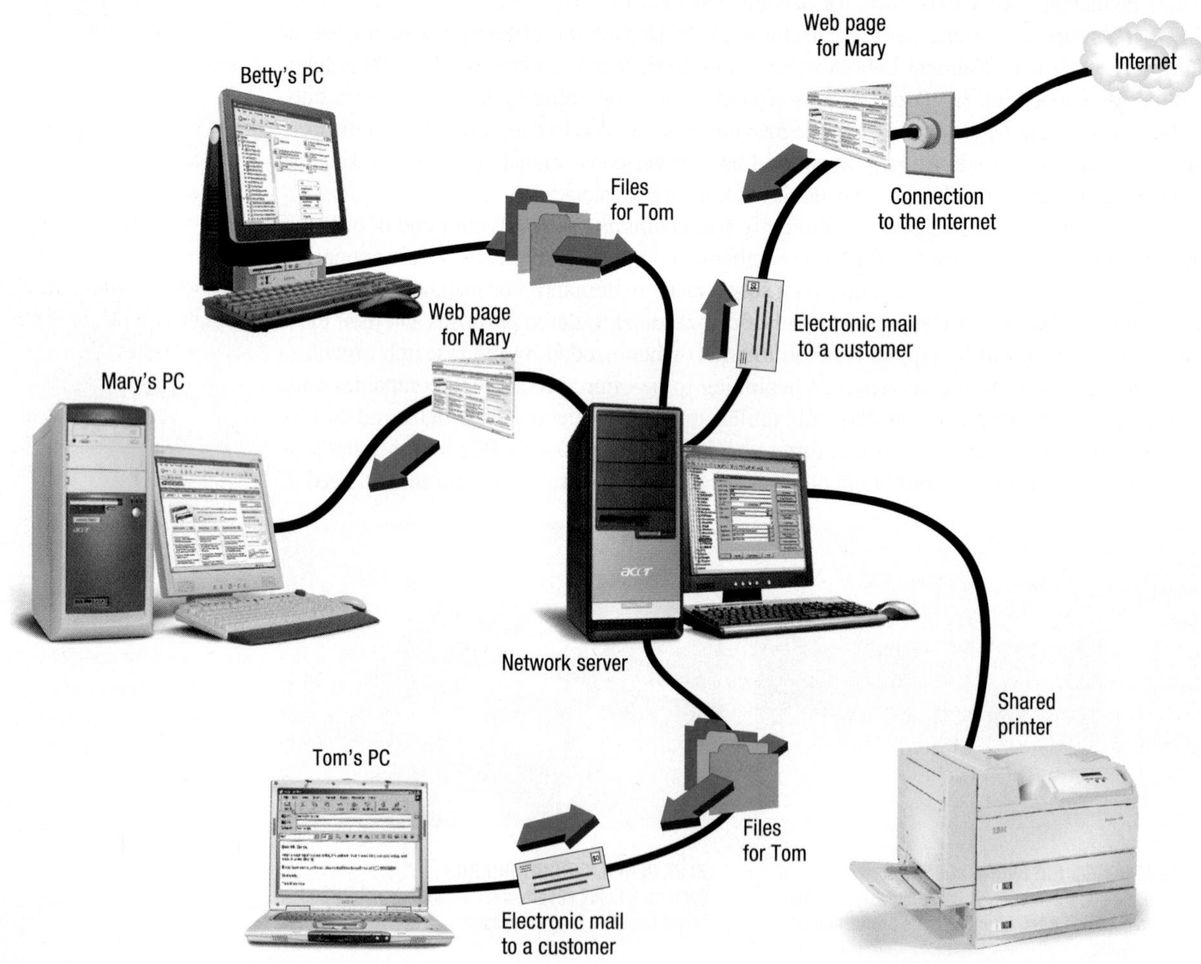

>**Computer network.** A collection of computers and other hardware devices that are connected together to share hardware, software, and data, as well as to communicate electronically with one another.

What Are the Internet and the World Wide Web?

The **Internet** is the largest and most well-known computer network in the world. It is technically a network of networks, since it consists of thousands of networks that can all access each other via the main *backbone* infrastructure of the Internet. Typically, individual users connect to the Internet by connecting to computers belonging to an **Internet service provider (ISP)**—a company that provides Internet access, usually for a fee. ISP computers are continually connected to a larger network, called a *regional network*, which, in turn, is connected to one of the major high-speed networks within a country, called a *backbone network*. Backbone networks within a country are connected to each other and to backbone networks in other countries. Together they form one enormous network of networks—the Internet. ISPs function as a gateway or onramp to the Internet, providing Internet access to their subscribers. Most ISPs charge a monthly fee for Internet access, although there are some ISPs that offer free Internet access in exchange for onscreen advertising. If you connect to the Internet using a school or company network, the school or company acts as your ISP. If you connect using a smart phone, PDA, or other handheld device, your wireless provider is usually your ISP. Home PC users typically use a national ISP (such as *America Online (AOL)*, *EarthLink*, *AT&T WorldNet*, *StarBand*, or *RoadRunner*) that provides Internet service to a large geographical area, or a local ISP that has a more limited service area. Tips for choosing and getting set up with an ISP are included in Chapter 8.

Millions of people and organizations all over the world are connected to the Internet. Two of the most common Internet activities today are exchanging e-mail and accessing the *World Wide Web (WWW)*. While the term "Internet" refers to the physical structure of that network, the **World Wide Web** refers to one resource—a collection of documents called **Web pages**—available through the Internet. A group of Web pages belonging to one individual or company is called a **Web site**. Web page files are stored on computers (called **Web servers**) that are continually connected to the Internet, so they can be accessed at any time by anyone with a computer (or other Web-enabled device) and an Internet connection. A wide variety of information is available via Web pages, such as news, weather, airline schedules, product information, government publications, music downloads, maps, telephone directories, movie trailers, and much, much more. You can also use Web pages to shop, bank, trade stock, and perform other types of online financial transactions, as well as to listen to music, play games, and perform other entertainment-oriented activities. Web pages are viewed using a **Web browser**, such as *Internet Explorer*, *Netscape Navigator*, *Safari*, *Opera*, or *Firefox*.

TIP

Although some people use the terms "Internet" and "Web" interchangeably, technically the Web–the collection of Web pages available over the Internet–is only one resource available via the Internet.

FURTHER EXPLORATION

For links to information about Web browsers, go to www.course.com/uc11/ch01

Accessing a Network or the Internet

To access a computer network (such as a home network, company network, or the Internet), you need a modem or a network adapter to physically connect your computer to the network. Communications software (either built into your operating system or installed as a separate program) allows you to connect to and *log on* to the network, if needed, so that you can access network resources. Sometimes a *username*, *user ID*, or *login ID* and a password are required to log on to a network—typically you will be asked to supply them each time you boot the computer. After providing the correct information, you will have access to network resources, and you can select the program you want to run.

To access the Internet, you must be connected to it. Many computers today are continually connected to the Internet (called a *direct* or *always-on connection*), in which the computer or other device being used to access the Internet is continually connected to the ISP's computer. With a direct connection, you only need to open your browser (using the desktop icon for your browser, the desktop icon for your ISP, or the appropriate Start menu item) to

---

>**Internet.** The largest and most well-known computer network, linking millions of computers all over the world. >**Internet service provider (ISP).** A business or other organization that provides Internet access to others, typically for a fee. >**World Wide Web.** The collection of Web pages available through the Internet. >**Web page.** A document, typically containing hyperlinks to other documents, located on a Web server and available through the World Wide Web. >**Web site.** A collection of related Web pages usually belonging to an organization or individual. >**Web server.** A computer that is continually connected to the Internet and hosts Web pages that are accessible through the Internet. >**Web browser.** A program used to view Web pages.

begin using the Internet. With a *dial-up connection*, the PC or device must dial up and connect to the ISP's computer via a telephone line when Internet access is needed. Most national dial-up ISPs include a desktop icon or Start menu item that opens your browser and dials your telephone together as a single step; smaller, regional dial-up ISPs may require you to open your browser and start the *dialing program* installed on your PC as two separate steps. You may also be asked to enter your username and password before being connected to the Internet; these will have been assigned or chosen during your ISP setup procedure. Once connected to the Internet, you can open a Web browser program and begin to view Web pages.

TIP

To see if a particular domain name is available for registration, visit the InterNIC Web site at www.internic.net and use the *Whois* search function.

In order to request a Web page or other resource located on the Internet, you need to use its *Internet address*. **Internet addresses** are numerical or text-based addresses used to identify resources accessible through the Internet, such as computers, Web pages, and people. Each Internet address is unique and is assigned to one—and only one—person or thing. The most common types of Internet addresses are *IP addresses* and *domain names* (to identify computers); *URLs* (to identify Web pages); and *e-mail addresses* (to identify people).

IP Addresses and Domain Names

IP addresses and their corresponding **domain names** are used to identify computers available through the Internet. IP (short for *Internet Protocol*) addresses are numeric, such as *207.46.138.20*, and are commonly used by computers to refer to other computers. A computer that hosts information available through the Internet (such as a Web server hosting Web pages) usually has a unique text-based domain name (such as *microsoft.com*) that corresponds to the host computer's IP address to make it easier for people to remember the address to use to access that information. IP addresses and domain names are unique; that is, there cannot be two computers on the Internet using the exact same IP address or exact same domain name. To ensure this, specific IP addresses are allocated to each network to be used with the computers on that network, and there is a worldwide registration system for domain name registration. Domain names are typically registered on an annual basis; the required fee varies from registrar to registrar. When a domain name is registered, the IP address of the computer that will be used with that domain name is also registered, so the computer can either be accessed using its domain name or corresponding IP address.

Domain names typically identify who owns that computer and either the type of entity (such as a school, a commercial business, the government, or an individual person) or the computer's location. A period separates the different parts of a domain name. The rightmost part of the domain name (beginning with the rightmost period) identifies the type of the organization or its location and is called the *top-level domain* (*TLD*). There were seven original TLDs used in the United States (see Figure 1-23). Since then, over 240 additional two-letter *country code TLDs* have been created to represent countries or territories (*.us* for United States and *.jp* for Japan, for instance). Because of the high demand for domain names, new top-level domains are periodically proposed to *ICANN* (*Internet*

FIGURE 1-23
Some top-level domains (TLDs).

ORIGINAL TLDS	INTENDED USE
.com	Commercial businesses
.edu	Educational institutions
.gov	Government organizations
.int	International treaty organizations
.org	Noncommercial organizations
.net	Network providers and ISPs
.mil	Military organizations
NEW TLDS	**INTENDED USE**
.biz	Businesses
.info	Resource sites
.name	Individuals
.museum	Museums
.pro	Licensed professionals
.aero	Aviation industry
.coop	Coop organizations

>**Internet address.** What identifies a computer, person, or Web page on the Internet, such as an IP address, domain name, or e-mail address. >**IP address.** A numeric Internet address used to uniquely identify a computer on the Internet. >**Domain name.** A text-based Internet address used to uniquely identify a computer on the Internet.

Corporation for Assigned Names and Numbers), the nonprofit organization responsible for Internet IP address allocation and domain name management. Seven new TLDs have been approved and recently implemented; there are also 10 additional TLDs under consideration.

Some TLDs—such as .gov, .edu, and .mil—are *restricted TLDs* and can only be registered by a qualifying organization; *unrestricted TLDs*—such as .com, .net, .biz, .name, and .us—can be registered by any person or type of organization. However, only the legitimate holder of a trademarked name can use that trademarked name as a domain name. Some sample domain names are shown in Figure 1-24. Although many domain names consist solely of two parts, additional parts can be used to identify an organization more specifically, as in the last example in Figure 1-24. When this occurs, all of the pieces of the domain name are separated by periods.

DOMAIN NAME	ORGANIZATION	TYPE/LOCATION OF ORGANIZATION
microsoft.com	Microsoft Corporation	Commercial business
stanford.edu	Stanford University	Educational institution
fbi.gov	Federal Bureau of Investigation	Government organization
navy.mil	United States Navy	Military organization
royal.gov.uk	The British Monarchy	Government organization in the United Kingdom

FIGURE 1-24 Examples of domain names.

INT

Uniform Resource Locators (URLs)

Similar to the way an IP address or domain name uniquely identifies a computer on the Internet, a **uniform resource locator** (**URL**) uniquely identifies a Web page. URLs consist of information identifying the Web server hosting the Web page (typically the *computer name* assigned to that computer by the organization's system administrator to uniquely identify that computer within the organization's domain name), the name of any folders in which the Web page file is stored, and the Web page's filename. For example, looking at the URL for the Web page shown in Figure 1-25 from right to left, we can see that the Web page is called *index.html*, and that file is stored in a folder called *arthur* on a Web server named *www* in the *pbskids.org* domain.

Some characteristics of the URL shown in Figure 1-25 are common to most URLs. The letters *http* stand for *Hypertext Transfer Protocol*—the protocol typically used to display Web pages. Web pages are the most common Internet resource accessed with a Web browser. If a different type of Internet resource is requested, a different protocol indicator is used. For example, URLs beginning with *ftp://* use *File Transfer Protocol*—a protocol used to upload and download files—and URLs beginning with *https://* use *Secure Hypertext Transfer Protocol*—the protocol used to display *secure Web pages*; that is, Web pages that can safely be used to transmit sensitive information, such as credit card numbers. The *www* at the beginning of the domain name in Figure 1-25 is a very common computer name for a Web server. The file extension *.html* stands for *Hypertext Markup Language*—the language usually used to create Web pages. Other file extensions,

FIGURE 1-25 A Web page URL.

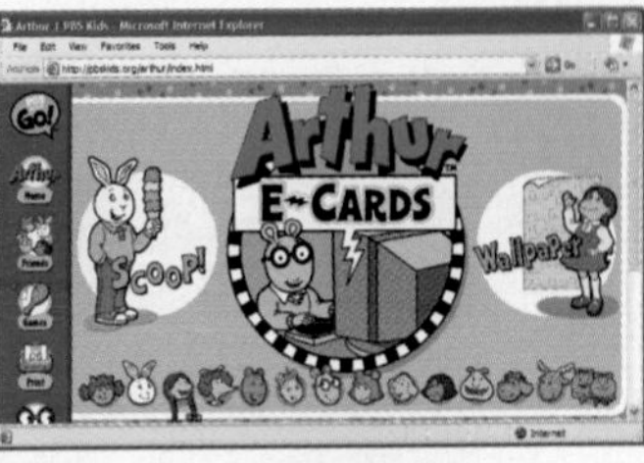

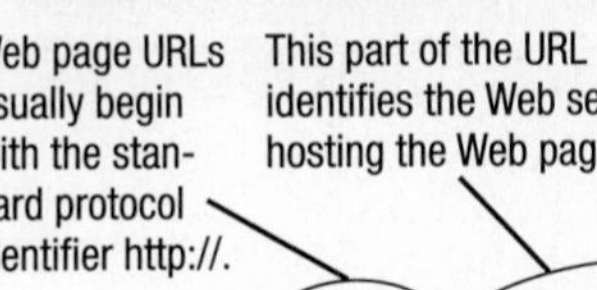

Web page URLs usually begin with the standard protocol identifier http://.

This part of the URL identifies the Web server hosting the Web page.

Next comes the folder(s) in which the Web page is stored, if necessary.

This is the Web page document that is to be retrieved and displayed.

http://www.pbskids.org/arthur/index.html

>**Uniform resource locator (URL).** An Internet address, usually beginning with http://, that uniquely identifies a Web page.

TIP

Be sure that any Web page used to send sensitive data (such as your social security number or credit card information) is secure. Look for a URL that starts with *https* instead of *http* and a locked padlock icon on the browser status bar.

such as *.htm* (another abbreviation for Hypertext Markup Language) and *.asp* (for *Active Service Pages*, which are commonly used with Web pages that are created dynamically based on user input), are also frequently used with Web pages.

E-Mail Addresses

To contact people using the Internet, you most often use their **e-mail addresses**. An e-mail address consists of a **username** (an identifying name), followed by the @ symbol, followed by the domain name for the computer that will be handling that person's e-mail (called a *mail server*). For example,

jsmith@thomson.com
maria_s@thomson.com
sam.peterson@thomson.com

are the e-mail addresses assigned respectively to jsmith (John Smith), maria_s (Maria Sanchez), and sam.peterson (Sam Peterson), three hypothetical employees at Thomson Learning, the publisher of this textbook. Usernames are typically a combination of the person's first and last names and sometimes include periods, underscores, and numbers, but cannot include blank spaces. To ensure a unique e-mail address for everyone in the world, usernames must be unique within each domain name. So, even though there could be a *jsmith* at Thomson Learning using the e-mail address *jsmith@thomson.com* and a *jsmith* at Stanford University using the e-mail address *jsmith@stanford.edu*, the two e-mail addresses are unique. It is up to each organization with a registered domain name to ensure that one—and only one—exact same username is assigned under its domain. Using e-mail addresses to send e-mail messages is discussed later in this chapter.

Pronouncing Internet Addresses

Because Internet addresses are frequently given verbally, it is important to know how to pronounce them. A few guidelines are listed next, and Figure 1-26 shows some examples of Internet addresses and their proper pronunciations.

- If a portion of the address forms a recognizable word or name, it is spoken; otherwise, it is spelled out.
- The @ sign is pronounced *at*.
- The period (.) is pronounced *dot*.
- The forward slash (/) is pronounced *slash*.

FIGURE 1-26
Pronouncing Internet addresses.

TYPE OF ADDRESS	SAMPLE ADDRESS	PRONUNCIATION
Domain name	berkeley.edu	berkeley dot e d u
URL	microsoft.com/windows/ie/default.asp	microsoft dot com slash windows slash i e slash default dot a s p
E-mail address	president@whitehouse.gov	president at whitehouse dot gov

>**E-mail address.** An Internet address consisting of a username and computer domain name that uniquely identifies a person on the Internet.
>**Username.** A name that uniquely identifies a user on a particular network.

INT

Surfing the Web

Once you have an Internet connection, you are ready to begin *surfing the Web*—that is, using a Web browser to view Web pages. In addition to being used to display Web pages, most Web browsers today can be used to perform other Internet tasks, such as downloading files, exchanging e-mail, accessing *discussion groups*, and participating in *chat sessions*. The ability to perform a variety of Internet tasks, either as part of the browser program itself or using a separate companion program that is opened automatically when needed, has made the Web browser a universal tool for exploring and using the Internet.

The first page that your Web browser displays when it is opened is your browser's starting page—or *home page*. Often this is the home page for the Web site belonging to your browser, school, or ISP. However, you can change your browser's home page to any page—such as a *search site* (a Web site that helps you find Web pages containing the information that you are seeking) or a news site—that you plan to visit regularly. The browser's *Options* or *Preferences* dialog box typically includes an option for changing the browser's home page. From your browser's home page, you can move to any Web page you desire, as discussed next.

TIP

The *home page* for a Web site is the starting page of that particular site; the *home page* for your browser is the Web page designated as the first page you see each time the browser is opened.

Using URLs and Hyperlinks

To navigate to a new Web page for which you know the URL, type that URL in the browser's *Address bar* and press Enter (see Figure 1-27). You can either edit the existing URL or delete it and type a new one, but be sure to match the spelling, capitalization, and punctuation exactly. If you do not know the exact URL to type, you can type the URL for a *search site* to display the search site's home page and then use that site to search for the Web page, as discussed shortly.

Web pages are connected by hyperlinks, which can be graphics or text. When a hyperlink is clicked with the mouse, the Web page associated with that hyperlink is displayed (when you point to a hyperlink, the *status bar* displays the URL of the page that will load if the hyperlink is clicked, as shown in Figure 1-27). Hyperlinks can be either text-based or image-based and are often underlined, although hyperlinks may also be displayed in a different color than the rest of the text on the page or underlined only when the mouse points to them. To more easily identify hyperlinks, the mouse pointer typically changes to a pointing hand when a hyperlink is pointed to; the pointing hand pointer indicates that the item being pointed to is, indeed, a hyperlink. When a hyperlink is clicked, the Web page associated with

TIP

If you get an error message when trying to load a Web page, check the spelling of the URL and then press Enter to try to load the page again. As a last resort, edit the URL to remove any folder or filenames and press Enter to try to load the home page of that site.

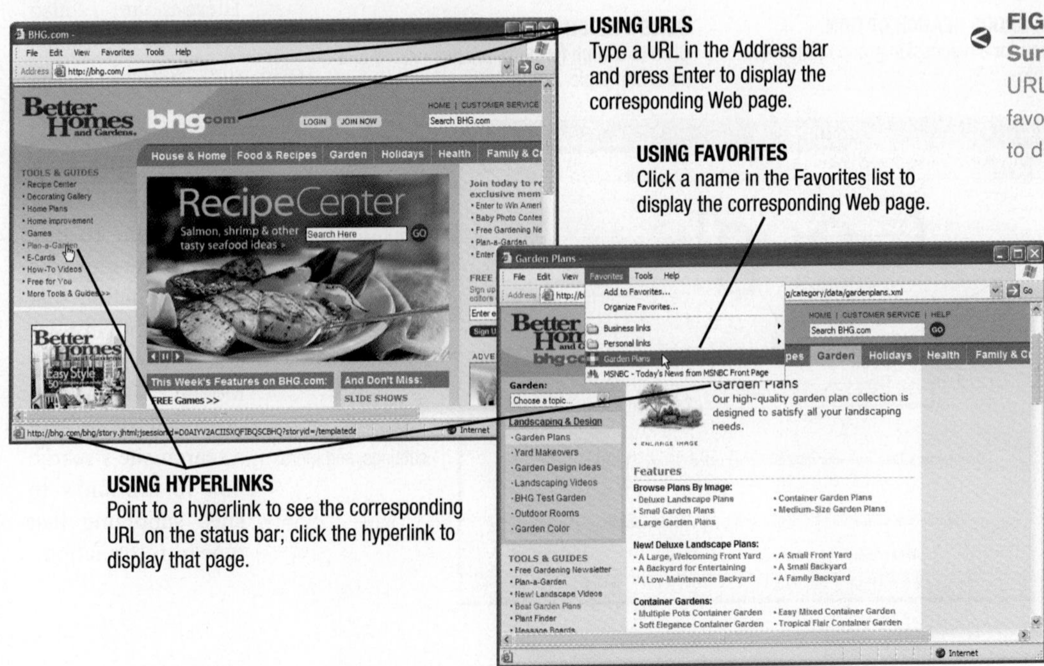

USING URLS
Type a URL in the Address bar and press Enter to display the corresponding Web page.
USING FAVORITES
Click a name in the Favorites list to display the corresponding Web page.
USING HYPERLINKS
Point to a hyperlink to see the corresponding URL on the status bar; click the hyperlink to display that page.
RecipeCenter
Garden Plans

FIGURE 1-27
Surfing the Web.
URLs, hyperlinks, and favorites can be used to display Web pages.

that hyperlink is displayed, regardless of whether the new page is located on the same Web server as the original page, or on a Web server in an entirely different state or country. In addition to Web pages, hyperlinks can also be linked to other types of files, such as to enable Web visitors to view or download images, listen to or download music files, view video clips, or download software programs.

To return to the previous Web page, you can use the Back button on your browser's toolbar. To print the current Web page, click the browser's Print button or select *Print* from the browser's File menu.

TIP

To save time when browsing on your own PC, add the URL for any Web page you plan to visit regularly to your *Favorites* list.

Using Favorites and the History List

Virtually all browsers have a feature (called *Favorites* in Internet Explorer and *Bookmarks* in Netscape Navigator) that you can use to save Web page URLs. This feature allows you to return to Web pages easily at a later time. To add the URL for the page you are currently viewing to your Favorites list, select the *Add to Favorites* option from your browser's Favorites menu. Once the URL for a page is saved as a favorite, you can redisplay that page again by selecting its link from the Favorites list (see Figure 1-27). Because a *Favorites list* can get large and unwieldy, typically an option on the Favorites menu allows you to delete outdated items from the list or move items into folders to keep them organized.

Most browsers also maintain a *History list*, which is a record of all Web pages visited in the last few weeks (how long a page stays in the History list depends on your browser settings). If you want to revisit a page you have been to recently that is not on your Favorites list, click the History button (if one is available on your browser), or look for a *History* option on the menu to display the History list, and then select the desired page.

FURTHER EXPLORATION

For links to further information about search and reference Web sites, go to www.course.com/uc11/ch01

Searching the Web

While casual surfing is a popular Web pastime, people often turn to the Internet to find specific types of information. When you know generally what you want but do not know which URL to use to find that information, one of your best options is to perform an *Internet search*. There are a number of special Web pages, called *search sites*, available to help you locate what you are looking for on the Internet. One of the most popular search sites—Google—is shown in Figure 1-28. Searching the Web is discussed in more detail in Chapter 8, but you typically type one or more *keywords* into the search box on a search site, and a list of links to Web pages matching your search criteria will be displayed. There are also numerous *reference sites* available on the Web to look up addresses, telephone numbers, ZIP codes, maps, and other information. To find a reference site, type the information that you are looking for (such as "ZIP code lookup" or "topographical maps") in a search site's search box to see links to sites supplying that type of information.

FIGURE 1-28
The Google search site.

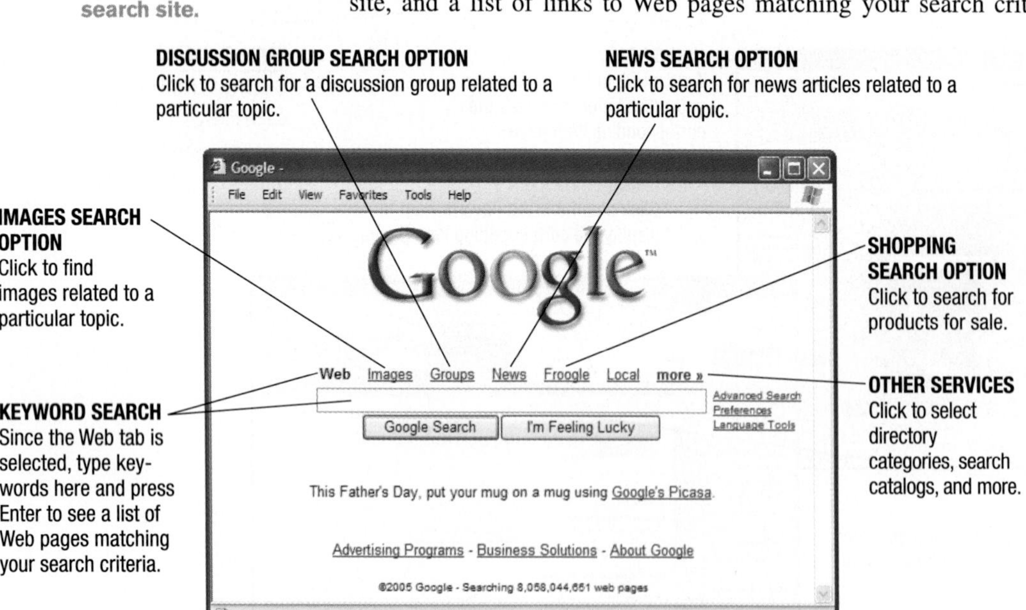
DISCUSSION GROUP SEARCH OPTION
Click to search for a discussion group related to a particular topic.
NEWS SEARCH OPTION
Click to search for news articles related to a particular topic.
IMAGES SEARCH OPTION
Click to find images related to a particular topic.
SHOPPING SEARCH OPTION
Click to search for products for sale.
KEYWORD SEARCH
Since the Web tab is selected, type keywords here and press Enter to see a list of Web pages matching your search criteria.
OTHER SERVICES
Click to select directory categories, search catalogs, and more.
Google -
File Edit View Favorites Tools Help
Google
Web Images Groups News Froogle Local more »
Advanced Search
Preferences
Language Tools
Google Search
I'm Feeling Lucky
This Father's Day, put your mug on a mug using Google's Picasa.
Advertising Programs - Business Solutions - About Google
©2005 Google - Searching 8,058,044,651 web pages
Internet

E-Mail

Electronic mail (more commonly called **e-mail**) is the process of exchanging electronic messages between computers over a network—usually the Internet. It is one of the most widely used Internet applications—Americans alone send billions of e-mail messages daily. If you are connected to the Internet (via a desktop computer, portable computer, or mobile device), then you can send an e-mail message to anyone who has an Internet e-mail address. As illustrated in Figure 1-29, e-mail messages typically travel from the sender's PC to his or her ISP, and then through the Internet to the recipient's ISP. When the recipient logs on to the Internet and requests his or her e-mail, it is sent to the PC he or she is currently using. Because e-mail is stored for an individual until he or she requests it, the sender and the receiver do not have to be online at the same time to exchange e-mail. In addition to text, e-mail messages can include attached files, such as photos and other documents. Some e-mail systems today allow for video transmission, as well—sometimes called *video e-mail*.

In order to send or receive e-mail, you typically use an *e-mail program* (such as *Netscape Mail*, *Microsoft Outlook Express*, *Microsoft Outlook*, or a proprietary mail program used by your ISP) that is set up with your name, e-mail address, incoming mail server, and outgoing mail server information. Once your e-mail program has been set up successfully, you do not need to specify this information again, unless you want to retrieve

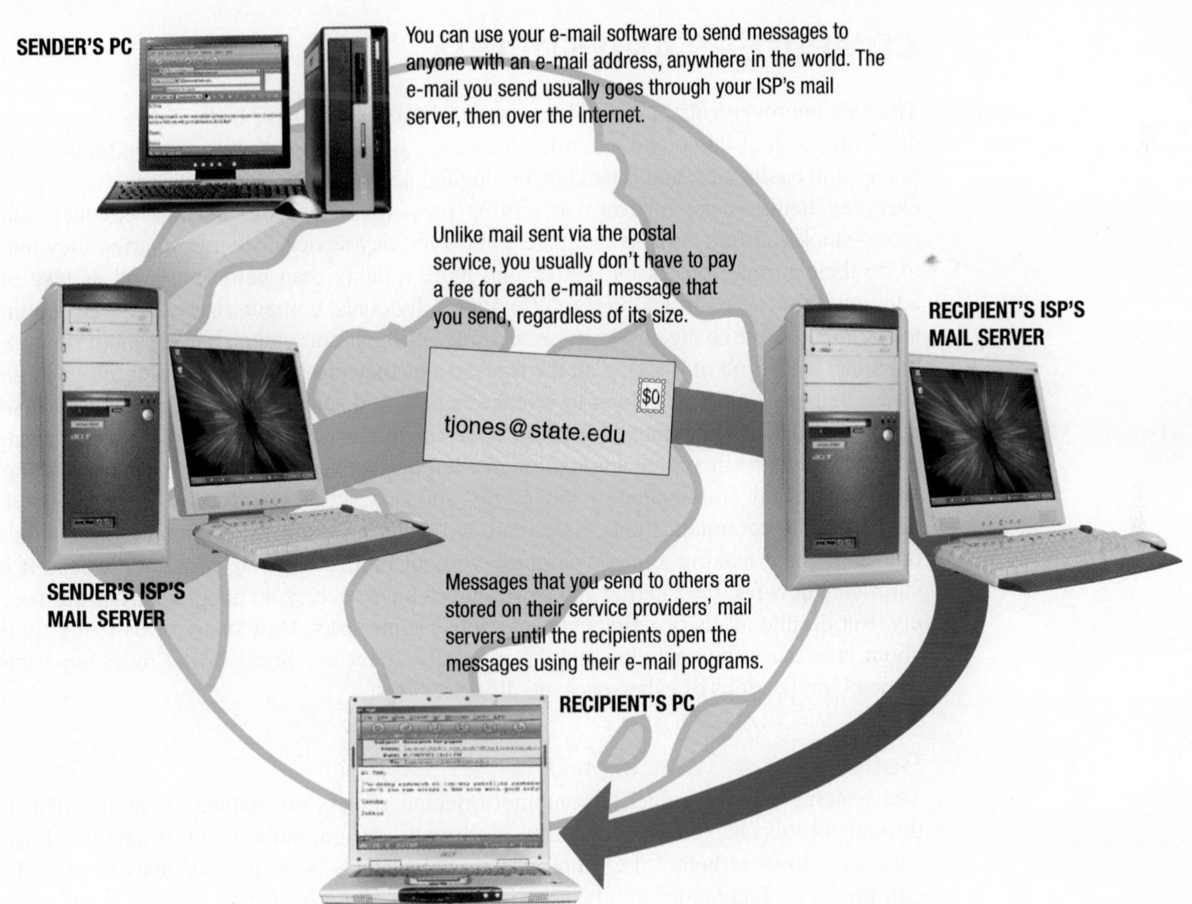

SENDER'S PC
You can use your e-mail software to send messages to anyone with an e-mail address, anywhere in the world. The e-mail you send usually goes through your ISP's mail server, then over the Internet.
Unlike mail sent via the postal service, you usually don't have to pay a fee for each e-mail message that you send, regardless of its size.
$0
tjones@state.edu
RECIPIENT'S ISP'S MAIL SERVER
SENDER'S ISP'S MAIL SERVER
Messages that you send to others are stored on their service providers' mail servers until the recipients open the messages using their e-mail programs.
RECIPIENT'S PC

FIGURE 1-29
How conventional e-mail works.

>**Electronic mail (e-mail).** Electronic messages sent from one user to another over the Internet or other network.

TIP

For a closer look at how to send, receive, and manage e-mail messages, see the "E-Mail Fundamentals" section of the References and Resources Guide located at the end of this book.

e-mail sent to a different e-mail account, you want to check your e-mail from a different PC, or you change ISPs. Some browsers allow multiple e-mail accounts (such as both a personal and school account) to be set up at one time. Others support only one e-mail account at a time, so the settings must be changed to check a different e-mail account.

Virtually all ISPs used with desktop and portable PCs include e-mail service in their monthly fee and do not charge additional fees for sending or receiving e-mail messages. However, many plans from wireless providers (such as those used with handheld PCs and smart phones) include a limited number or size of e-mail messages that can be sent or received during a billing period; messages after that point result in additional fees. With conventional e-mail, messages are usually downloaded to the user's PC and viewed using an e-mail program. With *Web-based e-mail*, e-mail messages stay on the mail server and are viewed using a Web browser. Web-based e-mail is offered by some ISPs, and free Web-based e-mail is available from some Web-based e-mail providers, such as *Hotmail*, *Yahoo! Mail*, and *Google Gmail*. Web-based e-mail is more flexible than conventional e-mail, since a user's e-mail can be accessed from any computer with an Internet connection. The user does not have to change his or her e-mail settings in order to view e-mail messages from a different PC, and all e-mail messages in the user's Inbox can be viewed from any computer. However, Web-based e-mail is typically slower than conventional e-mail and raises some privacy concerns, since your e-mail messages are stored on a Web server instead of on your PC.

COMPUTERS AND SOCIETY

The vast improvements in technology over the past decade have had a distinct impact on daily life, both at home and at work. Computers have become indispensable tools in our homes and businesses, and related technological advancements have changed the way our everyday items—cars, microwaves, coffee pots, toys, exercise bikes, telephones, and more—look and function. As computers and everyday devices become smarter, they tend to do their normal jobs faster, better, and more reliably than before, as well as take on additional functions. In addition to affecting individuals, computerization and advancing technologies have changed society as a whole. Without computers, banks would be overwhelmed by the job of tracking all the transactions they process, moon exploration and the space shuttle would still belong to science fiction, and scientific advances, such as DNA analysis and gene mapping, would be nonexistent. In addition, individuals are getting accustomed to the increased automation of everyday activities, such as shopping, banking, and travel. Many also depend on having fast and easy access to information via the Internet, and rapid communications via e-mail and instant messaging. And many of us would not think about making a major purchase without first researching it online. In fact, it is surprising how fast the Internet and its resources have become an integral part of our society. But despite all its benefits, *cyberspace* has some risks. How many of us really think about how our online activities might adversely affect us? Some of the most important societal implications of cyberspace are discussed next.

Benefits of a Computer-Oriented Society

The benefits of having such a computer-oriented society are numerous, as touched on throughout this chapter. The capability to virtually design, build, and test new buildings, cars, and airplanes before the actual construction begins helps professionals create safer end products. Technological advances in medicine allow for earlier diagnosis and more effective treatment of diseases than ever before. The benefit of beginning medical students performing virtual surgery using a computer instead of performing actual surgery on a patient is obvious. The ability to shop, pay bills, research products, participate in online courses, and look up vast amounts of information 24 hours a day, 7 days a week, 365 days a year via the Internet is a huge convenience. In addition, a computer-oriented society generates new opportunities. For example, technologies, such as speech recognition software and Braille input and output devices, enable physically or visually challenged individuals to perform necessary job tasks and communicate with others more easily.

In general, technology has also made a huge number of tasks in our lives go much faster. Instead of experiencing a long delay for a credit check, an applicant can get approved for a loan or credit card almost immediately. Documents and photographs can be e-mailed or faxed in mere moments, instead of taking at least a day to be physically mailed. And you can download information, programs, music files, and more on demand when you want or need them, instead of having to order them and then wait for delivery or physically going to a store to purchase the desired items.

Risks of a Computer-Oriented Society

Although there are a great number of benefits from having a computer-oriented society and a *networked economy*, there are risks as well. A variety of problems have emerged in recent years, ranging from stress and health concerns, to personal security and privacy issues, to ethical dilemmas. Many of the security and privacy concerns stem from the fact that so much of our personal business takes place online—or at least ends up as data in a computer database somewhere—and the potential for misuse of this data is enormous. Another concern is that we may not have had time to consider all the repercussions of collecting such vast amounts of information. Some people worry about creating a "Big Brother" situation, in which the government or another organization is watching everything that we do. Although the accumulation and distribution of information is a necessary factor of our networked economy, it is one area of great concern to many individuals. And some Internet behavior, such as downloading music or movies from an unauthorized source or viewing pornography on a school or office PC, can even get you sued or fired.

Security Issues

One of the most common online security risks today is your PC becoming infected with a *computer virus*—a malicious software program designed to change the way a computer operates. Computer viruses often cause damage to the infected PC, such as erasing data or bogging down the computer so it does not function well. Viruses can be attached to a program (such as one downloaded from the Internet), as well as attached to, or contained within, an e-mail message. To help protect your computer from viruses, never open e-mail attachments from someone you do not know or that have an executable *file extension* (the last three letters in the filename preceded by a period), such as *.exe*, *.com*, or *.vbs*, without first checking with the sender to make sure the attachment is legitimate. It is also crucial to install an *antivirus program* on your PC and set it up to scan all e-mail messages, attachments, and files before they are downloaded to make sure they are virus-free, as well as to scan your entire PC periodically for viruses. If a virus is found in an e-mail message (see Figure 1-30), the antivirus program will delete the infected file before the message appears in your Inbox; if a virus is found on your PC, the antivirus program will try to remove it.

Another growing security problem is *identity theft*—in which someone else uses your identity, typically to purchase goods or services. Identity theft can stem from personal information discovered from offline means—like discarded papers—or from information found online. *Phishing*—in which identity thieves send fraudulent e-mails to people masquerading as legitimate businesses to obtain social security numbers or other information needed for identity theft—is also a major security issue today. Common security concerns and precautions, such as protecting your PC from viruses and protecting yourself from identity theft, are discussed in more detail in Chapter 9.

FIGURE 1-30
Antivirus software. Antivirus software is crucial for protecting your PC from computer viruses.

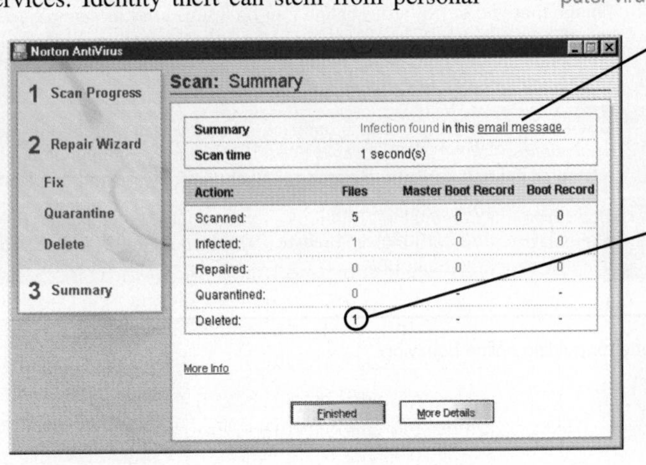

Privacy Issues

Some individuals view the potential risk to personal privacy as one of the most important issues regarding our networked society. As more and more data about our everyday activities is collected and stored in databases, our privacy is at risk because the potential for privacy violations increases. Today, data is collected about practically anything we buy online or offline, although offline purchases may not be associated with our identity unless we use a credit card or a membership or loyalty card. At issue is not that data is collected—with virtually all organizations using computers for recordkeeping, that is just going to happen—but rather how the collected data is used and how secure it is. Data collected by businesses may be used only by that company or, depending on the businesses' *privacy policy*, may be shared with others. Data shared with others often results in *spam*—unsolicited e-mails. Spam is an enormous problem for individuals and businesses today, and it is considered by many to be a violation of personal privacy. Privacy concerns and precautions are discussed in more detail in Chapter 15.

TIP

Use a *throw-away e-mail address*–a free e-mail address from Yahoo! or another free e-mail provider that you can change easily when shopping. This will help protect your privacy and cut back on the amount of spam delivered to your regular e-mail account.

Differences in Online Communications

There is no doubt that e-mail, instant messaging, and other online communications methods have helped speed up both personal and business communications and have made them more efficient (no more telephone tag, for instance). As you spend more and more time communicating online, you will probably notice some differences between online communications methods (e-mail, chat, and discussion groups, for example) and traditional communications methods (such as telephone calls and written letters). In general, online communications tend to be much less formal. This may be because people usually compose e-mail messages quickly and just send them off, without taking the time to reread and consider their message content or check their spelling or grammar. However, you need to be careful not to be so casual—particularly in business—that your communications appear unprofessional or become too personal with people you do not know.

To help in that regard, a special etiquette—referred to as **netiquette**—has evolved to guide online behavior. A good rule of thumb is always to be polite and considerate of others and to refrain from offensive remarks. This holds true whether you are asking a question via a company's e-mail address, posting a discussion group message, or chatting with a friend. When the communication involves business, you should also be very careful with your grammar and spelling, to avoid embarrassing yourself. Some specific guidelines are listed in Figure 1-31.

Another trend in online communications is the use of abbreviations and *emoticons*. Abbreviations or *acronyms*, such as BTW for "by the way," are commonly used to save time in all types of communications today. They are being used with increased frequency in text messaging and e-mail exchanged via

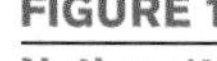

FIGURE 1-31
Netiquette. Use these netiquette guidelines and common sense when communicating online.

RULE	EXPLANATION
Use descriptive subject lines	Use short, descriptive titles for e-mail messages and discussion group posts. For example, "Question regarding MP3 downloads" is much better than a vague title, such as "Question."
Don't shout	SHOUTING REFERS TO TYPING YOUR ENTIRE E-MAIL MESSAGE OR DISCUSSION GROUP POST USING CAPITAL LETTERS. Use capital letters only when it is grammatically correct to do so or for emphasizing a few words.
Watch what you say	Things that you say or write online can be interpreted as being sexist, racist, ethnocentric, xenophobic, or in just general bad taste. Also check spelling and grammar–typos look unprofessional and nobody likes wading through poorly written materials.
Avoid e-mail overload	Don't send *spam mail*, which is unsolicated bulk e-mail and the Internet equivalent of junk mail. The same goes for forwarding e-mail chain letters or every joke you run across to everyone in your address book.
Be cautious	Don't give out personal information–such as your real name, telephone number, or credit card information–to people you meet in a chat room or other online meeting place.

>**Netiquette.** An etiquette for guiding online behavior.

wireless phones to speed up the text entry process. Emoticons—also sometimes called *smileys*—allow people to add an emotional tone to written online communications. Without these symbols, it is sometimes difficult to tell if the person is serious, joking, or being facetious, since you cannot see the individual's face or hear his or her tone of voice. Emoticons are illustrations of faces showing smiles, frowns, and other expressions that are created with keyboard symbols, such as the popular smile emoticon :-) (tilt your head to the left to view it). With some programs, emoticons are changed into actual faces, such as ☺. While most people would agree that these abbreviations and symbols are fine to use with personal and casual communications, they are not usually viewed as appropriate for formal business communications.

The Anonymity Factor

By their very nature, online communications lend themselves to *anonymity*. Since recipients usually do not hear senders' voices or see their handwriting, it is difficult to know for sure who the sender is. Particularly in discussion groups and chat rooms, where individuals use made-up names instead of real names, there is an anonymous feel to being online.

Being anonymous gives many individuals a sense of freedom, which makes them feel able to say or do anything online. This sense of true freedom of speech can be beneficial. For example, a reserved individual who might never complain about a poor product or service in person may feel comfortable lodging a complaint by e-mail. In political newsgroups or chat discussions, many people feel they can be completely honest about what they think and can introduce new ideas and points of view without inhibition. Anonymous e-mail is also a safe way for an employee to blow the whistle on a questionable business practice, or for an individual to tip off police to a crime or potential terrorist attack.

But, like all good things, online anonymity can be abused. Using the Internet as their shield, some people use rude comments, ridicule, profanity, and even slander to attack people, places, and things they do not like or agree with. Others may use multiple online identities (such as assuming two or more different usernames in a discussion group) to give the appearance of increased support for their points of view. Still others, feeling that their identities are protected, may use multiple identities to try to manipulate stock prices (by posting multiple negative messages or false information about a company to drive the price down, for instance), to get buyers to trust an online auction seller (by posting fictitious positive feedback comments about themselves), or to commit other types of illegal or unethical acts.

It is possible to hide your true identity while browsing or sending e-mail by removing personal information from your browser and e-mail program or by using a cloaking service, such as the *Anonymizer* service available for about $30 per year. But, in fact, even when personal information is removed, ISPs and the government may still be able to trace communications back to a particular computer when a crime has occurred, so it is difficult—perhaps impossible—to be completely anonymous online.

Information Integrity

As stated time and time again, the World Wide Web contains a vast amount of information on a wide variety of topics. While much of the information is factual, other information may be misleading, biased, or just plain wrong. As more and more people turn to the Web for information, it is crucial that they take the time to determine if the information they obtain and pass on to others is accurate. There have been numerous cases of information intended as a joke being restated on a Web site as fact, statements being quoted out of context, which changed the meaning from the original intent, and hoaxes circulated via e-mail. Consequently, use common sense when evaluating what you read online, and double-check information before passing it on to others.

One of the most direct ways of evaluating online content is by considering the source. If you obtain information from a news source that you trust, you should feel confident that the accuracy of its online information is close to that of its offline counterpart. For information about a particular product or technology, go to the originating company. For government information, government Web sites have more objective information than other Web sites that may have a bias.

TIP

To check if a story you hear about or receive via e-mail is a hoax or chain letter, try the Hoaxbusters site at hoaxbuster.ciac.org.

SUMMARY

COMPUTERS IN YOUR LIFE

Chapter Objective 1:
Explain why it is essential to learn about computers today and discuss several ways computers are integrated into our business and personal lives.

Computers appear almost everywhere in today's world, and most people need to use a computer or a computerized device frequently on the job, at home, at school, or while on the go. **Computer literacy**, which is being familiar with basic computer concepts, helps individuals feel more comfortable using computers and is a necessary skill for everyone today.

Computers abound in today's homes, schools, workplaces, and other locations. Increasingly, students and employees need to use a computer for productivity or research. Individuals often use computers at home and/or carry portable computers or devices with them to remain in touch with others or to use Internet resources on a continual basis.

WHAT IS A COMPUTER AND WHAT DOES IT DO?

Chapter Objective 2:
Define a computer and describe its primary operations.

Chapter Objective 3:
List some important milestones in computer evolution.

Chapter Objective 4:
Identify the major parts of a personal computer, including input, processing, output, storage, and communications hardware.

Chapter Objective 5:
Define software and understand how it is used to instruct the computer what to do.

A **computer** is a *programmable* electronic device that accepts **input**; performs **processing** operations; **outputs** the results; and provides **storage** for data, programs, or output when needed. Most computers today also have **communications** capabilities. This progression of input, processing, output, and storage is sometimes called the *information processing cycle*.

Data is the raw, unorganized facts that are input into the computer to be processed. Data that the computer has processed into a useful form is called **information**. Data can exist in many forms, representing *text*, *graphics*, *audio*, and *video*.

One of the first calculating devices was the *abacus*. Early computing devices that predate today's computers include the *slide rule*, the *mechanical calculator*, and Dr. Herman Hollerith's *Punch Card Tabulating Machine and Sorter*. *First-generation computers*, such as *ENIAC* and *UNIVAC*, were powered by *vacuum tubes*; *second-generation computers* used *transistors*; and *third-generation computers* were possible because of the invention of the *integrated circuit (IC)*. Today's *fourth-generation computers* use *microprocessors* and are frequently connected to the *Internet* and other *networks*. Some people believe that *fifth-generation computers* will likely be based on *artificial intelligence*.

A computer is made up of **hardware** (the actual physical equipment that makes up the computer system) and **software** (the computer's programs). Common hardware components include the *keyboard* and *mouse* (*input devices*), the *CPU* and *memory* (*processing devices*), *monitors* and *printers* (*output devices*), and *storage devices* and *storage media* (such as *floppy disks*, *CDs*, and *flash memory cards*). Most computers today also include a *modem* or other type of *communications device*.

All computers need *system software*, namely an **operating system** (usually *Windows*, *Mac OS*, or *Linux*), to function. The operating system assists with the **boot** process, and then controls the operation of the computer, such as to allow users to run other types of software and to manage their files. Most software programs today use a *graphical user interface (GUI)*, which typically displays information in **windows** on the **desktop**. The Windows **taskbar** contains the *Start button*, *taskbar buttons* and *taskbar toolbars*, and the *system tray*. Common features found on windows include **menus**, **toolbars**, **icons**, **dialog boxes**, and **sizing buttons**. **Hyperlinks**, sometimes found in windows, are clicked to display another document, Web page, or other information.

Application software consists of programs designed to allow people to perform specific tasks or applications, such as word processing, Web browsing, photo touch-up, and so on. Software programs are written using a *programming language*. Programs are written by **programmers**; **computer users** are the people who use the computer system.

COMPUTERS TO FIT EVERY NEED

Chapter Objective 6:
List the five basic types of computers, giving at least one example of each type of computer and stating what that computer might be used for.

Mobile devices are small devices typically used for accessing Web page data and e-mail. Mobile devices are used by individuals to maintain communications with the office while on the road, as well as for quick checks of weather forecasts, stock prices, flight information, and other Internet resources available for that particular device.

Small computers used by individuals at home or work are called **personal computers (PCs)** or **microcomputers**. Most PCs today are either **desktop PCs** (with a *desktop*, *tower*, or *all-in-one case*) or **portable PCs (notebook computers**, **tablet PCs**, or **handheld computers)** and typically conform to either the *PC-compatible* or *Macintosh* standard. Tablet PCs come in both *slate* and *convertible* tablet *PC* formats. **Thin clients** are designed solely to access a network; **Internet appliances** are designed specifically for accessing the Internet and e-mail.

Medium-sized computers, or **midrange servers**, are used in small- to medium-sized businesses to host data and programs that can be accessed by the company network. The powerful computers used by most large businesses and organizations to perform the information processing necessary for day-to-day operations are called **mainframe computers**. The very largest, most powerful computers, which typically run one application at a time, are classified as **supercomputers**.

COMPUTER NETWORKS AND THE INTERNET

Chapter Objective 7:
Explain what a network, the Internet, and the World Wide Web are, as well as how computers, people, and Web pages are identified on the Internet.

Computer networks are used to connect individual computers and related devices so that users can share hardware, software, and data as well as communicate with one another. The **Internet** is a worldwide collection of networks. Typically, individual users connect to the Internet by connecting to computers belonging to an **Internet service provider (ISP)**—a company that provides Internet access, usually for a fee. One resource available through the Internet is the **World Wide Web**—an enormous collection of **Web pages** located on **Web servers**. The starting page for a **Web site** (a related group of Web pages) is called the *home page* for that site. Web pages are viewed with a **Web browser**, are connected with hyperlinks, and can be used to retrieve news and product information, download music and movies, play online games, shop, and a host of other activities.

To access a computer network, you need some type of *modem* or *network adapter*. To access the Internet, an *Internet service provider* (*ISP*) is also used.

Chapter Objective 8:
Describe how to access a Web page.

Internet addresses are used to identify resources on the Internet and include numerical **IP addresses** and text-based **domain names** (used to identify computers), **uniform resource locators** or **URLs** (used to identify Web pages), and **e-mail addresses** (a combination of a **username** and domain name that is used to send an individual e-mail messages).

Once you are connected to the Internet and have opened your browser, Web pages can be displayed by clicking hyperlinks or by typing the appropriate URLs in the browser's *Address bar*. *Search sites* can be used to locate Web pages matching certain criteria, and **electronic mail (e-mail)** is used to send electronic messages over the Internet.

COMPUTERS AND SOCIETY

Chapter Objective 9:
Discuss the societal impact of computers, including some benefits and risks related to their prominence in our society.

Computers and devices based on related technology have become indispensable tools for modern life, making ordinary tasks easier and quicker than ever before and helping make today's worker more productive than ever before. However, there are many societal implications related to our heavy use of the Internet and the vast amount of information available through the Internet. Issues include privacy and security risks and concerns, the differences in online and offline communications, the anonymity factor, and the amount of unreliable information that can be found on the Internet. In addition, a special etiquette—referred to as **netiquette**—has evolved to guide online behavior.

REVIEW ACTIVITIES

KEY TERM MATCHING

Instructions: Match each key term on the left with the definition on the right that best describes it

a. computer
b. hardware
c. hyperlink
d. Internet
e. operating system
f. software
g. storage
h. supercomputer
i. uniform resource locator (URL)
j. Web site

1. ______ A collection of related Web pages usually belonging to an organization or individual.

2. ______ An Internet address, usually beginning with http://, that uniquely identifies a Web page.

3. ______ A programmable, electronic device that accepts data input, performs processing operations on that data, and outputs and stores the results.

4. ______ A type of system software that enables a computer to operate and manage its resources and activities.

5. ______ Text or an image located on a Web page or other document that is linked to a Web page or other type of document.

6. ______ The operation of saving data, programs, or output for future use.

7. ______ The fastest, most expensive, and most powerful type of computer.

8. ______ The instructions, also called computer programs, that are used to tell a computer what it should do.

9. ______ The largest and most well-known computer network, linking millions of computers all over the world.

10. ______ The physical parts of a computer system, such as the keyboard, monitor, printer, and so forth.

SELF-QUIZ

Instructions: Circle **T** if the statement is true, **F** if the statement is false, or write the best answer in the space provided. **Answers for the self-quiz are located in the References and Resources Guide at the end of the book.**

1. **T F** A mouse is one common input device.
2. **T F** Software includes all the physical equipment in a computer system.
3. **T F** A computer can run without an operating system if it has good application software.
4. **T F** One of the most common types of home computers is the midrange server.
5. **T F** An example of a domain name is *microsoft.com*.
6. ______ is the operation in which data is entered into the computer.
7. A(n) ______ PC can come in convertible or slate form.
8. Web pages are connected using ______, which can be either text or images.
9. Electronic messages sent over the Internet that can be retrieved by the recipient at his or her convenience are called ______.

10. Write the number of the term that best matches each of the following descriptions on the blank to the left of its description.

a. ______ Allows access to resources located on the Internet.
b. ______ Supervises the running of all other programs on the computer.
c. ______ Helps prepare written documents, such as letters and reports.
d. ______ Allows an individual to create application programs.

1. Word processing program
2. Operating system
3. Programming language
4. Web browser

EXERCISES

1. For the following list of computer hardware devices, indicate the principal function of each device by writing the appropriate letter—I (input device), O (output device), S (storage device), P (processing device), or C (communications device)—in the space provided.

a. CPU ______	d. Keyboard ______	g. Speakers ______
b. Monitor ______	e. Hard drive ______	h. DVD drive ______
c. CD drive ______	f. Modem ______	i. Microphone ______

2. Supply the missing words to complete the following statements.

a. The starting page for a Web site is called the site's ______.

b. For the e-mail address *jsmith@course.com*, *jsmith* is the ______ and *course.com* is the ______ name.

c. The e-mail address pronounced *bill gee at microsoft dot com* is written ______.

d. One of the most common online security risks today is a computer becoming infected with a(n) ______, which is a software program designed to change the way a computer operates without the permission or knowledge of the user and which often causes damage to the PC.

3. What is the difference between a tablet PC and a notebook PC?

4. List two reasons why a business may choose to network its employees' computers.

5. If a computer manufacturer called Apex created a home page for the Web, what would its URL likely be? Also, supply an appropriate e-mail address for yourself, assuming that you are employed by that company.

DISCUSSION QUESTION

The ubiquitous nature of cell phones today brings tremendous convenience to our lives, but will misuse of new improvements to this technology result in the loss of that convenience? For instance, camera phones being used to take photos in changing rooms has resulted in a ban on camera phones in many fitness centers, park restrooms, and other similar facilities. Cell phones being used to cheat on exams by taking photos of the exam to give to other students in a later class or to exchange answers during the test via text messaging has led to a ban on cell phones in many classrooms during exam periods. Do you think these reactions to cell phone misuse are justified? Is there another way to ensure the appropriate use of cell phones without banning their use for all individuals? Should there be more stringent consequences for those who use technology for illegal or unethical purposes?

PROJECTS

HOT TOPICS

1. **Mobile TV** As discussed in the Trend box, TV is one of the newest entertainment options available for cell phones. From live TV shows to video clips to reruns of TVs shows and movies, mobile TV is taking off.

   For this project, investigate the mobile TV options available today. Find at least two services and compare features, such as cost, compatibility, channels, and programming. Do your selected services offer live TV, video-on-demand, or both? If you have a cell phone, are any of the services available through your cellular provider? Have you ever watched TV on a cell phone? Would you want to? Why or why not? At the conclusion of your research, prepare a one-page summary of your findings and submit it to your instructor.

SHORT ANSWER/ RESEARCH

2. **24 Hours** Computers have a tremendous impact on our daily lives. They can be used to generate information or facilitate transactions. They can also be embedded in devices or appliances. On a daily basis, many computers are used by consumers, or on behalf of consumers, to carry out everyday tasks.

   For this project, take notice of and record all encounters you have with computing devices for the next 24 hours. Be sure to include both the computers that you use and ones that are used on your behalf. You should note both positive and negative impacts of these devices, and what your daily routine might be like without them. At the conclusion of the 24 hours, prepare a one-page summary of your observations and submit it to your instructor.

3. **Your ISP** As discussed in the chapter, ISPs are used to connect to the Internet. You may have a limited number of options for an ISP, depending on where you live and how much you are willing to spend on Internet service.

   For this project, research what options you have to connect to the Internet from where you live. For conventional dial-up Internet service, either call a local service provider listed in your telephone book or go to the Web site for America Online, EarthLink, Juno, or another large ISP and determine which ones have a local telephone access number for your area. For faster Internet service, your telephone company should be able to tell you if they offer any types of Internet service (such as *DSL* or *ISDN*) in your area and what the costs are. If you have access to cable, check with your local cable provider for information on cable Internet. If DSL, ISDN, and cable are not available to you, check into satellite service (such as from StarBand or DirecPC). After you have completed your research, summarize your findings in a one-page paper, including the cost and estimated speed for each service, any limitations on e-mail (such as number of e-mail addresses, mailbox size, or size of attachments), and whether or not each service ties up your telephone line. Be sure to include your opinion as to which service you would choose to use and why.

HANDS ON

4. **Buying a New PC** New PCs are widely available directly from manufacturers, as well as in retail, computer, electronic, and warehouse stores. Some stores carry only standard configurations as set up by the manufacturers; others allow you to customize a system.

   For this project, assume that you are in the market for a PC for your personal use. Make a list of your hardware and software requirements (refer to the "Guide for Buying a PC" in the References and Resources Guide at the end of this textbook, if needed), being as specific as possible. By researching newspaper ads, manufacturer Web sites, and/or systems for sale at local stores, find three systems that meet your minimum requirements. Prepare a one-page comparison chart, listing each requirement and how each system meets or exceeds it. Also include any additional features each system has, and information regarding the brand, price, delivery time, shipping, sales tax, and warranty terms for each system. On your comparison sheet, mark the system that you would prefer to buy and write one paragraph explaining why. Turn in your comparison sheet and summary to your instructor, stapled to copies of the printed ads, specifications printed from Web sites, or other written documentation that you collected during this project.

5. **The Internet** The Internet and World Wide Web are handy tools that can help you research topics covered in this textbook, complete many of the projects, and perform the online activities located on the textbook's Web site.

   For this project, find an Internet-enabled computer on your campus, at home, or at your public library. Follow the directions provided by your instructor or lab aide to access the Understanding Computers Web site located at www.course.com/uc11. Once you are at the site, note the types of information and activities that are available to you as a student and select a few of them by using your mouse to click the hyperlinks—usually underlined or otherwise highlighted text or graphical buttons—corresponding to the options you want to explore. At the conclusion of this task, prepare a one-page summary describing the resources available through this textbook's Web site and submit it to your instructor.

WRITING ABOUT COMPUTERS

6. **Online Education** The amount of distance learning available through the Internet and World Wide Web has exploded in the last couple of years. A few years ago, it was possible to take an occasional course online—now, a college degree can be earned online.

   For this project, look into the online education options available at your college or university and at least two other colleges or universities. Compare and contrast the programs in general, including such information as whether or not the institution is accredited, the types of courses available online, whether or not an entire certificate or degree can be earned online, and the required fees. After you have completed your general research, select one online course that interests you and research it more closely. Find out how the course works in an online format, including whether or not any face-to-face class time is required, whether assignments and exams are submitted online, which software programs or *plug-ins* (programs that give extra capabilities to a Web browser) are required, and other class requirements. Summarize your findings in a two- to three-page paper. Be sure to include your opinion as to whether or not you would be interested in taking an online course and why.

PRESENTATION/ DEMONSTRATION

7. **E-Mail Options** If you have access to the Internet, you can exchange electronic messages—including digital photos and other types of files—with any other person who has an e-mail address. This exchange can be accomplished using your computer or a PC available through your home, school, public library, or other location, provided that computer is connected to the Internet.

   For this project, research what e-mail options are available to the students at your school through the school's e-mail server as well as through free e-mail services available online, such as Hotmail, Yahoo! Mail, or Google Gmail. Compare features, such as mailbox size and any limitations on attachments, of the available services. Select one free online e-mail provider and sign up for an account. Send yourself one e-mail to experience the service and evaluate the features available through that online e-mail provider. Share your findings with the class in the form of a short presentation. The presentation should not exceed 10 minutes and should make use of one or more presentation aids, such as the chalkboard, handouts, overhead transparencies, or a computer-based slide presentation (your instructor may provide additional requirements). If possible, demonstrate the e-mail service you selected to the class. You may also be asked to submit a summary of the presentation to your instructor.

GROUP DISCUSSION

8. **New Technology: Benefits vs. Risks** As illustrated throughout this chapter, new technology adds convenience to our daily lives, helps many employees become more productive, and can increase the length and quality of our lives. However, there is usually a positive side and a negative side to each new technological improvement. Agricultural advancements help farmers grow more food more economically, but many people are concerned that heavy pesticide use and genetic engineering of crops and animals are dangerous to their health. Nuclear energy generates a very clean source for power, but it also has the possibility of tremendous destruction. The Internet allows users to obtain information very quickly and efficiently and to communicate with others at their convenience, but it also permits unscrupulous individuals to find out private information about others and commit fraud in ways that are easier than any that existed before. It is good to carefully consider the benefits vs. the risks of new technologies as they are made available to you.

   For this project, think of a technology, product, or service that you use (such as desktop PCs, handheld computers, cell phones, distance learning, online shopping, online banking, ATM machines, e-mail, electronic signature devices, music CDs, digital cameras, or DVD players). Consider the following questions: What benefits does this technology offer me? Does it bring any potential risks to my health, privacy, or security? If so, what can I do to minimize these risks? If this product or service did not exist, how would my life be different? If I don't use this technology, will I be at a disadvantage? Form an opinion about the benefits and risks of using this product or service and be prepared to discuss your position (in class, via an online class discussion group, or in a class chat room, depending on your instructor's directions). You may also be asked to write a short paper expressing your opinion.

WEB ACTIVITIES

ıe *Understanding Computers* Web site located at **www.course.com/uc11** features many resources help reinforce your understanding of the chapter content and help you prepare for exams. Your structor may also assign specific activities to be completed that will count toward your final grade the course.

ıstructions: Go to **www.course.com/uc11/ch01** to work the following online activities.

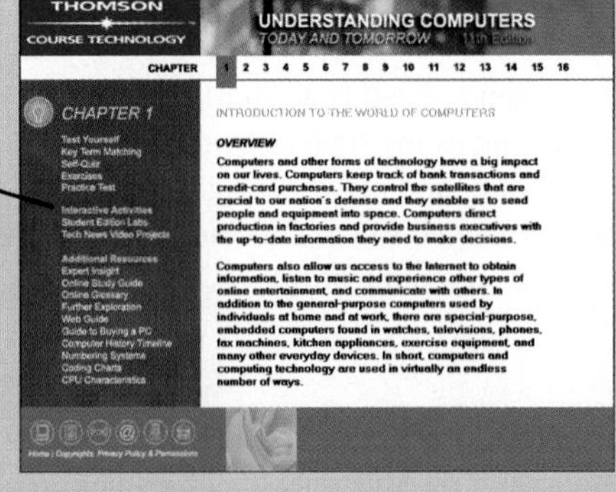

Click any link in the navigation bar on the left to access any of the online resources described below.

INTERACTIVE ACTIVITIES

1. **Crossword Puzzle** Practice your knowledge of the key terms in Chapter 1 by completing the interactive Crossword Puzzle.
2. **Tech News Video Project** Watch the **"High-Tech Climbing"** video clip that features professional mountain climber Ed Viesturs who brings a variety of high-tech gear (such as a notebook computer, digital camera, satellite phone, solar panels to recharge the equipment, and an all-in-one digital barometer, thermometer, altimeter, and wind gauge) on his climbs. After watching the video online, complete the corresponding project.
3. **Student Edition Labs** Reinforce the concepts you have learned in this chapter by working through the interactive **Using Windows** and **E-Mail** labs.

Student Edition Labs

TEST YOURSELF

1. **Key Term Matching** Test your knowledge of selected chapter key terms by matching the terms with their definitions.
2. **Self-Quiz** Test your retention of chapter concepts by taking the Self-Quiz.
3. **Exercises** Work these short exercises to review the concepts and terms covered in the chapter.
4. **Practice Test** Test how ready you are for an upcoming exam by completing the online Practice Test.

STUDY TOOLS/ ADDITIONAL RESOURCES

ıe Understanding Computers Web site has a wide range of additional resources, including an **ıline Study Guide** (containing study tips, a chapter outline with room to add your own notes, and chapter checklist of the activities to complete when the chapter is covered in class and when you e preparing for a test) and an **Online Glossary** for each chapter; **Further Exploration** links; a **'eb Guide**, a **Guide to Buying a PC**, and a **Computer History Timeline**; more information about **ımbering Systems**, **Coding Charts**, and **CPU Characteristics**; and much, much more!

EXPERT INSIGHT ON . . .
Personal Computers

NOKIA

A conversation with **VIPUL MEHROTRA**

Director, Technology and Portfolio Management for Nokia North America

My Background . . .

From an early age I was very interested in science (Dad is an Aeronautical Engineer). In undergraduate college I took Information Sciences Engineering as my field of study. I have been lucky enough to work with computers, workstations, services, software, and networks right from the beginning of my career. I gained experience in the IT industry before I moved to the telecom industry which attracted me due to the immense growth potential of mobility and communication.

"The power of mobility has transformed the way people live their lives, in addition to the way they communicate."

It's Important to Know . . .

The different kinds of computers available today. Computers are rapidly evolving, and new technology and terminology is surfacing faster than before. The risk is that people can get lost. Chapter 1 gives students a clear understanding and a good starting point to navigate through the world of computers.

What the Internet can be used for. I think this is a key point because our society today revolves around the Internet and we are highly dependent on it. The Internet is increasingly going mobile and in five years we will see mobile Internet becoming more popular.

The power of mobile devices. Mobile devices have expanded from just voice capabilities to imaging, games, entertainment, media, and many other exciting applications. Today a cellular phone can be built with a computer-like functionality to take pictures, play games, read news, stream videos, and much more. The power of mobility has transformed the way people live their lives, in addition to the way they communicate. People are more connected to their friends and family, as well as to information, media, entertainment, etc., while they are mobile. Students should understand how they can use this power to their advantage, such as to become better informed, communicate more easily, and share information.

How I Use this Technology . . .

I regularly use computers to search for information, to read and write e-mail including remote e-mail (when I am traveling), to share pictures, to keep in touch with family and friends, to pay bills, etc. I use my mobile phone (Nokia 9300 and Nokia 6682) to be connected (via voice and text messaging) with my friends, family, colleagues, and customers, as well as to read the news, exchange e-mail, share images, and download video clips. I also use my mobile phone as an alarm clock and calculator.

Vipul Mehrotra is currently the Director, Technology and Portfolio Management for Nokia North America. He is part of the Customer and Market Operations team engaged in technology marketing with key customers and the analysts, and portfolio analysis and development. In his 12 years working in this industry, he has worked for Nokia in the United States, Finland, and India. Vipul holds college degrees in both Engineering and Business.

"... the mobile phone has the potential to become the one personal device with which one can communicate, share information, transact, stream video and music, and so forth."

What the Future Holds . . .

Computers will be faster, smaller, full of rich media applications, will use wireless connections instead of cables, and could be the main information and entertainment device at home. As cellular phones are evolving from a voice only device to a voice device combined with a rich software platform, the mobile phone has the potential to become the one personal device with which one can communicate, share information, transact, stream video and music, and so forth. It will be the preferred device while on the go. Future evolution of mobile devices will see them interoperate with other devices at home—for example, to share images with TVs or PCs via Wi-Fi. Mobile video applications (such as video sharing, video streaming, video downloads, and video phone calls) have a lot of potential for the future as mobile devices and the communications infrastructure continue to become increasingly capable of handling such powerful applications/services.

Computers in general have transformed our society and today we are a digital society. Mobile devices will transform the society further and our life will be increasingly mobile. Students today should embrace mobility and use it for more than voice. They should use mobility to become a more informed person and to connect with other people and applications.

My Advice to Students . . .

Use technology to become a better informed person and use the information gained to become a responsible person. Use technology as an enabler to achieve your goals and improve your life and the lives of others.

Discussion Question

Vipul Mehrotra views the mobile phone as the platform of choice for the future. Think about which computing tasks you use your mobile phone for today and which ones you cannot. What changes need to be made in the future in order to perform all of these tasks on a mobile phone? Will the changes be primarily hardware changes? Software changes? Is the mobile phone the computer of the future? Be prepared to discuss your position (in class, via an online class discussion group, or in a class chat room, depending on your instructor's directions). You may also be asked to write a short paper expressing your opinion.

>For more information on Nokia and Nokia products, visit www.nokia.com.

MODULE HARDWARE

When most people think of computer systems, images of hardware usually fill their minds. Hardware includes the keyboard, monitor, and all of the other interesting pieces of equipment you take out of the box when you buy a computer system. This module explores the rich variety of computer hardware available today. But as you already know, hardware needs guidance from software in order to function. Hardware without software is like a car without a driver or a canvas and paintbrush without an artist.

This module divides coverage of hardware into three subject areas. Chapter 2 describes the hardware located inside the main box of the computer, which is called the system unit—the location where most of the work of a computer is performed. Chapter 3 discusses storage devices, which are the types of hardware that provide an indispensable library of resources for the computer. Chapter 4 covers the wide variety of hardware that can be used for input and output.

"Computers will get woven, invisibly in many cases, into many more aspects of life, such as in maintaining a healthy lifestyle, education, the environment, and government services."

For more comments from Guest Expert John Janakiraman of HP Labs, see the Expert Insight on . . . Hardware feature at the end of the module.

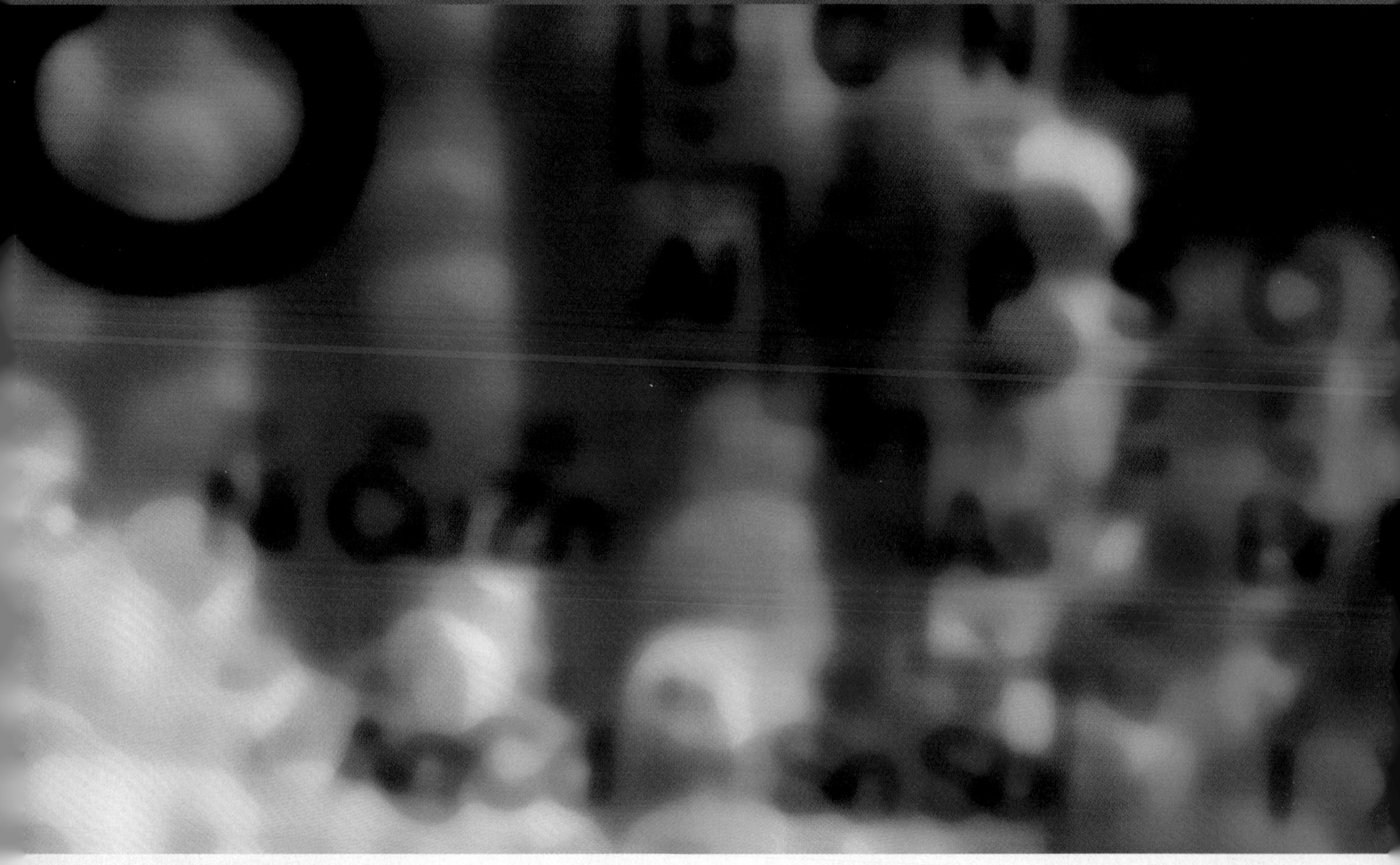

IN THIS MODULE

The System Unit: Processing and Memory

OUTLINE

LEARNING OBJECTIVES

After completing this chapter, you will be able to:

1. Understand how data and programs are represented to a computer and be able to identify a few of the coding systems used to accomplish this.
2. Explain the functions of the hardware components commonly found inside the system unit, such as the CPU, memory, buses, and expansion cards.
3. Describe how peripheral devices or other hardware can be added to a PC.
4. Understand how the computer system's CPU and memory components process program instructions and data.
5. Name and evaluate several strategies that can be used today for speeding up the operations of a computer.
6. List some technologies that may be used in future PCs.

OVERVIEW

The system unit of a computer is sometimes thought of as a mysterious "black box" that makes the computer work, and often the user does not have much understanding of what happens inside the computer. In this chapter, we demystify the system unit by looking inside the box and closely examining the functions of the parts inside. In doing so, the chapter gives you a feel for how the CPU, memory, and other devices commonly found within the system unit work together to process data into meaningful information.

To start, we discuss how a computer system represents data and program instructions. Here we talk about the codes that computers use to translate data back and forth from symbols that the computer can manipulate to symbols that people are accustomed to using. These topics lead into a discussion of how the CPU and memory are arranged with other processing and storage components inside the system unit, and then how a CPU carries out processing tasks. Finally, we look at strategies that are used today to speed up a computer, plus some strategies that may be used to create faster and better computers in the future.

While most of you reading this chapter will apply its contents to conventional personal computer systems–such as desktop and notebook PCs–keep in mind that the principles and procedures discussed in this chapter cover a broad range of computer products. These products include microprocessors embedded in toys, household appliances, and other devices, as well as processors located in powerful servers, mainframes, and supercomputers. ■

DATA AND PROGRAM REPRESENTATION

In order to be understood by a computer, data and programs need to be represented appropriately. There are *coding systems* (also called *coding schemes*) that are used to represent numeric, text-based, and multimedia data, as well as to represent programs. These concepts are discussed in the next few sections.

Digital Data Representation

Most computers today—such as the mobile devices, microcomputers, midrange servers, mainframes, and supercomputers discussed in Chapter 1—are *digital computers*. Digital computers can understand only two states, usually thought of as *off* and *on* and represented by the digits 0 and 1. Consequently, all data processed by a computer must be in digital form (0s and 1s) for it to be processed and stored. The process of representing data in digital form so it can be used by a digital computer is called *digital data representation*.

The 0s and 1s used with digital devices can be represented in a variety of ways, such as with an open or closed circuit, the absence or presence of an electronic charge, the absence or presence of a magnetic spot or depression on a storage medium, and so on. This two-state, or *binary*, nature of electronic devices is illustrated in Figure 2-1. Regardless of their physical representations, these 0s and 1s are commonly referred to as *bits*, a

FIGURE 2-1
Ways of representing 0 and 1. Digital computers recognize only two states–off and on–usually represented by 0 and 1.

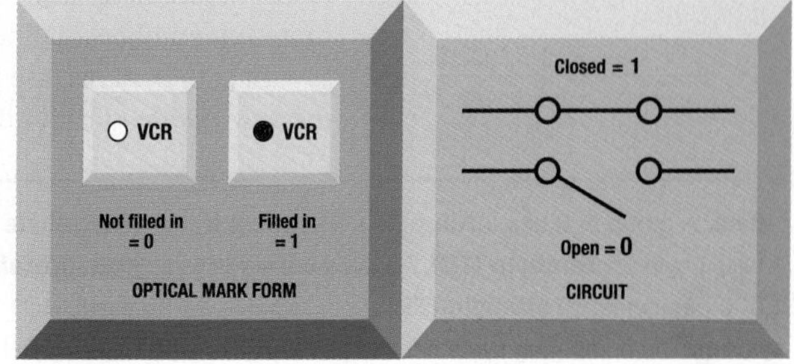

computing term derived from the phrase *binary digits*. A bit is the smallest unit of data that a digital computer can recognize, so the input you enter via a keyboard, the software program you use to play your MP3 files, and the term paper stored on your PC are all just groups of bits. Consequently, binary can be thought of as the computer's "native language."

People, of course, do not speak binary language. For example, you are not likely to go up to a friend and say,

0100100001001001

which translates into the word "HI" using one binary coding system. People communicate with one another in their *natural languages*, such as English, Chinese, Spanish, and French. For example, this book is written in English, which uses a 26-character alphabet. In addition, most countries use a numbering system with 10 possible symbols—0 through 9. As already mentioned, however, computers understand only 0s and 1s. For us to interact with a computer, a translation process from our natural language to 0s and 1s and then back again is required. When we enter data into a computer system, the computer translates the natural-language symbols we input into binary 0s and 1s. After processing the data in digital form, the computer translates and outputs the resulting information in a form that can be understood by the user.

A bit by itself typically represents only a fraction of a piece of data. Consequently, bits are usually grouped together to form letters and other characters, documents, program files, graphics files, and more. Eight bits grouped together are collectively referred to as a **byte**. It is important to be familiar with this concept because "byte" terminology is frequently used in a variety of computer contexts. For example, document size and storage capacity are measured in bytes, based on the amount of data that is contained in the document or that can be stored on the storage medium. In fact, the size of any item—such as a computer program, written document, photograph, or music file—stored on a storage medium is measured in bytes. Prefixes are commonly used with the term *byte* to represent larger amounts of data (see Figure 2-2). A **kilobyte (KB)** is equal to 1,024 bytes, but is usually thought of as approximately 1,000 bytes. A **megabyte (MB)** is about 1 million bytes; a **gigabyte (GB)** is about 1 billion bytes; a **terabyte (TB)** is about 1 trillion bytes; a **petabyte (PB)** is about 1,000 terabytes (2^{50} bytes); an **exabyte (EB)** is about 1,000 petabytes (2^{60} bytes); a **zettabyte (ZB)** is about 1,000 exabytes (2^{70} bytes); and a **yottabyte (YB)** is about 1,000 zettabytes (2^{80} bytes). Therefore, 5 KB is about 5,000 bytes, 10 MB is approximately 10 million bytes, and 2 TB is about 2 trillion bytes.

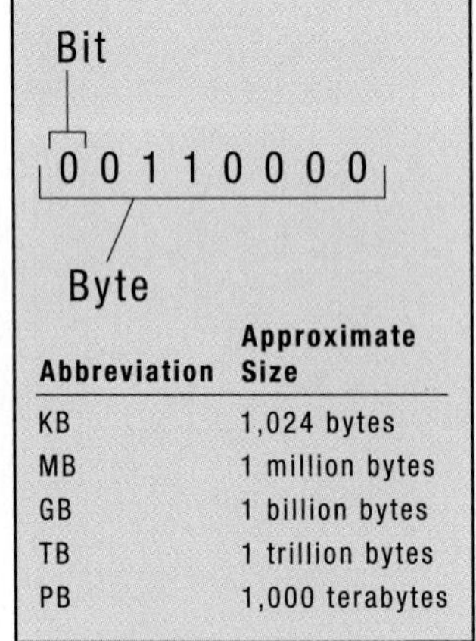

Abbreviation	Approximate Size
KB	1,024 bytes
MB	1 million bytes
GB	1 billion bytes
TB	1 trillion bytes
PB	1,000 terabytes

FIGURE 2-2
Bits and bytes.
Document size, storage capacity, and memory capacity are all measured in bytes.

Computers represent programs and data through a variety of binary-based coding schemes. The coding system used depends primarily on the type of data needing to be represented. Coding systems for numerical, text-based, and a few other types of data are discussed in the next few sections.

Representing Numerical Data: The Binary Numbering System

A *numbering system* is a way of representing numbers. The numbering system we commonly use is called the *decimal* (or *base 10*) *numbering system* because it uses 10 symbols—the digits 0, 1, 2, 3, 4, 5, 6, 7, 8, and 9—to represent all possible numbers. Numbers greater than nine, such as 21 and 683, are represented using combinations of these 10 symbols. The **binary numbering system** uses only two symbols—the digits 0 and 1—to represent all possible numbers. Consequently, computers use the binary numbering system to represent numbers and perform math computations.

In both systems, the position of each digit determines the power, or exponent, to which the *base number* (10 for decimal or 2 for binary) is raised. In the decimal numbering system,

>**Byte.** A group of 8 bits. >**Kilobyte (KB).** 1,024 bytes. >**Megabyte (MB).** Approximately 1 million bytes. >**Gigabyte (GB).** Approximately 1 billion bytes. >**Terabyte (TB).** Approximately 1 trillion bytes. >**Petabyte (PB).** Approximately 1,000 terabytes. >**Exabyte (EB).** Approximately 1,000 petabytes. >**Zettabyte (ZB).** Approximately 1,000 exabytes. >**Yottabyte (YB).** Approximately 1,000 zettabytes. >**Binary numbering system.** The numbering system that represents all numbers using just two symbols (0 and 1).

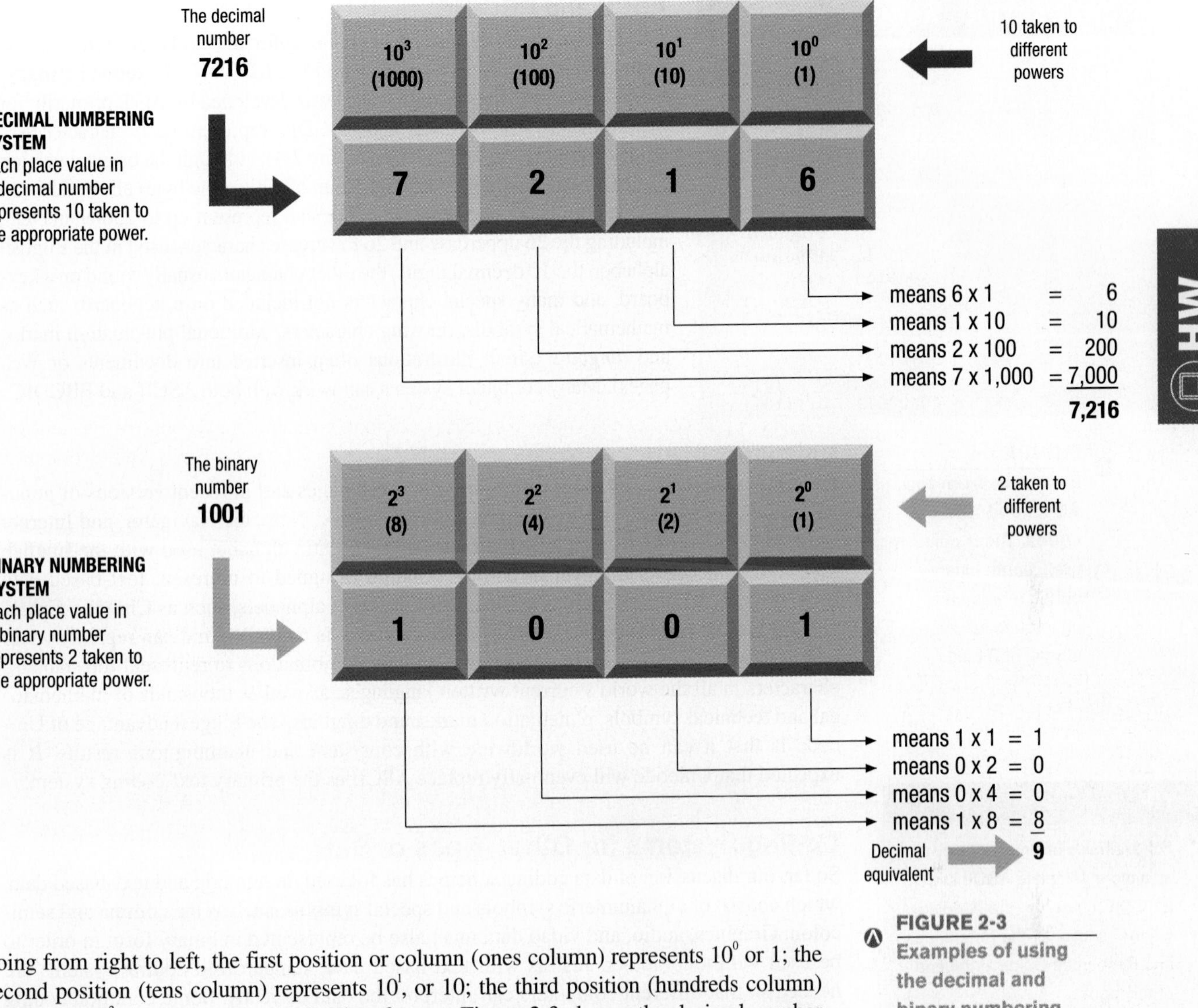

FIGURE 2-3
Examples of using the decimal and binary numbering systems.

oing from right to left, the first position or column (ones column) represents 10^0 or 1; the econd position (tens column) represents 10^1, or 10; the third position (hundreds column) epresents 10^2, or 100; and so forth. Therefore, as Figure 2-3 shows, the decimal number ,216 is understood as $7 \times 10^3 + 2 \times 10^2 + 1 \times 10^1 + 6 \times 10^0$ or 7,000 + 200 + 10 + 6 or 7,216. n binary, the concept is the same but the columns have different place values. For example, ne first column is the ones column (for 2^0), the second column is the twos column (2^1), the iird column is the fours column (2^2), and so on. Therefore, as illustrated in the bottom half f Figure 2-3, although 1001 represents "one thousand one" in decimal notation, in the inary numbering system 1001 equals "nine" ($1 \times 2^3 + 0 \times 2^2 + 0 \times 2^1 + 1 \times 2^0$ or 8 + 1 or 9).

FURTHER EXPLORATION

For links to further information about data representation, go to www.course.com/uc11/ch02

Coding Systems for Text-Based Data

Vhile numeric data is represented by the binary numbering system, text-based data is repesented by fixed-length binary coding systems specifically developed for text-based ata—namely, *ASCII*, *EBCDIC*, and *Unicode*. Such codes represent all characters on the eyboard that can appear in text data—numeric characters, alphabetic characters, and speial characters, such as the dollar sign ($) and period (.).

CHARACTER	ASCII	EBCDIC
0	00110000	11110000
1	00110001	11110001
2	00110010	11110010
3	00110011	11110011
4	00110100	11110100
5	00110101	11110101
A	01000001	11000001
B	01000010	11000010
C	01000011	11000011
D	01000100	11000100
E	01000101	11000101
F	01000110	11000110
+	00101011	01001110
!	00100001	01011010
#	00100011	01111011

FIGURE 2-4
Examples from the ASCII and EBCDIC codes. These common fixed-length binary codes represent all characters as unique strings of 8 bits.

ASCII and EBCDIC

ASCII (American Standard Code for Information Interchange) is the coding system traditionally used with PCs. **EBCDIC (Extended Binary-Coded Decimal Interchange Code)** was developed by IBM, primarily for mainframe use. Both ASCII and EBCDIC represent each character as a unique combination of 8 bits (see Figure 2-4), although the original version of ASCII was a 7-digit code. One group of 8 bits (one byte) allows 256 (2^8) unique combinations, so an 8-bit code can represent up to 256 characters, including the 26 uppercase and 26 lowercase characters used in the English alphabet, the 10 decimal digits, the other characters usually found on a keyboard, and many special characters not included on a keyboard, such as mathematical symbols, drawing characters, additional punctuation marks, and *dingbats* (small illustrations often inserted into documents or Web pages). Many computer systems can work with both ASCII and EBCDIC.

Unicode

Unicode is a newer code, now widely used for Web pages and in recent versions of popular software programs, such as Windows XP, Mac OS X, Netscape Navigator, and Internet Explorer. Unlike ASCII, which is limited to only the Latin alphabet used with the English language, Unicode is a universal coding standard designed to represent text-based data written in any language, including those with different alphabets, such as Chinese, Greek, and Russian. It is a longer code (32 bits per character is common) and can represent over one million characters—more than enough unique combinations to represent the standard characters in all the world's current written languages, as well as thousands of mathematical and technical symbols, punctuation marks, and dingbats. The biggest advantage of Unicode is that it can be used worldwide with consistent and unambiguous results. It is expected that Unicode will eventually replace ASCII as the primary text-coding system.

TIP

For examples of Unicode, as well as a more complete ASCII and EBCDIC chart, see the "Coding Charts" section in the References and Resources Guide at the end of this book.

Coding Systems for Other Types of Data

So far, our discussion of data coding schemes has focused on numeric and text-based data, which consist of alphanumeric symbols and special symbols, such as the comma and semicolon. Graphics, audio, and video data must also be represented in binary form in order to be used with a computer. Just as with text-based data, standardized coding systems are needed so that different computers can interpret the data correctly. Some common coding schemes used with these types of data are discussed next.

Graphics Data

Graphics data consists of still images, such as photographs or drawings. One of the most common methods for storing graphics data is in the form of a *bitmap*—a grid of hundreds of thousands of dots, called *pixels* (short for *picture elements*), arranged to represent an image. The color to be displayed at each pixel is represented by some combination of 0s and 1s, and the number of bits required to store the color for one pixel is called *bit depth*.

A *monochrome* graphic, which is the simplest type of bitmapped image, has only two possible colors. Suppose that these colors are black and white, and that the color white is represented by a 1 and the color black is represented by a 0. Using this scheme, the graphic would be represented to the PC as a black-and-white bitmap, such as the one shown in the top part of Figure 2-5, and the binary representation of that image would use a bit depth of 1 (and require one bit of storage space per pixel).

>**ASCII.** A fixed-length, binary coding system widely used to represent text-based data for computer processing on many types of computers. >**EBCDIC.** A fixed-length, binary coding system widely used to represent text-based data on IBM mainframe computers. >**Unicode.** A coding system for text-based data using any written language.

MONOCHROME GRAPHICS
With monochrome graphics, the color of each pixel is represented by a single bit, either 0 or 1.

ORIGINAL IMAGE

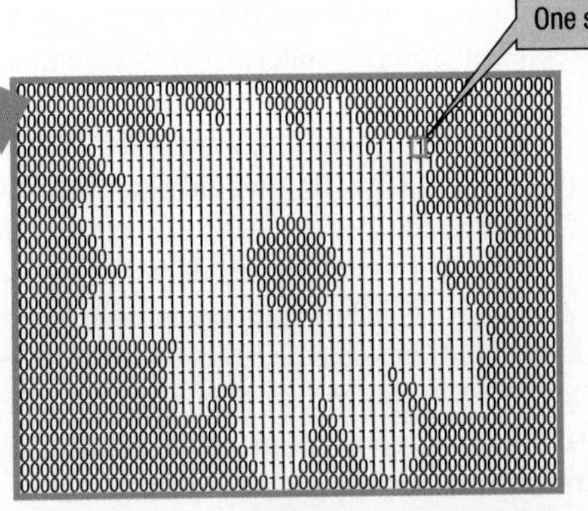

One sample pixel: 1

BITMAP

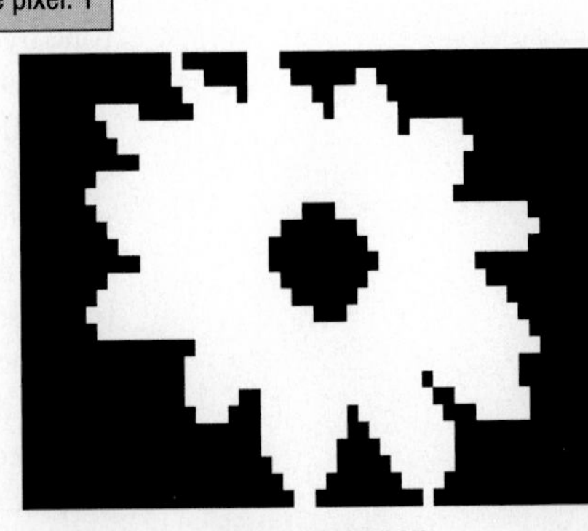

DISPLAYED IMAGE

GRAYSCALE GRAPHICS
With 256-shade grayscale graphics, the color of each pixel is represented by one byte, such as 01101110. Different byte values represent black, white, and 254 different shades of gray.

One sample pixel: 01101110

One sample pixel: 1110

16-COLOR IMAGE
The color of each pixel is represented using one half byte (4 bits).

One sample pixel: 01110110

256-COLOR IMAGE
The color of each pixel is represented using one byte (8 bits).

COLOR GRAPHICS
Color images can be 16-color, 256-color, or photographic quality. The more colors used, the better the image quality.

One sample pixel: 101001100100110111001011

PHOTOGRAPHIC-QUALITY (TRUE COLOR) IMAGE (16.8 million colors)
The color of each pixel is represented using three bytes (24 bits).

FIGURE 2-5
Representing graphics data. With bitmapped images, the color of each pixel is represented by bits; the more bits used, the better the image quality.

More realism can be achieved using a *grayscale* image. In grayscale images, each pixel can be not only pure black or pure white but also any of the 254 shades of gray in between. Therefore, each pixel could appear in any of 256 possible states. It takes 8 bits (one byte) to represent 256 (2^8) states, so grayscale images use a bit depth of 8 (and require one byte of storage per pixel). For example, 11111111 might represent one pure white pixel, 00000000 might represent one pure black pixel, and any byte pattern in between—such as 11001000 and 00001010—would represent one particular shade of gray (see the middle part of Figure 2-5).

With *color* images, a variety of bit depths are possible, including 4, 8, and 24 bits to represent 16, 256, or 16,777,216 colors respectively. In a 16-color image, one-half byte (4 bits, such as 0000, 1111, or some combination in between) is assigned to each pixel to represent the color to be displayed in that pixel. In a 256-color image, 1 byte (8 bits) is assigned to each pixel to represent its color. Finally, in a 16.8-million-color (called photographic quality or *true color*) image, 3 bytes (24 bits) are used to store the color data for each pixel in the image (see the bottom part of Figure 2-5). Some digital cameras today support 48-bit (6-byte) color images, in order to enable more precise color adjustments of digital photos taken with that camera.

Theoretically, the higher number of bits used in color coding, the higher the image quality. In practice, however, it is sometimes difficult for the human eye to tell much of a quality difference between low-end and high-end color images, unless the images have been enlarged. Because using fewer colors results in a smaller file size and a faster download time, Web developers often reduce true-color images to 256-color or 16-color images for use on Web pages. This is typically accomplished by a process called *dithering*. Dithering produces colors not available on a limited color palette by coloring neighboring pixels with two available colors that appear to blend together to make a different color. For example, your eye will see a lime green color on the screen when several yellow and green pixels are placed adjacent to one another.

TIP

Most Web page images today are 8-bit color images, and most digital cameras take 24-bit true color images.

Although bitmapped images are widely used, they are not the best choice when images need to be resized because the existing pixels are just made larger or smaller (no new pixels are added). This results in the image looking distorted or blurry. A better choice in this situation is *vector-based* images, which use mathematical formulas to represent images instead of a map of pixels; vector-based images can be resized without losing quality.

Audio Data

Like graphics data, *audio data*—such as a song or the sound of someone speaking—must be in digital form in order to be stored on a storage medium or processed by a PC. To convert analog sound to digital sound, several thousand *samples*—digital representations of the sound at a particular moment—are taken every second. When the samples are played back in order, they recreate the sound of the voice or music. For example, audio CDs record sound using 2-byte samples sampled at a rate of 44,100 times per second (the minimum number of times in order to maintain sound quality). When these samples are played back at a rate of 44,100 per second, the human ear cannot distinguish them, and they collectively sound like continuous voice or music. With so many samples per second, sound files take up a great deal of storage space—about 32 MB for a 2-minute stereo song (44,100 times × 2 bytes × 180 seconds × 2 channels).

Because of its large size, when audio data is transmitted over the Internet it is often compressed to shorten the download time. For example, files that are *MP3-encoded*—that is, compressed with the MP3 compression algorithm—are about 10 times smaller than their uncompressed digital versions, so they download 10 times faster and take up one-tenth of the storage space. For a look at how MP3 compression works, see the How It Works box.

HOW IT WORKS

MP3 Compression

The *MP3 format* is a compression system for music. It is used to reduce the number of bytes in a song without sacrificing musical quality. MP3 is officially *MPEG Audio Layer 3*, an *MPEG* (*Moving Pictures Experts Group*) compression standard. Each MPEG layer uses a different sampling rate to obtain different compression results. MP3 (Layer 3)–the norm for digital music today–typically compresses a CD-quality song to about one-tenth of its original size. For example, the 32 MB Norah Jones song shown in the accompanying illustration compresses to less than 3 MB after it is converted to an MP3 file. Because of its efficiency, the MP3 format is widely used for music downloaded from the Internet, as well as when music is copied from a CD to a PC or digital music player. Because of their smaller file sizes, MP3 files can be downloaded in minutes rather than hours, and hundreds of MP3 files can be stored on a single storage medium.

MP3 utilizes two compression techniques. The first technique uses the principle of *perceptual coding*; that is, removing the parts of the song that the human ear would not hear anyway, such as sounds that occur in frequencies too high or too low to be perceived by the human ear or soft sounds that are played at the same time as louder sounds. Although data is lost by this compression technique, the lost data is considered superfluous, so the size of the song is reduced without significantly altering the quality of the song. The second compression technique, called *Huffman coding*, substitutes shorter strings of bits for frequently used larger strings. Since the bits are reconstructed when the song is played, no information is lost during this process. The resulting MP3 file–saved with the file extension *.mp3*–can then be played on a PC using media player software, burned onto a CD, or copied to a digital music player.

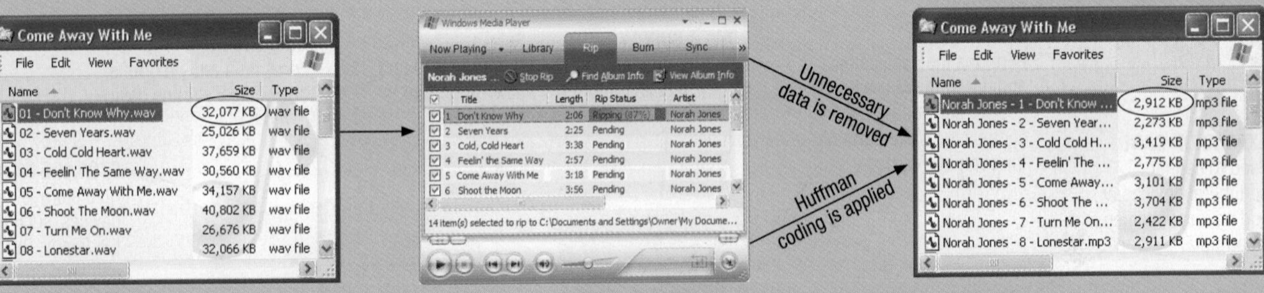

1. CD (WAV format) version of song: 32 MB.
2. Software removes the unnecessary parts of the song and codes the song in the MP3 format.
3. MP3 version of song: 2.9 MB.

Video Data

Video data—such as home movies, feature films, and television shows—is displayed using a collection of frames; each frame contains a still graphical image. When the frames are projected one after the other—typically at a rate of 30 frames per second—the illusion of movement is created. With so many frames, the amount of data involved in showing a two-hour feature film can be substantial. For instance, one frame containing a single 256-color image shown on a 640-by-480-pixel display requires 307,200 bytes. When you multiply that figure by 30 frames per second, 60 seconds per minute, and 120 minutes, you get more than 66 gigabytes of information for a typical two-hour movie. Fortunately, like audio data, video data can be compressed to reduce it to a manageable size. For example, a two-hour movie can be compressed to less than 8.5 GB to fit on a single DVD disc.

Representing Programs: Machine Language

Just like data, which must be represented by 0s and 1s, programs also need to be represented in binary form. Before a computer can execute any program instruction, such as requesting input from the user, moving a block of data from one place to another, or opening a new window on the screen, it must convert the instruction into a binary code known as **machine language**. An example of a typical machine language instruction is:

01011000011100000000000100000010

A machine language instruction might look like a meaningless string of 0s and 1s, but it actually represents specific operations and storage locations. The 32-bit instruction shown here, for instance, moves data between two specific memory locations on one type of computer system. Similar instructions transfer data from memory to other locations, add or subtract values in memory, and so on. Early computers required programs to be written in machine language, but today's programs are not. Instead, the programs are translated into machine language in order to be understood by the computer. Programming languages and *language translators* are discussed in more detail in Chapter 13.

INSIDE THE SYSTEM UNIT

The **system unit** is the main case of a computer. It houses the processing hardware for that computer, as well as a few other devices, such as disk drives, memory, the power supply, and cooling fans. The system unit for a desktop PC often looks like a rectangular box, although other shapes and sizes are available, such as the all-in-one PC illustrated in Figure 1-14 and the modified PCs shown in the Chapter 1 Inside the Industry box. The inside of a system unit for a typical desktop PC system is shown in Figure 2-6. In general, the system unit contains one or more *CPUs*, several types of *memory*, interfaces to connect external *peripheral*

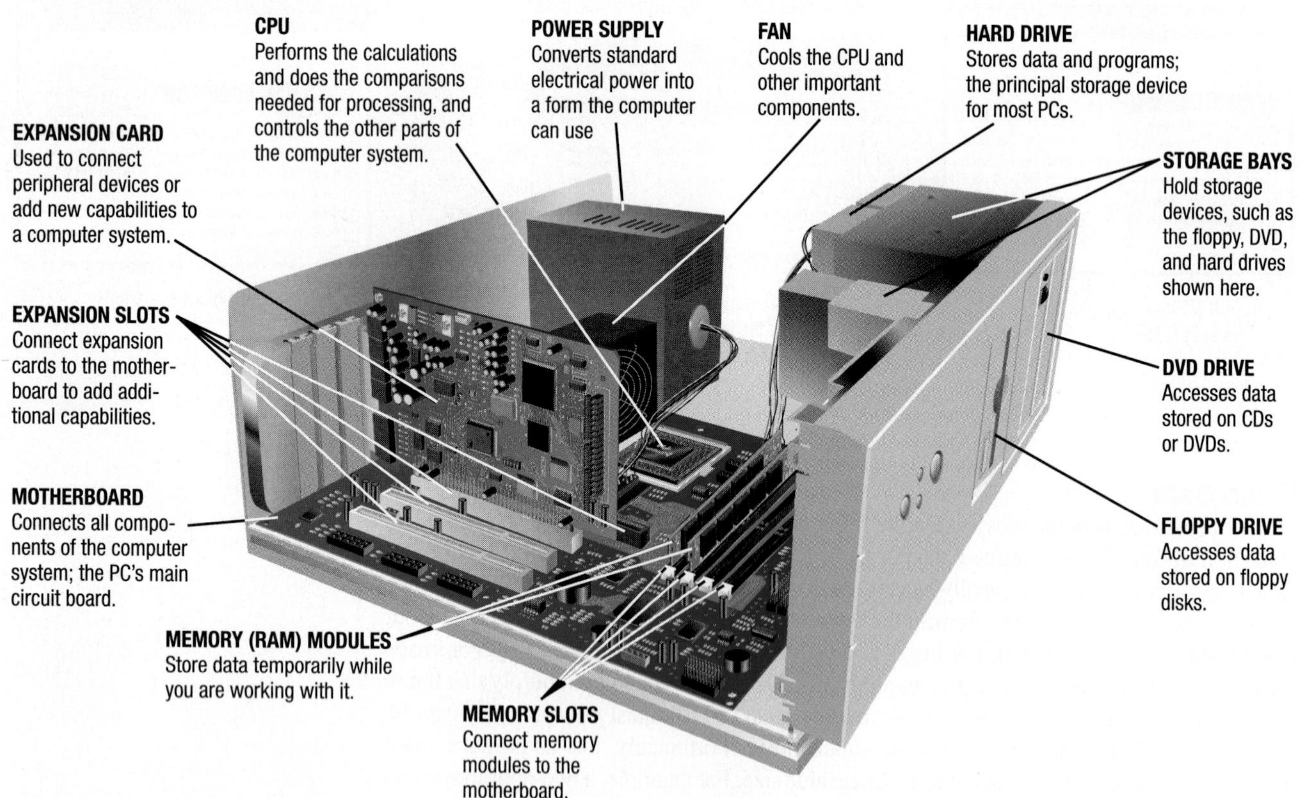
CPU
Performs the calculations and does the comparisons needed for processing, and controls the other parts of the computer system.
POWER SUPPLY
Converts standard electrical power into a form the computer can use
FAN
Cools the CPU and other important components.
HARD DRIVE
Stores data and programs; the principal storage device for most PCs.
EXPANSION CARD
Used to connect peripheral devices or add new capabilities to a computer system.
STORAGE BAYS
Hold storage devices, such as the floppy, DVD, and hard drives shown here.
EXPANSION SLOTS
Connect expansion cards to the motherboard to add additional capabilities.
DVD DRIVE
Accesses data stored on CDs or DVDs.
MOTHERBOARD
Connects all components of the computer system; the PC's main circuit board.
FLOPPY DRIVE
Accesses data stored on floppy disks.
MEMORY (RAM) MODULES
Store data temporarily while you are working with it.
MEMORY SLOTS
Connect memory modules to the motherboard.

FIGURE 2-6
Inside a typical system unit. The system unit houses the CPU, memory, and other important pieces of hardware.

>**Machine language.** A binary-based language for representing computer programs that the computer can execute directly. >**System unit.** The main box of a computer that houses the CPU, motherboard, memory, and other devices.

devices (such as printers), and other components all interconnected through sets of wires called *buses* on the *motherboard*. All of these components are discussed in the next few sections. Portable PCs have similar components, but many of the components are smaller and the system unit is typically combined with the computer screen to form a single piece of hardware.

The Motherboard

A *circuit board* is a thin board containing *chips*—very small pieces of silicon or other semiconducting material onto which *integrated circuits* are embedded—and other electronic components. The main circuit board inside the system unit is called the **motherboard** or *system board*. As shown in Figure 2-6, the motherboard has a variety of chips and boards attached to it; in fact, all devices used with a computer need to be connected in one way or another to the motherboard. Typically, *external* devices (such as monitors, keyboards, mice, and printers) connect to the motherboard by plugging into a *port*—a special connector exposed through the exterior of the system unit case. The port is either built directly into the motherboard, or it is created via an *expansion card* inserted into an *expansion slot* on the motherboard. A wireless device typically has a *transceiver* that plugs into a port to transmit data between the device and the motherboard. Ports and system expansion are discussed in more detail later in this chapter.

The CPU

The **central processing unit (CPU)** consists of a variety of circuitry and components packaged together on one chip, which is plugged directly into the motherboard. The CPU—also called the **microprocessor** (when talking about PCs) or just the **processor** (when speaking in general terms for any computer)—does the vast majority of the processing for a computer.

Most PCs today use CPUs manufactured by Intel or Advanced Micro Devices (AMD); some examples of their processors are shown in Figure 2-7. CPUs commonly used with desktop PCs include the Intel *Pentium 4* and AMD *Athlon 64*. Newer *dual-core CPUs* (CPUs that contain the processing components—or *cores*—of two separate, independent processors on a single CPU) include the Intel *Pentium D* and AMD *Athlon 64 X2*. Lower-end home PCs may use a CPU belonging to the Intel *Celeron* or AMD *Sempron* microprocessor families. Typically, portable computers use either desktop PC CPUs or similar microprocessors designed for portable PC use, such as the Intel *Pentium M* or AMD *Turion 64*. Among other things, processors designed for portable PC use typically run a little slower than comparable desktop CPUs, but run cooler and consume less power to allow the portable PCs to run

FIGURE 2-7

CPUs. Shown here are the Pentium D and Athlon 64 (for desktop PCs) and the Pentium M (for portable PCs).

INTEL PENTIUM D

AMD ATHLON 64

INTEL PENTIUM M

>**Motherboard.** The main circuit board of a computer, located inside the system unit, to which all computer system components connect.
>**Central processing unit (CPU).** The chip located inside the system unit of a computer that performs the processing for a computer.
>**Microprocessor.** A central processing unit (CPU) for a microcomputer. Also called processor. >**Processor.** Another name for central processing unit (CPU).

TECHNOLOGY AND YOU

CPUs and Running Shoes

We all know that CPUs are incorporated into all PCs and many other electronic devices, but running shoes?

Yes, if the new Adidas smart running shoe takes off. This shoe—called the *Adidas 1*—uses a processor in conjunction with a sensor and motorized system (see the accompanying photo) to automatically adjust the shoes' cushioning to adapt to the surface the runner is currently on. For example, the cushion becomes more rigid on dirt trails and softer on pavement or when the runner is walking. Sensor readings are taken on a continual basis (at a rate of about 1,000 readings per second), and the cushioning is adjusted when the shoe is in midair. The shoe's processor is capable of making five million calculations per second and is controlled by software also built into the shoe.

The Adidas 1 runs on replaceable batteries that are estimated to have a life of about 100 hours of running. Users can override or turn off the shoe's adjustment feature, when desired. The shoe also stops adjusting the cushioning if the runner walks more than 10 minutes. According to Adidas, the changes are so gradual and automatic that they are not noticeable to the runner—he or she just notices that the shoe feels right during an entire run. Now that is one smart shoe.

longer on battery power without a recharge. Powerful *workstations* (powerful PCs designed for users running engineering and other applications requiring extra processing capabilities) and servers use more powerful microprocessors, such as Intel's *Xeon* and *Itanium 2*, AMD's *Opteron*, IBM's *Power5*, and Sun's *UltraSPARC* microprocessors. Apple Macintosh computers traditionally use *PowerPC* processors—CPUs, such as the *G5*, that were originally developed through the cooperative efforts of Apple, Motorola, and IBM. However, Apple has announced that it will begin using Intel microprocessors for at least some Macs beginning in 2006. Selected CPUs introduced since 2000 are summarized in Figure 2-8; the characteristics listed in Figure 2-8 are discussed next.

FURTHER EXPLORATION

For links to further information about CPUs, go to www.course.com/uc11/ch02

In addition to computers, CPUs are incorporated into a number of other devices, such as appliances, cars, game boxes, and more. These CPUs are typically different from the ones used in computers. For instance, the CPU designed for the Sony PlayStation 3 is a powerful new processor named *Cell*. Cell is designed to process large volumes of high-definition content. It has nine cores and operates at 256 billion *floating point operations per second* (256 *gigaflops*)—as fast as a 1990's era supercomputer and 40 times faster than the CPU in the Sony PlayStation 2. The Cell microprocessor is not initially expected to be used for conventional PCs, but Sony and Toshiba have announced plans to incorporate the Cell processor into high-definition TVs and other home entertainment and media devices. For a look at an unusual product that uses a CPU—running shoes—see the Technology and You box.

Processing Speed

One measurement of the speed of a CPU is the *CPU clock speed*, which is rated in *megahertz (MHz)* or *gigahertz (GHz)*. A higher CPU clock speed means that more instructions can be processed per second than the same CPU with a lower CPU clock speed. For instance, a Pentium 4 microprocessor running at 3.6 GHz would be faster than a Pentium 4 running at 2.8 GHz, if all other components remained the same. CPUs for the earliest PCs ran at less than 5 MHz; today's fastest CPUs run at 3.8 GHz. Although CPU clock speed is

Read-Only Memory (ROM)

ROM (read-only memory) consists of nonvolatile chips that permanently store data or programs. Like RAM, these chips are attached to the motherboard inside the system unit, and the data or programs are retrieved by the computer when they are needed. An important difference, however, is that you can neither write over the data or programs in ROM chips (which is the reason ROM chips are called *read-only*), nor destroy their contents when you shut off the computer's power.

FURTHER EXPLORATION

For links to further information about memory, go to www.course.com/uc11/ch02

Flash Memory

Flash memory (sometimes called *flash RAM*) is a type of nonvolatile memory into which data can be stored and retrieved. Data is stored in flash memory in blocks, which are erased in a single action or *flash*. Flash memory chips (see Figure 2-11) have begun to replace ROM for storing system information, such as a PC's *BIOS* or *basic input/output system*—the sequence of instructions the PC follows during the boot process. For instance, one of the computer's first activities when you turn on the power is to perform a *power-on self-test* or *POST*. The POST takes an inventory of system components, checks each component for proper functioning, and initializes system settings, which produces the beeps you hear as your PC boots. Traditionally, the instructions for the POST have been stored in ROM. By storing this information in flash memory instead of ROM, the BIOS information can be updated as needed.

FIGURE 2-11
Flash memory chips.

In addition to PCs, devices such as portable PCs, cell phones, digital cameras, MP3 players, and other small devices can contain built-in flash memory. While some built-in flash memory chips are used only by the computer, other flash memory chips are designed to be used by the user for storage purposes. Flash memory chips used for storage are either built directly into a device (such as a PC, cell phone, digital cameras, MP3 player, or other small device) or incorporated into removable *flash memory cards* or *flash memory drives*. Flash memory storage devices and media are discussed in more detail in Chapter 3.

Fans, Heat Sinks, and Other Cooling Components

One byproduct of packing an increasing amount of technology in a smaller system unit is heat, a continuing problem for CPU and computer manufacturers. Since heat can damage components and cooler chips can run faster, virtually all computers today employ *fans*, *heat sinks* (small components typically made out of aluminum with fins that help to dissipate heat), or other methods to cool the CPU and system unit. One of the newest cooling methods being used with PCs uses liquid-filled tubes that act as radiators to draw heat away from processors. For example, *water cooling systems* are now available. Although initially expensive, difficult to install, and complicated to use, these systems are now available in simpler and less expensive formats. An added bonus of water-cooled PCs is that they are quieter than conventional systems.

Expansion Slots and Cards

Most desktop PCs have **expansion slots** located on the motherboard into which **expansion cards** (also called *add-in boards*, *interface cards*, and *adapter boards*) can be inserted. Expansion cards are used to give the PC additional capabilities, such as to add network or Internet connectivity or to connect a monitor or set of speakers to the computer. Today, many basic capabilities are being integrated directly into the motherboard. When this occurs—such as with *integrated sound* or *integrated graphics*—an expansion card is not

>**Read-only memory (ROM).** Nonerasable chips located on the motherboard into which data or programs have been permanently stored.
>**Flash memory.** A type of nonvolatile memory that can be erased and reprogrammed; commonly implemented in the form of sticks or cards.
>**Expansion slot.** A location on the motherboard into which expansion cards are inserted. >**Expansion card.** A circuit board that can be inserted into an expansion slot on a PC's motherboard to add additional functionality or to attach a peripheral device.

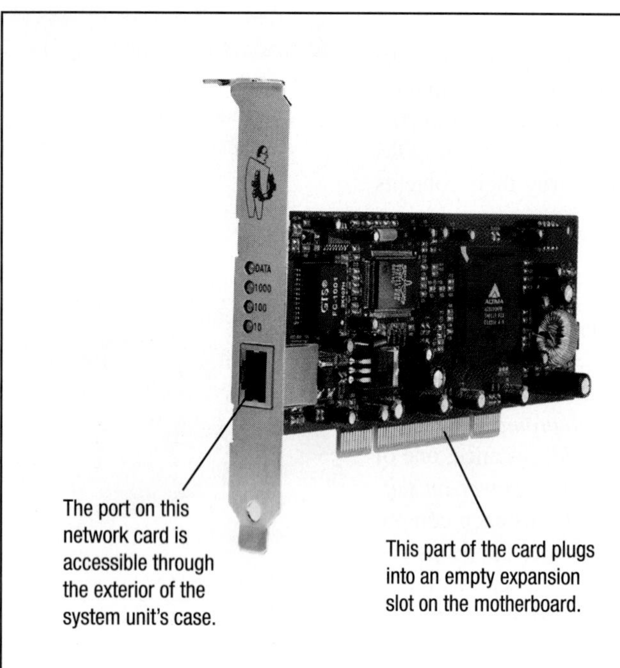

The port on this network card is accessible through the exterior of the system unit's case.
This part of the card plugs into an empty expansion slot on the motherboard.

COMMON EXPANSION CARDS

Card Type	Purpose
Accelerator board	Uses specialized processor chips that speed up overall processing.
Disk controller card	Enables a particular type of disk drive to interface with the PC.
Modem card	Provides communications capabilities to connect to a network or the Internet.
Network interface card	Enables a PC to connect to a network.
Sound card	Enables users to attach speakers to a PC and provides sound capabilities.
TV tuner card	Allows a PC to pick up television signals.
USB or FireWire card	Adds one or both of these ports to the PC.
Video capture board	Allows video images to be input into the computer from a video camera.
Video graphics board	Enables the connection of a monitor; may provide additional graphics capabilities.

FIGURE 2-12
Expansion cards for desktop PCs.

needed. Most new desktop PCs come with a few empty expansion slots on the motherboard so that new capabilities can be added, when needed. Figure 2-12 shows a typical expansion card and lists some examples of common expansion cards. As shown in this figure, expansion cards designed to connect external devices (such as a monitor, printer, scanner, or networking cable) have a *port* that is exposed through the case of the system unit to connect that device. Ports are discussed in more detail shortly.

Buses

As already discussed, a bus is an electronic path within a computer over which data travels. A variety of buses are used to tie the CPU to memory and to peripheral devices. The bus that moves data back and forth between the CPU and memory is typically called the *system bus*. Usually a *chipset* is used between the CPU and RAM (see Figure 2-13); if so, the part of the system bus between the CPU and the chipset is called the *frontside bus* (*FSB*). If external cache exists, the *backside bus* (*BSB*) transfers data between that cache and the CPU. Many CPUs today have 64-bit system buses, although the speed of the system bus varies. Generally a faster system bus indicates a faster PC, and a faster frontside bus creates less of a bottleneck in the overall performance of the system.

The buses that connect the CPU to peripheral (typically input and output) devices are usually referred to as **expansion buses**. Expansion buses are etched onto the motherboard and vary in width and speed. They either connect the CPU directly to *ports* on the system unit case or to expansion slots on the motherboard (some of the most common expansion buses and expansion slots are illustrated in Figure 2-13). It is important to realize that expansion slots are not interchangeable—each type of expansion slot is designed for a specific type of expansion card, such as *PCI*, *PCI Express* (*PCIe*), or *AGP*. Some of the most common types of expansion buses are discussed next.

TIP

The various PCI and PCI Express expansion slots are different sizes, and neither the slots nor the cards are interchangeable. Be sure to check the format of any empty expansion slot in your PC before buying a new expansion card.

>**Expansion bus.** A bus that connects the CPU to peripheral devices.

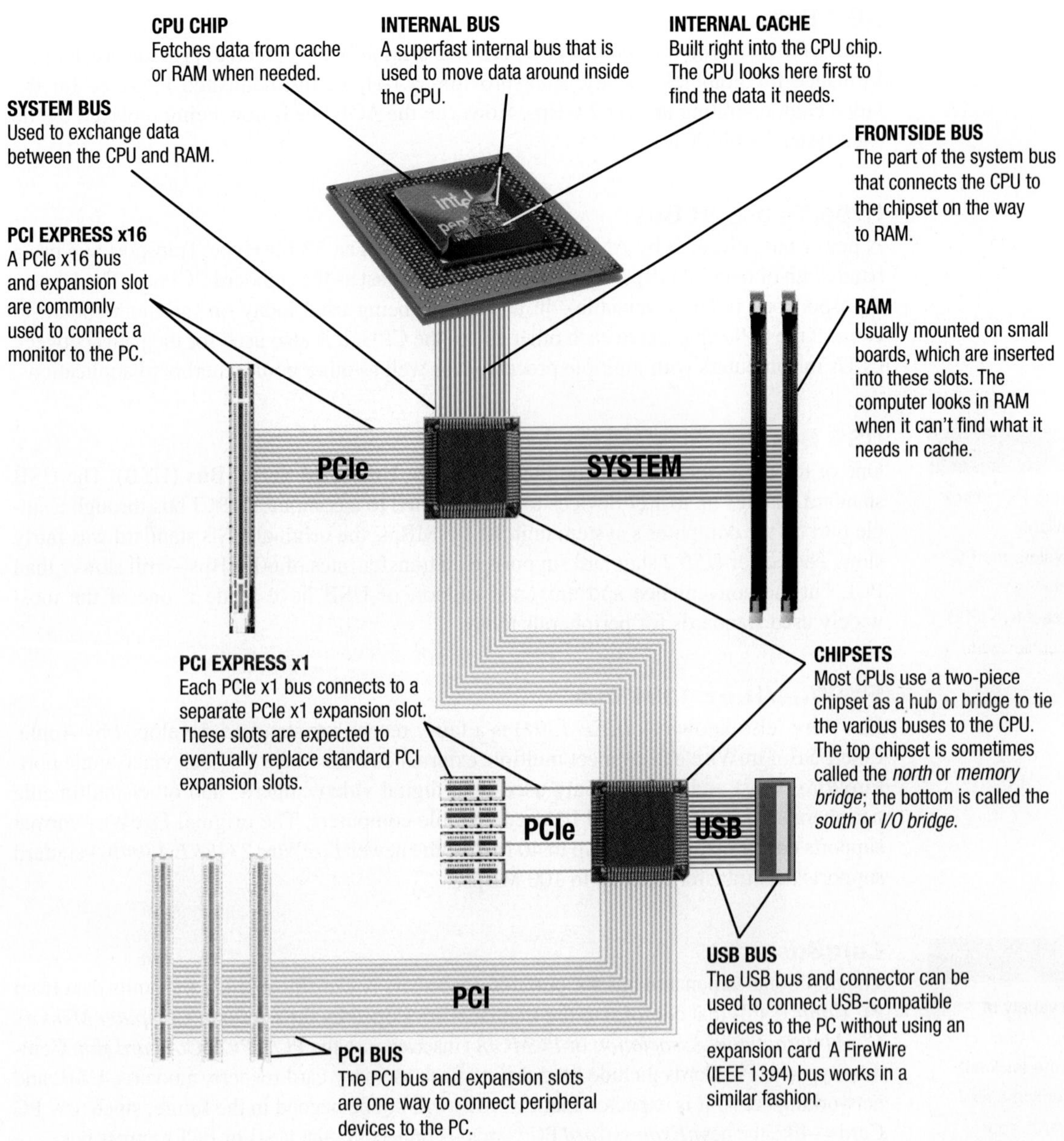

CPU CHIP
Fetches data from cache or RAM when needed.
INTERNAL BUS
A superfast internal bus that is used to move data around inside the CPU.
INTERNAL CACHE
Built right into the CPU chip. The CPU looks here first to find the data it needs.
SYSTEM BUS
Used to exchange data between the CPU and RAM.
FRONTSIDE BUS
The part of the system bus that connects the CPU to the chipset on the way to RAM.
PCI EXPRESS x16
A PCIe x16 bus and expansion slot are commonly used to connect a monitor to the PC.
RAM
Usually mounted on small boards, which are inserted into these slots. The computer looks in RAM when it can't find what it needs in cache.
PCIe
SYSTEM
PCI EXPRESS x1
Each PCIe x1 bus connects to a separate PCIe x1 expansion slot. These slots are expected to eventually replace standard PCI expansion slots.
CHIPSETS
Most CPUs use a two-piece chipset as a hub or bridge to tie the various buses to the CPU. The top chipset is sometimes called the north or memory bridge; the bottom is called the south or I/O bridge.
PCIe
USB
USB BUS
The USB bus and connector can be used to connect USB-compatible devices to the PC without using an expansion card A FireWire (IEEE 1394) bus works in a similar fashion.
PCI
PCI BUS
The PCI bus and expansion slots are one way to connect peripheral devices to the PC.
HW

FIGURE 2-13

Buses. Buses transport bits and bytes from one component to another, including the CPU, cache, RAM, and peripheral devices.

PCI and PCI Express Bus

The *PCI* (*Peripheral Component Interconnect*) bus has been one of the most common types of expansion buses in past years. It can be implemented as a 64-bit bus, but most PCs use a 32-bit PCI bus that has a bandwidth of 133 *MBps* (*megabytes per second*). The newest version of PCI is called **PCI Express (PCIe)**, formally known as *3GIO* for *third-generation input output*. A 16-bit version of PCIe (referred to as *PCIe x16*) is commonly used with *video cards* (to connect a monitor to a PC); other peripherals usually use a 1-bit PCIe bus (referred to as *PCIe x1*). PCIe is extremely fast—the 1-bit PCIe bus, at 500 MBps, is approximately four times faster than a regular PCI; PCIe x16 is significantly faster at 8 GBps.

>**PCI Express (PCIe).** One of the buses most commonly used to connect peripheral devices.

AGP Bus

The *AGP* (*Accelerated Graphics Port*) bus was originally developed to provide greater performance for graphics display. AGP provides a fast, 32-bit, dedicated interface for the video card, operating at over 2 GBps. However, the AGP bus is now being replaced by the even faster 16-bit PCIe.

HyperTransport Bus

A newer bus, invented by AMD, is *HyperTransport*. The 32-bit HyperTransport bus has a bandwidth of over 22 GBps—roughly 165 times as fast as the standard PCI bus. The HyperTransport bus is fairly versatile—in addition to being used today on the motherboard to connect the CPU chipsets to each other and to the CPU, it is also used for the paths between CPUs in computers with multiple processors as well as other nonmotherboard applications.

TIP

When buying a desktop PC, check to see how many available (nonused) expansion slots the PC has and what types they are. You should also have at least two USB ports to add additional hardware available in USB format.

USB Bus

One of the more versatile bus architectures is the **Universal Serial Bus (USB)**. The USB standard enables up to 127 devices to be connected to a computer's PCI bus through a single port on the computer's system unit. At 1.5 MBps, the original USB standard was fairly slow. The newer *USB 2* standard supports data transfer rates of 60 MBps—still slower than PCI, but the convenience and universal support of USB have made it one of the most widely used standards for peripherals today.

FireWire/IEEE 1394 Bus

FireWire (also known as *IEEE 1394*) is a fairly recent bus standard developed by Apple. Like USB, FireWire can connect multiple external devices to the PCI bus via a single port. FireWire is fast and is commonly used with digital video cameras and other multimedia peripherals for both Apple and IBM-compatible computers. The original FireWire format supports data transfer rates of up to 40 MBps; the newer *FireWire 2* (*IEEE 1394b*) standard supports data transfer rates up to 100 MBps.

TIP

PC Cards come in a variety of thicknesses–from *Type I* (the thinnest) to *Type III* (the thickest). It is a good idea to verify the size and number of PC Cards your notebook computer can support before buying a PC Card.

CardBus

The traditional expansion bus for portable computers is *CardBus*, which transmits data from *PC Cards* (cards that conform to the standards developed by the *Personal Computer Memory Card International Association* or *PCMCIA*) inserted into the PC's *PCMCIA card slot*. Common types of PC Cards include hard drives, flash memory card readers, modems, USB, and networking cards. It is expected that CardBus will not be needed in the future, since new PC Cards—like the new *ExpressCard* PC Cards—connect via the USB or PCI Express bus.

Ports

As already mentioned, **ports** are the connectors located on the exterior of the system unit that are used to connect external hardware devices. Each port is attached to the appropriate bus on the motherboard so that when a device is plugged into a port, the device can communicate with the CPU. Typical ports for a desktop PC are shown in Figure 2-14. As shown in this figure, there are unique connectors for each type of port on a computer system. When connecting cables to the system unit, it is important to pay attention to the *gender* of the port, in addition to the shape, pin count, and pin configuration. *Male* connectors have the pins extended and connect to *female* connectors with matching holes. If a port is of the proper

>**Universal Serial Bus (USB).** A universal bus used to connect up to 127 peripheral devices to a computer without requiring the use of additional expansion cards. >**FireWire.** A bus standard often used to connect digital video cameras to a PC. >**Port.** A connector on the exterior of a PC's system unit to which a device may be attached.

type (such as serial), but is the wrong gender or has the wrong number of pins, adapters or special cables can sometimes be used to convert the connector to the desired configuration.

If you want to add a new device to your PC and there is an available port for the device you want to add, then you just need to plug it in (shut down the computer first, unless the device uses a USB or FireWire port). Most computers today support the *Plug and Play* standard, in which the computer automatically configures new devices as soon as they are installed. If the appropriate port is not available, you need to either insert the appropriate expansion card to create one or use a USB or FireWire version of the device, if you have one of those two ports available on your PC. Because a wide variety of hardware is available in USB format today, most recent PCs come with at least two USB ports. In fact, it is becoming common to see multiple USB ports located on the front of a system unit for easier access, such as to connect a digital camera or USB flash memory drive on a regular basis. Front slots for the flash memory cards used with digital music players and digital cameras are also common today (see Figure 2-15). USB and FireWire devices can be plugged into USB and FireWire ports while the computer is powered up; they are recognized by the computer as soon as they are connected to it and can be used right away.

Some of the most common ports are discussed next; some of the oldest types—such as *serial* and *parallel* ports—are increasingly being referred to as *legacy ports* and are being phased out on newer PCs.

- *Serial ports* can transmit data only a single bit at a time. However, they use very inexpensive cables, and they can send data over long distances reliably. Serial ports can be used for such devices as keyboards, mice, and modems, although most systems today come with dedicated ports to attach the mouse and keyboard, as shown in Figure 2-14. *Serial connectors* typically have 9 or 25 pins and are referred to as *DB-9* or *DB-25 connectors*, respectively.

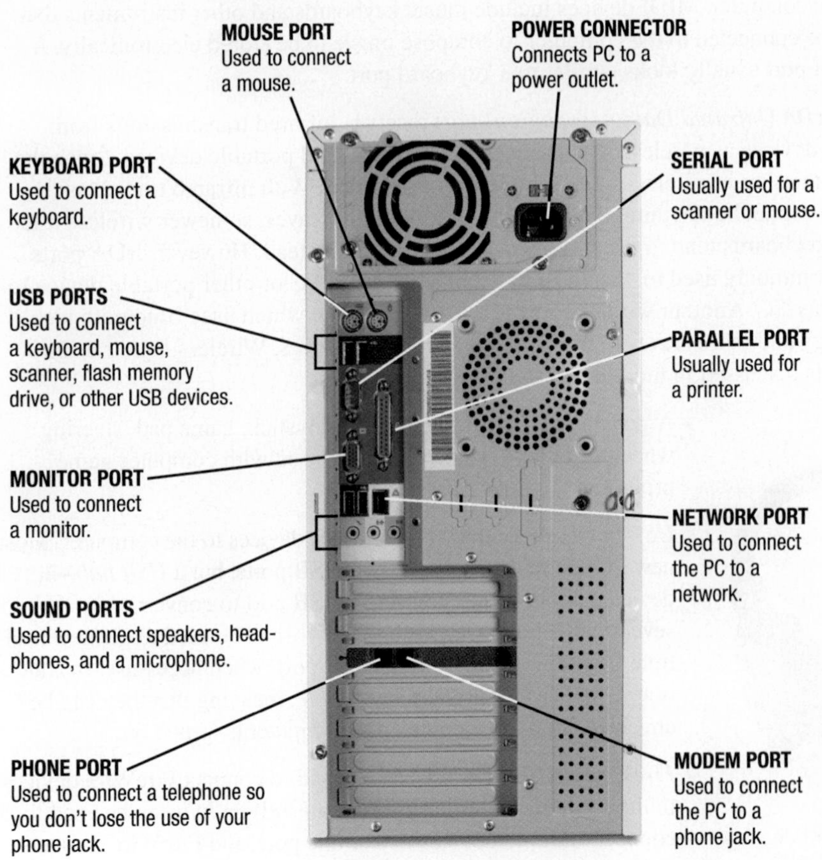
MOUSE PORT
Used to connect a mouse.
POWER CONNECTOR
Connects PC to a power outlet.
KEYBOARD PORT
Used to connect a keyboard.
SERIAL PORT
Usually used for a scanner or mouse.
USB PORTS
Used to connect a keyboard, mouse, scanner, flash memory drive, or other USB devices.
PARALLEL PORT
Usually used for a printer.
MONITOR PORT
Used to connect a monitor.
NETWORK PORT
Used to connect the PC to a network.
SOUND PORTS
Used to connect speakers, headphones, and a microphone.
PHONE PORT
Used to connect a telephone so you don't lose the use of your phone jack.
MODEM PORT
Used to connect the PC to a phone jack.

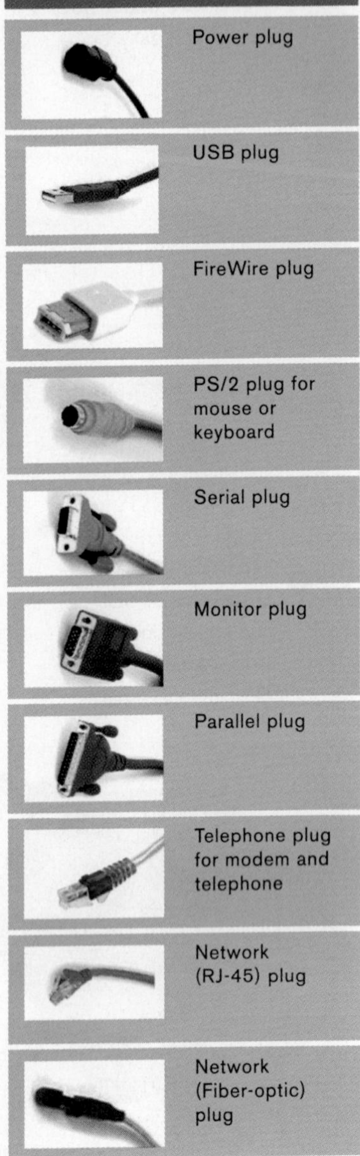
CONNECTORS
Power plug
USB plug
FireWire plug
PS/2 plug for mouse or keyboard
Serial plug
Monitor plug
Parallel plug
Telephone plug for modem and telephone
Network (RJ-45) plug
Network (Fiber-optic) plug

FIGURE 2-14
Typical ports and connectors for a desktop PC.

HW

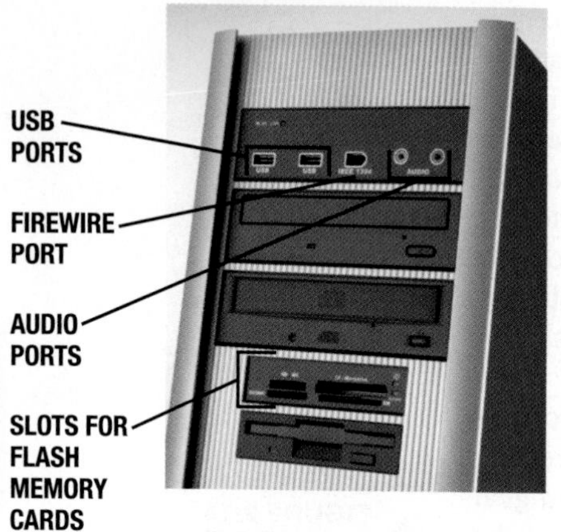

FIGURE 2-15
Front ports. Many computers today come with a variety of ports on the front of the system unit for easy access.

- *Parallel ports* can transmit data one byte (8 bits) at a time—making data transfers several times faster than those through serial ports—but they require more expensive cables and cannot send data reliably across distances greater than 50 feet. Consequently, parallel ports typically connect nearby printers to a PC. Newer types of parallel ports include the *Enhanced Parallel Port* (*EPP*) and the *Extended Capabilities Port* (*ECP*). These ports look like conventional parallel ports and accept the same size and shape of plug as the conventional parallel port (a 25-pin connector), but are more than 10 times faster when used with an appropriate cable.
- *Network ports* are used to connect a PC to a local area network. Most network cards contain a port that accepts an *RJ-45 connector*, which looks similar to a telephone connector but is larger. Coaxial cable or fiber optic connectors can be used for network connections, as well. Networks are discussed in more detail in Chapter 7.

- The *keyboard port* and the *mouse port* typically use a *PS/2 connector* and are used to connect the keyboard and mouse to the system unit. Some mice and keyboards today connect via a USB port instead.
- The *monitor port* is used to connect the monitor to a PC. Some computers also come with an *S-video* port that can be used to connect the computer to a television or other S-video device.
- The *modem port* and *phone port* are used to connect the PC to a phone outlet and then connect a telephone to the phone jack, respectively.
- *SCSI* (*Small Computer System Interface*) *ports* are high-speed parallel ports generally used to attach printers, scanners, and hard drives.
- A *MIDI port* is used to connect a *MIDI* (*musical instrument digital interface*) device to the computer. MIDI devices include music keyboards and other instruments that can be connected to the computer to compose music to be stored electronically. A MIDI port usually looks similar to a keyboard port.
- An *IrDA* (*Infrared Data Association*) *port* receives infrared transmissions from such devices as wireless keyboards, wireless mice, and portable devices. Since the transmission is wireless, the port does not use a plug. With infrared transmission, there cannot be anything blocking the infrared light waves, so newer wireless mice and keyboards tend to use radio wave transmission instead. However, IrDA ports are commonly used to "beam" data from a handheld PC or other portable device to another PC. Another wireless port is a *Bluetooth port*, which uses Bluetooth technology and radio waves to transmit data between devices. Wireless data transmission is discussed in more detail in Chapter 7.

FIGURE 2-16
USB hubs. A USB hub can be used to connect multiple USB devices to a single USB port.

- A *game port* is used to connect a joystick, game pad, steering wheel, or other device commonly used with computer game programs.
- *USB ports* are used to connect USB devices to the computer. Most new PCs come with at least two USB ports, but a *USB hub*—a device that plugs into your PC's USB port to convert one port into several USB ports (see Figure 2-16)—can be used to connect multiple USB devices to a single USB port, when necessary. In addition, USB devices are *hot-swappable*, meaning that they can be attached and removed while the computer is turned on.
- *FireWire* (*IEEE 1394*) *ports* are used to connect FireWire devices to the computer. Similar to USB, a *FireWire hub* can be used to connect multiple devices to a single port, and FireWire devices are hot-swappable.

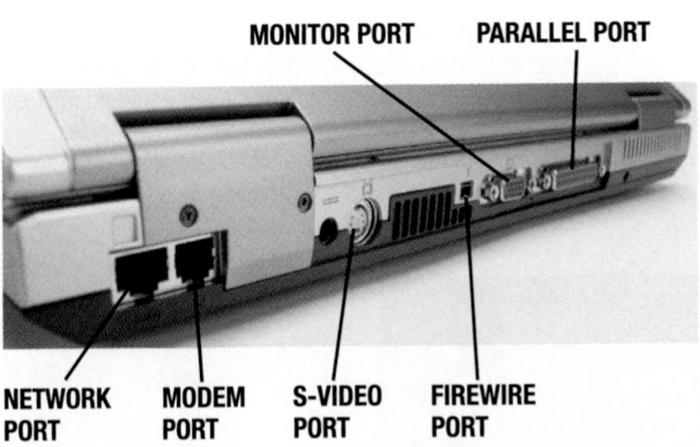

FIGURE 2-17

Notebook ports. Shown here are typical ports on the back (left) and side (right) of a typical notebook PC.

Notebook computers have ports similar to desktop PCs, but usually they do not have as many. One type of port found on notebook computers but not on desktop PCs is a port used to connect a *port replicator*. A port replicator is a hardware device containing additional ports (such as serial, parallel, PS/2, USB, and networking ports) that can be used with the notebook computer whenever the port replicator is connected to it (some port replicators connect via a USB or PC card slot instead). Some typical notebook ports are illustrated in Figure 2-17.

Most handheld PCs and mobile devices have a limited amount of expandability, but usually come with at least one built-in expansion slot that can be used to attach peripheral devices, such as modems, networking adapters, MP3 players, digital cameras, fingerprint readers, barcode scanners, and GPS receivers. Most often, the expansion slot is an *SD slot*, which can be used with both the postage-stamp-size *Secure Digital* (*SD*) flash memory cards and with hardware adhering to the *Secure Digital Input/Output* (*SDIO*) standard (see Figure 2-18). Some handheld PCs support additional types of flash memory cards or have a proprietary expansion slot designed only for hardware made for that device; a few include a PC card slot. More commonly, portable PCs are coming with an *ExpressCard port* that supports the new type of ExpressCard PC cards that are expected to eventually replace PCMCIA PC cards. Many portable PCs and some smart phones also have a port to connect a special portable keyboard designed for the device.

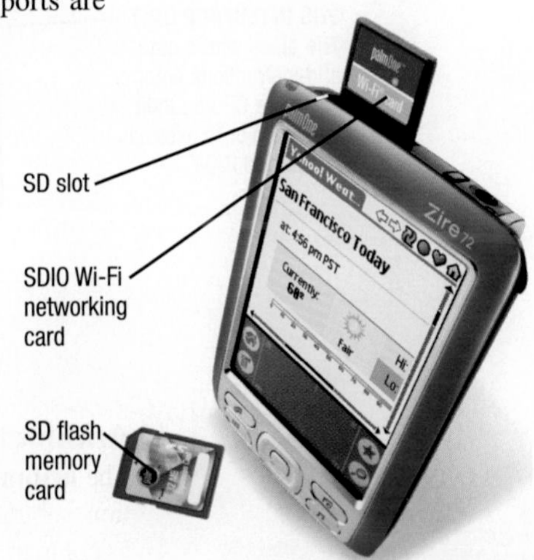

FIGURE 2-18

Handheld PC expansion. Most handheld PCs and smart phones have at least an SD-compatible expansion slot for expansion.

HOW THE CPU WORKS

As already discussed, a CPU consists of a variety of circuitry and components packaged together. The key element of the microprocessor is the *transistor*—a device made of semiconductor material that acts like a switch controlling the flow of electrons inside a chip. Today's CPUs contain hundreds of millions of transistors, and the number doubles approximately every 18 months. This phenomenon is known as *Moore's Law* and is explained in the Inside the Industry box. The primary components of a typical CPU are discussed next.

Typical CPU Components

To begin to understand how a CPU works, you need to know how the CPU is organized and what components it includes. This information will help you understand how electronic impulses move from one part of the CPU to another to process data. The architecture and components included in a CPU (referred to as *microarchitecture*) vary from microprocessor to microprocessor. A simplified example of the principal components that might be included in a typical CPU is shown in Figure 2-19 and discussed next. For a look at the companies that are used to examine the parts of a CPU or other computer component to gather evidence for patent lawsuits, see the Trend box.

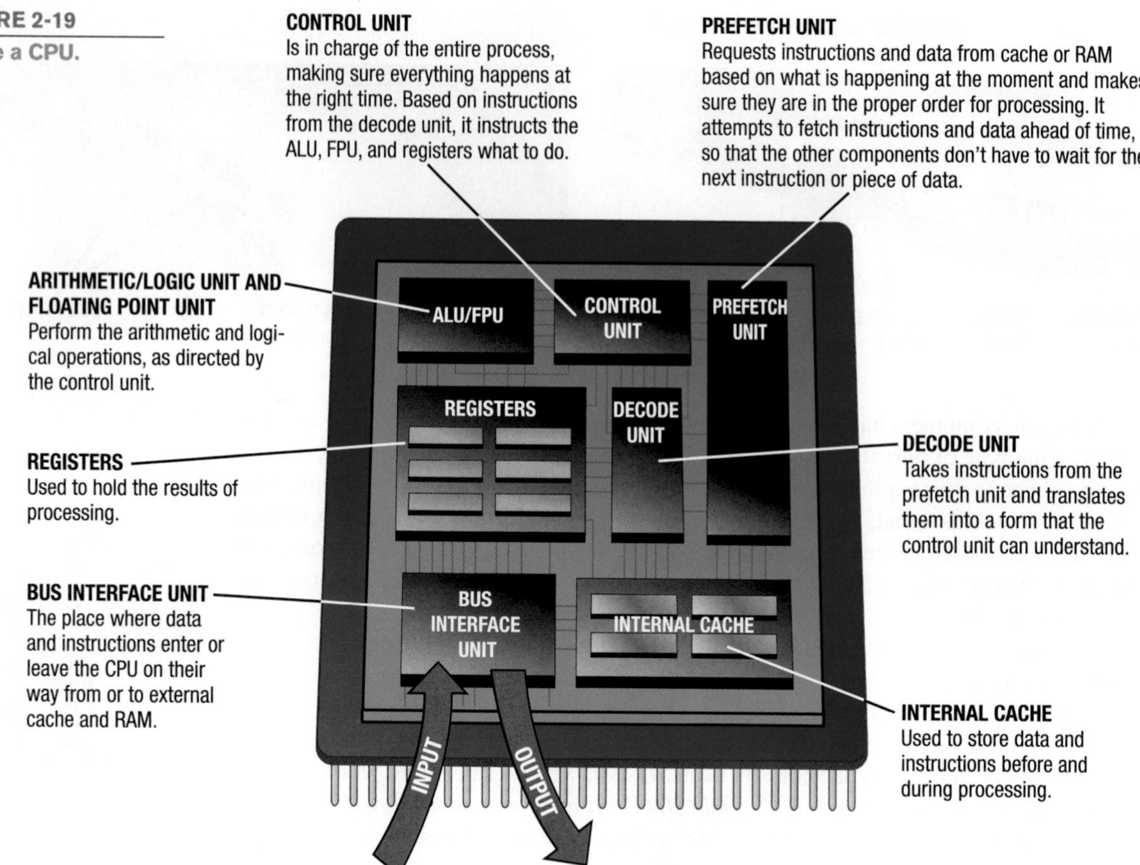
CONTROL UNIT
Is in charge of the entire process, making sure everything happens at the right time. Based on instructions from the decode unit, it instructs the ALU, FPU, and registers what to do.
PREFETCH UNIT
Requests instructions and data from cache or RAM based on what is happening at the moment and makes sure they are in the proper order for processing. It attempts to fetch instructions and data ahead of time, so that the other components don't have to wait for the next instruction or piece of data.
ARITHMETIC/LOGIC UNIT AND FLOATING POINT UNIT
Perform the arithmetic and logical operations, as directed by the control unit.
REGISTERS
Used to hold the results of processing.
BUS INTERFACE UNIT
The place where data and instructions enter or leave the CPU on their way from or to external cache and RAM.
DECODE UNIT
Takes instructions from the prefetch unit and translates them into a form that the control unit can understand.
INTERNAL CACHE
Used to store data and instructions before and during processing.
ALU/FPU
CONTROL UNIT
PREFETCH UNIT
REGISTERS
DECODE UNIT
BUS INTERFACE UNIT
INTERNAL CACHE
INPUT
OUTPUT

FIGURE 2-19
Inside a CPU.

Arithmetic/Logic Unit (ALU) and Floating Point Unit (FPU)

The **arithmetic/logic unit** (ALU) is the section of the CPU that performs arithmetic (addition, subtraction, multiplication, and division) involving integers and logical operations (such as comparing two pieces of data to see if they are equal or determining if a specific condition is true or false). Arithmetic requiring decimals is usually performed by the **floating point unit (FPU)** instead. Arithmetic operations are used both for actual mathematical calculations requested by the user, as well as for other everyday tasks. For example, editing a digital photograph in an image editing program, running the spelling checker in a word processing program, and burning a music CD are all performed by the ALU, with help from the FPU when needed, using only arithmetic and logical operations. Most CPUs today have multiple ALUs and FPUs that work together to perform the necessary operations.

Control Unit

The **control unit** coordinates and controls the operations and activities taking place within the CPU, such as retrieving data and instructions and passing them on to the ALU or FPU for execution. In other words, it directs the flow of electronic traffic within the CPU, much like a traffic cop controls the flow of vehicles on a roadway. Essentially, the control unit tells the ALU and FPU what to do and makes sure that everything happens at the right time in order for the appropriate processing to take place.

>**Arithmetic/logic unit (ALU).** The part of the CPU that performs logical operations and integer arithmetic. >**Floating point unit (FPU).** The part of the CPU that performs decimal arithmetic. >**Control unit.** The part of the CPU that coordinates its operations.

INSIDE THE INDUSTRY

Moore's Law

In 1965, Gordon Moore, the cofounder of Intel, observed that the number of transistors per square inch on chips had doubled every year since the integrated circuit was invented. He then made a now-famous prediction–that this doubling trend would continue for at least 10 more years. Here we are, 40 or so years later, and, although the pace has slowed down a bit, transistor density still doubles about every 18 months (see the accompanying figure). Due to technological breakthroughs, *Moore's Law* has been maintained for far longer than the original prediction and most experts, including Moore himself, expect the doubling trend to continue for at least another decade. In fact, Intel states that the mission of its technology development team is to continue to break barriers to Moore's Law.

Interestingly, other computer components also follow Moore's Law. For example, storage capacity doubles approximately every 20 months, and chip speed doubles about every 24 months. Consequently, the term "Moore's Law" has been expanded and is now used to describe the amount of time it takes components to double in capacity or speed.

Many experts predict that, eventually, a physical limit of the number of transistors that can be crammed onto a chip will end Moore's Law. But the end is not yet in sight.

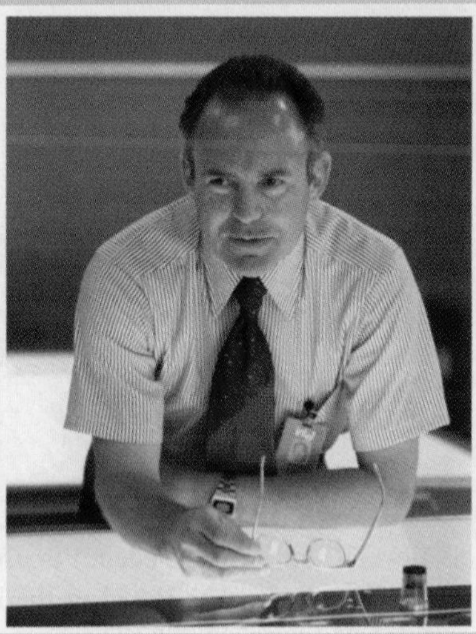

GORDON MOORE (1970)

Microprocessor	Year of Introduction	Transistors
4004	1971	2,300
8008	1972	2,500
8080	1974	4,500
8086	1978	29,000
Intel286	1982	134,000
Intel386™ processor	1985	275,000
Intel486™ processor	1989	1,200,000
Intel® Pentium® processor	1993	3,100,000
Intel® Pentium® II processor	1997	7,500,000
Intel® Pentium® III processor	1999	9,500,000
Intel® Pentium® 4 processor	2000	42,000,000
Intel® Itanium® processor	2001	25,000,000
Intel® Itanium® 2 processor	2003	220,000,000
Intel® Itanium® 2 processor (9MB cache)	2004	592,000,000

TRANSISTOR GROWTH

Prefetch Unit

The **prefetch unit** orders data and instructions from cache or RAM based on the task at hand. The prefetch unit tries to predict what data and instructions will be needed and retrieves them ahead of time, in order to help avoid delays in processing.

Decode Unit

The **decode unit** takes the instructions fetched by the prefetch unit and translates them into a form that can be understood by the control unit, ALU, and FPU. The decoded instructions go to the control unit for processing.

>**Prefetch unit.** The part of the CPU that attempts to retrieve data and instructions before they are needed for processing, in order to avoid delays. >**Decode unit.** The part of the CPU that translates instructions into a form that can be processed by the ALU.

TREND

High-Tech Investigators

With the high value of technology today and claims of stolen technology and patent infringements happening all the time, what can companies in the computer industry do to find out the truth? Increasingly, they turn to reverse engineering companies, such as Taeus International. Short for "Tear Apart Everything Under the Stars," Taeus is a leader in the area of applying engineering skills and industry knowledge to analyze products to evaluate patent claims. In a nutshell, companies like Taeus tear products apart to hunt for patented technologies that should not be there. Just as with criminal investigations, patent infringement claims require physical proof, and Taeus engineers inspect and photograph critical elements of a product (see the accompanying photo) to compare that product to existing patents.

In just the past few years, Taeus has helped to settle numerous patent infringement claims. For instance, it helped Intel avoid litigation when they were sued by Digital Equipment Corporation (DEC) for a share of its Pentium CPU profits. After Taeus found patented Intel technology inside DEC's servers, the case was settled with no money changing hands. They also do preemptive work helping tech companies avoid patent liabilities by searching through existing patents to determine which technology patents are enforceable before a problem arises.

At a rate of $100,000 to reverse engineer one computer chip, services such as the one Taeus provides are not cheap, but with patent lawsuits often exceeding $100 million, for tech companies that use Taeus services and avoid litigation, it is money well spent.

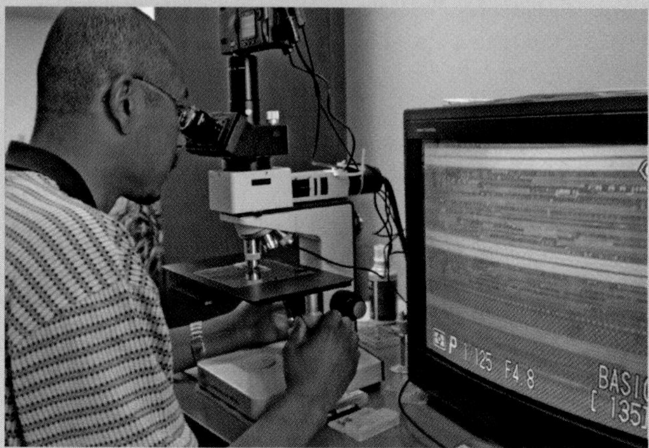

A Taeus engineer at work.

Internal Cache and Registers

As mentioned earlier, internal cache (such as Level 1 and Level 2 cache) is used to store instructions and data for the CPU, to avoid retrieving them from RAM or the hard drive, and registers are groups of high-speed memory located within the CPU that are used during processing. The ALU and FPU use registers to temporarily store data, intermediary calculations, and the final results of processing. CPUs today typically have a variety of registers—for example, the Intel Itanium 2 has a total of 328 different registers. As directed by the control unit after processing, the results located in the registers can be sent from the CPU to RAM or an output device, depending on the instructions received.

Bus Interface Unit

The **bus interface unit** is the place where instructions and data flow in and out of the CPU. It connects the CPU to the system bus so it can communicate with external cache, RAM, and the rest of the computer.

The System Clock and the Machine Cycle

As mentioned at the beginning of this chapter, every instruction that you issue to a computer—either by typing a command or clicking something with the mouse—is converted

>**Bus interface unit.** The part of the CPU where instructions and data flow in and out of the CPU.

into machine language. In turn, each machine language instruction in a CPU's *instruction set* (the collection of basic machine language commands that the CPU can understand) is broken down into several smaller, machine-level instructions called *microcode*. Microcoded instructions, such as moving a single piece of data from one part of the computer system to another or adding the numbers located in two specific registers, are built into the CPU to provide its basic instructions.

In order to synchronize the computer's operations, a **system clock**—a quartz crystal located on the motherboard—is used. The system clock sends out a signal on a regular basis to all other computer components, similar to a musician's metronome or a person's heartbeat. Each signal is referred to as a *cycle*. The number of cycles per second is measured in *hertz* (*Hz*). One megahertz (MHz) is equal to one million ticks of the system clock. Many PCs today have a system clock that runs at 200 MHz, and all devices that are synchronized with the system clock can run at this speed or can run faster or slower by running at a multiple of or a fraction of the system clock speed. For example, to reach a CPU clock speed of 2 GHz, a multiplier of 10 is used, meaning that the CPU clock essentially "ticks" 10 times during each system clock tick. During each CPU clock tick, the CPU usually executes one or more pieces of microcode. Most computers today can process more than one piece of microcode at one time—a characteristic known as *superscalar* or being able to process multiple *instructions per cycle* (*IPC*). A CPU with a higher clock speed processes more instructions per second than the same CPU using a lower clock speed.

Whenever the CPU processes a single piece of microcode, it is referred to as a **machine cycle**. Each machine cycle consists of the four general operations illustrated in Figure 2-20 and discussed next.

1. *Fetch*—the program instruction is fetched.
2. *Decode*—the instructions are decoded so the control unit, ALU, and FPU can understand them.
3. *Execute*—the instructions are carried out.
4. *Store*—the original data or the result from the ALU or FPU execution is stored either in the CPU's registers or in memory, depending on the instruction.

Because a machine cycle processes only a single instruction, many seemingly simple commands (such as multiplying two numbers) might require more than one machine cycle, and a computer might need to go through thousands, millions, or even billions of machine cycles to complete a user command or program instruction. A simplified example of how a CPU might process the command *2 + 3* is illustrated in Figure 2-21. In this example, four machine cycles are used, as follows:

1. The number 2 is fetched from RAM using the appropriate address and is sent to the decode unit, where it is determined that the number needs to be stored in register X. The control unit then stores the number in register X.

FIGURE 2-20
A machine cycle. A machine cycle is typically accomplished in four steps.

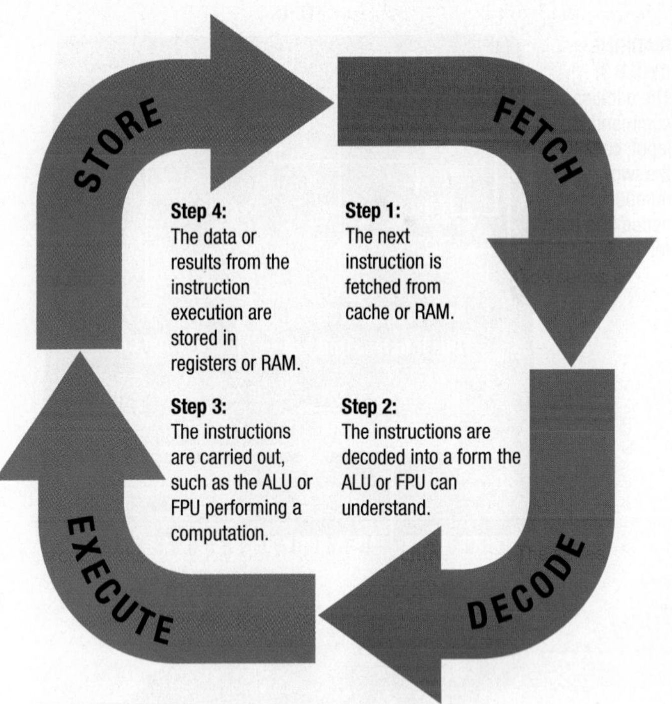
STORE
FETCH
Step 4:
The data or results from the instruction execution are stored in registers or RAM.
Step 1:
The next instruction is fetched from cache or RAM.
Step 3:
The instructions are carried out, such as the ALU or FPU performing a computation.
Step 2:
The instructions are decoded into a form the ALU or FPU can understand.
EXECUTE
DECODE

HW

>**System clock.** The timing mechanism within the computer system that synchronizes the computer's operations. >**Machine cycle.** The series of operations involved in the execution of a single machine level instruction.

MACHINE CYCLE 1: The number 2 is input and stored.

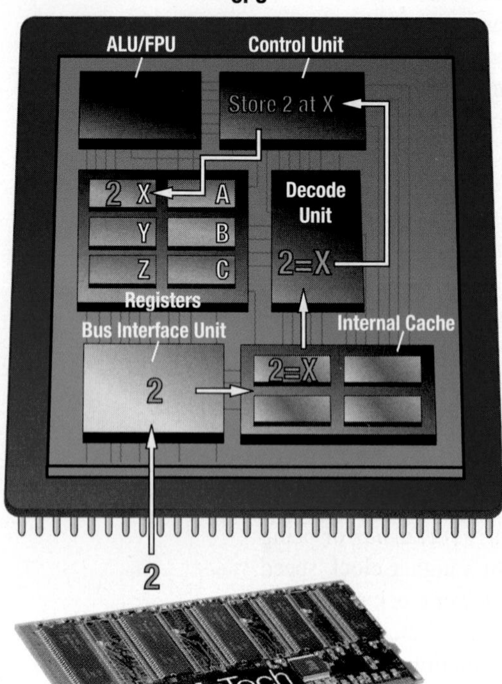

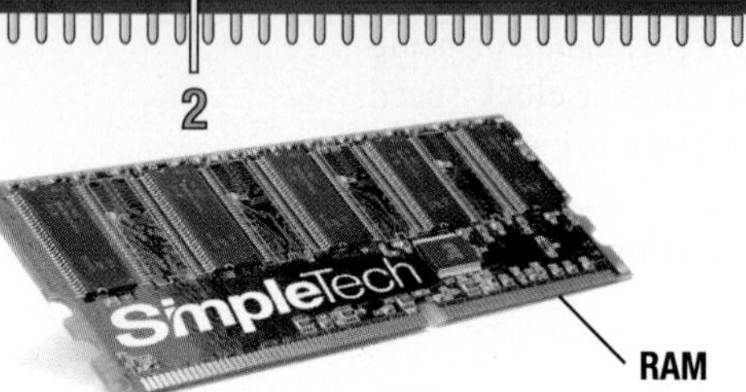

MACHINE CYCLE 2: The number 3 is input and stored.

CPU

ALU/FPU

Control Unit

Store 3 at Y

2 X

A

3 Y

B

Z

C

Registers

Decode Unit

3=Y

Bus Interface Unit

3

Internal Cache

2=X

3=Y

3

SimpleTech

RAM

MACHINE CYCLE 3: The addition command is input, causing the two numbers to be added and the result stored.

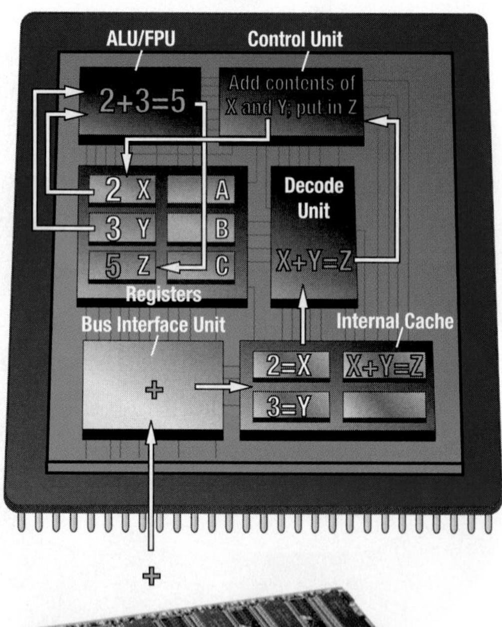

MACHINE CYCLE 4: The equal sign is input, causing the sum to be output.

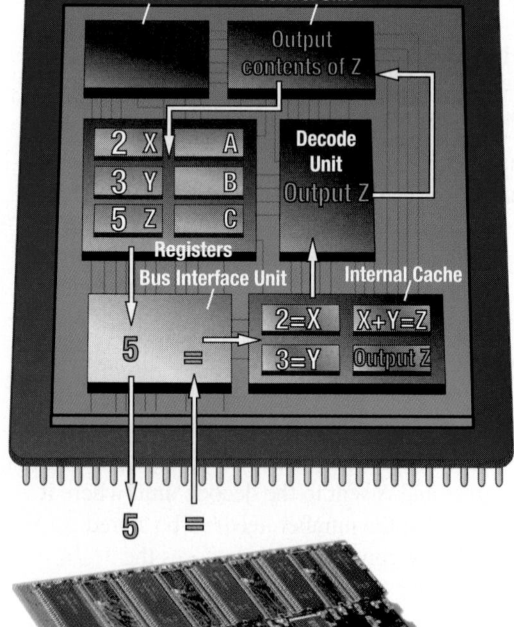

FIGURE 2-21
Machine cycle examples. This example, adding two numbers, requires 4 machine cycles.

2. The number 3 is fetched from RAM using the appropriate address and is sent to the decode unit, where it is determined that the number needs to be stored in register Y. The control unit then stores the number in register Y.
3. The addition symbol is fetched from RAM using the appropriate address and is sent to the decode unit, where it is determined that the numbers in registers X and Y need to be added and the sum stored in register Z. The control unit then instructs the ALU to add the two numbers, and then stores the result in register Z.
4. The equal sign is fetched from RAM using the appropriate address and is sent to the decode unit, where it is determined that the sum in register Z needs to be output. The control unit then sends the sum located in register Z to the appropriate location in RAM.

MAKING COMPUTERS FASTER AND BETTER NOW AND IN THE FUTURE

Over the years, computer designers have developed a number of strategies to achieve faster, more powerful, and more reliable computing performance. Researchers are also constantly working on ways to improve the performance of computers of the future. There are several ways computer users can speed up their computers today, and a number of technologies being developed by manufacturers to improve computers both today and in the future.

Improving the Performance of Your System Today

Several strategies you can use to try to improve the performance of your current computer are discussed next.

Add More Memory

With today's graphic-intensive interfaces and applications, much more memory is required than was necessary even a couple of years ago. If your computer is just a few years old and slows down significantly when you have multiple programs open, you should consider adding more memory to your system to bring it up to a minimum of 512 MB. Be sure to check inside your PC first to determine if there is room for more memory modules, and then check with your PC manufacturer to determine the appropriate type and speed of RAM that your PC uses. Some memory modules must be added in pairs. If you do not have enough empty RAM slots in your PC, you will need to remove some of the old modules and replace them with newer, higher capacity ones, in order to add more memory to your system.

TIP

Before opening your PC's system unit, be sure to turn it off and unplug it, then carefully remove the cover. Before touching any components inside the PC, touch the power supply to discharge any static electricity contained within your body.

Perform System Maintenance

As you work and use your hard drive to store and retrieve data, and as you install and uninstall programs, most PCs tend to become less efficient. One reason for this is because as large documents are stored, retrieved, and then stored again, they often become *fragmented*—that is, not stored in contiguous (adjacent) storage areas. Because the different pieces of the document are physically located in different places, it takes longer for the computer to retrieve or store it. Another reason a computer might become inefficient is that when programs are uninstalled, pieces of the program are sometimes left behind or references to these programs are left in operating system files. Yet another reason is that as a hard drive begins to get full, it takes longer to locate and manipulate the data stored on the drive. All of these factors can result in a system performing more slowly than it should.

FURTHER EXPLORATION

For links to further information about system maintenance, go to www.course.com/uc11/ch02

FIGURE 2-22
Uninstalling programs. Always uninstall programs properly, such as by using the Windows Control Panel *Add or Remove Programs* option.

To avoid some of these problems, regular *system maintenance* should be performed. Some system maintenance tips every computer user should be aware of are as follows:

- Uninstall any programs that you no longer want on your computer in order to free up space on your hard drive. Be sure to use the designated removal procedure for your operating system, such as the Add/Remove Programs option in the Windows Control Panel (see Figure 2-22) or an "Uninstall" option for that program located on the Start menu, to remove the program for Windows PCs.
- If you have large files (such as digital photos or other graphical images) stored on your computer that you do not need on a regular basis, consider moving them to a removable storage medium, such as a CD or DVD disc. Once copied onto the new medium, the files can be deleted from your hard drive to free up space. If the files are important, you might want to make two copies, just to be safe. Be sure to open the files from the storage medium to confirm that the transfer was successful before deleting the files from your hard drive, and store multiple discs containing the same files in different locations. Copying files, deleting files, and types of storage media will be discussed in more detail in later chapters.
- Delete the temporary files stored by your Web browser (choose *Internet Options* from the Tools menu, if you are using Internet Explorer; select *Preferences* from the Edit menu, and then choose *Advanced* and *Cache* in Netscape Navigator). Web browsers tend to store a large amount of data—it is not unusual to have over 1,000 temporary Internet files, including your browsing history and copies of Web pages you have recently visited. If you no longer need this information, deleting the files will make room on your hard drive. Deleting temporary Internet files can also speed up your Internet browsing. There are also *utility programs*, such as the Windows Disk Cleanup program, that can help you locate and delete temporary files left over from installing programs, uninstalling programs, and browsing the Internet.
- Open the Recycle Bin (or similar location holding deleted files on your PC) and empty it. As long as you are sure that none of the files in the Recycle Bin need to be restored, those files are taking up room on your hard drive needlessly.

FIGURE 2-23
The Windows Task Manager. The Windows Task Manager can be used to shut down processes manually, if necessary.

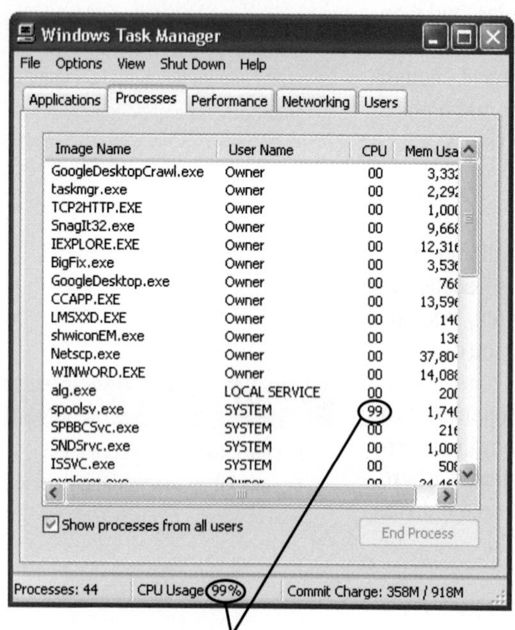

- Scan for *computer viruses* and *spyware* regularly. A computer that suddenly slows down might be the result of extra workload created by a computer virus, spyware program, or other threat. *Antivirus* and *antispyware programs* can help detect and correct these problems and are discussed in more detail in Chapter 9. If you are using Windows XP, you can also check the current CPU load any time by pressing the Ctrl+Alt+Delete key combination one time. The resulting Windows Task Manager screen can be used to view all open programs and processes, as shown in Figure 2-23. If the CPU load stays very high for a long period of time, look for a process with a high CPU percentage. Some processes, such as *print spoolers*, occasionally *hang* (stay running) after they should be finished; if this happens, the process can be shut down manually using this screen. But be sure you know what a process does (use an Internet search site to research it, if needed) before shutting it down to avoid creating problems with your PC.
- Use a utility program, such as the Windows Disk Defragmenter program, to arrange the files on your hard drive more efficiently. On large hard drives, this may need to be done during the night because of the time required to defragment the drive. Utility programs are discussed more in Chapter 5.

Buy a Larger or Second Hard Drive

As already mentioned, hard drives get less efficient as they fill up. If your hard drive is almost full and you do not have any data or programs that you can remove, you should consider buying and installing a second hard drive. The new drive can be an internal hard drive if you have an empty storage bay inside your computer. It can also be an external USB hard drive if you have a free USB port. Alternatively, you can replace your existing hard drive with a larger one, although the data transfer process will be a little more complicated. Hard drives are discussed in more detail in Chapter 3.

Upgrade Your Internet Connection

If your system seems slow primarily when you are on the Internet, the culprit might be your Internet connection. If you are using standard dial-up access, you may wish to investigate the faster connection options available in your area. Switching to cable, satellite, DSL, or another fast type of Internet service is more expensive than dial-up, but is significantly faster. The differences between these and other types of Internet connections are described in Chapters 7 and 8.

TIP

Using an external USB hard drive to store your data makes it very fast and easy to move your data to a different computer, when needed. It also protects your data from being lost if the main hard drive on your PC stops working or if you need to restore your computer's main hard drive back to its original state.

Upgrade Your Video Card

If you are a gamer, computer artist, graphical engineer, or otherwise use 3D-graphic-intensive applications, consider upgrading your video card to one that better supports 3D graphics or has more memory (called *video memory*) located on the card. If you do not use 3D applications, upgrading your video card may not improve your speed. However, if your PC uses integrated video (in which some of your computer's RAM is used for video memory), installing a separate video card, if the motherboard allows it, may speed up your system since it will free up the RAM currently being used for video memory.

Strategies for Making Faster and Better Computers

There are several strategies that researchers and manufacturers are using today to continue to build faster and better PCs. Some relate to technology in general; others are techniques used specifically to speed up the CPU. Some of these strategies are described in the next few sections.

Improved Architecture

Computer manufacturers continually work on improving the basic architecture of the PC, such as to make it faster, cooler, quieter, more energy efficient, and more reliable. For example, new designs for motherboards and CPUs are being developed, and computer components are continually being built smaller, so more power and capabilities can be contained in the same size package. In fact, today's CPUs—which are formed using a process called *lithography* that imprints patterns on semiconductor materials—typically contain transistors that are 50 *nanometers* (*nm*) in size; transistors as small as 10 nm have been created in lab settings. As lithography techniques continue to improve, transistors will likely continue to shrink, allowing more transistors to fit on the same-sized CPU. Creating components smaller than 100 nm fits the definition of *nanotechnology*, which is discussed in more detail shortly.

Other improvements include faster memory and faster bus speeds to help speed up processing and to help reduce or eliminate bottlenecks, and creating CPUs with multiple cores (such as the dual-core CPUs that are currently available and the *quad-core* CPUs that are expected by 2007). Improvements to CPU instruction set designs are also being made to expand the instruction set design for new applications—particularly growing multimedia applications, such as editing digital movies and photos, burning music CDs, and more—are continually being developed. For example, *MMX* (*Multimedia Extensions*) is a set of 57 multimedia instructions for handling many common multimedia operations, and *streaming SIMD extensions* (*SSEs*), *SSE2*, and *SSE3* help CPUs perform floating-point-intensive applications (such as video and audio handling, 3D modeling, and physical simulations) much more quickly than before, provided the software being used supports the extensions being used.

Improved Materials

Traditionally, CPU chips used aluminum circuitry etched onto a silicon backing. As the limit of the number of aluminum circuits that can be packed onto a silicon chip without heat damage or interference approached, chip makers began to look for alternate materials. Copper was one of the next choices since it is a far better electrical conductor, and it can produce chips containing more circuitry at a lower price. A more recent development is *SOI* (*silicon on insulator*). SOI chips use a thin layer of insulating material over the silicon to reduce heat and power consumption. This results in being able to place the circuits closer together than is possible without the insulating material. Another possibility sometimes used today in conjunction with SOI is *strained silicon*. With this technique, the silicon is "stretched out" or "strained" so that the atoms in silicon are further apart. Because of this, the electrons experience less resistance and flow up to 70% faster, which can lead to chips that are up to 35% faster without changing the size of the transistors.

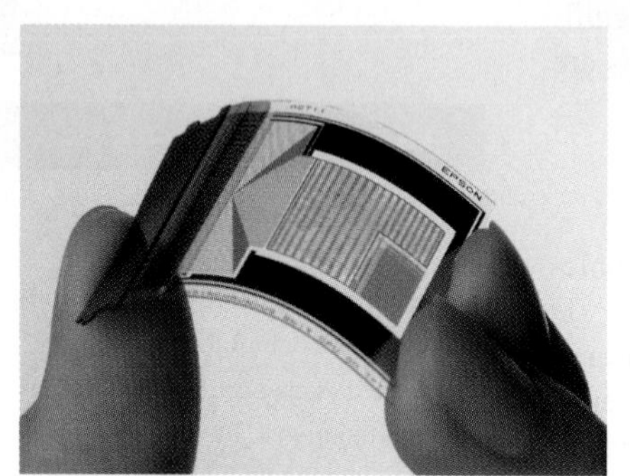

FIGURE 2-24
Flexible microprocessors.

For integration into clothing and other flexible materials, a number of companies are developing flexible electronic components, such as the flexible microprocessor shown in Figure 2-24. In addition to the ability to be bent without damaging the circuitry, flexible microprocessors are thinner, lighter, generate little heat, and consume significantly less energy than conventional microprocessors.

Another possibility currently in the testing stages is replacing the CPU entirely with *field-programmable gate arrays* (*FPGAs*). An FPGA is a type of chip that can be programmed and reprogrammed as needed. To replace a CPU, groups of FPGA chips would need to work together to process several tasks at the same time. While it is possible that FPGAs will replace CPUs in future PCs, they are currently being used in storage devices, networking hardware, cell phones, and digital cameras.

Pipelining

In older PC systems, the CPU had to completely finish processing one instruction before starting another. Today's PCs, however, can process multiple instructions at one time. One way this is accomplished is through **pipelining**. With pipelining, a new instruction begins executing as soon as the previous one reaches the next stage of the machine cycle. Figure 2-25 illustrates this process with a 4-stage pipeline. Notice that while the pipelined CPU is executing one instruction, it is simultaneously fetching and getting the next instruction ready for execution. Without a pipeline, the ALU and FPU would be idle while an instruction is being fetched and decoded.

Pipelines for CPUs today usually have between 10 and 20 stages, and the machine cycle is broken down in as many parts as needed to match the number of stages used. For example, with a 10-stage pipeline, the 4 steps of the machine cycle would be broken down into a total of 10 steps so that all stages of the pipeline can be used at one time. Pipelining increases the number of machine cycles completed per second, which increases the number of instructions performed per second, which improves performance.

>**Pipelining.** A CPU feature designed to begin processing a new instruction as soon as the previous instruction completes the first stage of the machine cycle.

Stages

Fetch Instruction 1	Decode Instruction 1	Execute Instruction 1	Store Result Instruction 1	Fetch Instruction 2	Decode Instruction 2	Execute Instruction 2

WITHOUT PIPELINING
Without pipelining, an instruction finishes an entire machine cycle before another instruction is started.

Stages

Fetch Instruction 1	Fetch Instruction 2	Fetch Instruction 3	Fetch Instruction 4	Fetch Instruction 5	Fetch Instruction 6	Fetch Instruction 7
	Decode Instruction 1	Decode Instruction 2	Decode Instruction 3	Decode Instruction 4	Decode Instruction 5	Decode Instruction 6
		Execute Instruction 1	Execute Instruction 2	Execute Instruction 3	Execute Instruction 4	Execute Instruction 5
			Store Result Instruction 1	Store Result Instruction 2	Store Result Instruction 3	Store Result Instruction 4

WITH PIPELINING
With pipelining, a new instruction is started when the preceding instruction moves to the next stage of the machine cycle.

FIGURE 2-25
Pipelining. Pipelining streamlines the machine cycle by executing different stages of multiple instructions at the same time, so the different parts of the CPU are idle less often.

HW

Multiprocessing and Parallel Processing

While the vast majority of desktop PCs are still driven by single CPUs, using more than one CPU is becoming more common, such as dual-core PCs that have the processing components of two CPUs contained on a single CPU. When two or more CPUs are located within a single computer, techniques that perform operations simultaneously—such as *multiprocessing* (most often used with desktop PCs, midrange servers, and mainframe computers) and *parallel processing* (most often used with supercomputers)—are possible.

With **multiprocessing**, each CPU typically works on a different job. Because multiple jobs are being processed simultaneously, they are completed faster than with a single processor. With **parallel processing**, multiple processors work together to make one single job finish sooner; as shown in Figure 2-26, a *control processor* assigns a portion of the processing for that job to each CPU. Two of the most common designs are *symmetric multiprocessing (SMP)* and *massively parallel processing (MPP)*. With SMP, a single copy of the operating system is in

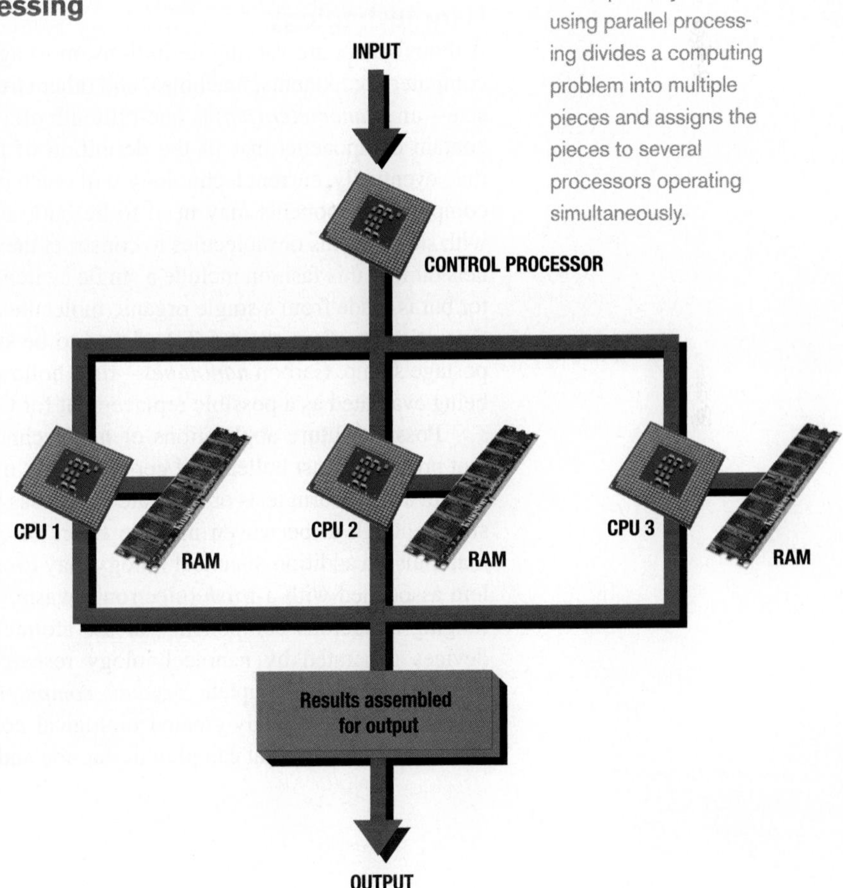

FIGURE 2-26
Parallel processing. A computer system using parallel processing divides a computing problem into multiple pieces and assigns the pieces to several processors operating simultaneously.

>**Multiprocessing.** The capability of an operating system to use multiple processors in a single computer, usually to process multiple jobs at one time faster than could be performed with a single processor. >**Parallel processing.** A processing technique that uses multiple processors simultaneously in a single computer, usually to process a single job as fast as possible.

charge of all the processors and the processors share memory. Typically, SMP systems do not exceed 64 processors. MPP systems, in contrast, can use hundreds or thousands of microprocessors and each processor has its own copy of the operating system and its own memory. MPP systems are typically more difficult to program than SMP systems.

The use of multiprocessing and parallel processing can increase astronomically the number of calculations performed in any given time period. For example, IBM's Blue Gene/L supercomputer (shown in Figure 1-21 in Chapter 1) uses 131,072 processors and will operate at approximately 360 teraflops when fully installed. In other words, it will be able to process about 360 trillion operations per second (most desktop PCs today operate slightly faster than 1 gigaflop).

A concept related to multiprocessing is *Hyper-Threading Technology*—a technology developed by Intel to enable software to treat a single processor as two processors. Since it utilizes processing power in the chip that would otherwise go unused, this technology lets the chip operate more efficiently, resulting in faster processing, provided the software being used supports Hyper-Threading.

Future Trends

Some of the strategies discussed in the prior sections are currently being used, but some ideas are further from being implemented. Selected trends we will likely see more of in the near future are discussed next.

Nanotechnology

Although there are varying definitions, most agree that **nanotechnology** involves creating computer components, machines, and other structures that are less than 100 nanometers in size—one *nanometer* (*nm*) is one-billionth of a meter. As already discussed, today's CPUs contain components that fit the definition of nanotechnology. But some experts believe that, eventually, current technology will reach its limits. At that point, transistors and other computer components may need to be built at the atomic and molecular level—starting with single atoms or molecules to construct the components. Prototypes of computer products built in this fashion include a single switch that can be turned on and off like a transistor but is made from a single organic molecule and tiny nickel-based *nanodots* that would, theoretically, allow about 5 TB of data to be stored on a hard drive roughly the size of a postage stamp. Carbon *nanotubes*—tiny, hollow tubes made up of carbon atoms—are also being evaluated as a possible replacement for CPU transistors.

Possible future applications of nanotechnology include improved military uniforms that protect against bullets and germ warfare, microscopic robots that can enter the bloodstream and perform tests or irradiate cancerous tumors, and computers and sensors that are small enough to be woven into the fibers of clothing or embedded into paint and other materials. In addition, nanotechnology may eventually solve much of the toxic waste problem associated with *e-trash* (electronic waste, such as old computer equipment) by rearranging dangerous components, at the atomic level, into inert substances. Some of the devices generated by nanotechnology research may contain or be constructed out of organic material. Complete *organic computers* are a long way off in the future, but researchers have already created biological computing devices—such as one interactive DNA-based system that can play tic-tac-toe and has never lost at that game.

>**Nanotechnology.** The science of creating tiny computers and components by working at the individual atomic and molecular levels.

Quantum Computing

The idea of **quantum computing** emerged in the 1970s, but it has received renewed interest lately. Quantum computing applies the principles of quantum physics and quantum mechanics to computers, going beyond traditional physics to work at the subatomic level. Quantum computers differ from conventional computers in that they utilize atoms or nuclei working together as quantum bits or *qubits*. Qubits function simultaneously as both the computer's processor and memory, and each qubit can represent more than just the two states (one and zero) available to today's electronic bits; a qubit can even represent many states at one time. Quantum computers can perform computations on many numbers at one time, making them, theoretically, exponentially faster than conventional computers. Physically, quantum computers in the future might consist of a thimbleful of liquid whose atoms are used to perform calculations as instructed by an external device.

While quantum computers are still in the pioneering stage, working quantum computers do exist. For instance, in 2001 the researchers at IBM's Almaden Research Center created a 7-qubit quantum computer (see Figure 2-27) composed of the nuclei of seven atoms that can interact with each other and be programmed by radio frequency pulses. This quantum computer successfully factored the number 15—not a complicated computation for a conventional computer, but the fact that it was possible to supply a quantum computer with the problem and have it compute the correct answer is viewed as a highly significant event in the area of quantum computer research. Hewlett-Packard scientists have developed a *crossbar latch*—a switch just a single molecule thick that can store binary data and might one day function as a transistor in a quantum computer.

Quantum computing is not well suited for general computing tasks but is ideal for, and expected to be widely used in, the areas of encryption and code breaking.

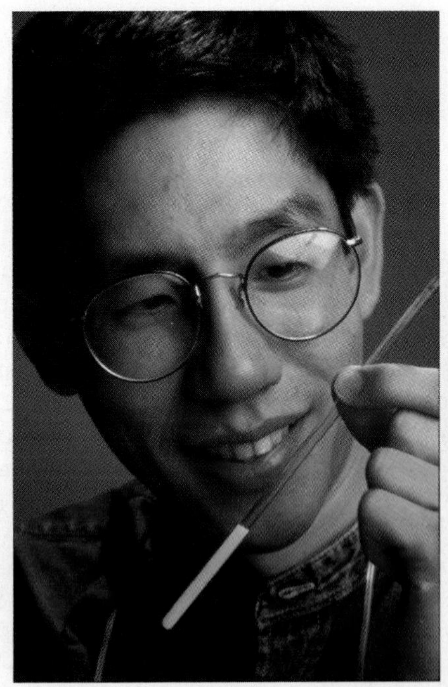

FIGURE 2-27
Quantum computers. The vial of liquid shown here contains the 7-qubit computer used by IBM researchers in 2001 to perform the most complicated computation by a quantum computer to date–factoring the number 15.

Optical Computing

Optical chips, which use light waves to transmit data, are also currently in development. A possibility for the future is the **optical computer**—a computer that uses light, such as from laser beams or infrared beams—to perform digital computations. Because light beams do not interfere with each other, optical computers can be much smaller and faster than electronic PCs. For instance, according to one NASA senior research scientist, an optical computer could solve a problem in one hour that would take an electronic computer 11 years to solve. While some researchers are working on developing an all-optical computer, others believe that a mix of optical and electronic components—or an *opto-electronic computer*—may be the best bet for the future. Opto-electronic technology is already being used to improve long-distance fiber-optic communications. Initial opto-electronic PC applications are expected to be in the area of speeding up communications between PCs and other devices, as well as between PC components. In fact, prototypes of chips that have both optical and electrical functions combined on a single silicon chip—a feat that was thought to be impossible until recently—already exist.

3D Chips

Three-dimensional (3D) chips are another technique for packing an increasing number of components onto small chips. With 3D chips, the transistors are layered, which cuts down on the surface area required. 3D chips are now available for some applications—such as video cards—and are expected to be used for other multimedia applications in the near future.

>**Quantum computing.** A technology that applies the principles of quantum physics and quantum mechanics to computers to direct atoms or nuclei to work together as quantum bits (qubits), which function simultaneously as the computer's processor and memory. >**Optical computer.** A computer that uses light, such as from laser beams or infrared beams, to perform digital computations.

SUMMARY

DATA AND PROGRAM REPRESENTATION

Chapter Objective 1:
Understand how data and programs are represented to a computer and be able to identify a few of the coding systems used to accomplish this.

The electronic components of a *digital computer* work in a two-state, or *binary*, fashion. It is convenient to think of these binary states in terms of 0s and 1s. Computer people refer to such 0s and 1s as *bits*. Converting data to these 0s and 1s is called *digital data representation*.

Computers use the **binary numbering system** to represent numbers and perform numeric computations. Text-based data can be represented with one of several fixed-length binary codes. Two popular coding schemes are **ASCII (American Standard Code for Information Interchange)** and **EBCDIC (Extended Binary-Coded Decimal Interchange Code)**. These systems represent single characters of data—a numeric digit, alphabetic character, or special symbol—as strings of eight bits. Each string of bits is called a **byte**. **Unicode** is another binary code used with text-based data that can represent text in all written languages, including those that use alphabets different from English, such as Chinese, Greek, and Russian.

The storage capacity of computers often is expressed in **kilobytes (KB)**, or thousands of bytes; **megabytes (MB)**, millions of bytes; **gigabytes (GB)**, billions of bytes; and **terabytes (TB)**, trillions of bytes. Other possibilities are the **petabyte (PB)**, about 1,000 terabytes; the **exabyte (EB)**, about 1,000 petabytes; the **zettabyte (ZB)**, about 1,000 exabytes; and the **yottabyte (YB)**, about 1,000 zettabytes.

The binary system can represent not only text but graphics, audio, and video data, as well. **Machine language** is the binary-based code through which computers represent program instructions. A program must be translated into machine language before the computer can execute it.

INSIDE THE SYSTEM UNIT

Chapter Objective 2:
Explain the functions of the hardware components commonly found inside the system unit, such as the CPU, memory, buses, and expansion cards.

PCs typically contain a variety of hardware components located inside the **system unit**. For instance, *chips* are mounted onto *circuit boards*, and those boards are positioned in slots on the **motherboard** or *system board*—the main circuit board for a PC. Every PC has a **central processing unit (CPU)**—also called a **processor** or **microprocessor** when referring to PCs—attached to its motherboard that performs the processing for the computer. CPU chips differ in many respects, such as what types of PCs the CPU is designed for, its *clock speed*, and *word size*. Another difference is the amount of **cache memory**—memory located on or very close to the CPU chip to help speed up processing. Other important differences are the general architecture of the CPU and the bus speed and width being used. The overall *processing speed* of the computer determines its performance. One of the most consistent measurements of overall performance is a **benchmark test**.

The main memory chips for a PC are commonly referred to as **RAM (random access memory)**. RAM is volatile and used to temporarily hold programs and data while they are needed. RAM is available in different types and speeds. **ROM (read-only memory)** are memory chips that store nonerasable programs. **Flash memory** is nonvolatile memory that can be erased and reprogrammed in blocks. Flash memory chips can be found in PCs and mobile devices; flash memory chips can also be used for storage with portable PCs, digital cameras, and other smaller devices. **Registers** are memory built into the CPU chip to hold data before or during processing.

Most desktop PCs contain internal **expansion slots**, into which users can insert **expansion cards** to give the computer added functionality. A computer **bus** is an electronic path along which bits are transmitted. The *system bus* moves data between the CPU and RAM, and **expansion buses** connect the CPU to peripheral devices. Common buses include *PCI*, **PCI Express (PCIe)**, *AGP*, *HyperTransport*, **USB (Universal Serial Bus)**, **FireWire**, and *CardBus*.

Chapter Objective 3:
Describe how peripheral devices or other hardware can be added to a PC.

System units typically have external **ports** that are used to connect peripheral devices to the computer. Notebook and tablet PCs may have fewer ports than desktop PCs. Handheld PC and mobile device users often add new capabilities with *Secure Digital* (*SD*) *cards* or other types of flash memory cards. In addition, some handheld PCs and mobile devices include a PC card slot or proprietary expansion system.

HW

HOW THE CPU WORKS

CPUs include at least one **arithmetic/logic unit (ALU)**, which performs integer arithmetic and logical operations on data, and at least one **floating point unit (FPO)**, which performs decimal arithmetic. The **control unit** directs the flow of electronic traffic between memory and the ALU/FPU and also between the CPU and input and output devices. Registers—high-speed temporary holding places within the CPU that hold program instructions and data immediately before and during processing—are used to enhance the computer's performance. The **prefetch unit** requests data and instructions before or as they are needed, the **decode unit** decodes the instructions input into the CPU, internal cache stores frequently used instructions and data, and the **bus interface unit** inputs data and instructions from RAM.

Chapter Objective 4:
Understand how the computer system's CPU and memory components process program instructions and data.

The CPU processes instructions in a sequence called a **machine cycle**, consisting of four basic steps. Each machine language instruction is broken down into several smaller instructions called *microcode*, and each piece of microcode corresponds to an operation (such as adding two numbers located in the CPU's registers) that can be performed inside the CPU. The computer system has a built-in **system clock** that synchronizes all of the PC's activities.

MAKING COMPUTERS FASTER AND BETTER NOW AND IN THE FUTURE

There are several possible remedies for a computer that is performing too slowly, including adding more memory, performing system maintenance to clean up the PC's hard drive, buying a larger or additional hard drive, and upgrading the computer's Internet connection or video card, depending on the primary role of the computer and where the processing bottleneck appears to be. To make computers work faster over all, computer designers have developed a number of strategies over the years, and researchers are continually working on new strategies. Some of the strategies already being implemented include improved architecture, **pipelining**, **multiprocessing**, **parallel processing**, and the use of improved materials.

Chapter Objective 5:
Name and evaluate several strategies that can be used today for speeding up the operations of a computer.

One possibility for future computers is **nanotechnology** research, which focuses on building computer components at the individual atomic and molecular levels. **Quantum computing** and **optical computers** are other possibilities being researched, along with *three-dimensional* (*3D*) *chips*.

Chapter Objective 6:
List some technologies that may be used in future PCs.

REVIEW ACTIVITIES

KEY TERM MATCHING

Instructions: Match each key term on the left with the definition on the right that best describes it.

a. ASCII

b. binary numbering system

c. byte

d. central processing unit (CPU)

e. control unit

f. motherboard

g. nanotechnology

h. parallel processing

i. random access memory (RAM)

j. Universal Serial Bus (USB)

1. ______ A processing technique that uses multiple processors simultaneously in a single computer, usually to process a single job as fast as possible.

2. ______ A fixed-length, binary coding system widely used to represent text-based data for computer processing on many types of computers.

3. ______ A group of 8 bits.

4. ______ A universal bus used to connect up to 127 peripheral devices to a computer without requiring the use of additional expansion cards.

5. ______ Chips connected to the motherboard that provide a temporary location for the computer to hold data and program instructions while they are needed.

6. ______ The chip located inside the system unit of a computer that performs the processing for a computer.

7. ______ The main circuit board of a computer, located inside the system unit, to which all computer system components connect.

8. ______ The numbering system that represents all numbers using just two symbols (0 and 1).

9. ______ The part of the CPU that coordinates its operations.

10. ______ The science of creating tiny computers and components by working at the individual atomic and molecular levels.

SELF-QUIZ

Instructions: Circle **T** if the statement is true, **F** if the statement is false, or write the best answer in the space provided. **Answers for the self-quiz are located in the References and Resources Guide at the end of the book.**

1. **T F** A storage medium that can hold 256 GB can hold about 256 billion characters.
2. **T F** ASCII is the coding system used by a computer to perform mathematical computations.
3. **T F** Cache memory is typically built into a CPU.
4. **T F** A bus is a pathway, such as on the motherboard or inside the CPU, along which bits can be transferred.
5. **T F** Computers that process data with light are referred to as quantum computers.
6. The binary number 1101 is equivalent to the decimal number ______.
7. The main memory the computer uses to temporarily store programs and data it is working with is ______.
8. A(n) ______ is a connector on the exterior of a computer's system unit into which a peripheral device may be plugged.
9. With ______, the CPU is able to begin executing a new instruction as soon as the previous instruction finishes the first stage of the machine cycle.

10. Number the following terms from 1 to 10 to indicate their size from smallest to largest.

a. _____ Petabyte		d. _____ Yottabyte		g. _____ Zettabyte	
b. _____ Kilobyte		e. _____ Exabyte		h. _____ Terabyte	
c. _____ Gigabyte		f. _____ Byte		i. _____ Megabyte	

EXERCISES

1. What do each of the following acronyms stand for?

   a. KB _____
   b. RAM _____
   c. ROM _____
   d. USB _____
   e. PCIe _____
   f. CPU _____

2. Using the ASCII code chart in this chapter or in the References and Resources Guide at the end of the book, decode the following word. What does it say?

   01000011 01000001 01000110 01000101

   _____ _____ _____ _____

3. Assume you have a USB mouse, USB keyboard, and USB printer to connect to a PC, but you have only two USB ports. Explain one solution to this problem that does not involve buying a new mouse, keyboard, or printer.

4. If your PC seems sluggish, list two things you could do to try to speed it up without resorting to purchasing an entirely new system.

5. Match the picture to its name and write the corresponding number in the blank to the left of each name.

   a. _____ memory module
   b. _____ expansion card
   c. _____ keyboard port
   d. _____ USB port

1. 2. 3. 4.

DISCUSSION QUESTION

In addition to being used with computers and consumer products, there are also processors and other similar components designed to be implanted inside the human body. One of the most prominent is the *VeriChip*—a tiny chip about the size of a grain of rice that is implanted under a person's skin. The VeriChip is intended to be used in conjunction with a database to provide identification data, such as to provide hospital emergency room personnel with health information about an unconscious patient. Another implantable device that is currently in development uses an implantable wafer containing medication in conjunction with a processor to deliver the medication at the appropriate time and dosage without patient intervention. And *brain-to-computer interfacing (BCI)* involves implanting electrodes directly into the human brain to restore lost functionality or to facilitate the communications of severely disabled individuals, such as by enabling them to move a mouse cursor or direct it to click an object using only their thoughts. What do you think about these implantable chip applications? Are the benefits worth the risk of something going wrong with the chips implanted inside your body? Are there any privacy risks? Would you consider using an implanted device? Why or why not?

PROJECTS

HOT TOPICS

1. **USB Gadgets** As discussed in the chapter, computers today usually come with several USB ports, often on the front of the PC for easy access. In addition to being used with conventional peripheral devices and external storage devices, a growing number of gadgets are being developed for use with an empty USB slot. Some—such as keyboard vacuums and ionizers—have practical applications; others—such as fake aquariums and disco balls—are more for entertainment purposes.

   For this project, locate several USB gadgets that are currently on the market. Research these products to determine their purpose and cost, and classify the gadgets as practical or entertaining. At the conclusion of your research, prepare a one- to two-page summary of your findings and submit it to your instructor. Be sure to mention which gadgets you think are worthwhile and which ones you would choose not to use and why.

SHORT ANSWER/ RESEARCH

2. **Adding Memory** Adding additional RAM to a PC is one of the most common computer upgrades. Before purchasing additional memory, however, a little research is in order to make sure that the purchased memory is compatible with the PC.

   For this project, select a computer to which you might want to add memory. It does not matter if you own the computer or not, but it needs to be one you can find out information about, such as your own PC, a school PC if there is someone to whom you can ask questions about the computer, or a computer for sale at a local store. For your selected PC, determine the following: manufacturer and model number, CPU, current amount of memory, total memory slots, and the number of available memory slots. (If you look inside the PC, be sure to unplug the power cord first and do not touch any components inside the system unit.) For a school PC, you may be able to find some of the information on the front of the PC; you will have to ask someone in charge of that PC for the rest of the information. For a PC at a local store, determine what you can from an advertisement or by looking at the PC in a store, then ask a salesperson (either in person or over the telephone) questions to determine any missing information. Once you have the necessary information, call a local store or use your information and a memory supplier's Web site to determine the appropriate type of memory needed for your selected PC. What choices do you have in terms of capacity and configuration? Can you add just one memory module, or do you have to add memory in pairs? Can you keep the old memory modules, or do they have to be removed? At the conclusion of your research, prepare a one-page summary of your findings and submit it to your instructor.

3. **In Review** It is a good idea to start the process of expanding or upgrading your computer by reading hardware reviews in offline or online computer journals, such as Computerworld, PC World, or MacWorld, or on tech news sites, such as CNET.com or ZDNet.com. Reviews available online are often organized by category, providing you with the latest information about compatibility, performance, cost, reliability, and overall value.

   For this project, select a piece of hardware that you would like to upgrade on your PC or add to your computer system (if you do not have a PC, just assume that you do). Some possible options include adding a new video board, modem, sound card, scanner, digital camera, printer, DVD drive, CD-R drive, network interface, or flash memory reader. Research specific brands and models of your selected product, then select the one that would best suit your needs, noting why you selected the model you did over its competitors. In your findings, be sure to identify how the device will be connected to your PC. If an expansion card is required, identify which slot the card would need to be inserted into and make certain that there is an empty slot of that type on your PC. If there is not an available slot, check whether the product is available in a format compatible with your PC, such as in a USB format. At the conclusion of your research, prepare a one-page summary of your findings and submit it to your instructor.

HANDS ON

4. **Ports** As mentioned in the chapter, external hardware connects to the computer via ports located on the exterior of the system unit. Conventional ports include parallel, serial, PS/2 (keyboard/mouse), sound, and monitor ports. Newer ports include USB 2 and FireWire (IEEE 1394) ports. Many PCs today also have a modem and/or networking port. Some of the older ports—particularly parallel and serial—are beginning to be referred to as "legacy ports." They are being omitted from some new computers today, and many people predict that they will eventually be replaced by newer types of ports.

   For this project, select one computer (such as at home, your school, public library, or a computer store) and make sure you can look at the exterior of the entire system unit. Draw a sketch of all four sides of the PC case, including all of its ports. On your sketch, label each port with a note about what that port is being used for (for the ports in use) or might be used for (for the available ports) on that particular PC. Does the PC you selected use legacy ports? If you wanted to add a flash memory drive or reader that plugs into a USB port, would you be able to use it with your selected PC? Why or why not? Turn in your labeled sketch along with the answers to these questions to your instructor.

5. **Intel Museum Tour** Intel Corporation has a great deal of interesting information about microprocessors and related technology on its Web site, including information available through its online museum.

   For this project, go to the Intel Museum at www.intel.com/museum/index.htm (if this URL no longer works at the time you do this project, go to the Intel home page at www.intel.com and search for "Intel Museum" using the site's search feature). Once you are at the Intel Museum home page, select an Online Exhibit related to microprocessors, such as *How the Transistor Works*, *How the Microprocessor Works*, *How Chips Are Made*, or *Clean Room*, and then tour the exhibit. As you tour, make a note of at least three interesting facts you learned. At the conclusion of this task, prepare a short summary listing the tour you took and the interesting facts you recorded and submit it to your instructor.

WRITING ABOUT COMPUTERS

6. **Wearable PCs** As mentioned in Chapter 1, wearable computers are computers that are small enough to be worn on a belt or wrist, like a portable MP3 player or Walkman. Although they have been available in some form for commercial applications for several years, their entry into the consumer market is just beginning. Some current features of wearable PCs, such as corded components and using an eye-piece display device that some individuals view as unattractive, may make today's wearable PCs less desirable than those that are expected to become available in the future.

   For this project, write a short essay expressing your opinion about wearable computers. Try to find a photo of a wearable computer geared toward consumer use—would you be willing to wear one in public today? Why or why not? If not, how (if at all) would wearable computers need to be changed in order for you to be willing to wear one? As they become smaller, wireless, and controllable by your voice, do you think their use by consumers will increase? Will their use be looked at as any different from wearing a Walkman or MP3 player in public? Think about your chosen profession—is wearable or portable computer use needed or useful today? What advantages and disadvantages do you see regarding wearable computer use in that profession? Submit your opinion on this issue to your instructor in the form of a short paper, not more than two pages in length.

PRESENTATION/ DEMONSTRATION

7. **Binary Conversions** As discussed in the chapter, all numbers processed by the CPU must be represented in a binary format. The conversion from decimal (base 10) to and from true binary (base 2) format is a fairly straightforward process and can be accomplished with basic arithmetic. The conversion from true binary format to hexadecimal (base 16) format is also a fairly straightforward process and is generally used to conserve memory whenever possible.

   For this project, research how to convert a three-digit decimal number to both binary and hexadecimal and back again, without the use of a calculator (refer to the "A Look at Numbering Systems" feature located on this book's Web site at www.course.com/uc11 if needed). Next, use your knowledge of binary and decimal numbering systems to determine how to represent the decimal number 10 in base 3. Share your findings with the class in the form of a short presentation, including a demonstration of the conversions between binary and hexadecimal and the representation of the decimal number 10 in base 3. The presentation should not exceed 10 minutes and should make use of one or more presentation aids such as the chalkboard, handouts, overhead transparencies, or a computer-based slide presentation (your instructor may provide additional requirements). You may also be asked to submit a summary of the presentation to your instructor.

GROUP DISCUSSION

8. **People Chips** The *VeriChip* is a tiny chip about the size of a grain of rice that is designed to be implanted under a person's skin, such as on the forearm. Each VeriChip contains a unique verification number that can be read when a proprietary scanner is passed over the implanted chip. Although the VeriChip does not contain any personal data at the present time, it can be used in conjunction with a database to access data, such as to provide hospital emergency room personnel with health information about an unconscious patient. According to the company that invented VeriChip, future versions could be used for access control to secure facilities, personal computers, cars, and homes, as well as to authenticate users for ATM and credit card transactions. Versions of the VeriChip with GPS capabilities could also be used to find missing individuals, such as kidnap victims and lost Alzheimer's patients. These VeriChip versions would be similar to the clip-on and wristwatch monitoring systems available today that allow for continuous location information to be broadcast to a proprietary receiver. Electronic payments are also another possibility—for example, one version of the VeriChip is already being used by some regular patrons at a nightclub in Barcelona, Spain, to charge their food and beverages to their house accounts. Although privacy-rights advocates worry that a chip like the VeriChip could someday be used by the government to track citizens, others view the chip no differently than a medical ID bracelet, and they are not concerned because it is available on a purely voluntary basis. What do you think? Would you be willing to have a VeriChip implanted under your skin if it made some tasks (such as unlocking your home or car) easier or some types of transactions (such as withdrawing money from your bank account or shopping online) more secure? Do you think it would make these tasks easier or more secure?

   For this project, form an opinion of the use of human-implantable chips and be prepared to discuss your position (in class, via an online class discussion group, or in a class chat room, depending on your instructor's directions). You may also be asked to write a short paper expressing your opinion.

WEB ACTIVITIES

The *Understanding Computers* Web site located at **www.course.com/uc11** features many resources to help reinforce your understanding of the chapter content and help you prepare for exams. Your instructor may also assign specific activities to be completed that will count toward your final grade in the course.

Instructions: Go to **www.course.com/uc11/ch02** to work the following online activities.

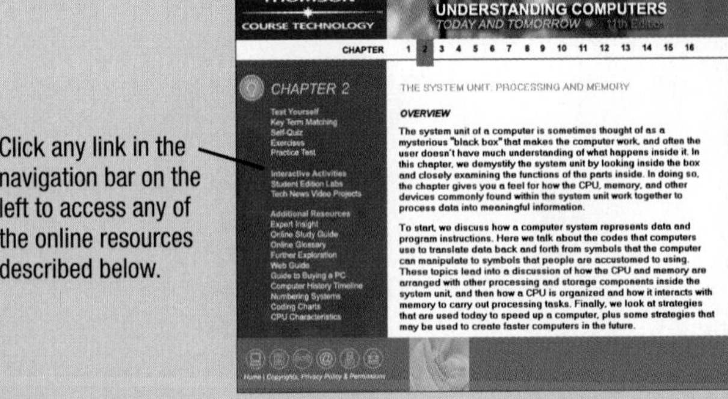
Click any link in the navigation bar on the left to access any of the online resources described below.
THOMSON
COURSE TECHNOLOGY
UNDERSTANDING COMPUTERS
TODAY AND TOMORROW
CHAPTER 2
OVERVIEW

INTERACTIVE ACTIVITIES

1. **Crossword Puzzle** Practice your knowledge of the key terms in Chapter 2 by completing the interactive Crossword Puzzle.
2. **Tech News Video Project** Watch the **"High-Tech Helmets"** video clip that features a new helmet sensor system developed by sports medicine researchers at Virginia Tech University. The sensors measure the physical impacts (in G-forces) experienced by each player to evaluate his condition on an on-going basis in order to help make football a little safer. After watching the video online, complete the corresponding project.
3. **Student Edition Labs** Reinforce the concepts you have learned in this chapter by working through the interactive **Binary Numbers** and **Understanding the Motherboard** labs.

Student Edition
Labs

TEST YOURSELF

1. **Key Term Matching** Test your knowledge of selected chapter key terms by matching the terms with their definitions.
2. **Self-Quiz** Test your retention of chapter concepts by taking the Self-Quiz.
3. **Exercises** Work these short exercises to review the concepts and terms covered in the chapter.
4. **Practice Test** Test how ready you are for an upcoming exam by completing the online Practice Test.

STUDY TOOLS/ ADDITIONAL RESOURCES

The Understanding Computers Web site has a wide range of additional resources, including an **Online Study Guide** (containing study tips, a chapter outline with room to add your own notes, and a chapter checklist of the activities to complete when the chapter is covered in class and when you are preparing for a test) and an **Online Glossary** for each chapter; **Further Exploration** links; a **Web Guide**, a **Guide to Buying a PC**, and a **Computer History Timeline**; more information about **Numbering Systems**, **Coding Charts**, and **CPU Characteristics**; and much, much more!

CHAPTER 3 Storage

OUTLINE

LEARNING OBJECTIVES

After completing this chapter, you will be able to:

1. Explain the difference between storage systems and memory.
2. Name several general characteristics of storage systems.
3. Identify the two primary types of magnetic disk systems and describe how they work.
4. Discuss the various types of optical disc systems available and how they differ from each other and from magnetic systems.
5. Explain what flash memory media and flash memory drives are and how they are used today.
6. List at least three other types of storage systems.
7. Summarize the storage alternatives for a PC, including which storage systems should be included on a typical PC and for what applications other storage systems are appropriate.

OVERVIEW

In Chapter 2, we discussed the role of RAM, the computer's main memory. RAM *temporarily* holds program instructions, data, and output while they are needed by the computer. For instance, when you first create a letter or other word processing document on your computer, the word processing program and the document are both temporarily stored in RAM. But when the word processing program is closed, the computer no longer needs to work with the program or the document, and so they are erased from RAM. Consequently, anything (such as your word processing document) that needs to be preserved for future use needs to be stored on a more permanent medium. *Storage systems* fill this role.

We begin this chapter with a look at the characteristics common among storage systems. Then, storage systems based on magnetic disks (namely floppy disks and hard drives) are discussed. From there, we turn to optical discs and discuss how optical discs work and the various types of CDs and DVDs available today. Next, we discuss flash memory storage systems, followed by a look at other types of storage systems that can be used for some applications, such as remote storage, smart cards, holographic storage, and storage systems used with large computer systems and networks. The chapter concludes with a summary and comparison of the portable storage devices covered in the chapter. ■

STORAGE SYSTEMS CHARACTERISTICS

All storage systems have specific characteristics, such as consisting of a *storage device* and a *storage medium*, *portability*, *volatility*, how data is accessed and represented, the type of storage technology used, and so on. These characteristics are discussed in the next few sections.

Storage Devices and Storage Media

There are two parts to any storage system: the **storage device** and the **storage medium**. A storage medium is the hardware where data is actually stored (for example, a *floppy disk*, *CD*, or *flash memory card*); a storage medium is inserted into the appropriate storage device (such as a *floppy drive*, *CD drive*, or *flash memory card reader*) to be read from or written to. Usually the storage device and storage medium are two separate pieces of hardware (that is, the storage medium is *removable*), although with some systems—such as a *hard drive*—the two parts are permanently sealed together to form one piece of hardware (called a *fixed-media* storage system). Fixed-media storage systems generally provide higher speed and better reliability at a lower cost than removable-media alternatives, but removable-media storage systems have the advantages of a virtually unlimited storage capacity (by purchasing more of the proper storage medium), being able to be easily transported from one location to another (to share data with others, transfer data between a

FURTHER EXPLORATION

For links to further information about removable storage devices and media, go to www.course.com/uc11/ch03

>**Storage device.** A piece of hardware, such as a floppy drive or CD drive, into which a storage medium is inserted to be read from or written to.

>**Storage medium.** The part of a storage system where data is stored, such as a floppy disk or CD disc.

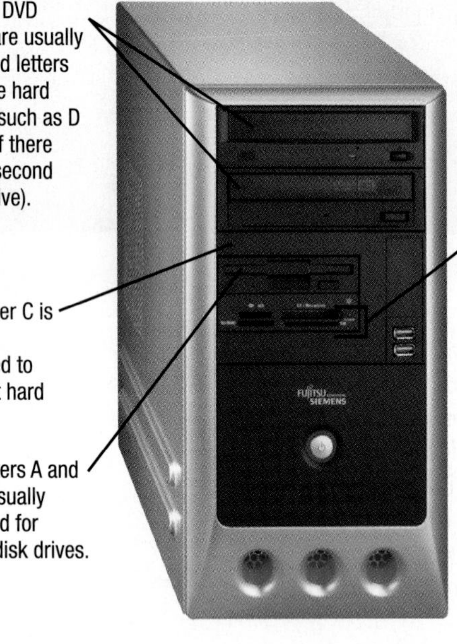
CD and DVD drives are usually assigned letters after the hard drives (such as D and E, if there isn't a second hard drive).
The letter C is usually assigned to the first hard drive.
The letters A and B are usually reserved for floppy disk drives.
The various slots in a built-in flash memory card reader are typically assigned next, such as the letters F, G, H, and I, in this example.
Other letters, beginning with J in this example, would be used for any other drives attached to the PC.

FIGURE 3-1
Storage device identifiers. To keep track of storage devices in an unambiguous way, the computer system assigns letters of the alphabet or names to each of them.

work and home PC, or take digital photos to a photo store, for instance), and being able to be stored in a secure area, such as for backup purposes or to protect sensitive data.

Storage devices can be *internal* (located inside the system unit), *external* (plugged into an external port on the system unit), or *remote* (located on another computer, such as a network server). Internal devices have the advantage of requiring no additional desk space and are often faster than their external counterparts. External devices can be used with multiple computers or added to a PC that has no room left inside its system unit. Remote devices are accessed over a network; in the case of the *online storage systems* accessed via the Internet, they have the additional advantage of being able to be accessed from any PC that has an Internet connection.

Regardless of how storage devices are connected to a computer, letters of the alphabet and/or names are typically assigned to each storage device, so the devices can be identified when they need to be used (see Figure 3-1). Some drive letters, such as for a floppy drive (*A*) and the first hard drive (*C*), are typically consistent from computer to computer and do not usually change even if more storage devices are added to a PC. The rest of the drive letters on a PC may change as new devices are added either permanently (like when an additional hard drive is installed inside the PC) or temporarily (like when a flash memory drive or digital camera is connected to the PC)—the computer just assigns and reassigns drive letters as needed, as often as needed.

Volatility

Storage media are **nonvolatile**. This means that when you shut off power to a storage device, the data stored on that device's storage medium will still be there when you turn the device back on. This feature contrasts with RAM, which is **volatile**. As discussed previously, programs and documents held in RAM are erased once they are no longer needed or the power to the computer is turned off.

Random vs. Sequential Access

When the computer system receives an instruction that requires data or programs located in storage, it must go to the designated location on the appropriate storage medium and retrieve the requested data or programs. This procedure is referred to as access. Two basic access methods are available: random and sequential.

Random access, also called *direct access*, means that data can be retrieved directly from any location on the storage medium, in any order. Most PC storage devices—including hard disk drives, floppy disk drives, and CD/DVD drives—are random access devices. They work like audio CD players or movie DVD players—the user can jump directly to a particular selection or location on the CD or DVD, as needed. Media that allow random access are sometimes referred to as *addressable* media. This means that the storage system can locate each piece of stored data or each program at a unique *address*, which is determined by the computer system. With *sequential access*, however, the data can only be retrieved in the

>**Nonvolatile.** Describes a storage medium that retains its contents when the power is shut off. >**Volatile.** Describes a medium whose content is erased when the power is shut off.

order in which it is physically stored on the medium. One type of PC storage device that uses sequential access is a *tape drive*. Computer tapes work like audio cassette tapes or videotapes—to get to a specific location on the tape, you must play or fast forward through all of the tape before it.

Logical vs. Physical Representation

Anything (such as a program, letter, digital photograph, or song) stored on a storage medium is referred to as a **file**. Data files are also sometimes called *documents*. When a document that was just created (such as a memo or letter in a word processing program) is saved, it is stored as a new file on the storage medium that the user designates. During the storage process, the user is required to give the file a name, called a **filename**; the user uses that filename whenever he or she wants to open the file again.

To keep files organized, related documents are often stored in **folders** (also called *directories*) located on the storage medium. For example, one folder might contain memos to business associates while another might hold a set of budgets for a specific project (see Figure 3-2). To further organize files, you can create *subfolders* (*subdirectories*) within a folder. For instance, you might create a "Letters" folder that contains one subfolder for letters sent to friends and a second subfolder for letters sent to potential employers. In Figure 3-2, both *Budgets* and *Memos* are subfolders inside the *My Documents* folder.

Although both the user and the computer use drive letters, folder names, and filenames to save and retrieve documents, a user typically views how data is stored (what has been discussed so far in this section and what appears in the *Windows Explorer* file management program screen shown in Figure 3-2) using *logical file representation*. That is, individuals view a document stored as one complete unit in a particular folder on a particular drive. Computers, however, use *physical file representation*; that is, they access data stored on the storage media using its physical locations. For example, the ABC Industries Proposal Memo file shown in Figure 3-2 is *logically* located in the Memos folders in the My Documents folder on the hard drive C, but the content of this file could be *physically* stored in many different pieces scattered across that hard drive. When this occurs, the computer keeps track of the various physical locations as well as the logical representations (filename, folder names, and drive letter) used to identify that file. Fortunately, users do not have to be concerned with how files are physically stored on a storage medium because the computer keeps track of that information and uses it to retrieve files whenever they are requested.

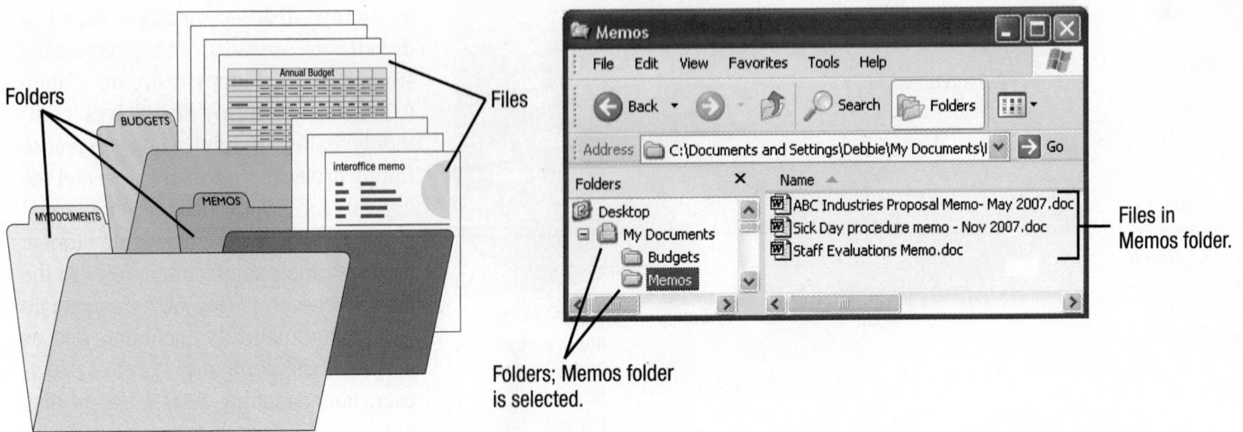

FIGURE 3-2
Organizing data.
Folders can be used to organize related items on a storage medium.

>**File.** Something stored on a storage medium, such as a program, document, or image. >**Filename.** A name given to a file by the user that is used to retrieve the file at a later time. >**Folder.** A named place on a storage medium into which files can be stored to keep the files stored on that medium organized.

TIP

Use the term *discs* when referring to optical media; use the term *disks* when referring to magnetic media.

Magnetic Disks vs. Optical Discs

Data is stored *magnetically* or *optically* on most storage media. With magnetic media, such as floppy disks, data is stored magnetically, which means the data (0s and 1s) is represented using different magnetic alignments. The magnetic alignment on the disk can be changed, so the data on magnetic disks can be erased and overwritten as needed. Optical storage media (such as CDs and DVDs) store data optically using laser beams. On some optical media, the laser burns permanent marks into the surface of the medium so the data cannot be erased or rewritten. With *rewritable* optical media, the laser changes the reflectivity of the medium but does not permanently alter the disc surface so that the reflectivity of the medium can be changed back again. Consequently, the data stored on the disc can be erased or overwritten.

Some storage systems use a combination of magnetic and optical technology. Others use a different technology altogether, such as flash memory media that represent data using *electrons*. Some of the most widely used storage systems are discussed in the remainder of the chapter.

MAGNETIC DISK SYSTEMS

Speedy access to data, relatively low cost, and the ability to erase and rewrite data make **magnetic disks** one of the most widely used storage media on today's computers. With magnetic storage systems, data is written by *read/write heads* which magnetize particles a certain way on a medium's surface to represent the data's 0s and 1s. The particles retain their magnetic orientation until the orientation is changed again, so files can be stored, rewritten to the disk, and erased, as needed. Storing data on a magnetic disk is illustrated in Figure 3-3. The most common type of magnetic disk is the *hard disk*; another common type of magnetic disk is the *floppy disk*.

FIGURE 3-3
Storing data on magnetic disks.

Read/write head
Disk surface
1. Prior to data storage, magnetic particles are not aligned.
2. The read/write head inscribes data by aligning each of the magnetic particles in one of two ways.
3. Particles aligned one way represent binary 0s; the other way represents binary 1s.

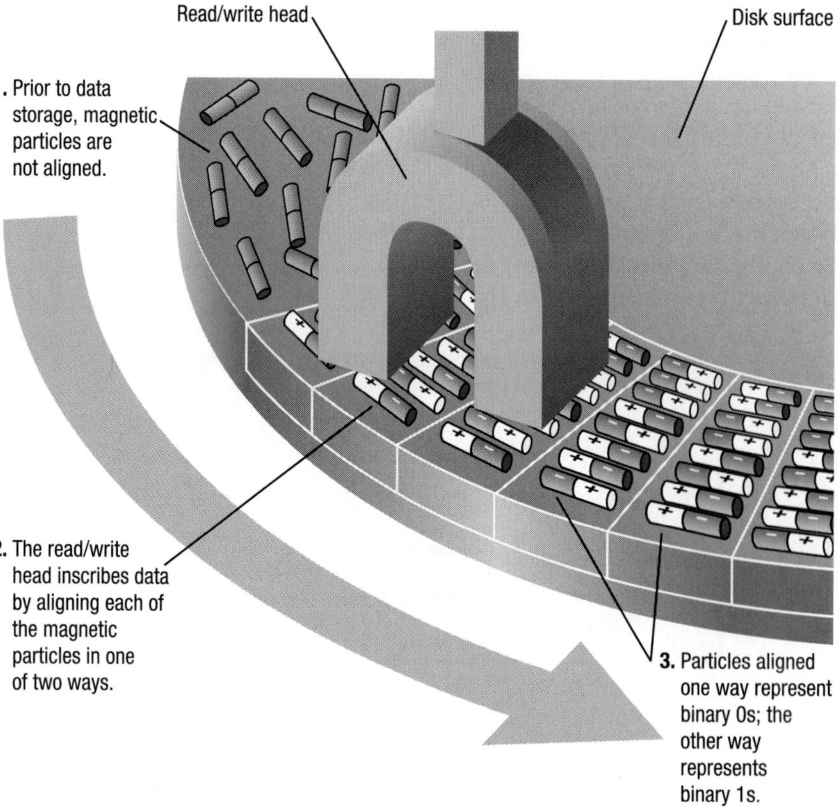

Floppy Disks and Drives

PCs have traditionally been set up to use a **floppy disk**—sometimes called a *diskette* or *disk*—to meet removable storage needs. Floppy disks are written to and read by **floppy disk drives** (commonly called *floppy drives*). Because floppy drives are relatively slow and the capacity of floppy disks is very small compared to newer removable storage media, some manufacturers refer to the floppy drive as a *legacy drive* and are no longer automatically including one as part of their computer systems. However, understanding how a floppy disk works will help you to understand how magnetic disks in general work.

>**Magnetic disk.** A storage medium that records data using magnetic spots on disks made of flexible plastic or rigid metal. >**Floppy disk.** A low-capacity, removable magnetic disk made of flexible plastic permanently sealed inside a hard plastic cover. >**Floppy disk drive.** A storage device that reads from and writes to floppy disks.

Floppy Disk Characteristics

A floppy disk consists of a round piece of flexible plastic (hence the name "floppy disk") coated with a magnetizable substance. The disk is protected by a square, rugged plastic cover lined with a soft material that wipes the disk clean as it spins (see Figure 3-4). The surface of a floppy disk is organized into circular rings, called **tracks**, and pie-shaped **sectors**. On most PC systems, the smallest storage area on a disk is a **cluster**—the part of a track that crosses a specific number of adjoining sectors (see Figure 3-5). Tracks, sectors, and clusters are numbered by the computer so it can keep track of where data is stored. The PC uses a *file system* to record where each file is physically stored and what filename the user has assigned to it. When the user requests a document (always by filename), the computer uses its file system to retrieve it. Since a cluster is the smallest addressable area on a disk, everything stored on a disk always takes up at least one cluster of space on the disk.

A write-protect square can prevent accidentally writing to the disk; the square's plastic window can be opened (for write-protection) and closed (for data storage) with your fingernail.

A hard plastic cover protects the disk from dirt and damage.

A spring-loaded shutter exposes the surface of a disk so it can be read from.

Liners remove dirt from the disk's surfaces as it spins.

A label can be placed on the disk to indicate its contents.

The plastic surfaces of the disk are coated with a magnetizable substance so that data can be recorded.

A metal hub at the center of the disk is used to spin the disk inside the drive.

FIGURE 3-4
The anatomy of a floppy disk.

Most floppy disks in use today measure 3½ inches in diameter and can store 1.44 MB of data, which is sufficient to store about 500 pages of double-spaced text or one or two digital photos, depending on the photo settings used. Floppy disks typically cost about 25 cents each. Music files, large numbers of digital photos, and documents containing a lot of images usually require a higher-capacity removable storage media—such as a CD, a DVD, or flash memory media; these types of storage media are discussed shortly.

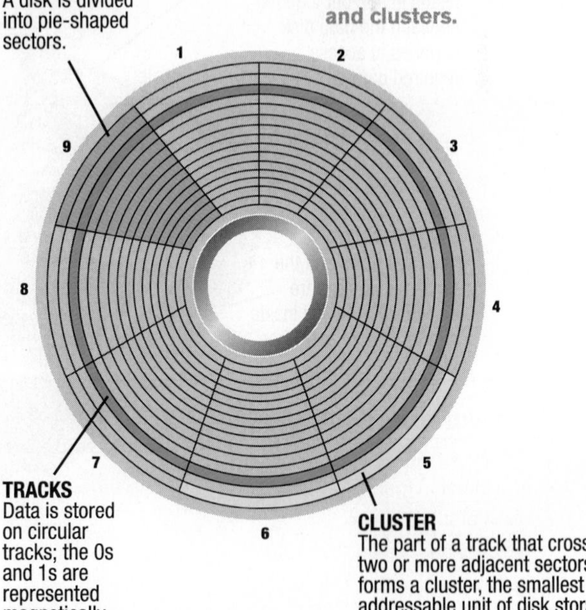

SECTORS
A disk is divided into pie-shaped sectors.
1
2
3
4
5
6
7
8
9
TRACKS
Data is stored on circular tracks; the 0s and 1s are represented magnetically.
CLUSTER
The part of a track that crosses two or more adjacent sectors forms a cluster, the smallest addressable unit of disk storage.

FIGURE 3-5
Magnetic disks (such as floppy disks) are organized into tracks, sectors, and clusters.

Using Floppy Disks

To use a floppy disk, it must first be inserted into a floppy drive (face up and with the disk shutter closest to the drive door, as illustrated in Figure 3-6). When it is completely inserted, the disk clicks into place, the metal shutter is moved aside to expose the surface of the disk, and the *eject button* on the front of the drive pops out. Before data can be stored on a floppy disk, the disk must be *formatted*. Most floppy disks sold today are already formatted for either IBM-compatible or Macintosh computers and are, therefore, ready to use. If a disk is not formatted, the user must format it first before it can be used. Users can also format floppy disks to quickly erase them for reuse—formatting a disk that already contains data erases everything on the disk.

>**Track.** A concentric path on a disk where data is recorded. >**Sector.** A pie-shaped area on a disk surface. >**Cluster.** The part of a track on a disk that crosses a fixed number of contiguous sectors; it is the smallest addressable area of a disk.

FIGURE 3-6
Inserting a floppy disk into a floppy drive. Disks go into a drive only one way–right side up, with the disk shutter facing the drive door.

When the floppy disk in the floppy drive needs to be accessed, the drive begins to rotate the disk within its plastic cover. The drive's read/write head can read (retrieve) data from or write (store) data onto the actual surface of the disk while the disk is spinning. The read/write heads move in and out over the surface of the disk, allowing the read/write heads access to all tracks on that disk. While the disk is spinning, the drive's indicator light goes on—do not remove the floppy disk while this light is on. To remove the disk, wait until the light goes off, and then press the eject button to remove the disk.

Hard Disk Drives

With the exception of computers designed to use only network storage devices (such as network computers and some Internet appliances), virtually all PCs come with a **hard disk drive** (commonly referred to as a **hard drive**) that is used to store most programs and data. *Internal hard drives* (those located in the system unit) are not designed to be removed, unless they need to be repaired or replaced. *External hard drives* typically connect to a computer via a USB port. In addition to being used with computers, hard drives are also increasingly being incorporated into other consumer products, such as *digital video recorders (DVRs)*, *game consoles*, *portable media players*, digital camcorders, cars, and more.

Hard Drive Characteristics

Similar to floppy drives, hard drives store data magnetically; they use read/write heads to store and retrieve data; and their disks are organized into tracks, sectors, and clusters. However, the disks used with a hard drive are made out of metal and are permanently sealed (along with the read/write heads and access mechanisms) inside the hard drive to avoid contamination and to enable the disks to spin faster. One drive may contain a stack of several hard disks, as shown in Figure 3-7.

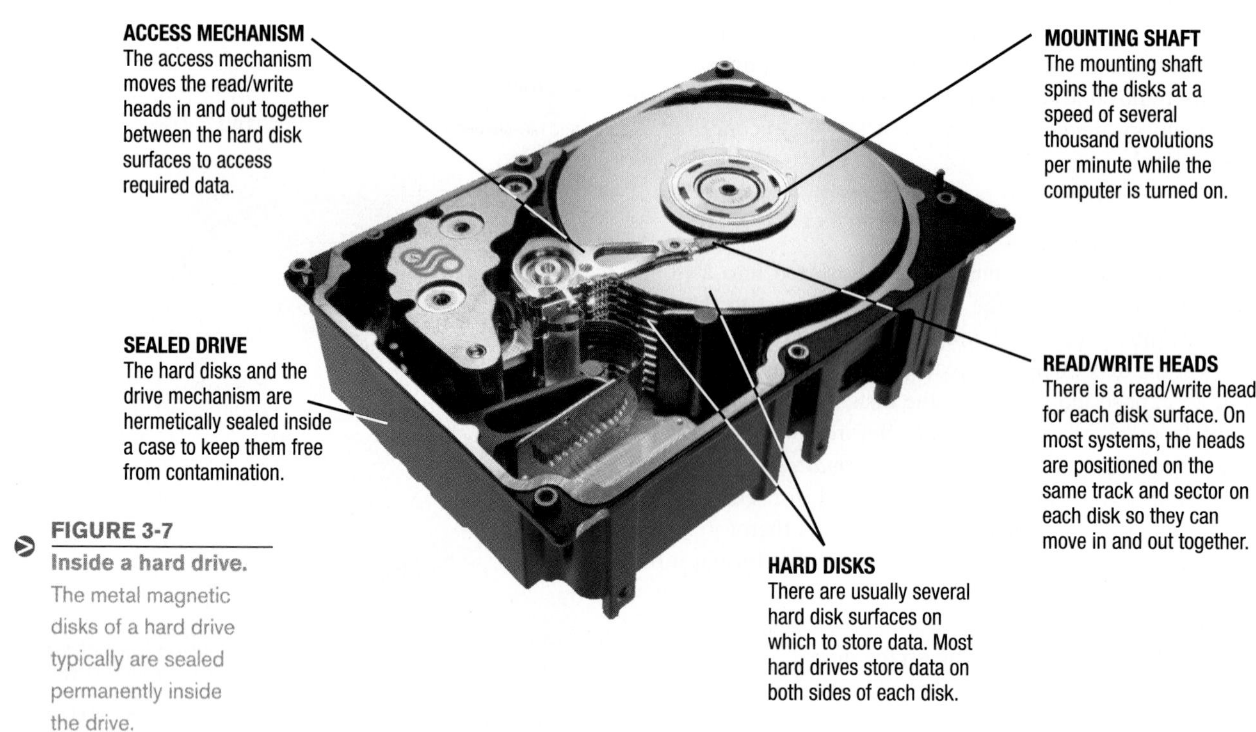

ACCESS MECHANISM
The access mechanism moves the read/write heads in and out together between the hard disk surfaces to access required data.
MOUNTING SHAFT
The mounting shaft spins the disks at a speed of several thousand revolutions per minute while the computer is turned on.
SEALED DRIVE
The hard disks and the drive mechanism are hermetically sealed inside a case to keep them free from contamination.
READ/WRITE HEADS
There is a read/write head for each disk surface. On most systems, the heads are positioned on the same track and sector on each disk so they can move in and out together.
HARD DISKS
There are usually several hard disk surfaces on which to store data. Most hard drives store data on both sides of each disk.

FIGURE 3-7
Inside a hard drive. The metal magnetic disks of a hard drive typically are sealed permanently inside the drive.

>**Hard disk drive.** A storage system consisting of one or more metal magnetic disks permanently sealed with an access mechanism inside its drive. Also called a **hard drive**.

In addition to tracks, sectors, and clusters, hard drives also have **cylinders**. A cylinder is the collection of one particular track, such as the first track or the tenth track, on each disk surface. In other words, it is the area on all of the hard disks inside the hard drive that can be accessed without moving the read/write access mechanism, once it has been moved to the proper position. For example, the four-disk system in Figure 3-8 contains eight possible recording surfaces (using both sides of each disk), so a cylinder on that system would consist of eight tracks, such as track 13 on all eight surfaces. Hard drives commonly have anywhere from a few hundred to a few thousand cylinders. The number of tracks on a single disk is equal to the number of cylinders in the disk system.

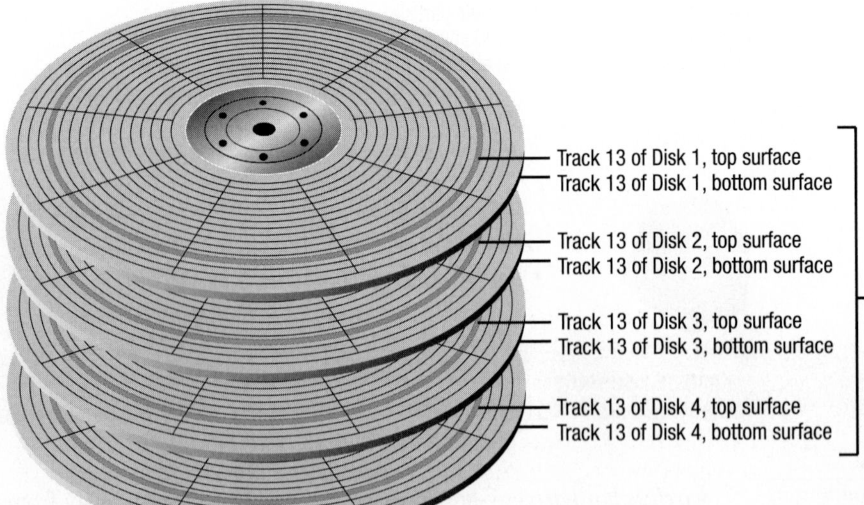

FIGURE 3-8
A disk cylinder. Hard drives use cylinders, in addition to tracks, sectors, and clusters, to keep track of where data is stored.

Virtually all hard drives are formatted at the factory before they are sold, so they are ready to be used as soon as they are installed. Because reformatting a disk erases everything on the disk, hard drives are rarely reformatted. This task is only performed if errors are preventing the hard drive from operating properly and there is no other option. To retrieve or store data, most hard drives have at least one read/write head for each recording surface. These heads are mounted on an *access mechanism*; this mechanism moves the heads in and out over the tracks together, similar to the way the heads move over a floppy disk. Because all the heads move together, all the tracks in the cylinder containing the data can be accessed at the same time.

TIP

Be very careful when formatting any type of storage media, since formatting erases all data stored on the media.

It is important to realize that a hard drive's read/write heads never touch the surface of the hard disk at any time, even during reading and writing. If the read/write heads do touch the surface—such as if the PC is bumped while the hard drive is spinning or a foreign object gets onto the surface of the disk, a *head crash* occurs, which may do permanent damage to the hard drive. Because the heads are located extremely close to the surface of the disk—less than one millionth of an inch above the surface—the presence of a foreign object the width of a human hair or even a smoke particle (about 2,500 and 100 millionths of an inch, respectively) on the surface of a hard disk is like placing a huge boulder on a road and then trying to drive over it with your car (see Figure 3-9). One never knows when a hard drive will crash—there may be no warning whatsoever—which is a good reason for keeping the drive backed up regularly. *Backing up* a computer system—that is, creating a second copy of important files—is discussed in more detail in Chapter 5. When hard drives containing critical data become damaged, *data recovery firms* may be able to help out, as discussed in the Inside the Industry box.

Internal PC hard drives today hold between 80 to 500 GB, and their storage capacity is continually growing. External hard drive storage capacity is even larger—up to 2 TB at the time of this writing. Some hard drives today come with built-in security features, such as a *fingerprint reader* that allows only authorized users access to the drive. Others—called

>**Cylinder.** The collection of tracks located in the same location on a set of hard disk surfaces.

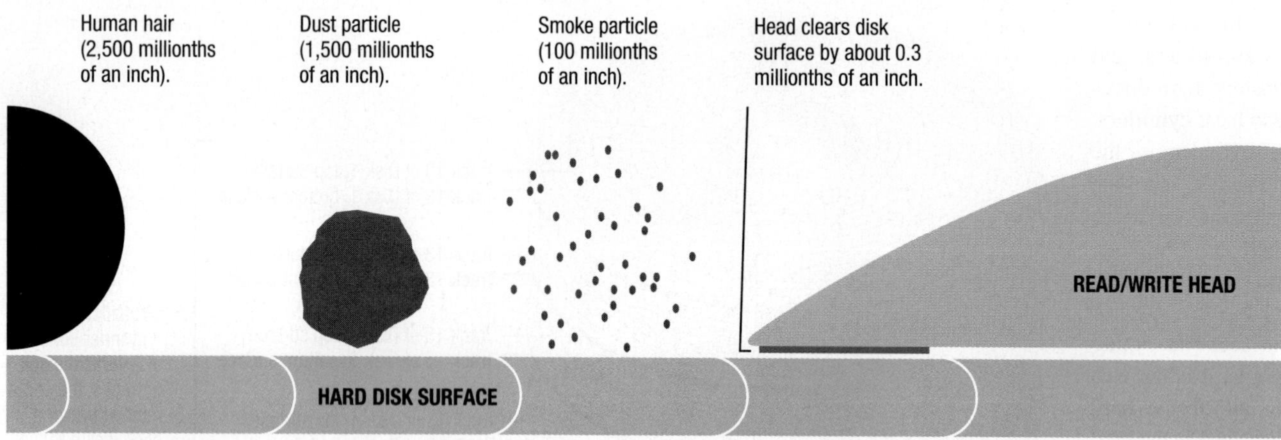

FIGURE 3-9

Obstacles on a hard disk surface. A human hair or even a smoke particle on a fast-spinning hard disk surface can damage both the surface and the read/write head.

wireless hard drives—are accessed from up to 100 yards away from the computer using a *Wi-Fi* wireless networking connection.

Hard Drive Speed and Caching

Because of their construction and the fact that their disks typically spin continually at a rate of 5,400 to 15,000 revolutions per minute, hard drives provide fast access to data. The total time that it takes for a hard drive to read or write data is called the **disk access time** and requires the following three steps:

1. Move the read/write heads to the cylinder that contains (or will hold) the desired data—called *seek time*.
2. Rotate the disks into the proper position so that the read/write heads are located over the part of the cylinder to be used—called *rotational delay*.
3. Move the data, such as reading the data from the disk and transferring it to memory, or transferring the data from memory and storing it on the disk—called *data movement time*.

A typical disk access time is around 10 milliseconds (ms). To minimize disk access time, drives usually store related data on the same cylinder. This strategy sharply reduces the seek-time component and improves the overall access time. Another strategy for speeding up hard drive performance is *disk caching*.

A *cache* (pronounced *cash*) is a place to store something temporarily. For instance, in Chapter 2 we learned that *cache memory* is a group of very fast memory chips used by the CPU to store data and instructions that might be needed in order to speed up processing. *Disk caching* is similar in concept—it stores data or programs that might be needed soon in memory chips in order to avoid having to retrieve the data or programs from the hard drive when they are requested. Since retrieving data from memory is much faster than from the hard drive, disk caching can speed up performance.

The memory used for disk caching can be a designated portion of RAM or memory chips located on the circuit board inside the hard drive. In either case, it is called the **disk cache**. When a hard drive uses disk caching (as most do today), any time the hard drive is accessed the computer copies the requested program and data, as well as extra programs or data located in neighboring areas of the hard drive (such as the entire track or cylinder), to the disk cache. The theory behind disk caching is that neighboring data will likely have to be read soon anyway (research indicates that there is an 80% to 90% chance the next

>**Disk access time.** The time it takes to locate and read data from (or position and write data to) a storage medium. >**Disk cache.** A dedicated part of RAM used to store additional data adjacent to data retrieved during a disk fetch to improve system performance.

INSIDE THE INDUSTRY

Data Recovery Experts

It happens far more often than most people imagine. A hard drive quits working the day before a big report is due, a laptop is dropped in the parking lot and then run over by a car, or a business burns down taking the PC containing the only copy of the company records with it. If the data on the drive was recently backed up, the data can be installed on a new drive with just a little expense and a short delay. When critical data was not backed up and is located on a potentially destroyed hard drive, it is time to seek a professional data recovery expert.

Data recovery firms, such as DriveSavers in California, specialize in recovering data from severely damaged storage media (see the accompanying photos). The damaged drives are taken apart in a clean room (an airtight room similar to the ones in which computer chips are manufactured), cleaned, put back together, and the data is copied onto a server. Then, if the file directory is not recovered, engineers try to match the jumbled data to file types in order to reconstruct the original files. DriveSavers clients have included Barbara Mandrell, whose musical director's hard drive containing several months of work and more than 1,200 orchestra charts needed for a concert nine days away stopped working; the executive producer of "The Simpsons," whose computer crashed taking scripts for 12 episodes of the show with it; an individual whose notebook PC was trapped for two days beneath a sunken cruise ship in the Amazon River; and a Fortune 500 company, which lost all its financial data and stockholder information when its Unix server went down. In all four cases, DriveSavers was able to recover all of the lost data.

Data recovery firms stress the importance of backing up data. According to Scott Gaidano, president of DriveSavers, "The first thing we tell people is back up, back up, back up. It's amazing how many people don't back up." It is also important to make sure the backup procedure is working. For instance, the Fortune 500 company mentioned previously performed regular backups and kept the backup media in a fire-resistant safe, but when they went to use the backup after their server crashed, they discovered that the backup media were all blank.

Because potentially losing all the data on a drive can be so stressful and traumatic, DriveSavers has its own data-crisis counselor, a former suicide hotline worker. Fortunately for their clients, DriveSavers has a 90% recovery rate. The services of data recovery experts are not cheap, but when the lost data is irreplaceable, they are a bargain.

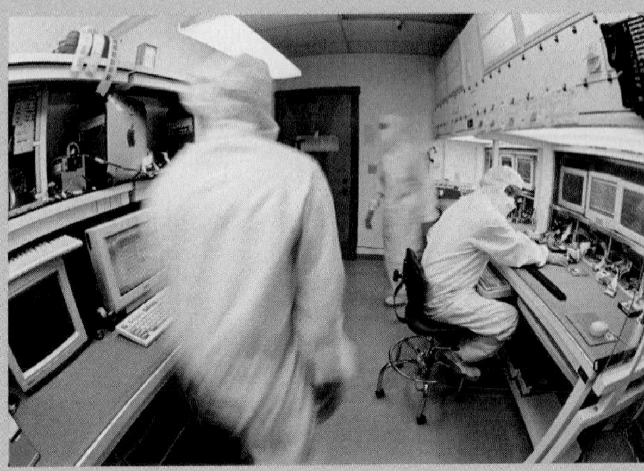

Data recovery. All the data located on the hard drive of this computer (left) that was virtually destroyed in a fire was recovered by data recovery experts in less than 24 hours. Recovery takes place in a clean room (right).

request will be for data located adjacent to the data last read), so the computer reduces the number of times the hard drive is accessed by copying that data into the disk cache before it is needed. When the next data is requested, the computer checks the disk cache first to see if the data it needs is already there. If it is, the data is retrieved for processing; if not, the computer retrieves the requested data from the hard drive (see Figure 3-10). Disk caching saves not only time but also wear and tear on the hard drive. In portable computers, it can also extend battery life.

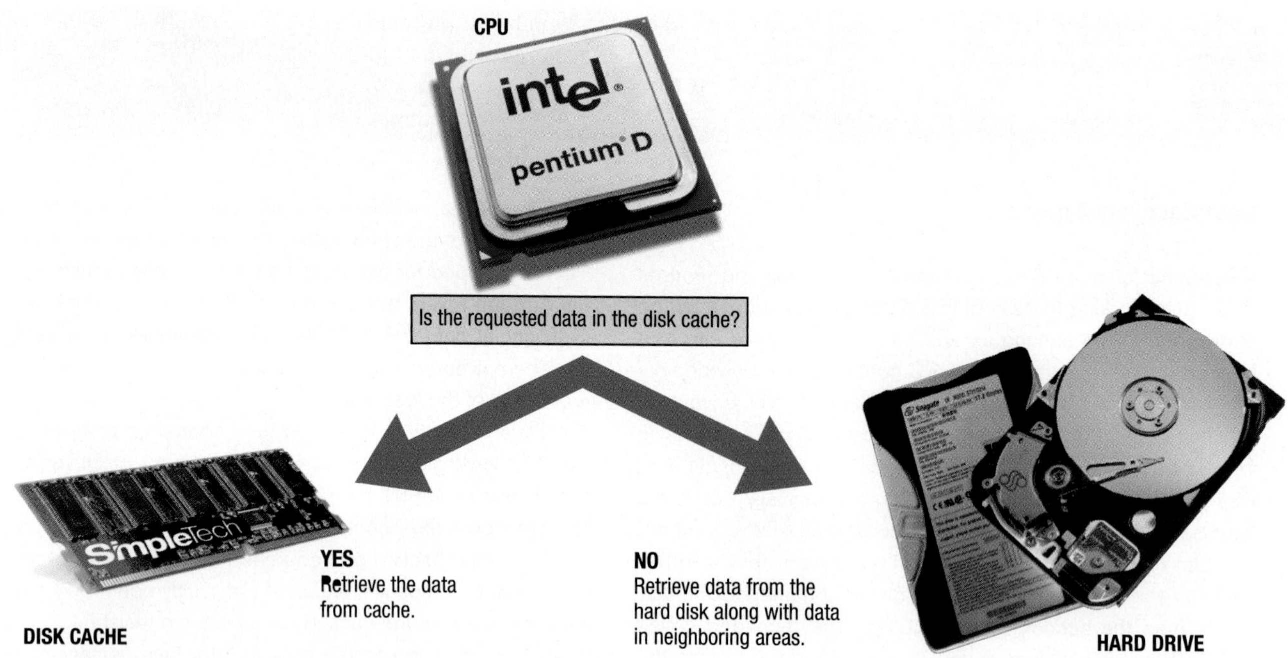
CPU
intel
pentium D
Is the requested data in the disk cache?
SimpleTech
DISK CACHE
YES
Retrieve the data from cache.
NO
Retrieve data from the hard disk along with data in neighboring areas.
HARD DRIVE

FIGURE 3-10
Disk cache. Disk cache is either a special area of RAM or memory chips located inside the hard drive case used to store small amounts of hard drive data, in order to speed up the retrieval of that data.

Partitioning and File Systems

Partitioning a hard drive enables you to logically divide the physical capacity of a single drive into separate areas, called *partitions*. Partitions look and act like independent disk drives and are sometimes referred to as *logical drives* since they are labeled as separate drives, such as a C drive and a D drive, but they are still physically one drive. One or more partitions are created when a hard drive is first formatted. Users can create additional partitions if desired, although this action usually destroys any data in the partitions being changed. Consequently, you should back up data stored on that drive to another storage medium before you repartition that hard drive, and then copy the data back onto the repartitioned hard drive. Some operating systems have a limit to the number of partitions that can be used.

While today's PCs do not usually need partitions to function (older operating systems could only address hard drives up to 512 MB, so hard drives larger than that limit had to use multiple partitions), partitioning a large drive can make it function more efficiently. This is because operating systems typically use a larger cluster size with a larger hard drive. When a large cluster size is used, disk space is often wasted because even tiny files have to use up one entire cluster of storage space. When a hard drive is partitioned, each logical drive can use a smaller cluster size, since each logical drive is smaller than the original drive. The cluster size, maximum drive size, and maximum file size are determined by the file system being used. For instance, the Windows *FAT32 file system* is more efficient than the original FAT system because FAT32 systems allow smaller cluster sizes, which cuts down on wasted storage space. The FAT32 file system also supports larger hard drives than the FAT file system. The recommended file system for Windows XP computers is the newer *NTFS* file system, which supports much larger drives and files than either the FAT or the FAT32 file systems, and includes better security capabilities.

Many computers today are set up with one partition for the main hard drive and another partition for a *recovery partition* that contains the data necessary to restore the hard drive back to its state at the time of purchase, if the computer malfunctions. Another reason for partitioning a hard drive is to be able to use two different operating systems on the same hard drive—such as Windows and Linux. You can then decide which operating system you will run each time you boot your computer. Creating the appearance of having separate hard drives for file management, multiple users, or other purposes is another common reason for partitioning a hard drive. Some users choose to install their programs on one partition of the hard drive (usually the one named C) and to store their data on a second partition (such as D). Storing data files on one partition and program files on a different partition makes it easier for the user to locate data files. It also enables users to back up all data files simply by backing up the entire data partition. Operating systems and backing up data are discussed in more detail in Chapter 5.

FURTHER EXPLORATION

For links to further information about hard drives, go to www.course.com/uc11/ch03

Hard Drive Interface Standards

Hard drives connect, or interface, with a computer using one of several different standards. These standards determine performance characteristics, such as the density with which data can be packed onto the disk, the disk access speed, the storage capacity, and the way the disk drive interfaces with other hardware.

The most common *hard drive interface standards* for desktop PCs today are *serial ATA* (*SATA*) and *serial ATA II* (*SATA II*), which are replacing earlier parallel standards, such as *parallel ATA* and *IDE*. The *SCSI* (for *small computer system interface* and pronounced "skuzzy") and the newer *serial attached SCSI* (*SAS*) standards are commonly used with servers. Another hard drive interface standard used with high-end servers is *Fibre Channel*—a reliable, flexible, and very fast standard geared for long-distance, high-bandwidth applications (hard drives used with larger computers and networks are discussed later in this chapter). Emerging standards for storage devices that are accessed via the Internet or another network that uses the *TCP/IP* networking standard to communicate include *Internet SCSI* (*iSCSI*) and *Fibre Channel over IP*. *External hard drives* today typically connect instead via a USB or FireWire port.

External and Portable Hard Drive Systems

Although hard drives are typically located inside the system unit, *external hard drives* (see Figure 3-11)—which typically connect to a PC via a USB port, a FireWire port, or a wireless networking connection—are also available. External hard drives can be used to transport a large amount of data from one PC to another (by moving the entire drive to another PC) or can be used with a single PC for backup or as a second hard drive.

While external drives can be moved from PC to PC when needed, *portable hard drives* are specifically designed for that purpose. One example of a portable *mini hard drive* is shown in Figure 3-11. This 1-inch portable hard drive—also referred to as a *pocket hard drive*—holds 5 GB. Because of their small physical size, portable mini hard drives are designed to be used with handheld PCs, digital music players, and other portable devices, in addition to being used to transfer data from one PC to another. *Internal mini hard drives* are also beginning to be built into portable devices to increase

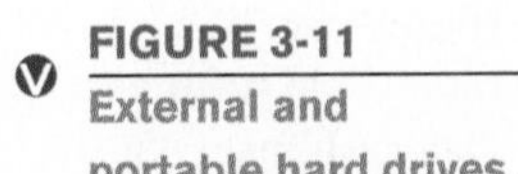

FIGURE 3-11
External and portable hard drives.

USB EXTERNAL HARD DRIVE
This drive holds 250 GB and connects via a USB port.

WI-FI EXTERNAL HARD DRIVE
This hard drive holds 160 GB and connects via a wireless Wi-Fi connection.

USB POCKET HARD DRIVE
This hard drive holds 5 GB, connects via a USB port, and can be carried in a pocket.

PC CARD HARD DRIVE
This hard drive holds 5 GB and connects via a PC Card slot.

their storage capacity. For instance, the Apple iPod comes with either a 20 GB or a 60 GB built-in mini hard drive and Palm's new LifeDrive handheld computer contains a 4 GB built-in mini hard drive. Notebook PCs can have built-in internal conventional or mini hard drives, but often use a removable *PC Card hard drive* (such as the one shown in Figure 3-11) instead.

High-Capacity Removable Magnetic Disks and Cartridges

There are some high-capacity removable magnetic storage systems available for users who need portability or the ability to store media in a secure location. These products fall into two categories: *superdiskettes* and *hard disk cartridges.*

Superdiskettes

Superdiskettes are high-capacity removable storage media that are usually *proprietary*; that is, can only be used with their respective drives. The most widely used type of superdiskette is the *Zip disk*, introduced by Iomega Corporation in 1995. Zip disks are high-capacity magnetic disks that can be read from and written to using only *Zip drives.* Zip disks are similar in size and in appearance to floppy disks (see Figure 3-12), but they have a capacity of 100, 250, or 750 MB and cannot be used in a conventional floppy disk drive. Zip drives can be internal or external and are *downward compatible*, meaning the higher-capacity Zip drives can read Zip disks with a matching or lower storage capacity. Zip drives are most appropriate for users who need to back up large files or transfer large files between PCs or other users that have a Zip drive. Because Zip drives were one of the first high-capacity removable storage solutions, they are still in use, although it is likely that they will eventually be replaced by other types of high-capacity removable media, such as optical discs and flash memory drives, that are not proprietary.

FIGURE 3-12
High-capacity removable magnetic disk systems.

ZIP DISKS
Zip disks can be used only with Zip drives and hold up to 750 MB per disk.

REV HARD DISK CARTRIDGES
REV cartridges can be used only with REV drives and hold up to 35 GB (or up to 90 GB of compressed data) per cartridge.

Hard Disk Cartridges

Some hard drive systems are designed to use removable *hard disk cartridges.* With these systems, the hard drive remains attached to the PC and the hard disk cartridges are inserted into and removed from the drive, similar to a floppy disk or superdiskette system. The advantage over other types of removable storage media is capacity—for instance, the Iomega REV system shown in Figure 3-12 holds 35 GB (or up to 90 GB with compression). Like superdiskettes, hard disk cartridges are proprietary, so they can only be used with their respective drives. Consequently, they are not appropriate for sharing data with a large group of users, but they are useful for storing and backing up very large files, transporting large files from one PC to another, and for exceptionally secure facilities—such as government and research labs—that require all hard drives to be locked up when not in use. They are also commonly used for complete system backups.

OPTICAL DISC SYSTEMS

Optical discs (such as *CDs* and *DVDs*) store data *optically*—using laser beams—instead of magnetically, like floppy and hard disks. Optical discs are made out of plastic and are typically 4½ inches in diameter, although smaller discs are sometimes used. Data can be stored on one or both sides of an optical disc, depending on the disc, and some discs use multiple layers to increase capacity. To keep data organized, optical discs are divided into tracks and sectors like magnetic disks but use a single grooved spiral track beginning at the center of the disc (see Figure 3-13), instead of a series of concentric tracks. (To avoid confusion with the *tracks* or songs on an audio CD, the track on an optical disc is sometimes referred to as a *groove*.) Data is written to an optical disc by stamping or molding the surface of the disc (for commercial CDs and DVDs) or by changing the reflectivity of the disc with a laser (for CDs and DVDs that are recorded using a CD or DVD drive). In either case, the disc is read with a laser and the reflection of the laser off of the disc indicates the data's 1s and 0s.

To accomplish this with molded or stamped CD and DVD discs, tiny depressions (when viewed from the top side of the disc) or bumps (when viewed from the bottom) are molded into the disc's surface. These bumps are called *pits*; the areas on the disc that are not changed are called *lands*. Although many people believe that each individual pit and land represents a 1 or 0, that is not completely accurate—it is the transition between a pit and land that represents a 1. When the disc is read, the angle of reflection of the laser beam inside the CD or DVD drive changes when it reaches a transition between a pit and a land, and when the drive detects a transition, it is interpreted as a 1; no transition for a specific period of time indicates a 0. With a CD or DVD that is recorded using a CD or DVD drive, the recording laser beam changes the reflectivity of the appropriate areas on the disc to represent the data stored there—dark, nonreflective areas are pits; reflective areas are lands, as illustrated in Figure 3-13—but the transition between a pit and a land still represents a 1 and no transition represents a 0.

The process of recording data onto an optical disc is called *burning*. To burn a CD-R or DVD-R disc, special hardware and software is needed. Many commercial burning programs are available, and many recent operating systems, such as Windows XP, include CD burning capabilities.

Optical discs can be made into a variety of sizes and shapes—such as a heart, triangle, irregular shape, or the hockey-rink shape commonly used with *business card CDs*—because the track starts at the center of the

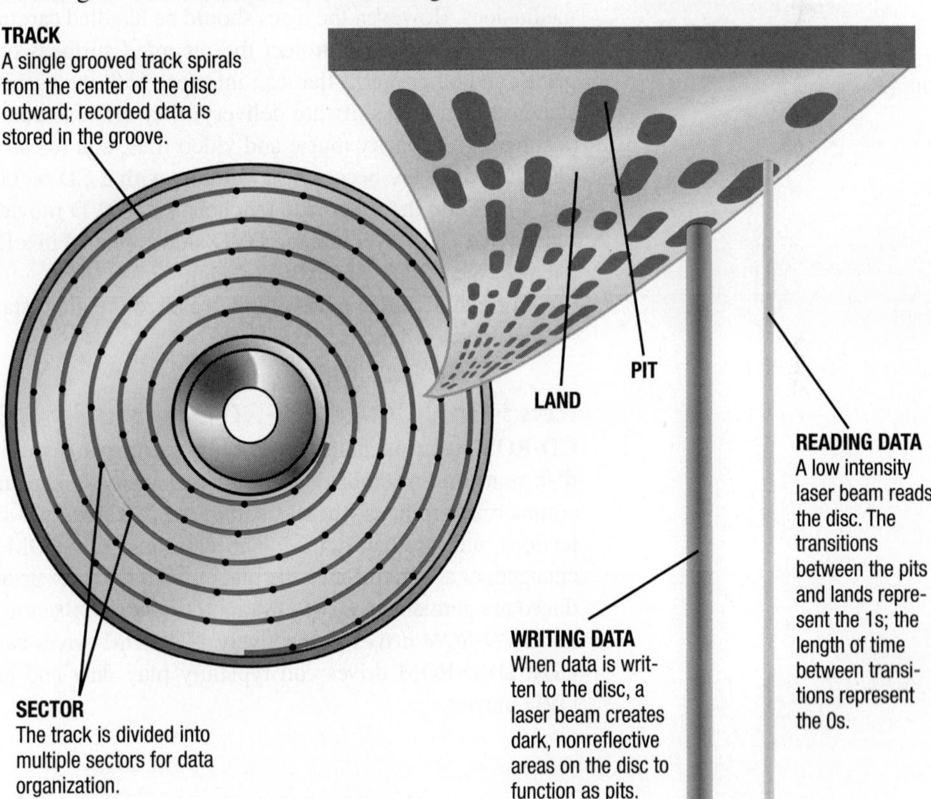

TRACK
A single grooved track spirals from the center of the disc outward; recorded data is stored in the groove.
SECTOR
The track is divided into multiple sectors for data organization.
LAND
PIT
WRITING DATA
When data is written to the disc, a laser beam creates dark, nonreflective areas on the disc to function as pits.
READING DATA
A low intensity laser beam reads the disc. The transitions between the pits and lands represent the 1s; the length of time between transitions represent the 0s.

FIGURE 3-13
How recorded optical discs work.

>**Optical disc.** A type of storage medium read from and written to using a laser beam.

FIGURE 3-14
Custom shaped optical discs. Optical discs can be made in a variety of shapes and sizes, such as the business card CD shown here.

disc and the track just stops when it reaches the outer edge of the disc. Standard shapes are molded and less expensive; custom shapes—such as those that match a key product or service being sold (a soda can, musical instrument, saw blade, candy bar, or house, as in Figure 3-14)—are custom cut and are more costly. The practice of using optical discs to replace ordinary objects, such as business cards, is becoming more common. For a closer look at business card CDs and DVDs, see the How it Works box.

CD and DVD discs are read by *CD* and *DVD drives*. The speed of a CD or DVD drive is rated as a number followed by the "×" symbol to indicate how fast the drive is compared to the first version of that drive. For instance, a 52× CD drive is 52 times faster than the original CD drive, and a 16× DVD drive is 16 times faster than the original DVD drive. Drives that can both read and write to discs typically state the speed for each type of operation separately. Many optical discs have a title and other text printed on one side; if so, they are inserted into the drive with the printed side facing up, and the data is stored on the bottom, nonprinted side of the disc.

One of the biggest advantages of CDs and DVDs is their large capacity—standard-sized 4½-inch CD discs hold either 650 MB or 700 MB, standard-sized DVD discs can hold 4.7 GB (single-layer discs) or 8.5 GB (double-layer discs), 3-inch mini CD discs hold about 200 MB, business-card-sized CD discs hold 50 MB, and business-card-sized DVD discs hold 325 MB. Other advantages include their small size and durability—optical discs are more durable than magnetic media and don't degrade with use, like some magnetic media does. However, the discs should be handled carefully and stored in *jewel cases* when they are not in use, to protect the recorded surfaces of the discs from scratches, fingerprints, and other marks that can interfere with the usability of a disc. Optical discs are the standard today for software delivery; they are also commonly used for storing and transporting high-capacity music and video files, and for backup. For added versatility, *hybrid CD/DVD* discs are becoming available, with a CD on one side (such as for audio content) and a DVD on the other side (such as for a DVD movie). The CD side of a hybrid disc is played in a CD player and the DVD side is played in a DVD player. Specific types of optical discs are discussed next.

For a look at one new way to organize the giant stacks of CDs and DVDs many individuals have on hand, see the Trend box.

Read-Only Discs: CD-ROM and DVD-ROM Discs

CD-ROM (compact disc read-only memory) discs and **DVD-ROM (digital versatile disc read-only memory) discs** are *read-only* storage media and come prerecorded with commercial products, such as software programs, clip art and other types of graphics collections, and product demos. The data on a CD-ROM or DVD-ROM cannot be erased, changed, or added to, since the pits molded into the surface of the disc when the disc is produced are permanent. CD-ROM and DVD-ROM discs are designed to be read by *CD-ROM* and *DVD-ROM drives*, respectively. CD-ROM drives can usually play both data and audio CDs; DVD-ROM drives can typically play data and audio CDs, DVD-ROM discs, and DVD movies.

>**CD-ROM (compact disc read-only memory) disc.** An optical disc, usually holding about 650 MB, that can be read from, but not written to, by the user. >**DVD-ROM (digital versatile disc read-only memory) disc.** An optical disc, usually holding 4.7 GB, that can be read from, but not written to, by the user.

HOW IT WORKS

Business Card CDs and DVDs

With computers so common in businesses and homes today, use of business card CDs is on the rise. Business card CDs are similar to conventional CDs, but they are physically smaller, come in different shapes, and hold less data. They can, however, be played using CD and DVD drives, just like any other CD. Business card CD-R discs can be recorded using a standard recordable CD or DVD drive, but are more commonly mass-produced once a master CD has been developed. For higher capacity, business card DVDs can be used.

Business card CDs and DVDs today can contain a wide variety of content, such as résumés in Word or PDF format, multimedia presentations, portfolio material (such as copies of ad campaigns created by advertising executives, digital images created by graphic artists, Web sites created by Web site designers, or photographs of an artist's or architect's work), catalogs, and copies of the company Web site–virtually any type of information an individual wants to distribute to others. The accompanying figure takes a closer look at one business card CD; as in this example, it is becoming common for business card CD content to be developed using a multimedia authoring program so that the content, along with animated effects to catch the user's interest, can be incorporated into a professional-looking presentation that is automatically played after the CD is inserted into a PC's CD or DVD drive. Blank business card CD-R discs cost about 50 cents each; professionally prepared business card CDs and DVDs cost between 50 cents and $2 each, depending on format, capacity, and shape.

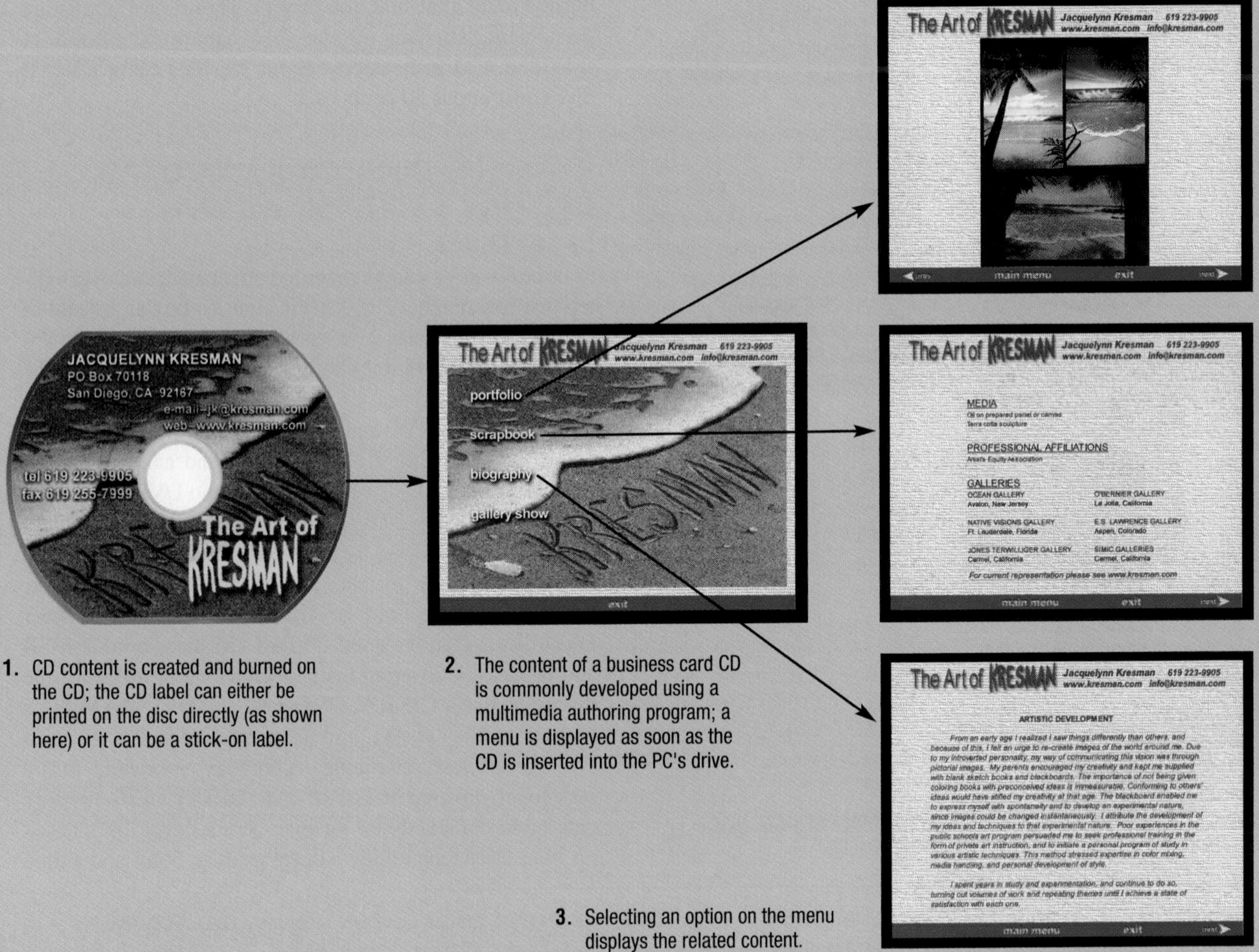

1. CD content is created and burned on the CD; the CD label can either be printed on the disc directly (as shown here) or it can be a stick-on label.

2. The content of a business card CD is commonly developed using a multimedia authoring program; a menu is displayed as soon as the CD is inserted into the PC's drive.

3. Selecting an option on the menu displays the related content.

Recordable Discs: CD-R, DVD-R, DVD+R, and DVD+R DL Discs

Recordable discs can be written to, but the discs cannot be erased and reused. Recordable CDs are typically **CD-R discs**; recordable DVDs are either **DVD-R discs** or **DVD+R discs**. Recordable CDs and DVDs are written to using an appropriate optical drive, such as a *CD-R drive* for CD-R discs and a *DVD-R drive* for DVD-R discs. Some optical drives support multiple types of discs; for instance, a drive might be able to record on both DVD-R and DVD+R discs. Virtually all recordable DVD drives can record on recordable CDs, in addition to recordable DVD discs. Once recorded, CD-R discs can be read by most types of CD and DVD drives; recorded DVD-R and DVD+R discs can be read by most DVD drives.

Recordable CDs are commonly used for backing up files, sending large files to others, and creating custom music CDs (for example, from MP3 files legally downloaded from the Internet or from songs on CDs the user owns). DVD-Rs can be used for similar purposes when more storage space is needed, such as for large backups and for storing home movies and other video files. The newest recordable DVDs (**DVD+R DL discs**) are *dual-layer* discs (also called *double-layer* discs), which means they use two recording layers on a single disc, resulting in a capacity of 8.5 GB (see Figure 3-15). One company has developed a similar six-layer DVD disc that holds 15 GB, but this product is not yet on the market.

Instead of having physically molded pits, recordable discs contain an organic light-sensitive dye located in the spiral grooved track and embedded between the plastic and reflective layers. When data is written to the disc, the recording laser inside the CD-R or DVD-R drive burns the dye, creating nonreflective burned areas that function as pits. These burn marks are permanent, so data on the disc cannot be erased or rewritten. CD-R discs cost about 15 cents each; DVD-R discs cost about 50 cents each.

FIGURE 3-15
Recordable and rewritable CDs and DVDs.

RECORDABLE DVD+R DL DISC
Dual-layer disc—holds 8.5 GB.

REWRITABLE CD-RW DISC
Single-layer disc—holds 650 MB.

REWRITABLE DVD-RAM DISC
Holds 9.4 GB.

REWRITABLE BLU-RAY DISC
Holds 23.3 GB.

Rewritable Discs: CD-RW, DVD-RW, DVD+RW, DVD-RAM, and Blue Laser Discs

Rewritable discs can be recorded on, erased, and overwritten just like magnetic disks (the How To box at the end of Chapter 6 illustrates how to store data—such as downloaded music or digital photos—on rewritable discs). The most common types of rewritable optical media are **CD-RW**, **DVD-RW**, and **DVD+RW discs**. CD-RW discs are written to using a *CD-RW drive* and can be read by most CD and DVD drives. DVD-RW and DVD+RW discs are recorded using a *DVD-RW* or *DVD+RW drive*, respectively, and can be read by most DVD drives. An additional rewritable DVD format is DVD-RAM. Single-layer **DVD-RAM** discs hold 4.7 GB and look similar to other DVD discs. Double-sided DVD-RAM discs hold 9.4 GB and need to be inserted inside a cartridge in order for the disc to be used. CD-RW, DVD-RW, and DVD-RAM discs cost about 50 cents, $1, and $3, respectively.

The newest rewritable technology uses *blue lasers* instead of *infrared* (CDs) or *red* (DVDs) *lasers* to store data more compactly on the disc. Single-layer discs based on blue laser technology—developed by Sony and called

>**CD-R disc.** A recordable CD. >**DVD-R/DVD+R discs.** Recordable DVDs. >**DVD+R DL disc.** A dual-layer recordable DVD. >**CD-RW.** A rewritable CD. >**DVD-RW/DVD+RW/DVD-RAM discs.** Rewritable DVDs.

TREND

Automated Optical Disc Carousels

Have you ever wasted valuable time searching for a CD or DVD? If you are like most people, the answer would be a resounding "Yes!" New products–such as the *automated disc carousel*–are becoming available to take care of this growing problem.

Automated disc carousels are CD and DVD storage systems that typically hold about 100 discs each. The carousel is connected to a PC and inserting a disc into the carousel launches an interface program that records the name, description, and user-supplied data about the disc. The disc is then allocated a storage slot inside the carousel. Once a disc has been inserted, retrieving it again is easy. Using the interface, the user browses or searches for the desired disc, and then the carousel ejects that disc so the user can insert it in his or her CD or DVD drive. When the user inserts the disc back into the carousel, the carousel stores the disc again, so it is ready for the next time it is requested. Automated carousels usually work with all kinds of optical discs, including computer, music, movie, and game discs.

One available product–Imation's *Disc Stakka*–is shown in the accompanying photograph. Each Disc Stakka holds up to 100 discs, and up to five units can be stacked for a total capacity of 500 discs without needing additional cabling or desk space. In addition to organizing your disks, the Disc Stakka and other similar products protect discs from the damage that can be caused by mishandling, such as stacked on a shelf, stored without a jewel case, or piled on a desk.

Blu-ray Discs (*BD*)—hold 23 GB. Dual-layer BD discs that hold 50 GB are in development, and a prototype of a four-layer BD disc that holds 100 GB was demonstrated in 2005. A similar, but competing, blue laser format developed by Toshiba and NEC is *high-definition DVD* (*HD-DVD*). This format, previously known as *Advanced Optical Disc* (*AOD*), is currently capable of storing up to 30 GB of data on a dual-layer disc and 45 GB on a triple-layer disc.

Blue laser discs were originally developed to enable recording, rewriting, and playback of high-definition content (such as HDTV shows and high-definition movies HD), as well as for storing large amounts of data. Blu-ray and HD-DVD are not compatible, and it has yet to be determined which format will be supported most by PC manufacturers and movie studios. But it is certain that a high-capacity optical disc format will be needed as high-definition content increases. Although recordable and rewritable conventional DVD drives are now available to record television shows and store home movies, a high-definition movie requires three or four of today's regular DVD discs. With blue laser discs, the same content would fit on a single disc. Blue laser discs are viewed by many as the next generation DVD format; in fact, Sony has announced that the upcoming PlayStation 3 game console will have a Blu-ray drive. Although originally only a rewritable format, read-only and recordable Blu-ray Discs (*BD-ROM* and *BD-R discs*, respectively) are also in development.

FURTHER EXPLORATION

For links to further information about DVD technology, go to www.course.com/uc11/ch03

To record and erase rewritable optical discs, *phase-change* technology is used. With this technology, the recordable CD or DVD disc is coated with layers of a special metal alloy compound that has two different appearances once it has been heated and then cooled, depending on the temperature reached during the heating process. With one temperature, the surface is reflective; with a higher temperature, it is not. Before any data is written to a disc, the disc is completely reflective. To record data on the disc, the recording laser heats the metal alloy in the appropriate spots on the spiral grooved track to the appropriate temperature to create nonreflective areas (pits); unburned areas (lands) remain reflective. To erase the disc, the appropriate temperature is used to change the areas to be erased back to their original reflective state.

It is important to realize that recordable and rewritable DVDs have not yet reached a single standard, so there are competing formats that are not necessarily compatible with each other. Luckily, most DVD drives today support more than one format. It is expected that, eventually, some type of DVD drive will replace the CD drive.

FLASH MEMORY SYSTEMS

Unlike magnetic and optical storage systems, **flash memory storage systems** have no moving parts—a property that makes them a *solid-state storage system*. Because they have no moving parts, flash memory storage systems require much less power than conventional drives, and they are resistant to shock and vibration. In addition, flash memory media (which consist of chips and other circuitry) are very small and so are especially appropriate for use with digital cameras, digital music players, handheld PCs, notebook computers, smart phones, and other types of portable devices (see Figure 3-16), as well as for transporting data from one place to another in a briefcase or pocket. Flash memory media is rewritable and has a longer expected life than removable magnetic media. Although flash memory media are relatively expensive per gigabyte, their convenience and universal compatibility make them an appealing storage option for many purposes. Today, flash memory

FIGURE 3-16
Flash memory uses.
Flash memory media are used in conjunction with a variety of devices, such as digital cameras, digital music players, PCs, smart phones, and more.

Flash memory stick

DIGITAL CAMERAS

Flash memory drive

DIGITAL MUSIC PLAYERS

Secure Digital (SD) card

DESKTOP COMPUTERS

PC Card flash memory reader

Flash memory cards

NOTEBOOK COMPUTERS

Secure Digital (SD) card

HANDHELD COMPUTERS

MultiMedia Card (MMC)

CELL PHONES

>**Flash memory storage system.** A storage system that uses flash memory media.

is most often found in the form of *flash memory media* and *flash memory drives*. Flash memory chips are also integrated directly into a variety of consumer products—such as portable computers, digital music players, and even sunglasses—to store MP3 files.

Flash Memory Media

The main type of *flash memory media* is the **flash memory card**—a small card containing flash memory chips and metal contacts to connect the card to the device or reader that it is being used with. Flash memory cards can be inserted into computers or other devices (such as handheld PCs, digital cameras, portable music players, and so forth) for storage purposes and come in a variety of formats, such as *CompactFlash*, *Secure Digital* (*SD*), *MultiMedia Card* (*MMC*), *xD*, and *Memory Stick* (see Figure 3-17). CompactFlash and Secure Digital (SD) cards are the most widely used type of flash memory media at the present time. Many computers and mobile devices today contain a built-in *flash memory card reader* that can read and write to at least one type of flash memory media; when an appropriate port is not built into the device, an external flash memory card reader can be used. Typically, flash memory media is purchased blank, but some flash memory-based software is available, such as games, encyclopedias, language translators, and more. The capacity of flash memory cards is continually growing and ranges from 64 MB to 8 GB at the present time.

Flash memory media can be inserted into a reader only one way, similar to a floppy disk. To help with this, many flash memory readers have directional hints imprinted next to each slot—look for these before inserting a flash memory card to insure you are using the proper card orientation and also make sure the slot is the proper size.

HW

FIGURE 3-17
Flash memory cards.
Shown here are four of the most widely used types of flash memory cards and a multicard reader.

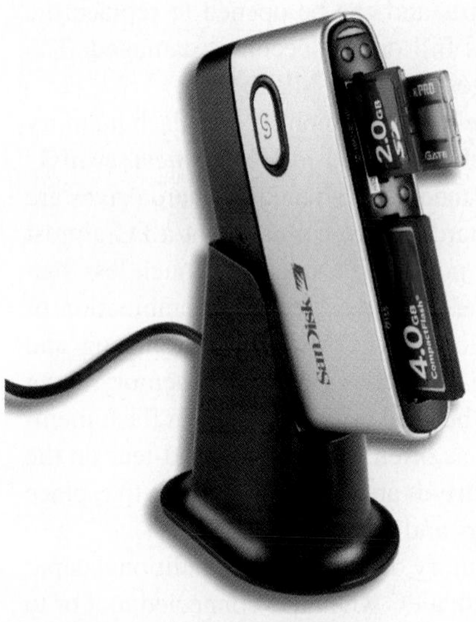

FLASH MEMORY CARD READER
This reader connects to a USB port and can be used with several different types of flash memory media.

COMPACTFLASH CARD

XD PICTURE CARD

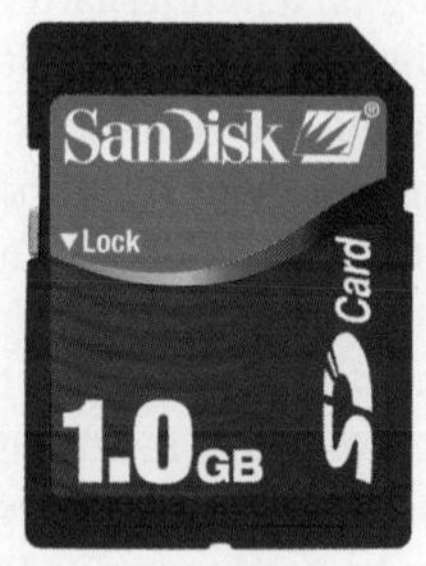

SECURE DIGITAL (SD) CARD

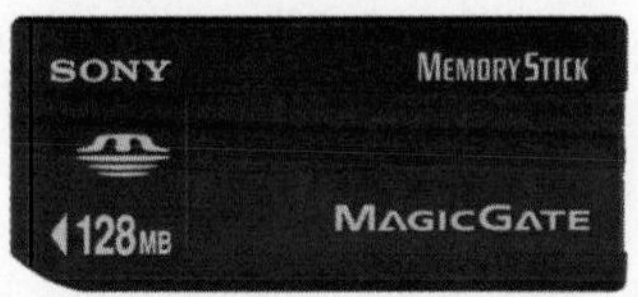

MEMORY STICK

>**Flash memory card.** A small, rectangular flash memory media, such as a CompactFlash or Secure Digital card.

FLASH MEMORY DRIVE WITH NECKCHAIN

CONVENTIONAL FLASH MEMORY DRIVE

FLASH MEMORY WATCH

FIGURE 3-18
Flash memory drives. USB flash memory drives are becoming increasingly popular for portable personal storage.

TIP

To avoid data loss when you are finished using a flash memory drive, first double-click the Safely Remove Hardware icon in the system tray, and then stop the drive before removing it from the USB slot.

Flash Memory Drives

Flash memory drives (sometimes called *USB mini drives*, *USB flash drives*, *thumb drives*, *jump drives*, and *key drives*) consist of flash memory media and a reader in a single self-contained unit. Most flash memory drives are designed to be very portable and so are small enough to fit in a pocket or be carried on a keychain or around the neck (see Figure 3-18). Some flash memory drives today are built into watches (a retractable cord is used to connect the watch to a PC when needed); one is even built into a Swiss Army knife. To read from or write to a flash memory drive, the user plugs it into a PC's USB port, and then the flash memory drive is assigned a drive letter by the computer, like any other type of drive attached to a PC. Files can be read from or written to the drive until it is unplugged from the USB port. Some flash memory drives have their flash memory media permanently sealed inside; others use standard flash memory cards and can be opened to replace the drive with a new memory card when the original is full or if it becomes damaged. The capacity of flash memory drives today typically ranges from 128 MB to 8 GB.

While portable USB flash memory drives are the most common type of flash memory drive, there are also *flash memory hard drives* (sometimes called *solid state memory disks* or *SSDs*) that use flash memory instead of magnetic media. Flash memory hard drives are much more expensive than conventional magnetic hard drives, but can boot a PC almost instantly, use much less battery power when used in portable PCs, and are much less susceptible to physical damage. *Hybrid hard drives* (*HHDs*), consisting of a combination of magnetic disks and flash memory, are under development. For instance, Samsung and Microsoft are collaborating on a hybrid hard drive that includes 1 GB flash memory along with the usual magnetic disks. Data to be written to the hard drive is cached in flash memory so the magnetic disks don't have to be accessed as often, saving wear-and-tear on the disks, as well as extending battery life. Hybrid hard drives are expected to begin to replace conventional hard drives in some notebook computers and tablet PCs by 2006.

In addition to convenient file transfers, flash memory drives can have additional capabilities, such as to automatically synchronize files with a PC when it is connected to it or to recreate the user's PC environment (including appearance, e-mail, contact lists, calendar, browser favorites, documents, and other designated files) on any PC to which the drive is connected. Some can even be used to lock a PC, password-protect data stored on the drive, issue Web site passwords, and even delete all Web-usage history when the user issues the command to stop the device. Others include *biometric features*—such as a built-in fingerprint reader—to allow only authorized individuals access to the data stored on the drive or to the PC the flash drive is being used with.

>**Flash memory drive.** A small drive that usually plugs into a PC's USB port and contains flash memory media.

OTHER TYPES OF STORAGE SYSTEMS

Other types of storage systems include *remote storage*, *smart cards*, and *holographic storage*. There are also storage systems and technologies designed for large computer systems and networks.

Remote Storage Systems

Remote storage refers to using a storage device that is not connected directly to the user's PC system; instead, the device is accessed through a local network or through the Internet. Using remote storage devices and media works similarly to using *local storage* (the storage devices and media that are directly attached to the user's PC)—the user just selects the appropriate remote storage device (such as a hard drive attached to a network server), and then stores data on or retrieves data from it. When the remote device is accessed through a local network, it is sometimes referred to as *network storage*; the term *online storage* most commonly refers to storage accessed via the Internet. Two examples of online storage sites are shown in Figure 3-19.

ONLINE PHOTO SHARING COMMUNITY
This site is designed to host online photo albums to be shared with others. Although albums can be password protected, many, such as the one shown here, are set up to be viewed by anyone.

LOGGING ON
This site requires users to log on before seeing their personal files stored on the site's server.

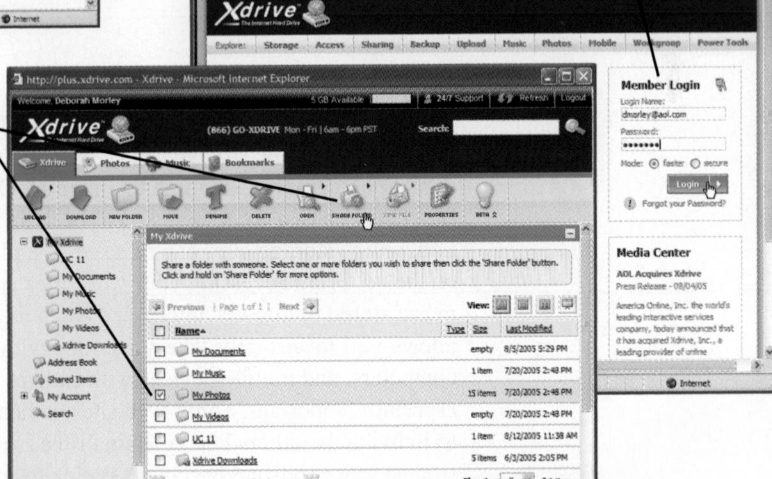

SHARING FILES
The contents of the marked folder will be shared with a specific individual, once his or her e-mail address is supplied.

SECURE ONLINE STORAGE
This site is designed to securely store files for backup or to be shared with others. After logging on, users can upload, download, or delete files, as well as designate who is allowed to access files.

FIGURE 3-19
Online storage.
Online storage services allow you to upload and download files from any PC or device with Internet access; some services have the option of password protecting access to your files.

>**Remote storage.** A storage device that is not directly a part of the PC being used, such as network storage or online storage.

TECHNOLOGY AND YOU

Smart Card IDs

At Pikeville College in Kentucky, the traditional school ID card has become much more than just an ID card. It has gotten smart. The new student ID cards are smart cards, which contain a built-in chip (see the accompanying photograph) that can hold digital cash values to be used at vending machines, printers, in the cafeteria, and at other places on campus to make purchases. When the cash stored in the card is depleted, the card can be reloaded at a card value center. Other uses for the Pikeville smart ID card include identifying students for exams and meal service, and providing access to secure areas, such as labs and residence halls. It may also be used as an ATM card in the future.

Smart card ID systems like this are not unique on college campuses today. Many colleges and universities across the country have either replaced or augmented their conventional student ID cards with smart card technology. The convenience of smart ID cards is a good fit with college students. They need to carry their student ID around anyway, and this smart card ID allows students to buy lunch, a soda, do laundry, or make copies without having to worry about how much cash they have on hand. In 2005, a college in Japan became the first college to use a smart card in conjunction with a *vein recognition system* (a noncontact biometric authentication system that verifies an individual's identity based on the veins in his or her palm) to authorize access to personal data, such as academic transcripts.

Other ID cards that are beginning to use smart card technology are national ID cards, driver's licenses, passports, and other important documents. Following the terrorist attacks in the United States on 9/11 and the subsequent attacks in other countries, there has be a strong push to create more secure identification documents to strengthen national security. In the United States, it is expected that new revamped driver's licenses will be used as a national ID card, and smart passports are being considered by both the United States and the United Kingdom. Hospitals in the United Kingdom are also beginning to use smart cards to restrict access to patient records to authorized individuals.

The Pikeville College smart ID card can be used for a wide variety of on-campus activities.

Individuals and businesses can use online storage Web sites for a variety of purposes. For instance, online storage can be used by individuals who want to share files—particular digital photographs—through the Internet. Online storage sites can also be used to transfer files between two computers and to back up files in case of a fire or other disaster. In addition, online storage sites can be used as a place to store content you want to access while on the go. From accessing your work files and contact information, to playing your digital music stored online via any device (such as a portable PC or smart phone), online storage allows you to virtually take your files with you. For some Internet appliances, network computers, and mobile devices with little or no local storage capabilities, online storage is especially important. Some Web sites dedicated to online storage offer the service for free to individuals; others charge a small fee, such as $5 or $10 per month for up to 5 GB of storage space (business accounts typically cost more).

Although some sites allow access to anyone, most online storage sites require users to log on with usernames and passwords to limit access to authorized individuals. Some sites allow you to e-mail links to others to download specific files in your online collection without having to supply a password. Other online storage sites contain an automatic back up option in which the files in designated folders on your PC are uploaded to your online account at regular specified intervals.

Smart Cards

A **smart card** is a credit card-sized piece of plastic that contains some computer circuitry—typically a processor, memory, and storage. Smart cards today are used to store a small amount of data (typically about 256 KB or less) for payment or identification purposes. For example, a smart card can store a prepaid amount of *digital cash* for purchases using a smart card-enabled vending machine or PC, and the amount of cash available on the card will be reduced as the card is used. Smart cards are also commonly used with national and student ID cards (see the Technology and You box); credit and debit cards; and cards that store loyalty system information (frequent flyer points, for example), identification data for accessing facilities or computer networks, or an individual's medical history and insurance information for fast treatment and hospital admission in an emergency. Although these applications have used conventional *magnetic stripe* technology in the past, the microprocessor in a smart card can perform computations—such as to authenticate the card and *encrypt* the data on the card to protect its integrity and secure it against unauthorized access—and data can be added to the card or modified on the card as needed.

To use a smart card, it must be inserted into a *smart card reader* built into or attached to a PC, keyboard, vending machine, or other device (see Figure 3-20). Once a smart card has been verified by the card reader, the transaction—such as making a purchase or unlocking a door—can be completed. For an even higher level of security, some smart cards today store *biometric data*—such as the characteristics of a fingerprint—in the card and use that data to ensure the authenticity of the card's user before authorizing the smart

CONVENTIONAL SMART CARDS
Used to store and retrieve personal information, as well as pay for items using digital cash loaded onto the card.

Smart card

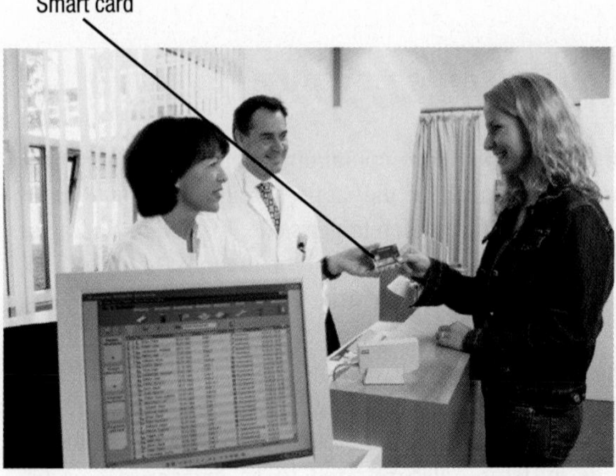

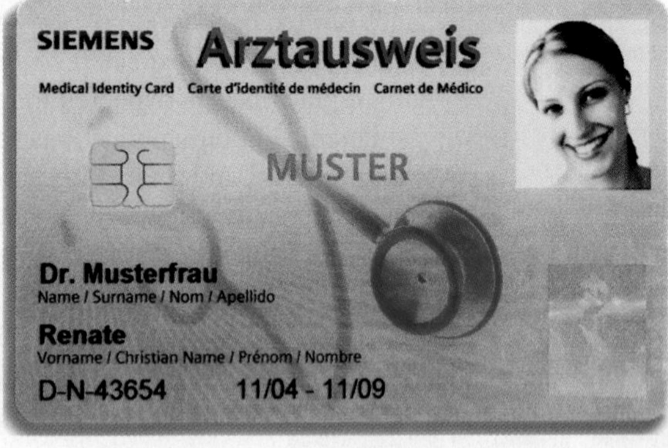

HIGH-CAPACITY SMART CARDS
The StorCard smart card shown here contains a magnetic disk inside the card to increase storage capacity to 100 MB.

>**Smart card.** A credit card-sized piece of plastic containing a chip and other circuitry into which data can be stored.

card transaction (biometrics, encryption, and other security procedures are discussed in more detail in Chapter 9). For applications that require more data storage, smart cards with an embedded magnetic disk are now available. For instance, the *StorCard* smart card shown in Figure 3-20 can be read by standard smart card readers, but holds 100 MB; storage capacities up to 5 GB are expected in the future.

FIGURE 3-21
Holographic storage. This recordable holographic drive and disc is expected to become available in 2006; each disc holds 300 GB.

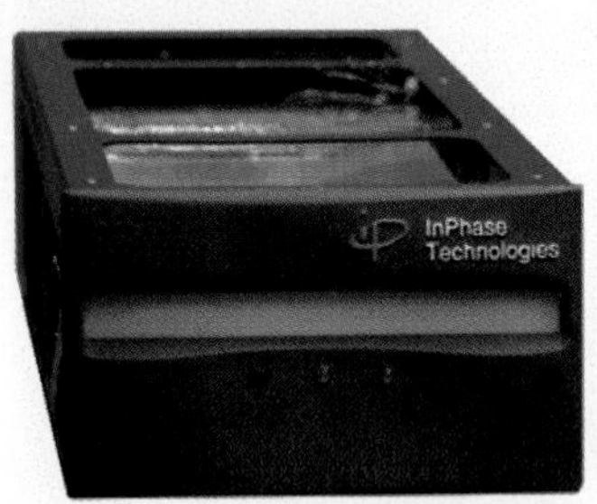

HOLOGRAPHIC DRIVE

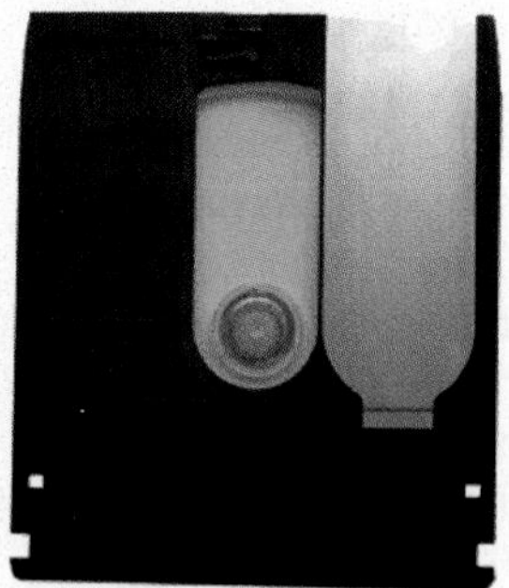

HOLOGRAPHIC DISC

Holographic Storage

Storing information in three dimensions is far from a new idea. DVDs use multiple layers to store more data on the same size disc as a CD, and 3D memory chips have been developed. One technology for 3D storage systems that, after many years of research and development, is now a reality is **holographic storage**. Holographic storage systems use two intersecting blue laser beams to store data through the entire thickness of the medium, which means that much more data can be stored on a holographic disc than on a CD of the same physical size. In fact, thousands of holographic files can be stored in an overlapping manner in the same area of the disc—a different angle or wavelength is used for each file so that each individual file can be retrieved when needed. The first generation of holographic drives (see Figure 3-21) is scheduled to be released by InPhase Technologies in 2006 and will utilize recordable discs with a capacity of 300 GB—enough room for almost 150 million pages of text, or 300,000 photos, or 21 hours of high-definition video. Rewritable holographic drives are expected to become available by early 2008, and the capacity of holographic discs is expected to reach 1.6 TB by 2009.

Potential initial applications for holographic data storage systems include high-speed digital libraries and image processing for medical, video, and military purposes—that is, for any application in which data needs to be stored or retrieved quickly in large quantities but rarely changed.

FIGURE 3-22
Storage servers for larger computer systems. Storage systems for larger computers are usually scalable so additional hard drives can be added as needed.

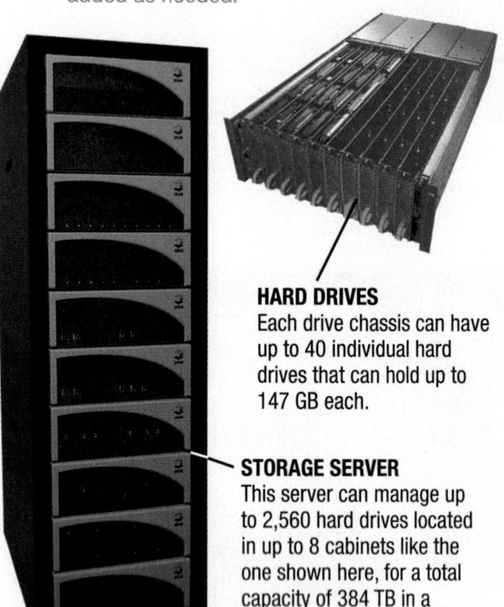

HARD DRIVES
Each drive chassis can have up to 40 individual hard drives that can hold up to 147 GB each.

STORAGE SERVER
This server can manage up to 2,560 hard drives located in up to 8 cabinets like the one shown here, for a total capacity of 384 TB in a single system.

Storage Systems for Large Computer Systems and Networks

Large computer systems (such as those containing mainframe computers and midrange servers) utilize much of the same storage hardware, standards, and principles as PCs but on a much larger scale. Instead of finding a single hard drive installed within the system unit, you are most likely to find a **storage server**—a separate piece of hardware containing multiple high-speed hard drives—connected to the computer system. Large storage servers typically contain racks of hard drives for a large total capacity. For instance, the storage server shown in Figure 3-22 can include up to 2,560 hard drives that hold 147 GB each for a total capacity of over 384 TB. These types of storage systems—also referred to as *enterprise storage systems*—typically use fast Fibre Channel connections and are *scalable*, meaning that more racks of drives can be added as needed up to the maximum capacity. In addition to being used as stand-alone storage for large computer systems, storage servers may also be used in *network attached storage* (*NAS*), *storage area network* (*SAN*), and *redundant arrays of independent disks* (*RAID*) storage systems. Most storage systems are based on magnetic disks, although *magnetic tape storage systems* are also possible.

>**Holographic storage.** An emerging type of storage technology that uses multiple blue laser beams to store data in three dimensions.
>**Storage server.** A hardware device containing multiple high-speed hard drives.

Network Attached Storage (NAS) and Storage Area Networks (SANs)

Storage servers are often used to provide storage for computer networks. With the vast amounts of data that many companies need to manage and store today, network-based storage has become increasingly important. One possibility is a **network attached storage (NAS)** device. NAS devices are high-performance storage servers that are individually connected to a network to provide storage for the computers connected to that network. **Storage area networks (SANs)** also provide storage for a network, but consist of a separate network of hard drives or other storage devices. That storage area network is, in turn, attached to the main network. The primary difference between NAS and SANs is how the storage devices interface with the network—that is, whether the storage devices act as individual network nodes, just like PCs, printers, and other devices on the network (NAS), or whether they are located in a completely separate network of storage devices that is accessible to the main network (SAN). However, in terms of functionality, the distinction between NAS and SANs is blurring, since they both provide storage services to the network. Both NAS and SAN systems are usually scalable, so new devices can be added as more storage is needed, and devices can be added or removed without disrupting the network.

RAID

RAID (redundant arrays of independent disks) is a method of storing data on two or more hard drives that work in combination to do the job of a larger drive (see Figure 3-23). Although RAID can be used to increase performance, it is most often used to protect critical data on a storage server. Because RAID usually involves recording redundant (duplicate) copies of stored data, the copies can be used, when necessary, to reconstruct lost data. This helps to increase the *fault tolerance*—the ability to recover from an unexpected hardware or software failure, such as a system crash—of a storage system.

There are six different RAID designs or levels (0 to 5) that use different combinations of RAID techniques. For example, RAID level 0 uses *disk striping*, which spreads files

FIGURE 3-23

RAID. The two main benefits of RAID are increased speed and the ability to recover easily from a disk crash.

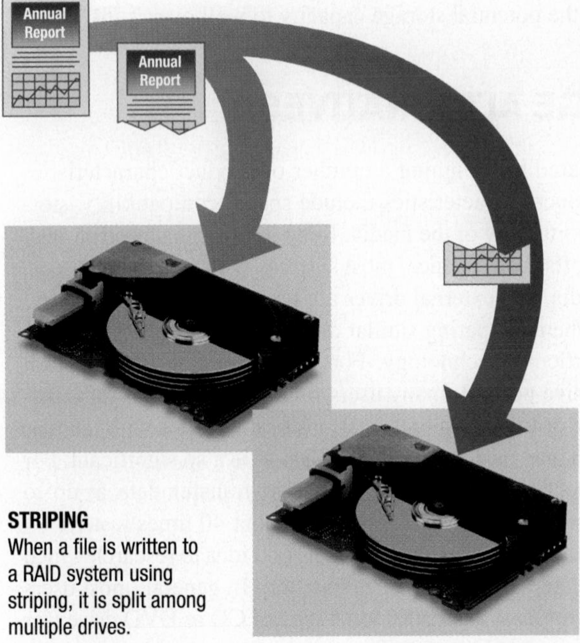

STRIPING
When a file is written to a RAID system using striping, it is split among multiple drives.

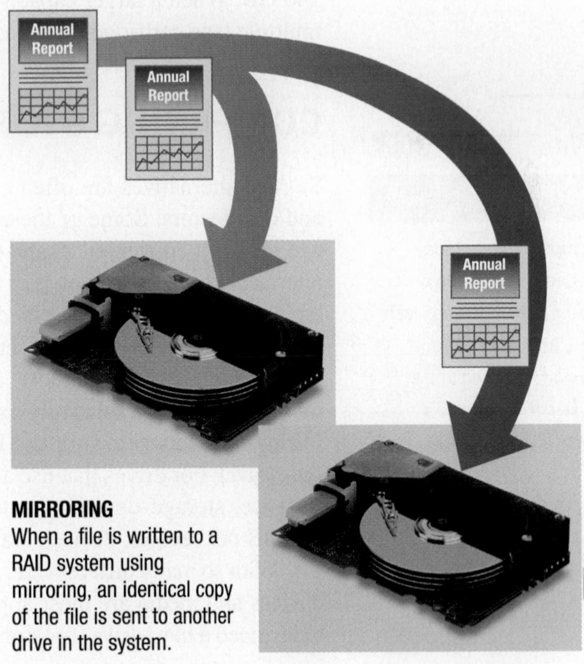

MIRRORING
When a file is written to a RAID system using mirroring, an identical copy of the file is sent to another drive in the system.

>**Network attached storage (NAS).** A high-performance storage server individually connected to a network to provide storage for computers on that network. >**Storage area network (SAN).** A network of hard drives or other storage devices that provide storage for another network of computers. >**RAID (redundant arrays of independent disks).** A storage method that uses several small hard disks in parallel to do the job of a larger disk.

over several disk drives (see the leftmost part of Figure 3-23). Although striping improves performance, since multiple drives can be accessed at one time to store or retrieve data, it does not provide fault tolerance. Another common RAID technique is *disk mirroring*, in which data is written to two duplicate drives simultaneously (see the rightmost part of Figure 3-23). The objective of disk mirroring is to increase fault tolerance—if one of the disk drives fails, the system can instantly switch to the other drive without any loss of data or service. RAID level 1 uses disk mirroring. Levels beyond level 1 use some combination of disk striping and disk mirroring, with different types of error correction provisions.

Because using RAID is significantly more expensive than just using a traditional hard drive storage system, it has traditionally been reserved for use with network and Internet servers. However, recently RAID has become more popular with PC users looking for increased performance. One test by *PC World* magazine showed that two RAID-connected drives completed some tasks in 40% less time than one drive of the same type. To implement RAID on a desktop PC, a RAID expansion card must be used.

Magnetic Tape Systems

Magnetic tape consists of plastic tape coated with a magnetizable substance that represents the bits and bytes of digital data, similar to magnetic disks. Although tape is no longer used for everyday storage applications because of its sequential-access property, it is still used today for data archiving and backup. One advantage of magnetic tape is its low cost per megabyte.

Most computer tapes today are in the form of *cartridge tapes*, which look similar to video or audio tapes. Computer tapes are read by *tape drives*, which can be either an internal or an external piece of hardware. Tape drives contain one or more read/write heads over which the tape passes to allow the drive to read or write data. Just as with other magnetic storage technologies, the 1s and 0s stored on magnetic tape are represented magnetically.

There are a variety of sizes and formats of cartridge tapes, and sizes and formats of tapes are not generally interchangeable. A typical tape cartridge holds between 40 GB and 240 GB. When a larger capacity is needed, some tape drives are designed to be used with multiple tape cartridges, increasing the potential storage capacity to well over 2 TB.

COMPARING STORAGE ALTERNATIVES

Storage alternatives are often compared by weighing a number of product characteristics and cost factors. Some of these product characteristics include speed, compatibility, storage capacity, convenience, and the portability of the media. Keep in mind that each storage alternative normally involves trade-offs. For instance, most systems with removable media are slower than those with fixed media, and external drives are typically slower than internal ones. Although cost is a factor when comparing similar devices, it is often not the most compelling reason to choose a particular technology. For instance, although the flash memory drives are relatively expensive per GB, many users find them essential for transferring files between work and home or for taking presentations or other files with them as they travel. For drives that use a USB interface, the type of USB port is also significant. For instance, storage devices that connect via the original USB port transfer data at up to 1.5 MB per second; devices that connect via a USB 2.0 port are about 40 times faster.

TIP

Virtually all computer users today need at least one USB port, in order to connect external hard drives, flash memory drives, and other storage hardware. If your PC doesn't have one, you can install an expansion card to add a USB port.

With so many different storage alternatives available, it is a good idea to research which devices and media are most appropriate for your personal situation. In general, most users today need a hard drive (for storing programs and data), some type of CD or DVD drive (for

>**Magnetic tape.** A plastic tape with a magnetizable surface that stores data as a series of magnetic spots; typically comes as a cartridge.

installing programs, backing up files, and sharing files with others), and a flash memory card reader (for transferring photos, music, and other content between portable devices and the PC). Some users may choose to include an additional drive for a particular type of high-capacity removable media, such as Zip disks, if they only need to use the disks in their PC or a PC that has a drive compatible with that medium. Users who plan to transfer music, digital photos, and other multimedia data on a regular basis between several different devices—such as a PC, digital camera, handheld PC, and printer—will want to select and use the flash memory media that is most compatible with the devices they are using and obtain the necessary adapter for their PC, if it does not include a built-in flash memory port. Some of the most common types of portable storage media are compared in Figure 3-24.

FIGURE 3-24
Portable storage alternatives. When comparing portable storage media, look at storage capacity, speed, cost, and device compatibility.

Media	Maximum Capacity	Approximate Cost (each)*	Approximate Cost (per GB)*	Can Be Read By	Best For
Conventional 3½-inch floppy disk	1.44 MB	$0.25	$175.00	Conventional floppy drive, SuperDisk drive	Transferring small files between users
Zip 750 disk	750 MB	$12.50	$17.00	Zip 750 drive	Archiving files or transferring large files between Zip users
CD-R disc	700 MB	$0.15	$0.20	Most CD and DVD drives	Transferring large files between users; archiving large files; making music CDs
CD-RW disc	700 MB	$0.50	$0.70	CD-RW drives, some other CD drives, most DVD drives	Transferring large files between users; archiving large files
DVD-R disc	4.7 GB	$0.50	$0.10	Most DVD drives	Transferring large files between users; archiving large files; backup; making home movie DVDs
DVD+RW	4.7 GB	$1.00	$0.20	Most DVD drives	Transferring large files between users; archiving large files; backup; making home movie DVDs
DVD+R DL	8.5 GB	$5.00	$0.60	DVD+R DL drives	Transferring large files between users; archiving large files; backup; making home movie DVDs
DVD-RAM	4.7 GB	$3.00	$0.60	DVD-RAM drives	Transferring large files between DVD-RAM users; archiving large files; backup
Flash memory drive (USB)	8 GB	**	$30.00	Any device with a USB port	Transferring small to medium-sized files between users or PCs
REV hard disk cartridge	35 GB	$40.00	$1.00	Proprietary drive to which that cartridge belongs	Archiving large files; securing sensitive data; backup
Portable hard drive (USB or PC card)	2 TB	**	$0.50	Any device with a USB port or PC card slot, respectively	Extending PC storage; securing sensitive data; backup
Flash memory cards	8 GB	**	$40.00	Compatible flash memory reader	Transferring small- to medium-sized files between users, PCs, or multimedia devices (digital cameras, MP3 players, etc.)

*Cost as of 2005 **Varies with capacity

SUMMARY

STORAGE SYSTEM CHARACTERISTICS

Chapter Objective 1:
Explain the difference between storage systems and memory.

Chapter Objective 2:
Name several general characteristics of storage systems.

Storage systems make it possible to save programs, data, and processing results for later use. They provide **nonvolatile** storage, so when the power is shut off, the data stored on the storage medium remains intact. This differs from RAM, which is **volatile**.

All storage systems involve two physical parts: A **storage device** and a **storage medium**. The most common types of storage media are magnetic disks and optical discs, which are read by the appropriate type of drive. Drives can be *internal*, *external*, or *remote*. Drives are typically assigned letters by the computer; these letters are used to identify the drive. Storage devices can record data either on *removable* media, which provide access only when inserted into the appropriate storage device, or *fixed media*, in which the media is permanently located inside the storage device. Removable media provide the advantages of unlimited storage capacity, transportability, safer backup capability, and security. Fixed media have the advantages of higher speed, lower cost, and greater reliability.

Sequential access allows a computer system to retrieve the records in a file only in the same order in which they are physically stored. *Random access* (also called *direct access*) allows the system to retrieve records in any order. In either case, **files** (sometimes called *documents*) stored on a storage medium are given a **filename** and can be organized into **folders**. This is referred to as *logical file representation. Physical file representation* refers to how the files are physically stored on the storage medium by the computer.

MAGNETIC DISK SYSTEMS

Chapter Objective 3:
Identify the two primary types of magnetic disk systems and describe how they work.

Magnetic disk storage is most widely available in the form of *hard disks* and *floppy disks*. Computer systems originally used **floppy disks** because they provided a uniform removable storage system at a low cost. Each side of a floppy disk holds data and programs in concentric **tracks** encoded with magnetized spots representing 0s and 1s. **Sector** boundaries divide a floppy disk surface into pie-shaped pieces. The part of a track crossed by a fixed number of contiguous sectors forms a **cluster**. To use a floppy disk, it is inserted into a **floppy disk drive**.

Hard disk drives (also called **hard drives**) are the main storage medium for most PCs. They offer faster access than floppy disks and much greater storage capacity. A hard drive contains one or more *hard disks* permanently sealed inside along with an *access mechanism*. A separate read/write head corresponds to each disk surface, and the access mechanism moves the heads in and out among the tracks to read and write data. All tracks in the same position on all surfaces of all disks in a hard drive form a disk **cylinder**. Hard drives can be divided into multiple *partitions* (logical drives) for efficiency or to facilitate multiple users or operating systems. Hard drives can be *internal* or *external*.

The total time it takes for a hard drive to read from or write to disks is called **disk access time**. A **disk cache** strategy, in which the computer fetches program or data contents in neighboring disk areas and transports them to RAM whenever disk content is retrieved, can help to speed up access time. Hard drives connect to a computer using one of several standards, such as *serial ATA* (*SATA*), *serial ATA II* (*SATA II*), or USB. If portability is required, portable hard drives, in which either the entire drive or a removable hard drive cartridge can be moved to another PC, are available. Hard drives for notebook PCs can be internal, external, or in a PC card format. *Mini hard drives* are commonly integrated in mobile devices and consumer electronic products.

OPTICAL DISC SYSTEMS

Optical discs store data *optically* using laser beams, and they can store data much more densely than magnetic disk technology. They are divided into tracks and sectors like magnetic disks, but use a single grooved spiral track instead of concentric tracks. Optical discs are available in a wide variety of *CD* and *DVD* formats and are read by *CD* or *DVD drives*. **CD-ROM (compact disc read-only memory) discs** come with data already stored on the disc. Data is represented by *pits* and *lands* permanently formed in the surface of the disk. CD-ROM discs cannot be erased or overwritten—they are *read-only*. **DVD-ROM (digital versatile disc read-only memory) discs** are similar to CD-ROM discs, but they hold much more data (4.7 GB instead of 700 MB). *Recordable discs* (**CD-R**, **DVD-R**, **DVD+R**, and **DVD+R DL discs**) and *rewritable disks* (**CD-RW**, **DVD-RW**, **DVD+RW**, **DVD-RAM**, and *blue laser discs*) can all be written to, but only recordable discs can be erased and rewritten to, similar to a floppy disk or hard drive. Recordable CDs and DVDs store data by burning permanent marks onto the disc, similar to CD-ROM and DVD-ROM discs; rewritable discs typically use *phase-change* technology to temporarily change the reflectivity of the disc to represent 1s and 0s. It is expected that, eventually, some form of DVD disc will eventually replace CDs as the optical disc standard.

Chapter Objective 4:
Discuss the various types of optical disc systems available and how they differ from each other and from magnetic systems.

FLASH MEMORY SYSTEMS

Flash memory storage systems have no moving parts. **Flash memory cards**, the most common type of *flash memory media*, are commonly used with digital cameras, portable PCs, and other portable devices, as well as with desktop PCs. Flash memory cards come in a variety of formats—the most common are *CompactFlash* and *Secure Digital (SD) cards*. **Flash memory drives** typically connect to a PC via a USB port and are a convenient method of transferring files between computers.

Chapter Objective 5:
Explain what flash memory media and flash memory drives are and how they are used today.

OTHER TYPES OF STORAGE SYSTEMS

Remote storage—using a storage device that is not directly a part of your PC system—typically involves using a *network storage* device or an *online storage service*. Online storage services enable users to share files with others over the Internet, access files while on the road, and backup documents. **Smart cards** are credit card-sized pieces of plastic that contain a chip or other circuitry usually used to store data or a monetary value. **Holographic storage**, which uses multiple blue laser beams to store data in three dimensions, is becoming available for high-speed data retrieval applications.

Storage systems for larger computers implement many of the same standards as PC-based hard drives. Instead of finding a single set of hard disks inside a hard drive permanently installed within a system unit, however, a **storage server** is often used. **Network attached storage (NAS)** and **storage area networks (SANs)** are commonly used to provide storage for a business network. **RAID (redundant arrays of independent disks)** technology can be used to increase *fault tolerance* and performance. **Magnetic tape** systems store data on plastic tape coated with a magnetizable substance. Magnetic tapes are usually enclosed in cartridges and are inserted into a *tape drive* in order to be accessed.

Chapter Objective 6:
List at least three other types of storage systems.

COMPARING STORAGE ALTERNATIVES

Most PCs today include a hard drive, some type of CD or DVD drive, and a flash memory card reader. The type of optical drive and any additional storage devices are often determined by weighing a number of product characteristics and cost factors. These characteristics include speed, compatibility, capacity, removability, and convenience.

Chapter Objective 7:
Summarize the storage alternatives for a PC, including which storage systems should be included on a typical PC and for what applications other storage systems are appropriate.

REVIEW ACTIVITIES

KEY TERM MATCHING

a. disk cache

b. DVD-ROM disc

c. file

d. flash memory card

e. flash memory drive

f. folder

g. hard disk drive

h. nonvolatile

i. RAID

j. remote storage

Instructions: Match each key term on the left with the definition on the right that best describes it.

1. _______ A dedicated part of RAM used to store additional data adjacent to data retrieved during a disk fetch to improve system performance.

2. _______ A named place on a storage medium into which files can be stored to keep the files stored on that medium organized.

3. _______ An optical disc, usually holding 4.7 GB, that can be read from, but not written to, by the user.

4. _______ A small drive that usually plugs into a PC's USB port and contains flash memory media.

5. _______ A small, rectangular flash memory media, such as a CompactFlash or Secure Digital card.

6. _______ A storage device that is not directly a part of the PC being used, such as network storage or online storage.

7. _______ A storage method that uses several small hard disks in parallel to do the job of a larger disk.

8. _______ A storage system consisting of one or more metal magnetic disks permanently sealed with an access mechanism inside its drive.

9. _______ Describes a storage medium that retains its content when the power is shut off.

10. _______ Something stored on a storage medium, such as a program, document, or image.

SELF-QUIZ

Instructions: Circle **T** if the statement is true, **F** if the statement is false, or write the best answer in the space provided. **Answers for the self-quiz are located in the References and Resources Guide at the end of the book.**

1. **T** **F** A computer system with a C drive and a D drive must have two physical hard drives.

2. **T** **F** The smallest amount of space a file on a disk can take up is one cluster.

3. **T** **F** External hard drives typically connect via a flash memory reader.

4. **T** **F** A CD-R is a type of read-only optical disc.

5. **T** **F** Most PCs today include a hard disk drive.

6. A storage medium is _______ if it loses its content when the power is shut off.

7. A single-sided, single-layer DVD disc typically holds _______.

8. A(n) _______ looks similar to a credit card but contains a chip and other circuitry into which data can be stored.

9. Secure Digital (SD) cards are one type of _______ medium.

10. Match the storage device to the drive letter that it would most likely be assigned on a typical PC, and write the corresponding number in the blank to the left of each drive letter.

a. ______ A:	1. CD/DVD drive
b. ______ C:	2. Floppy disk
c. ______ D:	3. Hard drive

EXERCISES

1. Assume, for simplicity's sake, that a kilobyte is 1,000 bytes, a megabyte is 1,000,000 bytes, and a gigabyte is 1,000,000,000 bytes. You have an 80-gigabyte hard drive with the following content:

ITEM	STORAGE SPACE USED
Operating system	65 MB
Office suite	85 MB
Other software	250 MB
Digital photos	3.5 GB
Other documents	10 MB

Approximately how much room is left on the drive? ______

2. Match the image to its name, and write the corresponding number in the blank to the left of its name.

a. ______ Hard drive	c. ______ Optical disc	e. ______ Flash memory drive
b. ______ Floppy disk	d. ______ Smart card	f. ______ Flash memory card

1.

2.

3.

4.
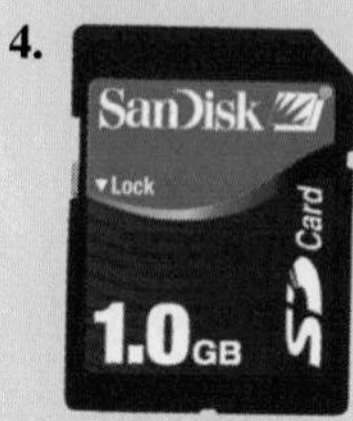

5.

6.

3. Explain why CD-ROM discs are not erasable, but CD+RW discs are.

4. What does the term "solid-state drive" mean? List one storage device to which this term applies.

5. Which types of storage media would be appropriate for someone who needed to exchange large (5 MB to 75 MB) files with another person? List at least three different types, stating why each might be the most appropriate under specific conditions.

DISCUSSION QUESTION

People send their digital photos over the Internet in different ways. For instance, digital photos are often e-mailed to others, posted on an online storage site, or uploaded to a server (such as one belonging to SnapFish, Walmart, or Costco) in order to order prints, enlargements, or other photo-based items. If you have ever sent photos over the Internet, were you concerned about someone other than the intended recipient intercepting or viewing your photo files? If you have ever uploaded files to a processing service for printing, did you check to see if the Web server being used was secure? Should individuals be concerned about sending their personal photos over the Internet? There are a number of advantages, but are there privacy risks, as well?

PROJECTS

?OT TOPICS

1. **Blue Laser Discs** As mentioned in the chapter, an emerging optical technology that uses blue lasers can increase the capacity of a standard-sized DVD disc significantly. At the time of this writing, Sony Blu-ray DVD drives were only available in Japan and were extremely expensive. Another blue laser standard, competing against and incompatible with Blu-ray, is Advanced Optical Disc.

   For this project, research the current state of blue laser DVDs. Are there any products available in the United States? Has the blue laser standard war been settled, or is there still more than one competing standard? What is the current capacity of discs using blue laser technology? At the conclusion of your research, prepare a one- to two-page summary of your findings and submit it to your instructor.

SHORT ANSWER/ RESEARCH

2. **Smart IDs** The chapter Technology and You box discusses the growing use of smart cards as campus ID cards. Some credit cards are now being issued as smart cards, and smart cards have been proposed to replace conventional drivers' licenses, medical insurance cards, and other important documents. Some countries have already implemented smart-card-based national ID cards. The ability of a smart card to hold a larger amount of personal data than a conventional magnetic stripe card and to confirm online credit card orders via a smart card reader attached to your PC is viewed as a benefit by some. The additional information potentially available through a card (such as an individual's medical history or purchasing record), however, is viewed as a privacy risk to others.

   For this project, consider the points raised in the previous paragraph and write a short essay expressing your opinion about using smart cards to replace conventional magnetic stripe cards. If it is not already, would you want your campus ID card to be a smart card? Why or why not? Do you think smart cards will be used any differently by consumers in the future than conventional magnetic stripe cards are used at the present time? List any pros and cons of replacing magnetic stripe cards with smart cards and provide a concluding paragraph stating other possible uses for smart cards that would be beneficial and/or accepted by the general public. Submit your opinion on this issue to your instructor in the form of a one-page paper.

3. **Auto Backup** For those of us who forget to back up our files on a regular basis, there is an alternative—using an automatic backup utility that performs this task for you on a regular basis. Many backup programs offer this option, and some online storage sites have the option of uploading your designated files or folders to the online storage site on a regular basis. In addition, some companies that sell storage devices with removable media include this software for free with the purchase of the device.

   For this project, research a few of the options that are available for performing automatic backups, and summarize the alternatives that you find. At the conclusion of your research, prepare a one-page summary of your findings and submit it to your instructor.

HANDS ON

4. **Storage Evaluation** Most PCs have multiple storage devices, such as a hard drive, floppy drive, CD or DVD drive, and so on.

   For this project, find one computer (such as at home, your school, or a public library) that you are allowed to use, preferably the one you will use most often for this course. By looking at the outside of the PC, as well as by using a file management program (such as Windows

Explorer), identify each storage device on your selected PC. For each device, list the type of storage device (such as floppy disk drive, CD drive, or hard drive) and its assigned drive letter. In Windows Explorer, right-click each hard drive icon and select Properties to determine the size of the drive and how much room is left. At the conclusion of this task, prepare a one-page summary of your observations and submit it to your instructor.

5. **Online Storage** There are a number of online storage services (such as Xdrive, Yahoo! Briefcase, and IBackup) designed to allow users to backup and share files with others; specialty online storage services designed for digital photo sharing include Fotki and Yahoo! Photos.

For this project, visit at least one online storage site designed for backup and file exchange, and at least one site designed for digital photo sharing. You can try the sites listed above or use a search site to find alternative sites. Tour the sites you select to determine what features each service offers, what it costs, the amount of storage space available, and your options for sending your uploaded files to others. Do the sites you selected password protect your files, or are they available for anyone with an Internet connection to see? What are the benefits for using these types of online storage services? Can you think of any drawbacks? Would you want to use any of the online storage sites you visited? Why or why not? At the conclusion of this task, prepare a short summary containing the information and answers to the questions listed above, and then submit it to your instructor.

WRITING ABOUT COMPUTERS

6. **Storage Solutions** The selection of an appropriate storage solution is usually based on the computer being used and the individual's storage requirements.

For this project, consider the storage requirements for each of the following three scenarios, and determine an appropriate storage solution for each one.

Scenario 1: A home computer where several family members will be using the computer for homework, shopping, taxes, downloading and playing music, playing multimedia games, and surfing the Web.

Scenario 2: A small accounting company that has only one computer and is using it to support all the administrative and information needs of the company.

Scenario 3: A two-person video editing and multimedia production company that has two computers and specializes in recording and producing videos of weddings and other special occasions.

Feel free to modify or clarify the three scenarios defined above in order to make your storage solutions match more closely with the diverse number of possibilities and storage options available today. Submit your recommendations to your instructor in the form of a short paper, not more than two pages in length. Be sure to include why you choose each storage solution.

PRESENTATION/ DEMONSTRATION

7. **Flash Cards** The number of uses for flash memory cards has been growing at a tremendous rate. Primarily developed for use with digital cameras, today's possibilities include storage for portable and desktop PCs and a variety of other devices, as well as providing programs and peripheral devices for some PCs.

For this project, research the various uses for flash memory cards. Find at least two examples of flash memory products in each of the following three categories: user storage, software, and an interface for a peripheral device. Share your findings with the class in the form of a short presentation, including the products that you found and their specifications, as well as your opinion regarding the flash card market in the future. Be sure to include any current or potential application you find in your research in addition to the three categories listed here. The presentation should not exceed 10 minutes and should make use of one or more presentation aids, such as the chalkboard, handouts, overhead transparencies, or a computer-based slide presentation (your instructor may provide additional requirements). You may also be asked to submit a summary of the presentation to your instructor.

GROUP DISCUSSION

8. **Big Brother?** Some of the storage technology used today, such as smart cards, can help facilitate faster and more secure access to locked facilities, protect against the use of stolen credit card numbers, and, when used in conjunction with a biometric characteristic, unequivocally identify a user to a computer system. They can also be used for employee monitoring, informing a business where each employee carrying or wearing his or her smart card is located at all times. While some people find benefits to the applications just discussed, others worry that smart cards and other devices will be used to track our movements. Is the convenience of smart card technology worth the possibility that information about you and your actions will be recorded in a database somewhere? Do you think employers or the government have the right to track individuals' movements? If so, under what conditions do they have this right? What are some advantages and disadvantages for the government and your employer always knowing where you are? Have you ever used a smart card or been identified with a biometric system? If so, how do you rate the experience?

   For this project, form an opinion of the use of smart cards and similar technology to identify individuals for various applications and be prepared to discuss your position (in class, via an online class discussion group, or in a class chat room, depending on your instructor's directions). You may also be asked to write a short paper expressing your opinion.

WEB ACTIVITIES

The *Understanding Computers* Web site located at **www.course.com/uc11** features many resources to help reinforce your understanding of the chapter content and help you prepare for exams. Your instructor may also assign specific activities to be completed that will count toward your final grade in the course.

Instructions: Go to **www.course.com/uc11/ch03** to work the following online activities.

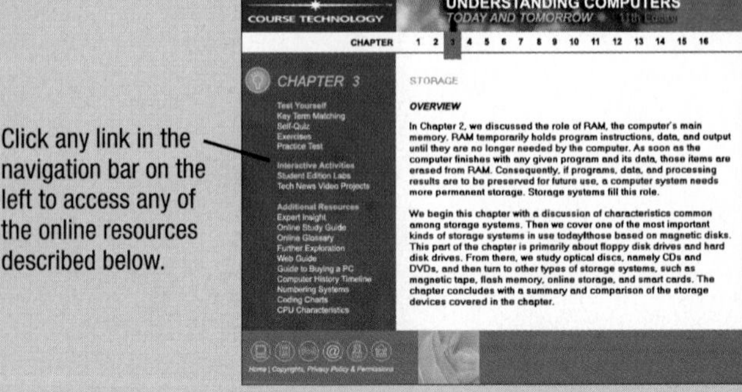

INTERACTIVE ACTIVITIES

1. **Crossword Puzzle** Practice your knowledge of the key terms in Chapter 3 by completing the interactive Crossword Puzzle.
2. **Tech News Video Project** Watch the **"Online Storage Options"** video clip that takes a look at the growing use of online storage, which allows you to upload files and then access them from any computer anywhere you have an Internet connection. After watching the video online, complete the corresponding project.
3. **Student Edition Labs** Reinforce the concepts you have learned in this chapter by working through the interactive **Managing Files** lab.

TEST YOURSELF

1. **Key Term Matching** Test your knowledge of selected chapter key terms by matching the terms with their definitions.
2. **Self-Quiz** Test your retention of chapter concepts by taking the Self-Quiz.
3. **Exercises** Work these short exercises to review the concepts and terms covered in the chapter.
4. **Practice Test** Test how ready you are for an upcoming exam by completing the online Practice Test.

STUDY TOOLS/ ADDITIONAL RESOURCES

The Understanding Computers Web site has a wide range of additional resources, including an **Online Study Guide** (containing study tips, a chapter outline with room to add your own notes, and a chapter checklist of the activities to complete when the chapter is covered in class and when you are preparing for a test) and an **Online Glossary** for each chapter; **Further Exploration** links; a **Web Guide**, a **Guide to Buying a PC**, and a **Computer History Timeline**; more information about **Numbering Systems**, **Coding Charts**, and **CPU Characteristics**; and much, much more!

CHAPTER 4 Input and Output

OUTLINE

Overview
Keyboards
Pointing Devices
- The Mouse
- Electronic Pens
- Touch Screens
- Other Pointing Devices

Scanners, Readers, and Digital Cameras
- Scanners
- Readers
- Digital Cameras

Audio Input
- Voice Input Systems
- Music Input Systems

Display Devices
- Display Device Characteristics
- Flat-Panel Display Technologies
- Data and Multimedia Projectors

Printers
- Printer Characteristics
- Laser Printers
- Ink-Jet Printers
- Special-Purpose Printers
- Multifunction Devices

Audio Output

LEARNING OBJECTIVES

After completing this chapter, you will be able to:

1. Explain the purpose of a computer keyboard and the types of keyboards widely used today.
2. List several different pointing devices and describe their functions.
3. Describe the purposes of scanners and readers and list some types of scanners and readers in use today.
4. Understand how digital cameras differ from conventional cameras.
5. Explain how audio input is accomplished.
6. Describe the characteristics of a display device.
7. List several types of printers and explain their function.
8. Understand which hardware devices are used for audio output.

OVERVIEW

In Chapter 2, we learned how data is processed by a computer. The focus of Chapter 4 is on the hardware designed for inputting data into the computer, and then outputting results to the user after the data has been processed. We begin with a look at input. First we discuss the most common *input devices* used with personal computers to enter commands or data into the PC–mainly, keyboards and pointing devices (such as a mouse). Next, hardware designed for capturing data in electronic form, such as scanners, barcode readers, and digital cameras, is discussed, followed by a look at two types of audio input.

The second part of this chapter explores the different types of *output devices*–hardware that can be used for output. Typically, output occurs on the screen (via a display device) or paper (via a printer). Display devices are covered first, including their basic properties and the various types of display devices in use today. Next, we discuss printers and devices used for audio output. Keep in mind that this chapter describes only a sample of the input and output equipment available today. In fact, there are thousands of input and output products, and they can be combined together in many ways to create a computer system to fit almost any conceivable need. ■

KEYBOARDS

Most PCs today are designed to be used with a **keyboard**. Virtually all desktop PCs are used in conjunction with either a wired or wireless keyboard. Wired keyboards are connected via a cable to the computer's system unit; *wireless keyboards* are powered by batteries and send wireless signals to a receiver that is usually plugged into the computer's serial or USB port. Although earlier wireless keyboards used *infrared signals* and needed to be within *line of sight* of their receivers, newer models use *radio waves* and, therefore, do not require line of sight transmission, although there is a limit on the allowable distance between the keyboard and the receiver. Some of the newest wireless keyboards are *Bluetooth-compliant*, meaning they communicate with the PC via a Bluetooth wireless networking connection. Bluetooth and wireless networking are covered in more detail in Chapter 7.

Most keyboards today (refer to the typical desktop PC keyboard shown in Figure 4-1) contain the standard alphanumeric keys found on all keyboards and typewriters along with a *numeric keypad* (used for entering numbers), *function keys* (used to issue commands in some programs), *Delete* and *Backspace keys* (used to delete characters from the screen), *Control* and *Alternate keys* (used in conjunction with other keys on the keyboard to issue commands, such as Ctrl+S to save the current document, in some programs), and *directional keys* (used to move around within a document). Some keyboards also contain additional keys for a specific purpose or software program, such as to open the Windows Start menu, control the speaker volume, launch an e-mail program or favorite Web site, or

TIP

Some keys on a keyboard, like the Caps Lock and Number Lock keys, are *toggle* keys, which are pressed once to turn the feature on and again to turn the feature off. If you ever find yourself typing in all caps or the numeric keypad does not work, check the status of these keys.

>**Keyboard.** An input device containing numerous keys, arranged in a configuration similar to that of a typewriter, that can be used to input letters, numbers, and other symbols.

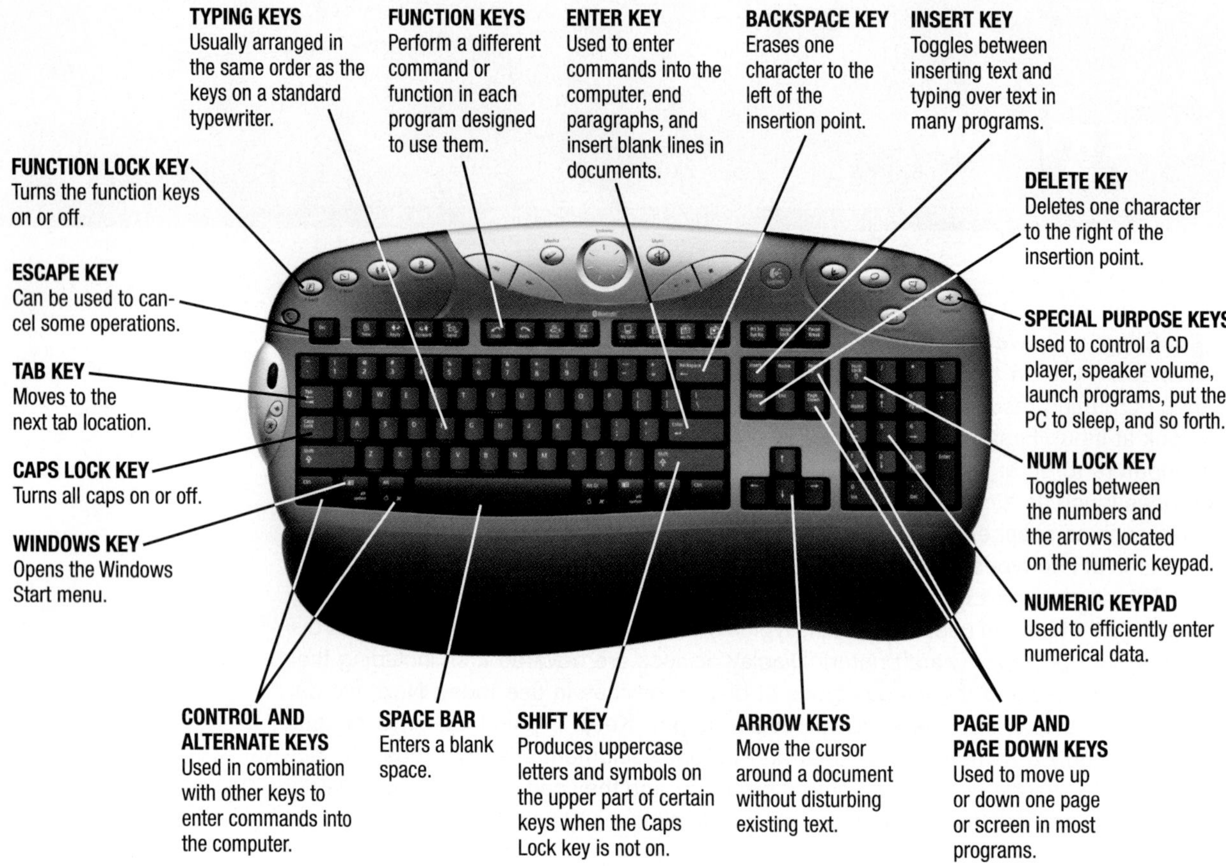

TYPING KEYS
Usually arranged in the same order as the keys on a standard typewriter.
FUNCTION KEYS
Perform a different command or function in each program designed to use them.
ENTER KEY
Used to enter commands into the computer, end paragraphs, and insert blank lines in documents.
BACKSPACE KEY
Erases one character to the left of the insertion point.
INSERT KEY
Toggles between inserting text and typing over text in many programs.
FUNCTION LOCK KEY
Turns the function keys on or off.
DELETE KEY
Deletes one character to the right of the insertion point.
ESCAPE KEY
Can be used to cancel some operations.
SPECIAL PURPOSE KEYS
Used to control a CD player, speaker volume, launch programs, put the PC to sleep, and so forth.
TAB KEY
Moves to the next tab location.
NUM LOCK KEY
Toggles between the numbers and the arrows located on the numeric keypad.
CAPS LOCK KEY
Turns all caps on or off.
WINDOWS KEY
Opens the Windows Start menu.
NUMERIC KEYPAD
Used to efficiently enter numerical data.
CONTROL AND ALTERNATE KEYS
Used in combination with other keys to enter commands into the computer.
SPACE BAR
Enters a blank space.
SHIFT KEY
Produces uppercase letters and symbols on the upper part of certain keys when the Caps Lock key is not on.
ARROW KEYS
Move the cursor around a document without disturbing existing text.
PAGE UP AND PAGE DOWN KEYS
Used to move up or down one page or screen in most programs.

FIGURE 4-1
A typical desktop keyboard.

perform specific tasks in the Microsoft Office software programs. When buying a PC or replacement keyboard, look carefully at the keyboard to be sure it fits your needs.

Notebook PCs usually have a keyboard that is smaller and contains fewer keys than a desktop PC keyboard, and the keys are typically placed closer together. Because of this, notebook buyers should try out the keyboard before buying, whenever possible, to ensure that the size, layout, and feel of the keyboard meet their needs. Notebook computer users can also connect and use a conventional keyboard, when needed, if the notebook contains a keyboard or USB port.

FIGURE 4-2
Keyboards for handheld PCs and mobile devices.

FLIP-OPEN THUMB PAD

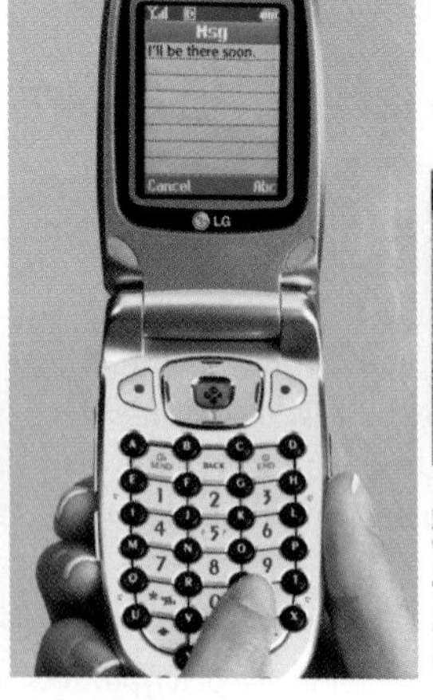

BUILT-IN KEYBOARD

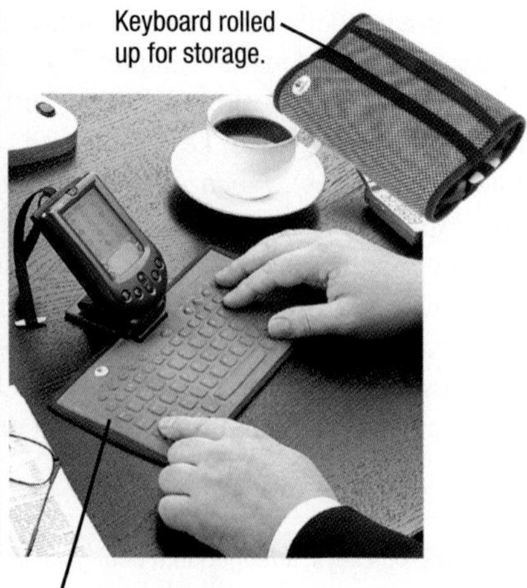

FOLDABLE KEYBOARD

Many handheld PCs and mobile devices today have a built-in keyboard or *thumb pad* (a keyboard designed to be pressed with just the thumbs, as shown in Figure 4-2), but the layout may be different than a conventional keyboard, and the keyboard layout may vary from device to device. For instance, some smart phones have several letters assigned to a single key, and the key is pressed multiple times to indicate the desired letter. Others, like the smart phone with a built-in keyboard shown in Figure 4-2, contain separate keys for each letter of the alphabet but they are in a different order than on a typical keyboard. If the device does not have a built-in keyboard, often a special *portable keyboard* or *portable thumb pad* can be used with the device for easier data entry. Portable keyboards designed for handheld PCs typically fold or roll up (see Figure 4-2); thumb pads slip over the bottom of a handheld PC or smart phone. Full-sized keyboards can also be used with portable computers, if the proper connector is built into the PC. Portable computers that do not support a keyboard or thumb pad typically rely on *pen input* or *touch input* instead, as discussed shortly.

POINTING DEVICES

In addition to a keyboard, most PCs today have some type of **pointing device**. Unlike keyboards, which are used to enter characters at the *insertion point* (sometimes called the *cursor*) location, pointing devices are used to move an onscreen *mouse pointer*—usually an arrow. Once that pointer is pointing to the desired object on the screen, that object can be selected (usually by pressing a button on the pointing device) or otherwise manipulated. Some common types of pointing devices are the *mouse*, *electronic pen*, and *touch screen*.

The Mouse

A **mouse** rests on the desk or other flat surface close to the user's PC and is moved across the surface with the user's hand in the appropriate direction to point to and select objects on the screen. Older *mechanical mice* have a ball exposed on the bottom surface of the mouse to control the pointer movement. Most mice today are *optical mice* that track movements with light. Newer *laser mice* (such as the one shown in Figure 4-3) use laser beams to track movement and are even more accurate—one study found them to be 20 times more accurate—than conventional optical mice. While mechanical mice require regular cleanings to operate properly, optical and laser mice do not. Mice are commonly used to start programs; open, move around, and edit documents; draw or edit images; and more. A list of common mouse commands is included in Figure 4-3.

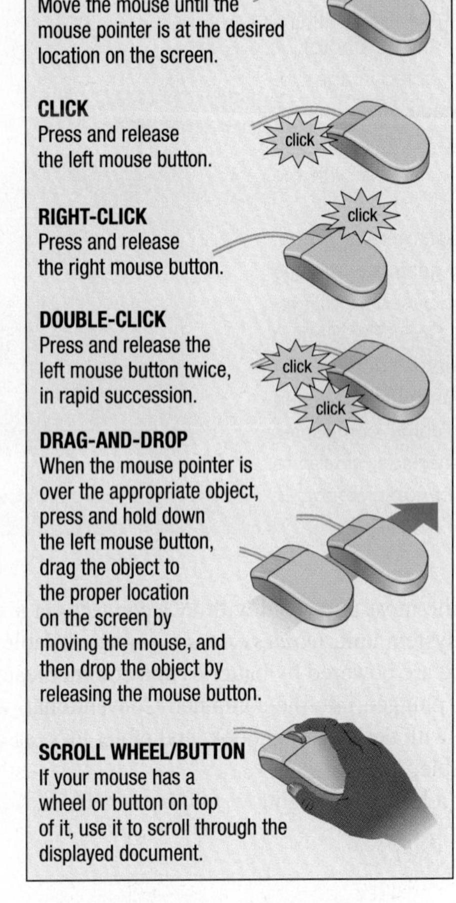

POINT
Move the mouse until the mouse pointer is at the desired location on the screen.
CLICK
Press and release the left mouse button.
click
RIGHT-CLICK
Press and release the right mouse button.
click
DOUBLE-CLICK
Press and release the left mouse button twice, in rapid succession.
click
click
DRAG-AND-DROP
When the mouse pointer is over the appropriate object, press and hold down the left mouse button, drag the object to the proper location on the screen by moving the mouse, and then drop the object by releasing the mouse button.
SCROLL WHEEL/BUTTON
If your mouse has a wheel or button on top of it, use it to scroll through the displayed document.

COMMON MOUSE OPERATIONS

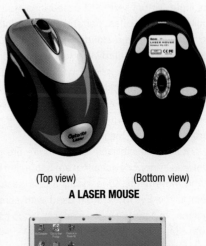

(Top view) (Bottom view)

A LASER MOUSE

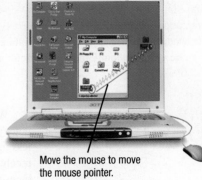

Move the mouse to move the mouse pointer.

USING A MOUSE

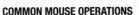

FIGURE 4-3
Using a mouse.

>**Pointing device.** An input device that moves an onscreen pointer, such as an arrow or insertion point, to allow the user to select objects on the screen. >**Mouse.** A common pointing device that the user slides along a flat surface to move a pointer around the screen and clicks its buttons to make selections.

TREND

Virtual Input Devices

There is an ongoing trend to continue to make input methods and devices easier and more natural to use. Voice recognition is one strong possibility. Other possibilities include more *virtual*, less physical, devices that use projections or gestures instead of more conventional methods of input.

One emerging input device being developed for use with portable PCs and mobile devices is the *virtual keyboard.* A virtual keyboard uses a projector and camera—the projector projects a keyboard image onto a flat surface and the camera translates motion on that projected image back to the computer as input. Virtual keyboard capabilities are expected to soon be built into cell phones, portable PCs, and other portable devices to allow input via a standard keyboard layout without requiring actual keyboard hardware (see the accompanying photo). A related emerging application is the use of projected images for consumer kiosks. Instead of requiring floor space, kiosk images are displayed on a wall or the floor using a wall-mounted projector and a camera tracks the user's interactions with the projected images as input.

Other possibilities for the future are *gesture-based input devices*—input devices that are controlled by gestures, such as hand movements. One example of a gesture-based input system is the EyeToy system used with some Sony PlayStation games. This system uses a special video camera in conjunction with software to enable the player to control the game using only body movements. For computer input, some companies are working toward a noncontact gesture interface, similar to the one used by Tom Cruise's character in *Minority Report* to change the images on his display by just gesturing with his hands. Although such an interface might be far in the future, more than one company has already developed a *motion-controlled* interface for mobile devices, in which users can rotate a smart phone or other device to change the orientation of the display image, tip the device forward or backward to zoom in or out, tip the device left or right to change songs on a music playlist, tilt the device to scroll, and more, allowing the user to operate the device with one hand. One interface even enables users to "write" in the air with the phone and have the phone recognize and input the letters or numbers being written.

A virtual keyboard.

While most mice sold with PCs connect via a serial, USB, or PS/2 port on the computer's system unit, *wireless mice* are also available. Similar to wireless keyboards, wireless mice are powered by batteries and communicate wirelessly with the system unit via a receiver plugged into the computer. Conventional, wireless, and small travel mice can all be used with desktop, notebook, and tablet PCs, as desired, as long as an appropriate port is available.

For a look at emerging *virtual input devices*, see the Trend box.

>**Electronic pen.** An input device that is used to write electronically on the display screen; also called a **stylus** or *digital pen*.

Electronic Pens

An **electronic pen** is a pointing device that can be used instead of a mouse to select objects, as well as to draw or write electronically on the screen. Also called a **stylus** or *digital pen*, electronic pens are typically wireless and look similar to a ballpoint pen. Handheld PCs, tablet PCs, and other devices that accept pen input typically use a stylus. *Pen-based PCs* and other devices that use electronic pens are discussed next. The idea behind pen-based input and *digital writing* in general is to make using a computer as convenient as writing with a pen, while adding the extra capabilities the computer can provide, such as converting the pen-based text input to editable typed text or retrieving handwritten electronic documents by keywords or the document contents.

Pen-Based PCs

Although their capabilities depend on the type of computer and software being used, electronic pens can be used with a variety of computer types (see Figure 4-4). Most often, electronic pens are used with handheld or tablet PCs to input handwritten text and sketches, as well as to manipulate objects (such as to select an option from a menu, select a group of text, or resize an image). Depending on the software being used, handwritten input can be stored as an image, stored as handwritten characters that can be recognized by the computer, or converted to editable, typed text. For the latter two options, software with **handwriting recognition** capabilities must be used.

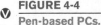

FIGURE 4-4
Pen-based PCs. Users of pen-based PCs can typically use their stylus to input handwritten data and instructions, as well as to select menu items, check boxes, and command buttons.

HANDHELD PC

TABLET PC

DESKTOP PC

Some handwriting recognition systems require the handwritten input to conform to a specific handwriting style (such as the *Palm Graffiti* alphabet used with Palm handheld PCs); others can accept handwritten input written in the users' personal style. Just as with *speech recognition*—in which the computer accepts spoken input—handwriting recognition usually requires some training for the PC to adjust to the particular style of the user, and the input is not always interpreted correctly. For a look at how handwriting recognition works, see Figure 4-5.

One area of recent growth is the use of *digital forms*—such as the patient assessment form shown in Figure 4-5—in conjunction with handwriting recognition. This application is expected to continue to grow in the near future as companies continue to move towards digital records and digital documents.

>**Handwriting recognition.** The ability of a device to identify handwritten characters.

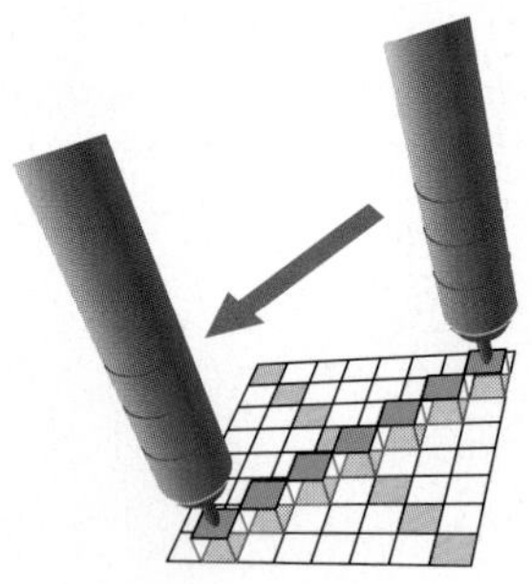

1. As the pen moves, the computer continually calculates its position, instructing the pixels it passes over to turn on.

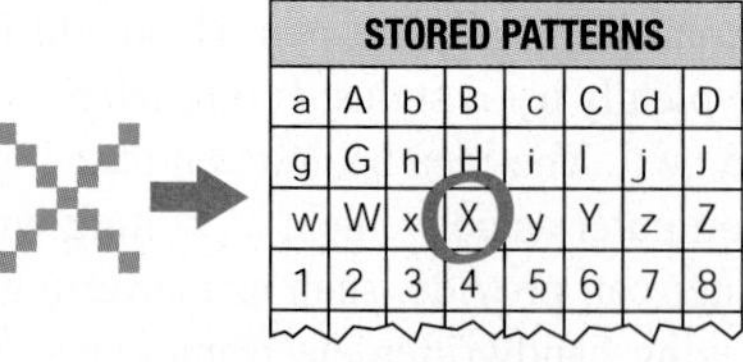

2. The computer then compares the pattern that was input to other patterns it has stored. It makes allowances within certain limits for imprecision.

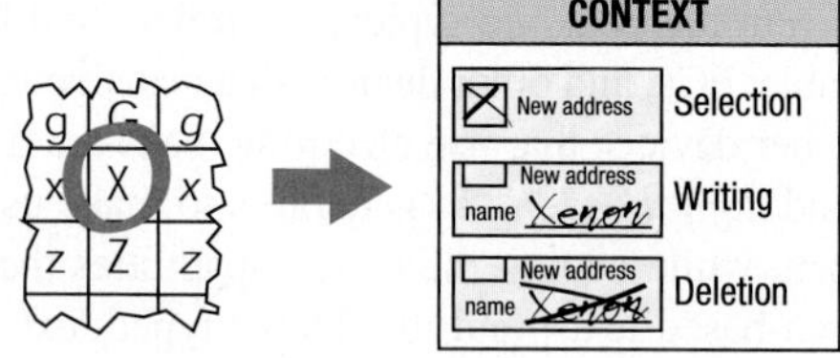

3. After a pattern is recognized, the computer looks at the context in which the pattern was made before it decides what to do. For instance, an "X" in a check box means selecting a certain action, whereas an "X" over filled-in text implies a deletion operation.

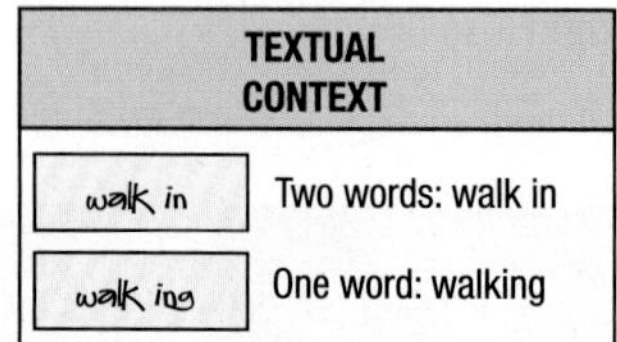

4. For text input, the computer looks at surrounding words, consults dictionaries, and uses grammar rules to determine the most likely intended input.

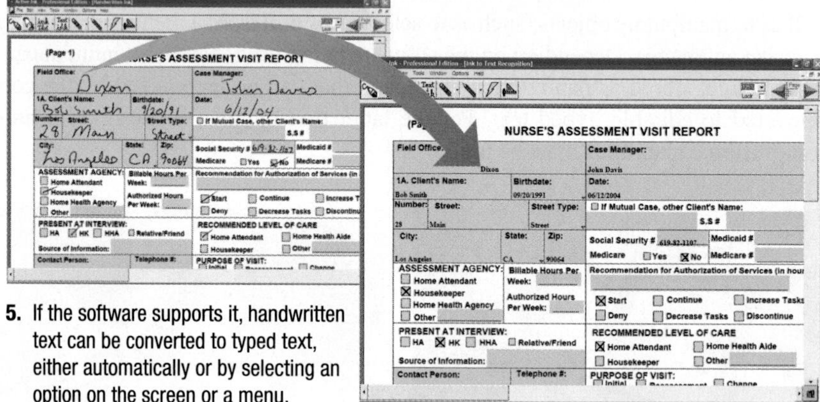

5. If the software supports it, handwritten text can be converted to typed text, either automatically or by selecting an option on the screen or a menu.

FIGURE 4-5
How handwriting recognition works. Pen-based computers usually use contextual clues, dictionaries, grammar rules, and more to make the best determination of what the user wrote, instead of strictly interpreting content letter by letter.

Digital Writing Systems

Other types of electronic pens used with PCs include those designed solely to capture handwritten input as it is written and then transfer that input to the PC after the pen is docked in its cradle attached to the PC. Alternatively, the input can be transmitted wirelessly to a PC as it is being written. Typically, these *digital writing systems* require the use of special paper, and anything written on that paper can be transferred to a PC (see Figure 4-6).

Graphics Tablets

A **graphics tablet**—also called a *digitizing tablet*—is a flat, touch-sensitive tablet used in conjunction with a stylus (see Figure 4-6). Anything drawn or written on the graphics tablet is automatically transferred to the connected PC in graphic form. Graphics tablets are often used by graphic artists, photographers, and other graphics professionals in conjunction with *image editing software* to create original images or to modify digital photographs.

Signature Capture Devices

Another type of pen-based input device is the *signature capture device* (see Figure 4-6). These devices are commonly attached to point-of-sale equipment, so they can electronically record signatures used to authorize credit card purchases. Delivery companies,

>**Graphics tablet.** A flat, rectangular input device that is used in conjunction with a stylus to transfer drawings, sketches, and anything written on the device to a PC in graphic form.

DIGITAL WRITING SYSTEM
When the Send box on the paper is selected, the document content is transferred wirelessly to the computer.

GRAPHICS TABLET
All input written on the graphics tablet is transferred in real time to the computer.

SIGNATURE CAPTURE DEVICE
When a signature is entered and the appropriate confirmation box is tapped, the signature is recorded.

FIGURE 4-6
Other uses for electronic pens.

restaurants, retail stores, and other service businesses may also use a signature capture device—or a handheld or tablet PC with appropriate software—to record authorizing signatures.

Touch Screens

As PCs have become more integrated into the lives of consumers, **touch screens** have become increasingly more prominent. With a touch screen, the user touches the screen with his or her finger to select commands or otherwise provide input to the computer with which the touch screen is being used (see Figure 4-7). Touch screen kiosks are found in a variety of locations—such as retail stores, movie theaters, courthouses, fast-food restaurants, and airports—to allow for more self-service applications, including self-check-in. According to the IHL Consulting Group, U.S. consumers spent $123 billion at consumer kiosks in 2003—an 80% jump from the year before—and purchases made via kiosks are expected to surpass $1 trillion by 2007. Touch screens are also used in *point-of-sale (POS) systems*—systems that record sales transaction data at the point where the product or service is purchased, such as a checkout or sales counter—and are useful for on-the-job applications (such as factory work) that require users to wear gloves, or where using a keyboard or mouse is otherwise impractical.

FIGURE 4-7
Touch screens. Touch screens are commonly used in consumer kiosks and point-of-sale systems.

Other Pointing Devices

A few other common pointing devices are described next and shown in Figure 4-8. There are also pointing devices specifically designed for users with limited mobility. These pointing devices—along with *ergonomic keyboards*, *Braille keyboards*, and other types of input devices designed for users with special needs—are discussed in Chapter 16.

AIRLINE SELF-CHECK-IN

RESTAURANT ORDER-ENTRY SYSTEM

>**Touch screen.** A display device that is touched with the finger to issue commands or otherwise generate input to the connected PC.

FIGURE 4-8
Other common pointing devices.

JOYSTICK
Used most often in computer games.

TRACKBALL
Takes up less desk space than a mouse and is easier for some users to manipulate.

POINTING STICK
Found on some notebook PCs. The stick is pushed in different directions to move the onscreen pointer.

TOUCH PAD
Commonly found on notebook PCs, keyboards, or as a stand-alone device.

Joysticks and Other Gaming Devices

A **joystick**, which looks similar to a car's gearshift, is most often used with computer games. The movement of the joystick's stick controls an onscreen object, such as a player or vehicle in a game. Buttons on the joystick are usually assigned functions, such as jumping or firing a weapon, by the program being used. Today, some games can be used with gloves containing built-in sensors, enabling the computer to detect hand movements directly. Other gaming input devices include *gamepads* that are held in the hand and contain buttons similar to those on a joystick and *steering wheels* for driving games.

Trackballs

Similar to an upside-down mechanical mouse, a **trackball** has the ball mechanism on top, instead of on the bottom. The ball is rotated with the thumb, hand, or finger to move the onscreen pointer. Because the device itself does not need to be moved, trackballs take up less space on the desktop than mice; they also are easier to use for individuals with limited hand or finger mobility.

>**Joystick.** An input device that resembles a car's gear shift and is often used for gaming. >**Trackball.** An input device, similar to an upside-down mouse, that can be used to control an onscreen pointer and make selections.

Pointing Sticks

A **pointing stick** (also called a *touch stick*) is the pencil eraser-shaped device found in the middle of many notebook computer keyboards. It works similarly to a trackball, except that the thumb or finger pushes the stick in the appropriate direction, instead of rolling the ball, and the stick is pushed down to perform mouse clicks.

Touch Pads

A **touch pad** is a rectangular pad across which a fingertip or thumb slides to move the onscreen pointer. The buttons that appear next to the touch pad surface are used to perform clicks and other mouse actions; often the pad can be tapped to make selections, as well. Although most often found on notebook computer keyboards, touch pads are also available as stand-alone devices to be used with desktop computers.

FIGURE 4-9

Source data automation. Recording data initially in digital form or capturing data directly from a source document can both help reduce data input errors and save time.

RECORDING DATA DIRECTLY INTO A PC

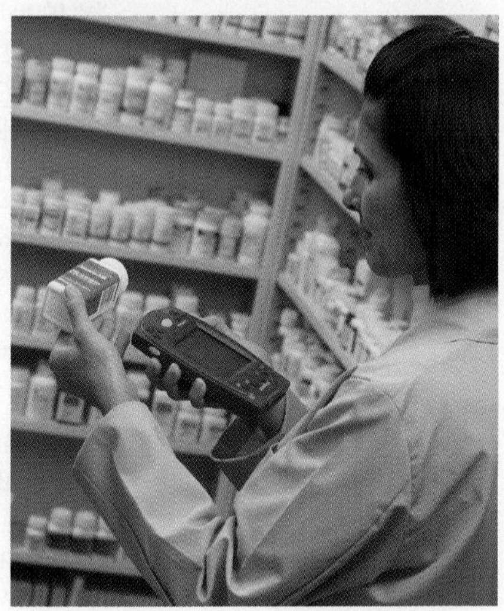

CAPTURING DATA FROM ITS SOURCE DOCUMENT

SCANNERS, READERS, AND DIGITAL CAMERAS

Some input devices are designed either to convert data that already exists in physical form to digital form or to capture data initially in digital form. Documents containing data that already exists in physical form—such as an order form, photograph, invoice, check, or price label—are referred to as *source documents*. There are various types of scanners and readers that can be used to capture data from a source document and convert it into input that the computer can understand. Capturing data directly from a source document (called *source data automation*) saves time and is usually more accurate than inputting the data via a keyboard or other manual input device. It also allows the people who know the most about the events that the data represents to be the ones who input the data, which helps ensure accuracy during the data-entry process. For instance, an insurance adjuster or auto mechanic entering data directly into a computer about the condition of a car involved in an accident will likely have fewer input errors than if he or she recorded that data on paper and then it was later keyed into a PC by an assistant; and a pharmacist electronically verifying the identity of a prescription medicine against a customer's record and prescription before giving it to the customer can help reduce prescription errors (see Figure 4-9).

Many of the most common devices used in source data automation are *scanning* or *reading devices*; that is, devices that read printed text, codes, or graphics, and then translate the results into digital form that can be used by a computer. The next few sections discuss several different types of scanning and reading devices, followed by a look at *digital cameras*, which capture data initially in digital form.

Scanners

A **scanner**, more officially called an *optical scanner*, captures the image of a usually flat object (such as a printed document, photograph, or drawing) in digital form and then transfers that data to a PC. Typically, the entire document (including both text and images) is input as a single graphical image that can be resized, inserted into other documents, posted on a Web page, e-mailed to someone, printed, or otherwise

>**Pointing stick.** An input device shaped like a pencil eraser that appears in the middle of some notebook computer keyboards and is used as a pointing device. >**Touch pad.** A small rectangular-shaped input device, often found on notebook computers, that is touched with the finger or thumb to control an onscreen pointer and make selections. >**Scanner.** An input device that reads printed text and graphics and transfers them to a computer in digital form.

treated like any other graphical image. The text in the image, however, cannot be edited unless **optical character recognition (OCR)** software is used in conjunction with the scanner to input the scanned text as individual text characters.

Types of Scanners

Scanners exist in a variety of configurations (see Figure 4-10). A **flatbed scanner** is designed to scan flat objects one page at a time. Flatbed scanners work in much the same way that photocopiers do—whatever is being scanned remains stationary while the scanning mechanism moves underneath it to capture the image. Some scanners can scan slides and film negatives, in addition to printed documents; scanners designed for high-volume processing come with automatic document feeders so that large quantities of documents can be scanned with one command. Businesses are increasingly converting their paper documents to electronic form for both archival purposes and to send electronically to clients. As more document processing is being carried out via e-mail and fax, high-volume scanning is becoming more important.

With a **sheetfed scanner**, documents are inserted into the top of the scanner, similar to the way paper is inserted into a fax machine. This design reduces the amount of desk space required. However, the feature also prevents the scanner from scanning bound-book pages or other items thicker or larger than a standard sheet of paper. Sheetfed scanners are most often used in mobile settings with a portable PC.

Handheld scanners are useful for capturing short newspaper or magazine articles, as well as Web addresses, names, and telephone numbers. Most handheld scanners (such as the *C-Pen* scanner shown in Figure 4-10) are designed to be used away from the computer. The scanned text is stored in the scanner and can be transferred to a PC (via a cable or a wireless connection) when needed. Data that will be needed while on the go (such as phone numbers, e-mail addresses, and so on) can also be stored in the scanner for retrieval at a later time. Other handheld scanners are designed to stay connected to the PC so that the user can scan data while working at his or her computer. Some handheld scanners can scan text in a variety of languages and come with built-in dictionaries to allow the text to be translated, or words defined, while the text is being scanned.

Applications requiring the most professional results may require the use of a *drum scanner*. A drum scanner is much more expensive and more difficult to operate than the other types of scanners discussed here. When a drum scanner is used, the documents to be scanned are mounted on a glass cylinder, which is then rotated at high speeds around a sensor located inside the scanner. Multimedia and medical applications may require the use of a *three-dimensional (3D) scanner*, which can scan an image or person in 3D. Task-specific scanners, such as *receipt scanners* and *business card scanners*, are also available.

For a look at how scanning is beginning to be used in conjunction with clothes shopping, see the Technology and You box.

Scanning Quality and Resolution

The quality of scanned images is indicated by *optical resolution*, typically measured in the number of *dots per inch (dpi)*. When a document is scanned using either an application program (such as a word processing program) or scanning software, the resolution to be used with the scanned image can often be specified. The resolution of scanned images can also be specified when the image is first saved or if it is modified at a later time using an *image editing program*. Scanners today usually scan at between 3,200 × 6,400 dpi and

>**Optical character recognition (OCR).** The ability of a scanning device to recognize handwritten or typed characters and convert them to electronic form as text, not images. >**Flatbed scanner.** An input device that scans flat objects one at a time. >**Sheetfed scanner.** A scanner that can accept a single sheet of paper at one time. >**Handheld scanner.** A small, handheld optical scanner.

FLATBED SCANNER
Used to input photos, sketches, slides, bound books, and other relatively flat documents into the computer.

HANDHELD SCANNER
Used to capture small amounts of text.

FIGURE 4-10
Optical scanners.

SHEETFED SCANNER
Used to scan one flat document at a time.

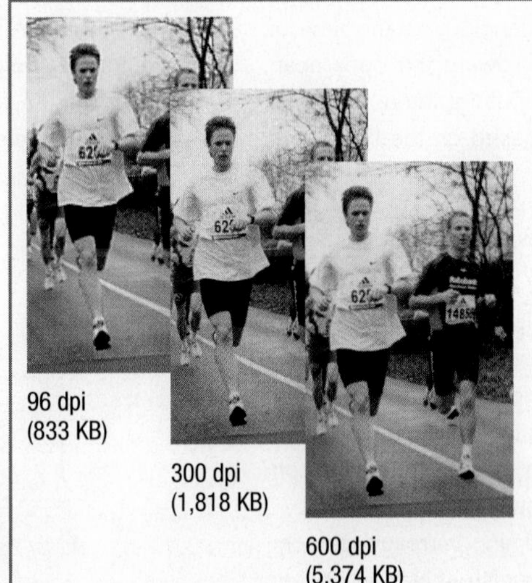

RESOLUTION
Most scanners let you specify the resolution (in dpi) at which you wish to scan. High-resolution images look sharper but result in larger file sizes.

4,800 × 9,600 dpi and use *48-bit color*; that is, they use 48 bits (or 6 bytes) to store the color for each **pixel** (*picture element*; that is, the smallest colorable area in an electronic image) for a possible 281 trillion colors. Higher resolution and a larger number of colors result in better images but also result in a larger file size, as illustrated in the lower-right image in Figure 4-10. Higher resolution is needed, however, if the image is to be enlarged significantly or if only one part of the image is to be extracted and enlarged.

The file size of a scanned image is also determined in part by the physical size of the image. To keep file size to a minimum, it is important to size the image to the desired size before saving it. It is also important to keep in mind the resolution of the output device to be used. Typically, 96 dpi is used for images to be displayed on a monitor (such as on a Web page), and 300 dpi or higher is used for images to be printed. Once an image has been scanned, it can usually be resized and then saved in the appropriate file format and resolution for the application with which the image is to be used. Scanners can cost anywhere from less than one hundred dollars to one thousand dollars or more.

FURTHER EXPLORATION

For links to further information about scanning documents and photographs, go to www.course.com/uc11/ch04

>**Pixel.** The smallest colorable area in an electronic image, such as a scanned document, digital photograph, or image displayed on a display screen.

TECHNOLOGY AND YOU

Body Scanners: Fitting Room of the Future?

One emerging scanning application that may be coming to a mall near you is *Intellifit*–an electronic fitting booth designed to help you quickly find clothes that fit. After walking into a see-though Intellifit booth (shown in the accompanying photo), radio waves use the moisture in your skin to take numerous, accurate measurements of your body. Unlike earlier body-scanning devices, you can remain dressed in your street clothes during the scanning procedure, which takes only about 10 seconds. The scan is safe and uses the same technology as the devices used to detect weapons in airports. Following the body scan, you are provided with a confidential computer printout listing the brands and sizes that will fit you best based on the body scan measurements.

Intellifit booths are already installed in some stores–such as Macy's, Levi's, David's Bridal, and Lane Bryant–nationwide. After being scanned once, you can use that information to shop for clothes both in stores and online. To help inform clothing manufacturers and retail stores about the current sizes of consumers today, a summary of the data from individuals scanned with the machine is compiled and provided to interested manufacturers and retailers. For privacy purposes, the summarized data contains no personally identifiable information–just statistics.

Systems such as Intellifit are becoming increasingly common as consumers' frustration with inconsistent sizing between and even within brands is mounting. According to a survey by Kurt Salmon Associates, 70% of women said they have difficulty finding clothes that fit them well, 81% saw a wide variation in size between brands, and 72% said a particular size within a brand is not even consistent. It is not uncommon for a particular individual's size to vary one, two, or even three sizes between clothing brands, making shopping a more time-consuming and frustrating activity than in the past. And jeans can be especially difficult to fit since there are so many different styles, and the shape of the individual often affects the size needed for a particular jeans style. Using a sizing system such as Intellifit solves this problem.

Another technology tool designed to help with clothes selection is the *virtual model*, such as the one used on the Land's End Web site. After the user selects options (such as body shape, height, weight, hair cut, complexion, and shape of eyes, nose, and lips), a virtual model of the user is created and can be saved. The user can then try on Land's End clothes on his or her virtual model to view what the item should look like on his or her body. If the user inputs his or her measurements, the system will also determine the appropriate size needed for that item.

Readers

A variety of *readers* are available to read the different types of codes and marks used today. Some of the most common are discussed next.

Barcode Readers

A **barcode** is an *optical code* that represents data with bars of varying widths. Barcodes are read with **barcode readers**. To read the data encoded in the barcode, light from the laser inside the barcode reader is reflected from the light spaces on the barcode (the dark bars absorb the light), and the barcode reader interprets the patterns of white space as the numbers or letters represented by the barcode. Then, data associated with that barcode—typically

>**Barcode.** A machine-readable code that represents data as a set of bars. >**Barcode reader.** An input device that reads barcodes.

identifying data, such as to uniquely identify a product, shipped package, or other item—can be retrieved. *Fixed* barcode readers are frequently used in point-of-sale (POS) systems (see Figure 4-11); *portable* barcode readers are also available. Portable barcode readers (either dedicated barcode reading devices or portable PCs with built-in barcode reading capabilities) are used by workers who need to scan barcodes while on the go, such as while walking through a warehouse or at a variety of different retail locations.

The most familiar barcode is *UPC* (*Universal Product Code*), the barcode commonly found on packaged goods in supermarkets. Businesses and organizations can also create and use custom barcodes to fulfill their unique needs. For instance, shippers, such as FedEx, UPS, and the U.S. Postal Service, use their own barcodes to mark and track packages; hospitals use custom barcodes to match patients with their charts and medicines; libraries and video stores use barcodes for checking out and checking in materials, such as books and movies; researchers use barcodes to tag and track the migration habits of animals; and law enforcement agencies use barcodes to mark evidence. In fact, any business with a barcode printer and appropriate software can create custom barcodes for use with its products or to classify items used within its organization, such as client or employee files, computers, office equipment, sales receipts, and more. The most popular barcode for these types of nonfood use is Code 39, which can encode both letters and numbers. Examples of a UPC code, Code 39 barcode, and POSTNET code (used by the U.S. Postal Service to represent a ZIP or postal code for sorting purposes) are shown in Figure 4-11.

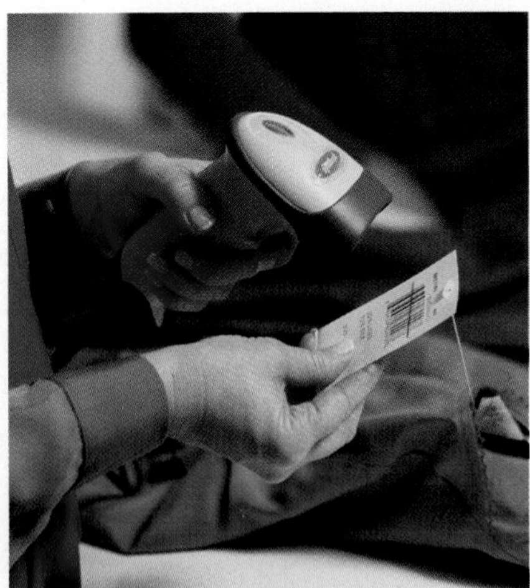

FIXED BARCODE READERS
Used most often in retail point-of-sale applications.

PORTABLE BARCODE READERS
Used when portability is needed.

INTEGRATED BARCODE READERS
Built into or added to portable PCs.

BARCODES
Uniquely identify a product or other item.

UPC (UNIVERSAL PRODUCT CODE)

CODE 39

POSTNET CODE

FIGURE 4-11
Barcode readers and barcodes.

Radio Frequency Identification (RFID) Readers

Radio frequency identification (RFID) is a technology that can store and transmit data located in **RFID tags**. RFID tags, which contain tiny chips and radio antennas, can be attached to objects that need to be tracked. Many RFID tags today are *passive*, which require a reader to "wake them up" so they can broadcast data; *active RFID tags* include a battery, so they broadcast data on a continual basis. Some RFID applications already in use include tracking the movement of inventory pallets and shipping containers, tracking or locating livestock and other animals, and tagging tractors and other large assets to keep

>**Radio frequency identification (RFID).** A technology used to store and transmit data located in RFID tags. >**RFID tag.** A device containing tiny chips and radio antennas that is attached to objects that will be identified using RFID technology.

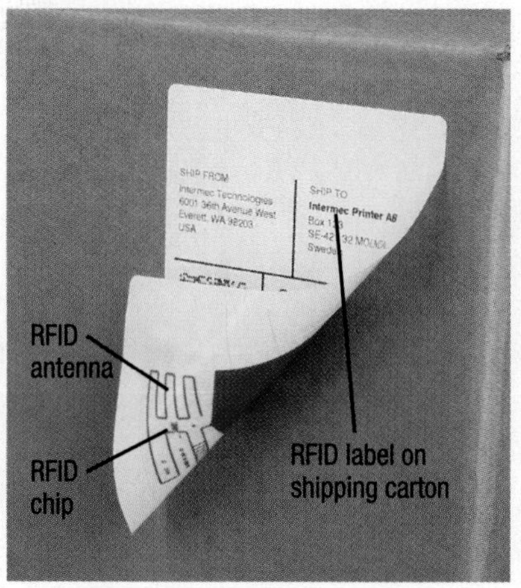

RFID TAGS
RFID tags, containing a built-in chip and an antenna, are often included in shipping labels today.

RFID READERS
This portal RFID reader reads all of the RFID tags on a palette at one time, as it passes between the readers.

FIGURE 4-12
RFID readers and tags.

track of their locations. Recently, the Department of Defense, Wal-Mart, Target, and a number of other major retailers across the globe began requiring suppliers to start using RFID tags on delivered items, the Social Security Administration (SSA) is beginning to use RFID tags to track orders for SSA forms and pamphlets, and the FDA has recommended the use of RFID tags for prescription drugs to prevent counterfeiting. In addition, Delta Air Lines has been testing RFID luggage tags with amazing results—baggage tagged with RFID tags arrived at the proper destination nearly 100% of the time, whereas barcoded luggage typically arrived with only 80% to 85% accuracy. RFID is also extensively used by the military, primarily for asset tracking, although the technology is also being used to track wounded soldiers, civilians, and POWs (via wristbands with built-in RFID chips) in at least one Navy hospital located in the Iraqi desert. The U.S. Army is also installing RFID tags on military vehicles located in Iraq to allow convoys to be tracked (via the tags and GPS technology), and redirected, if necessary.

Unlike barcode systems, data can be stored in an RFID tag before it is attached and that data can be updated via the antenna after the tag is attached to its designated item—for instance, to record information about the product's origin, shipping history, or final destination. RFID tags are also read by radio waves, instead of by light. This is an advantage over barcodes because radio waves do not require line of sight, can be read from a distance of up to 15 feet if an *ultra-high frequency RFID tag* is used, and can pass through materials such as cardboard and plastic. These characteristics enable all the RFID tags attached to all items located inside a shipping container to be read at one time as the container passes by a *portal RFID reader* or is picked up by an *RFID-enabled forklift* (an RFID tag and portal RFID reader are shown in Figure 4-12). RFID-equipped products and store shelves can even keep track of inventory, automatically reorder products (according to ordering criteria previously set up) when supplies run low, notify employees when items need restocking or wind up in the wrong aisle, and help employees quickly find recalled products.

RFID is also being used in conjunction with several types of electronic payment systems. Special key fobs or wands containing RFID chips allow customers to pay for gas or fast food by waving the wand close to a special reader (for security purposes, *high-frequency RFID chips* are used in electronic payment applications, so the wand has to be within a few inches of the reader), and the purchase amount is automatically deducted from a checking account or charged to a credit card, depending on the customer's preference when registering to use the RFID payment system. Some credit cards—such as Chase's *Blink* cards—are also RFID-enabled, allowing consumers to more quickly authorize credit card transactions by simply waving the card in front of a special reader. An increasing number of U.S. highways are using RFID tags placed on cars for automatic toll collection. Singapore has gone a step further by using the RFID tags to collect different toll prices at different times of the day, in the hope that this will encourage drivers to stay off busy roads during rush times.

For a closer look at how RFID technology works and a peek at its possible future, see the Inside the Industry box, beginning on page 150.

Optical Mark Readers (OMRs)

Optical mark readers (*OMRs*) input data from special forms to score or tally exams, questionnaires, ballots, and so forth. Typically, users use a pencil to fill in small circles or other shapes on the form to indicate their selections, and then the forms are inserted into an optical mark reader (see Figure 4-13) to be scored or tallied. Filled-in responses reflect the light, and those responses are recorded by the OMR. If it is an exam or some other type of objective instrument, a form containing the correct responses is input first, and then the OMR can indicate any wrong answers and print the total correct on each exam form; surveys and other subjective forms are usually just tallied and the results printed on a tally sheet. In either case, the results can be input to a computer system, or the data can be stored on a disk or other storage medium, if the optical mark reader is connected to a computer.

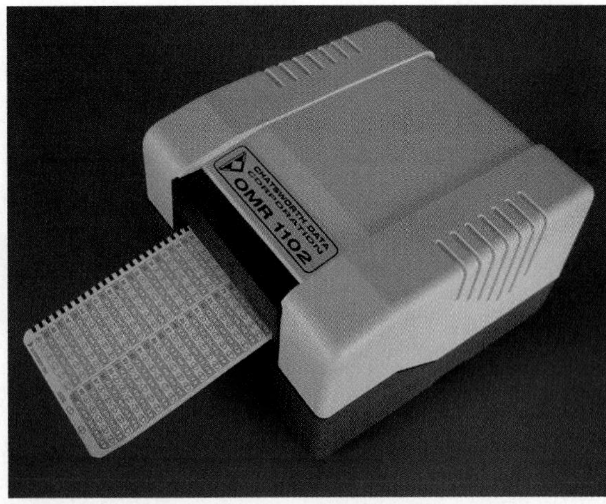
CHATSWORTH DATA CORPORATION
OMR 1102

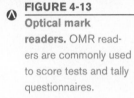

FIGURE 4-13
Optical mark readers. OMR readers are commonly used to score tests and tally questionnaires.

Optical Character Recognition (OCR) Devices

Optical characters are characters specifically designed to be identifiable by humans as well as by some type of *optical character recognition* (*OCR*) device. Optical characters conform to a certain font design, such as the one shown in Figure 4-14. The optical reader shines light on the characters and converts the reflections into electronic patterns that the machine can recognize. The OCR device can identify a character only if it is familiar with the font used. Today, most machines are designed to read several standard OCR fonts, even when these fonts are mixed in a single document.

Optical characters are widely used in processing *turnaround documents*, such as the monthly bills for credit card, utility, and cable-TV companies (see Figure 4-14 for a sample utility bill that uses OCR fonts). These documents contain optical characters in certain places on the bill to aid processing when consumers send it back with payment—or "turn it around." Sometimes it is easy to spot the optical characters on a document. Today, however, many OCR fonts look so much like normal text that it is hard for an ordinary person to tell which parts the computer system can read and which parts it cannot.

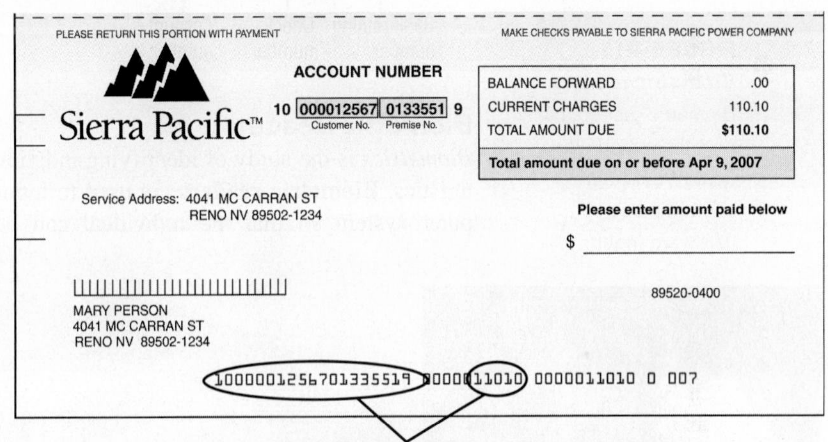

PLEASE RETURN THIS PORTION WITH PAYMENT

MAKE CHECKS PAYABLE TO SIERRA PACIFIC POWER COMPANY

Sierra Pacific™

ACCOUNT NUMBER
10 000012567 0133551 9
Customer No. Premise No.

BALANCE FORWARD	.00
CURRENT CHARGES	110.10
TOTAL AMOUNT DUE	$110.10
Total amount due on or before Apr 9, 2007	

Service Address: 4041 MC CARRAN ST
RENO NV 89502-1234

Please enter amount paid below
$

89520-0400

MARY PERSON
4041 MC CARRAN ST
RENO NV 89502-1234

1000001256701335519 0000011010 0000011010 0 007

OPTICAL CHARACTERS
These OCR characters indicate the customer account number and amount due and can be read by both computers and humans.

FIGURE 4-14
Optical characters. The most common use of optical characters is in turnaround documents, such as on the utility bill shown here.

Magnetic Ink Character Recognition (MICR) Readers

Magnetic ink character recognition (*MICR*) is a technology confined primarily to the banking industry, where it is used to facilitate high-volume processing of checks. Figure 4-15 illustrates a check encoded with MICR characters and a reader/sorter that processes such checks. The standard font adopted by the banking industry contains only 14 characters—the 10 decimal digits (0 through 9) and four special symbols. MICR characters are inscribed on checks with magnetic ink by a special machine. As people write and cash checks, the recipients deposit them in the banking system. At banks, reader/sorter machines magnetically read and identify the MICR-encoded bank and account information on the check, magnetically encode the amount of the check onto the check, and sort the checks. Images of the checks can then be captured and routed to the appropriate bank for processing.

FIGURE 4-15
Magnetic ink character recognition (MICR).

MICR READER
This device that reads and sorts checks and other MICR-encoded documents can process around 500 documents per minute (dpm); faster units can process up to 2,000 dpm.

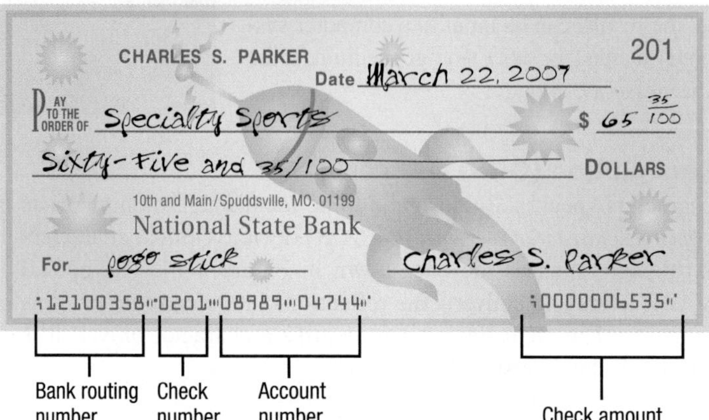

MICR-ENCODED CHECK
MICR characters on the bottom of the check respectively identify the bank, check number, account number, and check amount. The characters on the left are put on when checks are preprinted; the numbers representing the check amount are added when the check is cashed.

FIGURE 4-16
Biometric readers.
Biometric readers can be either stand-alone (left) or built into another piece of hardware (right).

Biometric Readers

Biometrics is the study of identifying individuals based on measurable biological characteristics. **Biometric readers** are used to input biometric data about a person into a computer system so that the individual can be identified based on a particular unique physiological characteristic (such as a fingerprint, hand geometry, face, or iris of the eye) or personal trait (such as a voice or signature). Emerging biometric readers can identify individuals by their skin, gait, or the veins in their hand. As shown in Figure 4-16, a biometric reader can be stand-alone or built into another piece of hardware, such as a keyboard or mouse. Some handheld computers, notebook PCs, and storage devices (such as external hard drives and flash memory drives) today have built-in fingerprint readers to allow only authorized users access to the PC or data stored on the device. Biometric input devices are increasingly being used to restrict access to facilities or computer systems, authorize electronic payments, log on to

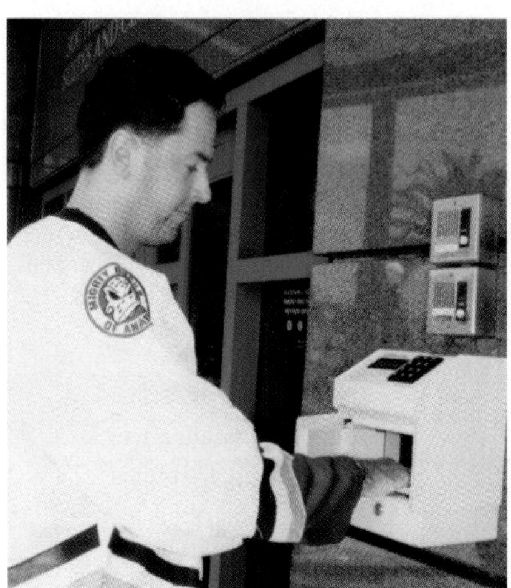

STAND-ALONE HAND GEOMETRY READER
Often used for access control, such as to authenticate NHL Mighty Ducks players at the Anaheim Pond arena shown here.

BUILT-IN FINGERPRINT READER
Often used for access control or to authorize electronic financial transactions.

>**Biometric reader.** A device used to input biometric data.

secure Web sites, punch in and out of work, and more. Biometrics for access control is covered in more detail in Chapter 9.

Digital Cameras

Digital cameras work much like conventional film cameras, but instead of recording images on film they record them on some type of digital storage medium, such as a flash memory card, digital tape cartridge, or DVD disc. Digital cameras are usually designated either as *still* cameras (which take individual still photos) or *video* cameras (which capture moving video images). Many still cameras can take a limited amount of video, and many video cameras can capture still images, but the quality may not be as good. This may change in the future, however, as digital camera manufacturers begin to design digital cameras that incorporate both capabilities. For example, Samsung's DuoCam digital camera, released in 2005, contains the technology (including two separate lenses) to take both high-quality still photos and high-quality video.

Digital Still Cameras

Digital still cameras are available in a wide variety of sizes and capabilities. For instance, you can get an inexpensive (less than $100) consumer stand-alone, point-and-shoot model; a professional digital camera with removable lenses; a *digital camera watch*; or a digital camera integrated into your handheld PC or mobile phone (see Figure 4-17). The primary appeal of digital still cameras is that the images are immediately available for viewing or printing, instead of having to have the film developed first. Digital still cameras typically use flash memory for storage, in the form of either removable flash memory cards or built-in flash memory chips. The number of digital photos that can be stored in the camera at one time depends on the capacity of the storage medium being used and the resolution of the photos being taken (many cameras let you select the resolution to be used). At any time, the photos can be transferred to a PC or printer, usually by removing the flash memory card and inserting it into the PC or printer, by connecting the camera to a PC via a cable, or by attaching the camera to a special docking station attached to the printer or PC. Once the photos have been transferred to a PC, they can be retouched with image editing software, saved, printed, posted to a Web page, or burned onto a CD or DVD disc, just like any other digital image. The images on the storage medium can be deleted at any time to make room for more photos.

FIGURE 4-17

Digital still cameras. Digital still cameras, which record images on digital media instead of on film, are available in many shapes and sizes.

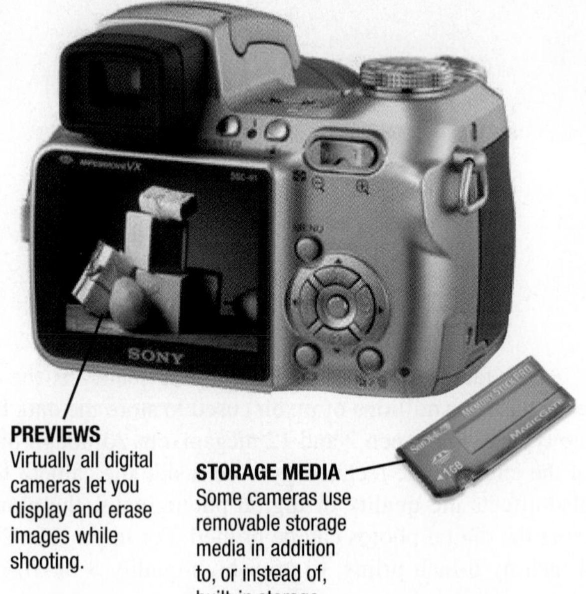

PREVIEWS Virtually all digital cameras let you display and erase images while shooting.

STORAGE MEDIA Some cameras use removable storage media in addition to, or instead of, built-in storage.

TYPICAL CONSUMER DIGITAL CAMERA

PROFESSIONAL DIGITAL CAMERA

DIGITAL CAMERA INTEGRATED INTO A MOBILE PHONE

>**Digital camera.** An input device that takes pictures and records them as digital data (instead of film or videotaped) images.

INSIDE THE INDUSTRY

RFID

RFID is a technology that uses radio waves to automatically identify objects. The RFID chip inside an RFID tag stores information about the object to which it is attached. One of the fastest-growing RFID applications is to identify retail goods. RFID tags can be made in a variety of shapes and sizes, including tags designed to be attached to end products, shipping palettes, and shipping labels (see the accompanying figure). Whenever an RFID-tagged item is within range of an RFID reader, the tag's built-in antenna allows the information located within the RFID chip to be sent to the reader. For supply chain applications, additional information can be stored in the RFID chip during the life of the product–such as manufacturing and origin data, shipping time, and the temperature range the item has been exposed to–which can be read at the final destination.

To use RFID as a replacement for barcodes, a unique identifying product code referred to as an *Electronic Product Code* (*EPC*) is typically assigned to each product and stored in its RFID tag. This code, currently in its second generation of development, can be used in conjunction with a database to determine additional product information, such as the pricing information needed in order for the RFID tag to be used at checkout. Because RFID technology can read numerous items at one time, it is possible that, someday, *low-frequency RFID tags* (tags with a reading range of approximately 3 feet) will be used to allow consumers to shop, bag their items, and have all the items rung up at the checkout station at one time.

Despite all its advantages, there are a number of privacy and security issues that need to be resolved before RFID gains widespread use at the consumer end. Precautions against fraudulent use–such as using high-frequency tags that need to be within a few inches of the reader and requiring a PIN code, signature, or other type of authorization when an RFID payment system is used–are being developed. Privacy advocates are concerned about linking RFID tag data with personally-identifiable data contained in corporate databases, as well as the possibility of using RFID tags to track the movements or shopping habits of consumers. A proposed solution to the latter concern is to allow consumers to either remove or deactivate a tag after purchase so it can no longer be read. In the meantime, at least two states have introduced legislation to place limits on the use of RFID technology.

TIP

When comparing the zoom capabilities of a digital camera, look for *optical zoom*, not *digital zoom*, specifications. Optical zoom specifications reflect how much the camera can zoom without losing image quality.

One factor affecting digital camera quality is the number of pixels (measured in *megapixels* or millions of pixels) used to store the data for each image. Today's cameras are typically between 2 and 12 megapixels. Although other factors—such as the quality of the lens and the technology used inside the camera to capture and process images—also affects the quality of digital photographs, the number of pixels does impact how large the digital photos can be printed. For instance, a 2-megapixel camera can produce 4-inch by 6-inch prints; to print high-quality 8-by-10-inch prints, a 3- or 4-megapixel camera is needed.

1. RFID tags are created in various formats and attached to end products, shipping cartons, or other items to be tracked. Some tags, such as the ones on the orange crates shown here, are reusable; others, such as the ones shown on the shipping label and tire, are designed to be disposable.

2. Data is stored in the RFID tag when the tag is created or attached and then can be updated as needed during the life of the product. Tags can be read automatically as palettes move through portal RFID readers or are lifted by RFID-enabled forklifts to keep track of products during shipping and to receive them easily into inventory at the final destination.

4. In the future, retail stores may use RFID-enabled checkout systems to ring up all of the products in a shopping cart at one time.

3. At the final destination, product history can be read and products can be restocked and reordered when supplies run low. If reusable RFID tags or RFID-tagged shipping containers are used (such as the orange crates shown here), they are cleaned and returned to the grower or supplier.

Some digital cameras today are Wi-Fi enabled, so digital photos can be e-mailed to others directly from the camera. Another recent improvement in digital cameras is a decrease in the delay between when the user presses the button and when the camera takes the photo, which is especially important when taking action shots. Although not yet as quick as conventional film cameras, the delay typically associated with digital cameras is continually being made shorter. Consumer digital cameras start at about $100; professional digital cameras cost $1,000 or more.

FURTHER EXPLORATION

For links to further information about digital cameras and digital photography, go to www.course.com/uc11/ch04

Digital Video Cameras

Digital video cameras include *digital camcorders* and small *PC video cameras* (see Figure 4-18). Digital camcorders are similar to conventional *analog* camcorders, but they store images on digital media—typically either on mini digital video (DV) tape cartridges or rewritable DVDs, although hard drive digital camcorders are now available. Once the video is recorded, it can be transferred to a PC, edited with software as needed, and saved to a DVD or other type of storage medium.

PC video cameras—commonly called PC cams—are designed to transmit video images over the Internet, such as during a *videoconference* or *video phone call.* Although video phone calls can be one-way (with only one person sending video and only one person receiving it), usually during a videoconference each person has a PC video camera attached to his or her PC to transmit images to the participant, as in Figure 4-18. Some one-way applications include PC cameras located in childcare centers that allow parents to watch live video of their children during the day, and surveillance cameras set up in homes and offices that broadcast images to the owner's PC so he or she can check for intruders and monitor the location remotely. PC cameras can also be used to broadcast images continually to a Web page, such as the cameras frequently found in zoo animal exhibits, on top of mountains, or other locations of interest to the general public. In this type of application, the video camera is referred to as a *Web cam.*

Digital video cameras can also be used for identification purposes, such as with face recognition technology to authorize access to a secure facility or computer resource. These and other types of security applications are discussed in more detail in Chapter 9.

DIGITAL CAMCORDER
Typically allows you to view video during and after it is recorded; digital media, such as the DVD shown here, are used for storage instead of videotape.

PC VIDEO CAMERA
Commonly used to deliver video over the Internet, such as in the family videoconference shown here.

FIGURE 4-18
Digital video cameras. Common types include digital camcorders and PC video cameras.

AUDIO INPUT

Audio input is the process of entering audio data into the computer. Types of audio input include voice and music.

Voice Input Systems

A system used to input spoken words and convert them to digital form is known as a **voice input system**. All voice input systems (also called *speech recognition systems* and *voice recognition systems*) consist of a *microphone* or *headset* (a set of *headphones* with a built-in microphone) and appropriate software, such as *IBM ViaVoice* or *ScanSoft NaturallySpeaking*. Voice input can also be used to dictate text or commands the computer will recognize, as an

>**Voice input system.** A system that enables a computer to recognize the human voice.

The patient exhibits signs of...

1. The user speaks into a microphone that cancels out background noise and inputs the speech into the computer.

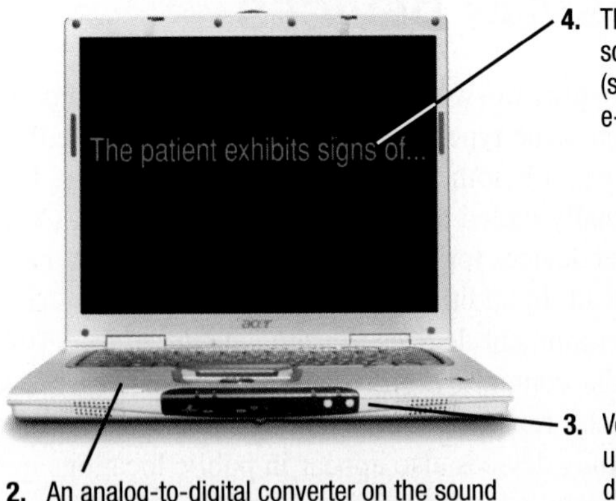
The patient exhibits signs of...

2. An analog-to-digital converter on the sound card located inside the PC converts the spoken words to phonemes, the fundamental sounds in the language being used, and digitizes them.

3. Voice recognition software matches up the phoneme combinations to determine the words that were spoken. Sentence structure rules are used to select one word if it is a questionable match or a word with a homonym.

4. The spoken words appear on the screen in the application program (such as a word processor or an e-mail program) being used.

FIGURE 4-19
How a voice input system works.

alternative to mouse or keyboard input. Voice input systems are used by individuals who cannot use a keyboard, as well as by individuals who prefer not to use a keyboard or who can generate input faster via a voice input system. For instance, medical and legal transcription is the most frequently used voice input application at the present time. Voice input systems are also increasingly being incorporated into portable PCs, mobile devices, cells phones, GPS systems, and so on for hands-free operation. Specialty voice recognition systems are also used to control machines, robots, and other electronic equipment, such as by surgeons during surgical procedures.

Here's a quick look at how a typical voice input system might work (see Figure 4-19). First, a microphone is used to input the spoken words into the PC, and then the sounds are broken into digital representations of *phonemes*—the basic elements of speech, such as *duh*, *aw*, and *guh* for the word "dog." (The English language contains about 50 phonemes.) Next, the voice recognition software analyzes the content of the speech to convert the phonemes to words. Once words are identified, they are displayed on the screen. If a match is questionable or a homonym is encountered (such as the choice between "their," "there," and "they're"), the program analyzes the context in which the word is used in an attempt to identify the correct word. If the program inserts an inappropriate word while converting the user's voice input to text, the user can usually override it. To increase accuracy, most voice recognition software can be trained by individual users to allow the program to become accustomed to the user's speech patterns, voice, accent, and pronunciation.

Music Input Systems

Musical input can be recorded for use in music arrangements, to accompany a multimedia presentation, or to create a custom music CD. Music can be input into a PC via a CD, a DVD, or a Web download. For original compositions, a *MIDI* (*musical instrument digital interface*) device, such as a MIDI keyboard with piano keys instead of, or in addition to, alphanumeric keys (see Figure 4-20), can be used. Once the music is input into the computer, it can be saved, modified, played, inserted into other programs, or burned onto a CD or DVD, as necessary.

FIGURE 4-20
A combination PC/MIDI keyboard.

DISPLAY DEVICES

A **display device**—the most common form of output device—presents output visually, such as on some type of computer screen. Because the output appears temporarily on a display device, it is sometimes referred to as *soft copy*. The display device for a desktop PC is more formally called a **monitor**. With all-in-one PCs, notebook computers, handheld PCs, and other devices for which the screen is built into the unit, the term **display screen** is often used instead. In addition to being used with computers, display screens are also built into home entertainment devices, *portable media players* (which play music, videos, and other multimedia content), *digital picture frames* (which display images uploaded via a PC or cell phone), remote controls, gaming devices, and other consumer products (see Figure 4-21). Display devices also appear in public locations in the form of electronic *e-paper* signs (see the How it Works box), on kiosks, and to target advertising to consumers when they are waiting in a check-out line, riding in an elevator or taxi, in the restroom, or some other location where they are captive for a few minutes—a trend referred to as *captive marketing*.

Display Device Characteristics

There are several characteristics and features that differentiate one type of display device from another. The following sections discuss a few of the most significant characteristics.

FIGURE 4-21
Uses for displays.

COMPUTERS

SMART PHONES

HOME ELECTRONICS

PORTABLE MEDIA PLAYERS

DIGITAL PICTURE FRAMES

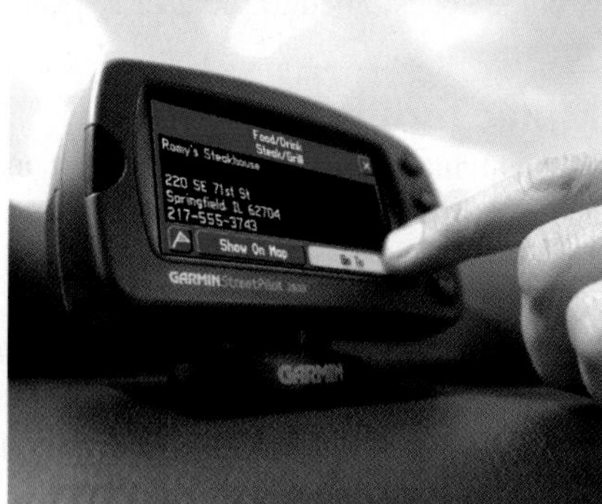

CAR NAVIGATION SYSTEMS

>**Display device.** An output device that contains a viewing screen. >**Monitor.** A display device for a desktop PC. >**Display screen.** A display device built into a notebook computer, handheld PC, or other device.

Color vs. Monochrome Displays

Display devices form images by lighting up the proper configurations of *pixels*. *Monochrome displays* use only two colors (usually black and white or black and green) and are not commonly used today as monitors although they still appear on some consumer products. *Color displays* are the norm and form colors by mixing combinations of only three colors—red, green, and blue (see Figure 4-22). When a display device blends red, green, and blue light of varying intensities, it can produce an enormous spectrum of colors.

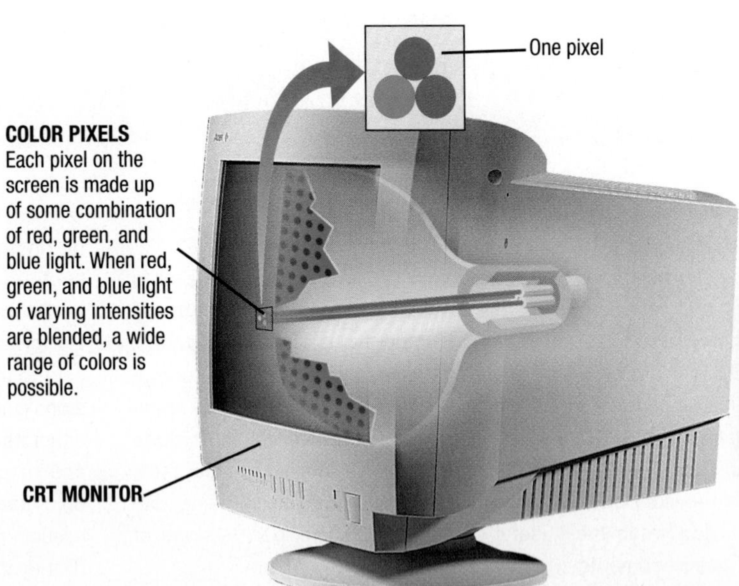

One pixel
COLOR PIXELS
Each pixel on the screen is made up of some combination of red, green, and blue light. When red, green, and blue light of varying intensities are blended, a wide range of colors is possible.
CRT MONITOR

FIGURE 4-22
A color CRT monitor.

CRT vs. Flat-Panel Monitors

The traditional type of monitor for a desktop PC is the **CRT monitor**, such as the one shown in Figures 4-22. CRTs use *cathode-ray tube* technology to display images, so they are large, bulky, and heavy like conventional televisions. To form images on the screen of a CRT monitor, an electron gun sealed inside a large glass tube fires at a phosphor-coated screen to light up the appropriate pixels in the appropriate color to display the images, similar to a conventional television. Because the phosphors glow for only a limited amount of time, the monitor image must be redrawn (*refreshed*) on a continual basis, relighting each pixel in the appropriate color—typically this occurs between 60 and 85 times per second.

Thinner and lighter *flat-panel displays* form images by manipulating electronically charged chemicals or gases sandwiched between thin panes of glass (or other transparent material) instead of firing a bulky electron gun (flat-panel technology is discussed in more detail shortly). Flat-panel displays are almost always used on portable computers and mobile devices, and they are frequently also used with desktop PCs. In fact, the sale of flat-panel monitors surpassed that of CRT monitors for the first time in 2004, and, according to the research firm IDC, flat-panel monitors are expected to make up about 80% of the display market by 2007. Flat-panel monitors have the advantage of taking up less desk space and consuming less power, although the images displayed on a flat-panel display sometimes cannot be seen clearly when viewed from certain angles. As shown in Figure 4-23, the smaller footprint of a flat-panel display makes it possible to use multiple monitors working together to increase the amount of data the user can view at one time.

Another difference between CRT monitors and flat-panel displays is that most flat-panel displays use digital signals to display images, while CRT monitors use analog signals. Digital signals allow for much sharper images.

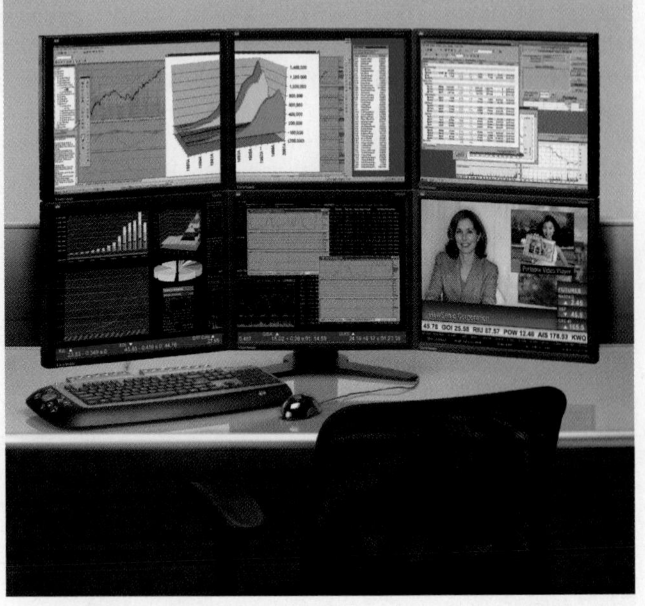

FIGURE 4-23
Flat-panel displays.
The smaller footprint of a flat-panel display makes it possible to use multiple monitors together to increase productivity.

>**CRT monitor.** A display device that projects images onto a display screen using a technology similar to the one used with conventional TVs.

HOW IT WORKS

E-Paper

Electronic paper (*e-paper*) consists of a display device onto which written content is displayed in electronic form, but that is thinner and more paper-like than other types of display devices. E-paper products are being developed by a number of companies, such as Gyricon Media, Xerox, and E Ink. Practical applications for e-paper from an environmental standpoint include any documents that only need to be kept for a short time, such as newspapers and retail display signs. Instead of being discarded when their useful life has ended, e-paper versions of these documents could be erased and then reused.

Electronic paper is becoming a viable replacement for some traditional paper and ink applications. For instance, one of the first areas in which e-paper has been applied is retail signs, such as those found in department stores and other retail establishments, as well as hotels, conference centers, schools, and more. These *e-signs* look like ordinary paper signs, but their text can be changed wirelessly (two examples of e-signs are included in the accompanying photographs). Consequently, instead of continually having to print new paper signs, e-signs can be changed electronically to be reused, which saves the time and expense of printing, delivering, and setting up new signs, as well as the time, cost, and waste associated with disposing of the old ones. Their low power consumption means that e-signs can run off of battery power for an extended period of time without attention. Other retail applications currently in development include e-paper shelf price tags that can electronically communicate with the store's database to always display the current price, and newspaper dispenser boxes that are updated periodically during the day to reflect the latest headlines or a featured section of the newspaper.

So how does e-paper work? One type of e-paper technology uses two sheets of very thin transparent plastic with millions of very small beads sandwiched between them. Each bead is smaller than a grain of sand and sealed inside a tiny pocket surrounded by liquid (these beads and their liquid are sometimes referred to as *electronic ink* or *e-ink*). Each bead (see the close up photo of e-ink in the accompanying photos) has two colors–such as half white and half black–and can rotate within its pocket only when an electrical signal is received. To change the text or images displayed on the e-paper, electronic signals are sent to the e-paper via a wireless transmission. These electronic signals instruct each bead to rotate appropriately to display either its black side or white side in order to form the proper text and images, similar to the way pixels are used to display images on a monitor. The content remains displayed until another transmission changes the pattern, such as changing all the beads to display their white sides to "erase" the e-paper. Current e-paper products can be written to and erased electronically thousands of times, but in the near future that number is expected to increase to several million times.

As e-paper technology improves, it is expected that the e-paper will more easily support the smaller text needed for personal printouts. Types of e-paper expected in the future include regular-sized e-paper that can be inserted into a special computer printer to be printed electronically and then reused over and over again; regular and newspaper-sized e-papers that can wirelessly download new content from the Internet; and *e-books* that look and feel like real paper books, but whose content can be rewritten to display the content of a different book when directed by the user.

Improvements that need to be made before e-paper and other e-ink applications become more commonplace include color capabilities, lower cost, and increased life span, as well as thinner and more flexible e-paper. Future possibilities for e-ink include its use on billboards, T-shirts, and even paint for easy redecorating. *Conductive e-ink* currently in development can carry electricity after it is printed; conductive e-ink will potentially enable keyboards to be printed onto military uniform sleeves, light switches to be printed onto wallpaper, and radio circuitry and controls to be printed onto clothing and other everyday objects.

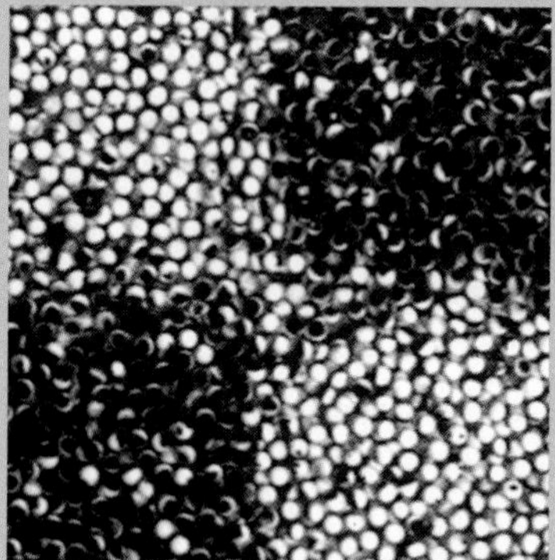

E-paper products, such as the e-signs shown here (right) are written electronically using tiny beads (left) and can be erased and rewritten over and over again.

Size

Monitor size is measured diagonally from corner to corner, similarly to the way TV screens are measured. It is important to realize, however, that the actual viewing area of a CRT monitor is almost always smaller than the stated monitor size. For example, one 17-inch monitor might have a *viewable image size* (*VIS*) of 16 inches, while another 17-inch monitor might have a viewable image size of 15.7 inches. Although 0.3 inches may not sound like much of a difference in size, small size variations can be noticeable and are important to keep in mind when comparing the quality and price of two CRT monitors (there typically is no difference between the stated size and the VIS of flat-panel displays). Most desktop PC monitors today are between 15 and 24 inches for desktop PCs; notebook and tablet displays are usually between 13 and 17 inches. To better view DVDs and other multimedia content, some monitors today are *widescreen displays*, which conform to the 16:9 aspect ratio of widescreen televisions, instead of the conventional 4:3 aspect ratio.

HW

Screen Resolution

Regardless of the technology used, the screen of a display device is divided into a fine grid of small areas or dots—pixels. The number of pixels used on a display screen determines the *screen resolution*, which affects the amount of information that can be displayed on the screen at one time. When a high resolution is selected, such as 1,280 pixels horizontally by 1,024 pixels vertically (written as 1,280 × 1,024 and read as *1280 by 1024*), more information can fit on the screen, but everything will be displayed smaller than with a lower resolution, such as 800 × 600 or 1,024 × 768 (see Figure 4-24). The screen resolution on most computers today can be changed by users to match their preferences and the software being used (on Windows PCs, display options are changed using the Control Panel). Very high-resolution monitors are available for special applications, such as viewing digital X-rays.

FIGURE 4-24

Screen resolution. A higher screen resolution (measured in pixels) displays everything smaller than a lower screen resolution.

800 × 600

1,024 × 768

1,280 × 1,024

Video Cards and Ports

The video card or integrated video component built directly into the motherboard on a PC is used to connect a display device to the computer. The type of video card or component used determines such display characteristics as the screen resolutions available, the number of bits used to store color information about each pixel (called the *bit depth*), the total number of colors that can be used to display images, how many monitors can be connected to the PC, the types of connectors that can be used to connect the monitor to the PC, whether or not you can receive TV broadcasts or connect a digital video recorder (DVR) to the computer, and so forth.

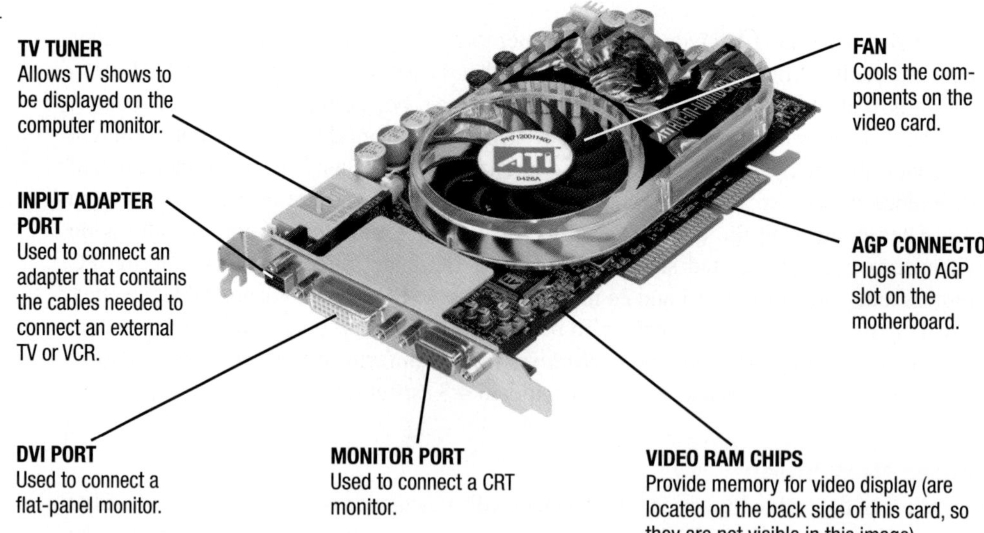

TV TUNER
Allows TV shows to be displayed on the computer monitor.
INPUT ADAPTER PORT
Used to connect an adapter that contains the cables needed to connect an external TV or VCR.
FAN
Cools the components on the video card.
AGP CONNECTOR
Plugs into AGP slot on the motherboard.
DVI PORT
Used to connect a flat-panel monitor.
MONITOR PORT
Used to connect a CRT monitor.
VIDEO RAM CHIPS
Provide memory for video display (are located on the back side of this card, so they are not visible in this image).

FIGURE 4-25
Video cards. Video cards provide a connection to a monitor, as well as determine video capabilities.

Video cards also contain memory chips (typically called *video RAM* or *VRAM*) to support graphics display, although some systems use a portion of the PC's regular RAM as video RAM instead. To support higher resolutions, higher bit depths, and a greater number of colors, a sufficient amount of video RAM is required. Most video cards today contain between 128 and 256 MB of video RAM.

CRT monitors typically connect to a video card via a conventional monitor port and connector. Flat-panel displays usually have the option of connecting via a *Digital Visual Interface* (*DVI*) port, if that port exists on the video card being used. A DVI connection allows the flat-panel monitor to receive digital signals directly from the computer, creating a clearer, more reliable signal than if the conventional monitor connection was used. For the video card shown in Figure 4-25, a monitor can connect via either a conventional monitor port or a DVI port. This video card also has a built-in TV tuner, which can be used to display TV shows as well as enable the computer to act as a digital video recorder (DVR). It also can connect to an external VCR or TV, has 256 MB of video RAM, can support screen resolutions of 640 × 480 up to 2,048 × 1,536, and can display screen images in true color (16.7 million colors).

Wired vs. Wireless Monitors

Most monitors today are *wired monitors*; that is, monitors that are physically connected to the system unit via a cable. Some monitors, however, are designed to be wireless. *Wireless monitors*—sometimes called *smart displays*—are portable monitors that are wirelessly connected to a desktop PC, so they can access that PC from anywhere within a home or office, as long as the monitor is within the required range of the PC. Although similar in appearance to a tablet PC, an important difference is the location of the computing hardware. Unlike a tablet PC, which contains all processing hardware inside the tablet and is independent of any other device, a smart display is designed to always be used in conjunction with its associated PC and cannot function independently when the PC is off or the monitor is too far away from the PC. Smart displays typically use a wireless *Wi-Fi* networking connection (discussed in more detail in Chapter 7) to connect the display to the system unit whenever both pieces of hardware are within range of the same wireless network. Wireless monitors often come with some type of stand or docking station. Typically, the mouse and keyboard attached to the docking station are used when the smart display is connected to its docking station, and touch or pen input is used when the smart display is undocked.

FURTHER EXPLORATION

For links to further information about display devices, go to www.course.com/uc11/ch04

3D FLAT-PANEL DISPLAY
This 3D monitor uses multiple layers to display images in different depths at one time and can display input from more than one PC at one time.

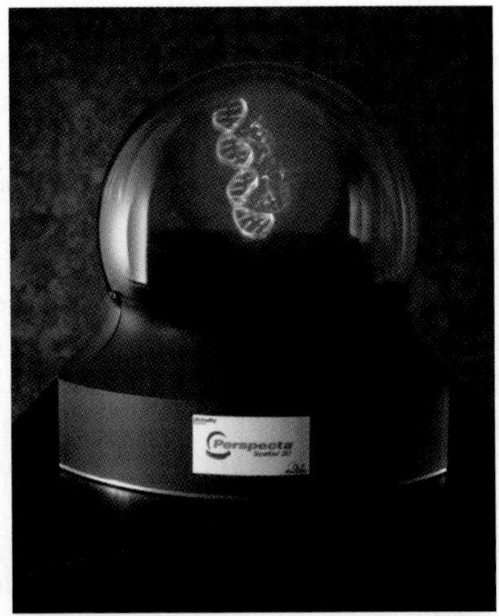

3D DOME DISPLAY
This 20-inch dome allows a 360° view of images, such as the DNA image shown here.

WEARABLE PERSONAL DISPLAY
The sunglasses shown here include a display screen that projects images: the images appear equivalent to those projected on a 14-inch monitor.

FIGURE 4-26
3D output devices.

2D vs. 3D Displays

Recent improvements in flat-screen display technology and graphics processing have led to several emerging *three-dimensional* (*3D*) output devices, including *3D display screens* for computers (see Figure 4-26), as well as cell phones, digital cameras, car navigation systems, and other small devices. Unlike traditional 3D applications that require special 3D glasses, the newest 3D products use filters, prisms, and other techniques to create the 3D effect using only the display screen. In addition to their appeal for games, movies, and other consumer PC applications, 3D displays are an important improvement for scientists, physicians, architects, and other professionals who routinely view detailed graphics or diagrams in the course of their work.

In addition to conventionally shaped and sized 3D displays, alternative 3D display shapes—such as the dome-shaped 3D display shown in Figure 4-26—are beginning to become available. *3D projectors*, such as those used to display *holograms*, are also in the works. In fact, researchers at Tokyo University have developed a holographic device that uses a 360-degree digital camera to scan a person's head and then that data can be sent over telephone lines to a special display device that projects a 3D image of the person. Another emerging display option is the *wearable personal display*, such as the display sunglasses shown in Figure 4-26. Similar to the *head-mounted displays* used by soldiers, surgeons, and other individuals who require a hands-free display while working, wearable personal displays project the image from a PC or other device with video output (such as a digital camera or portable DVD player) to a display screen located close to the eye, but the display screen is built into the glasses and the glasses are designed for personal use.

Digital TV and HDTV

Digital television (*DTV*) is a set of 18 broadcasting standards for delivering TV programming using digital signals, instead of conventional analog TV signals. In the United States, all commercial broadcasters are required today to broadcast some programs in digital form, but they must continue analog broadcasts until the end of 2006. At this time, analog broadcasts are scheduled to be replaced completely with digital broadcasts, but this deadline is expected to be extended in at least some areas of the United States until 85% of the homes in that area have TV sets capable of displaying digital TV programming.

In addition to increased quality, digital TV technology can also be used to transmit large amounts of other data into the home to be accessed via a computer or television set. Possibilities include *video-on-demand* (renting movies online that are downloaded to your PC or DVR instead of physically picking them up at a movie rental store) and *interactive TV* (television with some interactive activities that you can perform while watching the show). These applications, currently delivered via the Internet, are discussed in more detail in Chapter 8.

HDTV (*high-definition television*) is a high-resolution type of digital television that results in an even clearer, sharper picture than regular digital TV. Computer monitors and televisions that have a built-in HD tuner and can receive HDTV broadcasts today are referred to as *HD-capable* or *HD-integrated*. All TV sets that are sold after July 1, 2006 and are larger than 24" are required to have a built-in HD tuner, and it is expected that similar requirements will be set for computer monitors. *HD-ready* or *HD-compatible* computer monitors and TVs require an external HD source (such as an HD receiver or a cable or satellite set-top box containing an HD tuner) in order to receive digital TV broadcasts. To watch digital TV broadcasts on an older analog TV set, a digital-to-analog converter is required, and the quality will be analog quality.

TIP

The term *HDTV monitor* is another name for an HD-ready display device and does not refer to its ability to be used as a computer monitor.

Flat-Panel Display Technologies

Flat-panel displays form images by manipulating electronically charged chemicals or gases sandwiched between thin panes of glass instead of using a bulky electron gun like CRT monitors. The most common flat-panel technologies are *liquid crystal display* (*LCD*), *organic light emitting diode* (*OLED*), and *gas plasma*. Monitors using each of these technologies are shown in Figure 4-27.

Liquid Crystal Displays (LCDs)

A **liquid crystal display (LCD)** uses charged liquid crystals located between two sheets of clear material (usually glass or plastic) to light up the appropriate pixels to form the image on the screen. Several layers of liquid crystals are used, and, in their normal state, the liquid crystals are aligned so that light passes through the display. When an electrical charge is applied to the liquid crystals (via an electrode grid layer contained within the LCD panel), the liquid crystals change their orientation or "twist" so that light cannot pass through the display, and the liquid crystals at the charged intersections of the electrode grid

FIGURE 4-27
Flat-panel displays.

LCD DISPLAYS
The most common type of computer monitor and flat-panel television.

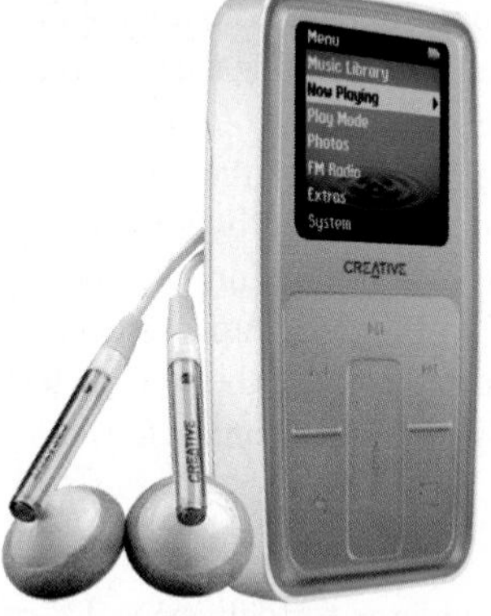

OLED DISPLAYS
Used primarily with smaller displays, like digital cameras and handheld PCs.

PLASMA DISPLAYS
Used primarily with large computer monitors and TVs.

>**Flat-panel display.** A slim type of display device that uses electronically charged chemicals or gases instead of an electron gun to display images. >**Liquid crystal display (LCD).** A type of flat-panel display that uses charged liquid crystals to display images.

appear dark. Color LCD displays use a color filter that consists of a pattern of red, green, and blue *subpixels* for each pixel, and the voltage used controls the orientation (twisting) of the liquid crystals and the amount of light that gets through, affecting the color and shade of that pixel—the three different colors blend to make the appropriate colored pixel.

Just as with other products (such as digital watches and appliances) that use LCD display technology, unless light is built into the display, it can be viewed only with reflective light. Consequently, LCD panels used with computer monitors typically include at least one fluorescent light inside the panel, usually at the rear of the display—a technique referred to as *backlighting*. LCDs are the most common type of flat-panel technology used for small- to medium-sized computer monitors (typically up to only about 23 inches). Larger flat-panel displays typically use another type of technology (such as *gas plasma* today) and it is expected that, someday, LCD monitors may be completely replaced by newer technologies, such as *OLED*, discussed next.

TIP

Display devices and printers designed for visually impaired PC users and other users with special needs are discussed in Chapter 16.

HW

Organic Light Emitting Diode (OLED) Displays

Organic light emitting diode (OLED) displays also use layers, but there is a distinct difference between OLEDs and LCDs. While LCDs are *nonemissive*, which means they do not produce light and so they require backlighting, OLEDs use a layer of organic material which, when electric current is applied, emits a visible light. Therefore, OLEDs do not use backlighting, which makes them more energy efficient and lengthens the battery life of portable devices using OLED displays. In order to produce color output, there must be blue, red, and green organic material, as shown in Figure 4-28. In addition, there are other advantages of OLEDs over LCDs. For instance, OLEDs are even thinner (Samsung unveiled a 40-inch OLED television in 2005 that is only about one inch thick), they have a wider viewing angle visible from virtually all directions, and their images are brighter and sharper. OLED displays are beginning to be incorporated into digital cameras and mobile phones; over the next few years, their use is expected to be expanded to other portable consumer electronic devices, as well as car dashboard displays, television sets, and other products.

There are also a few special types of OLEDs, which lead to applications not possible with CRT or LCD technology. For instance, *flexible OLED (FOLED)* displays—a technology developed by Universal Display Corporation—are OLED displays built on flexible surfaces, such as plastic or metallic foil. Flexible displays using FOLED technology—such as displays that can roll up when not in use—are being developed by several companies. Other possible uses for flexible screens include making lighter desktop and portable PC monitors, enabling pullout displays

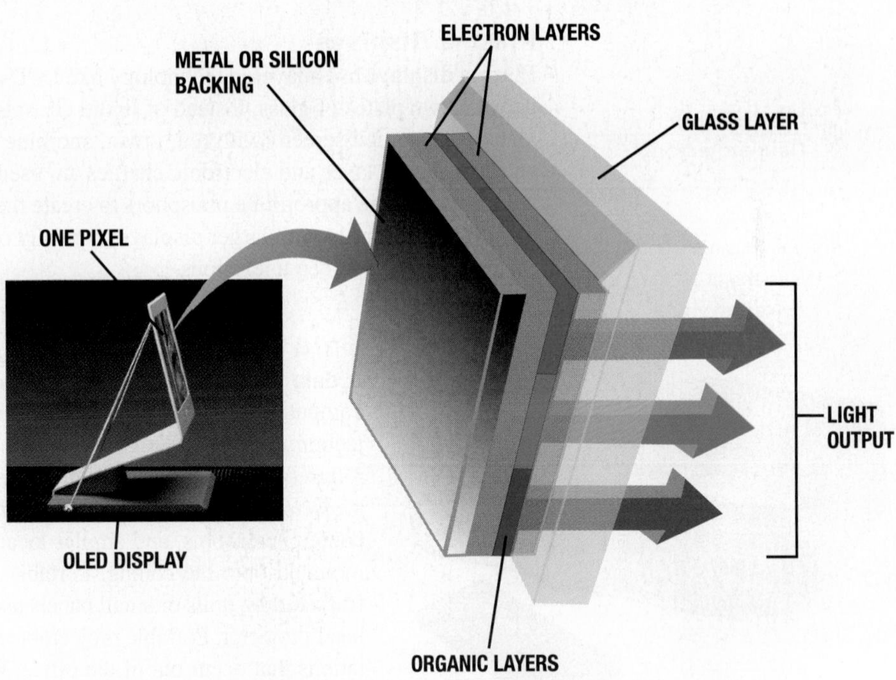

FIGURE 4-28
How OLED displays work. Each pixel on an OLED display emits light in the appropriate color.

>**Organic light emitting diode (OLED) display.** A type of flat-panel display that uses emissive organic material to display brighter and sharper images.

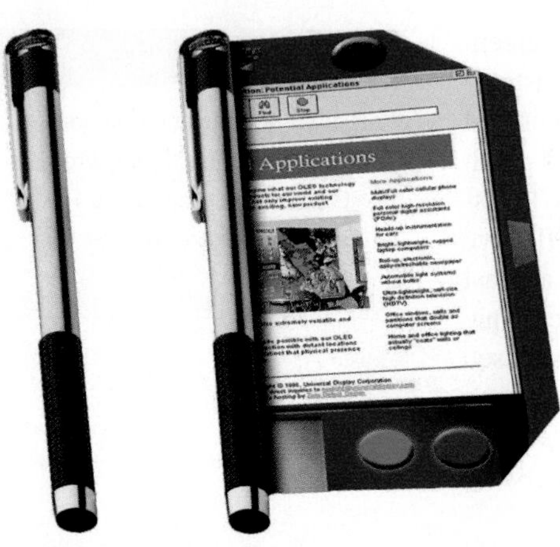

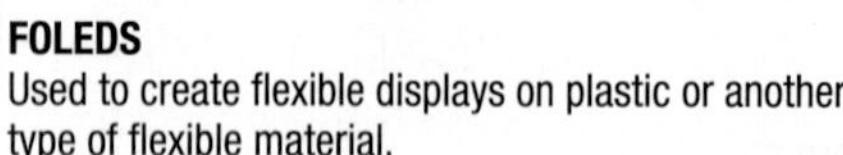

FOLEDS
Used to create flexible displays on plastic or another type of flexible material.

TOLEDS
Used to create transparent displays.

FIGURE 4-29
Special types of OLEDs.

(see Figure 4-29) to be used in conjunction with handheld PCs and mobile devices, integrating displays on military uniform sleeves, and allowing retractable wall-mounted big screen televisions and monitors. The flexibility of FOLED displays also adds to their durability, and their thinness makes FOLED technology extremely suitable for mobile devices.

Another form of OLED developed by Universal Display Corporation is *transparent OLED (TOLED)*. TOLED displays are transparent and can emit light towards the top and bottom of the display surface. The portion of the display that does not currently have an image displayed (and the entire display device when it is off) is nearly as transparent as glass, so the screen can be seen through (see Figure 4-29). TOLEDs open up the possibility of displays on home windows, car windshields, helmet face shields, and other transparent items. A third type of OLED is *Phosphorescent OLED* or *PHOLED*. The term *phosphorescence*, also referred to as *electrophosphorescence*, is a process that results in much more conversion of electrical energy into light instead of heat. When used with PHOLEDs, this process makes the efficiency of a PHOLED up to four times higher than a conventional OLED. Consequently, PHOLED technology is very appropriate for use on mobile devices, consumer electronics, and other devices where power consumption is an important concern.

Plasma Displays

Plasma displays use a layered technology like LCD and OLEDs, but they use a layer of gas between two plates of glass, instead of liquid crystals or organic material. Similar to CRTs, a phosphor-coated screen (with red, green, and blue phosphors for each pixel) is used, but an electron grid layer and electronic charges are used (as in LCD displays) to make the gas atoms light up the appropriate phosphors to create the image on the screen. Plasma technology is used primarily with larger displays (typically over 40 inches), such as large computer monitors and big screen televisions.

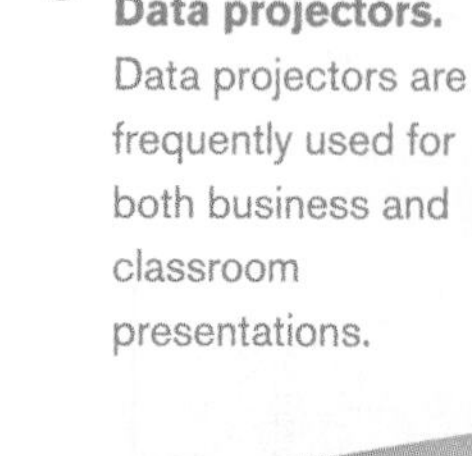

FIGURE 4-30
Data projectors.
Data projectors are frequently used for both business and classroom presentations.

Data and Multimedia Projectors

A **data projector** connects to a computer, and any output that is sent to the computer monitor is also projected through the projector onto a wall or projection screen (see Figure 4-30). Most data projectors today (sometimes referred to as *data/video projectors*, *multimedia projectors*, or *digital projectors*) can project video, in addition to computer output. In classrooms, conference rooms, and similar locations, projectors are often permanently mounted onto the ceiling. Portable projectors are also available, either as freestanding units or small panels used in conjunction with a standard overhead projector. Portable projectors are commonly used for business presentations that occur out of the office. While most data projectors connect via cable to a PC, *wireless projectors* that use a Wi-Fi connection are available.

>**Plasma display.** A type of flat-panel display that uses layers of gas to display images; most often used on large displays. >**Data projector.** A display device that projects all computer output to a wall or projection screen.

PRINTERS

Instead of the temporary, ever-changing soft copy output that a monitor produces, **printers** produce *hard copy*; that is, a permanent copy of the output on paper. Most desktop PCs are connected to a printer; portable PCs can use printers as well.

Printer Characteristics

Printers differ in a number of important respects, such as the technology used, size, speed, and quality. Some general printer characteristics are discussed next, followed by a look at the most common types of printers.

Impact vs. Nonimpact Printing

Printers produce images through either impact or nonimpact technologies. *Impact printers*, like old ribbon typewriters, have a print mechanism that actually strikes the paper to transfer ink to the paper. For example, a *dot-matrix printer* uses a print head consisting of pins that strike an inked ribbon to transfer the ink to the paper. As illustrated in Figure 4-31, the appropriate pins are extended (and, consequently, strike the ribbon) as the print head moves in order to form the appropriate words or images. When the pins press into the ribbon, dots of ink are transferred onto the paper. Impact printers are primarily used today for producing multipart forms, such as invoices, packing slips, and credit card receipts.

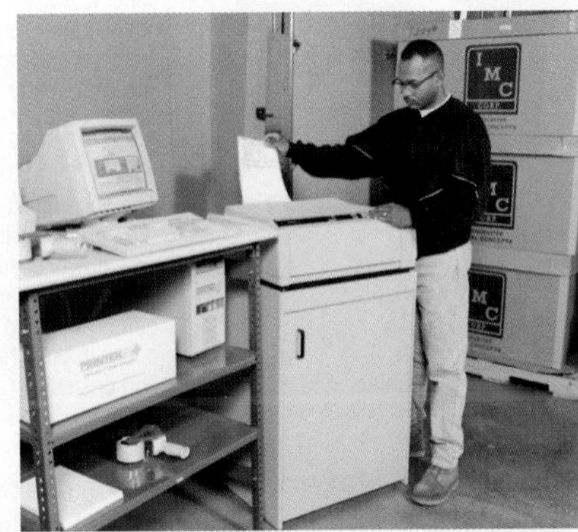

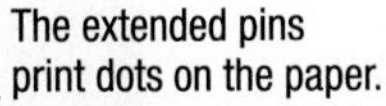

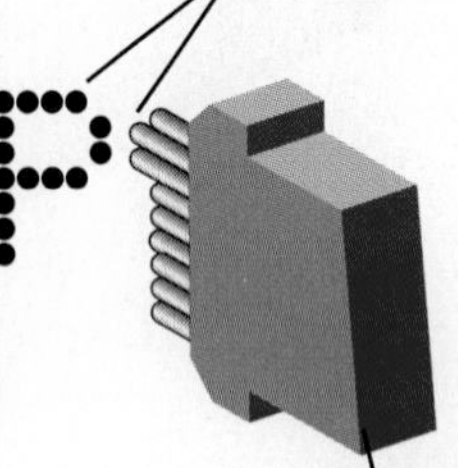

The extended pins print dots on the paper.
As the print head moves from left to right, specific pins are extended to form the text and images.

FIGURE 4-31
Dot-matrix printers.
Dot-matrix printers are impact printers; today they are typically high-speed printers used in manufacturing, shipping, or similar applications.

Most printers today are *nonimpact printers*, meaning they form images without the print mechanism actually touching the paper. Nonimpact printers (such as the *laser* and *ink-jet printers* discussed shortly) usually produce higher-quality images and are much quieter than impact printers. Both impact and nonimpact printers form images with dots, similarly to the way monitors display images with pixels. Because of this, printers are very versatile and can print text in virtually any size, as well as print photos and other graphical images. In addition to paper, both impact and nonimpact printers can print on transparencies, envelopes, mailing labels, and more.

Color vs. Black and White

Both *color printers* and *blank-and-white printers* are available. Color printers work similarly to black-and-white printers, except they use at least four different colors of ink—cyan (blue), magenta (red), yellow, and black—instead of only black ink. Color printers either apply all of the colors in one pass, or they go through the entire printing process multiple times, applying one color during each pass. Color printers are often used in homes (to print photographs, greeting cards, flyers, and more); businesses may use black-and-white printers for output that does not need to be in color (since it is less expensive and faster to print in black and white) and color printers for output that needs to be in color.

>**Printer.** An output device that produces output on paper.

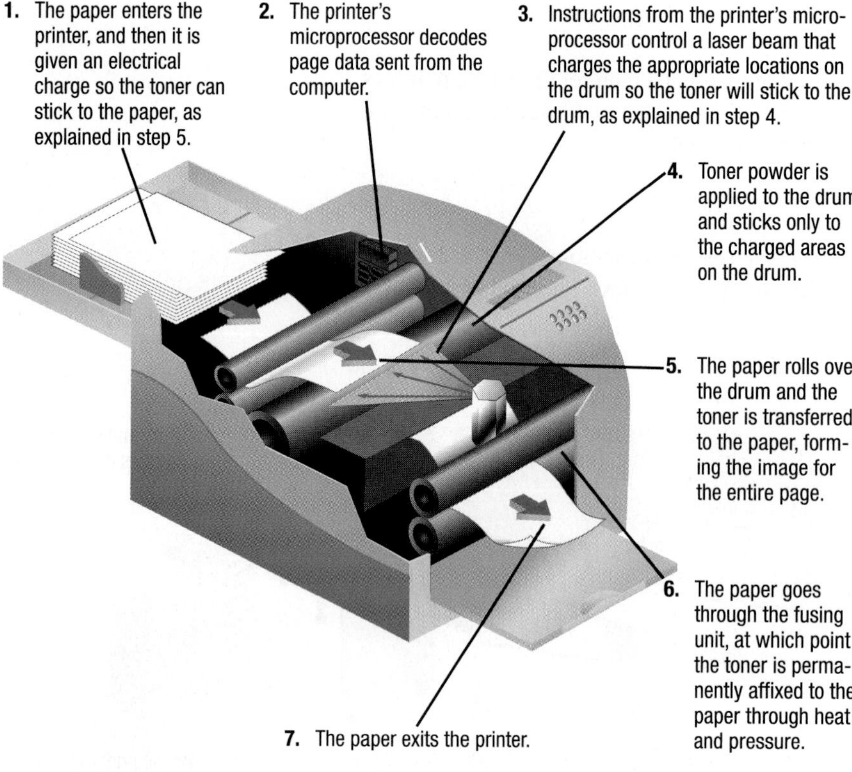

1. The paper enters the printer, and then it is given an electrical charge so the toner can stick to the paper, as explained in step 5.
2. The printer's microprocessor decodes page data sent from the computer.
3. Instructions from the printer's microprocessor control a laser beam that charges the appropriate locations on the drum so the toner will stick to the drum, as explained in step 4.
4. Toner powder is applied to the drum and sticks only to the charged areas on the drum.
5. The paper rolls over the drum and the toner is transferred to the paper, forming the image for the entire page.
6. The paper goes through the fusing unit, at which point the toner is permanently affixed to the paper through heat and pressure.
7. The paper exits the printer.

NETWORK LASER PRINTER

PERSONAL LASER PRINTER

FIGURE 4-32
How laser printers work.

TIP

To save money, consider buying *recharged* (refilled) toner cartridges when your laser printer cartridge runs out of toner powder. Recharged cartridges typically cost about one-third less than new cartridges and last at least as long.

Personal vs. Network Printers

Most printers found in homes and small businesses today are commonly referred to as *personal printers*—that is, printers designed to be connected to one computer and not shared with others. *Network printers*, in contrast, are printers designed to be shared by multiple users. Although multiple users can share a personal printer through a home or office network, network printers are specifically designed for high-volume, high-speed printing (both a personal printer and a network printer are shown in Figure 4-32), network printers are usually larger than personal printers, work up to about 10 times faster than personal printers, and cost anywhere from $500 to $10,000 or more. Some network printers are *line printers* (which print one line of text at a time), but most are *page printers* (which print a full page of output at a time). Some high-end network printers can also collate and staple.

Print Resolution

Most printing technologies today form images with dots of liquid ink or flecks of ink toner powder. The number of *dots per inch* (*dpi*)—called the *print resolution*—affects the quality of the printed output. Printers with a higher print resolution tend to produce sharper and cleaner text and images than printers with a lower resolution. Although other factors (such as the technology and number of colors used) affect the quality of a printout, guidelines for acceptable print resolution are typically 300 dpi for general-purpose printouts, 600 dpi for higher-quality documents, 1,200 dpi for photographs, and 2,400 dpi for professional applications.

Print Speed

Print speed is typically measured in *pages per minute* (*ppm*). How long it takes a document to print depends on the actual printer being used, the selected print resolution, and the content being printed. For instance, pages containing photographs or other images typically take longer to print than pages containing only text, and full-color pages take longer to print than black-and-white pages. Common speeds for personal printers today range from about 6 to 25 ppm; network printers typically print from 45 to 100 ppm.

Laser Printers

Laser printers are the standard for business documents and come in both personal and network styles. To print a document, the laser printer first uses a laser beam to charge the appropriate locations on a drum to form the page's image, and then *toner powder* (powdered ink) is released from a *toner cartridge* and sticks to the drum. The toner is then transferred to a piece of paper when the paper is rolled over the drum, and a heating unit fuses the toner powder to the paper to permanently form the image (see Figure 4-32). Laser printers print one entire page at a time and are typically faster and have better quality output than *ink-jet printers*, discussed next. Common print resolution for laser printers is between 600 and 2,400 dpi; speeds for personal laser printers range from about 6 to 25 ppm. Black-and-white laser printers start at about $150; color laser printers start at about $400.

Ink-Jet Printers

Ink-jet printers form images by spraying tiny drops of liquid ink onto the page, one printed line at a time (see Figure 4-33). Some printers print with one single-sized ink droplet; others print using different-sized ink droplets by using multiple nozzles or varying electrical charges for more precise printing. Because they are relatively inexpensive, have

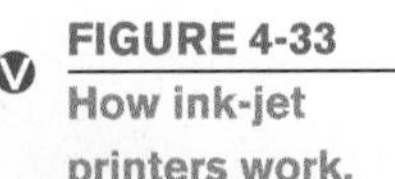
FIGURE 4-33
How ink-jet printers work.

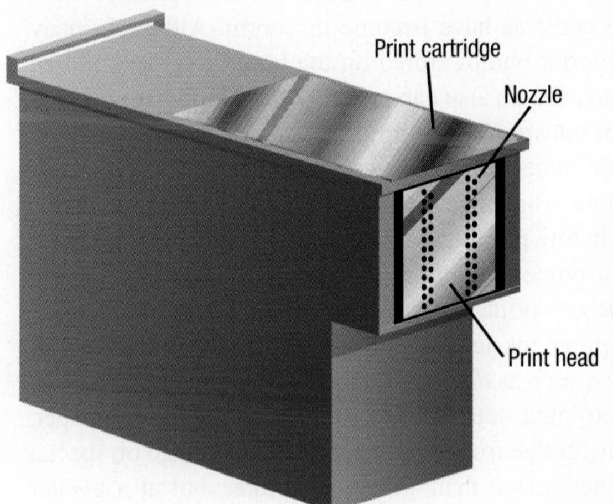

HOW INK-JET PRINTERS WORK
Color ink-jet printers create colors by mixing different combinations of four colors of ink—magenta, cyan, yellow, and black. The different colors can be in one or multiple cartridges. Each cartridge is made up of 300 or more tiny ink-filled firing chambers, each attached to a nozzle smaller than a human hair. To print images, the appropriate color ink is ejected through the appropriate nozzle.

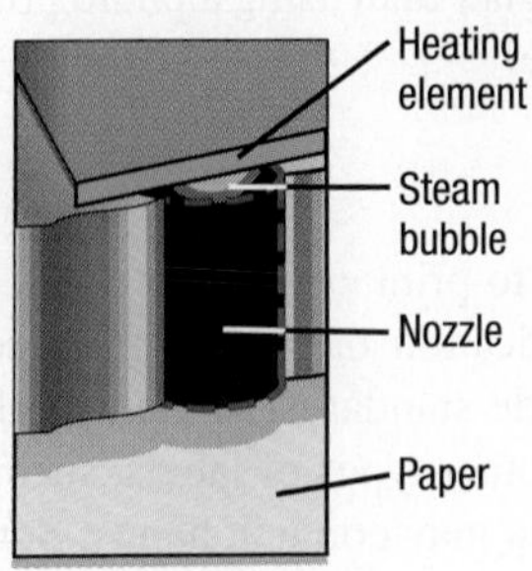

1. A heating element makes the ink boil, which causes a steam bubble to form.

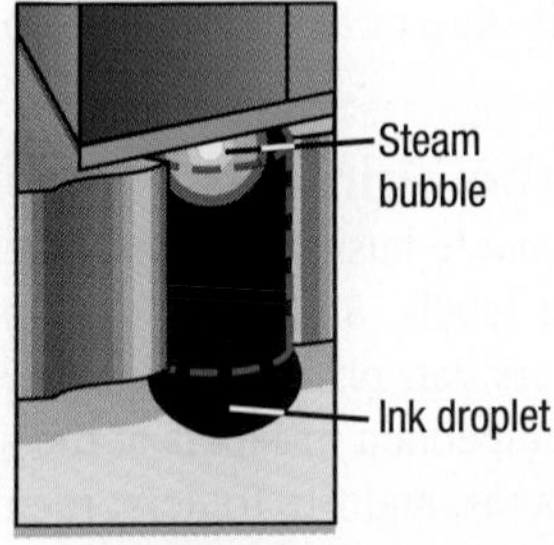

2. As the bubble expands, it pushes ink through the nozzle.

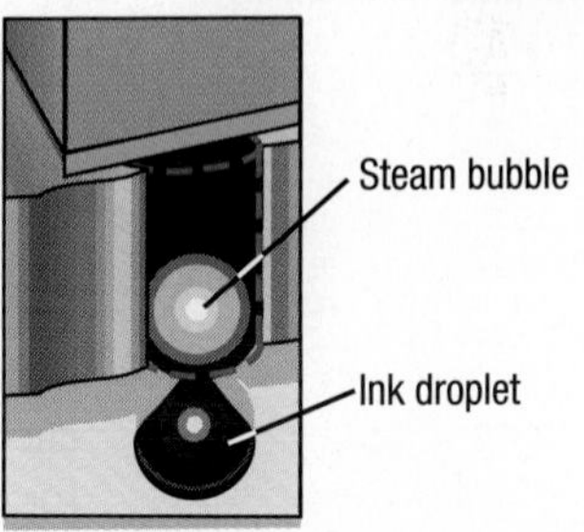

3. The pressure of the bubble forces an ink droplet to be ejected onto the paper. When the steam bubble collapses, more ink is pulled into the print head, so it is ready for the next steam bubble.

>**Laser printer.** An output device that uses toner powder and technology similar to that of a photocopier to produce images on paper. >**Ink-jet printer.** An output device that sprays droplets of ink to produce images on paper.

good-quality output, and can print in color, ink-jet printers are usually the printer of choice for home use. With the use of special photo paper, *photo-quality ink-jet printers* can also print photograph quality digital photos. At around $100 or less for a simple home printer, ink-jet printers are affordable, although the cost of the replaceable ink cartridges can add up, especially if you do a lot of color printing.

In addition to being used in computer printers, ink-jet technology is also being used in the development of a number of emerging applications unrelated to current ink-jet printers, such as dispensing liquid metals, aromas, computer chips and other circuitry, and even "printing" human tissue and other organic materials for medical purposes.

Special-Purpose Printers

Although printers can typically print on a variety of media, such as sheets of labels, envelopes, transparencies, photo paper, and even fabric, some printers are designed for a particular purpose. Some of the most common *special-purpose printers* are discussed next and illustrated in Figure 4-34.

Photo Printers

Photo printers are color printers designed to print photographs. Photo printers have become increasingly popular as digital cameras have become the norm. Although many photo printers are connected to a PC to print photos stored on the hard drive or modified using image editing software, most photo printers also can print photos directly from a digital camera or a storage medium without transferring them first to a computer, typically by using a cable, flash memory card slot, or camera docking station to connect the camera or storage medium to the printer. Often, photo printers have a preview screen (see Figure 4-34) to allow for minor editing and cropping before printing, but it is usually more efficient to do extensive editing via a PC. Some photo printers can print a variety of photo paper sizes; others—sometimes called *snapshot printers*—print only on standard 4 × 6-inch photo paper.

Photo printers today usually use either ink-jet technology, like conventional ink-jet printers, or a *thermal-transfer* technology, such as *thermal-wax transfer* or *dye-sublimation*. Thermal-wax transfer printers use heat to melt dots of wax from a ribbon onto the paper. Dye-sublimation printers use heat to transfer dye from a ribbon to form the image on special paper. Both technologies produce a better image than an ink-jet printer, but at a greater expense. Although photo printers offer the convenience of printing digital photos at home and whenever the need arises, the cost per photo is typically higher than using a photo printing service at a retail store or an Internet photo printing service.

TIP

In addition to printing digital photo prints, many retail and Internet photo services can print your digital photos on shirts, mugs, playing cards, calendars, mouse pads, even valid U.S. postage stamps.

Barcode and Label Printers

Barcode printers enable businesses and other organizations to print custom barcodes on price tags, shipping labels, and other documents for identification or pricing purposes. Most barcode printers can print labels in a variety of barcode standards; some can also encode RFID tags embedded in labels at the same time. For other types of labels, such as for envelopes, packages, and file folders, regular *label printers* may come in handy. Some special-purpose label printers can print *electronic postage* (sometimes called *e-stamps* or *PC postage*). E-stamps are valid postage stamps that can be printed once a postage allotment has been purchased via the Internet or from an e-stamp vendor; postage values are deducted from your allotment as you print the e-stamps. Some e-stamp services also allow stamps to be printed directly onto shipping labels and envelopes using laser or ink-jet printers, as well.

>**Photo printer.** An output device designed for printing digital photographs. >**Barcode printer.** An output device that prints barcoded documents.

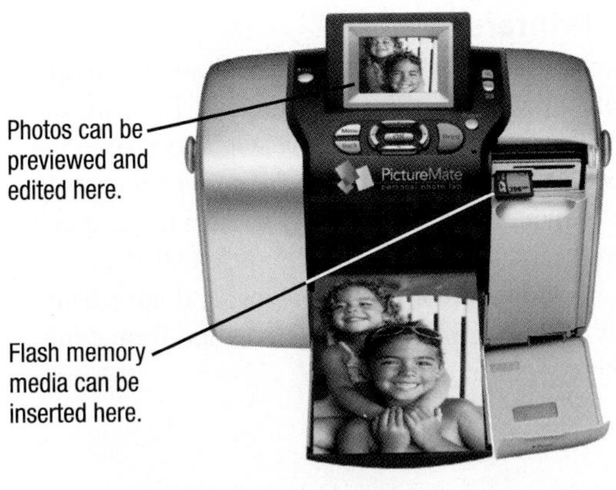

Photos can be previewed and edited here.
Flash memory media can be inserted here.
PictureMate

PHOTO PRINTERS
Used to print digital photographs, such as those taken with a digital camera.

BARCODE PRINTERS
Used to print barcoded labels. This printer can also program RFID tags, when they are embedded inside the barcoded labels.

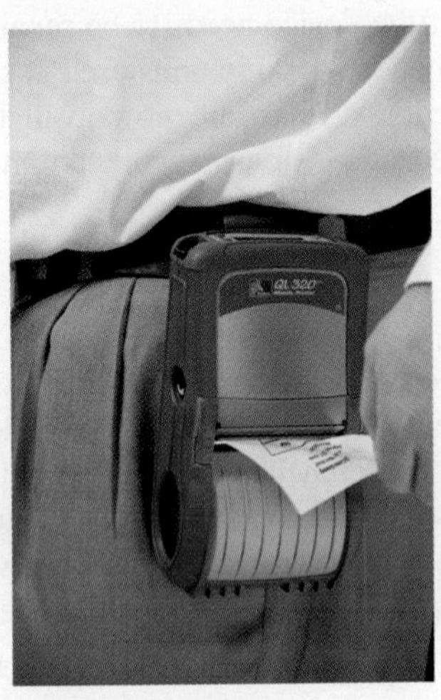

PORTABLE PRINTERS
Used to print from a portable PC or while on the go.

WIDE-FORMAT PRINTERS
Used for printouts that are too big for a standard-sized printer.

FIGURE 4-34
Special-purpose printers.

Portable Printers

Portable printers are small, lightweight printers that can be used on the go, such as with a notebook computer, handheld PC, or smart phone. Some portable printers need to be physically connected to the computer; others can receive documents to be printed using wireless transmission. Portable printers are used by businesspeople while traveling, as well as to print receipts and other needed documents while on the job. Some snapshot printers today are also small enough to be considered portable. The portable printer featured in Figure 4-34 is designed for printing receipts, barcodes, and other small items; some portable printers can print on regular-sized (8½-by-11-inch) paper.

Plotters and Wide-Format Ink-Jet Printers

A *plotter* is an output device that is designed primarily to produce charts, drawings, maps, blueprints, three-dimensional illustrations, and other forms of large documents. *Electrostatic plotters* create images using toner in conjunction with a matrix of tiny wires to charge the paper with electricity. When the charged paper passes over the toner bed, the toner adheres to it and produces an image. While these types of plotters were commonly used in the past and a few are still available, it is more common today to use an *ink-jet plotter* (also called a *wide-format ink-jet printer*) for large documents, including color posters, signs, and advertising banners (see Figure 4-34). Although typically used to print on paper, some wide-format ink-jet printers can print directly on fabric and other types of materials.

Multifunction Devices

A **multifunction device** (sometimes called a *multifunction printer*) is a device that offers some combination of printing, copying, scanning, and faxing capabilities. Most commonly, these types of devices are based on color ink-jet printer technology, although laser multifunction devices are available. The advantage of using a multifunction device is that it takes up less space and is less expensive than purchasing multiple machines. The disadvantages include possibly not being able to find a multifunction device that has exactly the components you would get if you bought them separately, and the risk that when the device breaks down, you will lose all of its functions if the device needs to be repaired off site. Although multifunction devices have traditionally been desktop units used in small offices and home offices, larger workgroup multifunction devices are now available that are designed for multiple users, either as stand-alone stations or as networked units.

AUDIO OUTPUT

Audio output is output in the form of voice or music. *Speakers* and *headsets* are the most common types of audio output hardware. **Speakers** connect to a PC and provide audio output for computer games, music, video, TV, videoconferencing, and other applications that have audio output. *Voice output* can also occur when a computer (such as your PC or the Web server hosting a Web page you are viewing) talks to you. These types of voice output systems—sometimes also referred to as *text-to-speech systems*—typically either use prerecorded sentences stored in digital form (such as a greeting or instruction) or prerecorded

>**Multifunction device.** A device that offers multiple functions (such as printing, scanning, and faxing) in a single unit. >**Speakers.** Output devices that produce sound.

words or sounds used to create sentences extemporaneously (such as when quoting an account balance).

Computer speaker systems resemble their stereo system counterparts and are available in a wide range of prices. Some speaker systems consist of only a pair of speakers. Others include a subwoofer for better bass tones (see Figure 4-35), and still others are capable of surround sound effects. Many speakers have a *headphone jack*, which allows a *headphone* or *headset* to be used so the sound will not disturb others (such as in a school computer lab or public library); if not, there is almost always a headphone port on the outside of the system unit (coming from the sound card or integrated sound component). Instead of being standalone units, the speakers for some desktop PCs are built directly into, or permanently attached to, the monitor. Portable PCs and mobile devices almost always have speakers and headphone jacks integrated into the device, but there are external speakers designed for these devices to boost their sound when at home or another fixed location. For instance, a speaker system designed to be used with the iPod digital music player is shown in Figure 4-35.

FIGURE 4-35
Speakers.

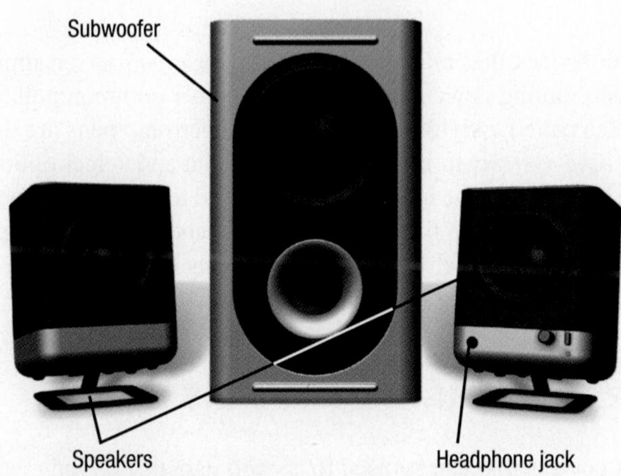

COMPUTER SPEAKERS
Many speaker systems today come with a subwoofer, in addition to the standard two speakers.

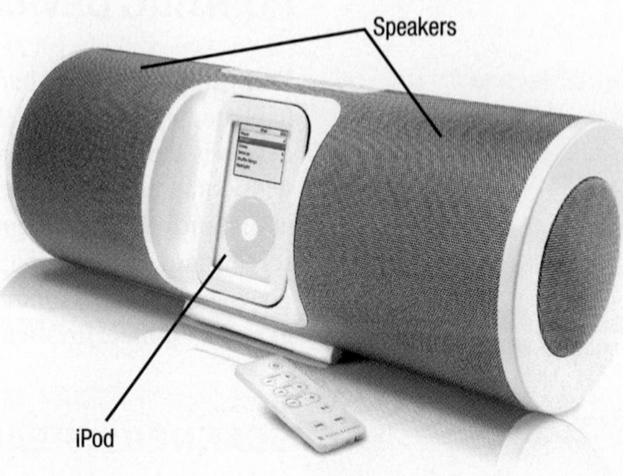

IPOD SPEAKERS
External speakers are also available for use with mobile devices to increase quality, such as the iPod speakers shown here.

HW

SUMMARY

KEYBOARDS

Chapter Objective 1: Explain the purpose of a computer keyboard and the types of keyboards widely used today.

Most people use a **keyboard** as one of the two main sources of computer input. Keyboards typically include the standard alphanumeric keys, plus a variety of other keys for special purposes. Some handheld PCs and mobile devices include a keyboard or a *thumb pad*—if not, a *portable keyboard* or *portable thumb pad* can often be used. *Wireless keyboards* are also available.

POINTING DEVICES

Chapter Objective 2: List several different pointing devices and describe their functions.

Pointing devices are hardware devices that move an onscreen *mouse pointer* or similar indicator. The most widely used pointing device is the **mouse**. Another common pointing device is the **electronic pen** (also called a **stylus** or *digital pen*). Electronic pens are used with computers and *digital writing systems* to input handwritten data and select options; with **handwriting recognition** technology, the input can be converted to typed text. **Touch screens** are monitors that are touched with the finger to select commands or provide input. Touch screens are commonly used in consumer kiosks. Other pointing devices include the **graphics tablet**, **joystick**, **trackball**, **pointing stick**, and **touch pad**.

SCANNERS, READERS, AND DIGITAL CAMERAS

Chapter Objective 3: Describe the purposes of scanners and readers and list some types of scanners and readers in use today.

There are many different input devices that can be used to convert data that already exists (such as on *source documents*) to digital form or to initially capture data in digital form. A **scanner** allows users to input data that exists in physical form, such as photographs, drawings, and printed documents, into a computer system. Most scanners are **flatbed scanners**, **sheetfed scanners**, or **handheld scanners**. *Drum*, *3D*, *receipt*, and *business card scanners* are also available. When used with **optical character recognition (OCR)** software, the computer system recognizes scanned text characters and stores them digitally so they can be manipulated by the computer. If not, the scanned data is input as an image.

Barcode readers read **barcodes**, such as the *UPC codes* used to identify products in many retail stores. **Radio frequency identification (RFID)** readers read and store data in **RFID tags**, which contain tiny chips and antennas and which are attached to packages and other items for identification purposes. RFID tags today are most often used in conjunction with shipping containers and other large assets, though their use is expanding and is expected to grow in the near future.

Optical mark readers read specific types of marks on certain forms, such as on testing forms and voter ballots. *Optical character recognition* (*OCR*) *devices* read specially printed *optical characters*, such as those on bills and other *turnaround documents*; *magnetic ink character recognition* (*MICR*) is used by the banking industry to rapidly sort, process, and route checks to the proper banks; and **biometric readers** identify individuals by their fingerprint, hand geometry, face or other *biometric* characteristic.

Chapter Objective 4: Understand how digital cameras differ from conventional cameras.

Digital cameras work much like regular cameras, but record digital images on some type of digital storage medium, instead of on conventional film or videotape. The images can later be transferred to a PC for manipulation or printing, as desired. *Digital still cameras* take still photos; *digital video cameras* consist of *digital camcorders*; and *PC cams* are used to capture video images for videoconferencing, video phone calls, or to broadcast via a Web site.

AUDIO INPUT

Voice input systems, which enable computer systems to recognize spoken words, are one means of audio input. Voice input technologies offer tremendous work-saving potential in the legal and medical fields, such as for transcription. *MIDI* devices can be used to input original music compositions into a PC. Music can also be input via a CD, DVD, or Web download.

Chapter Objective 5:
Explain how audio input is accomplished.

DISPLAY DEVICES

Display devices (also called **monitors** and **display screens**) are the most common of the output devices for a computer; they are also incorporated into a wide variety of other electronic devices. Monitors are available in a wide variety of sizes and are generally either **CRT monitors** or **flat-panel displays**. Flat-panel displays are most often **liquid crystal displays (LCDs)** or **plasma displays**, but these technologies are expected to be someday replaced by **organic light emitting diode (OLED) displays**. OLED displays generate their own light so they do not require *backlighting*, are more energy efficient, and produce sharper and brighter images. Special types of OLEDs (such as *flexible*, *transparent*, and *Phosphorescent OLEDs*) are emerging for special applications. Regardless of the technology used, the screen of a display device is divided into a fine grid of small areas or dots—**pixels**. Monitors can be *wired* or *wireless*, some support 3D images, and some can display *HDTV* broadcasts and other types of *digital television*. **Data projectors** connect to a PC and project any output sent to the PC's monitor through the projector onto a wall or projection screen.

Chapter Objective 6:
Describe the characteristics of a display device.

PRINTERS

Printers produce *hard copy* output through either *impact* or *nonimpact* printing technology. Most printers today form images as matrices of dots, although with many technologies, the dots are too small to be visible. Quality of printers is usually measured in *dots per inch* (*dpi*); speed is typically measured in *pages per minute* (*ppm*). Both *personal* and *network printers* are available; some printers print in color and others in just black and white.

The most common printers are **laser printers** and **ink-jet printers**. Special-purpose printers include **photo printers**, **barcode printers**, *portable printers*, *plotters*, and *wide-format ink-jet printers*. **Multifunction devices** incorporate the functions of multiple devices—typically a printer, scanner, and fax machine—into a single unit.

Chapter Objective 7:
List several types of printers and explain their function.

AUDIO OUTPUT

Audio output devices include **speakers**, to output music or spoken voice, and *voice output* systems, which enable computer systems to play back or compose spoken messages from digitally stored words, phrases, and sounds. *Headphones* or *headsets* can be used to prevent the sound from disturbing other people.

Chapter Objective 8:
Understand which hardware devices are used for audio output.

REVIEW ACTIVITIES

KEY TERM MATCHING

Instructions: Match each key term on the left with the definition on the right that best describes it.

a. digital camera

b. electronic pen

c. handwriting recognition

d. laser printer

e. mouse

f. optical character recognition (OCR)

g. OLED display

h. RFID tag

i. scanner

j. touch screen

1. _____ A common pointing device that the user slides along a flat surface to move a pointer around the screen and clicks its buttons to make selections.

2. _____ A device containing tiny chips and radio antennas that is attached to objects that will be identified using RFID technology.

3. _____ A display device that is touched with the finger to issue commands or otherwise generate input to the connected PC.

4. _____ An input device that reads printed text and graphics and transfers them to a computer in digital form.

5. _____ An input device that is used to write electronically on the display screen; also called a stylus or digital pen.

6. _____ An input device that takes pictures and records them as digital data (instead of film or videotaped) images.

7. _____ An output device that uses toner powder and technology similar to that of a photocopier to produce images on paper.

8. _____ A type of flat-panel display that uses emissive organic material to display brighter and sharper images.

9. _____ The ability of a device to identify handwritten characters.

10. _____ The ability of a scanning device to recognize handwritten or typed characters and convert them to electronic form as text, not images.

SELF-QUIZ

Instructions: Circle **T** if the statement is true, **F** if the statement is false, or write the best answer in the space provided. **Answers for the self-quiz are located in the References and Resources Guide at the end of the book.**

1. **T F** A keyboard is an example of a pointing device.
2. **T F** Most digital cameras store photos on conventional floppy disks.
3. **T F** UPC is a type of barcode.
4. **T F** Consumer kiosks located in retail stores commonly use touch screens for input.
5. **T F** An ink-jet printer normally produces a better image than a laser printer.
6. With _____ software, pen-based PCs can convert handwritten text into editable, typed text.
7. A(n) _____ can be used to convert flat printed documents, such as a drawing or photograph, into digital form.
8. The smallest colorable area in an electronic image (such as a scanned document, digital photograph, or image displayed on a display screen) is called a(n) _____.

9. Portable PCs virtually always use ________ displays, while desktop PCs may use the larger, more bulky ________ monitors.

10. Match each input device to its input application, and write the corresponding number in the blank to the left of the input application.

a. ________ Gaming		1. RFID tag
b. ________ Pen-based computing		2. Keyboard
c. ________ Consumer kiosk		3. Stylus
d. ________ Text-based data entry		4. Joystick
e. ________ Access a secure facility		5. Biometric reader
f. ________ Tracking goods		6. Touch screen

EXERCISES

1. For the following list of computer input and output devices, write the appropriate abbreviation (I or O) in the space provided to indicate whether each device is used for input (I) or output (O).

a. ________ Biometric reader	f. ________ Digital camera
b. ________ Graphics tablet	g. ________ Pointing stick
c. ________ Speaker	h. ________ Microphone
d. ________ Photo printer	i. ________ OLED monitor
e. ________ Flat-panel display	j. ________ Joystick

2. Write the number of the type of printer that best matches each of the printing applications in the blank to the left of each printing application. Note that all types of printers will not be used.

a. ________ To print inexpensive color printouts for a wide variety of documents.
b. ________ To print all output for an entire office.
c. ________ To print receipts for jet-ski rentals at the beach.
d. ________ To print high-quality black-and-white business letters and reports at home.

1. Personal laser printer	5. Barcode printer
2. Network laser printer	6. Plotter
3. Color laser printer	7. Ink-jet printer
4. Photo printer	8. Portable printer

3. List three advantages of RFID technology over barcode technology.

4. Would an OLED display or an LCD display use more battery power? Explain why.

5. List one personal or business application that you believe is more appropriate for a dot-matrix printer, instead of another type of printer, and explain why.

DISCUSSION QUESTION

The choice of an appropriate input device for a product is often based on both the type of device being used and the target market for that device. For instance, a device targeted to college students and one targeted to older individuals may use different input methods. Suppose that you are developing an Internet appliance being marketed to senior citizens. What type of hardware would you select as the primary input device? Why? What are the advantages and disadvantages of your selected input device? How could the disadvantages be minimized?

PROJECTS

HOT TOPICS

1. **E-Paper** The chapter Trend box discusses electronic paper (e-paper)—an erasable, reusable alternative to traditional paper and ink for computer output. Although currently in its early stages, some experts predict that it will become a viable product for many personal applications in the very near future. One of the first widespread applications for e-paper is retail signs. The obvious benefit of e-paper is reducing the use of traditional paper and ink and the resources needed to create and dispose of paper and ink. Two disadvantages at the current time are longevity (the medium is not designed to display an image for long periods of time) and expense.

   For this project, research the current state of e-paper. What products are available now? Are additional products expected to become available in the near future? When more products become available, do you think businesses or individuals will choose to use these types of products if the only incentive is a cleaner environment? Or will there need to be an economic incentive, such as savings on the cost of paper and ink surpassing the cost of using e-paper? What applications do you think are the most appropriate and exciting for the use of e-paper technology? At the conclusion of your research, prepare a one-page summary of your findings and submit it to your instructor.

SHORT ANSWER/ RESEARCH

2. **New Keyboards** The design and capability of keyboards continue to evolve to meet new user needs. Newer keyboards offer special features, such as ergonomic design, Internet buttons, wireless connections, multimedia control buttons, and built-in fingerprint and smart card readers.

   For this project, research a variety of keyboards designed for use with a desktop PC that are currently for sale. Select at least three different models and identify the special features and cost of each. At the conclusion of your research, prepare a one-page summary of your findings and submit it to your instructor. Be sure to include whether or not you would consider purchasing one of your selected keyboards and why.

3. **Printer Shopping** Printers today have many more features than a few years ago. These features may include improved quality, more memory, photo printing capabilities, digital camera connectivity, built-in flash memory card readers, and faster speed.

   For this project, suppose you are in the market for a new printer, primarily for personal and school applications. Make a list of the most important features needed to meet your needs, and then research printers currently on the market to identify which one you feel would be the best printer for your needs. Be sure to take into consideration both the price of the printer and the price of consumables (such as paper, ink cartridge/toner—both the cost and disposal of) in your evaluation process. At the conclusion of your research, prepare a one-page summary of your findings and submit it to your instructor.

HANDS ON

4. **Will it Fit?** Many new PCs today come with very large—such as 17-inch or 19-inch—monitors. Although they make output much easier to see, sometimes it may be difficult to get the monitor to fit on your desk.

   For this project, find two 17-inch and two 19-inch CRT monitors made by different manufacturers and determine their physical size (most manufacturers have size and other specifications listed by model on their Web sites, although you may also use newspaper or magazine ads or research systems for sale at your local stores). Next, select the desk or table at home that you would use for your PC and measure it. Draw a sketch to scale of the top surface of the desk (bird's-eye view) and then add each monitor (drawn to scale) to your sketch to illustrate how well each one would fit. Are there any significant size differences among the models sold by the manufacturers you selected? Would you need to eliminate any of these models due to lack of space? Next, find two 17-inch and two 19-inch flat-panel monitors made by different manufacturers and determine their physical size. How much difference is there between these models and the CRT models you researched earlier? Compare the prices of the eight monitors. Do you think the price difference justifies a larger monitor size? The convenience of a smaller footprint? Prepare a summary of your findings to turn in to your instructor along with your sketch.

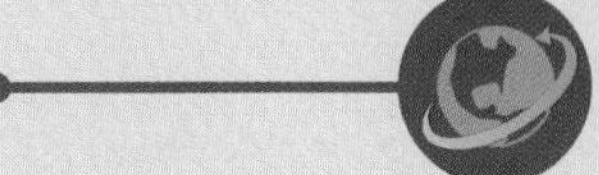

HW

5. **Keyboarding Speed Test** Although voice input and other alternative means of input are emerging, most of the time input is a matter of entering large amounts of data via the keyboard. Proper keyboarding technique and practice can help increase both your speed and accuracy. Keyboarding tests are available online to evaluate your keyboarding ability; keyboarding tutorials are available both online and in software form.

   For this project, find a site (such as Typingtest.com) that offers a free online typing test (often the test requires your browser to have Java compatibility). Take the available typing test to test your keyboarding speed and accuracy. At the conclusion of the test, rate your keyboarding ability and determine whether a keyboarding course or tutor program, or just keyboarding experience, will help bring you up to speed if you do not already keyboard at least 20 correct words per minute (cwpm). Take the test one more time to see if your speed improves now that you are familiar with how the test works. If your speed is fast, but your accuracy is low, take the test one more time, concentrating on accuracy. If you test less than 20 correct words per minute on all tests, use a search site to locate a site with a free typing tutor and evaluate it to see if it would be helpful to increase your speed and accuracy. At the conclusion of this task, prepare a short summary of your experience, including the typing test site used and your best score.

WRITING ABOUT COMPUTERS

6. **Assistive Computing** In addition to the conventional input and output hardware mentioned in the chapter, there are a variety of *assistive* input and output devices that physically challenged individuals can use to make computing easier and more efficient.

   For this project, select one type of disability, such as being blind, deaf, paraplegic, quadriplegic, or having the use of only one arm or hand. Research the hardware and software options that could be used with a new PC for someone with the selected disability. Make a list of potential limitations of any standard PC hardware and the assistive hardware and software that would be appropriate for this individual to use to overcome the limitation of that hardware. Research each possibility, comparing such factors as ease of use, cost, and availability and then prepare a recommendation for the best computer system for your selected hypothetical situation. Summarize your findings in a two- to three-page paper.

PRESENTATION/ DEMONSTRATION

7. **Instant Photos** Digital cameras are becoming very common for both consumers and professionals, and there are many options for printing digital photographs.

   For this project, research the options for printing photos taken with digital cameras. Select one personal printer capable of printing good-quality photos and determine the cost of the printer, as well as the printing cost per photograph (include the cost of ink and photo-quality paper). Also locate two businesses (either physical stores in your area or online services) that will print digital photos. For each location, determine the cost per photo, waiting time, and options available for submitting the photos. Share your findings with the class in the form of a short presentation. The presentation should not exceed 10 minutes and should make use of one or more presentation aids, such as the chalkboard, handouts, overhead transparencies, or a computer-based slide presentation (your instructor may provide additional requirements). You may also be asked to submit a summary of the presentation to your instructor.

GROUP DISCUSSION

8. **Biometrics and Personal Privacy** Biometric input devices, such as the use of fingerprint readers, hand geometry readers, or iris scanners, are increasingly being used for security purposes. Common activities that some employees are required to use at work include using a biometric reader to clock in and out of work or to obtain access to locked facilities, a computer, or a computer network. Other uses of biometric technology are more voluntary, such as expedited airport-screening programs used by some frequent travelers. While viewed as a time-saving tool by some, other individuals may object to their biometric characteristics being stored in a database for this purpose. Is convenience worth compromising some personal privacy? What about national security? Would you be willing to sign up for a voluntary program, such as an airport-screening system or a payment system that enabled you to purchase goods and services (automatically charged to your credit card or deducted from your bank account) at retail stores and restaurants using only your fingerprint? Would you work at a job that required you to use a biometric input device on a regular basis? Do you think a national ID card (such as a standard hard-to-forge national driver's license containing a thumbprint or other biometric data) could help prevent terrorist attacks, such as the September 11, 2001 attacks? If so, do you think most Americans would support their use?

   For this project, form an opinion of the use of biometric input devices and any potential impact their use may have on personal privacy. Be sure to consider the questions mentioned in the previous paragraph and be prepared to discuss your position (in class, via an online class discussion group, or in a class chat room, depending on your instructor's directions). You may also be asked to write a short paper expressing your opinion.

WEB ACTIVITIES

The *Understanding Computers* Web site located at **www.course.com/uc11** features many resources to help reinforce your understanding of the chapter content and help you prepare for exams. Your instructor may also assign specific activities to be completed that will count toward your final grade in the course.

Instructions: Go to **www.course.com/uc11/ch04** to work the following online activities.

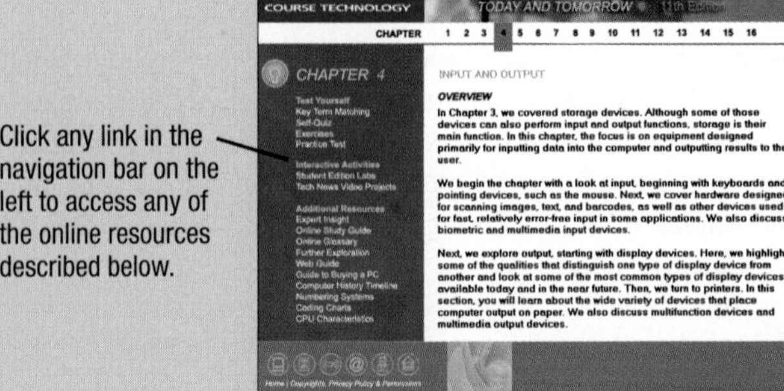

INTERACTIVE ACTIVITIES

1. **Crossword Puzzle** Practice your knowledge of the key terms in Chapter 4 by completing the interactive Crossword Puzzle.
2. **Tech News Video Project** Watch the **"Predicting Huge Surf"** video clip that features a system that uses various types of input regarding weather and the surf to determine, often only hours in advance, when the surf will be huge so that the Mavericks Surf Contest can take place. After watching the video online, complete the corresponding project.
3. **Student Edition Labs** Reinforce the concepts you have learned in this chapter by working through the interactive **Using Input Devices** and **Peripheral Devices** labs.

TEST YOURSELF

1. **Key Term Matching** Test your knowledge of selected chapter key terms by matching the terms with their definitions.
2. **Self-Quiz** Test your retention of chapter concepts by taking the Self-Quiz.
3. **Exercises** Work these short exercises to review the concepts and terms covered in the chapter.
4. **Practice Test** Test how ready you are for an upcoming exam by completing the online Practice Test.

STUDY TOOLS/ ADDITIONAL RESOURCES

The Understanding Computers Web site has a wide range of additional resources, including an **Online Study Guide** (containing study tips, a chapter outline with room to add your own notes, and a chapter checklist of the activities to complete when the chapter is covered in class and when you are preparing for a test) and an **Online Glossary** for each chapter; **Further Exploration** links; a **Web Guide**, a **Guide to Buying a PC**, and a **Computer History Timeline**; more information about **Numbering Systems**, **Coding Charts**, and **CPU Characteristics**; and much, much more!

EXPERT INSIGHT ON . . .

Hardware

A conversation with JOHN JANAKIRAMAN

Research Manager for Data Center Architecture, HP Labs

My Background . . .

I studied engineering since I always enjoyed solving problems. I got fascinated by the creativity in building electronic/computing devices and pursued graduate studies in computer science to prepare for a career in this field. I now lead a team researching how the next generation of servers must be architected and managed. My primary responsibility is to create a future where the architecture and management of servers enable a range of applications (e.g., digital movie rendering, searching the Web, and voice-over-IP) to be performed much more reliably, efficiently, and easily.

“Students in all fields should become computer-literate and keep abreast of developments in the field of computing.”

It's Important to Know . . .

Basic computer concepts. For instance, that the engine of the computer is the processor that executes computer instructions provided by the programmer. Storage such as disks maintain all permanent data in the computer, while memory and caches are actually used to temporarily store instructions and data close to the processor. All computer users should be aware of these concepts.

Computer designers are not focused only on the performance of computers these days. Their designs increasingly focus on non-performance objectives such as lowering power consumption, improving reliability, and improving usability. The industry is also envisioning new ways of using processors to improve the way we live. Computers can be embedded in medicines for health applications, in the environment for ecological applications, and so on.

Computing appliances must be able to interact with each other. For instance, a PDA must be able to communicate with a PC. So, computer hardware and software vendors must actively develop standards in every aspect of computing so that computers can work together. Creating standards while simultaneously building unique products is an important business challenge for the computer industry.

How I Use this Technology . . .

I use my computers at home to interact with family and friends (e.g., through e-mail and VoIP phone calls), to follow news, to shop and pay bills, to work from home, and to maintain my personal content (e.g., photos and financial documents). I maintain a wireless network which allows me to roam around the house while still being connected to the Internet through my broadband provider. I maintain most of my content on storage devices and back them up periodically. I use a photo-quality printer to print photos and other documents. In addition to my digital camera/camcorder, I use my computer to record audio

John Janakiraman is currently the Research Manager for the Data Center Architecture group at HP Labs. He is leading research on the architecture and management of the server infrastructure in data centers, where his team is researching virtualization and automation techniques to improve the efficiency, reliability, and manageability of data centers. He and his team have developed many technologies that have influenced HP products, industry standards, and open-source community projects. John has a Ph.D. in Computer Science.

Future advances in hardware technology and their decreasing costs can have a beneficial impact on society in many ways, such as to improve the quality of personal life, improve economic opportunity in developing regions, and improve environment management.

and video of my family. Like other individuals, I also invisibly use computers integrated into devices, such as in cars and in the garden sprinkler system.

What the Future Holds . . .

Computer hardware will decrease in cost while becoming more powerful, compact, and power-efficient. Advances in computer hardware will enable pervasive wireless connectivity, permit more of the human experience to be captured in digital form, and provide richer entertainment. Computers will get woven, invisibly in many cases, into many more aspects of life, such as in maintaining a healthy lifestyle, education, the environment, and government services.

Future advances in hardware technology and their decreasing costs can have a beneficial impact on society in many ways, such as to improve the quality of personal life, improve economic opportunity in developing regions, and improve environment management. Technology also imposes some societal responsibilities, such as the appropriate handling of used computer parts (e.g., recycling) so that they do not contaminate the environment.

My Advice to Students . . .

A career in the intersection between technology and some other field (as diverse as, for example, medicine, library management, or geology) can give you an edge. Getting real-world experience through internships in related jobs is also key. To rise to a position of leadership, solid verbal and written communication skills and the ability to influence people's thinking are also critical.

Students in all fields should become computer-literate and keep abreast of developments in the field of computing. This knowledge can enable them to use computing to advance their field by conceiving new solutions and tools. It will also equip them to reason about the risks and rewards of specific computing applications and to influence the development of governance policies.

Discussion Question

John Janakiraman views the appropriate handling of used computer parts so that they do not contaminate the environment one of the responsibilities involved with the use of technology. Think about all of the computing refuse you create—such as old printouts, depleted toner cartridges, broken hardware, and so forth. What do you feel is your responsibility for making sure this refuse is disposed of properly? Does the manufacturer share any of that responsibility? Some states—such as California—are beginning to charge a recycling fee on some hardware, such as computer monitors, to help pay for the cost of properly disposing of that hardware. Do you agree with this trend? What should individuals be required to do to help alleviate the computing refuse problem? Is there a long-term solution to this problem? Be prepared to discuss your position (in class, via an online class discussion group, or in a class chat room, depending on your instructor's directions). You may also be asked to write a short paper expressing your opinion.

>For more information on HP, visit www.hp.com. For more information on HP Labs, visit www.hpl.hp.com. Some good industry association references are www.acm.org and www.ieee.org.

MODULE SOFTWARE

In Chapter 1, we looked at the basic software concepts needed to get a computer system up and running. We continue that focus in this module, discussing in more depth both system software—the software used to run a computer—and application software—the software that performs the specific tasks that users want to accomplish using a computer.

System software, the subject of Chapter 5, consists of the programs that enable the hardware of a computer system to operate and run application software. Chapter 6 offers a brief introduction to some of the most common types of application software, such as word processing, spreadsheet, database, presentation graphics, and multimedia software.

“. . . eventually we'll stop talking about how computers are changing our society, and focus more on using them to get on with our lives and be part of society.”

For more comments from Guest Expert Aaron Weber of Novell, Inc., see the Expert Insight on . . . Software feature at the end of the module.

IN THIS MODULE

CHAPTER 5 System Software: Operating Systems and Utility Programs

OUTLINE

Overview
System Software vs. Application Software
The Operating System
- Functions of an Operating System
- Processing Techniques for Increased Efficiency
- Differences Among Operating Systems

Operating Systems for Desktop PCs and Servers
- DOS
- Windows
- Mac OS
- UNIX
- Linux
- NetWare
- Solaris

Operating Systems for Handheld PCs and Mobile Devices
- Embedded and Mobile Versions of Windows
- Palm OS
- Embedded Linux
- Symbian OS

Operating Systems for Larger Computers
Utility Programs
- File Management Programs
- Search Tools
- Diagnostic and Disk Management Programs
- Uninstall Utilities
- File Compression Programs
- Backup and Recovery Utilities
- Antivirus, Antispyware, Firewalls, and Other Security Programs

The Future of Operating Systems

LEARNING OBJECTIVES

After completing this chapter, you will be able to:

1. Understand the difference between system software and application software.
2. Explain the different functions of an operating system and discuss some ways that operating systems can differ from one another.
3. List several ways in which operating systems enhance processing efficiency.
4. Name today's most widely used operating systems for desktop PCs and servers.
5. State several devices other than desktop PCs and servers that require an operating system and list one possible operating system for each type of device.
6. Discuss the role of utility programs and outline several duties that these programs perform.
7. Describe what the operating systems of the future might be like.

OVERVIEW

All stand-alone computers require some sort of software to run the computer system. For instance, software is needed to translate your commands into a form the computer can understand, to open and close other software programs, to manage your stored files, to help to keep your computer running smoothly and efficiently, and to locate and set up new hardware as it is added to the PC.

The type of software used to perform these tasks is system software–the focus of this chapter. System software runs in the background at all times, making it possible for you to use your computer. It is also responsible for a variety of tasks that need to be carried out as you work. For example, when you issue the command for your PC to store a document on your hard drive, the system software must make sure that such a drive exists, look for adequate space on the hard drive, write the document to this space, and finally update the hard drive's directory with the filename and disk location so that the document can be retrieved again when needed. When you click an icon to start a software program, the system software must first determine which program is associated with that icon and where the program is stored on the hard drive in order to verify that the program file exists in that location, and then it launches that program. In addition to managing your local computer, the system software may perform additional tasks if you are connected to a network, such as checking the validity of your user ID or password before granting you access to network resources and ensuring that you have permission to access the data or programs you are requesting.

System software is usually divided into two categories: operating system software and utility programs. We begin this chapter by taking a look at the difference between system software and application software, and then examining the operating system–the primary component of system software. We discuss what operating systems do, in general, and then explore the operating systems most widely used today. Next, we cover utility programs. Utility programs typically perform support functions for the operating system, such as allowing you to manage your files, perform maintenance on your computer, check your PC for viruses, or uninstall a program you no longer want on your PC. Chapter 5 closes with a look at what the future of operating systems may hold. ■

SYSTEM SOFTWARE VS. APPLICATION SOFTWARE

Computers run two general types of software: system software and application software.

- **System software** consists of the "background" programs (namely, the operating system and utility programs) that run a computer system and allow you to use your computer. These programs enable the computer to boot, to launch application programs, and to facilitate important jobs, such as transferring files from one storage medium to another, configuring your computer system to work with a specific brand

>**System software.** Programs, such as the operating system, that control the operation of a computer and its devices, as well as enable application software to run on the PC.

of printer or monitor, managing files on your hard drive, and protecting your computer system from unauthorized use.

- **Application software** includes all the programs that allow a user to perform certain specific tasks on a computer, such as writing a letter, preparing an invoice, viewing a Web page, listening to an MP3 file, checking the inventory of a particular product, playing a game, preparing financial statements, designing a home, and so forth. Application software is discussed in detail in Chapter 6.

In practice, the difference between system and application software is not always clear cut. Some programs, such as those used to burn DVDs, were originally viewed as utility programs. Today, these programs typically contain a variety of features (including the ability to transfer videos and digital photos to a PC, edit videos and photos, create DVD movies, copy CDs and DVDs, and create slide shows) in addition to burning CDs and DVDs, and so now more closely fit the definition of an application program. Also, system software often contains application software components. For example, the *Microsoft Windows* operating system contains several application programs, including a Web browser, calculator, painting program, and text editor. A program's classification as system or application software usually depends on the principal function of the program, and the distinction between the two categories is not always clear.

FIGURE 5-1
The intermediary role of the operating system. The operating system acts as a middleman between the user and the computer, as well as between application software programs and the computer system's hardware.

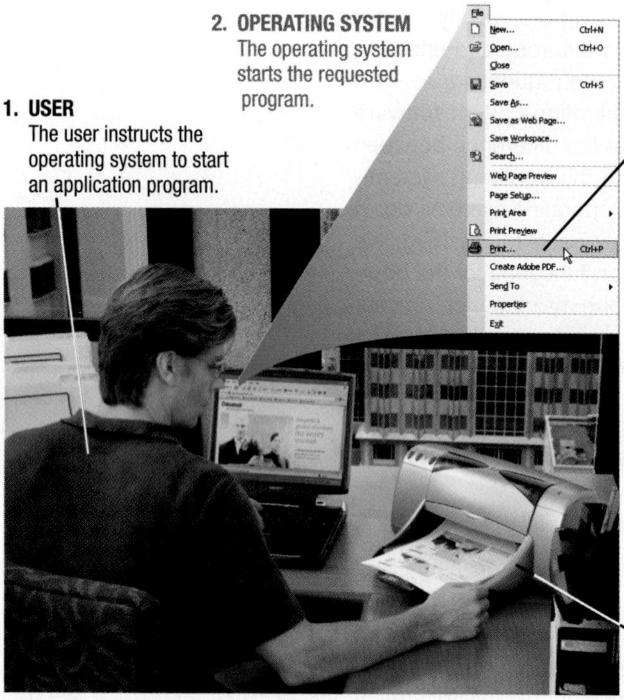

1. USER
The user instructs the operating system to start an application program.

2. OPERATING SYSTEM
The operating system starts the requested program.

3. USER
The user instructs the application program to print the current document.

4. APPLICATION PROGRAM
The application program hands the document over to the operating system for printing.

5. OPERATING SYSTEM
The operating system sends the document to the printer.

6. PRINTER
The printer prints the document.

THE OPERATING SYSTEM

A computer's **operating system** is a collection of programs that manage and coordinate the activities taking place within a computer system. The operating system boots the computer, launches application software programs, and ensures that all actions requested by a user are valid and processed in an orderly fashion. It also manages the computer system resources to perform those operations with efficiency and consistency, and it facilitates connections to the Internet and other networks. When you are ready to print a document or save it onto your hard drive, the operating system assists with those tasks, as well.

In general, the operating system serves as an intermediary between the user and the computer (see Figure 5-1) and is the most critical piece of software installed on the computer. Without an operating system, no other program can run, and the computer cannot function. Many tasks performed by the operating system, however, go unnoticed by the user because the operating system works in the background much of the time.

>**Application software.** Programs that enable users to perform specific tasks on a computer, such as writing a letter or playing a game.

>**Operating system.** The main component of system software that enables the computer to manage its activities and the resources under its control, run application programs, and interface with the user.

Functions of an Operating System

Operating systems have a wide range of functions—some of the most important are discussed next.

> **TIP**
>
> Press Ctrl+Alt+Delete to bring up the Task Manager screen shown in Figure 5-2.

Interfacing with Users

As Figure 5-1 suggests, one of the principal roles of every operating system is to translate user instructions into a form the computer can understand. In the other direction, it translates any feedback from the hardware—such as a signal that the printer has run out of paper or the scanner is turned off—into a form that the user can understand. The means by which an operating system or any other program interacts with the user is called the *user interface*; user interfaces can be *text-based* or *graphics-based*, as discussed in more detail shortly. Most, but not all, operating systems today use a *graphical user interface* or *GUI*.

Booting the Computer

As discussed in Chapter 1, the first task your operating system performs when you power up your PC is to *boot* the PC. During the boot process, certain parts of the operating system (called the *kernel*) are loaded into memory. The kernel remains in memory the entire time the PC is on so that it is always available; other parts of the operating system are retrieved from the hard drive and loaded into memory when they are needed. Before the boot process ends, the operating system determines which hardware devices are connected and properly configured, and it reads an opening batch of instructions. These instructions—which the user can customize to some extent when necessary—assign tasks for the operating system to carry out before the current session begins; for instance, checking for computer viruses or starting up a few programs (such as a security program or instant messaging program) to continually run in the background. Typically, many programs are running in the background at any one time, even before the user launches any application software (see Figure 5-2). In Windows, the system configuration information is stored in the *registry* files, which should be modified only by the Windows program itself or advanced Windows users.

FIGURE 5-2
Even with no application programs open, many programs–launched by the operating system during the boot process–run in the background.

TASK MANAGER
These programs are running, even before any application programs are launched by the user.

SYSTEM TRAY ICONS
These programs were launched during the boot process and will show up in the system tray unless they are closed by the user.

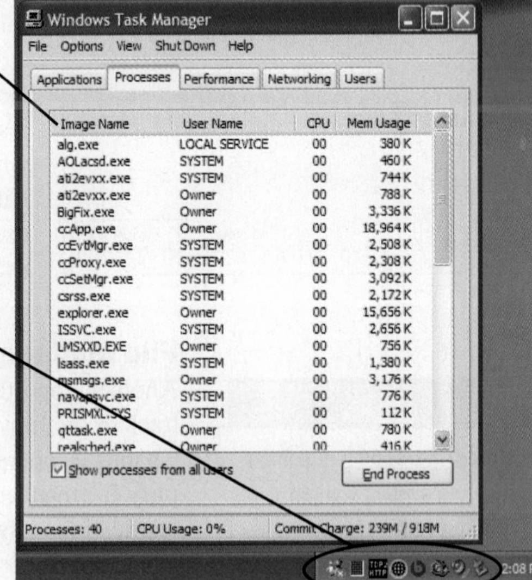

Configuring Devices

The operating system is also used to configure the devices connected to a computer system. Small programs called **device drivers** (or just *drivers*) are used to communicate with peripheral devices, such as monitors, printers, and scanners. Most operating systems today include the drivers needed for the most commonly used peripheral devices. In addition, drivers often come on a disk or a CD packaged with the peripheral device, or they can be obtained from the manufacturer's Web site. Most operating systems today look for new devices each time the PC boots and recognize new devices as they are connected to the PC. If a new device is found, the operating system will typically try to install the appropriate driver automatically in order to get the new hardware ready to use (see Figure 5-3)—a feature called *Plug and Play*. Because USB and FireWire devices can be connected to a PC when the computer is running, those devices will be recognized and configured, as needed, whenever they are plugged into the PC.

FIGURE 5-3
Finding new hardware. Most operating systems are designed to detect new hardware and automatically try to configure it.

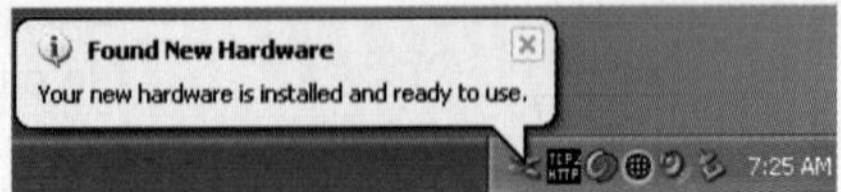

>**Device driver.** A program that enables an operating system to communicate with a specific hardware device.

SW

Once a device and its driver have been properly installed, they usually work fine. If the device driver file gets deleted or becomes corrupted, however, it will no longer work. Usually, the operating system detects this during the boot process and notifies the user that the driver needs to be reinstalled. The user can then reinstall the driver either by using the initial installation disk for that hardware or by downloading a new installation file from the manufacturer's Web site. Device drivers also frequently need to be updated after you *upgrade* your operating system to a newer version. Some operating systems, such as *Windows*, have options to automatically check for operating system updates—including updated driver files—on a regular basis.

Managing and Monitoring Resources and Jobs

As you work on your PC, the operating system is in charge of managing *system resources* (such as software, disk space, and memory) and making them available to devices and programs when they are needed. If a problem occurs—such as a program stops functioning or too many programs are open for the amount of memory available—the operating system notifies the user and tries to correct the problem, sometimes by closing the offending program (see Figure 5-4). If the problem cannot be corrected by the operating system, the user typically needs to reboot the computer.

FIGURE 5-4

Program malfunctions. When a problem occurs, most operating systems attempt to close only the programs or tasks causing the problem, rather than requiring a full reboot.

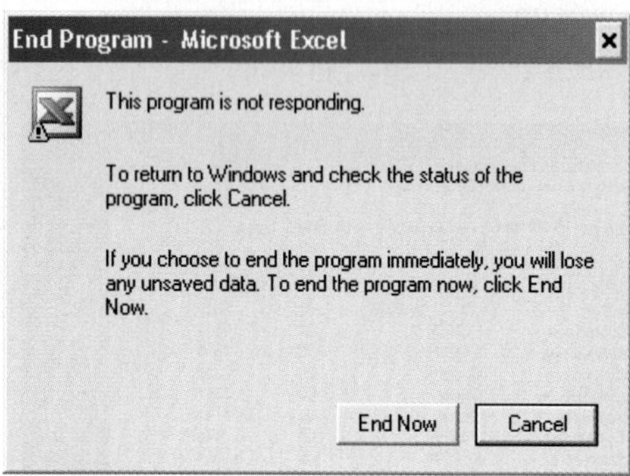

Along with assigning system resources, the operating system performs a closely related process: scheduling user jobs to be performed using those resources. *Scheduling routines* in the operating system determine the order in which jobs (such as documents to be printed and files to be retrieved from a hard job) are carried out, as well as which commands get executed first if the user is working with more than one program at a time or if the computer being used supports multiple users.

TIP

When a program stops functioning in an operating system with an error reporting system (such as Windows or Linux), click the option to report the problem, if you are connected to the Internet. After doing so, you may be given a link to information available to correct that problem, such as a software patch or update.

File Management

Another important task that the operating system performs is *file management*—keeping track of the files stored on a PC so that they can be retrieved when needed. As discussed in Chapter 3, operating systems organize the files on a disk or hard drive into *folders* to simplify file management. Usually the operating system files are stored in one folder, and each application software program is stored in its own separate folder. Other folders may be created by the user for storing and organizing files. Folders can contain both files and other folders (called *subfolders*).

Files and folders are usually viewed in a hierarchical format; the top of the hierarchy for any storage medium is called the *root directory* (such as C:\ for the root directory of the hard drive C shown in Figure 5-5). The root directory almost always contains both files and folders. To access a file, you generally navigate to the folder containing that file by opening the appropriate drive, folder, and subfolders. Alternatively, you can type the *path* to a file's exact location. For example, as Figure 5-5 shows, the path

C:\My Documents\Letters\Mary

leads through the root directory of the C drive and the *My Documents* and *Letters* folders to a file named *Mary*. A similar path can also be used to access the files *John* and *Bill*. As discussed in Chapter 3, users specify a filename for each file when they initially save the file on a storage medium; there can be only one file with the exact same filename in any particular folder on a storage medium.

Filename rules vary with each operating system. For instance, all current versions of Windows support filenames that are from 1 to 255 characters long and may include numbers, letters, spaces, and any special characters except \ / : * ? " < > and |. Filenames almost always contain a *file extension* at the end of the filename. File extensions are generally three characters preceded by a period and are automatically added to a filename by the program in which that file was created, although sometimes the user may have a choice of file extensions supported by a program. Some common file extensions are listed in Figure 5-6.

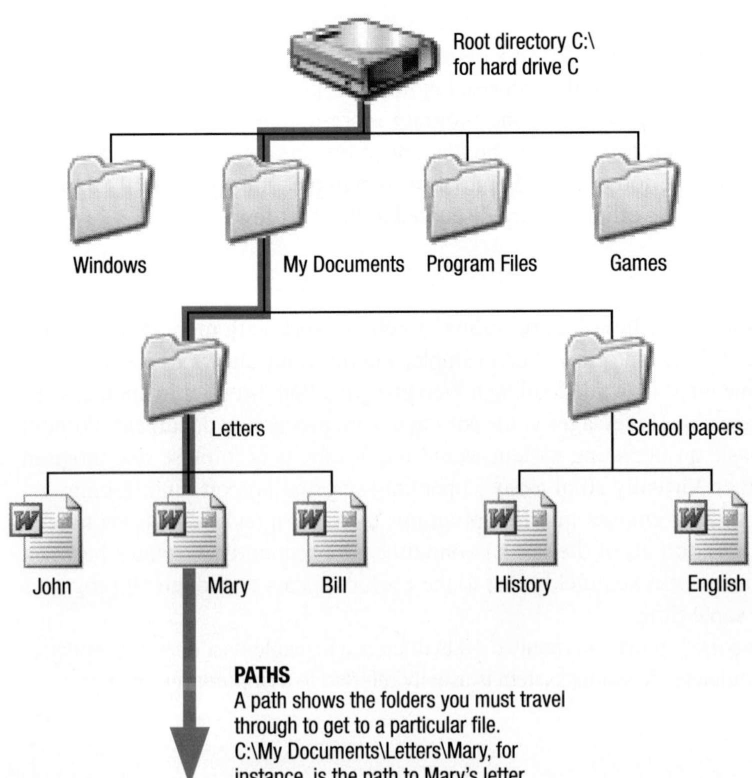

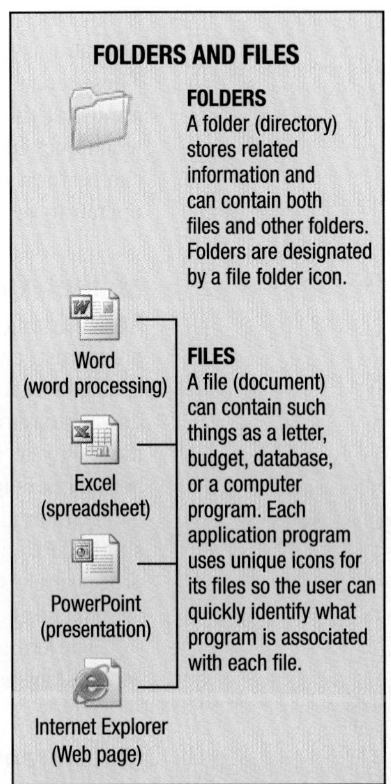

FOLDERS AND FILES
FOLDERS
A folder (directory) stores related information and can contain both files and other folders. Folders are designated by a file folder icon.
Word
(word processing)
Excel
(spreadsheet)
PowerPoint
(presentation)
Internet Explorer
(Web page)
FILES
A file (document) can contain such things as a letter, budget, database, or a computer program. Each application program uses unique icons for its files so the user can quickly identify what program is associated with each file.

FIGURE 5-5
A sample hard drive organization.

File extensions should not be changed by the user because the operating system uses them to identify the program that should be used to open the document. For instance, if you give the command in a *file management program* (a program, such as *Windows Explorer*, that allows you to perform file management) to open a file named *Letter to Mom.doc*, the document will open using the Microsoft Word program because the *.doc* file extension is typically associated with the Microsoft Word word processing program. Depending on how your PC and file management program are set up, you may or may not be able to see file extensions; they are typically hidden by default, although that setting can be changed by the user. If the file to be opened does not have a file extension that your operating system recognizes, the operating system will ask you which program should be used to open the file.

File management programs can be used to open, move, copy, rename, or delete files, and to create new folders. The Windows Explorer file management program and other utilities typically included in an operating system are discussed near the end of this chapter.

FIGURE 5-6
Common file extensions.

WIDELY USED FILE EXTENSIONS
DOCUMENTS
.doc .txt .htm .html .mht .mhtml .xml .xls .mdb .ppt .rtf .pdf
PROGRAMS
.com .exe
GRAPHICS
.bmp .tif .jpg .eps .gif .png .pcx .svg
AUDIO
.wav .au .mp3 .snd .aiff .midi .aac .wma .ra
VIDEO
.mpg .mov .avi .mpeg .rm .wmv .asf
COMPRESSED FILES
.zip .sit .sitx .tar

Security

A computer's operating system can protect against unauthorized access by using *passwords*, *biometric* characteristics (such as fingerprints), or other security procedures to prevent outsiders from accessing system resources that they are not authorized to access. Most operating systems have other security features available, such as an integrated *firewall* to protect against unauthorized access via the Internet or an option to automatically download and install *security patches* (small program updates that correct known security problems) from the operating system's manufacturer on a regular basis. Operating system passwords can also be used to set up different accounts on a single PC to control access and capabilities; for example, to control children's access so they cannot install programs or change system settings. Passwords, biometrics, and other security issues related to networks and the Internet are discussed in much more detail in Chapter 9.

Processing Techniques for Increased Efficiency

Operating systems often utilize various processing techniques to operate more efficiently. These techniques usually involve either processing multiple programs at the same time or almost at the same time, or processing one program more quickly. Consequently, these techniques increase system efficiency and the amount of processing the computer system can perform in any given period of time. Some of the techniques most commonly used by operating systems to increase efficiency are discussed in the next few sections.

Multitasking

Multitasking refers to the ability of an operating system to work with more than one program (also called a *task*) at one time. For example, multitasking allows a user to edit a spreadsheet file in one window while loading a Web page in a Web browser in another window, or to retrieve new e-mail messages while editing a word processing document. Without the ability to multitask, an operating system would require the user to close one program before opening another. Virtually all of today's operating systems support multitasking.

Although multitasking enables multiple programs to be open and used at one time, a single CPU cannot work on all of the tasks at one time. Consequently, it rotates between processing tasks, but it works so quickly that to the user it appears as though all programs are executing at the same time.

The term *multitasking* is most commonly used in reference to single-user operating systems. Multitasking with a multiuser operating system is usually referred to as *multiprogramming*.

Multithreading

A *thread* is a sequence of instructions within a program that is independent of other threads. Examples might include spell checking, printing, and opening documents in a word processing program. Operating systems that support *multithreading* have the ability to run multiple threads for a program at one time (similar to the way multitasking is used to run multiple programs at one time) so that processing is completed faster and more efficiently. Most current operating systems support multithreading. Some CPU architectures—such as Intel's Hyper-Threading Technology—are designed to take advantage of multithreading.

Multiprocessing, Parallel Processing, and Coprocessing

As discussed in Chapter 2, both **multiprocessing** and **parallel processing** involve using two or more CPUs in one computer system to perform work more efficiently. The primary difference between these two techniques is that, with multiprocessing, each CPU typically works on a different job; with parallel processing, the processors usually work together to make one job finish sooner. In either case, all CPUs perform tasks *simultaneously* (at precisely the same instant), in contrast with multitasking and multithreading, which use a single CPU and process programs or tasks *concurrently* (by taking turns). Figure 5-7 illustrates the difference between concurrent and simultaneous processing.

Multiprocessing is supported by most operating systems and is traditionally used with servers and mainframe computers, although the *dual-core CPUs* discussed in Chapter 2 are bringing multiprocessing to the desktop PC user. Parallel processing is used most often with supercomputers and supercomputer clusters.

Coprocessing is another way of increasing processing efficiency. Coprocessing utilizes special-purpose processors (called *coprocessors*) to assist the CPU with specialized chores. For example, a *math coprocessor* performs mathematical computations, and a *graphics coprocessor* performs high-speed calculations for fast screen graphics display.

>**Multitasking.** The capability of an operating system to work with more than one programs at one time. >**Multiprocessing.** The capability of an operating system to use multiple processors in a single computer, usually to process multiple jobs at one time faster than could be performed with a single processor. >**Parallel processing.** A processing technique that uses multiple processors simultaneously in a single computer, usually to process a single job as fast as possible.

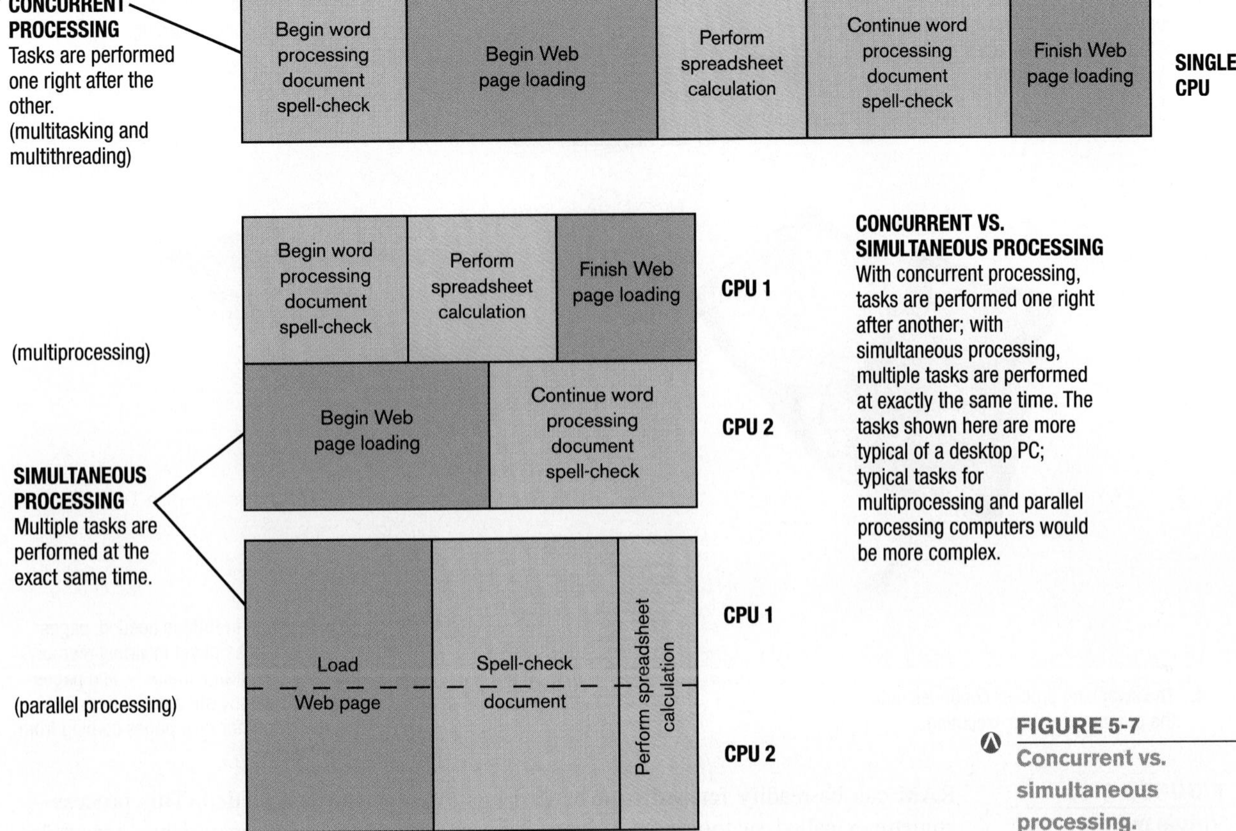

FIGURE 5-7
Concurrent vs. simultaneous processing.

Memory Management

Another key function of the operating system is *memory management*, which is optimizing the use of main memory (RAM). The operating system allocates RAM to programs as needed and then reclaims that memory when the program is closed. With today's memory-intensive programs (Windows XP requires a minimum of 64 MB of RAM, although 128 MB is recommended, and each open program requires additional RAM), good memory management can help speed up processing.

One memory management technique frequently used by operating systems is **virtual memory**, which uses a portion of the computer's hard drive as additional RAM. Programs and data ready for processing are stored in the virtual memory area of the hard drive (sometimes called the *swap file*). There, the content of virtual memory is divided into either fixed-length *pages* or variable-length *segments*, depending on the operating system being used. For example, a program that requires 20 MB of memory might be divided into 10 pages of 2 MB each. As the computer executes the program, it stores only some of the pages in RAM and the rest in virtual memory. As it requires other pages during program execution, it retrieves them from virtual memory and writes over the pages in RAM that are no longer needed (pages in RAM containing data not yet in virtual memory are copied to virtual memory before they are overwritten in RAM). All pages remain intact in virtual memory as the computer processes the program, so any page that was overwritten in

TIP

Although memory used by a program or process is supposed to be released when it is no longer needed, this does not always happen. Referred to as *memory leaking*, this problem can cause your computer to run out of memory temporarily. When this occurs, reboot the computer to refresh your RAM.

>**Virtual memory.** A memory-management technique that uses hard drive space as additional RAM.

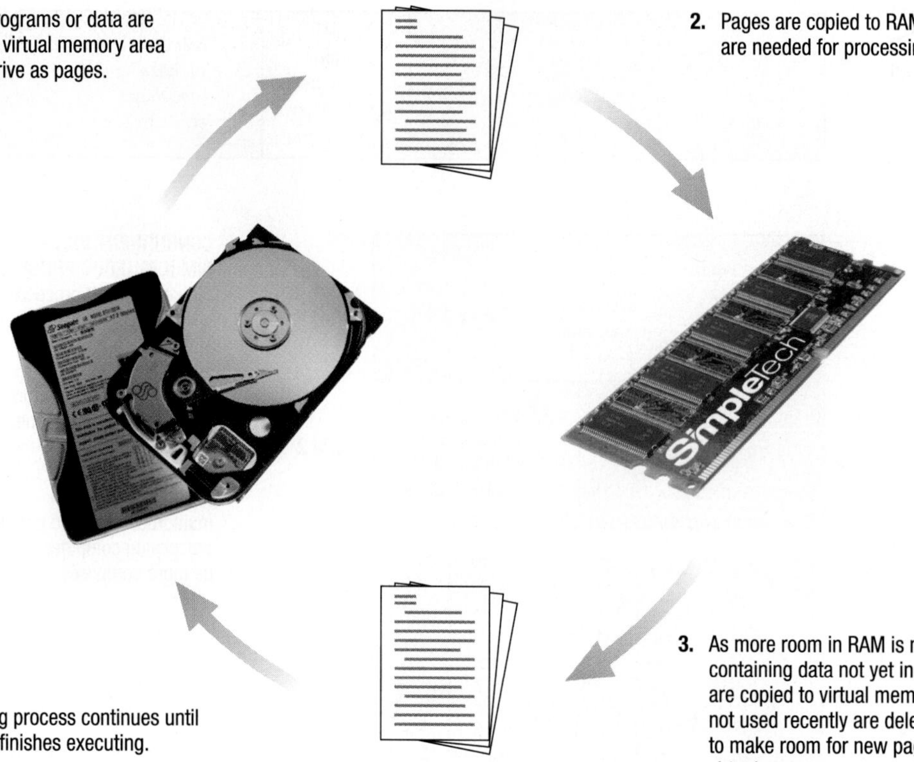

1. Portions of programs or data are copied to the virtual memory area of the hard drive as pages.

2. Pages are copied to RAM as they are needed for processing.

3. As more room in RAM is needed, pages containing data not yet in virtual memory are copied to virtual memory, and pages not used recently are deleted from RAM to make room for new pages coming from virtual memory.

4. The swapping process continues until the program finishes executing.

FIGURE 5-8
Virtual memory. With virtual memory, the operating system uses a portion of the hard drive as additional RAM.

RAM can be readily fetched from virtual memory again when needed. This process—sometimes called *swapping* or *paging*—continues until the program finishes executing (see Figure 5-8). Virtual memory allows you to use more memory than is physically available on your computer, but using virtual memory is slower than just using RAM. Most operating systems today allow the user to specify the total amount of hard drive space to be used for virtual memory.

Buffering and Spooling

Some input and output devices are exceedingly slow, compared to today's CPUs. If the CPU had to wait for these slower devices to finish their work, the computer system would face a horrendous bottleneck. For example, suppose a user just sent a 50-page document to the printer. Assuming the printer can output 10 pages per minute, it would take 5 minutes for the document to finish printing. If the CPU had to wait for the print job to be completed before performing other tasks, the PC would be tied up for 5 minutes.

To avoid this problem, most operating systems use two techniques—buffering and spooling. A **buffer** is an area in RAM or on the hard drive designated to hold input and output on their way in or out of the system. For instance, a *keyboard buffer* stores a certain number of characters as they are entered via the keyboard, and a *print buffer* stores documents that are waiting to be printed. The process of placing items in a buffer so they can be retrieved by the appropriate device when needed is called **spooling**. The most common use of spooling and buffering is for print jobs. It allows multiple documents to be sent to the printer at one time, and they will print, one after the other, in the background while the computer and user are performing other tasks. The documents waiting to be printed are said to be in a *print queue*, which designates the order the documents will be printed. While in the

>**Buffer.** An area in RAM or on the hard drive designated to hold input and output on their way in or out of the system. >**Spooling.** The process of placing items in a buffer so they can be retrieved by the appropriate device (such as a printer) when needed.

print queue, some operating systems allow the order of the documents to be rearranged, as well as the cancellation of a print job (see Figure 5-9).

Although originally used primarily for keyboard input and print jobs, most PCs and operating systems today use several other buffers to speed up operations. For instance, it is common today to use buffers to assist in redisplaying screen images and buffers in conjunction with burning CDs and DVDs.

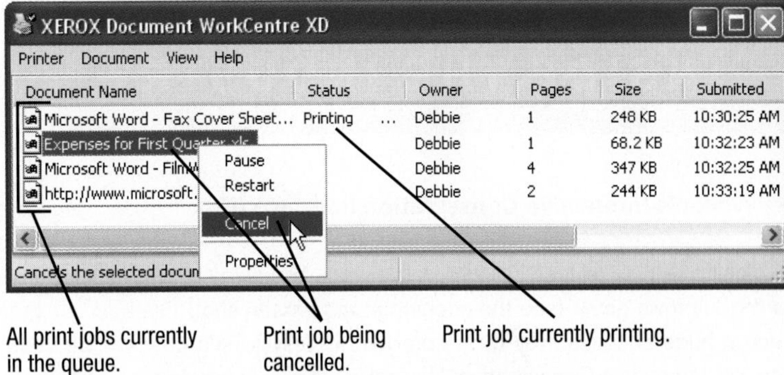

FIGURE 5-9
A print queue.

Differences Among Operating Systems

There are different types of operating systems available to meet different needs. Some of the major distinctions between operating systems include the type of user interface utilized, whether the operating system is targeted for personal or network use, and what type of processing and CPU the operating system is designed for.

Command Line vs. Graphical User Interface

Most PC operating systems today use a **graphical user interface** (**GUI**). The older *DOS* operating systems and some versions of the *UNIX* and *Linux* operating systems use a **command line interface** (see Figure 5-10), although graphical versions of UNIX and Linux are available. With a command line interface, commands to the computer are typed using the keyboard; as explained in Chapter 1, graphical user interfaces allow the user to issue commands by selecting icons, buttons, menu items, and other graphical objects with a mouse or other pointing device. Operating systems for larger computers, such as mainframes, tend to use command line interfaces.

For a look at the interactive graphical user interface used in the popular *You Don't Know Jack* computer game, see the Inside the Industry box.

FIGURE 5-10
Command line vs. graphical user interfaces.

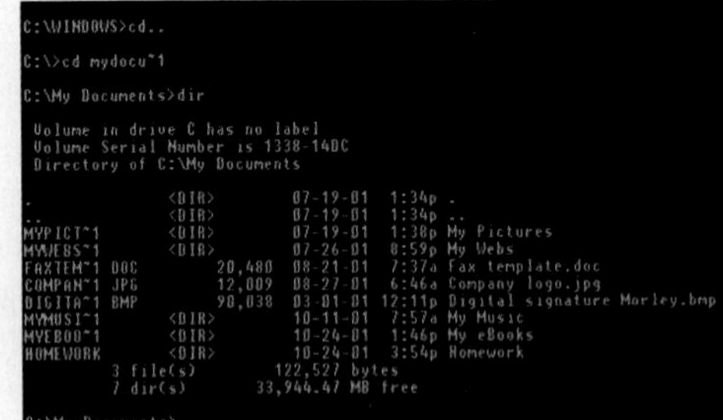

COMMAND LINE INTERFACE
Commands are entered using the keyboard.

GRAPHICAL USER INTERFACE
Icons, buttons, menus, and other objects are selected with the mouse to issue commands to the PC.

Personal vs. Server Operating Systems

Most operating systems are designated as either single-user **personal** (*desktop*) **operating systems** or multiuser **server** (*network*) **operating systems**. Although most personal operating systems today include some networking capabilities—such as to create a home network—they are designed to be installed on user PCs; server operating systems are designed to be installed on network servers. Many operating systems—such as Windows, *Mac OS*, and Linux—come in both a personal version and a server version (see Figure 5-11).

On a server-based network, a server operating system is installed on the server, and each PC attached to the network has its own personal operating system installed, just as with a stand-alone PC. The PCs may also need special *client* software to access the network and issue requests to the server. The server operating system—*Novell NetWare*, for example—controls access to network resources, while the personal operating system (such as Microsoft Windows, Mac OS, or Linux) controls the activity on the local PC. For instance, when you boot a PC connected to the network, the server operating system asks for your username and password, verifies your identity based on

>**Graphical user interface (GUI).** A graphically based interface that allows a user to communicate instructions to the computer easily. >**Command line interface.** A user interface in which commands are typed on a keyboard. >**Personal operating system.** A type of operating system designed to be installed on a PC. >**Server operating system.** A type of operating system designed to be installed on a network server.

INSIDE THE INDUSTRY

Jellyvision's Interactive Conversation Interface (iCi)

Beginning with its release in 1995, Jellyvision's *You Don't Know Jack* adult trivia game (see the accompanying screen shot) has been a huge success. Key to the program is Jellyvision's concept of "Interactive Conversation" that relies on a user interface called the *Interactive Conversation Interface* (*iCi*). The goal of iCi is to create the illusion of conversation between the player (a person) and the game host (a software program). To accomplish this, writers, designers, and other individuals work together to script and record realistic answers to every possible situation the player will encounter during the game and every response he or she will make to a question, and then they develop the program so that the proper responses will be delivered for each possible player action. Several factors crucial to the success of this process include ensuring the dialog is appropriate and doesn't repeat, giving the user only one task to do at a time with a limited number of choices, and keeping the pace steady by responding appropriately if the user does not answer a question. For instance, not answering a question quickly enough in the *You Don't Know Jack* program might cause the host's next assigned line to be "OK, sleepy, let's try that again" or "Excuse me, we've got a game to play!"–in the same manner as a real game show host would prod a contestant who failed to act in a timely manner during a live game show. Adding to the appeal of the *You Don't Know Jack* program is the chatty background atmosphere of a game show studio, catchy music and graphics, lots of animation, funny trivia questions, and a host whose casual, but intimate, conversation is funny, as well as sarcastic at times.

In addition to being used with computers games, iCi can be used for a variety of other applications, such as for an interactive tour with a guide who gives you advice via a cell phone as you travel by asking and responding to questions, for customized news delivery, for interactive customer service support, for educational applications, and more.

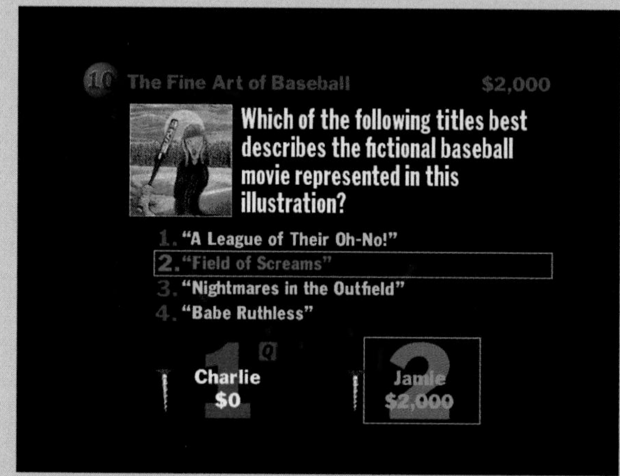

Jellyvision's best-selling YOU DON'T KNOW JACK games use iCi to create realistic conversations between the player and the host.

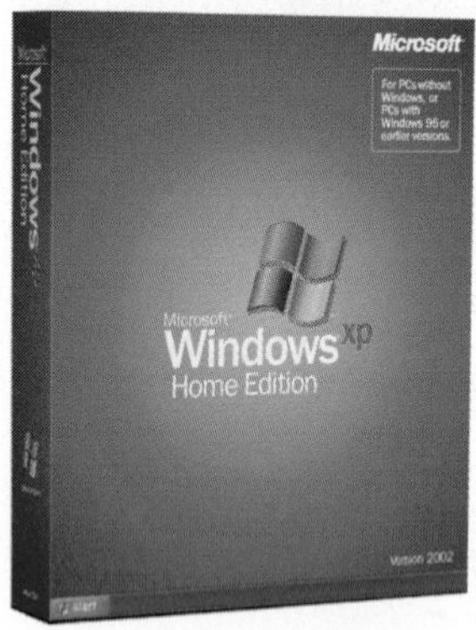

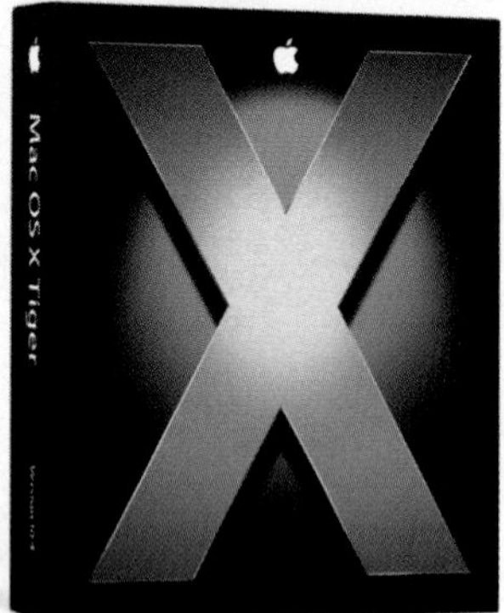

PERSONAL VERSIONS
Windows (left) and Mac OS (right)

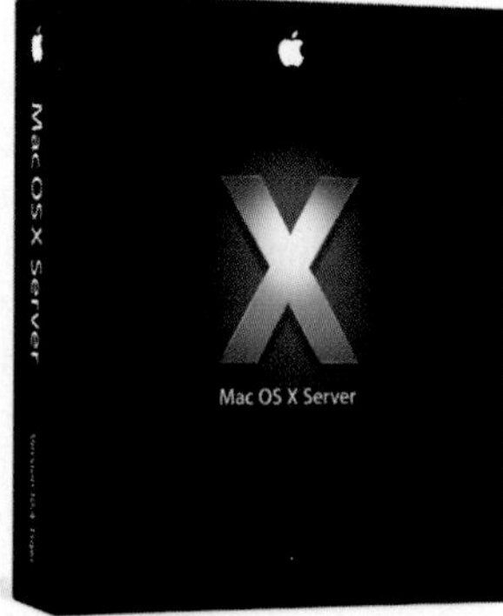

SERVER VERSIONS
Windows (left) and Mac OS (right)

FIGURE 5-11
Many operating systems have both a personal version and a server version.

2. NetWare provides a shell around your desktop operating system. The shell program enables you to communicate with NetWare, which is located on a network computer called a file server.

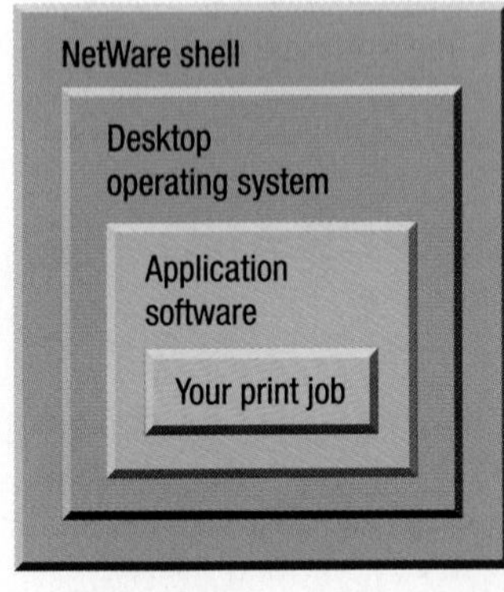

3. When you request a network activity, such as printing a document using a network printer, your application program passes the job to your desktop operating system, which sends it to the netWare shell, which sends it on to NetWare, Which is located on the network server.

Network file server running NetWare server software

4. NetWare then sends your job to a computer known as a print server, which lines up your job in its print queue and prints the job when its turn comes.

Your print job

Network print server

Your print job

Desktop PC running Windows and NetWare client software

4. Your print job
3. Job C
2. Job B
1. Job A
Print queue

1. When you log on to the network, you gain access to network resources, such as application programs, shared data files, and printers. Once logged on, you can access files, print, and more.

Network printer

FIGURE 5-12
How a server operating system works. This example uses NetWare; other server operating systems work in a similar manner.

this supplied data, and then grants you access to the network resources you are authorized to access, such as launching programs or opening documents stored on the network server, or printing a document on a shared printer. Network resources (such as a shared network hard drive or printer) generally look like local (non-network) resources. For instance, a network hard drive would be listed with its own identifying letter (such as F or G) along with the drives included on your PC, and a network printer would be included on your list of available printers whenever you open a Print dialog box, provided you are connected to and logged on to the network. If you do not log on to the network or if the network is down, you cannot access network resources, such as to launch a program located on the network server, save a document to a network hard drive, or print using a shared printer. However, the personal operating system installed on your PC will allow you to work locally on that computer, just as you would on a stand-alone PC.

An overview of a typical NetWare scenario is illustrated in Figure 5-12; many other server operating systems work in a manner similar to this example. In addition to personal operating systems and server operating systems, there are also *mobile operating systems* and *embedded operating systems*. These operating systems are usually based on a personal operating system and are installed on consumer kiosks, cars, cash registers, cell phones, handheld PCs, and other non-PC-based devices.

The Types of Processors Supported

Most operating systems today are designed to be used with specific types of processors, such as Intel and AMD desktop CPUs, or Intel's Itanium processor. In addition, most operating systems today are designed for either 32-bit or 64-bit CPUs. As discussed in Chapter 2, typical desktop PC microprocessors are 32-bit processors, but the use of 64-bit processors is growing. Because their word size is twice as large, 64-bit processors can process up to twice as much data per clock cycle as a 32-bit processor (depending on the extent to which the application being used supports 64-bit processing), and they can address more than 4 GB of RAM. Both of these factors help to speed up processing in some applications, if a 64-bit operating system is being used. Operating systems that support 64-bit CPUs often include other architectural improvements that together may result in a more efficient operating system and, consequently, faster operations. At least some versions of Windows, Mac OS, Linux, and other widely used operating systems are 64-bit operating systems. Details about these and other operating systems are discussed next.

OPERATING SYSTEMS FOR DESKTOP PCS AND SERVERS

As previously discussed, operating systems today are usually designed either for desktop PCs or network servers and many operating systems are available in both personal and server versions. The most widely used personal and server operating systems are discussed next.

DOS

During the 1980s and early 1990s, **DOS (Disk Operating System)** was the dominant operating system for microcomputers. DOS traditionally used a command line interface, although newer versions of DOS support a menu-driven interface. A sampling of DOS commands is provided in Figure 5-13.

There were two primary forms of DOS: *PC-DOS* and *MS-DOS*. Both were originally developed by Microsoft Corporation, but PC-DOS was created originally for IBM microcomputers (and is now owned by IBM), whereas MS-DOS was used with IBM-compatible PCs. Neither version is updated any longer, but an alternative version of DOS originally created by Digital Research and called *DR-DOS* is still available and being marketed for use with thin clients and devices that use embedded operating systems. DOS, in any of its forms, is not widely used with personal computers today because it does not utilize a graphical user interface and does not support modern processors and processing techniques.

Windows

There have been many different versions of the Microsoft **Windows** operating system over the last several years. The next few sections chronicle the main developments of the Windows operating system.

Windows 1.0 through Windows 2000

Microsoft created the original version of Windows—*Windows 1.0*—in 1985 in an effort to meet the needs of users frustrated by having to learn and use DOS commands. Windows 1.0 through *Windows 3.x* (*x* stands for the version number of the software, such as Windows 3.0, 3.1, or 3.11) were not, however, full-fledged operating systems. Instead, they were *operating environments* for the DOS operating system; that is, graphical shells that operated around the DOS operating system designed to make DOS easier to use. Windows 3.0 was the first widely used version of Windows and allowed DOS to address more than 1 MB of RAM, perform multitasking, and run several built-in utility applications—such as a card file, calendar, and paint program. Still, the shortcomings of DOS limited the effectiveness of Windows 3.x.

>**DOS (Disk Operating System).** The operating system designed for and widely used on early IBM and IBM-compatible PCs. >**Windows.** The primary PC operating system developed by Microsoft Corporation; the most recent version is Windows XP.

```
C:\WINDOWS>cd..

C:\>cd mydocu~1

C:\My Documents>dir

 Volume in drive C has no label
 Volume Serial Number is 1338-14DC
 Directory of C:\My Documents

.              <DIR>        07-19-01  1:34p .
..             <DIR>        07-19-01  1:34p ..
MYPICT~1       <DIR>        07-19-01  1:38p My Pictures
MYWEBS~1       <DIR>        07-26-01  8:59p My Webs
FAXTEM~1 DOC        20,480  08-21-01  7:37a Fax template.doc
COMPAN~1 JPG        12,009  08-27-01  6:46a Company logo.jpg
DIGITA~1 BMP        90,038  03-01-01 12:11p Digital signature Morley.bmp
MYMUSI~1       <DIR>        10-11-01  7:57a My Music
MYEBOO~1       <DIR>        10-24-01  1:46p My eBooks
HOMEWORK       <DIR>        10-24-01  3:54p Homework
         3 file(s)         122,527 bytes
         7 dir(s)       33,944.47 MB free

C:\My Documents>
```

COMMAND	DESCRIPTION	EXAMPLE	EXPLANATION
COPY	Copies individual files	**COPY BOSS A:WORKER**	Makes a copy of the file BOSS located in the current directory on the current disk and stores it on the disk in the A drive using the filename WORKER.
DIR	Displays the names of files on a disk	**DIR A:**	Displays names of files stored on the disk in the A drive.
DEL	Deletes individual files	**DEL A:DOLLAR**	Deletes the file DOLLAR from the disk in the A drive.
REN	Renames individual files	**REN SAM BILL**	Changes the name of the file SAM located in the current directory on the current disk to BILL.
CD	Changes to a new directory	**CD HOMEWORK**	Changes the current directory to HOMEWORK, located one level down from the current location on the current disk.
FORMAT	Prepares a disk for use, erasing what was there before	**FORMAT A:**	Formats the disk in the A drive.

FIGURE 5-13

DOS. Even though DOS has become technologically obsolete, some PCs still use it. This table lists some of the most commonly used DOS commands, and the screen shows DOS in action.

SW

In 1994, Microsoft announced that all versions of Windows after 3.11 would be full-fledged operating systems instead of just operating environments. The next several versions of Windows are listed next:

- *Windows 95* (released in1995) and *Windows 98* (released in 1998)—both used a similar GUI to the one used with Windows 3.x, but they were easier to use, and supported multitasking, long filenames, a higher degree of Internet integration, more options for customizing the desktop user interface, improved support for large hard drives, and support for both DVD and USB devices.
- *Windows 98 Second Edition* (*SE*)—an update to Windows 98 released in 1999. Although Windows 98 is no longer sold, there is still an installed base of older PCs running Windows 98 SE.
- *Windows NT* (*New Technology*)—the first 32-bit version of Windows designed for high-end workstations and servers. Windows NT was built from the ground up using a different basic code base or kernel than the other versions of Windows.

TIP

When a new version of a program that you use (such as an operating system or application program) becomes available, you can typically buy an *upgrade* version of that program that installs over your existing version, if you want to move to the new version. Upgrades are almost always less expensive than buying a new full version.

- *Windows Me (Millennium Edition)*—the replacement for Windows 98 and Windows 98 SE. Designed for home PCs, Windows Me supported improved home networking and a shared Internet connection; it also featured improved multimedia capabilities, better system protection, a faster boot process, and more Internet-ready activities and games. Windows Me was the last version of Windows that used the original Windows 95 kernel.
- *Windows 2000*—released in 2000 to replace Windows NT for workstation use. Windows 2000 was geared towards high-end business workstations and servers and included support for wireless devices and other types of new hardware.

These earlier versions of Windows have all been replaced by *Windows XP* (a personal operating system) and *Windows Server 2003* (a server operating system). Versions of *Windows Vista*, when available, will replace both Windows XP and Windows Server 2003. These three versions of Windows are discussed next.

Windows XP

Windows XP is the latest personal version of Windows and replaces both Windows 2000 (for business use) and Windows Me (for home use). It is based on Windows NT technology and is more stable and powerful than earlier versions of Windows built on the Windows 9x kernel. Windows XP has a slightly different appearance than earlier versions of Windows (see Figure 5-14), but the basic elements (Start menu, taskbar, menu bars, and so forth) are still present. In addition, users have the option of using the classic Windows interface—the one used in Windows 2000, Me, and 98—instead of the new interface, if they prefer. Some of the newest features of Windows XP are related to multimedia and communications, such as improved photo, video, and music editing and sharing; the ability to switch between user accounts without closing open windows; the ability to access a PC remotely via a network; improved networking capabilities; and support for handwriting and voice input.

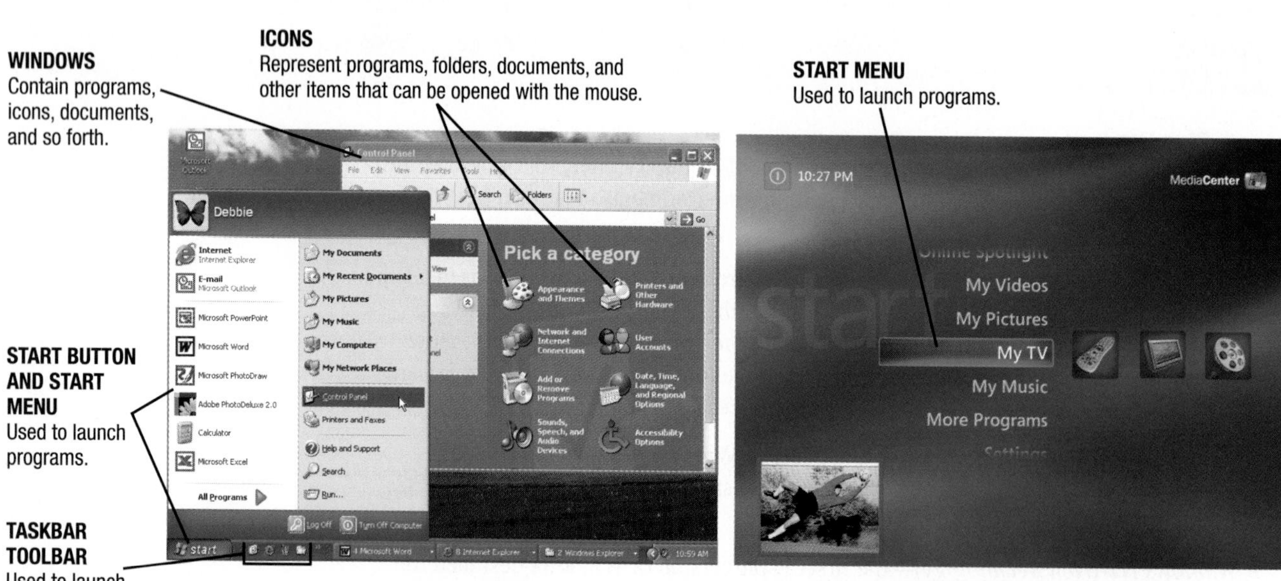
WINDOWS
Contain programs, icons, documents, and so forth.
ICONS
Represent programs, folders, documents, and other items that can be opened with the mouse.
START MENU
Used to launch programs.
START BUTTON AND START MENU
Used to launch programs.
TASKBAR TOOLBAR
Used to launch programs.
WINDOWS XP PROFESSIONAL
WINDOWS XP MEDIA CENTER EDITION
Control Panel
Pick a category
Debbie
10:27 PM
My Videos
My Pictures
My TV
My Music
More Programs

FIGURE 5-14
Windows XP. Most versions of Windows XP look like the Professional edition (left); Windows XP Media Center (right), however, has a different appearance.

>**Windows XP.** The latest personal version of Windows; designed to replace both Windows Me and Windows 2000.

Windows XP is available in the five different versions listed next. All of the versions except *Windows XP Media Center Edition* use a similar interface (refer again to Figure 5-14). In addition, there are special versions of Windows XP Home Edition that contain fewer features and are designed for first-time home users with lower-end PCs in a variety of countries other than the United States. One of these *Windows XP Starter Editions* is shown in Figure 5-15.

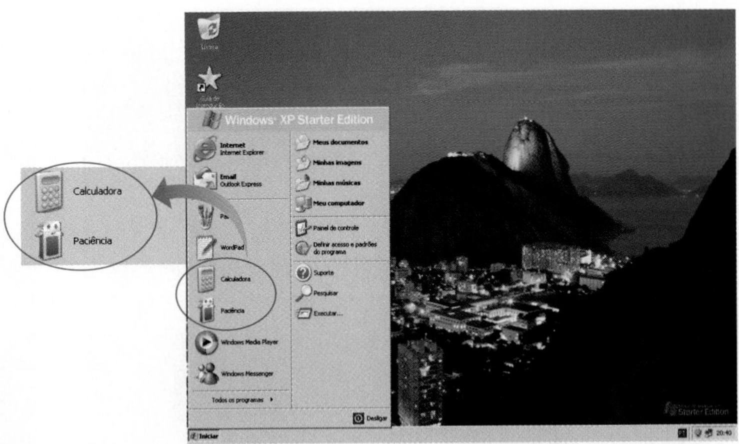

FIGURE 5-15
Windows XP Starter Editions. There are Windows XP Starter Editions for a variety of countries, such as the Brazilian version shown here.

- *Windows XP Home Edition*—designed for home PCs. Includes improvements for working with digital photographs, playing digital music, making home movies, and communicating with others.
- *Windows XP Professional*—designed for business users and advanced home computing. In addition to the features included in the Home Edition, Windows XP Professional has additional security and privacy features, improved ability to connect to large networks, and the ability to remotely access one PC from another.
- *Windows XP Professional x64 Edition*—designed specifically for high-end business PCs using 64-bit CPUs and users who require large amounts of memory and processing speed, such as for movie special effects, 3D, animation, engineering, and scientific applications.
- *Windows XP Tablet PC Edition*—designed for use with tablet PCs and includes extended pen and speech input capabilities, as well as improved wireless connectivity. This version of Windows is only available already installed on a tablet PC.
- *Windows XP Media Center Edition*—designed for living room PCs and other PCs designated as Windows Media Center PCs. Combines computing, television, and multimedia capabilities; incorporates additional features for watching live TV, recording TV shows, watching DVDs, and managing music, video, and photo collections on a PC or TV display. This version of Windows is only available already installed on a Windows Media Center PC.

Windows Server 2003

Windows Server 2003 is the most recent version of Windows designed for server use. It builds on the server version of Windows 2000 but is designed to be easier to deploy, manage, and use. It also incorporates Microsoft *.NET* technology for connecting information, people, systems, and devices. Windows Server 2003 comes in four versions: *Standard Edition* for small to medium networks with standard workloads; *Enterprise Edition* for larger, more mission-critical servers; *Datacenter Edition* for high-level servers requiring the highest levels of scalability and reliability; and *Web Edition* for dedicated Web servers. In 2005, Microsoft released 64-bit *x64* versions of the Standard, Enterprise, and Datacenter editions.

>**Windows Server 2003.** The most recent version of Windows designed for server use.

FIGURE 5-16
Windows Vista. The beta version shown here reveals some slight differences in appearance from Windows XP, but the core functionality seems to remain the same.

Windows Vista

The next major release of Windows is **Windows Vista** (previously code-named *Longhorn*). Beta testing of Windows Vista began in 2005, and both a personal and server version of the new Windows is expected to be available by 2007. Previews of Windows Vista reveal a new graphical interface that has the core functionality of the Windows XP interface but a slightly different appearance (see Figure 5-16). Windows Vista is expected to include more visual features and to have intuitive file management capabilities that allow documents to be created or organized based on characteristics, such as author, subject, keyword, category, artist, song title, and so forth. Beta versions of Vista also include improved search capabilities and better support for peer-to-peer searches and file sharing. In addition, Vista is expected to directly support DVD burning, and Microsoft has announced that it will be more secure, easier to manage and update, and it will support advanced document technologies, such as *XML* (*extensible markup language*). XML is discussed in more detail in Chapter 10.

Mac OS

Mac OS is the proprietary operating system for computers made by Apple Corporation. It is based on the UNIX operating system (discussed shortly) and originally set the standard for graphical user interfaces. Many of today's operating systems follow the trend that Mac OS started and, in fact, use interfaces that highly resemble the one used with Mac OS.

There have been a number of different versions of Mac OS since the original Apple Macintosh computer debuted in 1984. The latest personal and server versions of the operating system are version 10.4 of **Mac OS X**, also known as *Tiger*. Like earlier versions of Mac OS X, Tiger (see Figure 5-17) allows multithreading and multitasking; it also supports dual 64-bit processors and a high level of multimedia functions and connectivity. New features include a new search feature, called *Spotlight*, which allows users to search through documents, folders, e-mail messages, and programs based on a variety of criteria, and then continues to update those searches and add related files as the user works. A new *Dashboard* feature hosts a variety of mini applications called *widgets* that can be used to receive timely information from the Internet, such as stock quotes, weather forecasts, flight updates, phone numbers, and more. Tiger also supports handwritten and voice input.

>**Windows Vista.** The upcoming version of Windows (previously known as Longhorn) that is designed to replace Windows XP. >**Mac OS X.** The most recent version of the operating system used on Apple computers.

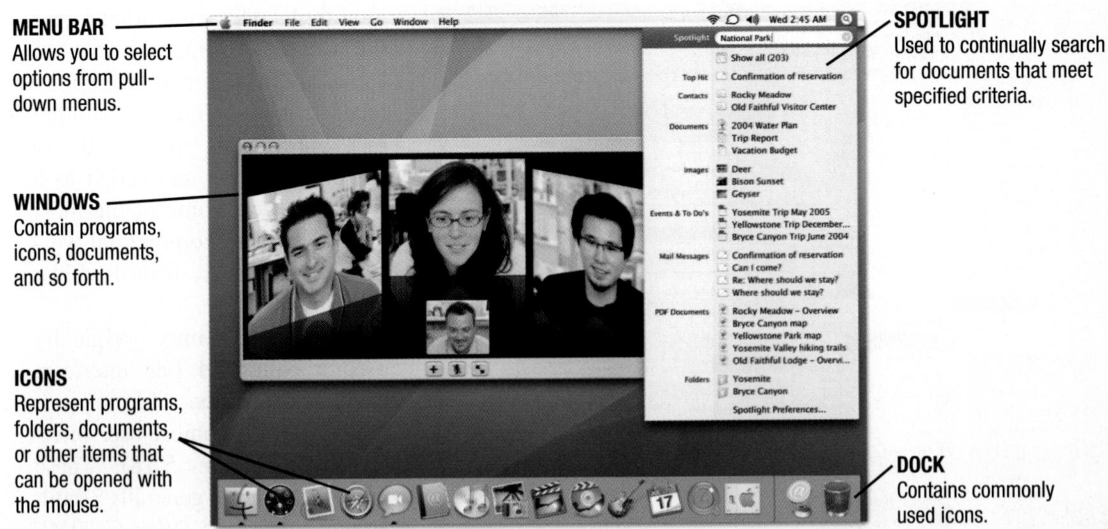

MENU BAR
Allows you to select options from pull-down menus.
WINDOWS
Contain programs, icons, documents, and so forth.
ICONS
Represent programs, folders, documents, or other items that can be opened with the mouse.
SPOTLIGHT
Used to continually search for documents that meet specified criteria.
DOCK
Contains commonly used icons.

FIGURE 5-17
Mac OS X Tiger.

UNIX

UNIX was originally developed in the late 1960s at AT&T Bell Laboratories as an operating system for midrange servers. UNIX is a multiuser, multitasking operating system. Computer systems ranging from microcomputers to mainframes can run UNIX, and it can support a variety of devices from different manufacturers. This flexibility gives UNIX an advantage over competing operating systems for many types of applications. However, UNIX is more expensive, requires a higher level of PC knowledge, and tends to be harder to install, maintain, and upgrade than most other commonly used operating systems.

There are many versions of UNIX available and many operating systems based on UNIX. These operating systems—such as Mac OS and Linux—are sometimes referred to as *UNIX flavors*. In fact, the term "UNIX," which initially referred to the original UNIX operating system, has evolved to refer today to a group of similar operating systems based on UNIX. Many UNIX flavors are not compatible with each other, which creates some problems when a program written for one UNIX computer system is moved to another computer system running a different flavor of UNIX. A new universal UNIX specification is expected to be used with upcoming versions of UNIX-based operating systems to alleviate this incompatibility problem. In fact the *Open Group* open source consortium is a working group dedicated to the development and evolution of the *Single UNIX Specification*—a standardized programming environment for UNIX applications. Both personal and server versions of UNIX-based operating systems are available.

Linux

Linux is a flavor of UNIX originally developed by Linus Torvalds in 1991 when he was a student at the University of Helsinki in Finland. The operating system was released to the public as *open source software*; that is, a program whose *source code* is available to the public and can be modified to improve it or to customize it to a particular application. Over the years, Linux has obtained a loyal band of followers, and volunteer programmers from all over the world have collaborated to improve it, sharing their

>**UNIX.** An operating system developed in the 1970s for midrange servers and mainframes; many variations of this operating system are in use today. >**Linux.** A version (flavor) of UNIX that is available without charge over the Internet and is increasingly being used with PCs, servers, mainframes, and supercomputers.

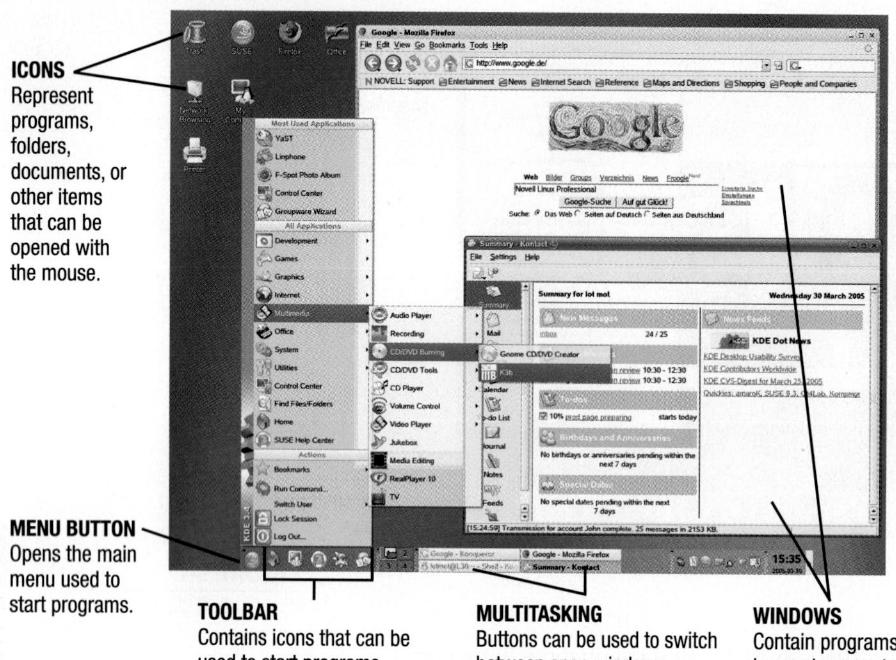

ICONS
Represent programs, folders, documents, or other items that can be opened with the mouse.
MENU BUTTON
Opens the main menu used to start programs.
TOOLBAR
Contains icons that can be used to start programs.
MULTITASKING
Buttons can be used to switch between open windows.
WINDOWS
Contain programs, icons, documents, and so forth.

FIGURE 5-18

Linux. Linux is a rapidly growing alternative to Windows and Mac OS that is available free of charge over the Internet. Purchased versions are also available, such as the one shown here.

modified code with others over the Internet. Some versions of Linux are available as free downloads from the Internet; companies are also permitted to customize Linux and sell it as a retail product. Some of the most widely known commercial versions of Linux are from Red Hat and Novell.

Although Linux originally used a command line interface, most recent versions of Linux programs use a graphical user interface (see Figure 5-18). These interfaces are generally built around either the *KDE* or *GNOME* desktop environments, products of the KDE Internet project and the GNOME project and foundation, respectively. Both organizations are committed to developing free, easy-to-use desktop environments and powerful application frameworks for Linux and other operating systems based on UNIX. Purchased Linux operating systems usually come with more support materials than the versions downloaded for free. Linux is available in personal, professional, and server versions.

In the past few years, Linux has grown from an operating system used primarily by computer techies who disliked Microsoft to a widely accepted operating system with strong support from mainstream companies, such as Sun, IBM, HP, and Novell. For instance, many large companies, including Charles Schwab & Co, use Linux to run their data centers; the city of Munich, Germany, has switched to Linux; and several large cities in Brazil are running only Linux software. The primary reason companies are switching to Linux and other open source software is cost. Typically, using the Linux operating system and a free or low-cost office suite, Web browser program, and e-mail program can enable a business to work competitively while at the same time saving several hundreds of dollars per computer user. For instance, Microsoft Windows XP Professional Edition retails for $299 while Linux can be downloaded for free or a retail version purchased for around $50, and the standard edition of Microsoft Office 2003 retails for $400 while the similar *OpenOffice.org* office suite is free and Sun's *StarOffice 7* costs $80. Although most of these programs do not incorporate as many features as Microsoft Office, many users find them adequate for their needs, and the cost savings can be significant. Another reason some companies are moving to Linux is dissatisfaction with Microsoft products, the need for only a limited number of employee applications (such as retail store computers that are set up to do a limited number of tasks), as well as companies employing programmers, engineers, and other technical workers who are already familiar with Linux or UNIX. Many Linux supporters maintain that personal computers running Linux crash less often, are more secure and less prone to viruses and other security hazards, and are easier to run on older equipment. In addition to the growing use on servers and desktop PCs, it has been suggested that the next biggest growth area for the Linux operating system might be in lower-end personal computers, Internet appliances, and point-of-sale terminals.

NetWare

NetWare—developed by Novell during the mid-1980s—is one of the most widely used operating systems today for networks and competes directly with the server versions of Windows and Mac OS. As discussed earlier and illustrated in Figure 5-12, NetWare provides a shell around your personal desktop operating system through which you can interact with network resources, such as a shared hard drive or printer. The latest version of NetWare is *NetWare 6.5*. NetWare is also incorporated in Novell's new Open Enterprise Server product that combines NetWare and Novell's server version of Linux (*SUSE Linux Enterprise Server*) into a single suite to allow businesses to use NetWare, Linux, or a combination of both technologies.

FURTHER EXPLORATION

For links to further information about operating systems, go to www.course.com/uc11/ch05

Solaris

Solaris is a UNIX-based operating system developed by Sun Microsystems for Sun computers. The Solaris operating system can run on desktop systems and servers, as well as on some supercomputers. There is also a Solaris operating environment that can be used to bring enhanced stability and functionality to UNIX machines. The latest version of Solaris—*Solaris 10*—is designed to run across a variety of platforms in a safe, efficient, and stable manner. Some new features include diagnostic tools to detect and fix bottlenecks and errors before they cause a failure and a new *container* system that allows a server to be partitioned into as many as 8,000 secure partitions. In 2005, Sun released some of the Solaris code to create a new open source project called *OpenSolaris*.

OPERATING SYSTEMS FOR HANDHELD PCS AND MOBILE DEVICES

Handheld PCs, as well as smart phones, pagers, and other mobile devices, usually require a different operating system than a desktop PC. Typically, the operating system used is one designed for mobile devices in general or is a proprietary operating system designed solely for that specific device. In many mobile devices, the operating system is embedded into the device using flash RAM chips or similar hardware. Operating systems are also embedded into everyday objects, such as home appliances, game boxes, digital cameras, toys, watches, navigation systems, home medical devices, voting terminals, portable media players, and cars. The most widely used operating systems for handheld PCs and mobile devices are discussed next.

Embedded and Mobile Versions of Windows

There are both embedded and mobile versions of Windows targeted for handheld PCs, smart phones, and other mobile devices, called *Windows Embedded* and *Windows Mobile*, respectively.

Windows Embedded

Windows Embedded is a family of operating systems based on Windows that is designed primarily for nonpersonal computer-based devices, such as cash registers, ATM machines, thin clients, and consumer electronic devices. The Windows Embedded family includes *Windows CE 5.0* (designed for devices requiring multimedia capabilities, such as DVD

>**NetWare.** A widely used operating system for PC-based networks. >**Windows Embedded.** A family of operating systems based on Windows and designed for nonpersonal computer devices, such as cash registers and consumer electronic devices.

TECHNOLOGY AND YOU

Smart Cars

Computers have been integrated into cars for years to perform tasks such as regulating fuel consumption, controlling emissions, assisting with gear shifting and braking, and more. Lately, however, the use of computers in cars has skyrocketed. It is estimated that over 20% of the components in today's cars are electronic, and that figure is expected to reach 40% in the near future. Essentially, cars are getting smart and these new digital improvements help to make cars smarter and safer. Some features, such as GPS navigation systems and smart air bag systems that adjust the deployment of an air bag based on the weight of the occupant, are fairly standard today. Some new and emerging trends in smart cars include the following:

- Volvo has developed a *blind spot information system (BLIS)* that uses a digital camera mounted on the driver's side mirror to detect vehicles in the driver's blind spot (see the accompanying photo). The camera takes 25 photos per second and an onboard computer analyzes the photos to determine when there is a moving car or motorcycle in the blind spot—a yellow warning light near the mirror tells the driver that something is in the blind spot. This feature is available as an option on 2006 models.
- Select Audi models now have the option of a *keyless entry and ignition system*, in which the user's fingerprint is used to unlock and start the car.
- Ford, BMW, and Mercedes are all working to develop *adaptive cruise control systems*. These systems, available now on select Mercedes models, use a radar system installed on the front of the car to detect the speed and distance of the vehicle ahead of it, and then automatically decrease or increase the speed of the car up to the driver's selected cruise control speed to maintain a safe distance from the vehicle ahead of it.
- IBM has developed a *voice recognition system* that uses both video and audio input to understand more accurately the driver's voice commands. In tests, the dual-input system improved performance by 80%.
- In addition to being used to lock, unlock, arm, and disarm the car, the remote for Dodge Viper's new security system is a *two-way remote* that blinks and chimes to notify the owner whenever the car's alarm system goes off.

One of the biggest challenges for smart car technologies is the safe use of all the smart gadgets being incorporated into cars. The concern stems from studies consistently showing that distracted drivers are the cause of the vast majority of crashes—nearly 80%, according to a 2005 study. Voice controlled digital dashboards, cell phones, and other devices help because they are hands-free, although studies have found that your risk of an accident requiring a trip to the hospital quadruples when you are talking on a cell phone—hands-free or not.

1. A digital camera takes 25 photos per second to identify moving vehicles in the driver's blind spot.
2. A light indicates that a moving vehicle is in the driver's blind spot.

Volvo's BLIS system. This system notifies the driver when a moving vehicle is in the driver's blind spot.

players, digital cameras, and other consumer electronic devices) and *Windows XP Embedded* (a more powerful operating system used with retail point-of-sale terminals, thin clients, and advanced gaming boxes). There is also a version of Windows CE called *Windows Automotive*, which is an embedded operating system used in cars. For a look at some of the features now available in *smart cars*, see the Technology and You box.

Windows Mobile

Windows Mobile is the version of Windows designed for handheld PCs, smart phones, and portable media players. Windows Mobile has some of the look and feel of the larger desktop versions of Windows (see Figure 5-19) and can be used with *pocket* versions of a number of Microsoft desktop computer software products, such as Word, Excel, Outlook, Messenger, Internet Explorer, and more. The most recent version is *Windows Mobile 5.0*.

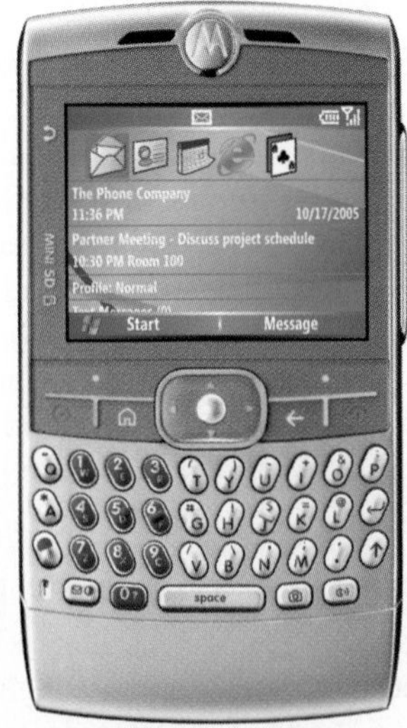

HANDHELD PC

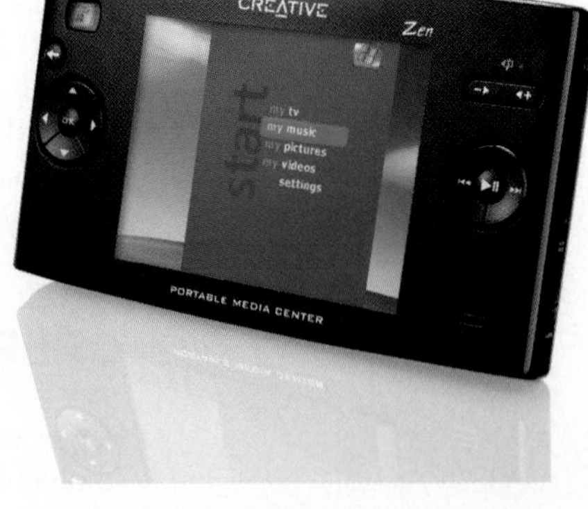

PORTABLE MEDIA PLAYER

FIGURE 5-19
Windows Mobile. Mobile versions of Windows resemble desktop versions of Windows, but on a smaller scale.

Palm OS

Palm OS is the operating system designed for Palm handheld devices (see Figure 5-20). The philosophy behind Palm OS was to design an operating system specifically for mobile devices, instead of trying to convert an entire desktop operating system into a smaller package. Consequently, Palm OS was designed to use memory and battery power very efficiently. Palm OS is developed by PalmSource, a subsidiary of Palm, Inc., and the latest version is *Palm OS Cobalt 6.1*. In addition to being used on Palm handheld PCs, Palm OS has been increasingly used by other manufacturers of handheld PCs, smart phones, and mobile devices.

Embedded Linux

Embedded Linux is another alternative for use with handheld PCs and mobile devices. In addition to existing versions of embedded Linux, Palm announced in 2005 the intent to develop a version of the Palm OS based on a version of embedded Linux. A Wi-Fi Internet tablet using embedded Linux is shown in Figure 5-20. This product, from Nokia, connects to the Internet via a Wi-Fi network or a Bluetooth-compatible mobile phone. Other embedded Linux products include the TiVo DVR and the TouchTunes touch screen digital jukeboxes.

FIGURE 5-20
Palm OS, embedded Linux, and Symbian OS.

A HANDHELD PC RUNNING PALM OS

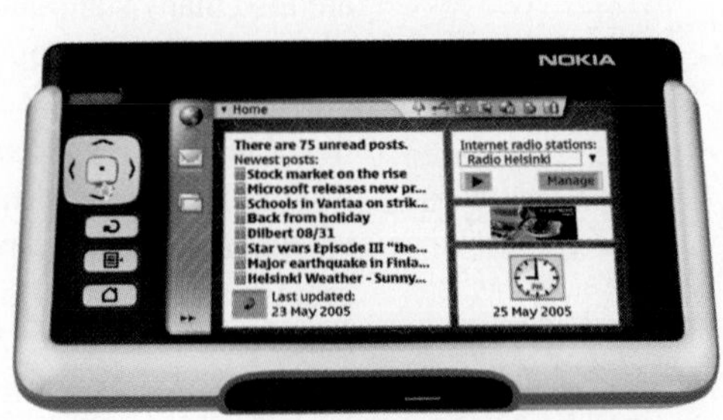

A WI-FI INTERNET TABLET RUNNING EMBEDDED LINUX

A SMART PHONE RUNNING SYMBIAN OS

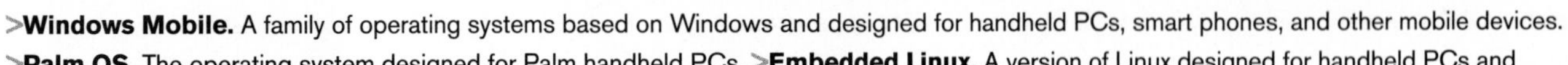

>**Windows Mobile.** A family of operating systems based on Windows and designed for handheld PCs, smart phones, and other mobile devices. >**Palm OS.** The operating system designed for Palm handheld PCs. >**Embedded Linux.** A version of Linux designed for handheld PCs and mobile devices.

Symbian OS

Symbian OS is one of the leading operating systems for smart phones, and it is based on the *EPOC* operating system developed by the UK technology company Psion. Symbian OS was initially released in 1998 by the private company Symbian, which was established by Psion and several wireless industry leaders, including Nokia, Ericsson, and Motorola. Symbian OS is an advanced, multithreaded, multitasking operating system that includes support for Web browsing, e-mail, handwriting recognition, synchronization, and a range of other applications designed for mobile communications and computing. Symbian OS has a flexible user interface framework that enables mobile phone manufacturers to develop and customize user interfaces to meet the needs of their customers. A smart phone using Symbian OS Version 7.0 and one possible user interface is shown in Figure 5-20.

OPERATING SYSTEMS FOR LARGER COMPUTERS

Larger computer systems—such as high-end servers, mainframes, and supercomputers—sometimes use operating systems designed solely for that type of system. For instance, IBM's *z/OS*, *OS/390*, and *MVS* operating systems are designed for their various mainframes, and many larger Sun computers are powered by the Solaris operating system. Conventional operating systems, such as Windows, UNIX, and Linux, are also used with both mainframes and supercomputers. Linux is increasingly being used with both mainframes and supercomputers; often a group of Linux PCs are linked together to form what is referred to as a *Linux supercluster* supercomputer. For example, the world's fastest supercomputer—Blue Gene/L (shown in Figure 1-21 in Chapter 1)—runs Linux. Larger computer systems may also use a customized operating system based on a conventional operating system; for instance, many IBM mainframes use *AIX*, a version of UNIX developed by IBM.

UTILITY PROGRAMS

A **utility program** is a type of software program that performs a specific task, usually related to managing or maintaining the computer system. Many utility programs—such as programs for finding files, diagnosing and repairing system problems, cleaning up a hard drive, viewing images, playing multimedia files, and backing up files—are built into operating systems. There are also many stand-alone utility programs available as an alternative to the operating system's utility programs (such as a *search tool* or *backup program* containing additional features) or to provide additional utility features not usually built into operating systems (such as an *antivirus* or *file compression* program). Stand-alone utility programs are often available in a *suite* of related programs (such as a collection of security programs or maintenance programs, as shown in Figure 5-21). Some of the most commonly used integrated and stand-alone utility programs are discussed next. For a look at how to download and install a new utility program from the Internet, see the How it Works box.

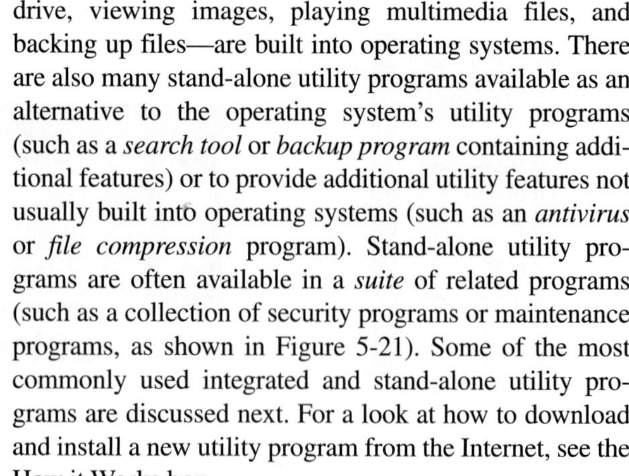

Includes:
Norton AntiVirus™
Norton Utilities™
Norton GoBack™
CheckIt® Diagnostics

FIGURE 5-21
Utility suites. Utility suites contain a number of related utility programs.

>**Symbian OS.** A leading operating system for smart phones. >**Utility program.** A type of software that performs a specific task, usually related to managing or maintaining the computer system.

HOW IT WORKS

Downloading and Installing Programs

Many software programs are available to download via the Web. To download a program, generally a hyperlink is clicked and then the file is downloaded to your PC in the location that you specified. To start the installation process for a downloaded file, locate the file on your hard drive and open it. With some installations, you can specify the location in which the program will be installed on your PC. Many installations require that you accept the terms of a license agreement before the program will be installed; if the product was purchased, some also require you to type in the *registration code* that was provided after your payment was processed. Once the installation process has been completed, the program can be launched. This procedure is illustrated in the accompanying illustration.

DOWNLOADING THE PROGRAM

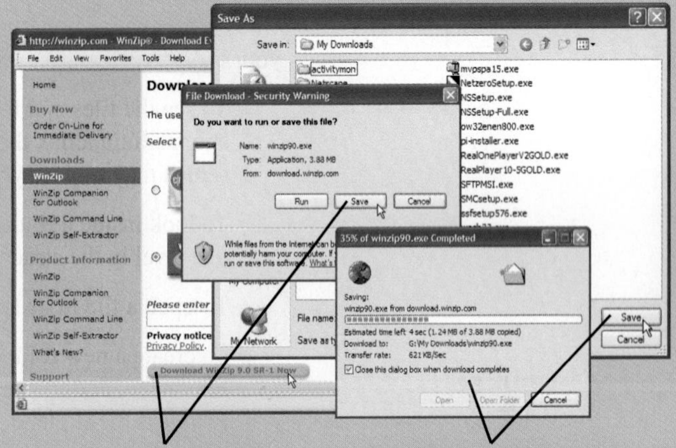

1. Click the download link, then click Save to download the program.
2. Specify the download location, then click Save to download the installation file.

INSTALLING THE PROGRAM

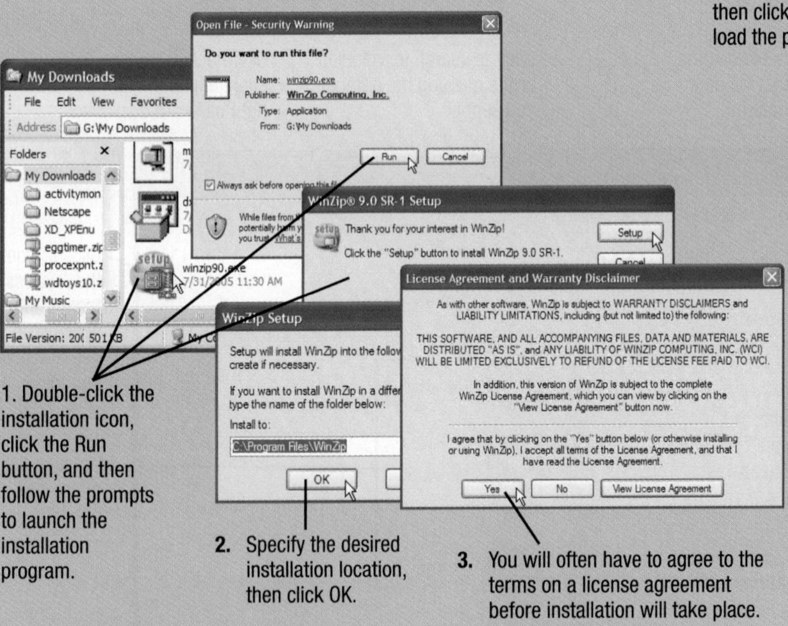

1. Double-click the installation icon, click the Run button, and then follow the prompts to launch the installation program.
2. Specify the desired installation location, then click OK.
3. You will often have to agree to the terms on a license agreement before installation will take place.

USING THE INSTALLED PROGRAM

Click the program name on the Start menu to launch the installed program

File Management Programs

File management programs allow you to perform such file management tasks as formatting a disk; looking at the contents of a storage medium; and copying, moving, deleting, and renaming folders and files. The primary file management program included with Windows XP is *Windows Explorer*. Common file management tasks using this program are summarized next; since there is generally more than one way to perform each of the following tasks, one commonly used method is described for each task.

Looking at the Contents of a PC

Once a file management program is open, you can look at the files and folders stored on your PC.

- To see the files and folders stored on your floppy disk, hard drive, or any other storage medium, click the appropriate letter or name for that medium (some programs or setups may require you to double-click instead of single-click); see Figure 5-22.
- To look inside a folder, double-click the folder. To close that folder and go back up one level in the structure, click the Up toolbar button.
- To open a file in its associated program, double-click it.
- To create a new folder in the current location, select *New* and then *Folder* from the File menu, and then enter the name for the new folder while the default name *New Folder* is highlighted.

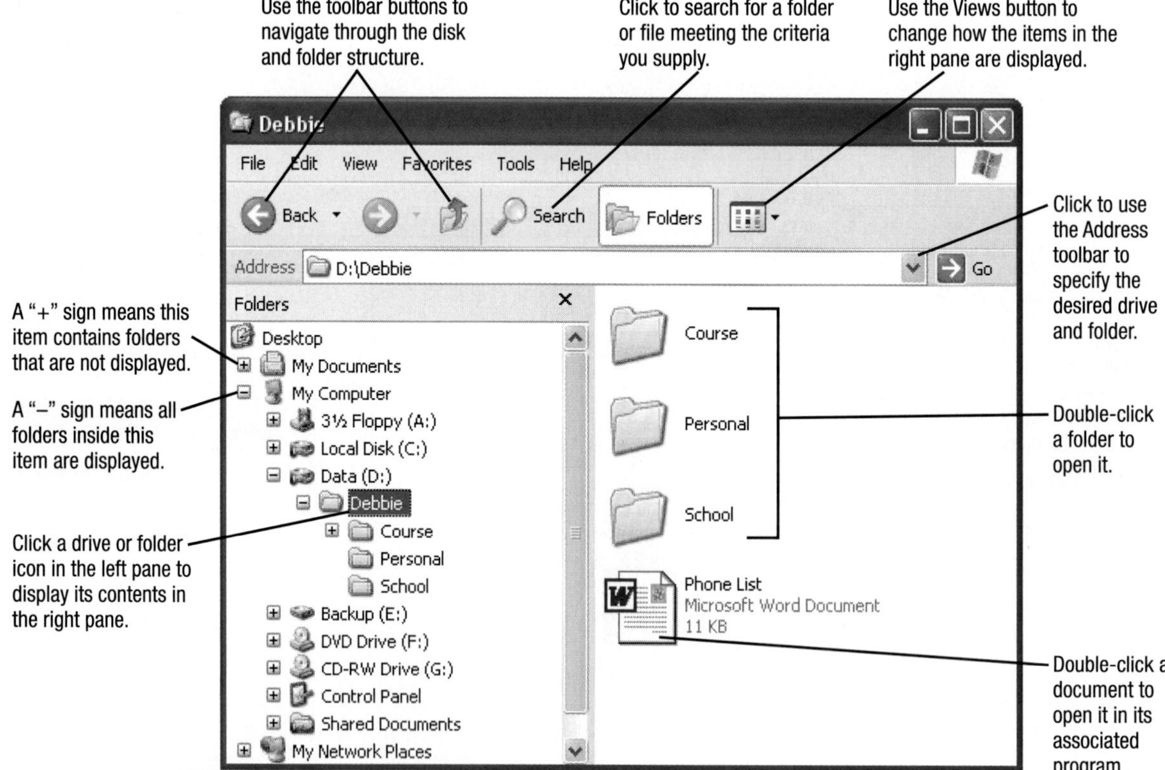
Use the toolbar buttons to navigate through the disk and folder structure.
Click to search for a folder or file meeting the criteria you supply.
Use the Views button to change how the items in the right pane are displayed.
Click to use the Address toolbar to specify the desired drive and folder.
A "+" sign means this item contains folders that are not displayed.
A "–" sign means all folders inside this item are displayed.
Click a drive or folder icon in the left pane to display its contents in the right pane.
Double-click a folder to open it.
Double-click a document to open it in its associated program.
Debbie
File Edit View Favorites Tools Help
Back
Search
Folders
Address D:\Debbie
Go
Folders
Desktop
My Documents
My Computer
3½ Floppy (A:)
Local Disk (C:)
Data (D:)
Debbie
Course
Personal
School
Backup (E:)
DVD Drive (F:)
CD-RW Drive (G:)
Control Panel
Shared Documents
My Network Places
Course
Personal
School
Phone List
Microsoft Word Document
11 KB

FIGURE 5-22
Using Windows Explorer to look at the contents of a PC.

>**File management program.** A utility program that enables the user to perform file management tasks, such as copying and deleting files.

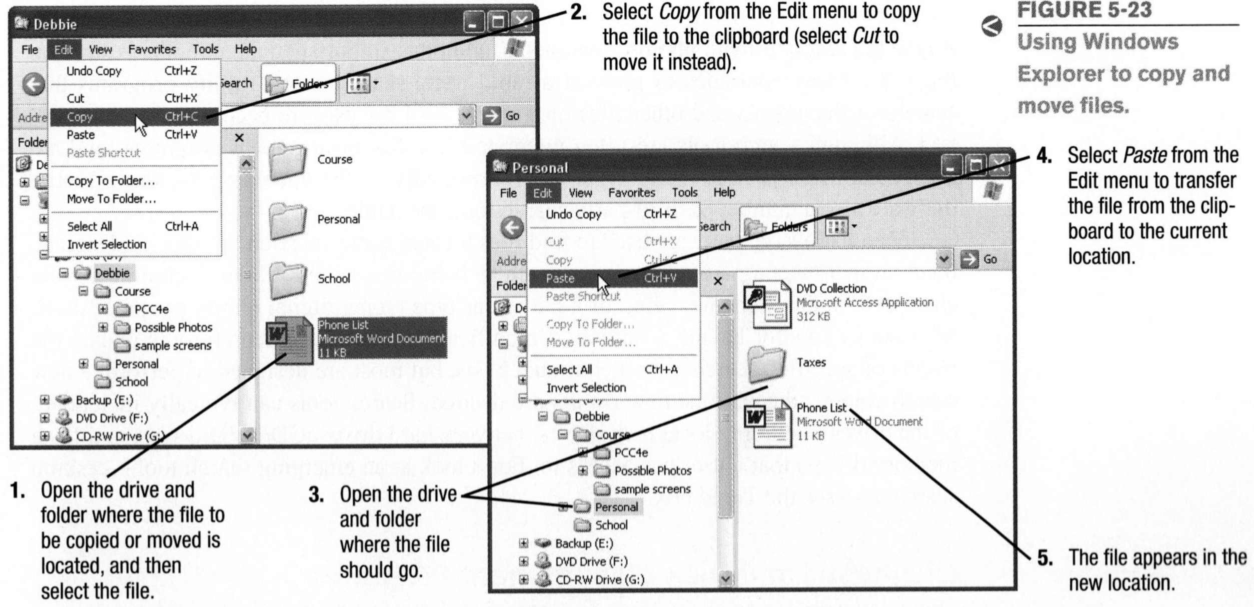

2. Select *Copy* from the Edit menu to copy the file to the clipboard (select *Cut* to move it instead).
4. Select *Paste* from the Edit menu to transfer the file from the clipboard to the current location.
1. Open the drive and folder where the file to be copied or moved is located, and then select the file.
3. Open the drive and folder where the file should go.
5. The file appears in the new location.
Debbie
Personal
Course
School
Phone List
Microsoft Word Document
11 KB
DVD Collection
Microsoft Access Application
312 KB
Taxes

FIGURE 5-23
Using Windows Explorer to copy and move files.

Copying, Moving, and Renaming Files and Folders

You can also copy or move files using a file management program. (To copy or move an entire folder, use the same procedure, but select the folder instead of a file.)

1. Open the drive and folder where the file is located.
2. Select the desired file.
3. Select *Copy* from the Edit menu (see Figure 5-23) to copy the file to a temporary storage area called the *clipboard*. (If you want to move the file instead of copying it, select *Cut* instead of *Copy*).
4. Open the drive and folder where you want the file to go, and then select *Paste* from the Edit menu to transfer the item from the clipboard to the new location.

To change the name of a file or folder:

1. Open the drive and folder where the item to be renamed is located.
2. Select the item you want to rename.
3. Choose *Rename* from the Edit menu, or click a second time on the filename or folder name.
4. When the name is highlighted, either type the new file or folder name or click the highlighted name to display an insertion point, and then edit the name.

Deleting Files and Folders

Files can be deleted using a file management program. (To delete an entire folder, use the same procedure, but select the folder instead of a file.)

1. Open the drive and folder where the item to be deleted is located.
2. Select the item you want to delete, and then press the Delete key on the keyboard.
3. At the Confirm File/Folder Delete dialog box, select *Yes* to delete the file or folder. (Deleting a folder will delete all the files and folders contained within the folder being deleted. To cancel the deletion of a file or folder, select *No* at the Confirm File/Folder Delete dialog box.)

TIP

You can also copy, move, rename, or delete a file or folder in Windows Explorer by right-clicking the item and selecting the desired action.

TIP

To *restore* a file or folder deleted from your PC's hard drive, open your PC's *Recycle Bin* and restore the file to its original location. Files and folders deleted from removable media cannot be restored in this manner, but there are special utility programs available to help you recover deleted files from flash memory cards and drives, as long as you have not written anything to the card or drive since the files were deleted.

SW

Search Tools

As the amount of e-mail, photos, documents, and other important data individuals store on their PCs today continues to grow at a rapid pace, **search tools**—utility programs that search for documents and other files on a user's hard drives—are becoming more important. Although search tools are often integrated into file management programs (and are highly improved in Mac OS X Tiger and, purportedly, in the upcoming Windows Vista), there are also a number of third-party search tools available.

Search tools typically are used to find files located somewhere on the specified storage medium that meet a particular pattern, such as being in a certain folder, including certain characters in the filename, being of a particular type (song, digital photo, or spreadsheet, for instance) and/or having a particular modification date. Some search tools update the results of specified searches on a continual basis, but most are designed to perform a new search command each time new results are desired. Search tools can typically include all of the drives (including local hard drives, network hard drives, CD/DVD drives, and flash memory drives) that a user has access to. For a look at an emerging search tool—desktop searching—see the Trend box.

Diagnostic and Disk Management Programs

Diagnostic programs evaluate your system, looking for problems and making recommendations for fixing any errors that are discovered. *Disk management programs* diagnose and repair programs related to your hard drive. Diagnostic and disk management utilities included in the Windows operating system can perform such tasks as checking the Windows registry for errors, cleaning out extra system files that are no longer needed, checking your hard drive for errors, recovering damaged or erased files, and optimizing your hard drive (by rearranging the data on the hard drive so all files are stored in contiguous locations—called *disk defragmentation*) so it works more efficiently.

File Compression Programs

File compression programs reduce the size of files so they take up less storage space on a storage medium or can be transmitted faster over the Internet. The most common format for user-compressed files in the Windows environment is the *.zip* format, created by file compression programs such as the *WinZip* program shown in Figure 5-24. Mac users typically use *StuffIt* or a similar program instead, although many file compression programs can open files compressed with other programs. A file compression program is required to both compress (*zip*) and decompress (*unzip*) files, unless the zipped file is made *executable*. Executable zipped files have the extension *.exe* and decompress automatically when they are opened, even if the appropriate file compression program is not installed on the recipient's PC. File compression programs can compress either a single file or a group of files into a single compressed file. When multiple files are compressed, they are separated back into individual files when the file is decompressed.

FIGURE 5-24
File compression. File compression can be used with both image and text files, though image files generally compress more efficiently.

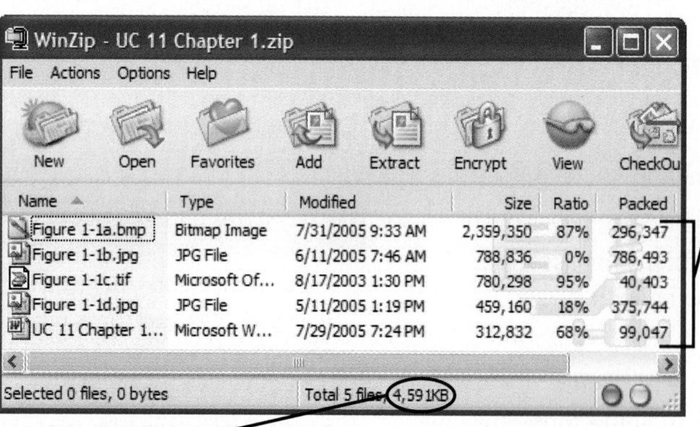

COMPRESSION RATIOS
Certain image file formats (such as *.bmp* and *.tif*) compress more than others (such as *.jpg*, which is already in a compressed format). Text files (such as *.doc*) fall somewhere in between.

FILE SIZE
The 5 files, totalling over 4.5 MB, are zipped into a single 1.6 MB *.zip* file.

>**Search tool.** A utility program designed to search for files on the user's hard drive.

TREND

Desktop Searching

Many Internet search companies—such as Google, Microsoft, Yahoo, AOL, and Ask Jeeves—are developing desktop search tools that apply the technology used in their Internet search tools. For example, the *Google Desktop Search* program (see the accompanying figure) is currently free and searches through files, e-mail and chat messages, cached Web pages, and other content stored on the user's hard drive to find the items that match the user's supplied search terms. Most of these search tools create an index of the content of the PC first, so that searches can be carried out quickly and efficiently. In fact, if you choose to have Google Desktop Search run in the background on a continuous basis, it will update the index anytime PC processing power is available to keep your searches up-to-the-moment current. An enterprise version of Google Desktop Search is also available that extends searching capabilities to the company network.

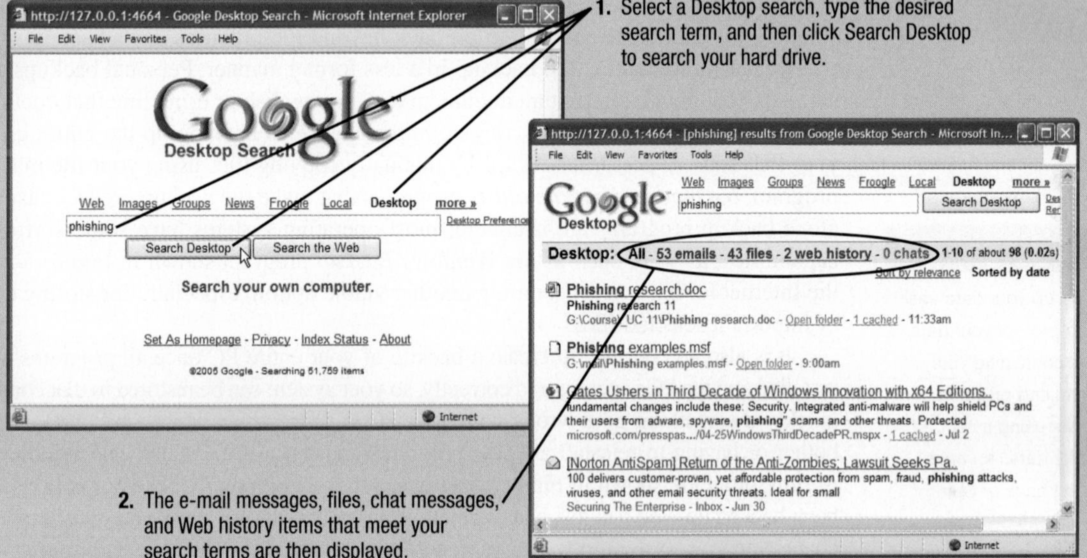
1. Select a Desktop search, type the desired search term, and then click Search Desktop to search your hard drive.
2. The e-mail messages, files, chat messages, and Web history items that meet your search terms are then displayed.
Google Desktop Search
phishing
Search Desktop
Search the Web
Search your own computer.
Desktop: All - 53 emails - 43 files - 2 web history - 0 chats
Phishing research.doc
Phishing examples.msf

Google's Desktop Search feature allows you to quickly find files, e-mail messages, cached Web pages, and other content stored on your PC.

Uninstall Utilities

When programs are *uninstalled* (removed from the hard drive), small pieces of the programs can be left behind on the hard drive or in system files unless an *uninstall utility* is used. If a user removes programs by deleting the program's folder (which is not the recommended method for removing programs), a large amount of extraneous data can accumulate on the hard drive over time. Uninstall utilities remove the programs themselves, along with all references to those programs in your system files. Some uninstall capabilities are built into most operating systems; uninstall utility programs are also available as stand-alone programs, and sometimes an uninstall option is included in a program's folder when that program is originally installed.

TIP

Windows users should be cautious when uninstalling programs; if an uninstall utility asks you whether to keep or delete a system file (such as a *.dll* file) that it says might be needed by another program, it is safer to keep it.

Backup and Recovery Utilities

TIP

Be sure to save your documents frequently as you work, in case the power goes out. Creating a copy of a document with a different filename (by using the *Save As* option of the File menu, for example) before editing a document is another good idea, so you can return to the original version, if needed.

Virtually every computer veteran will warn you that, sooner or later, you will lose some critical files. Maybe a storm will knock down power lines, causing your electricity to go out—shutting off your PC and erasing the document that you have not saved yet. Perhaps your PC will stop working in the middle of finishing that term paper that is due tomorrow. Or, more likely, you will accidentally delete or overwrite an important file or the file just will not open properly anymore. And do not forget major disasters—a fire or flood can completely destroy your PC and everything that is stored on it.

Creating a **backup** means making a duplicate copy of important files so that when a problem occurs, you can restore those files using the backup copy. You can back up your entire PC (so it can be restored at a later date, if needed) or you can just back up data files. Depending on their size, backup data can be placed on a floppy disk, recordable or rewritable CD or DVD disc, second hard drive, or virtually any other storage medium. Good backup procedures can help protect against data loss.

It is critical for a business to have backup procedures in place that back up all data on a frequent, regular basis—such as every night. A rotating collection of backup media should be used so it is possible to go back beyond the previous day's backup, if needed. Individuals, however, tend to back up in a less formal manner. Personal backups can be as simple as copying an important document to a floppy disk or e-mailing that document to a second PC you have access to, or as comprehensive as backing up the entire contents of your PC. You can perform backups by manually copying files using your file management program, but there are *backup utility* programs that make the backup process easier. Standalone backup programs are available; most operating systems have some sort of backup capabilities, as well, such as the *Windows Backup* program shown in Figure 5-25. Using the Internet for backup is becoming another viable option, especially for storing duplicates of important selected files.

TIP

To make backing up your data easier, as well as to protect your data if the hard drive containing your operating system and program crashes, consider using a second hard drive just for data. Your system can be rolled back or your operating system can be reinstalled without jeopardizing your data, and the data hard drive can be moved to a new PC, if a major PC problem occurs.

It is also a good idea to create a backup of your entire PC once all programs have been installed and the PC is configured correctly, so your system can be restored to that configuration quickly if something goes wrong with your PC at a later time, which saves you the time and bother of having to reinstall all your programs and settings manually. The Windows *System Restore* program, shown in Figure 5-25, exists for that purpose. Once your entire system has been backed up, you can just back up data from that point on, unless you make enough major changes to your system to warrant a new full system backup. For convenience, many backup programs can be scheduled to back up specified files, folders, or drives on a regular basis (such as every Friday night). To protect against fires and other natural disasters, backup media should be stored in a different physical location than your PC or inside a fire-resistant safe. Backups and *disaster recovery* are discussed in more detail in Chapter 15.

Antivirus, Antispyware, Firewalls, and Other Security Programs

A *computer virus* is a software program that is designed to cause damage to the computer system or perform some other malicious act, and *spyware* is a software program installed without the user's knowledge that secretly collects information and sends it to an outside party via the user's Internet connection. Other security concerns today include *phishing* schemes that try to trick users to supply personal information that can be used for credit card fraud, *identity theft*, and other criminal acts. Because of these threats, it is critical that all computer users today protect themselves and their computers—there are many *security utility programs* designed for this purpose. For instance, *antivirus* programs can protect against getting a virus in the first place (by checking files and e-mail messages being

>**Backup.** A duplicate copy of data or other computer content in case the original version is destroyed.

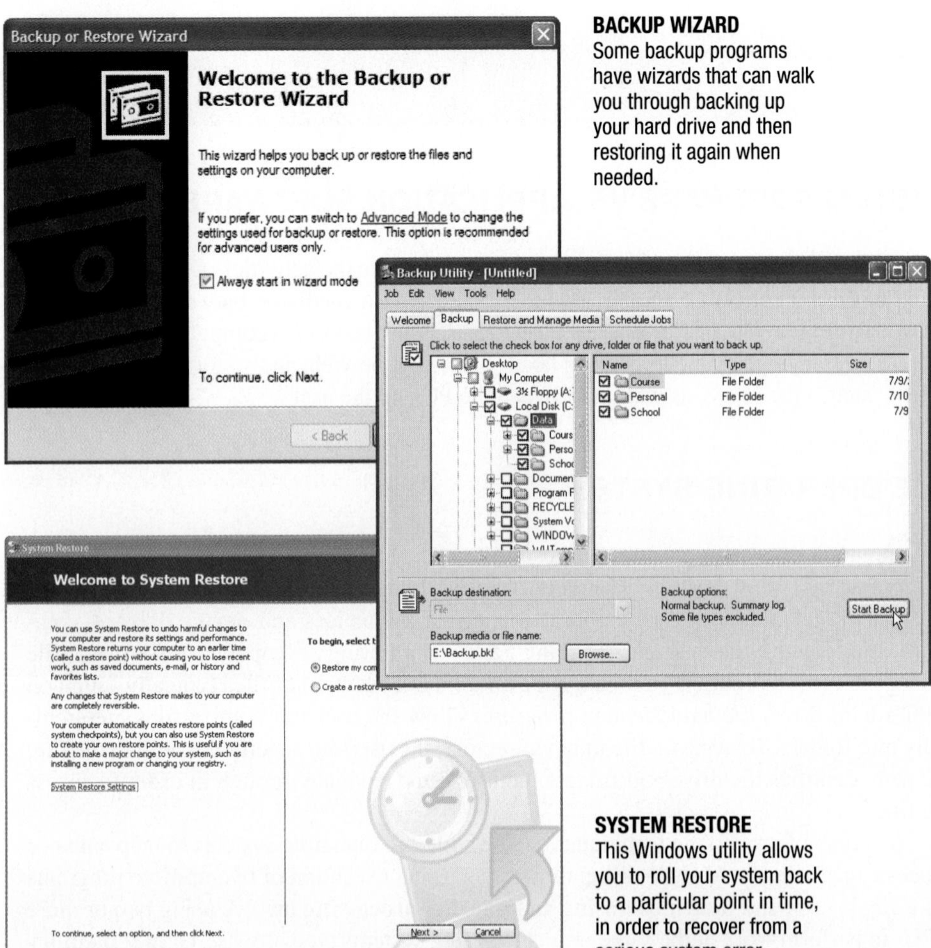

BACKUP WIZARD
Some backup programs have wizards that can walk you through backing up your hard drive and then restoring it again when needed.

MANUAL BACKUP
Many backup programs allow you to select just the files you want backed up. In this example, just the checked folders will be backed up to a CD+RW disc in the E drive.

SYSTEM RESTORE
This Windows utility allows you to roll your system back to a particular point in time, in order to recover from a serious system error.

FIGURE 5-25
Backup and recovery utilities. Most backup utilities, such as the Windows Backup program shown here, allow you to back up an entire hard drive or just specific folders and files; Windows XP also includes a System Restore utility.

downloaded to your PC before they are stored on your PC), as well as detect and remove any viruses that may find their way onto your PC; *antispyware programs* can detect and remove any spyware programs installed on your PC; and *firewalls* can protect against someone accessing your PC via the Internet. Because network and Internet security is such an important topic today, Chapter 9 is dedicated to these topics.

FURTHER EXPLORATION

For links to further information about utility programs, go to www.course.com/uc11/ch05

THE FUTURE OF OPERATING SYSTEMS

The future configuration of operating systems is anyone's guess, but it is expected that they will continue to become more user-friendly and, eventually, be driven primarily by a voice interface. Operating systems are also likely to continue to become more stable and self-healing, repairing or restoring system files as needed. In addition, they will likely continue to include improved security features and to support multiple processors and other technological improvements.

With the pervasiveness of the Internet, operating systems in the future may be used primarily to access software available through the Internet or other networks, instead of accessing software on the local device. Improvements will almost certainly continue to be made in the areas of synchronizing and coordinating data and activities between a person's various computing and communications devices, such as his or her desktop PC, handheld PC, and smart phone.

SUMMARY

SYSTEM SOFTWARE VS. APPLICATION SOFTWARE

Chapter Objective 1: Understand the difference between system software and application software.

System software consists of the programs that coordinate the activities of a computer system. The basic role of system software is to act as a mediator between **application software** (programs that allow a user to perform specific tasks on a computer, such as word processing, playing a game, preparing taxes, browsing the Web, and so forth) and the computer system's hardware, as well as between the PC and the user.

THE OPERATING SYSTEM

Chapter Objective 2: Explain the different functions of an operating system and discuss some ways that operating systems can differ from one another.

A computer's **operating system** is the primary system software program that manages the computer system's resources and interfaces with the user. The functions of the operating system include booting the computer, configuring devices and **device drivers**, communicating with the user, managing and monitoring computer resources, file management, and security. To manage the enormous collection of files typically found on a PC's hard drive, *file management programs* allow the user to organize files hierarchically into folders. To access a file in any directory, the user can specify the *path* to the file; the path identifies the drive and folders the user must navigate through in order to access the file.

Chapter Objective 3: List several ways in which operating systems enhance processing efficiency.

A variety of processing techniques can be built into operating systems to help enhance processing efficiency. **Multitasking** allows concurrent execution of two or more programs for a single user, and **multiprocessing** and **parallel processing** involve using two or more CPUs to perform work at the same time. Operating systems typically use **virtual memory** to extend conventional memory by using a portion of the hard drive as additional memory, and **spooling** frees up the CPU from time-consuming interaction with input and output devices, such as printers, by storing input and output on the way in or out of the system in a **buffer**.

Some of the differences among operating systems center around whether it uses a **graphical user interface (GUI)** or **command line interface**, whether it is a **personal operating system** designed for individual users or a **server** (*network*) **operating system** designed for multiple users, and the types and numbers of processors supported.

OPERATING SYSTEMS FOR DESKTOP PCS AND SERVERS

Chapter Objective 4: Name today's most widely used operating systems for desktop PCs and servers.

One of the original operating systems for PCs was **DOS (Disk Operating System)**, which is still in existence, but not widely used. Most desktop PCs today run a version of **Windows**. *Windows 3.x*, the first widely used version of Windows, was an *operating environment* that added a GUI shell to DOS, replacing the DOS command line interface with a system of menus, icons, and screen boxes called *windows*. *Windows 95*, *Windows 98*, *Windows 98 Second Edition* (*SE*), *Windows NT*, *Windows Me*, and *Windows 2000*—all successors to Windows 3.*x*—included an increasing number of enhancements, such as multitasking, a better user interface, and more Internet, multimedia, and communications functions. The current personal version of Windows is **Windows XP**, which has a variety of versions to meet specific needs and types of PCs. The successor to Windows XP and the current network version of Windows, **Windows Server 2003**, is **Windows Vista**, which is expected to be available by 2007.

Mac OS X is the most recent version of *Mac OS*, the operating system used on Apple computers. **UNIX** is a flexible, general-purpose server operating system that works on mainframes, midrange computers, PCs used as network servers, graphics workstations, and even desktop PCs. A *flavor* (version) of UNIX called **Linux** has gathered popularity because it is distributed free over the Internet and can be used as an alternative to Windows and Mac OS. Linux has earned support as a mainstream operating system in recent years and is being used in computer systems of all sizes, from desktop PCs to supercomputers. **NetWare** is a widely used server operating system, and *Solaris* is used on Sun computers.

OPERATING SYSTEMS FOR HANDHELD PCS AND MOBILE DEVICES

Handheld PCs and mobile devices usually require a different operating system than a desktop PC. For handheld PCs, mobile versions of Windows (such as **Windows Embedded** and **Windows Mobile**) and **Palm OS** (the operating system designed for Palm handheld PCs) are widely used. **Embedded Linux** is another operating system used with handheld PCs and mobile devices; smart phones sometimes use the **Symbian OS**, which is designed around the *EPOC* operating system. Other everyday devices—such as cars—that contain a computer use an operating system, as well.

Chapter Objective 5:
State several devices other than desktop PCs and servers that require an operating system and list one possible operating system for each type of device.

SW

OPERATING SYSTEMS FOR LARGER COMPUTERS

High-end servers, mainframes, and supercomputers may use an operating system designed specifically for that type of system, but are increasingly using customized versions of conventional operating systems, such as Windows, UNIX, and Linux.

UTILITY PROGRAMS

A **utility program** is a type of system software program written to perform specific tasks usually related to maintaining or managing the computer system. **File management programs** enable users to perform file management tasks, such as copying, moving, and deleting files. **Search tools** are designed to help users find files on their hard drives; *diagnostic* and *disk management programs* deal primarily with diagnosing and repairing PC problems, such as hard drive errors and accidentally deleted files, as well as maintenance tasks, such as performing *disk defragmentation*. *Uninstall utilities* allow programs to be removed from a hard drive without leaving annoying remnants behind, *file compression* programs reduce the stored size of files so they can be more easily archived or sent over the Internet, and **backup** programs make it easier for users to back up the contents of their hard drive. There are also a number of security-oriented utility programs, such as *antivirus*, *antispyware*, and *firewall* programs.

Chapter Objective 6:
Discuss the role of utility programs and outline several duties that these programs perform.

THE FUTURE OF OPERATING SYSTEMS

In the future, operating systems will likely become even more user-friendly, voice-driven, and stable, repairing themselves when needed and causing errors and conflicts much less frequently.

Chapter Objective 7:
Describe what the operating systems of the future might be like.

REVIEW ACTIVITIES

KEY TERM MATCHING

Instructions: Match each key term on the left with the definition on the right that best describes it.

a. backup
b. device drive
c. Linux
d. Mac OS X
e. multiprocessing
f. operating system
g. spooling
h. utility program
i. virtual memory
j. Windows Mobile

1. ______ A duplicate copy of data or other computer content for use in the event that the original version is destroyed.
2. ______ A family of operating systems based on Windows and designed for handheld PCs, smart phones, and other mobile devices.
3. ______ A memory-management technique that uses hard drive space as an extension to a PC's RAM.
4. ______ A program that enables an operating system to communicate with a specific hardware device.
5. ______ A type of software that performs a specific task, usually related to managing or maintaining the computer system.
6. ______ A version (flavor) of UNIX that is available without charge over the Internet and is increasingly being used with PCs, servers, mainframes, and supercomputers.
7. ______ The capability of an operating system to use multiple processors in a single computer, usually to process multiple jobs at one time faster than could be performed with a single processor.
8. ______ The main component of system software that enables the computer to manage its activities and the resources under its control, run application programs, and interface with the user.
9. ______ The most recent version of the operating system used on Apple computers.
10. ______ The process of placing items in a buffer so they can be retrieved by the appropriate device (such as a printer) when needed.

SELF-QUIZ

Instructions: Circle **T** if the statement is true, **F** if the statement is false, or write the best answer in the space provided. **Answers to the self-quiz are located in the References and Resources Guide at the end of the book.**

1. **T F** Microsoft Windows XP is an example of an operating system.
2. **T F** Most operating systems today use a command line interface.
3. **T F** The principal reason so many people like UNIX is that it is much easier to use than competing operating systems.
4. **T F** Solaris is an operating system designed for smart phones.
5. **T F** Linux can be used on mainframe and supercomputers, in addition to PCs and servers.
6. System software consists of ______ software and ______ programs.
7. ______ is a popular version of UNIX available for free over the Internet.
8. To decrease the size of a file, a(n) ______ utility program can be used.
9. To guard against losing your data if a computer problem occurs, you should ______ your data files on a regular basis.

10. Match each device to the most appropriate operating system and write the corresponding number in the blank to the left of the device.

a. ______ Home office PC	d. ______ Business network server
b. ______ Mainframe computer	e. ______ Handheld PC
c. ______ Smart phone	f. ______ Living room PC

1. Symbian OS	4. Windows XP Media Center Edition
2. NetWare	5. Palm OS
3. Windows XP Professional	6. UNIX

EXERCISES

1. For the following path, identify the drive the document is located on, the name of the file, and whether or not the document is stored inside a folder. If the file is stored inside one or more folders, list the folder name(s).

   C:\My Documents\Resume.doc

2. Match each program or processing technique with the appropriate term and write the corresponding number in the blank to the left of each term.

a. ______ Zipped file	e. ______ Printer
b. ______ Server operating system	f. ______ Simultaneous processing
c. ______ Swap file	g. ______ Command line interface
d. ______ Folder	h. ______ Fragmentation

1. DOS	5. Multiprocessing
2. NetWare	6. Spooling
3. File management program	7. File compression program
4. Virtual memory	8. Disk management program

3. Would a notebook PC typically have Windows 3.1, Windows XP, Windows Mobile, or Windows Server 2003 installed as its operating system? Explain your answer.

4. What type of utility program can be used to make a duplicate copy of your hard drive?

5. Identify the purpose of each of the following types of utility programs.

   a. File management program ______________________________
   b. Search tool ______________________________
   c. Uninstall utility ______________________________
   d. File compression program ______________________________
   e. Antivirus program ______________________________

DISCUSSION QUESTION

As discussed in the chapter, more and more everyday devices—including cars and other vehicles—are being controlled by operating systems. Even large transportation systems, such as subway trains, are increasingly becoming automated. There are advantages, such as avoiding possible driver errors and the ability to change the speed of or reroute trains to avoid collisions or to run the system more efficiently. But are there potential risks, as well? For example, Thailand's Finance Minister once had to be rescued from inside his limousine after the onboard computer malfunctioned, leaving the vehicle immobilized. With the door locks, power windows, and air conditioning not functioning, the Minister and his driver were in growing danger until a guard freed them by smashing one of the vehicle's windows with a sledgehammer 10 minutes later. Do you think the benefits of increased automation of devices that could put us in danger if they malfunction outweigh the risks? What types of safeguards do you think should be incorporated into computer-controlled cars, subway trains, and other automated vehicles? What about medication dispensers and other automated medical devices?

SW

PROJECTS

HOT TOPICS

1. **Autonomic Computing** *Autonomic computing* is a term coined by IBM to refer to computers that can operate on their own with little need of attention from a person. To facilitate this, autonomic computers are expected to have built-in self-diagnostics and other types of utilities, as well as other appropriate software. Autonomic computers will have the ability to recognize, isolate, and recover from problems, with as little human intervention as possible. Some see autonomic computing as a natural progression for computing, similar to the way the telephone system evolved from using a human switchboard operator to a system that automatically routes calls on its own; others are more skeptical.

   For this project, research the current state of autonomic computing. Has the definition of an autonomic computer changed since this project was written? How do the autonomic computing systems being tested today compare in terms of reliability and the ability to recover from errors to conventional computer systems? Are there any autonomic computer systems available in the United States? Do you think all computers in the future will be autonomic? Do you see any disadvantages of autonomic computing? At the conclusion of your research, prepare a one- to two-page summary of your findings and submit it to your instructor.

SHORT ANSWER/ RESEARCH

2. **Suit Happy** Beginning with the lawsuit filed against Microsoft by Apple Corporation in the late 1980s, claiming that the Windows interface stole the look and feel of the Apple OS, there have been a number of lawsuits involving operating systems. Some more recent legal actions include the antitrust lawsuit filed against Microsoft in 1998 by the Justice Department, the suit filed in 2002 against Microsoft by Sun Microsystems regarding the inclusion of their Java program in the Windows operating system, and the lawsuit filed in 2003 against IBM by the SCO Group (formerly Caldera Systems) regarding UNIX and Linux.

   For this project, select a lawsuit that involved an operating system product (either one of those mentioned in the previous paragraph or a more recent example) and research it. Be sure to find out what the initial claim was, the defending company's response, and the result of the lawsuit, if it was settled. If it hasn't yet been settled, provide an update of the current status of the suit. If it was settled, do you agree with the ruling? Why or why not? At the conclusion of your research, prepare a one-page summary of your findings and submit it to your instructor.

3. **Compression** As described in the chapter, compression programs can be used to make more efficient use of disk space and speed up the delivery of files over the Internet. They also come in handy for large files—such as digital photographs or other types of graphical images—that you want to archive. The most common compression programs create files with the file extensions *.zip*, *.sit*, and *.exe*. Compression programs usually allow you to create both compressed files and self-extracting compressed files. Self-extracting files automatically decompress when you download them, while compressed files must be decompressed by running a version of the program that compressed them.

   For this project, identify compression programs associated with each of the file extensions listed above and determine which extensions represent a self-extracting format, as well as which extensions are associated with the Windows and Mac OS operating systems. For the type of PC you use most often, find at least two compression programs that you might use and compare their costs and capabilities. At the conclusion of your research, prepare a one-page summary of your findings and submit it to your instructor.

4. **File Practice** As discussed in the chapter, all operating systems have at least one program you can use to manage your files; typically, they work similarly to the Windows Explorer program illustrated in Figures 5-22 and 5-23.

For this project, obtain a blank floppy disk or other removable storage medium (such as a USB flash memory drive) appropriate for the computer you will be using most often, insert it into the PC, and perform the following tasks.

   a. Open the file management program (such as Windows Explorer for Windows PCs). Once the program is open, click or double-click the icon for the removable storage medium being used (such as the letter *A* for a floppy drive) to display the content of your storage medium (if a message stating that the floppy disk needs to be formatted appears, select the option to format the disk and then continue with the rest of the steps in this project, provided you know the disk doesn't contain any data, since formatting will erase the disk). Are there any files on the storage medium? By looking at the status bar at the bottom of the file management program's window, or by right-clicking the drive icon and selecting *Properties*, determine how much room is available on the storage medium.

   b. Open any word processing program available on your PC (such as Word, WordPerfect, or WordPad). Create a new document consisting of just your name. By using the appropriate toolbar button or File menu option, save the document onto your storage medium (be sure to change the save location to the appropriate drive and give the document an appropriate name, such as your last name). Return to your file management program and view the content of your storage medium. Is your new document stored there? If so, how big is it and how much room is left on your storage medium now? If it is not there, use your word processor's *Save As* option to save the file again, making sure you are storing it on your storage medium.

   c. Prepare a short summary of your work to submit to your instructor, listing the software programs used, the name of the file you saved on your storage medium, the size of the file, and the amount of space left on your storage medium once the file was stored on it.

   d. Return to your file management program, display the content of your storage medium, and delete the file you stored there.

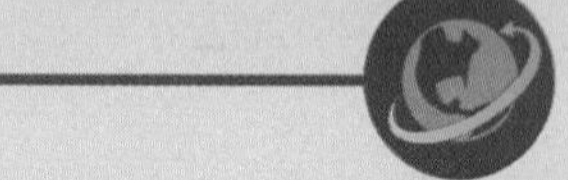

5. **How Stuff Works: System Software** The How Stuff Works Web site has a number of interesting articles and tutorials explaining how some computer-oriented hardware, software, and technologies work.

For this project, go to the How Stuff Works Web site at www.howstuffworks.com and use either the search option or browse through the computer topics to locate an article related to operating systems or utility programs, such as one explaining how operating systems, file compression, screensavers, virtual memory, or computer viruses work. Read through the article, making note of at least three new things you learned about your chosen topic. At the conclusion of the article, prepare a short summary for your instructor, including the name of the article and the new information you learned from reading it.

WRITING ABOUT COMPUTERS

6. **Operating System Bugs** Most software, including operating systems, is not error-free when it is first released. Some programs, in fact, contain thousands of problems, called *bugs*. Some are annoying; others leave security holes in your system that can make it vulnerable from attack by a computer virus or unscrupulous individual.

For this project, identify one recently discovered security hole in a current operating system or a program included with that operating system, such as a utility or Web browser. You may want to review recent computer journals or search the Internet for the information. Once you have identified your hole or bug, find out what the potential problem was, how the problem can be fixed, and where an individual would go to download the appropriate *security patch* or upgrade. Does the security patch fix just that one problem, or does it address multiple bugs? Is there a charge for it? If someone bought a PC today with that operating system installed, would it contain the bug? What is the easiest way for Windows users to keep their operating system up-to-date? Submit this project to your instructor in the form of a short paper, not more than two pages in length.

PRESENTATION/ DOCUMENTATION

7. **OS Support** No matter which operating system you have, it's likely you will eventually need to get some help resolving a system-related hardware or software problem. Support for most popular operating systems includes the following: searchable knowledge bases, technical support phone numbers and e-mail addresses, online support chat sessions, FAQs, and user discussion groups.

   For this project, first find out what type of help each support option listed in the previous paragraph can be used for. Next, select one operating system and research the support options available for that program, including the options available through the Web site of the program's manufacturer. Select one support option and determine in more detail how it would be used and what type of information can be obtained. Share your findings with the class in the form of a short presentation. The presentation should not exceed 10 minutes and should make use of one or more presentation aids, such as the chalkboard, handouts, overhead transparencies, or a computer-based slide presentation (your instructor may provide additional requirements). You may also be asked to submit a summary of the presentation to your instructor.

GROUP DISCUSSION

8. **Teaching Computer Viruses** When the University of Calgary announced plans to offer a new course in the Fall 2003 semester that included instruction on writing computer viruses, it unleashed a huge round of criticism and objections from the computer industry. Although the course was to delve into the ethics and legalities surrounding viruses, the students would also be coding actual viruses, which worried many industry leaders. At Calgary, planned precautions included only allowing fourth year students to take the course, not having a network connection in the classroom, and prohibiting the removal of disks from the classroom. Do you think these precautions are sufficient? Should virus-coding be allowed as part of a computer degree curriculum? The University's premise is that students need to know how viruses work to be able to develop antivirus software; however, the antivirus industry disagrees, and most antivirus professionals were never virus writers. Who do you think is right? Will including teaching illegal and unethical acts in college classes help to legitimize the behavior in society? Research whether or not the University of Calvary ever offered the class as planned. Do you agree with that decision?

   For this project, form an opinion of the inclusion of virus-writing instruction in college classes and its potential impact on society and the computer industry and be prepared to discuss your position (in class, via an online class discussion group, or in a class chat room, depending on your instructor's directions). You may also be asked to write a short paper expressing your opinion.

WEB ACTIVITIES

The *Understanding Computers* Web site located at **www.course.com/uc11** features many resources to help reinforce your understanding of the chapter content and help you prepare for exams. Your instructor may also assign specific activities to be completed that will count toward your final grade in the course.

Instructions: Go to **www.course.com/uc11/ch05** to work the following online activities.

Click any link in the navigation bar on the left to access any of the online resources described below.

INTERACTIVE ACTIVITIES

1. **Crossword Puzzle** Practice your knowledge of the key terms in Chapter 5 by completing the interactive Crossword Puzzle.
2. **Tech News Video Project** Watch the **"Emergency System Restore"** video clip that takes a look at the Windows System Restore option that can restore your system to a previous configuration if a problem occurs with your current settings. After watching the video online, complete the corresponding project.
3. **Student Edition Labs** Reinforce the concepts you have learned in this chapter by working through the interactive **Backing up Your Computer** and **Maintaining a Hard Drive** labs.

TEST YOURSELF

1. **Key Term Matching** Test your knowledge of selected chapter key terms by matching the terms with their definitions.
2. **Self-Quiz** Test your retention of chapter concepts by taking the Self-Quiz.
3. **Exercises** Work these short exercises to review the concepts and terms covered in the chapter.
4. **Practice Test** Test how ready you are for an upcoming exam by completing the online Practice Test.

STUDY TOOLS/ ADDITIONAL RESOURCES

The Understanding Computers Web site has a wide range of additional resources, including an **Online Study Guide** (containing study tips, a chapter outline with room to add your own notes, and a chapter checklist of the activities to complete when the chapter is covered in class and when you are preparing for a test) and an **Online Glossary** for each chapter; **Further Exploration** links; a **Web Guide**, a **Guide to Buying a PC**, and a **Computer History Timeline**; more information about **Numbering Systems**, **Coding Charts**, and **CPU Characteristics**; and much, much more!

CHAPTER 6 Application Software

OUTLINE

LEARNING OBJECTIVES

After completing this chapter, you will be able to:

1. Describe what application software is, the different types of ownership rights, and the difference between installed and Web-based software.
2. Detail some concepts and commands that many software programs have in common.
3. Discuss word processing and explain what kinds of documents are created using this type of program.
4. Explain the purpose of spreadsheet software and the kinds of documents created using this type of program.
5. Identify some of the vocabulary used with database software and discuss the benefits of using this type of program.
6. Describe what presentation graphics and electronic slide shows are and when they might be used.
7. List some types of graphics and multimedia software consumers frequently use.
8. Name other types of application software programs and discuss what functions they perform.

OVERVIEW

As discussed in previous chapters, **application software** consists of programs designed to perform specific tasks or applications. Today, a wide variety of application software is available to meet virtually any user need. Individuals and businesses can buy software to be used to write letters, keep track of their finances, participate in videoconferences, learn a foreign language, entertain themselves or their children, create music CDs or home movie DVDs, manage a business's inventory, create greeting cards and flyers, make business presentations, process orders, prepare payrolls and tax returns, touch up digital photos, teach their kids the ABCs, and hundreds of other applications.

This chapter begins with a look at some characteristics of application software in general. Then we take a look at five of the most widely used types of application software programs: word processing, spreadsheet, database, presentation graphics, and graphics and multimedia software. The chapter concludes with a look at a few other types of application software not discussed in other chapters in this book. ■

THE BASICS OF APPLICATION SOFTWARE

All computer users should be familiar with the basic characteristics and concepts related to application software; for instance, the different possible ownership rights and delivery methods, how software for desktop PCs and handheld PCs differ, and the basic software commands that are common to most types of application software. Although these topics are discussed next in the context of application software, they also apply to other types of software, such as system software (discussed in Chapter 5) and programming languages (discussed in Chapter 13).

Software Ownership Rights

Ownership rights of a software program specify the allowable use of the program. After a software program is developed, the developer holds the ownership rights for that program. Whether or not the program can be sold, shared with others, or otherwise distributed is up to that developer, typically an individual or an organization. When a software program is purchased, the buyer is not actually buying the software. Instead, the buyer is acquiring a **software license** that permits him or her to use the software. This license specifies the conditions under which a buyer can use the software, such as whether or not it may be shared with others and the number of computers on which it may be installed (many software licenses permit the software to be installed on just one PC). In addition to being included in printed form inside the packaging of most software programs, the licensing agreement is usually displayed and must be agreed to by the end user at the beginning of the software installation process (see Figure 6-1).

TIP

Ownership rights for original creative works are referred to as *copyrights* and are discussed in more detail in Chapter 16.

>**Application software.** Programs that enable users to perform specific tasks on a computer, such as writing a letter or playing a game.

>**Software license.** An agreement, either included in a software package or displayed on the screen during installation, that specifies the conditions under which a buyer of the program can use it.

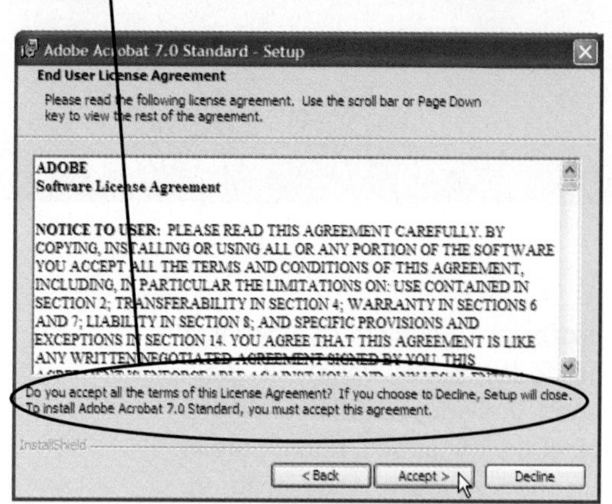

COMMERCIAL SOFTWARE PROGRAM

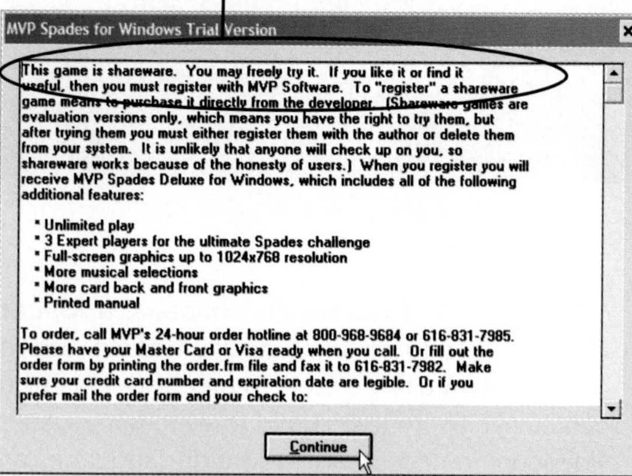

SHAREWARE PROGRAM

FIGURE 6-1
Software licenses. Most software programs display their licensing agreements at the beginning of the installation process.

There are four basic categories of software: *commercial software*, *shareware*, *freeware*, and *public domain software*. Each of these types of software has different ownership rights, as shown in Figure 6-2 and discussed next. In addition, some software is **open source software**—programs whose source code is available to the general public. Open source programs are copyrighted, but individuals and businesses are allowed to modify the program and redistribute it—the only restriction is that changes must be shared with the open source community, and the original copyright notice must remain intact. For more information about open source software, see the Inside the Industry box.

Commercial Software

Commercial software is software that is developed and sold for a profit. When you buy a commercial software program (such as Microsoft Office, TurboTax, or The Sims), it typically

FIGURE 6-2
Software ownership rights.

TYPE OF SOFTWARE	EXAMPLES	MOST COMMONLY OBTAINED FROM
Commercial software	Microsoft Office (office suite) Norton AntiVirus (antivirus program) Adobe Photoshop (image editing program) Flight Simulator (game)	Manufacturer's Web site, online stores, and physical stores
Shareware	WinZip (file compression program) Media Jukebox (media player and CD ripper) Image Shrinker (image optimizer) Rings of the Maji (game)	Manufacturer/author's Web site and download sites, such as Shareware.com and Tucows.com
Freeware	Internet Explorer (Web browser) Outlook Express (e-mail program) QuickTime Player (media player) Yahoo! Messenger (instant messaging program)	Manufacturer/author's Web site and download sites, such as Shareware.com and Tucows.com
Public domain software	Lynx (text-based Web browser) Pine (e-mail program)	Download, university, and government sites; open source and public domain organizations

>**Open source software.** Software programs whose source code is made available to the general public. >**Commercial software.** Copyrighted software that is developed, usually by a commercial company, for sale to others.

INSIDE THE INDUSTRY

Open Source Software

As discussed in Chapter 5, use of open source software has grown over the past few years, primarily for cost reasons. In addition to the open source operating system Linux, there are low-cost or no-cost alternatives for a wide selection of application programs today. For instance, the free *OpenOffice.org* office suite (see the accompanying screen shot) can be used instead of Microsoft Office; the free *GIMP* (*GNU Image Manipulation Program*) program can be used to retouch photos instead of Adobe Photoshop or another pricey image editing program; and the $495 *MySQL* database program is a much less costly, but viable, alternative to Oracle and other database programs that typically cost between $5,000 and $40,000. In addition to saving you money, these alternative programs typically require less disk space and memory. For instance, installing OpenOffice.org instead of Microsoft Office saves the user about 200 MB of hard drive space and about 128 MB of RAM.

Other benefits of using open source software include increased stability and security, and the ability to modify the application's source code. Perceived risks include lack of support and compatibility issues. However, both Linux and open source application programs are continuing to gain acceptance and their use is growing. For instance, more than 4 million copies of the OpenOffice.org program have been downloaded and there is a proposal in Massachusetts to have all documents in offices run by the state move from proprietary formats (like Word and WordPerfect) to the *OpenDocument* open source file standard. Some insiders feel that the open source movement is finally gathering the momentum that many predicted several years ago.

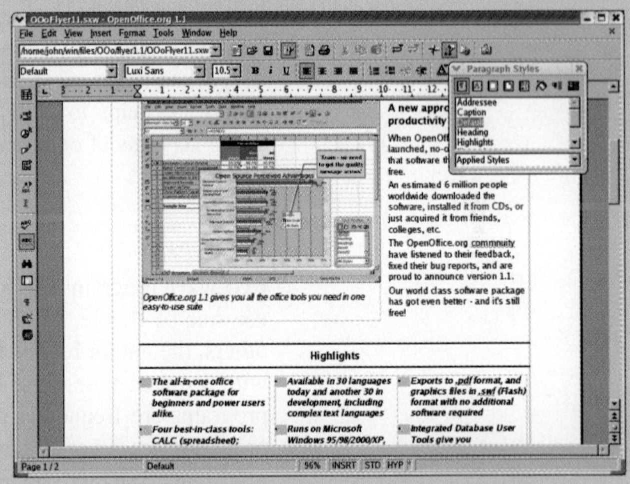

The OpenOffice.org word processing program.

comes with a *single-user license*, which means you cannot legally make copies of the installation CD to give to your friends, and you cannot legally install the software on their computers using your CD. You cannot even install the software on a second PC that you own, unless allowed by the license. For example, some software licenses state that the program can be installed on one desktop PC and one notebook PC; others allow installation on both a home and work PC, as long as the two computers will never be used at the same time. Schools or businesses that need to install software on multiple computers or need to have the software available to multiple users over a network can usually obtain *site licenses* or *network licenses* for the specified number of users. To determine which activities are allowable for a particular commercial software program, refer to the licensing agreement for that program.

In addition to their full versions, some commercial software is available as a *demo* or *trial version*. Typically, these versions can be used free of charge and distributed to others, but often they are missing some key features (such as the ability to save or print a document) or they will not run after the trial period expires. Since these programs are not designed as replacements for the fee-based version, it is ethical to use them only to determine if you would like to buy the full program. If the decision is made against purchasing the product, the demo or trial version should be uninstalled from your PC.

Shareware

Shareware programs are software programs that are distributed on the honor system. Most shareware programs are available to try free of charge, but the author usually requests that you pay a small fee if you intend to use the program regularly (see the shareware license in Figure 6-1). By paying the requested shareware fee, you become a registered user and can use the program for as long as you want to use it. Registered users may also be entitled to product support, documentation, and updates. Shareware programs are widely available from a variety of download sites on the Internet. You can legally and ethically copy shareware programs to pass along to friends and colleagues, but those individuals are expected to pay the shareware fee if they decide to keep the product.

Most shareware programs have a specified trial period, such as one month. Although it is not illegal to use shareware past the specified trial period, it is unethical to do so. Ethical use of shareware dictates either paying for the program or uninstalling it from your PC at the end of the trial period. Shareware is typically much less expensive than commercial versions of similar software because it is often developed by a single programmer and because it uses the shareware marketing system to sell directly to consumers with little or no packaging or advertising expenses. Shareware authors stress that the ethical use of shareware helps to cultivate this type of software distribution. Legally, shareware and demo versions of commercial software are similar, but shareware is typically not missing key features.

Freeware

Freeware programs are software programs that are given away by the author for others to use free of charge. Although freeware is available free of charge and can be shared with others, the author retains the ownership rights to the program, so you cannot do anything with it—such as sell it or modify it—that is not expressly allowed by the author. Freeware programs are frequently developed by students, professional programmers, and amateur programmers either as a programming exercise or as a hobby. Some freeware software programs are released by commercial companies as well, such as Microsoft's Internet Explorer and Netscape's Navigator. Like shareware programs, freeware programs are widely available over the Internet.

Public Domain Software

Public domain software is not copyrighted; instead, the ownership rights to the program have been donated to the public domain. Consequently, it is free and can be used, copied, modified, and distributed to others without restrictions.

Installed vs. Web-Based Software

Software also differs in how it is delivered to the end user. It can either be installed on and run from the end user's PC or delivered to the PC via the Internet.

Installed Software

Installed software—that is, software that is installed on a PC before it is run—is the most common type of software. Installed software programs are either purchased in physical form (such as in a shrink-wrapped box containing a CD, license agreement, and user's manual) or are downloaded from the Internet (see Figure 6-3). Whether or not downloaded software requires a fee depends on whether the program is a commercial program, demo

---

>**Shareware.** Copyrighted software that is distributed on the honor system; consumers should either pay for it or uninstall it after the trial period. >**Freeware.** Copyrighted software that may be used free of charge. >**Public domain software.** Software that is not copyrighted and may be used without restriction.

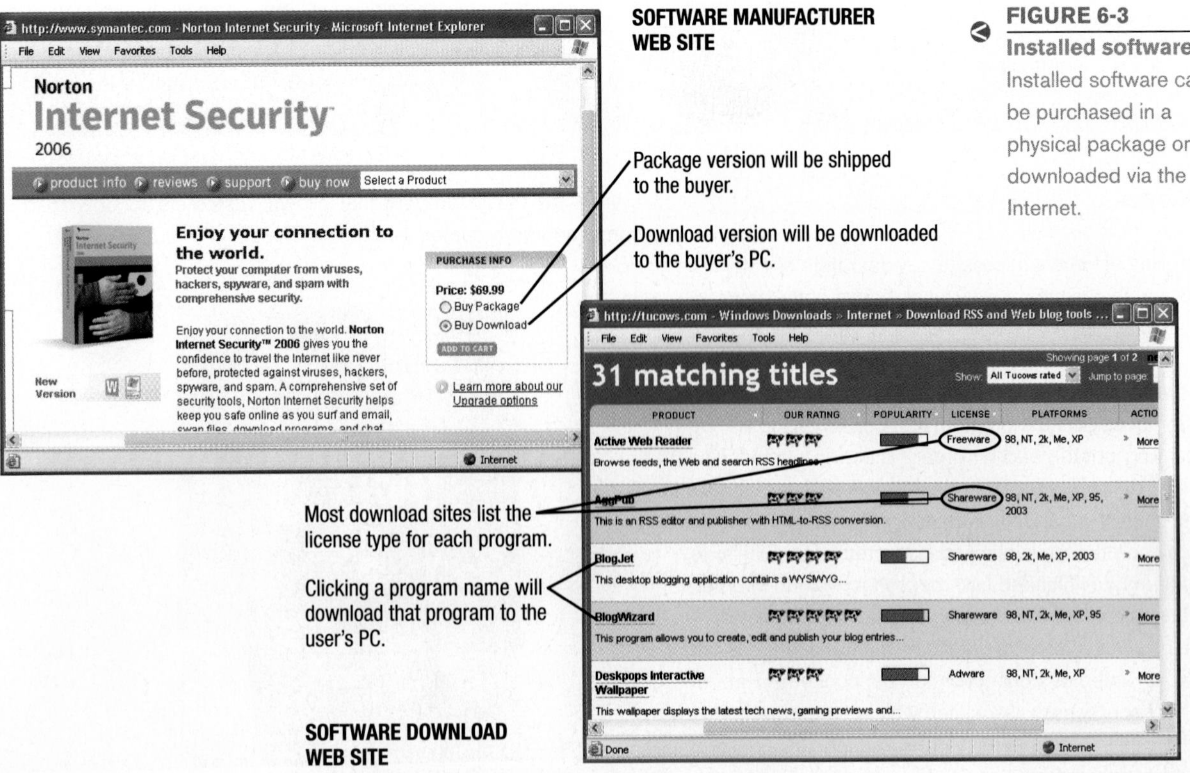
SOFTWARE MANUFACTURER WEB SITE
Norton
Internet Security
2006
Enjoy your connection to the world.
PURCHASE INFO
Price: $69.99
Buy Package
Buy Download
Package version will be shipped to the buyer.
Download version will be downloaded to the buyer's PC.
31 matching titles
Most download sites list the license type for each program.
Clicking a program name will download that program to the user's PC.
SOFTWARE DOWNLOAD WEB SITE

FIGURE 6-3

Installed software. Installed software can be purchased in a physical package or downloaded via the Internet.

SW

program, shareware, freeware, or public domain software. When you purchase software in a downloaded format, you usually place the order, the payment is processed, and then you are provided with a link to download the purchased program. To download free software, you just need to click the appropriate hyperlink (such as on the manufacturer's site or a shareware download site) to download the free program. In either case, downloaded programs typically need to be installed before they can be used. This either occurs automatically after the program is downloaded, or the user needs to launch the downloaded installation program to begin the installation process. With a downloaded program, you do not normally receive a CD containing the program, although some vendors will mail you one for an additional fee, and most allow you to back up the program onto a CD as soon as it is downloaded.

For a look at a new way to purchase software—via *software kiosks*—see the Trend box.

TIP

Some downloaded installation programs don't contain the entire program and so need Internet access during the installation process to download the remaining components. If you are installing a program and receive an error message about the Internet, check your Internet connection to be sure you are still connected and then run the installation program again.

Web-Based Software

Instead of being available in an installed format, some software is run directly from the Internet as *Web-based software*. A Web-based software program can only be accessed via the Internet, and it can be free (such as an interactive game available through a Web site) or fee-based (such as software available from an *application service provider* (*ASP*)—a company that manages and distributes software over the Internet, typically for a monthly or annual fee). There is a wide range of Web-based software available; one example is shown in Figure 6-4. One advantage of Web-based software over installed software is that the programs and your files can be accessed from any PC with an Internet connection regardless of the type of PC or operating system used. Many Web-based programs are available for handheld PCs and mobile devices, in addition to desktop PCs, as shown in Figure 6-4. This makes Web-based software especially appropriate for shared scheduling and other communication or collaboration applications, since documents and other data can be shared regardless of an individual's location or device. Another advantage of Web-based software is that the software may be updated on a regular basis for no additional cost to the

TREND

Software Kiosks

Designed to give customers access to a wider range of software without requiring shelf space, a new kiosk-based software delivery system—called *SoftwareToGo*—is now available in retail stores, such as CompUSA. SoftwareToGo currently offers about 1,500 software titles from nearly 250 publishers. To use the system, the customer selects the program at a consumer kiosk (see the accompanying photo), and an order receipt is printed. The customer brings the order receipt to a salesclerk and pays for the program, and then the salesclerk uses a separate machine to burn the discs and print the labels and documentation. Similar to software programs downloaded from publishers via the Internet, the price is the same as the corresponding shrink-wrapped program and the product is never out of stock, but the user does not have to have an Internet connection or be concerned about viruses or other security risks associated with Internet downloads to obtain the program. The creator of the *SoftwareToGo* system expects the same technology to be used soon to deliver music, movies, audio books, television content, and other digital media products, in addition to software. Starbucks already has a similar system for music delivery that allows customers to download songs and burn customized music CDs.

user. Some potential disadvantages are that the cost may eventually exceed the cost of buying a similar shrink-wrapped package, and you cannot access the program and your data when the server on which they reside goes down.

While Web-based software is typically hosted on a provider's PC (such as a Web server belonging to an ASP or an organization providing Web-based games or other services to the public), some Web-based software is designed to be installed on a company server. Because the software is available via the Web, it can be accessed by company employees and partners, regardless of their current locations. For example, IBM's widely used Lotus Notes product is designed to be installed on a company server and used to facilitate e-mail, calendaring, group scheduling, and collaboration for company employees via the Web. IBM has announced plans to integrate Lotus Notes into Workspace, another of IBM's server-based collaboration products, and to add a productivity suite to Workplace, in order to create a complete suite of private Web-based communication and collaboration tools designed to be delivered to employees and partners via a company network.

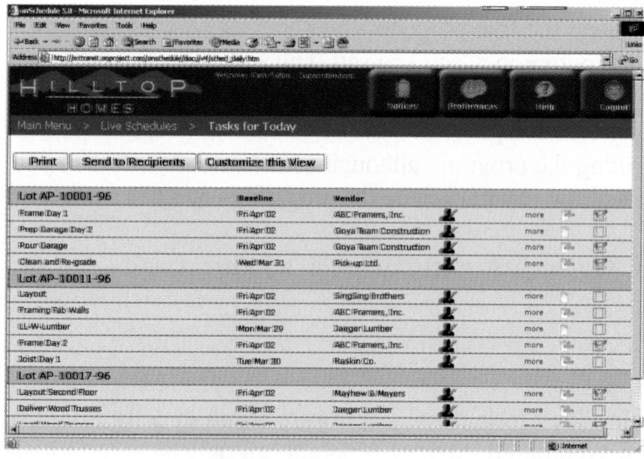

DESKTOP WEB-BASED PROGRAM

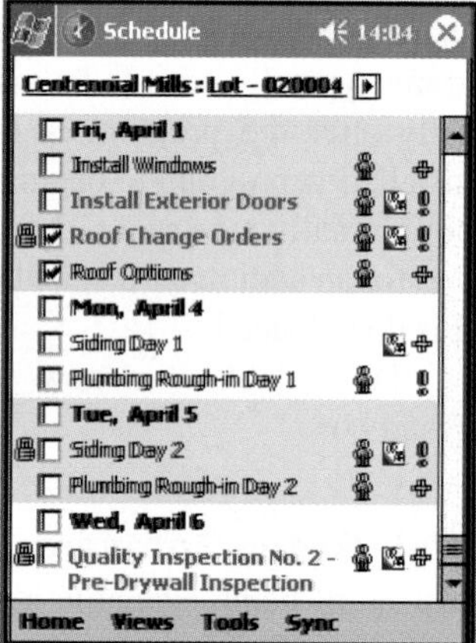

HANDHELD WEB-BASED PROGRAM

FIGURE 6-4
Web-based software. Web based software can be free or (like the programs shown here) fee-based.

Software Suites

Related software programs are sometimes sold bundled together as a **software suite**, such as a group of graphics programs, utility programs, or office-related software. *Office suites*, sometimes called *productivity software suites*, are used by most businesses and many individuals to produce written documents. Typically, office suites contain the programs discussed next; many also contain additional productivity tools—such as a calendar or a messaging program.

- *Word processing software*—allows users to efficiently create, edit, and print the type of documents that would have been created with a typewriter in the past.
- *Spreadsheet software*—provides users with a convenient means of creating documents containing complex mathematical calculations.
- *Database software*—allows users to store and organize vast amounts of data and retrieve specific information when needed.
- *Presentation graphics software*—allows users to create visual presentations to convey information more easily to others.

One of the most widely used office software suites is **Microsoft Office**. The latest versions are *Microsoft Office 2003* (for Windows users) and *Microsoft Office 2004 for Mac* (for Mac OS users); the next version—*Office 12*—is expected to be available sometime in 2006. Similar suites (see Figure 6-5) are available from Corel (*WordPerfect Office*), IBM (*Lotus SmartSuite*), and Sun (*StarOffice*). A free alternative suite similar to *StarOffice* is *OpenOffice.org*, which is available as a free download via the Internet from the OpenOffice.org Web site or on CD for a small fee from various distributors. Many suites are available in different versions, such as a home version containing fewer programs than a professional version. Not all of these suites are available for all operating systems. For example, Microsoft Office is available for both Windows and Mac OS, WordPerfect and SmartSuite are just for Windows users, and StarOffice can be used by Windows, Linux, or Solaris users.

The primary advantages of using a software suite include a total cost that is lower than buying the programs individually and a common interface. Although, as mentioned in an earlier chapter, most programs written for the same operating system (such as Windows or Mac OS) use similar interfaces and commands, a software suite goes one step further. Usually the menu and toolbar structure in the suite is very similar from program to program. This similarity is not just for the basic commands (such as *Save* and *Print*)—all commands

FIGURE 6-5

Office suites. The most common office suites are Microsoft Office, Corel WordPerfect Office, Lotus SmartSuite, and Sun StarOffice.

>**Software suite.** A collection of software programs bundled together and sold as a single software package. >**Microsoft Office.** One of the most widely used office software suites.

(such as adding borders and shading or inserting a row or column) that appear in more than one program in the suite are performed in the same manner. Once you have experience working with one program in a suite, this cross-program functionality makes it easier to learn another program in that suite.

Although you can often copy content from one program to another even if the two programs are not in the same suite—such as copying a drawing created in the Windows Paint program into a word processing document or copying word processing content into an e-mail message—with a software suite you can sometimes go a step further and *link* documents created within a suite together, such as displaying a spreadsheet document within a word processing document. When two documents are linked, the software will ask if you want to display the most recent version of the linked document (the spreadsheet document in this example) whenever the document containing the link (the word processing document in this example) is opened. If you choose to update the link, the spreadsheet displayed in the word processing document will be refreshed to show the most current version. This process of embedding and linking content from one program to another is called *object linking and embedding* (*OLE*).

Similar to software suites are *integrated software programs*—such as *Microsoft Works* and *AppleWorks*. Integrated software programs are similar to full suites, but contain fewer features and are one integrated program instead of a collection of separate programs. Integrated software programs often come installed on home PCs.

Desktop vs. Mobile Software

Unlike notebook and tablet PCs, which usually run the same application software as desktop PCs, handheld PCs and mobile devices require special application software designed for that type of device, sometimes called *mobile software*. A wide variety of mobile software is available today, such as calendars, e-mail and instant messaging programs, address books, language translators, games, reference software, media players, Web browsers, inventory and pricing programs, synchronization programs, and portable versions of popular productivity programs, like Word, Excel, PowerPoint, and Outlook (see Figure 6-6). Some software typically comes installed on the device when it is purchased; additional software can be purchased or downloaded as needed.

FIGURE 6-6

Mobile software.

There is a wide variety of software available today for handheld PCs and mobile devices.

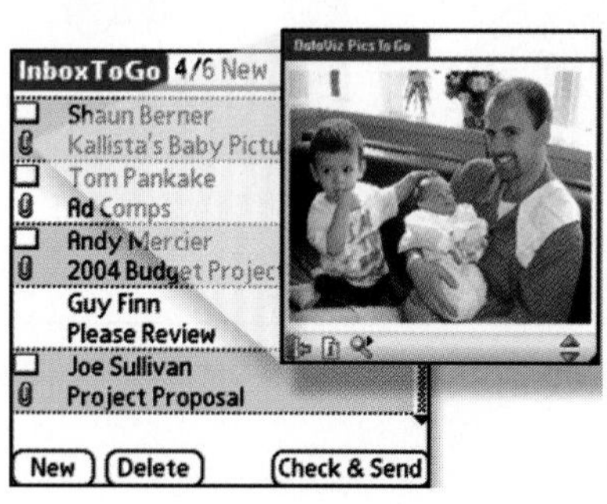

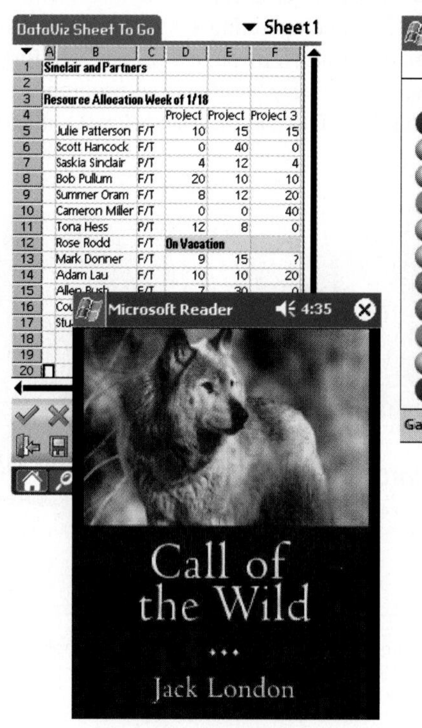

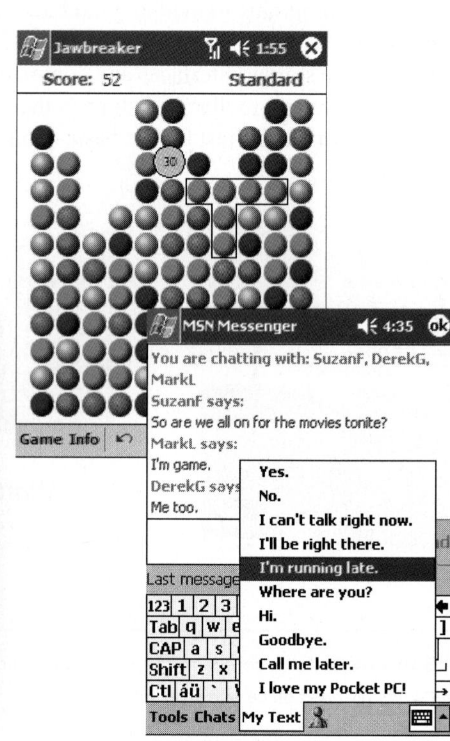

In addition to having a more compact, efficient appearance, many handheld applications include features for easier data input, such as an onscreen keyboard, a phrase list, or handwriting recognition capabilities. Some mobile software programs are designed to be compatible with popular *desktop software* to facilitate sharing documents between the two platforms. For example, both *Documents to Go* (for handheld PCs running Palm OS) and *Pocket Office* (for handheld PCs running Windows Mobile) are compatible with Microsoft Office documents created with a desktop PC. *Synchronization software* can also be used to synchronize the data stored on a desktop PC and a portable PC.

Common Software Commands

Application programs today have a number of concepts and commands in common. For example, many programs allow you to create a new document (such as a letter, drawing, house plan, or greeting card) and then *save* it. To reopen the document at a later time, you use the *open* command, and to print the document, you use the *print* command. One of the greatest advantages of using software instead of paper and pencil to create documents is that you can make changes without erasing or recreating the entire document because the document is created and then saved on a storage medium, instead of it being created directly on paper. Consequently, the document can be retrieved, modified, saved, and printed as many times as needed. Many programs also include tools to help you as you create documents, such as a *spelling and grammar check* feature to help you locate and correct spelling and grammatical errors in your documents, a built-in *thesaurus* to help you enhance the vocabulary used in your documents, a *styles* feature to allow you to apply a common format to a series of documents or a group of similar headings within a single document, and so forth.

Some of the most common application software commands are described in Figure 6-7, with examples of the toolbar buttons and keyboard shortcuts used to perform these operations in Microsoft Office. Many of these commands would be performed in the same manner in other Windows programs. Some of the most common basic software commands are discussed in more detail next.

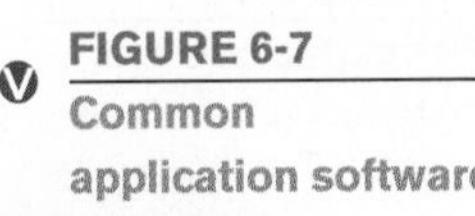
FIGURE 6-7
Common application software commands.

COMMAND	TOOLBAR BUTTON	KEYBOARD SHORTCUT	DESCRIPTION
New document		Ctrl+N	Creates a new blank document.
Open		Ctrl+O	Opens a previously saved document from a storage medium, usually for editing or printing.
Save		Ctrl+S	Saves the current version of the document to a storage medium.
Print		Ctrl+P	Prints the current version of the document onto paper.
Spelling and grammar		F7	Starts the spelling and grammar check for the entire document.
Cut		Ctrl+X	Moves the selected item to the clipboard.
Copy		Ctrl+C	Copies the selected item to the clipboard.
Paste		Ctrl+V	Pastes the contents of the clipboard to the current location.
Undo		Ctrl+Z	Undoes the last change to the document.
Close		Alt+F4	Closes the document. Any changes made to the document are lost if the document wasn't saved first.

SW

Editing a Document

Editing a document refers to changing the content of the document, such as adding or deleting text. Most application software programs that allow text editing have an **insertion point** displayed on the screen that usually looks like a blinking vertical line. An insertion point indicates the current location in the document; that is, where the next change will be made to that document. To insert text, just start typing and the text will appear at the insertion point location. To delete text, press the Delete key to delete one character to the right of the insertion point; press the Backspace key to delete one character to the left of the insertion point. If the insertion point is not in the proper location for the edit, it must be moved (by using the arrow keys on the keyboard or by pointing and clicking with the mouse) to the appropriate location in the document. To select an object or block of text, click the object or drag the mouse over the text. Usually, once an object or some text is selected, it can be manipulated, such as moved, deleted, copied, or *formatted*.

TIP

Once an object or block of text is selected, press *Ctrl+C* to copy it or *Ctrl+X* to cut (move) it, and then move the insertion point to the new location and press *Ctrl+V* to paste the object or text there. You can also delete selected objects or text by pressing the Delete key.

Formatting a Document

While editing changes the actual content of a document, *formatting* changes the appearance of the document. Common types of formatting include changing the *font face*, *font size*, *font style*, and *font color* of text; changing the *line spacing* or *margins* of a document; adding *page numbers*; and adding *shading* or *borders*. A font face or *typeface* is a named collection of text characters that share a common design, such as Arial or Times New Roman. The characters in a font face are usually available in a wide variety of font sizes, which are measured in *points*. All the characters in a particular font face and font size are referred to as a *font*; for example, 12-point Times New Roman is a font. *Font style* refers to formatting that adds additional features to the text, such as bold, italic, or underline, and *font color* refers to the color of the text (see Figure 6-8). Default fonts are installed on a PC with the operating system and some application programs; additional fonts also can be purchased and added specifically by the user. Most, but not all, application programs allow you to use any of the fonts installed on your PC.

TIP

When selecting font size in a document, 72 points equals one-inch-tall text.

FIGURE 6-8

Fonts. The face, size, style, and color of text can be specified in many application programs.

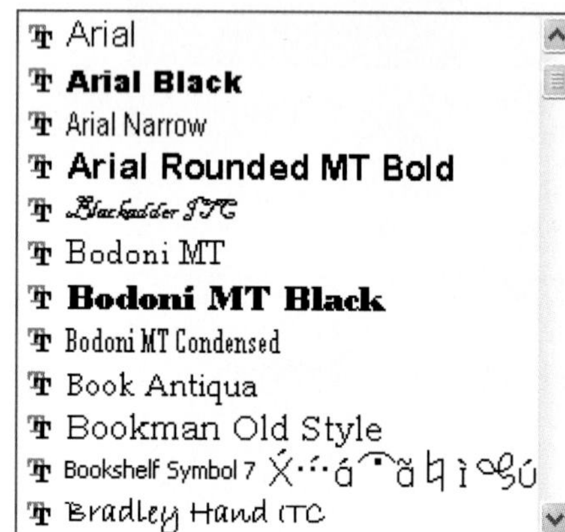

SAMPLE FONT FACES

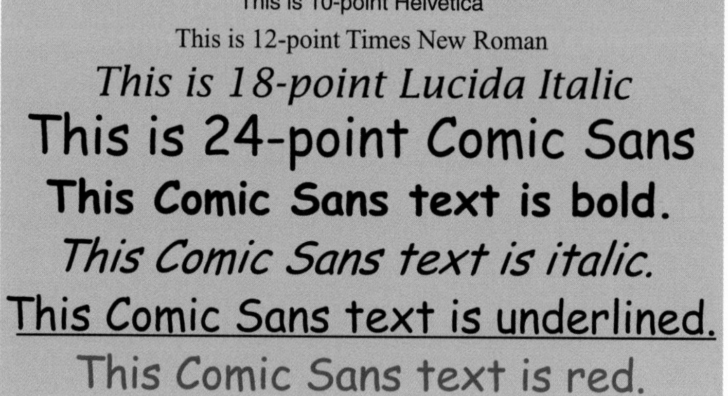

SAMPLE FONT SIZES, STYLES, AND COLORS

>**Insertion point.** An onscreen character that indicates the current location in a document, which is where the next change will be made to the document.

Getting Help

Most people run into problems or need some help as they work with a software program. There are various options for getting help when you need it. For instance, most application programs have a built-in help feature, typically available through a *Help* option on the menu bar. The type and amount of built-in help available varies from program to program, but some of the most common configurations are illustrated in Figure 6-9 and listed next. Help may also be available through resources on the Web.

- *Table of Contents*—works similarly to the table of contents in a book with related help topics organized under main topics. With most help systems, selecting a main topic reveals the help topics related to that main topic; selecting a help topic displays related information on the screen.
- *Index*—works similarly to an index in a book with all help topics organized as an alphabetical list. Typically typing the name of a help topic scrolls the index to that help topic if it is contained in the index; selecting a help topic displays the related information on the screen.

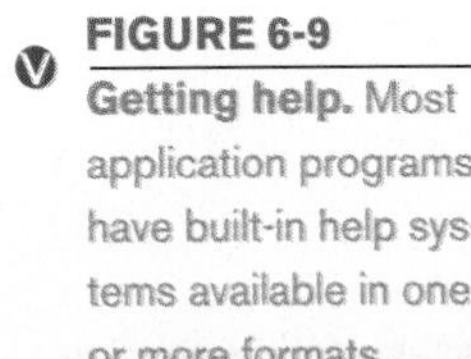

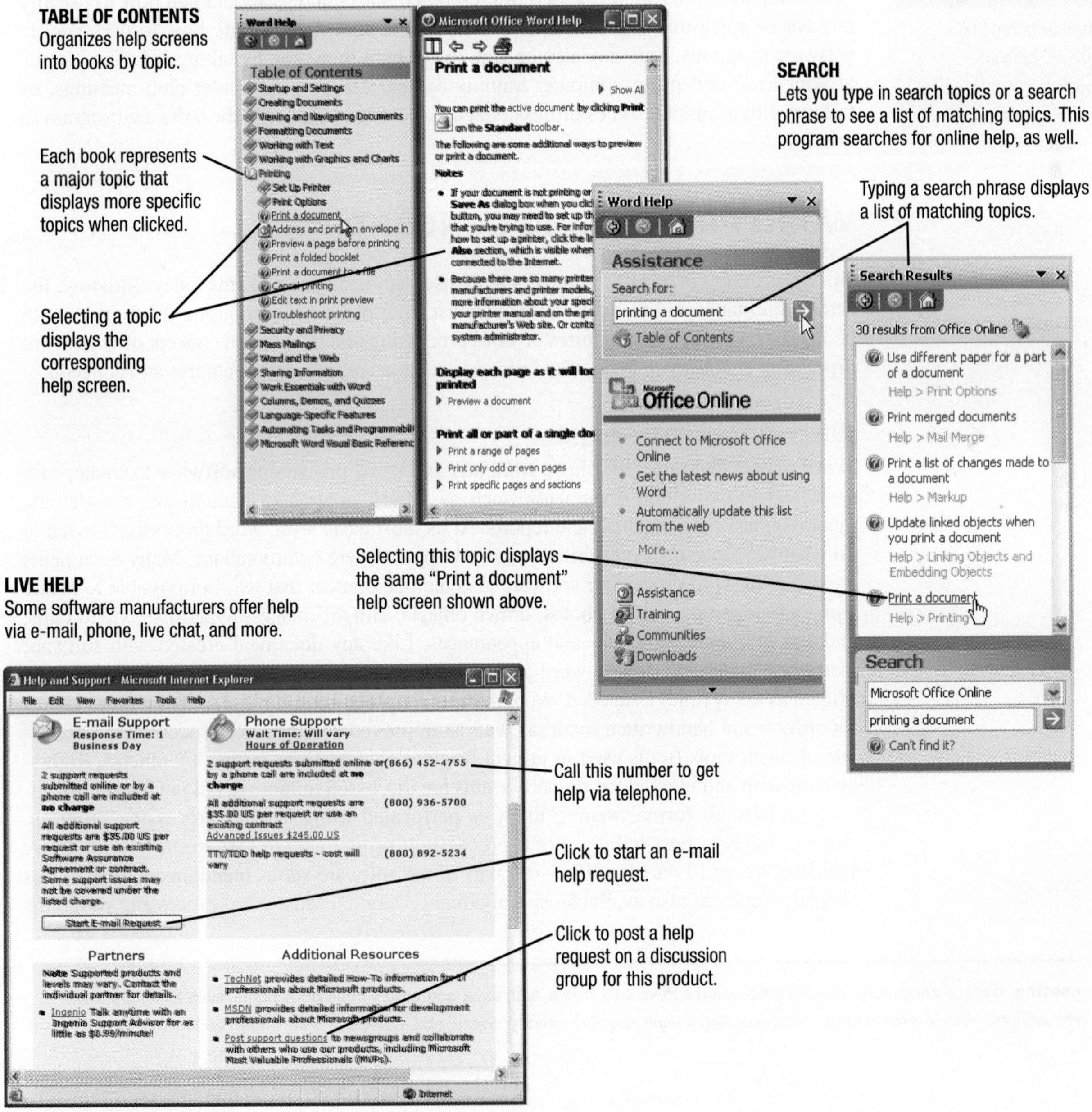

FIGURE 6-9

Getting help. Most application programs have built-in help systems available in one or more formats.

TABLE OF CONTENTS
Organizes help screens into books by topic.

Each book represents a major topic that displays more specific topics when clicked.

Selecting a topic displays the corresponding help screen.

SEARCH
Lets you type in search topics or a search phrase to see a list of matching topics. This program searches for online help, as well.

Typing a search phrase displays a list of matching topics.

Selecting this topic displays the same "Print a document" help screen shown above.

LIVE HELP
Some software manufacturers offer help via e-mail, phone, live chat, and more.

Call this number to get help via telephone.

Click to start an e-mail help request.

Click to post a help request on a discussion group for this product.

SW

- *Search*—allows you to search for help topics by typing a keyword or phrase (similar to a search site), and then the help system displays a list of possible matching help topics. Because a help search feature usually looks for all help screens containing the search term (not just all help topics containing the search term), a help search generally returns more help screens than searching for the same term using a help index feature.

Some help systems automatically search for online help from the manufacturer's Web site if the program detects an Internet connection. In addition, there is a vast amount of additional information about application software programs available via the Web. For instance, many software manufacturers offer online tutorials and lists of tips and tricks for their programs on their Web sites, as well as free or fee-based support via e-mail, telephone, or discussion group. There are also general-purpose software tutorial sites that provide online tutorials for a variety of programs, as well as sites dedicated to a particular application, such as desktop publishing or digital photo touch-up.

There are also numerous resources for offline help, including periodicals (such as magazines and journals) that often contain articles about how to most effectively use particular software programs, books (both reference books and textbooks) on how to use any number of software programs, and tutorial videos that demonstrate how to use specific software programs. You may also be able to get help in person by taking software classes at your local college or computer training center, attending computer club meetings, or talking with a computer sales professional at a local store that sells the software program in question.

FURTHER EXPLORATION

For links to further information about application software resources, go to www.course.com/uc11/ch06

WORD PROCESSING CONCEPTS

Word processing is one of the most widely used application programs today. Although the actual commands and features vary somewhat from program to program, it is important to be familiar with the basic features of word processing and the general concept of what word processing enables you to do. The following sections discuss these features and concepts.

What Is Word Processing?

Word processing refers to using a computer and **word processing software** to create, edit, save, and print written documents, such as letters, contracts, manuscripts, newsletters, invoices, marketing material, and reports. At its most basic level, word processing is used to do what was done on a typewriter before computers were commonplace. Many documents created with word processing software also include content that was not possible to create using a typewriter, such as photos, drawn objects, clip art images, hyperlinks, video clips, and text in a variety of sizes and appearances. Like any document created with software instead of paper and pencil, word processing documents can be retrieved, modified, and printed as many times as needed. Word processing programs today typically include support for speech and handwritten input, as well as improved collaboration, security, and *rights-management* tools (tools used to protect original content from misuse by others). Rights-management and intellectual property rights are discussed in more detail in Chapter 16.

Virtually all formal writing today is performed using a word processing program. Among today's best-selling word processing programs are *Microsoft Word*, *Corel WordPerfect*, and *Lotus WordPro*—all part of the software suites mentioned earlier in this chapter; some are also available as individual programs. Most word processing programs

>**Word processing.** Using a computer and word processing software to create, edit, save, and print written documents, such as letters, contracts, and manuscripts. >**Word processing software.** Application software used to create, edit, save, and print written documents.

offer hundreds of features, but virtually all support a core group of features used to create, edit, and format documents. Some of these basic features are described in the next few sections, using Microsoft Word as the example.

Creating a Word Processing Document

Every word processor contains an assortment of operations for creating and editing documents, including commands to insert both text and graphics and then move, copy, delete, or otherwise edit the content, as needed. Some features in a typical word processing program are shown in Figure 6-10.

When entering text in a word processing document, it is important to know when to press the Enter key. Word processing programs use a feature called **word wrap**, which means the insertion point automatically moves to the beginning of the next line when the end of the screen line is reached. Consequently, the Enter key should not be pressed until it

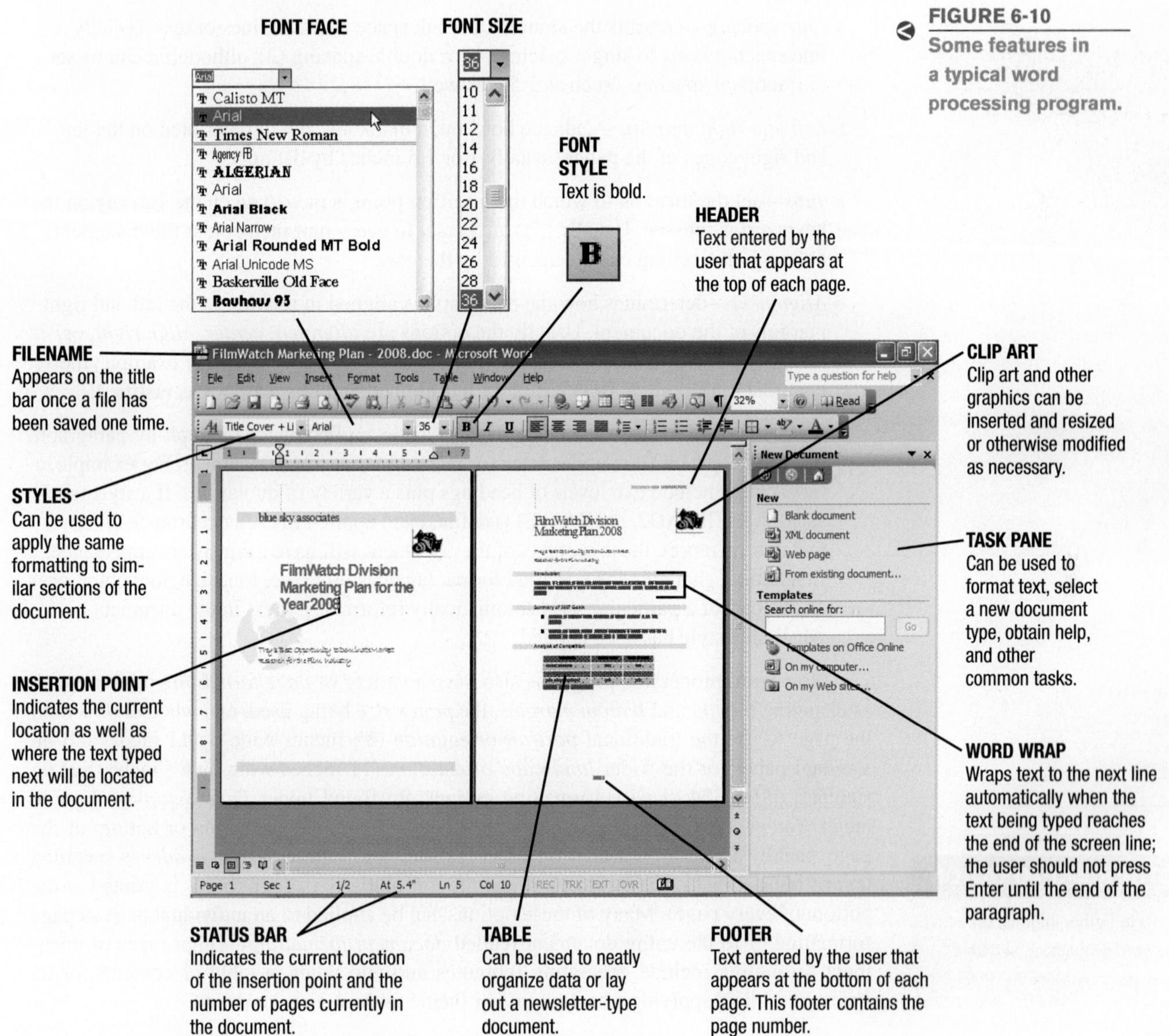

FONT FACE
FONT SIZE
FONT STYLE
Text is bold.
HEADER
Text entered by the user that appears at the top of each page.
FILENAME
Appears on the title bar once a file has been saved one time.
CLIP ART
Clip art and other graphics can be inserted and resized or otherwise modified as necessary.
STYLES
Can be used to apply the same formatting to similar sections of the document.
TASK PANE
Can be used to format text, select a new document type, obtain help, and other common tasks.
INSERTION POINT
Indicates the current location as well as where the text typed next will be located in the document.
WORD WRAP
Wraps text to the next line automatically when the text being typed reaches the end of the screen line; the user should not press Enter until the end of the paragraph.
STATUS BAR
Indicates the current location of the insertion point and the number of pages currently in the document.
TABLE
Can be used to neatly organize data or lay out a newsletter-type document.
FOOTER
Text entered by the user that appears at the bottom of each page. This footer contains the page number.
FilmWatch Marketing Plan - 2008.doc - Microsoft Word
FilmWatch Division Marketing Plan for the Year 2008

FIGURE 6-10
Some features in a typical word processing program.

SW

>**Word wrap.** The feature in a word processing program that automatically returns the insertion point to the next line when the end of the screen line is reached.

TIP

When typing text in a word processing program, you should only press Enter after a short line (like a title), at the end of a paragraph, and to leave a blank line between paragraphs.

is time to begin a new paragraph. When changes are made to the document—such as adding, modifying, or deleting text or changing the text size or page margins—the program will automatically adjust the amount of text on each screen line, as long as the Enter key is not pressed at the end of a line.

In most word processing programs, formatting can be applied at the character, paragraph, and document levels. Character *formatting* changes the appearance of individual characters, such as to change the font face, size, style, or color. To format characters, you usually select them with the mouse, and then apply the appropriate format using either toolbar buttons (refer again to Figure 6-10) or the *Font* option on the Format menu.

Paragraph formatting changes an entire paragraph at one time, such as specifying the line spacing for a particular paragraph. To format paragraphs, you usually select the paragraph with the mouse, and then apply the appropriate format using either toolbar buttons or the *Paragraph* option on the Format menu. The most common types of paragraph formatting are listed next.

- *Line spacing*—controls the amount of blank space between lines of text. Usually line spacing is set to single spacing (1) or double spacing (2), although it can be set to fractional spacing—such as 1.5—as well.
- *Left* and *right margins*—indicate how much blank space will be printed on the left and right edges of the paper (usually 1 or 1.5 inches by default).
- *Tabs*—set the location to which the insertion point is moved when the Tab key on the keyboard is pressed. Usually tabs are preset to every half inch across the document, although this setting can be changed by the user.
- *Alignment*—determines how the paragraph is aligned in relation to the left and right margins of the document. Usually the options are *align left*, *center*, *align right*, or *justify* (flush with both the left and right edges of the document). For example, the document in Figure 6-10 is primarily left-aligned and this textbook is justified.
- *Styles*—named format specifications that can be applied on a paragraph-by-paragraph basis to keep a uniform appearance for related sections in a document. For example, a report may include two levels of headings plus a variety of quotations. If a style (such as HEAD1, HEAD2, or QUOTE) is defined and applied to each occurrence of these parts of the report, those sections of the document will have a consistent appearance. In addition, changing the specified format (such as font face, font size, font color, or alignment) of a particular style automatically reformats all text in the document to which that style has been applied.

Most word processing programs also have a variety of *page formatting* options, such as changing the *top* and *bottom margins*, the *paper size* being used, and whether you want the page to use the traditional *portrait orientation* (8½ inches wide by 11 inches tall on standard paper) or the wider *landscape orientation* (11 inches wide by 8½ inches tall on standard paper). Most page formatting options are found under *Page Setup* on the File menu. You can also choose whether to include page numbers at the top or bottom of the page, usually as part of a header or footer (as shown in Figure 6-10, a *header* is specified text or images that print automatically at the top of every page; a *footer* is printed at the bottom of every page). Many of these options can be applied to an individual page as page formatting or to the entire document (called *document formatting*). Other types of document formatting include generating footnotes and end notes, a table of contents, or an index, as well as applying a background or theme to the entire document.

FURTHER EXPLORATION

For links to further information about word processing software, go to www.course.com/uc11/ch06

Tables, Graphics, and Templates

Most word processing programs today have advanced features to help users create documents or add special features to documents. For instance, a *table* feature allows content to be organized in a table consisting of *rows* and *columns*. It can be used for a basic data table, such as the one shown in Figure 6-10; tables can also be used for layout purposes, such as

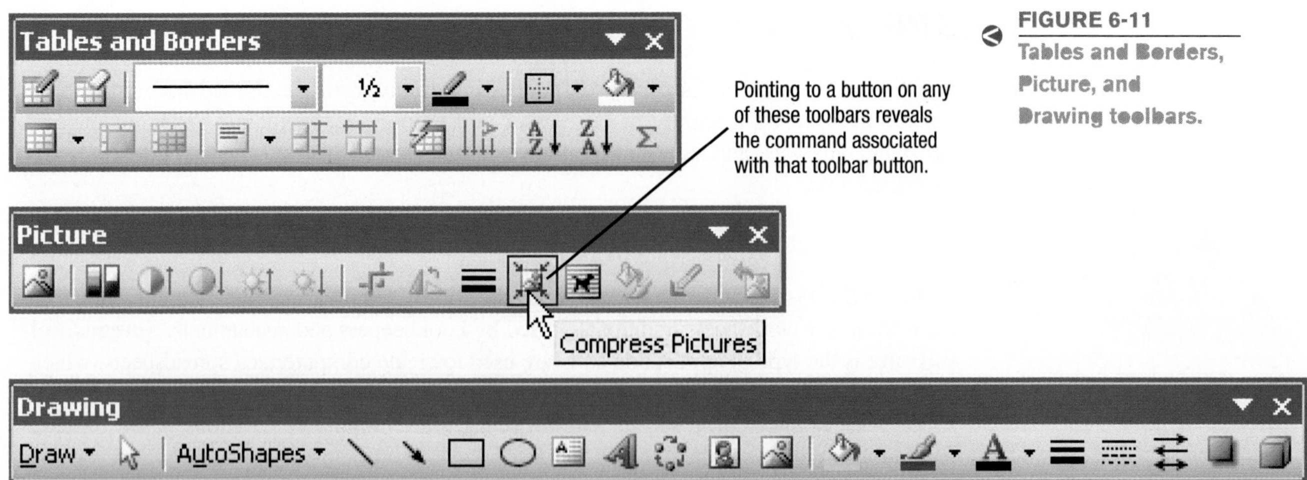
Tables and Borders
Picture
Compress Pictures
Drawing
Draw
AutoShapes
Pointing to a button on any of these toolbars reveals the command associated with that toolbar button.

FIGURE 6-11
Tables and Borders, Picture, and Drawing toolbars.

when creating a newsletter or Web page. Once a table has been created, shading, borders, and other formatting can be applied to the table and/or its contents, and rows and columns can be inserted or deleted, as needed. The *Tables and Borders toolbar* available in Word to help users create and modify tables is shown in Figure 6-11.

Graphics or *drawing* features are also commonly found in word processing programs. Virtually all word processing programs allow images (such as a photograph, a drawing from another program, or a *clip art image*, as in Figure 6-10) to be inserted into a document. Once an image is inserted into a document, it can be modified (such as changing the brightness or contrast of a digital photo, cropping an image, converting a color image to grayscale, compressing an image to reduce the file size of the document, or adding borders). The *Picture toolbar* used in Word for these purposes is shown in Figure 6-11 along with the *Drawing Toolbar* that can be used to create new images (such as arrows and other graphical shapes). Once images are inserted into a document, they can be copied, moved, deleted, or otherwise modified, just like any other object in the document.

To help users create new documents quickly, many word processing programs have a variety of *templates* available. A template is a document that is already created and formatted to fit a particular purpose, such as a fax cover sheet, résumé, memo, business card, calendar, business plan, newsletter, or Web page. Usually placeholder text is included for text that can be customized so that all the user needs to do is fill in the blanks on the template document. A similar tool is a *wizard*, which consists of a series of screens that prompt the user for the necessary information and then creates a particular type of document based on the users input. Wizards are typically available for creating documents, such as envelopes, legal pleadings, calendars, and agendas, as well as for tasks, such as sending a fax or publishing a Web page.

TIP

Additional templates are often available for free through software manufacturer Web sites, such as Microsoft's *Office Online* Web site.

Word Processing and the Web

Most word processing programs today include Web-related features, such as the ability to send a document as an e-mail message via the word processing program, the inclusion of Web page hyperlinks in documents, and the ability to create or modify Web pages. Optional file formats for Web pages created in many word processing programs include regular *Hypertext Markup Language* (*HTML*), the more versatile *Extensible Markup Language* (*XML*), and the *single file Web page* or *MHTML* (*MIME Hypertext Markup Language*) format that combines all the elements of a Web site (text, images, sound files, animated items, and other elements) into a single file so it can be more easily published to the Web or sent via e-mail to others.

TIP

When hyperlinks are included in a document, clicking the hyperlink opens the corresponding Web page, as long as the computer being used has an active Internet connection.

SW

SPREADSHEET CONCEPTS

Another widely used application program is *spreadsheet software*. Spreadsheet software is commonly used by a variety of businesses and employees, including CEOs, managers, assistants, analysts, and sales representatives. Basic spreadsheet concepts and features are described next.

What Is a Spreadsheet?

A **spreadsheet** is a group of values and other data organized into rows and columns, similar to the ruled paper worksheets traditionally used by bookkeepers and accountants. **Spreadsheet software** is the type of application software used to create computerized spreadsheets, which typically contain a great deal of numbers and mathematical calculations. Because spreadsheets are designed to be set up with *formulas* that compute calculations based on data entered into the spreadsheet, all formula results are automatically updated whenever any changes are made to the data. Consequently, no manual computations are required, which increases accuracy. In addition, the automatic recalculation of formulas allows individuals to modify spreadsheet data as often as necessary either to create new spreadsheets or to experiment with various possible scenarios to help make business decisions. Spreadsheet software typically also includes the ability to generate charts and perform detailed analysis based on the data in a spreadsheet.

The most widely used spreadsheet programs today are *Microsoft Excel*, *Corel Quattro Pro*, and *Lotus 1-2-3*—again, all part of the software suites mentioned at the beginning of this chapter; some are also available as individual programs. Some of the basic features supported by all spreadsheet programs are described in the next few sections, using Microsoft Excel as the example.

Creating a Spreadsheet

TIP

As with word processing programs, spreadsheet templates are available to help users quickly create common types of business documents, such as balance sheets, income statements, invoices, and purchase orders.

A single spreadsheet document is often called a **worksheet**. Most spreadsheet programs allow multiple worksheets to be saved together in a single spreadsheet file, called a **workbook**. Worksheets are divided into **rows** and **columns**. The intersection of a row and a column is called a **cell**. Each cell is identified by its *cell address*, which consists of the column letter followed by the row number, such as B4 or E22. The *cell pointer* is used to select a cell. The selected cell is called the *active cell* (also called the *current cell*) and has a border around it so it is easy to identify. You can enter content in the active cell, as well as apply formatting to content already in the active cell. The cell pointer can also be used to select more than one cell; if so, the selected cells are called a *range* or *block*. Ranges are always rectangular and are identified by specifying two opposite corners of the range, such as D8 through E9 (usually typed as *D8:E9* or *D8..E9*, depending on the spreadsheet program being used) for the four cells in the range shown in Figure 6-12.

TIP

Clip art, graphics, photographs, and other images can also be inserted into a cell–look for a *Picture* option on the Insert menu.

Data is entered directly into worksheet cells by clicking a cell to make it the active cell and then typing the data. Cell content can be erased by pressing the Delete key; typing new content replaces the old content of the active cell with the new content. The data entered into a cell is usually a *label*, a *constant value*, a *formula*, or a *function*. **Labels** are words, column headings, and other nonmathematical data, such as *Profit Statement* and *July* in Figure 6-12. **Constant values** are numbers, such as *105* or *12740.25*, and are entered into a cell without any additional characters, such as a dollar sign or comma. The *numeric format* or *style* applied to a cell (such as *Currency*, *Comma*, or *Percent*) determines how the

---

>**Spreadsheet.** A group of values and other data organized into rows and columns. >**Spreadsheet software.** Application software used to create spreadsheets, which typically contain a great deal of numbers and mathematical computations and are organized into rows and columns. >**Worksheet.** A document in a spreadsheet program. >**Workbook.** A collection of worksheets saved in a single spreadsheet file. >**Row.** In a spreadsheet program, a horizontal group of cells on a worksheet. >**Column.** In a spreadsheet program, a vertical group of cells on a worksheet. >**Cell.** The location at the intersection of a row and column on a worksheet into which data can be typed. >**Label.** A text-based entry in a worksheet cell that identifies data on the worksheet. >**Constant value.** A numerical entry in a worksheet cell.

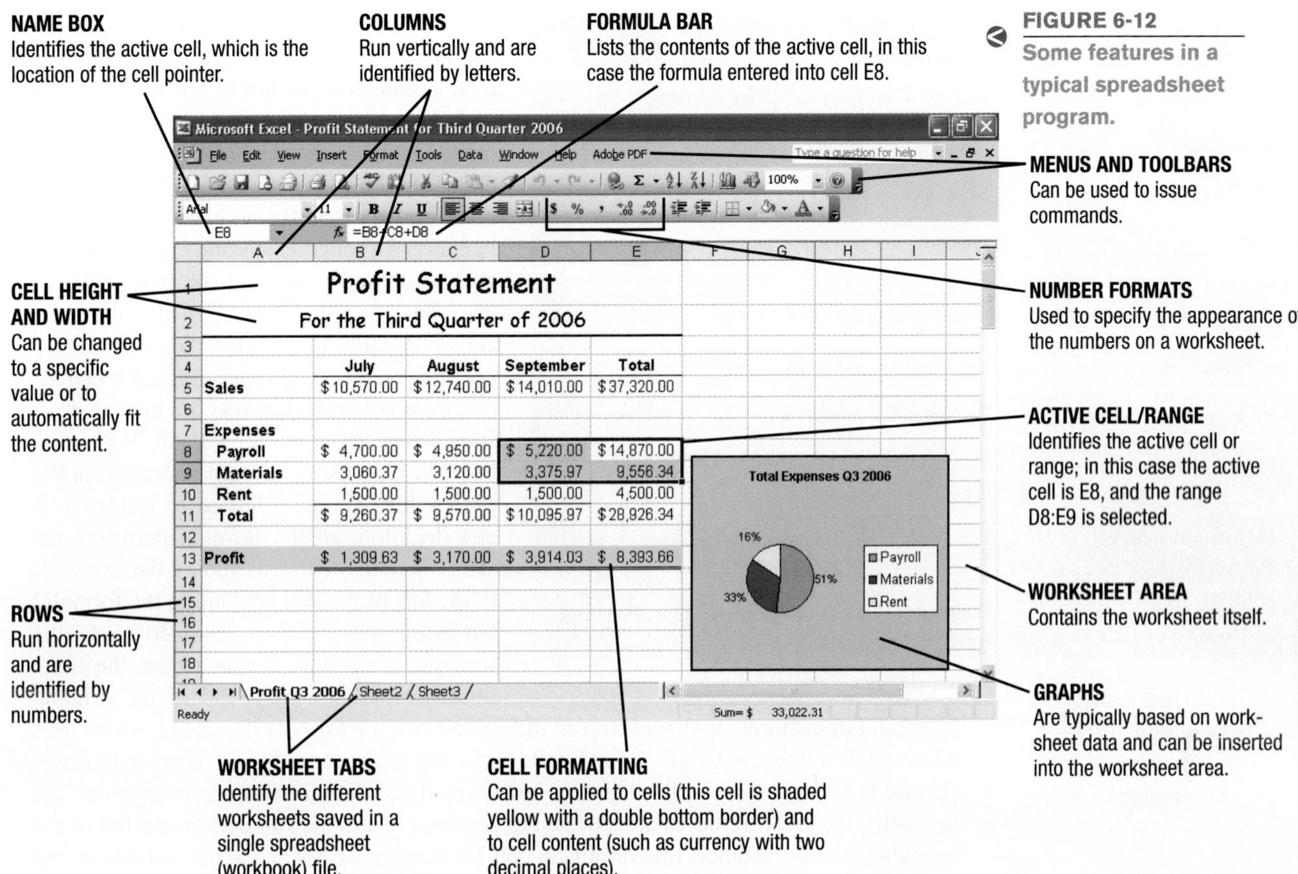
NAME BOX
Identifies the active cell, which is the location of the cell pointer.
COLUMNS
Run vertically and are identified by letters.
FORMULA BAR
Lists the contents of the active cell, in this case the formula entered into cell E8.
MENUS AND TOOLBARS
Can be used to issue commands.
CELL HEIGHT AND WIDTH
Can be changed to a specific value or to automatically fit the content.
NUMBER FORMATS
Used to specify the appearance of the numbers on a worksheet.
ACTIVE CELL/RANGE
Identifies the active cell or range; in this case the active cell is E8, and the range D8:E9 is selected.
ROWS
Run horizontally and are identified by numbers.
WORKSHEET AREA
Contains the worksheet itself.
GRAPHS
Are typically based on worksheet data and can be inserted into the worksheet area.
WORKSHEET TABS
Identify the different worksheets saved in a single spreadsheet (workbook) file.
CELL FORMATTING
Can be applied to cells (this cell is shaded yellow with a double bottom border) and to cell content (such as currency with two decimal places).
Microsoft Excel - Profit Statement for Third Quarter 2006
E8
=B8+C8+D8
Profit Statement
For the Third Quarter of 2006
July
August
September
Total
Sales
$ 10,570.00
$ 12,740.00
$ 14,010.00
$ 37,320.00
Expenses
Payroll
$ 4,700.00
$ 4,950.00
$ 5,220.00
$ 14,870.00
Materials
3,060.37
3,120.00
3,375.97
9,556.34
Rent
1,500.00
1,500.00
1,500.00
4,500.00
Total
$ 9,260.37
$ 9,570.00
$ 10,095.97
$ 28,926.34
Profit
$ 1,309.63
$ 3,170.00
$ 3,914.03
$ 8,393.66
Total Expenses Q3 2006
16%
33%
51%
Payroll
Materials
Rent
Profit Q3 2006
Sheet2
Sheet3
Ready
Sum= $ 33,022.31

FIGURE 6-12
Some features in a typical spreadsheet program.

numeric content of the cell will display. A **formula** performs mathematical operations on the content of other cells—such as adding or multiplying them—and displays the results in the cell containing the formula. A **function** is a named, programmed formula, such as to compute the average of a group of cells or calculate a mortgage payment amount. Common mathematical operators are listed in Figure 6-13; some commonly used spreadsheet functions are listed in Figure 6-14.

When entering a formula or function into a cell, most spreadsheet programs require that you begin with some type of mathematical symbol, usually the equal sign =. You can then enter the cell addresses and mathematical operators to create the formula, or you can type the appropriate function name and *arguments* (such as a cell or range address). When creating formulas and functions, it is important to always use the cell addresses of *where* the numbers you want to include in the calculation are located (such as =B8+C8+D8 for the formula used to calculate the value displayed in cell E8 in Figure 6-12), rather than the numbers themselves (such as =4700+4950+5220). If the actual numbers are used in the formula instead of the cell addresses, the result of that formula (such as the total in cell E8) will not be correctly updated if one of the numbers (such as July payroll expenses in cell B8) is changed. When a proper formula (using the cell references instead of the actual numbers) is used instead, the formula will be recomputed automatically every time any data in any of the cells used in that formula is changed.

FIGURE 6-13
Mathematical operators. These mathematical operators are universal operators used by most application programs that perform calculations, including spreadsheet programs.

SYMBOL	OPERATION
+	Addition
–	Subtraction
*	Multiplication
/	Division
^	Exponentiation

>**Formula.** An entry in a worksheet cell that performs computations on worksheet data and displays the results. >**Function.** A named formula that can be entered into a worksheet cell to perform some type of calculation or to extract information from other cells in the worksheet.

EXAMPLES OF FUNCTIONS	
= SUM (range)	Calculates the sum of all values in a range.
= MAX (range)	Finds the highest value in a range.
= MIN (range)	Finds the lowest value in a range.
= NOW ( )	Inserts the current date and time.
= COUNT (range)	Counts the number of nonempty cells containing numerical values in a range.
= AVERAGE (range)	Calculates the average of values in a range.
= ABS (cell or expression)	Calculates the absolute value of the cell or expression.
= FV (rate, number of payments, payment amount)	Calculates the future value of an annuity at a specified interest rate.
= PMT (rate, number of payments, loan amount)	Calculates the periodic payment for a loan.
= IF (conditional expression, value if true, value if false)	Supplies the values to be displayed if the conditional expression is true or if it is false

FIGURE 6-14
Common spreadsheet functions.

Because many spreadsheet columns contain similar formulas (such as to add the three columns to the left of the Total column in the spreadsheet shown in Figure 6-12), the copy command can be used to duplicate formulas to help create a spreadsheet much more quickly than typing each formula individually. Although labels and constant values will be copied exactly to the new location, the way formulas behave when they are copied depends on whether they use *relative cell referencing* or *absolute cell referencing*.

Relative cell references are used in most spreadsheet programs by default. With relative cell references, the cell addresses in the copied formula are adjusted to reflect their new location, so the formula performs the same operation (such as adding the two cells to the left of the cell containing the formula) but in the new location. In other words, the formula in the new location does the same *relative* operation as it did in the original location. For example, in the left screen in Figure 6-15, the formula in cell D2, which uses relative cell references to add the two cells to the left of the formula cell, is copied to cells D3 and D4. Because the cell references are all relative, when the formula is copied to the new cells, the cell references are adjusted to continue to add the two cells to the left of the formula cell. For instance, the formula in cell D3 became =B3+C3 and the formula in cell D4 became =B4+C4. Relative cell references are also adjusted accordingly when a row or column is inserted or deleted.

In contrast, when *absolute cell references* are used, formulas are copied exactly as they are written (see the rightmost screens in Figure 6-15). It is appropriate to use an absolute cell reference when you always want to use a specific cell address in all copies of

COPYING WITH RELATIVE CELL REFERENCES
In most formulas, cell addresses are relative and will be adjusted as the formula is copied.

D2 | =B2+C2

	A	B	C	D
1		Cones	Sundaes	Total
2	April	600	200	800
3	May	800	500	1300
4	June	1500	600	2100
5	Total			
6				

Formula for cell D2

Formula for cell D4 became =B4+C4

Results when the formula in cell D2 is copied to cells D3 and D4.

COPYING WITH ABSOLUTE CELL REFERENCES
A dollar ($) sign marks a cell reference as absolute; it will be copied exactly as it appears in the source cell.

D2 | =$B$2+$C$2

	A	B	C	D
1		Cones	Sundaes	Total
2	April	600	200	800
3	May	800	500	800
4	June	1500	600	800
5	Total			
6				

Formula for cell D2

Results when the formula in cell D2 is copied to cells D3 and D4.

Formula for cell D4 became =$B$2+$C$2.

IMPROPER USE

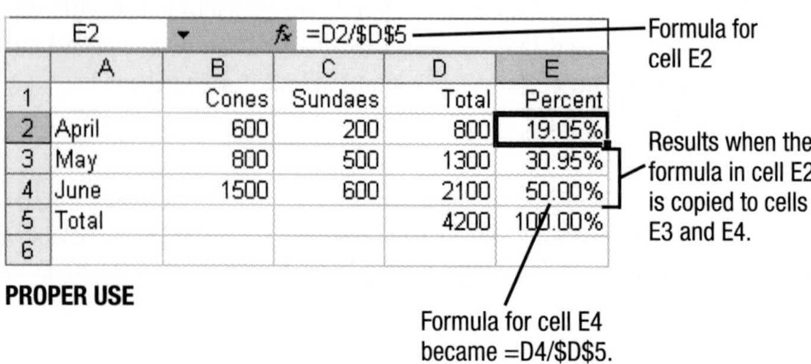

E2 | =D2/$D$5

	A	B	C	D	E
1		Cones	Sundaes	Total	Percent
2	April	600	200	800	19.05%
3	May	800	500	1300	30.95%
4	June	1500	600	2100	50.00%
5	Total			4200	100.00%
6					

Formula for cell E2
Results when the formula in cell E2 is copied to cells E3 and E4.
Formula for cell E4 became =D4/$D$5.

PROPER USE

FIGURE 6-15
Relative vs. absolute cell referencing.

the formula—such as always multiplying by a constant value (perhaps a sales tax rate or overtime rate located in a particular cell on the worksheet) or always dividing by a total in order to compute a percentage. In other words, whenever you do not want a cell address to be adjusted when the formula is copied, you must use an absolute cell reference in the formula. To make a cell reference in a formula absolute, a special symbol—usually a dollar sign ($)—is placed before each column letter and row number that should not change. For example, both of the cell references in the formula in cell D2 in the top right screen in Figure 6-15 are absolute, resulting in the formula =$B$2+$C$2 being placed in both cells (D3 and D4) when the formula is copied. Obviously, this is not the correct formula for these cells—the formulas in these cells need to use relative cell references in order to display the proper total. In cells E2 through E4 in the bottom right screen, however, an absolute cell reference is used for cell D5 (written as $D$5) in the formula to compute the percent of total sales by dividing the total sales for each month by the total sales for all three months (located in cell D5). In fact, an absolute reference for cell D5 is necessary if the formula in cell E2 is to be copied to cells E3 and E4, since the denominator in all three cells should be D5.

TIP

Some spreadsheet programs support a shortcut for quickly copying a cell to adjacent cells, such as dragging the bottom right corner of the original cell in Microsoft Excel.

Charts and What-If Analysis

Most spreadsheet programs include some type of *charting* or *graphing* capability. Because the data to be included in many business charts is often already located on a spreadsheet, using that program's charting feature eliminates reentering data. Instead, the cells containing the data to be charted are selected, and then the type of chart—as well as titles and other customizations—can be specified. The finished chart can usually be inserted into a range of cells on an existing worksheet (refer again to Figure 6-12) or placed in a blank worksheet by itself. Types of charts are discussed in more detail later in this chapter.

Because spreadsheet programs automatically recalculate all formulas on a worksheet every time a cell on the worksheet is edited, they are particularly useful for *what-if analysis* (also called *sensitivity analysis*)—a tool frequently used to help make business decisions. For example, suppose you want to know *what* profit would have resulted for July in Figure 6-12 *if* sales had been $15,000 instead of $10,570. You can simply enter the new value (15000) into Cell B5, and the spreadsheet program automatically recalculates all formulas, allowing you to determine (from looking at the new value in cell B13) that the profit would have been $5,739.63. This ability to enter new numbers and immediately see the results allows businesspeople to run through many more possibilities in a shorter period of time before making decisions than in the past when all such calculations had to be performed by hand. Another type of sensitivity analysis (called *goal seeking* in Microsoft Excel) involves having the spreadsheet compute the amount a constant value would need to be in order for the result of a particular formula to become a specified amount (such as the total sales required to obtain a July profit of $5,000 if all of the expenses stayed the same).

FURTHER EXPLORATION

For links to further information about spreadsheet software, go to www.course.com/uc11/ch06

Spreadsheets and the Web

As with word processors, most spreadsheet programs have built-in Web capabilities. Although they are less commonly used to create Web pages, many spreadsheet programs have an option on the File menu to save the current worksheet as a Web page, and hyperlinks can be inserted into worksheet cells. Ranges of cells can also be selected and copied to a Web publishing or word processing program to insert spreadsheet data into a Web page as a table.

DATABASE CONCEPTS

People often need to retrieve large amounts of data rapidly. For example, a customer service representative may need to locate a customer's order status quickly while the customer is on the telephone. The registrar at a university may have to look up a student's grade point average or rapidly determine if the student has any outstanding fees before processing his or her class registration. A clerk in a video store may need to determine if a particular movie is available for rental and, if not, when it is due to be returned. The type of software used for such tasks is a *database management system*. Computer-based database management systems are rapidly replacing the paper-based filing systems that people used in the past to find information. The most common type of database used on PCs today is a *relational database*. The basic features and concepts of PC-based relational database software are discussed next. Other types of database programs are discussed in Chapter 14.

What Is a Database?

A **database** is a collection of related data that is stored on a computer and organized in a manner enabling information to be retrieved as needed (see Figure 6-16). A *database management system* (*DBMS*)—also called **database software**—is the type of program

FIGURE 6-16 Paper-based vs. computerized databases. Data is organized into fields (columns), records (rows), and tables.

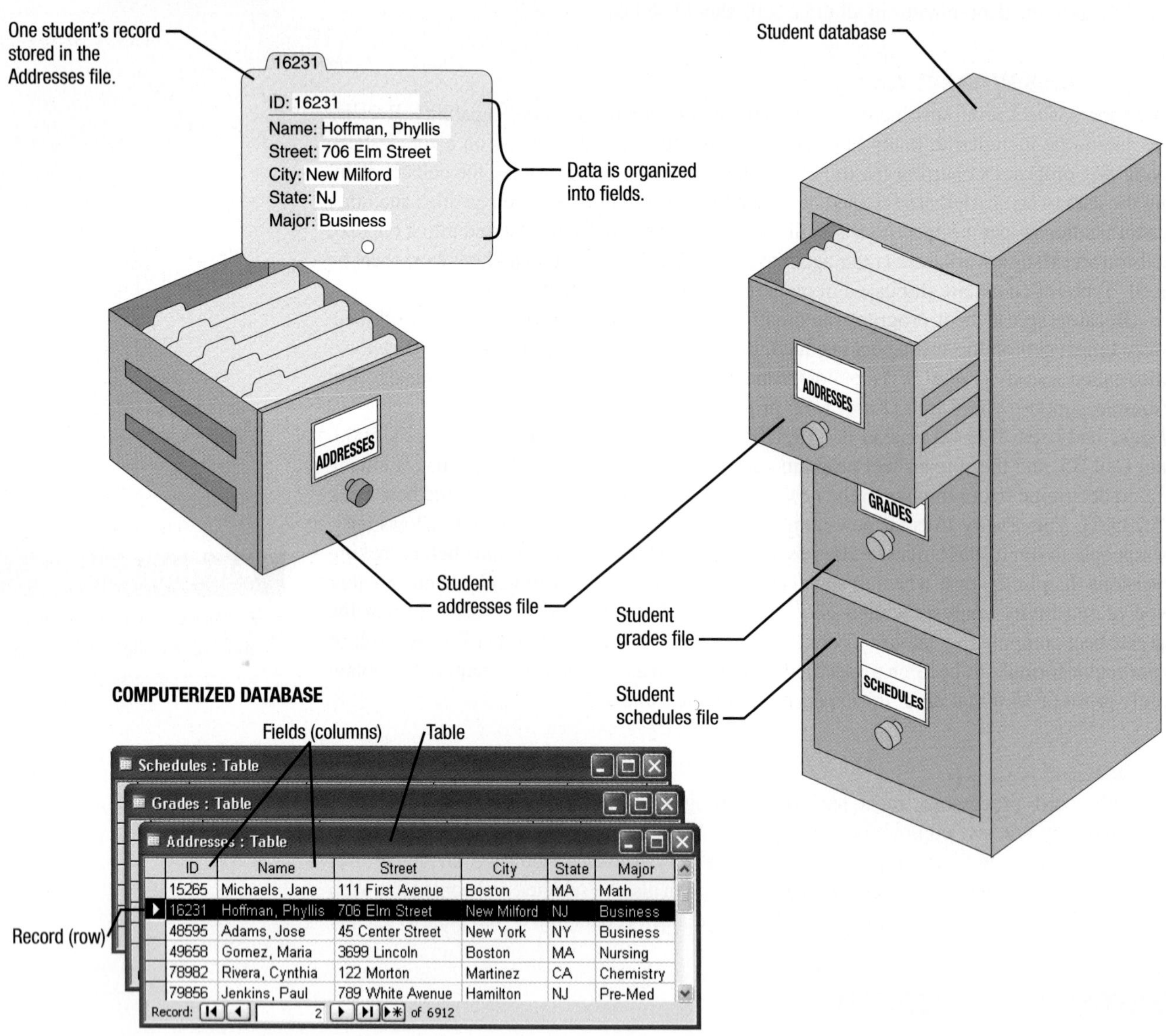

>**Database.** A collection of related data that is stored in a manner enabling information to be retrieved as needed; in a relational database, a collection of related tables. >**Database software.** Application software that allows the creation and manipulation of an electronic database.

used to create, maintain, and organize data in a database, as well as to retrieve information from it. Although not all databases are organized identically, most are organized into *fields*, *records*, and *files*. A **field** (today more commonly called a **column**) is a single type of data, such as a person's name or a person's telephone number, to be stored in a database. A **record** (today more commonly called a **row**) is a collection of related fields—for example the ID number, name, address, and major of Phyllis Hoffman (refer again to Figure 6-16). A **table** is a collection of related rows (such as all student address data, all student grade data, or all student schedule data). One or more related tables can be stored in a database file.

The most commonly used *relational database management systems* (*RDBMSs*) include *Microsoft Access*, *Corel Paradox*, and *Lotus Approach*—all part of their respective software suites—as well as the stand-alone *Oracle Database* product from Oracle Corporation. Some of the basic features of database programs in general are described in the next few sections, using Microsoft Access as the example.

FURTHER EXPLORATION

For links to further information about database software, go to www.course.com/uc11/ch06

Creating a Database

A database can contain a variety of *objects* (see Figure 6-17). The object that contains the data in a new database is the *table*; other objects (such as *forms*, *queries*, and *reports*, discussed shortly) can be created and used in conjunction with that table when needed. Unlike word processing documents and spreadsheets, you do not see the content of a database table or other object on the screen at all times—only when you request to see it.

To create a database table, the *structure* of the table is specified first. A table's structure includes a list of fields and their properties. As a minimum, each field needs to have a *field name* (an identifying name unique within the table) and a *data type* (the type of data to be contained in the field, for example text, a number, a date, or an object such as a photo) defined. Other possible properties include the *field size* (the maximum number of characters allowed for the content of that field), *default value* (the initial content of the field that remains until it is changed), the format identifying how the field content should be displayed, and whether or not the field is *required* (must contain some content). A table structure is shown in Figure 6-18.

After the table structure has been created, data is entered into the table. This can occur using either the table's *Datasheet view* or a *form* created to enter data into that table (refer again to Figure 6-18). Existing table data can be edited in the same manner. If the structure of the table needs to be changed, such as to change the size or type of a field, the table needs to be opened in *Design view*, which is the same screen used to originally create the table structure.

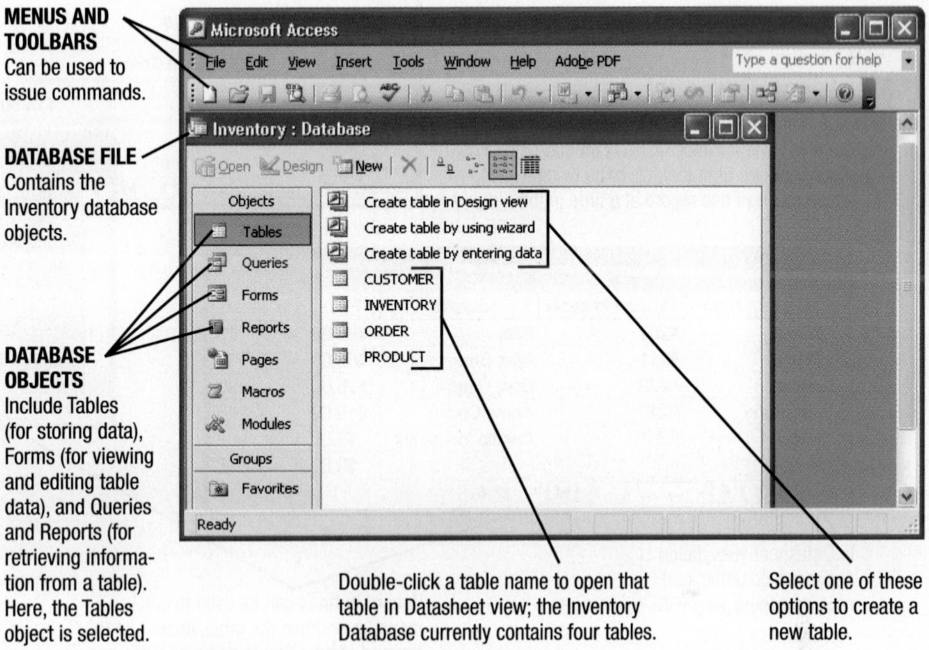

MENUS AND TOOLBARS Can be used to issue commands.

DATABASE FILE Contains the Inventory database objects.

DATABASE OBJECTS Include Tables (for storing data), Forms (for viewing and editing table data), and Queries and Reports (for retrieving information from a table). Here, the Tables object is selected.

Double-click a table name to open that table in Datasheet view; the Inventory Database currently contains four tables.

Select one of these options to create a new table.

FIGURE 6-17

Typical database objects. Common database objects include tables, forms, queries, and reports. The first object to be created is the table.

>**Field.** A single category of data to be stored in a database, such as a person's name or telephone number. Also called a column. >**Column.** In a database, a field. >**Record.** A collection of related fields in a database. Also called a row. >**Row.** In a database program, a record. >**Table.** In a relational database, a collection of related records or rows.

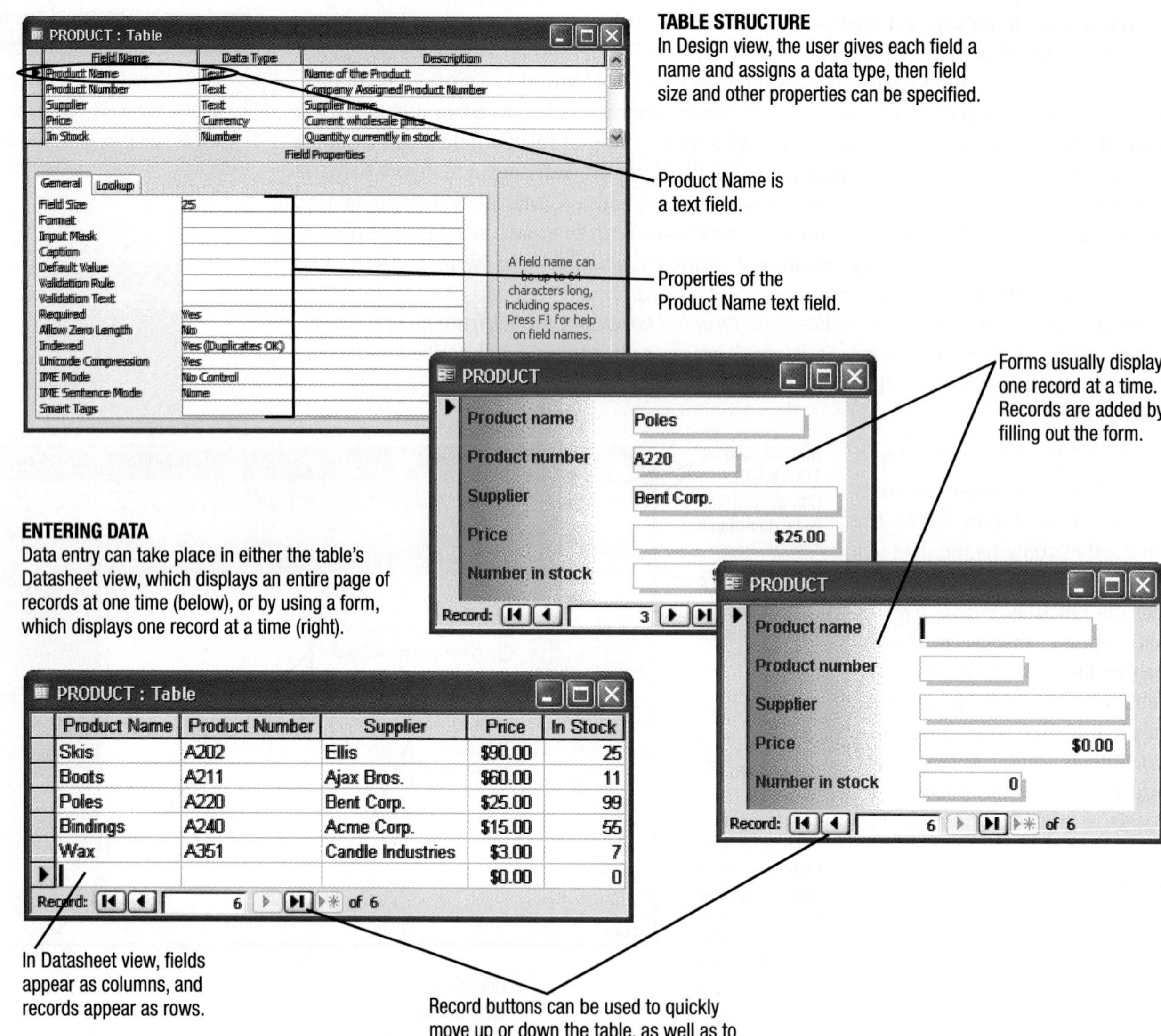

FIGURE 6-18
Creating a database in a typical database program.

Queries and Reports

To retrieve information from a database, *queries* and *reports* are used. A *query* is a question, or, in database terms, a request for specific information from the database. Each query object is created and saved under its own name in the database file. A query object contains *criteria*—specific conditions that must be met in order for a record (row) to be included in the query results—as well as instructions regarding which fields (columns) should appear in the query results. For instance, the criteria for the query shown in Figure 6-19 is all products with prices less than $25 and the query results should display only the Product Name, Product Number, and Price fields. Whenever the query is opened and the results displayed, only the specified three fields for only the records meeting the specified criteria at the time are displayed. Each time the query is opened, the query results will accurately reflect the current data in the database. For instance, the query results shown in Figure 6-19 contain only the two records from the table in Figure 6-18 that contain products with prices less than $25, but if a new product priced less than $25 was added to the database, three records would be displayed when the query was reopened.

TIP

Databases, queries, and reports are discussed in more detail in Chapter 14.

When a more formal output is required, *reports* are used. Report objects are typically created using a wizard and can contain page and column headings, as well as additional formatting and customized output. Whenever a report object is opened, the corresponding table data is displayed in the specified location on the report. Consequently, just as with queries, reports always display the data contained in a table at the time the report is generated. Many database programs allow reports to be created in a variety of styles and can incorporate text formatting, clip art, and other enhancements.

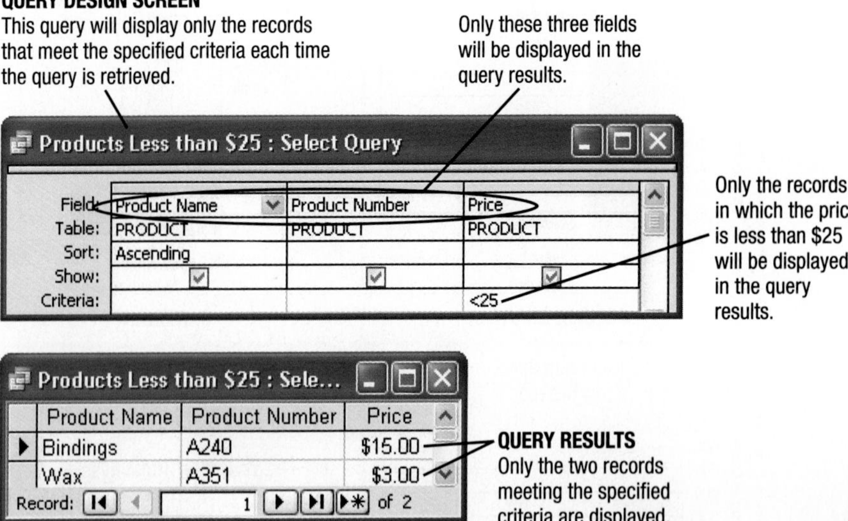
QUERY DESIGN SCREEN
This query will display only the records that meet the specified criteria each time the query is retrieved.
Only these three fields will be displayed in the query results.
Products Less than $25 : Select Query
Field: Product Name
Product Number
Price
Table: PRODUCT
PRODUCT
PRODUCT
Sort: Ascending
Show:
Criteria:
<25
Only the records in which the price is less than $25 will be displayed in the query results.
Products Less than $25 : Sele...
Product Name
Product Number
Price
Bindings
A240
$15.00
Wax
A351
$3.00
Record: 1 of 2
QUERY RESULTS
Only the two records meeting the specified criteria are displayed.

FIGURE 6-19
Creating and using a database query.

Databases and the Web

Databases are used often on the Web. Many Web sites use one or more databases to keep track of inventory; allow searching for people, documents, or other information; place real-time orders; and so forth. For instance, anytime you type keywords in a search site or hunt for a product on a retail store's Web site using its search feature, you are using a Web database. Web databases are explained in more detail in Chapter 14.

PRESENTATION GRAPHICS CONCEPTS

If you try to explain to others what you look like, it may take several minutes. Show them a color photograph, on the other hand, and you can convey the same information within seconds. The saying "a picture is worth a thousand words" is the cornerstone of *presentation graphics*. The basic concepts and features of presentation graphics are discussed in the next few sections.

What Is a Presentation Graphic?

A **presentation graphic** is an image designed to visually enhance a presentation, typically to convey information more easily to people. Presentation graphics can be used in *electronic slide shows*, as well as in printed handouts, overhead transparencies, word processing documents, and Web pages. Some examples of presentation graphics are shown in Figure 6-20.

To create presentation graphics, **presentation graphics software** is used. Some of today's most common presentation graphics programs are *Microsoft PowerPoint*, *Corel Presentations*, and *Lotus Freelance Graphics*. While some presentation graphics programs are designed to create stand-alone graphics, presentation graphics software is more often used to create electronic slide shows; that is, groups of electronic **slides**. Each slide—containing content such as text, images, video clips, or sound clips—is displayed one at a time, typically for a business presentation. Slide shows can be run on individual computers or presented to a large group using a computer projector. The next few sections discuss creating an electronic slide show, using Microsoft PowerPoint as the example.

>**Presentation graphic.** An image, such as a graph or text chart, designed to visually enhance a presentation. >**Presentation graphics software.** Application software used to create presentation graphics and online slide shows. >**Slide.** A one-page presentation graphic that can be displayed in a group with others to form an online slide show.

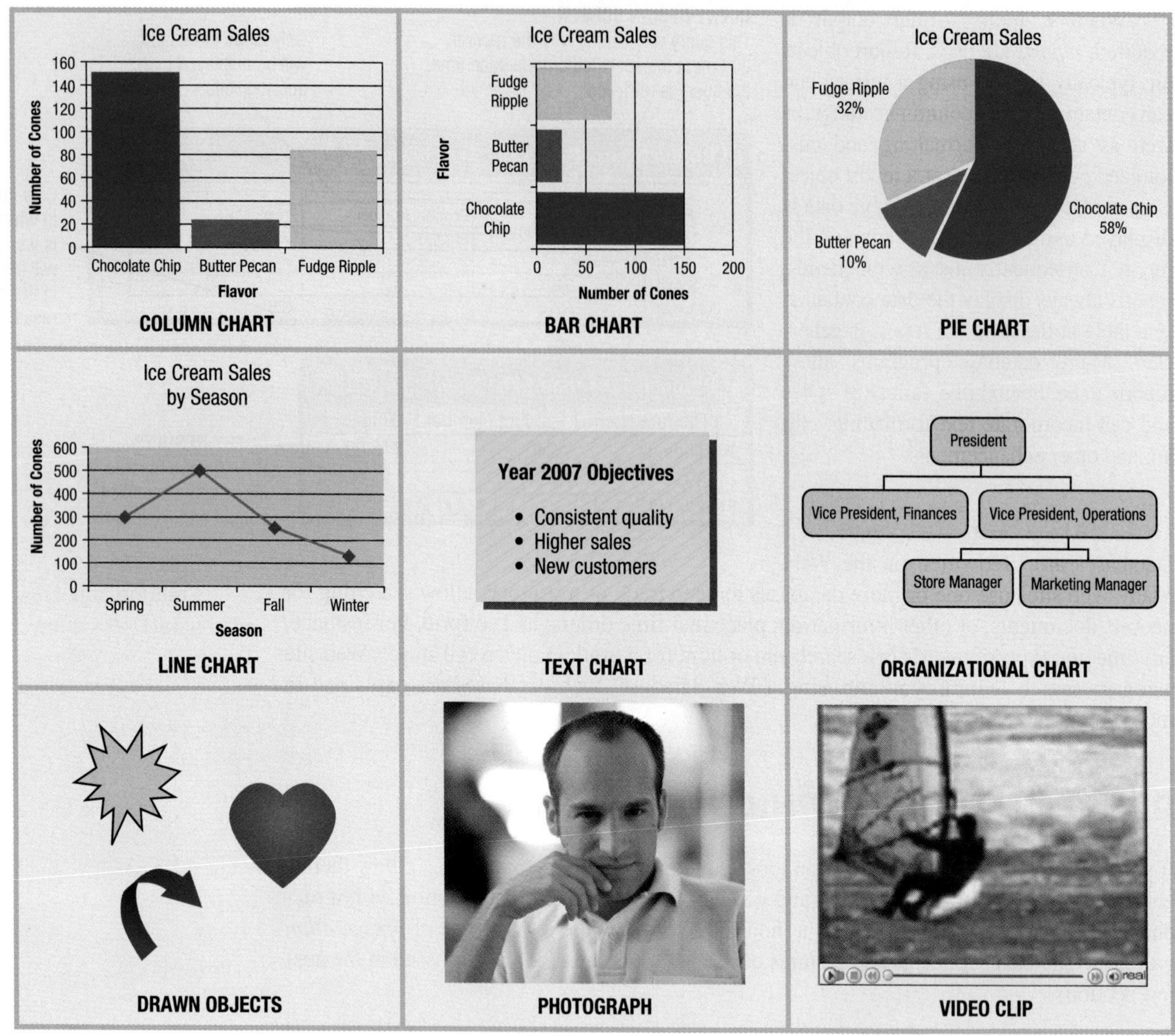

FIGURE 6-20
Examples of presentation graphics. Presentation graphics can include a variety of charts, text, images, video clips, and more.

TIP

Although transitions and other effects can make a presentation more interesting, remember that the most important part of a presentation is the content.

Creating a Presentation

Presentation graphics programs contain an assortment of tools and operations for creating and editing slides, including preformatted *slide layouts* containing placeholders for the various elements in the slide (such as text, images, or charts) that can be selected to quickly create a basic slide by replacing the placeholders with the proper content. Additional slides can be inserted into the presentation, photos or drawn objects can be added to slides, text can be formatted, and other modifications can be made until the presentation is completed. A typical presentation graphics program is shown in Figure 6-21.

To create more exciting and dynamic presentations, multimedia objects and animated effects can be used. For instance, video and audio clips can be inserted into a slide and set up to play automatically each time the slide containing those elements is displayed, or, alternatively, to play when their placeholders on the slide are clicked. Text or other objects can be *animated* so that a special effect, such as *flying* the text in from the edge of the screen or *dissolving* the text in from a blank slide, will be used to display that text or object each time the slide is viewed. Animation settings can be specified to indicate the sequence in which objects will be displayed (such as to build a bulleted list one item at a time), whether or not a video will loop continuously, and more. In addition, *transitions*—special effects used between slides—can also be applied to specific slides, or random transitions can be selected for the entire slide show.

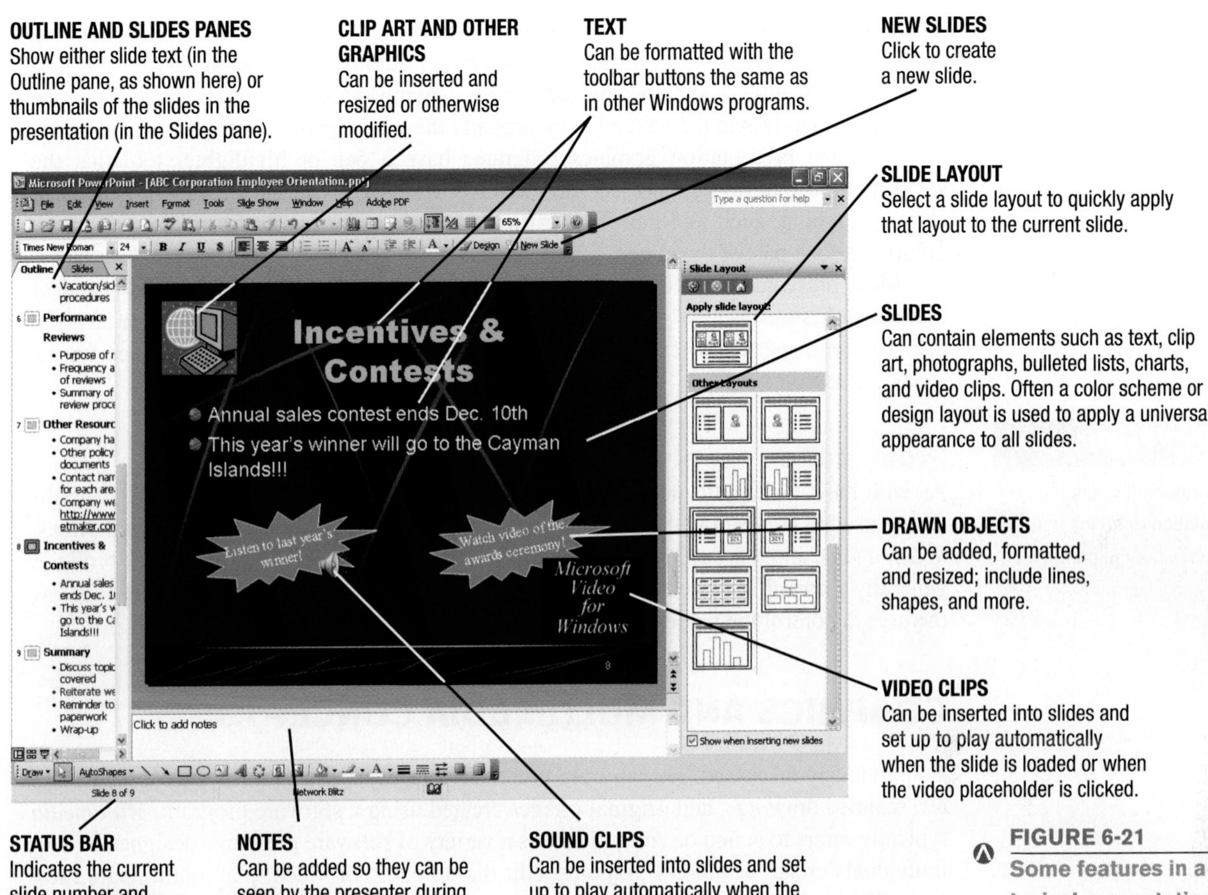

OUTLINE AND SLIDES PANES
Show either slide text (in the Outline pane, as shown here) or thumbnails of the slides in the presentation (in the Slides pane).

CLIP ART AND OTHER GRAPHICS
Can be inserted and resized or otherwise modified.

TEXT
Can be formatted with the toolbar buttons the same as in other Windows programs.

NEW SLIDES
Click to create a new slide.

SLIDE LAYOUT
Select a slide layout to quickly apply that layout to the current slide.

SLIDES
Can contain elements such as text, clip art, photographs, bulleted lists, charts, and video clips. Often a color scheme or design layout is used to apply a universal appearance to all slides.

DRAWN OBJECTS
Can be added, formatted, and resized; include lines, shapes, and more.

VIDEO CLIPS
Can be inserted into slides and set up to play automatically when the slide is loaded or when the video placeholder is clicked.

STATUS BAR
Indicates the current slide number and how many slides are in the presentation.

NOTES
Can be added so they can be seen by the presenter during the slide show or included on printouts.

SOUND CLIPS
Can be inserted into slides and set up to play automatically when the slide is loaded or when the sound placeholder is clicked.

FIGURE 6-21
Some features in a typical presentation graphics program.

Finishing a Presentation

Once all of the slides in a slide show have been created and the desired animation and transition effects have been applied, the slide show is ready to be run. To preview the slides and rearrange them if needed, presentation graphics programs typically have a special view, such as the *slide sorter view* shown in Figure 6-22. Using this view, slides can easily be rearranged by dragging them with the mouse to their new location in the presentation.

FIGURE 6-22
Electronic slide shows.

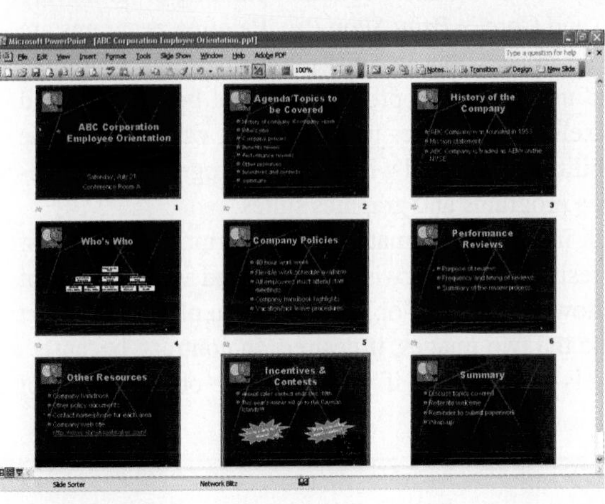

SLIDE SORTER VIEW
This view allows you to preview and rearrange the order that the slides in a presentation will be displayed.

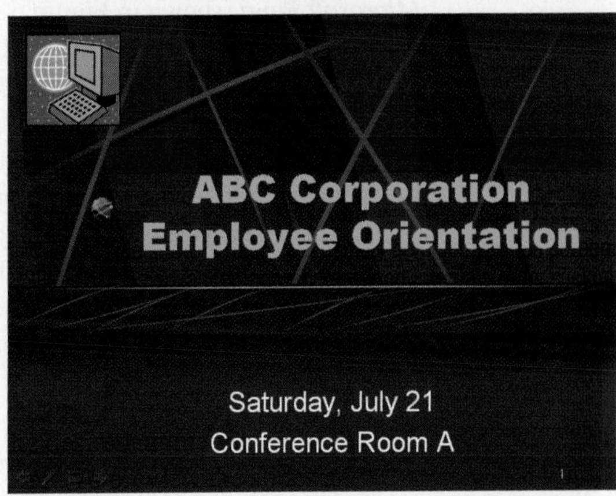

SLIDE SHOW
When a slide show is run, it will usually be displayed full screen. Slides can be advanced at predetermined intervals or by clicking the mouse or pressing the spacebar.

When the slide show is run, the slides are displayed in the designated order. Depending on how the presentation is set up, the slides either automatically advance after a specified period of time, or the speaker (or person viewing the slide show, for a stand-alone presentation) moves to the next slide by pressing the spacebar or clicking anywhere on the screen. Some presentation graphics programs have a pen or highlighter tool that the speaker can use during the presentation to temporarily write on the slides while the slide show is running, such as to circle a particular sentence for emphasis or draw an arrow pointing to one part of the slide.

Most presentation software programs can also print the slides (either full-sized or miniature versions printed several to a page) to create overhead transparencies or an audience handout; speaker notes or the presentation outline can also usually be printed for the speaker's use.

FURTHER EXPLORATION

For links to further information about presentation graphics software, go to www.course.com/uc11/ch06

Presentation Graphics and the Web

As with the other application programs discussed so far, presentation graphics programs can be used to generate Web pages or Web page content, and slides can include hyperlinks. When a slide show is saved as a series of Web pages and displayed using a Web browser, generally forward and backward navigational buttons are displayed on the slides to allow the user to control the presentation.

GRAPHICS AND MULTIMEDIA CONCEPTS

As previously discussed, *graphics* are graphical images, such as digital photographs, clip art, scanned drawings, and original images created using a software program. *Multimedia* typically refers to sound or video. There is a variety of software programs designed to help individuals create or modify graphics, edit digital audio or video, play multimedia files, burn CDs and DVDs, and so forth, as discussed next. Multimedia for Web sites are discussed in Chapter 10.

Graphics Software

Graphics software—also called *digital imaging software*—is used to create or modify images. Graphics programs are commonly distinguished by whether they are primarily oriented toward painting, drawing, or image editing, although these are general categories, not strict classifications.

Painting programs allow you to create *bit-mapped images*, which are created by coloring the individuals pixels in an image. Two of the most common painting programs are *Microsoft Paint* (shown in Figure 6-23) and Corel's *Paint Shop Pro*. Painting programs are often used to create and modify simple images, but use for these programs is limited because the bit-mapped images created using painting programs cannot be enlarged and still maintain their quality, since the pixels in the images just get larger, which makes the edges of the images look jagged. Capabilities associated with painting programs are sometimes included in other types of graphics programs and graphics suites.

Drawing programs typically create images using mathematical formulas, instead of by coloring pixels, so images can be resized and otherwise manipulated without loss of quality. Most drawing programs also allow you to *layer* objects so, if you place one object on top of another, you can later separate the two images, if desired. In contrast, because a painting program colors the actual pixels in an image, if you move one object on top of

>**Graphics software.** Application software used to create or modify images.

PAINTING PROGRAMS
Typically create images pixel by pixel so images cannot be layered or resized.

DRAWING PROGRAMS
Typically create images using mathematical formulas so images can consist of multiple objects that can be layered, and the images can be resized without distortion.

PHOTO EDITING PROGRAMS
Allow users to edit digital photos.

FIGURE 6-23
Graphics software.

another, the pixels are recolored and the objects cannot be separated. Drawing programs are used by individuals and small business owners to create original art, logos, business cards, and more; they are also used by professionals to create corporate images, Web site graphics, and so forth. Some popular drawing programs include *Adobe® Illustrator®* (see Figure 6-23), *Macromedia Freehand*, and *CorelDRAW*.

Image editing or *photo editing programs* are drawing or painting programs specifically designed for touching up or modifying images, such as custom images and digital photos. Editing options include correcting brightness or contrast, eliminating red eye, cropping, resizing, and applying filters or other special effects. Most programs also include options for *optimizing* images to reduce the file size. Optimization techniques include reducing the number of colors used in the image and converting the image to a more appropriate file format. Some of the most widely used consumer photo editing programs are *Adobe PhotoShop Elements*, *Ulead Photo Express*, *Apple iPhoto*, *Nero PhotoShow Elite*, *Nero PhotoSnap* (see Figure 6-23), and *Microsoft Photo Editor*. It is also common for graphics programs today to include photo editing capabilities, even if that is not the program's primary focus.

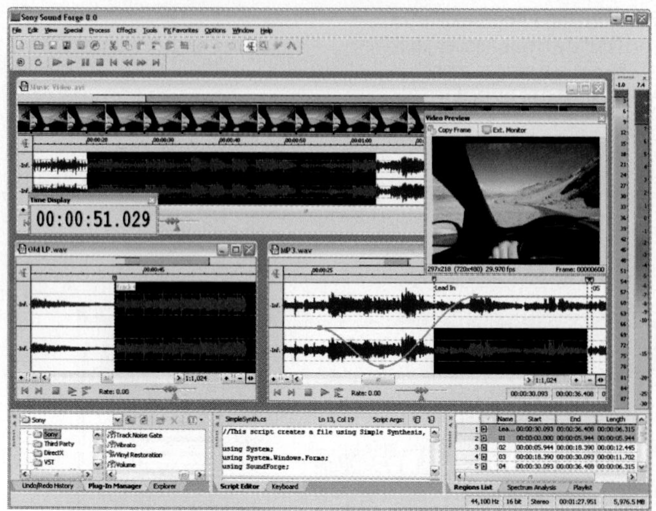
00:00:51.029

FIGURE 6-24
Audio editing software. Once sound has been captured in digital form, it can be edited as needed.

Audio Editing Software

For creating and editing audio files, *audio editing* software is used. To capture sound, a *sound recorder* can be used to capture input from a microphone or MIDI (musical instrument digital interface) device; to capture sound from a CD, *ripping software* is used. In either case, the audio file can then be modified, as needed. For instance, background noise or pauses may need to be removed, portions of the selection may need to be edited out, multiple segments may need to be spliced together, and special effects such as fade-ins and fade-outs may need to be applied. Some audio editing software is designed to create professional audio for products, Web pages, presentations, and so forth; others are designed for personal use. Common audio editing programs include *Windows Sound Recorder*, *Sony Media Software's Sound Forge® 8* software (shown in Figure 6-24), *Sony Media Software's ACID®* software products, and *Adobe Audition*.

Video Editing and DVD Authoring Software

It is common today for consumers to want to edit home movies and transfer them to DVDs; businesses also often find the need for *video editing*, such as to prepare video clips for presentations and Web sites. Video editing involves modifying existing videos, such as deleting or rearranging scenes or adding voice-overs and other special effects. *DVD authoring* refers to organizing the content to be transferred to DVD, such as importing video clips, creating the desired menu structure, and so forth. Today, these two capabilities are commonly found in a single program, such as *MyDVD Studio 6* (see Figure 6-25), *Adobe Premiere Elements*, *Ulead DVD MovieFactory*, and *Sony Media Software's Vegas® Movie Studio+DVD*. Most DVD authoring programs include *DVD burning* capabilities, as well, in order to transfer the finished DVD content to a DVD disc.

FIGURE 6-25
DVD authoring software. Today, these programs typically include video editing and DVD burning capabilities.

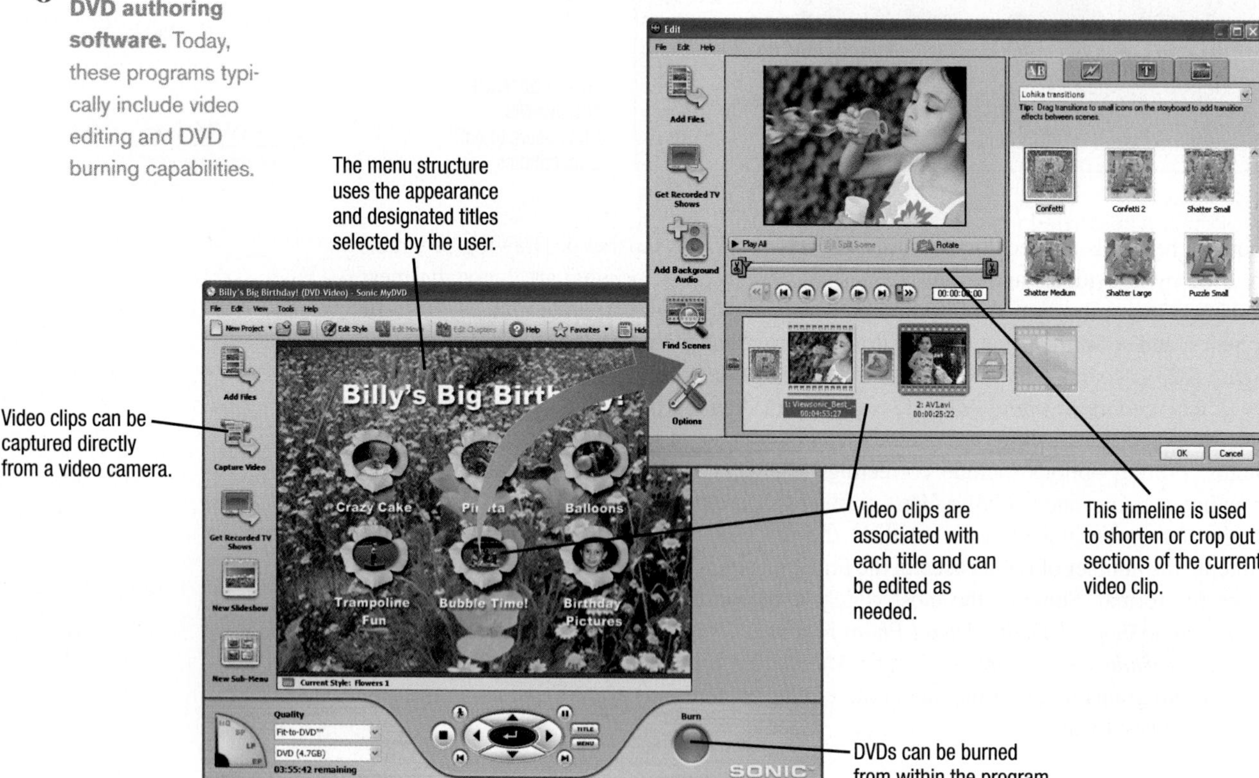
The menu structure uses the appearance and designated titles selected by the user.
Video clips can be captured directly from a video camera.
Video clips are associated with each title and can be edited as needed.
This timeline is used to shorten or crop out sections of the current video clip.
DVDs can be burned from within the program.
Billy's Big Birthday!
Crazy Cake
Balloons
Trampoline Fun
Bubble Time!
Birthday Pictures
Burn
SONIC

CD and DVD Burning Software

CD and *DVD burning software* is software used to record data on recordable or rewritable CDs and DVDs. CD or DVD burning software typically comes installed on a PC containing a recordable or rewritable drive; other CD or DVD burning software can be added if that software is not capable of everything the user wishes to do. Most programs can burn both CDs and DVDs; some include DVD authoring capabilities and other additional features. Two widely used programs are *Roxio Easy Media Creator* (now owned by Sonic) and *Nero Express*. CD and DVD burning software is widely used by consumers to burn custom music CDs, burn digital photos or movies onto DVDs, back up files, and more. With recordable CDs and DVDs, files cannot be erased later to make room for additional files. With rewritable CDs and DVDs, the files can be erased and new files stored on the disc, just like a floppy disk or hard drive. The How it Works box discusses how digital photos can be transferred to a PC and then backed up using DVD burning software.

Media Players

Media players are programs designed to play audio and video files. They are used to play media available via your PC—such as music CDs or downloaded music or video—as well as online audio and video clips. Some media players, such as the *RealOne Player* shown in Figure 6-26, can also be used to locate and play music from Internet radio stations. Another widely used media player is *Windows Media Player*. Media players typically allow you to arrange your stored music into *playlists*, and many allow you to transfer songs from your music collection to CDs or digital music players. Some also include a *music store* to allow you to select and purchase music files from within the media player program.

It is important when using digital music to adhere to copyright laws, such as only transferring music from CDs that you have purchased and only downloading MP3 files from sites that compensate the artists and record labels. While most music download sites today are legal and charge around $1 per title, illegal *peer-to-peer (P2P)* MP3 file exchanges do exist. Copyrights and P2P networks are discussed in more detail in later chapters.

FIGURE 6-26
A typical media player program.

Graphics, Multimedia, and the Web

Graphics and multimedia software is often used by individuals and businesses alike to create Web sites or content to be shared via the Web. In addition, games, tutorials, demonstrations, and other multimedia content available on the Web are often created with multimedia software. Professional graphics and multimedia software, along with creating multimedia Web sites, are the focus of Chapter 10.

FURTHER EXPLORATION

For links to further information about graphics and multimedia software, go to www.course.com/uc11/ch06

HOW IT WORKS

Managing and Archiving Digital Photos

With the proliferation of digital cameras today, it is becoming important to know how to organize a large collection of digital photos, as well as archive the photos for backup purposes. Typically, the first step is transferring the digital photos to your PC. After connecting a digital camera to or inserting a flash memory card into a Windows-based PC, the *Scanner and Camera Wizard* usually starts automatically. As shown in the accompanying figure, this wizard helps you copy the photos to a folder on your PC and assign all of the photos in the group a descriptive name—such as *July 2005* or *Hawaii 2006*—which is used in the filename for each photo (such as *July 2005 001*, *July 2005 002*, and so on). Using group names makes it much easier to locate a desired photo later on.

Once photos have been copied to your PC, you can edit them using photo editing software, move them into other folders to keep them organized or get ready to print them, view them, or archive them on CD or DVD. Burning a DVD +RW disc using the Roxio Easy Media Creator 7.5 Digital Media Suite is shown in the accompanying figure. Because digital photos only exist in digital form (no negatives, for instance), it is extremely important to back them up carefully to ensure you do not lose them if you have computer or hard drive problems.

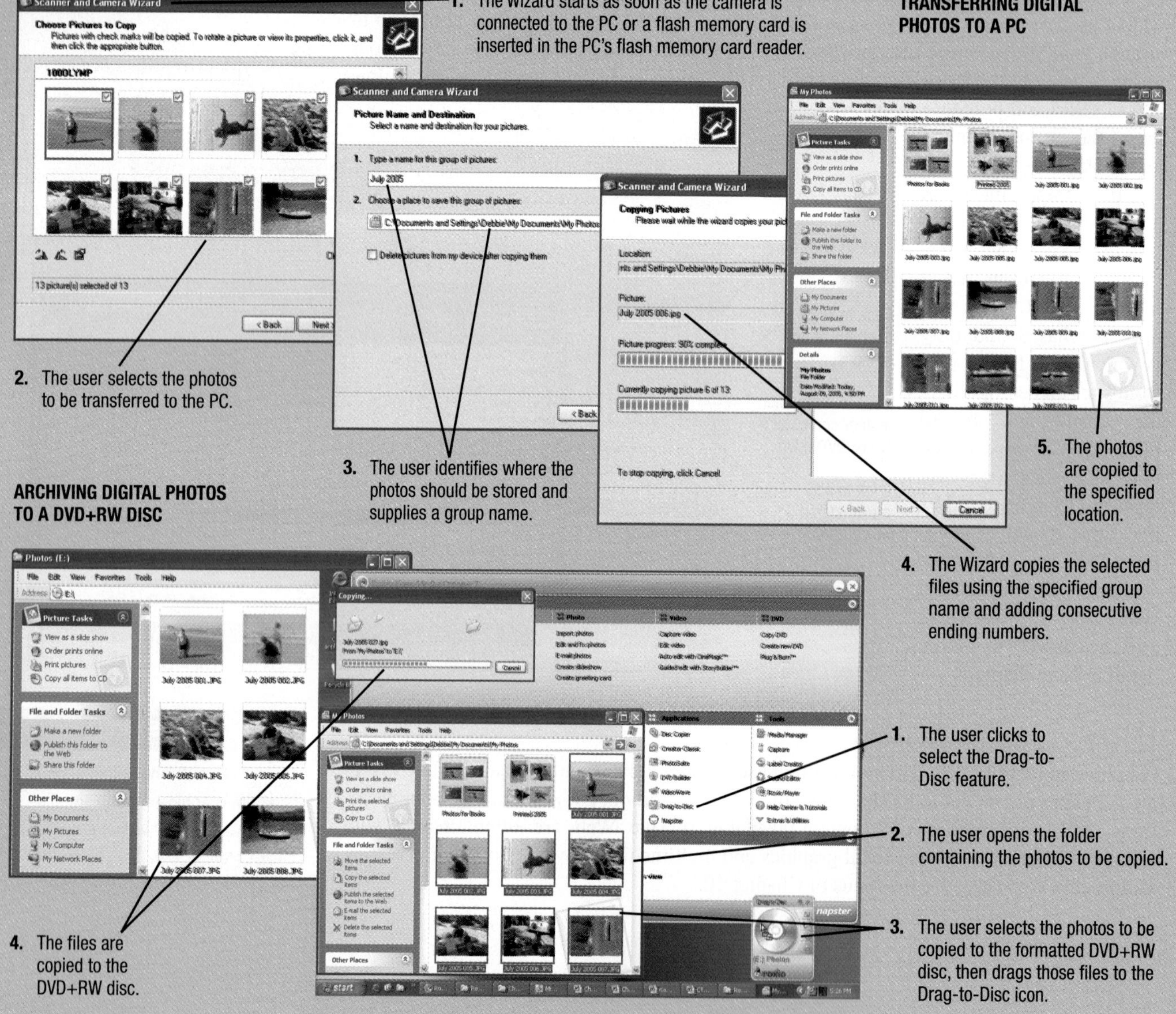

TRANSFERRING DIGITAL PHOTOS TO A PC
1. The Wizard starts as soon as the camera is connected to the PC or a flash memory card is inserted in the PC's flash memory card reader.
2. The user selects the photos to be transferred to the PC.
3. The user identifies where the photos should be stored and supplies a group name.
4. The Wizard copies the selected files using the specified group name and adding consecutive ending numbers.
5. The photos are copied to the specified location.
ARCHIVING DIGITAL PHOTOS TO A DVD+RW DISC
1. The user clicks to select the Drag-to-Disc feature.
2. The user opens the folder containing the photos to be copied.
3. The user selects the photos to be copied to the formatted DVD+RW disc, then drags those files to the Drag-to-Disc icon.
4. The files are copied to the DVD+RW disc.

OTHER TYPES OF APPLICATION SOFTWARE

There are many other types of application software available today. Some are geared for business or personal productivity; others are designed for entertainment or educational purposes. Still others are designed specifically for a particular business application, such as accounting or inventory. A few of the most common types of application software not previously covered are discussed next; some are shown in Figure 6-27.

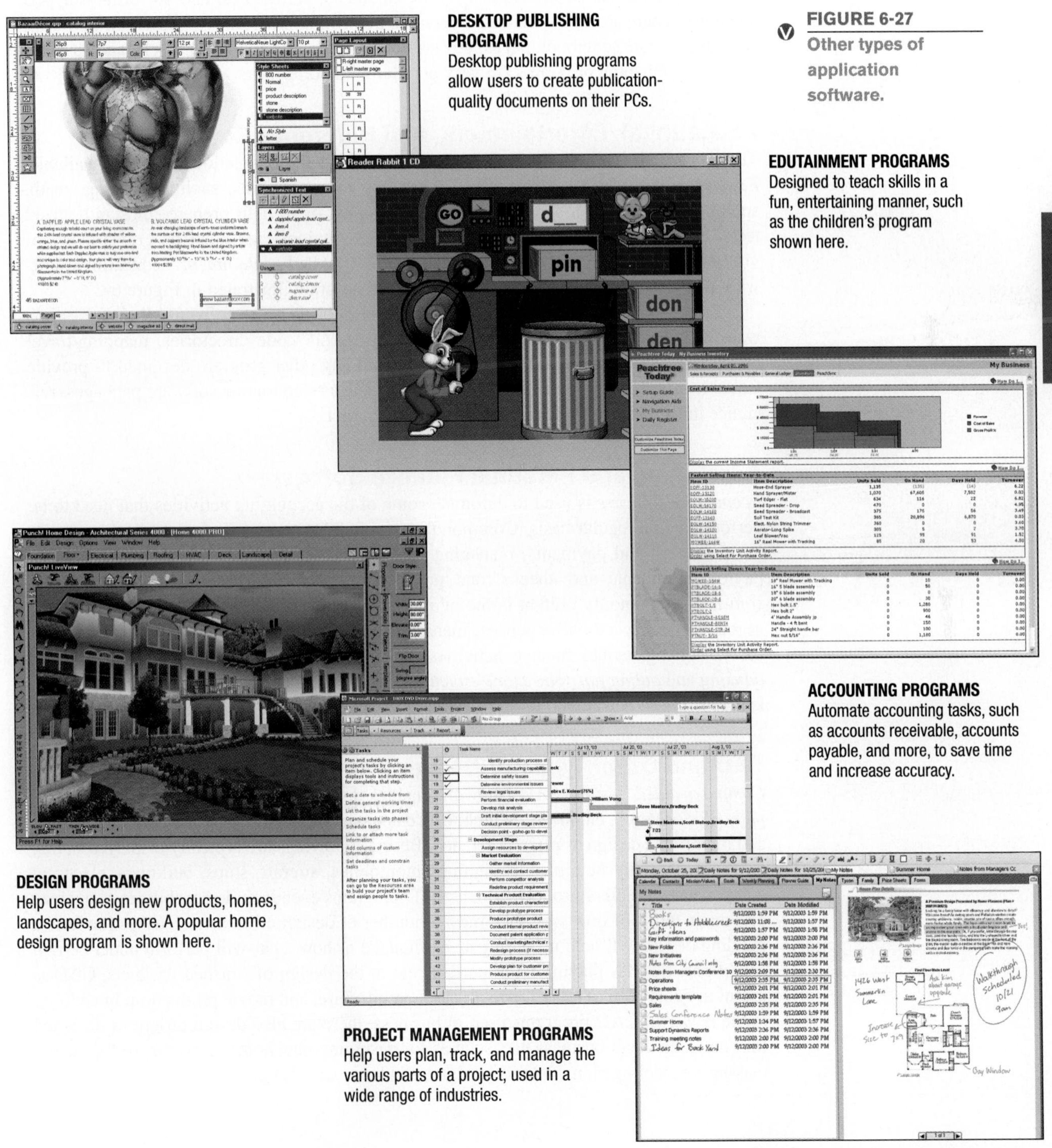

FIGURE 6-27 Other types of application software.

DESKTOP PUBLISHING PROGRAMS
Desktop publishing programs allow users to create publication-quality documents on their PCs.

EDUTAINMENT PROGRAMS
Designed to teach skills in a fun, entertaining manner, such as the children's program shown here.

ACCOUNTING PROGRAMS
Automate accounting tasks, such as accounts receivable, accounts payable, and more, to save time and increase accuracy.

DESIGN PROGRAMS
Help users design new products, homes, landscapes, and more. A popular home design program is shown here.

PROJECT MANAGEMENT PROGRAMS
Help users plan, track, and manage the various parts of a project; used in a wide range of industries.

PERSONAL PRODUCTIVITY PROGRAMS
Allow individuals to access schedules, contacts, notes, and more in one location.

Desktop and Personal Publishing Software

Desktop publishing refers to using a desktop PC to combine and manipulate text and images to create attractive documents that look as if they were created by a professional printer (see Figure 6-27). Although many desktop publishing effects can be produced using a word processing program, users who frequently create publication-style documents usually find a desktop publishing program a more efficient means of creating those types of documents. *Personal publishing* refers to creating desktop-publishing-type documents—such as greeting cards, invitations, flyers, calendars, certificates, and so forth—for personal use. There are also specialized personal publishing programs for particular purposes, such as to create scrapbook pages, cross stitch patterns, CD and DVD labels, and so forth. Personal publishing programs are very popular with home users.

Educational, Entertainment, and Reference Software

There is a wide variety of educational and entertainment application programs available. *Educational software* is designed to teach one or more skills, such as reading, math, spelling, a foreign language, and world geography, or to help prepare for standardized tests. *Entertainment software* includes games, simulations, and other programs that provide amusement. A hybrid of these two categories is called *edutainment*—educational software that also entertains—such as the children's program illustrated in Figure 6-27.

Reference software is another common type of application software. Reference software includes encyclopedias, dictionaries, atlases, ZIP code directories, mapping/travel programs, cookbook programs, legal guides, and any other program designed to provide valuable information. In addition to being available as stand-alone software packages, reference information is widely available on the Internet.

Accounting and Personal Finance Software

Accounting software is used to automate some of the accounting activities that need to be performed on a regular basis. Common tasks include writing and printing checks, recording purchases and payments, managing inventory (refer again to Figure 6-27), creating payroll documents and checks, and preparing financial statements. *Personal finance software* is commonly used at home by individuals to write checks and balance checking accounts, track personal expenses, manage stock portfolios, and prepare income taxes. Increasingly, personal finance activities are becoming Web-based, such as the *online banking* and *online portfolio management* services available through many banks and brokerage firms and discussed in more detail in Chapter 8.

CAD and Other Types of Design Software

Computer-aided design (CAD) software enables designers to design objects on the computer. For example, engineers or architects can create designs of buildings or other objects and modify the design as often as needed. Because drawings are typically displayed in 3D, CAD is especially helpful in designing automobiles, aircraft, ships, buildings, electrical components, and other products. Some CAD programs even include capabilities to analyze designs in terms of how well they meet a number of design criteria, such as testing how a building design will hold up during an earthquake or how a car will perform under certain conditions. Besides playing an important role in the design of finished products, CAD is useful in fields such as art, advertising, law, architecture, and movie production. In addition to the powerful CAD programs used in business, there are also design programs designed for home and small business use, such as for designing new homes (see Figure 6-27), and making remodeling plans, interior designs, and landscape designs.

TECHNOLOGY AND YOU

Taking Digital Classroom Notes

There are several options for digital note taking software, in addition to the standard handwriting software included with a tablet PC. For instance, Microsoft *OneNote* and Agilix Labs *GoBinder* programs (see the accompanying screen shot) are designed specifically to make note taking–and, particularly, retrieving information from the notes–easier. Like a paper notebook, tabbed sections can be created (such as one tab per course) and files, notes, Web links, and any other data are stored under the appropriate tabs. The built-in search tools allow you to find the information that you need quickly and easily. Some programs–such as GoBinder–are set up to integrate with Blackboard Learning System software, for classes using that system. Others–such as OneNote–can store and create links in your notes to audio recordings, such as recorded lectures. Digital note taking programs often include other helpful tools, such as a calendar and address book; some can sync calendars and contact information with the Microsoft Outlook program. As an extra plus, these programs typically save your notes to disk automatically, so you do not have to remember to save the file yourself.

Some examples of classroom note taking software in use include the University of Vermont School of Business Administration (which requires students to have a tablet PC and OneNote software in order to facilitate note taking and collaboration, as well as give students experience using the tools that they will need on the job) and Brigham Young University law school (which uses OneNote software to record audio and video of in-class exercises to help students refine their negotiation and legal counseling skills).

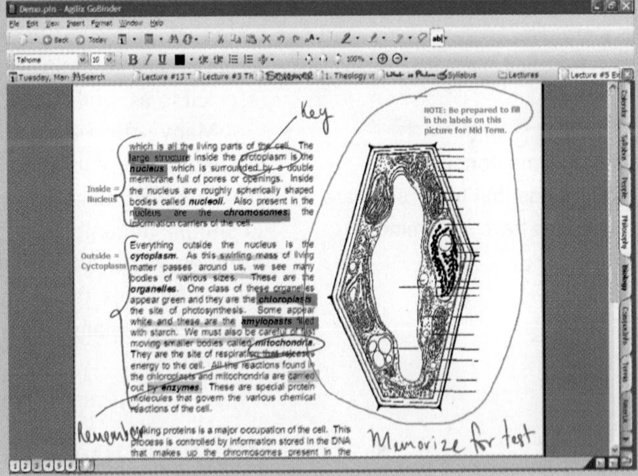

Project Management and Collaboration Software

Project management software, illustrated in Figure 6-27, is used to plan, schedule, track, and analyze the tasks involved in a project, such as the construction of a building or the schedule for preparing a large advertising campaign for a client. This type of software shows how project activities are related and when they must start and finish. Once created, schedules prepared by such software can be shared with others and updated as the project progresses. Project management capabilities are often included in *collaboration software*—software that enables a group of individuals to work together on a project.

Note Taking and Personal Productivity Software

Note taking software is used by both students and businesspeople to take notes during class lectures, meetings, and similar settings. Note taking software today typically supports handwritten input, which can be saved in its handwritten form as an image or converted to typed text. Drawings, typed text, and audio input are usually supported, as well. Some note taking software can even link a student's notes with an instructor's recorded lecture, as discussed in the Technology and You box.

Personal productivity software (sometimes also called *personal organizers* or *personal planners*) today typically also supports handwritten input (see Figure 6-27) and is designed to organize important data, such as appointments, notes, and contact information, in one central location for an individual.

SUMMARY

THE BASICS OF APPLICATION SOFTWARE

Chapter Objective 1:
Describe what application software is, the different types of ownership rights, and the difference between installed and Web-based software.

Application software is software designed to carry out a specific task. Common types of application software include games, Web browsers, word processing programs, multimedia software, utility programs, and more. Many application software programs on the market today are **commercial software** programs that are developed and sold for a profit. When a software program is purchased, individual users receive a **software license** authorizing them to use the software. Some commercial software is available in a *trial version*. Other software is available as **shareware**. Other classes of software are **freeware** and **public domain software**. **Open source software** is the term for programs whose source code is available to the general public. Most software is *installed* on a local PC or network server; other software is *Web-based*. Organizations that provide Web-based software are referred to as *application service providers* (*ASPs*).

Chapter Objective 2:
Detail some concepts and commands that many software programs have in common.

Many office-oriented programs are sold bundled together as a **software suite**. One of the most widely used software suites is **Microsoft Office**. Although different in purpose, most application software programs share some of the same concepts and functions, such as similar document-handling operations and help features. For instance, documents are commonly *opened*, *saved*, *printed*, and *edited* in a similar manner; the **insertion point** typically identifies the current position in a document. Many types of documents can be *formatted* to change their appearance. Handheld PCs require specially designed application software.

WORD PROCESSING CONCEPTS

Chapter Objective 3:
Discuss word processing and explain what kinds of documents are created using this type of program.

Word processing refers to using a PC and **word processing software** to create, manipulate, and print written documents, such as letters, contracts, and so forth. When creating or editing a word processing document, the **word wrap** feature automatically moves the insertion point to the next line when the end of the screen line is reached. Common types of *formatting* include changing the *font face*, *font size*, or *font style* of selected text; adjusting *line spacing*, *margins*, *indentation*, *tabs*, and *alignment*; changing the top and bottom margins, and paper size; and adding *headers* and *footers*. Other enhancements found in most word processing programs include the ability to include graphical images and *tables*, and to use *styles*, *templates*, or *wizards* for more efficient document creation. Documents can also include hyperlinks and be saved as Web pages in many programs. Most word processors also include a spelling and grammar check feature and other useful tools.

SPREADSHEET CONCEPTS

Chapter Objective 4:
Explain the purpose of spreadsheet software and the kinds of documents created using this type of program.

Spreadsheet software is used to create documents (**spreadsheets** or **worksheets**) that typically include a great deal of numbers and mathematical computations; a collection of worksheets stored in the same spreadsheet file is called a **workbook**. A worksheet is divided into **rows** and **columns** that intersect to form **cells**, each of which can be accessed through a *cell address*, such as B3. A rectangular group of cells is referred to as a *range*.

Content is entered into individual cells and may consist of **labels**, **constant values**, **formulas**, or **functions**. Formulas can be typed using *relative cell* or *absolute cell references*, depending on the type of computation required. Once created, the contents of individual cells may be edited and formatted. *Numeric formats* are used to change the appearance of numbers, such as adding a dollar sign or displaying a specific number of decimal places. Spreadsheet programs commonly include a *charting* or *graphing* feature and the ability to perform *what-if analysis*. Some spreadsheet programs allow worksheets to be saved in the form of a Web page and the inclusion of hyperlinks in cells.

DATABASE CONCEPTS

A *database management system* (*DBMS*) or **database software** program enables the creation of a **database**—a collection of related data stored in a manner so that information can be retrieved as needed. In a relational DBMS (the most common type found on PCs), a **field** or **column** is a collection of characters that make up a single piece of data, such as a name or phone number; a **record** or **row** is a collection of related fields; and a **table** is a collection of related records. One or more tables can be stored in a database file.

Chapter Objective 5: Identify some of the vocabulary used with database software and discuss the benefits of using this type of program.

A relational database typically contains a variety of *objects*, such as tables, *forms* to input or view data, *queries* to retrieve specific information, and *reports* to print a formal listing of the data stored in a table or the results of a query. When a table is created, the table fields are specified along with their characteristics, such as *field name*, *field size*, and *data type*. After this *structure* has been created, data can be entered into the table. Both the data in the table and the table structure can be modified. Databases are commonly integrated into the Web, such as to keep track of inventory and to facilitate online ordering.

SW

PRESENTATION GRAPHICS CONCEPTS

Presentation graphics are images used to visually enhance the impact of information communicated to other people. **Presentation graphics software** can be used to create presentation graphics and *online slide shows* consisting of electronic **slides**. Individual slides are created, and then they can be edited and formatted, as can the overall appearance of the slides. Multimedia elements, such as images and video clips, can also be included. After all slides have been created for a presentation, the order of the slides can be rearranged and *transitions* between the slides can be specified. It is becoming increasingly common to find slide-based presentations available through the Web. Web-based slide shows can include multimedia elements, as well as hyperlinks and other navigational buttons.

Chapter Objective 6: Describe what presentation graphics and electronic slide shows are and when they might be used.

GRAPHICS AND MULTIMEDIA CONCEPTS

Graphics are graphical images, such as digital photographs, clip art, and original art. *Multimedia* refers to applications that include more than one type of media, typically text, graphics, animation, and interactivity. To create graphics, **graphics software**—such as a *painting*, *drawing*, or *image editing program*—can be used. *Audio editing*, *video editing*, and *DVD authoring software* are common types of multimedia programs, as are the *media player* programs used to play audio and video files. *CD* and *DVD burning software* can be used to burn songs or other data on a CD or DVD disc.

Chapter Objective 7: List some types of graphics and multimedia software consumers frequently use.

OTHER TYPES OF APPLICATION SOFTWARE

Other types of application software include *desktop publishing* and *personal publishing* programs, *computer-aided design* (*CAD*) and other types of *design software*, *project management software*, *accounting software*, and *personal finance software*. The use of *collaboration*, *note taking*, and *personal productivity software* is growing. *Educational*, *entertainment*, and *reference software* are very popular with home users.

Chapter Objective 8: Name other types of application software programs and discuss what functions they perform.

REVIEW ACTIVITIES

KEY TERMS MATCHING

Instructions: Match each key term on the left with the definition on the right that best describes it.

a. cell

b. database

c. field

d. formula

e. label

f. public domain software

g. record

h. shareware

i. software license

j. workbook

1. ______ A collection of related data that is stored in a manner enabling information to be retrieved as needed; in a relational database, a collection of related tables.

2. ______ A collection of related fields in a database. Also called a row.

3. ______ A collection of worksheets saved in a single spreadsheet file.

4. ______ An agreement, either included in a software package or displayed on the screen during installation, that specifies the conditions under which a buyer of the program can use it.

5. ______ An entry in a worksheet cell that performs computations on worksheet data and displays the results.

6. ______ A single category of data to be stored in a database, such as a person's name or telephone number. Also called a column.

7. ______ A text-based entry in a worksheet cell that identifies data on the worksheet.

8. ______ Copyrighted software that is distributed on the honor system; consumers should either pay for it or uninstall it after the trial period.

9. ______ Software that is not copyrighted and may be used without restriction.

10. ______ The location at the intersection of a row and column on a worksheet into which data can be typed.

SELF-QUIZ

Instructions: Circle **T** if the statement is true, **F** if the statement is false, or write the best answer in the space provided. **Answers to the self-quiz are located in the References and Resources Guide at the end of the book**.

1. **T F** Microsoft Office is one example of a software suite.
2. **T F** Changing the font size in a document is an example of a formatting operation.
3. **T F** In a word processing document, the Enter key is always pressed at the end of each screen line to move down to the next line.
4. **T F** The formula =A2+B2 located in cell C2 would multiply the two cells to the left of cell C2.
5. **T F** One use for a media player program is to play downloaded music files.
6. With a(n) ______ program, the source code for the program is made available to the general public and so can be modified by others.
7. The blinking vertical line displayed onscreen that indicates the current location in a document, such as where the next change will be made to the document in a word processing program, is called the ______.
8. A named formula (such as @SUM) in a spreadsheet program is called a(n) ______.
9. In a relational database, the database object into which the actual data is entered is the ______.

10. Match each application with its type of application program and write the corresponding number in the blank to the left of each application.

a. _______ Creating a home movie DVD.		1. Media player
b. _______ Practicing multiplication tables.		2. Reference software
c. _______ Creating a child's birthday invitation.		3. Educational software
d. _______ Looking up the capital of Brazil.		4. DVD burning software
e. _______ Listening to a music CD.		5. Personal publishing software

EXERCISES

1. List the four main programs included in the Microsoft Office 2003 software suite and identify tasks for which each program is designed.

2. Would rearranging the paragraphs in a document using a word processing program use a cut operation or a copy operation? Explain your answer.

3. Match each spreadsheet element with its term and write the corresponding number in the blank to the left of each term.

a. _______ An absolute cell address	1. =SUM(A1:A2)
b. _______ A constant value	2. =B6*C6
c. _______ A formula	3. $D$4
d. _______ A relative cell address	4. 150
e. _______ A function	5. B6

4. Referring to the database table below, answer the following questions.

a. How many records are there?
b. How many fields are there?
c. How many records would be listed for a query with the criteria State is "CO" and the Balance is less than $10?

CUSTOMER NUMBER	NAME	STREET	CITY	STATE	ZIP	BALANCE
810	John T. Smith	31 Cedarcrest	Boulder	CO	80302	10.00
775	Sally Jones	725 Agua Fria	Santa Fe	NM	87501	0
690	William Holmes	3269 Fast Lane	Boulder	CO	80302	150.35
840	Artis Smith	2332 Alameda	Lakewood	CO	80215	3.50

5. Match each type of presentation graphic with its presentation and write the corresponding number in the blank to the left of each presentation.

a. _______ Adding an arrow to highlight a point located on a slide.	1. Pie chart
b. _______ Conveying the new company privacy policy.	2. Text chart
c. _______ Illustrating the percent of sales coming from each sales territory.	3. Photograph
d. _______ Showing what the latest prototype of an upcoming product looks like.	4. Drawn object

DISCUSSION QUESTION

Open source software is usually reviewed and improved by independent programmers who update the software products at no charge for fun, notoriety, or programming practice. Proponents of open source software believe that if programmers who are not concerned with financial gain work on an open source program, they will produce a more useful and error-free product much faster than the traditional commercial software development process. If open source use continues to grow as expected, it will impact software as we know it today. Will the growth force existing commercial software companies to streamline their development process in order to cut costs to better compete with open source products? Or will they feel the need to produce products that are better and more reliable than open source competitors? Or will commercial software companies simply go out of business? Will commercial software manufacturers be justified in raising their prices to make up for revenue lost to open source competitors? Do you think that strategy would be effective? Do you think open source software will have a positive or negative impact on the quality of software available for use? Would you prefer to use open source software? Why or why not?

PROJECTS

HOT TOPICS

1. **Natural Input** As pen and voice input technologies continue to improve, these types of more natural input methods are increasingly being supported by software programs.

   For this project, research the current state of either pen input or voice input, in conjunction with application software. What are the advantages of your selected method of input? The disadvantages? Select one office application program (such as a word processor or spreadsheet program) and one other application program and find out the extent that your chosen programs can be used with your selected method of input. Would you prefer to use a keyboard and mouse or your selected method of input with these programs? Explain. At the conclusion of your research, prepare a one- to two-page summary of your findings and submit it to your instructor.

SHORT ANSWER/ RESEARCH

2. **Software Search** Just as with toys, movies, and music, the price of a software program can vary tremendously, based on where you buy it, sales, rebates, and more. Although most packages claim a manufacturer's suggested retail price, it is almost always possible to beat that price—sometimes by a huge amount—with careful shopping.

   For this project, select one software program that you might be interested in buying and research it. Either by reading the program specifications in a retail store or on a Web page, determine the minimum hardware and software requirements (such as processor type and speed, amount of free hard drive space, amount of memory, and operating system) for your chosen program. By checking in person, over the phone, or via the Internet, locate a minimum of three price quotes for the program. Be sure to check availability and estimated delivery time, and include any sales tax and shipping charges. If any of the online vendors have the option to download the software, instead of sending a physical package, be sure to record that information, as well. At the conclusion of this task, prepare a one-page summary of your research and submit it to your instructor. Be sure to include a recommendation of where you think it would be best to buy your chosen product and why.

3. **CD Cards** CDs the approximate shape and size of a business card are increasingly being used to replace traditional business cards. Advantages include being able to include a complete multimedia presentation or Web site on the CD, as well as photographs, portfolio materials, and other useful content.

   For this project, research CD business cards. How much data can they contain? Can individuals or businesses create their own CD cards, or do they have to be purchased from a CD business card development agency? How much do the discs cost? Are they widely available? Locate one CD business card development agency (either a local business or an agency with a Web site) and determine what type of content they can supply for a custom card. What are the advantages and disadvantages of using a CD business card? Would you prefer to hand out a multimedia CD card or a traditional business card when meeting new business acquaintances? At the conclusion of your research, prepare a one-page summary of your findings and submit it to your instructor.

HANDS ON

4. **Templates and Wizards** Most word processing, spreadsheet, database, and presentation graphics software programs include a variety of templates, wizards, and other tools to help you create new documents faster and easier.

For this project, select one office suite program that you have access to (select one you will be using in this course, if applicable) and identify three tools included in the program that can be used to create a new document. For each tool, explain how it is accessed and what type of document is created with the tool. Next, pick one of your selected tools and use it to create a new document to evaluate how easy it is to work with and how useful the tool is. At the conclusion of your research, prepare a one-page summary of your findings and submit it to your instructor.

5. **Online Tours** There are many online tours and tutorials for widely used application programs. Some are available through the software company's Web site; others are located on third-party Web sites.

   For this project, locate a free online tour or tutorial for a program you are interested in (go to www.course.com/uc11/ch06 for access to the "Application Software Resources" Further Exploration links to tutorials for a variety of application programs) and work your way through one tour or tutorial. Be sure to take notes about those features that are of most interest to you, and evaluate how helpful you think the tutorial is for someone who is just learning how to use the program in question. At the conclusion of this task, prepare a one-page summary of your efforts and submit it to your instructor.

SW

WRITING ABOUT COMPUTERS

6. **Reference Tools** As described in the chapter, reference software includes encyclopedias, dictionaries, atlases, ZIP code directories, mapping/travel programs, and more. Many of these programs are available as commercial software that can be purchased; others are available over the Internet for free or with a paid subscription.

   For this project, identify two different types of reference tools that are available via the Internet (use a search site to search for Web sites offering particular reference tools until you find two that interest you). For each of your chosen online reference tools, try out the reference tool (if it is available at no cost) and see how helpful and easy to use it is. If the tool requires a fee or subscription, do not try it out—just make a note of what the service is supposed to consist of and the fee involved. Next, for each of your chosen reference tools, locate a similar offline version of the tool in the form of a hard copy book or an installable software program (visit a local software retailer, local bookstore, or search the Internet to find these non-Web-based alternative reference tools). Evaluate each offline reference tool, noting its capabilities, price, and how this version differs from the online version. At the conclusion of your research, submit this project to your instructor in the form of a short paper, not more than two pages in length. Be sure to include your opinion regarding the availability and usefulness of online versus offline reference tools, which of the tools you evaluated you would prefer to use, and why.

PRESENTATION/ DOCUMENTATION

7. **Compatibility** Files created by an application program are often upward-compatible, but not always downward-compatible. In other words, if you create a file using the most recent version of Microsoft Word and attempt to open the file using Word 95, you may get an error message. However, you would be able to open a Word 95 file in a later version of Word. In addition, you may be able to open a document created in a different program, if the program is of a similar type (such as opening a Word document in WordPerfect). Some application programs feature a "Save As" option to save the file in a format appropriate for an older version of the program, for an entirely different program, or for a more universal file format, such as *.rtf* (*Rich Text Format*), *.html* (*Hypertext Markup Language*), or *.xml* (*Extensible Markup Language*).

   For this project, select one widely used software program and determine the file formats in which the program can save documents and which file formats the program can open. If there are older versions of the program, are documents upward-compatible? Downward compatible? If the program can save a document in a plain text (*.txt*) file, is there a downside? In addition, research the *.rtf*, *.html*, and *.xml* formats and determine their purposes, the programs in which documents saved in each of these formats can be opened, and the programs in which documents saved in each of these formats can be edited. What about the *Portable Document Format* (*.pdf*)? Does your program support it? When might it be useful? Have you ever experienced a compatibility problem with a document? If so, how was the problem resolved? Share your findings with the class in the form of a short presentation. The presentation should not exceed 10 minutes and should make use of one or more presentation aids, such as the chalkboard, handouts, overhead transparencies, or a computer-based slide presentation (your instructor may provide additional requirements). You may also be asked to submit a summary of the presentation to your instructor.

GROUP DISCUSSION

8. **Emotion Recognition Software** An emerging application is *emotion recognition software*, which tries to read people's emotions. Similar to face recognition systems, emotion recognition systems use a camera and software to analyze individuals' faces, but instead of trying to identify the individual, the system attempts to recognize his or her current emotion. The first expected application of such a system is for ATM machines, which already have the necessary hardware (primarily cameras) installed. One expected feature is changing the advertising display to more specifically target each individual, based on the customer's emotional response to displayed advertising. Even more helpful applications would include rephrasing instructions if the customer appeared confused or enlarging the screen text if the customer appeared to be squinting. Emotion recognition applications for the future could include using this type of system to help therapists understand a patient's emotional state. It is not surprising that privacy advocates are concerned about the emotions of citizens being read in public locations without their consent. They also dislike the idea of customer emotions at an ATM machine being connected with their identity. Proponents of the technology argue that it is no different than when human tellers or store clerks interpret customers' emotions and modify their treatment of the customer accordingly. Is this a worthy new technology or just a potential invasion of privacy? What are the pros and cons of such a system from a business point of view, and then from a customer point of view? Are there any safeguards that could be implemented or specific ways of using an emotion-recognition system that would alleviate many of the disadvantages? What other potential uses for such a system might there be besides the ones mentioned in this project? Would you object to using an ATM machine with emotion-recognition capabilities?

   For this project, form an opinion of the use of emotion recognition systems in public locations, as well as in private situations, such as a therapist's office or in the home, and be prepared to discuss your position (in class, via an online class discussion group, or in a class chat room, depending on your instructor's directions). You may also be asked to write a short paper expressing your opinion.

WEB ACTIVITIES

The *Understanding Computers* Web site located at **www.course.com/uc11** features many resources to help reinforce your understanding of the chapter content and help you prepare for exams. Your instructor may also assign specific activities to be completed that will count toward your final grade in the course.

Instructions: Go to **www.course.com/uc11/ch06** to work the following online activities.

Click any link in the navigation bar on the left to access any of the online resources described below.

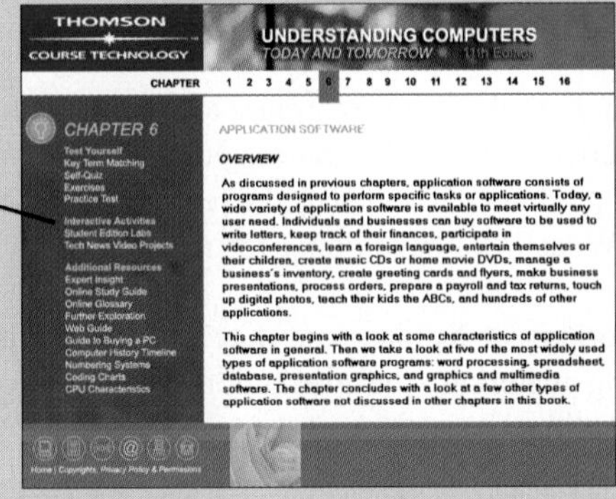

INTERACTIVE ACTIVITIES

1. **Crossword Puzzle** Practice your knowledge of the key terms in Chapter 6 by completing the interactive Crossword Puzzle.
2. **Tech News Video Project** Watch the **"Software Vending Machines"** video clip that takes a look at purchasing software via consumer kiosks, as an alternative to buying a shrink-wrapped package or downloading the software via the Internet. After watching the video online, complete the corresponding project.
3. **Student Edition Labs** Reinforce the concepts you have learned in this chapter by working through the interactive **Word Processing**, **Spreadsheets**, **Databases**, and **Presentation Software** labs.

TEST YOURSELF

1. **Key Term Matching** Test your knowledge of selected chapter key terms by matching the terms with their definitions.
2. **Self-Quiz** Test your retention of chapter concepts by taking the Self-Quiz.
3. **Exercises** Work these short exercises to review the concepts and terms covered in the chapter.
4. **Practice Test** Test how ready you are for an upcoming exam by completing the online Practice Test.

STUDY TOOLS/ ADDITIONAL RESOURCES

The Understanding Computers Web site has a wide range of additional resources, including an **Online Study Guide** (containing study tips, a chapter outline with room to add your own notes, and a chapter checklist of the activities to complete when the chapter is covered in class and when you are preparing for a test) and an **Online Glossary** for each chapter; **Further Exploration** links; a **Web Guide**, a **Guide to Buying a PC**, and a **Computer History Timeline**; more information about **Numbering Systems**, **Coding Charts**, and **CPU Characteristics**; and much, much more!

EXPERT INSIGHT ON . . .
Software

Novell.

A conversation with AARON WEBER
Product Marketing Manager for Novell Linux Desktop

My Background . . .

I was a Spanish major in college and I only took a computer class to get my math requirement out of the way, but I really enjoyed it, so I took a couple more. The courses pointed out to me what kinds of things could be done with technology. When I graduated, I'd managed to collect some Web development skills, but I wasn't an expert by any means. What I did have going for me was that I knew how to translate geek-speak into every-day English.

I knew a few people who were working at Ximian, and they needed a writer. I had to write Web pages, the business plan, the marketing materials, the instruction manuals, everything. After Novell bought Ximian, I began doing just marketing.

> **"Eventually, everyone will have terabytes of data and no idea where they put the particular file they're looking for. Applications are going to have to help them find it."**

It's Important to Know . . .

About open source software, such as Linux. It does a lot more than people think, and for a lot less than they're used to paying. Open source software allows people more control over what's going on inside their computer, and features are driven by user needs. For instance, people that speak a language that isn't supported by Microsoft Windows can create an open source equivalent interface in their native language. That's what keeps me in this business when I have a bad day at work—knowing that I'm building something that everybody will be able to use, even if they aren't rich and powerful.

About intellectual property and the ways that it's being used and misused. Not just that people are stealing songs via P2P networks, but that the music and movie industry and other rights-holders are trying to control the way that you use your data. I'd like people to ask questions like "Should it be illegal to play a DVD you buy in Europe on a DVD player you buy in the U.S., or print an e-book onto paper, or even read an e-book to a friend?

Who controls your data. Because in a very real sense, whoever controls your data controls you. For example, credit reports control a lot of what you can do, and the quality of that data is not really well regulated. It only takes a few pieces of data to impersonate someone, and then wreck their credit. On a smaller scale, what are you allowed to do with a music file you download? Remix? Copy to a CD? As computers and the data they store and retrieve become more and more central to our lives, individual consumers will need to be sure that they control the way those computers behave—not, say, the manufacturers or the music or movie industry, who are likely to demand that technology behave in ways that benefit industry and not individuals or consumers.

Aaron Weber is currently the Product Marketing Manager for Novell Linux Desktop. He writes materials about the Novell Linux Desktop operating system, does research on competing products to make recommendations about how Novell can best compete with them, and promotes the Novell Linux Desktop to resellers and hardware vendors. Aaron has worked as a technical writer and a Web developer, and has published several articles about Linux and open sources software for O'Reilly, Novell Connection Magazine, and Interex Enterprise Solutions Magazine.

> **"People like the idea of software that doesn't break and is easy to use, but given the choice between that and something with more power and complexity, they almost always go for the power and complexity."**

How I Use this Technology . . .

I'm using OpenOffice.org on Novell Linux Desktop right this very minute. I'm also using the Gaim instant messaging client to talk to my friend about news articles we're both reading with the Mozilla Firefox Web browser, and listening to music encoded in the Ogg format.

What the Future Holds . . .

There are two things that are really going to change the industry. One of them is a growing concern with intellectual property—all the Digital Rights Management (DRM) software out there is pretty flawed, but it's reflective of a general attitude that data and ideas have to be guarded. Students can prepare for this by learning as much as possible about fair use, patent restrictions, and copyright restrictions.

The other trend I see is shrinking profits on software. Some software products have huge profit margins that are just not sustainable. As the industry matures, base functionality is going to be available for less and less, and software companies are going to have to prove their worth, or die. That will put pressure on them to cut costs. Students will need to be prepared to learn new skills and apply old skills to new situations.

I also believe that, at some point, people are going to stop noticing the impact that software has on society, because its going to be part of society. We don't talk so much about the impact of, say, the standard-size screw on society these days, but machine screws used to be all different sizes depending on the manufacturer. Now there are a few standard sizes, and it's a lot cheaper to attach things to each other. It'll be that way with software—eventually we'll stop talking about how computers are changing our society, and focus more on using them to get on with our lives and be part of society.

Software in five years will also almost certainly be more complicated. People like the idea of software that doesn't break and is easy to use, but given the choice between that and something with more power and complexity, they almost always go for the power and complexity. And future applications will have to deal with a lot more data. Eventually, everyone will have terabytes of data and no idea where they put the particular file they're looking for. Applications are going to have to help them find it.

My Advice to Students . . .

Encrypt and back up your data. Encryption keeps it from prying eyes, and backing it up means you have a spare in case of disaster. (Don't keep the backup next to the original.)

Discussion Question

Aaron Weber views intellectual property rights as one of the more important issues for the future. He poses an interesting question: "Should it be illegal to print an e-book onto paper or even read an e-book to a friend?" Think about intellectual property rights as they relate to e-books. If you purchase an e-book, what should you be allowed to do with it? Is there any difference to your rights regarding the use of an e-book if you check the e-book out of the library instead of purchasing it? Be prepared to discuss your position (in class, via an online class discussion group, or in a class chat room. depending on your instructor's directions). You may also be asked to write a short paper expressing your opinion.

>For more information on Novell, visit www.novell.com. For general technical information, see www.oreillynet.com. For information about intellectual property rights, visit eff.org.

MODULE

NETWORKS AND THE INTERNET

Computer networks and the Internet play a critical role in our society today. Because of this, it is important for all individuals to be familiar with basic networking concepts and terminology, as well as with the variety of activities that are taking place today via the world's largest network—the Internet. It is also important for all individuals to be aware of the potential problems and dangers these technologies can bring.

Chapter 7 introduces basic networking principles, including networking and communications applications, what a computer network is, and how a computer network works. The Internet and World Wide Web are the topics of Chapter 8. Although they were introduced in Chapter 1, Chapter 8 explains how the Internet and World Wide Web originated, and looks more closely at common Internet activities and how to find information on the Web. Useful strategies, such as how to select an ISP and how to perform Internet searches, are some of the topics included in this chapter. Chapter 9 takes a look at some of the risks related to network and Internet use, as well as measures computer users can take to lessen these risks.

"If you do not understand the threats targeting your network and computing infrastructure, it can be very difficult to determine what types of protection strategies to employ."

For more comments from Guest Expert Jeff Bardin of The Hanover Insurance Group, see the Expert Insight on . . . Networks and the Internet feature at the end of the module.

IN THIS MODULE

CHAPTER 7 Computer Networks

OUTLINE

LEARNING OBJECTIVES

After completing this chapter, you will be able to:

1. Define a network and its purpose.
2. Describe several uses for communications technology.
3. Understand the various topologies and architectures a computer network might use.
4. Explain the difference between a LAN, a WAN, and a PAN, and between an intranet, an extranet, and a VPN.
5. Understand characteristics about data and how it travels over a network.
6. Name specific types of wired and wireless transmission media and explain how they transmit data.
7. Identify different protocols that can be used to connect the devices on a network.
8. List several types of networking hardware and explain the purpose of each.

OVERVIEW

The term **communications**, when used in a computer context, refers to *telecommunications*; that is, data sent from one device to another using communications media, such as telephone lines, privately owned cables, and the airwaves. Communications usually take place over a private (such as a home or business) network, the Internet, or a telephone network.

In business, communications networks are essential. For instance, business people throughout the world regularly use telephone, e-mail, and messaging systems to communicate with fellow employees, business partners, and customers. Documents can now be sent electronically in mere moments, instead of being physically delivered from person to person. Ordering systems allow ordering to take place in real time via the Internet or telephone, and inventory systems can communicate electronically with supplier ordering systems to facilitate deliveries of the necessary items at the appropriate time. Outside salespeople and traveling executives use portable computers and mobile devices to keep in constant touch with others, as well as to access real-time data located on the company network and Web site. The list of business communications applications is seemingly endless. Communications technology has also had a tremendous impact on our personal lives. It allows us to stay in constant touch with others, work from remote locations, locate useful information, and access services and entertainment.

The purpose of Chapter 7 is to introduce you to the concepts and terminology surrounding a computer network. First, a computer network is defined, followed by a look at some common communications and networking applications. Next, a number of technical issues related to networks are discussed, including the major types of networks, how data is transmitted over a network, and the types of transmission media involved. We then proceed to an explanation of the various ways networked devices communicate with one another, and the chapter closes with a look at the various types of hardware used in conjunction with a computer network. ■

WHAT IS A NETWORK?

A *network*, in general, is a connected system of objects or people. As discussed in Chapter 1, a **computer network** is a collection of computers and other hardware devices connected together so that network users can share hardware, software, and data, as well as electronically communicate with each other. The largest computer network in the world is the Internet. Another type of *communications network* is a *telephone network*. Computer networks and telephone networks are commonly used for a variety of purposes by both individuals and businesses. Some common uses for computer networks are listed in Figure 7-1.

FIGURE 7-1
Common uses for computer networks.

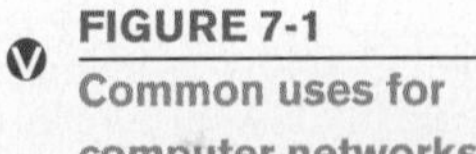

- Sharing a printer or an Internet connection among several users.
- Sharing application software (with a network license) so it can be purchased less expensively and needs to be installed and updated on only one computer.
- Working collaboratively, such as sharing a company database or using collaboration tools to create or review documents.
- Exchanging e-mail and files among network users and over the Internet.
- Connecting a home computer to the entertainment devices (such as a TV or stereo system) located within a home.

NET

>**Communications.** The transmission of data from one device to another. >**Computer network.** A collection of computers and other hardware devices that are connected together to share hardware, software, and data, as well as to communicate electronically with one another.

One area of recent growth is *home networks*. Today, there are approximately 30 million home networks worldwide, and that number is expected to increase to 71 million by 2007. According to the research firm NPD Group, home network use in the United States grew 20% in 2004, with home networks in over one-third of all households that have computers. Home networks are used to enable computers to share an Internet connection, to share digital photos and other files, and to connect computers and home entertainment devices (such as a television and stereo system) together to facilitate the delivery of downloaded music and movies. In business, networks are used extensively to facilitate communications and file sharing.

NETWORKING AND COMMUNICATIONS APPLICATIONS

Today, a wide variety of important business and personal networking and communications applications take place over some type of communications network, typically a company network, a telephone network, or the Internet. Two of the most widely used Internet applications—accessing Web pages and exchanging e-mail—were discussed in Chapter 1, and additional Internet-based applications are discussed in Chapter 8. The following sections take a look at some other types of networking and communications applications.

Mobile Phones

Mobile phones (also called *wireless phones*) are phones that use a wireless network for communications instead of being connected to the regular telephone network via a conventional telephone jack. The most common type of mobile phone is the *cellular (cell) phone*. Another, but less common, type of mobile phone is the *satellite phone* (see Figure 7-2). Both types of mobile phones allow people to communicate with other people using mobile phones, as well as with people using conventional *landline* phones. Although their use is similar, the technology driving each type of phone differs, as discussed later in this chapter. While cell phones can only be used in locations within a country where cellular service is available, satellite phone coverage is typically on a country-by-country basis, and some satellite services cover the entire earth. Consequently, satellite phones are most often used by individuals—such as soldiers, journalists, wilderness guides, and researchers—traveling in remote areas, who may not have continuous cellular service.

FIGURE 7-2
Mobile phones.

CELLULAR PHONE

SATELLITE PHONE

Mobile phones today can often be used for exchanging e-mail, text, and video messages; taking and exchanging digital photos; playing games; listening to music; watching TV and videos; and retrieving information from the Web. Mobile phones can even be used to take walking tours of certain cities in the United States and to pay for goods and services, as discussed in the Trend box. Mobile phones are widely used in many countries—there are around 180 million mobile phone users in the United States alone. Many

>**Mobile phone.** A cellular or satellite phone.

TREND

New Mobile Phone Applications: Celebrity Walking Tours and Park-by-Phone

You know you can use your cell phone to make phone calls, send text messages, even download ring tones and games, but many more cell phone applications are available today. From generating maps and driving directions, to allowing you to pay for goods and services, to acting as a personal tour guide, mobile phone applications abound. For instance, if you want to take a walking tour of Washington, D.C., Manhattan, or Boston, let your cell phone be your guide. A new service by Talking Street™ features celebrity tour guides, including Sigourney Weaver, Jerry Stiller, and Steven Tyler. To take a cell phone tour, you follow a map to designated historic locations. At each location, you dial the Talking Street phone number and enter the number of your current location to hear the corresponding narration (see the accompanying photo). You can visit the stops in any order, and can take the tour at your own pace–you can even spread out the tour over several days, if desired, for no additional fees. Tours cost about $5.95 each and take about 30 cell-phone minutes.

Another new cell phone application is Park-by-Phone—a no hassle way to pay for parking. Instead of needing correct change to feed a meter or to buy a parking permit, any individual who has signed up for the Park-by-Phone service can use his or her cell phone to pay for parking at designated parking places. All the Park-by-Phone participant needs to do is to dial the Park-by-Phone telephone number and then enter his or her member number and the parking meter number printed on a bright yellow sticker on the meter (see the accompanying photo). Once the call is completed, the parking fee is charged to his or her Park-by-Phone account.

New cell phone applications include cell phone walking tours (left) and Park-by-Phone (right).

individuals—around 9% of all U.S. adults, according to one estimate—are even dropping their landline telephone service completely in favor of using their mobile phones as their primary telephones. In developing countries and other locations with a poor traditional communications infrastructure, mobile phones may be the only telephone alternative.

An emerging type of cell phone is one designed for young children. These products, such as the Whereifone and Firefly, have limited features and built-in controls, such as to allow children to only call predesignated phone numbers. Some include *GPS* capabilities (discussed shortly) so parents can locate their children at any time via a Web site; others can alert parents by text message if the child carrying the cell phone leaves a prespecified area.

FIGURE 7-3

Pagers. Pagers are commonly used today for notification purposes.

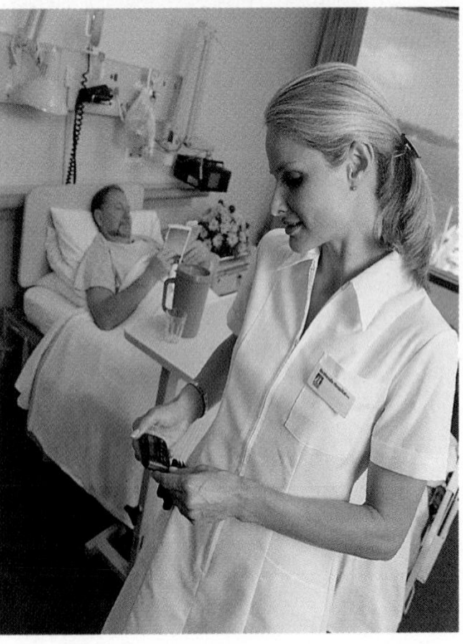

Paging and Messaging

Paging is the term generally used for sending short numeric or text messages to a person's pager from a phone or another pager. With two-way paging, generally referred to as *messaging*, text-based messages can be both sent and received. Messaging today most often takes place via a mobile phone, instead of a stand-alone messaging device. However, stand-alone one-way pagers are still used today, most often for *onsite paging* applications in which workers or patrons are supplied pagers so they can be notified when needed. For instance, one-way pagers are used by restaurants to notify patrons when their tables are ready, by childcare facilities to notify parents if there is an issue with their child, and by hospitals and other healthcare facilities to contact a patient's family members or to contact healthcare workers when they are needed in a particular location (see Figure 7-3).

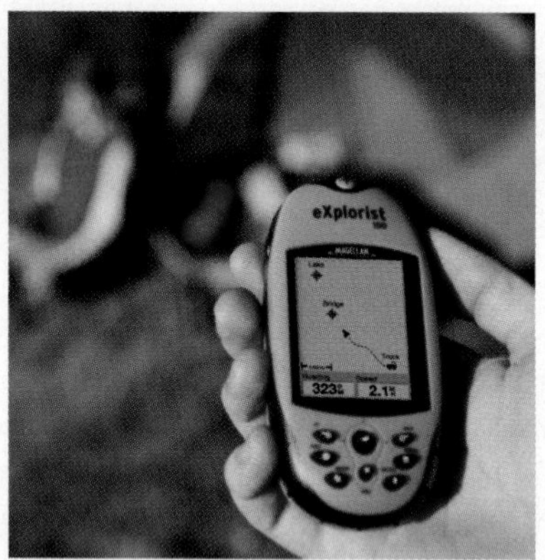

HANDHELD GPS RECEIVER

CAR-MOUNTED GPS RECEIVER

FIGURE 7-4
GPS receivers.
Global positioning systems can be used by people who need to know their exact geographical location, usually for safety or navigational purposes.

Global Positioning Systems (GPSs)

A **global positioning system** (**GPS**) is a satellite-based location and navigation system. It consists of *GPS receivers* (usually handheld or mounted in vehicles or boats) and a group of 24 Department of Defense *GPS satellites*. GPS receivers receive and interpret the data sent via GPS satellites to determine the receiver's exact geographic location, including the latitude, longitude, and altitude.

Although originally used solely by the military, GPS receivers are now widely available for business and personal use. GPS is commonly used by hikers, motorists, surveyors, farmers, fishermen, and other individuals who want or need to know their precise geographical position at specific times. In the past, the government, for national security reasons, required consumer GPS receivers to be less accurate than they were technologically capable of being. This restriction was discontinued in 2000, leading to more accurate GPS receivers, and today's GPS systems are accurate to within 3 meters (less than 10 feet). Handheld GPS receivers are about the size of a mobile phone (see Figure 7-4); wristwatch GPS devices are also available. Some mobile phones and handheld PCs have GPS capabilities built-in or available as an add-on feature. GPS capabilities are also commonly built into cars and can be used in conjunction with some monitoring systems to locate people or objects, as discussed shortly.

FURTHER EXPLORATION

For links to further information about GPS, go to www.course.com/uc11/ch07

In addition to their practical uses, GPS receivers can also be used for entertainment purposes. For example, *geocaching*, in which individuals use GPS receivers to locate secret caches hidden by others, is growing in popularity, particularly among families. To find the secret caches, participants follow the coordinates posted on a geocaching Web site.

Monitoring Systems

There are a number of communications systems available today for monitoring the status of or location of individuals, as well as vehicles or other assets. For instance, electronic *medical monitors* (see Figure 7-5) are available that take the vital signs of an individual (such as weight, blood-sugar readings, or blood pressure) or prompt individuals to answer questions (such as if he or she ate yet that day, took prescribed medication, or feels well). Other medical monitoring systems use pressure pads and motion sensors to track an individual's movement within his or her home, and electronic pill dispensers automatically dispense the proper medication at the proper time. These devices usually transfer readings and the individual's responses to questions to a healthcare provider automatically via the Internet or a telephone network so that potential problems can be detected early. Use of home medical monitoring systems is expected to continue to increase in the United States as the population ages.

Some monitoring systems are designed to locate or track an object, such as a vehicle. These systems typically use GPS satellites to determine the location of the object. Other monitoring systems are designed to monitor how an object is being used. For instance, some car monitoring systems can determine the location of a car if it is stolen; others can

>**Global positioning system (GPS).** A system that uses satellites and a receiver to determine the exact geographic location of the receiver.

HOME MEDICAL MONITORING
Used to transfer the vital signs of an individual and other health-related information to a medical professional.

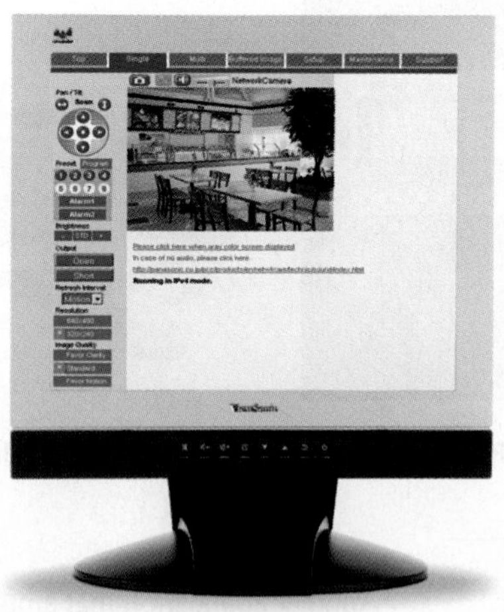

REMOTE LOCATION MONITORING
Used to monitor homes and businesses when they are unoccupied in order to detect breaks-in or other problems.

FIGURE 7-5
Examples of electronic monitoring systems.

record data about seat belt usage, speed, and other measures related to safe driving. Some rental car agencies use these latter types of monitoring systems to detect customer speeding and assess a fine accordingly, to both deter reckless driving and to compensate the agency for the cost of the extra wear-and-tear on the rental cars due to the excessive speed used. Progressive Insurance is exploring the use of these monitoring systems to track driver habits and then lower insurance rates for safer drivers. In addition, the data recorded by these types of monitoring systems can be used in accident investigations. Small home models are even available for parents to use to monitor the driving behavior of their children. Other *GPS-based monitoring systems* are used to monitor the location of repair workers and other employees who work outside the office. After the allowable work area for an employee is designated on the employer's computer, the monitoring system sends a notice to that PC if the employee exits that prescribed geographical area.

Some short-range monitoring systems today use *RFID technology*. As discussed in Chapter 4, *radio frequency identification* (*RFID*) is a technology that can store and transmit data located in *RFID tags*. RFID tags contain tiny chips and radio antennas. They can be permanently attached to objects, such as products, vehicles, shipping containers, pets—even people. They can be *passive RFID tags*, which require a reader to "wake them up" so they can broadcast data, or *active RFID tags*, which continually broadcast, allowing their locations to be displayed on a computer monitor in real time. When used in conjunction with a communications network, RFID tags can be used to locate the object the tag is attached to. For instance, hospitals can use their company network to continually monitor the location of equipment or even patients.

Other examples of electronic monitoring systems are those that use sensors or video cameras and the Internet to watch an individual (such as a parent watching his or her child in a daycare center or an individual monitoring the health of an elderly parent) or a location (such as an individual's home or place of business when it is unoccupied, as shown in Figure 7-5). For a look at an emerging type of monitoring system that uses sensors and communications media—*smart dust*—see the Inside the Industry box.

NET

CAR RECEIVER

HOME RECEIVER

PERSONAL RECEIVER

FIGURE 7-6
Satellite radio.
Satellite radio receivers are available for use in the car, at home, and on the go.

FIGURE 7-7
Videoconferencing.
Two of the simplest videoconferencing setups are via a PC or a video phone.

Satellite Radio

Another application that employs the use of satellites is *satellite radio*. Originally designed for the car, satellite radio offers delivery of clear digital music, news, and other radio content across an entire country, instead of just a limited broadcast area as with conventional radio stations. This means that one could drive from coast to coast without ever switching the radio station. And, because it is available on a subscription basis (such as $12.95 per month for about 150 channels), it is typically commercial free. Two popular satellite radio providers are SIRIUS and XM Radio. To receive satellite radio broadcasts, you need a satellite receiver (see Figure 7-6) and an antenna, if one is not built directly into the receiver. Since each satellite provider typically has its own set of two or three broadcast satellites, some satellite radio hardware is not interchangeable and so receivers and antennas need to be compatible with your chosen satellite radio provider. Satellite radio is becoming standard as a new car feature; personal and home receivers are also available to receive radio broadcasts at home or while on the go.

PC VIDEOCONFERENCE
Typically takes place via an Internet connection.

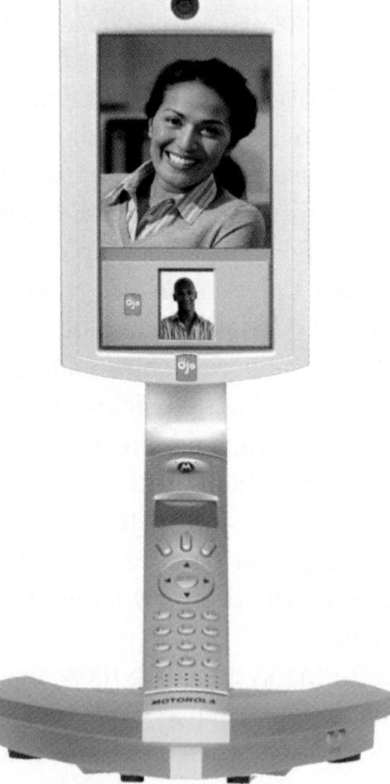
VIDEO PHONE CALLS
Typically take place via standard telephone lines.

Videoconferencing

Videoconferencing is the use of communications technology to conduct real-time, face-to-face meetings between individuals physically located in different places. Videoconferencing can take place via a PC and the Internet (sometimes called *online conferencing* or a *PC video conference*, and illustrated in Figure 7-7) or via a dedicated videoconferencing set up; it is also now available via conventional telephone lines. For example, the *video phone* shown in Figure 7-7 allows two individuals to have

>**Videoconferencing.** A real-time meeting that takes place between people in different locations via computers and communications media.

INSIDE THE INDUSTRY

Smart Dust

Motes—also known as *smart dust*—are tiny computers containing one or more sensors that are powered by a battery and that can communicate with other motes via miniscule radio transmitters. The sensors can perform a variety of measurements, such as assessing temperature, light, sound, position, acceleration, weight, and humidity. Multiple motes can work together to transmit data about their environment. For example, when scattered over a battlefield, motes can be used to detect enemy vehicles in the area and to transmit location information about the vehicles (via GPS coordinates) to neighboring motes, who relay the information to the military commander on an ongoing basis. This information allows the enemy vehicles to be tracked in real time. Currently, the mote circuitry is about the size of a postage stamp—with the necessary batteries, a mote is about the size of a deck of playing cards (see the accompanying figure)—and can run for three to five years on two AA batteries. As battery technologies improve—especially solar technologies for automatic recharging—the size of motes is expected to continue to shrink.

For nonmilitary applications, motes could be embedded into concrete foundations on bridges to take and relay periodic structural and salt readings to detect possible problems with structural damage due to salt or other factors. They could also be attached to power meters and water meters in homes to transmit readings to the utility company on a regular basis, and they could be scattered in vineyards, orange groves, and other agricultural fields to relay temperature and moisture settings to the farmer.

Motes (smart dust) use attached sensors to collect data and an antenna to transmit the data to the other motes on the network.

a video conference using just the video phone connected to their regular telephone lines. Online conferencing typically takes place via an individual's PC using video cameras, microphones, and either videoconferencing software (such as *CUseeMe*), a messaging or chat program that allows voice and video exchange (such as *Microsoft Messenger*, *MSN Messenger*, or *Apple iChat AV*), or the Web site of an *online conferencing service provider* (such as Infinite Conferencing or WebEx). In addition to audio and video, online conferencing typically includes other sharing options, such as a shared electronic whiteboard or workspace so that documents and suggested modifications can be viewed by all participants.

Videoconferencing has grown rapidly since the terrorist attacks on September 11, 2001, due to the initial closure of the airports and the resulting tighter security measures for travel. As businesses continue to discover that videoconferencing is a cost-effective and time-saving alternative for some types of business meetings, many believe that it will continue to grow as a business communications method, as well as for personal use.

Collaborative Computing

Another way of collaborating with others using a computer and communications technology is using collaborative software tools to work together on documents and other project components—often called *workgroup computing* or *collaborative computing*. There are many industries in which collaboration is a very important business tool. For example, engineers and architects commonly collaborate on designs; advertising firms and other businesses need to route proposals and other important documents to several individuals for comments before preparing the final version of a client presentation; and newspaper, magazine, and book editors must read and edit drafts of articles and books before they are published. Instead of these types of collaborations taking place on paper, as in the not-too-distant past, electronic *collaboration tools* are typically used. These tools, such as the revision tools available in Microsoft Office and specialized collaboration software, allow multiple individuals to edit and make comments in a document without destroying the original content. Documents are either stored on and accessed from a network server or routed to individuals via e-mail. When a document has been reviewed by all individuals and is returned to the original author, he or she can read the comments and accept or reject changes that others have made. Other collaboration programs may incorporate shared calendars, project scheduling, and other tools in addition to document sharing. Collaborative computing takes place via both private company networks and the Internet.

Telecommuting

The Internet, e-mail, videoconferencing, mobile phones, and collaborative computing have made **telecommuting** a viable option for some. With telecommuting, individuals work at home and communicate with their place of business and clients via communications technologies. Telecommuting allows the employee to be flexible, such as working nontraditional hours or remaining with the company after a relocation. It also enables a company to save on office and parking space as well as office-related expenses, such as utilities. As an environmental plus, telecommuting helps cut down on the traffic and pollution caused by traditional work commuting.

Digital Data Distribution

With the vast amount of digital data—including digital photos, music, movies, and medical imaging files—that need to be transferred from one location to another, *digital data distribution* is a growing communications application. For instance, the Yankee Group predicts that by 2007 about one in five U.S. households will have a *digital media receiver*—a device used to deliver an individual's digital photos, music, videos, and recorded TV shows from his or her PC to his or her home entertainment devices (such as a TV or stereo system) located anywhere in the house, typically via a wireless network. Digital data distribution can even be used to send television shows and other multimedia content from a user's home TV to his or her portable PC, as discussed in the Technology and You box.

Another digital data distribution application is *digital cinema*. With digital cinema, movies are created, distributed, and projected in digital form. The biggest proponent of digital cinema has been George Lucas, who was not satisfied with the way the digital effects used in his *Stars Wars: Episode 1* movie looked when the movie was transferred to film for distribution. When the movie was released, he set up four digital exhibition sites to show the film in digital format—the first public demonstration of a full-length motion picture from a major studio using digital electronic projectors in movie theatres to replace the normal film projectors—and digital cinema was born. Since then, digital projection equipment has been developed, and movies that are now filmed digitally can remain in digital format from creation through projection—the finished movies are sent to movie theaters in digital form via satellites. Distributing movies digitally saves the Hollywood studios about

>**Telecommuting.** The use of computer and electronic devices to enable an individual to work from his or her home.

TECHNOLOGY AND YOU

Multimedia Place Shifting

The increased use of broadband Internet connections and wireless networks has led to a new communications application—delivering media, such as television shows, music, and movies, from a user's home TV or DVR to the user's computer wherever she or he happens to be at the moment. Similar to the way the VCR allows consumers to *time shift* (watch recorded shows at a more convenient time), these emerging devices and services allow users to *place shift* (watch recorded shows at a more convenient location). One multimedia place-shifting product is Sling Media's *Slingbox* (see the accompanying figure). This product allows the user (via installed software on the PC being used and his or her Slingbox ID code) to remotely control his or her cable box, satellite receiver, or DVR and transfer that content to his or her PC or mobile phone via the Internet. For instance, he or she can watch local news while out of town, watch a recorded TV show while at the beach, or start recording a TV show from the office. In general, place shifting allows users to utilize their cable or satellite services, or access their favorite recorded shows, when they are away from home. Guest passwords can be assigned, such as to allow grandparents to watch home videos of their grandkids remotely; if security cameras are connected to the TV or VCR, home owners can even monitor the security of their home from out of town. It is expected that other uses for multimedia place shifting products will soon be available, such as to stream digital photos, downloaded music, and other multimedia content from a user's home PC to his or her current location.

The Slingbox (left) allows individuals to placeshift media from their home TVs and DVRs to their portable PCs or mobile devices (right).

$1,500 per film print. It also maintains quality, both for any digital special effects used in the film and for viewing, since the quality drop that occurs with a film print each time it is played is no longer a factor. Although the conversion to digital projection equipment is costly, it also allows movie theaters more flexibility, such as to add additional theaters for a popular film without the additional cost and time delay of ordering a new print. Digital cinema specifications are currently under development by a consortium consisting of the seven major Hollywood studios. Although specifications and security precautions need to be developed to avoid piracy and it is likely that film and digital distribution will coexist for some time (many movies, such as *Star Wars*, *Episode III*, are now distributed in both film format and digital format), it is also expected, that, someday, all movie distribution will be completely digital.

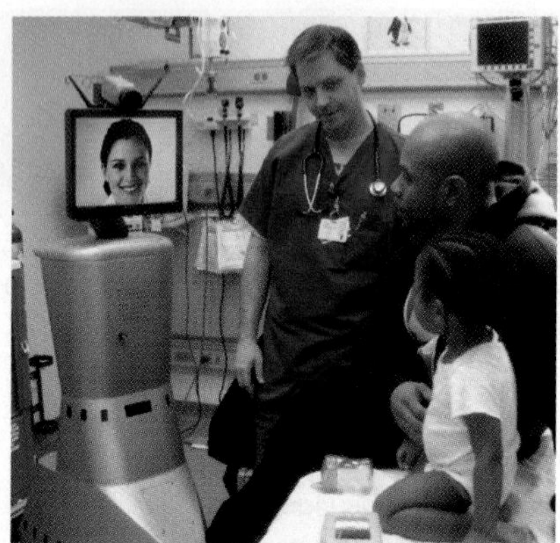

REMOTE CONSULTATIONS
Using remote-controlled teleconferencing robots, physicians can "virtually" consult with patients or other physicians in a different physical location; the robot transmits video images and audio to and from the doctor (via his or her PC) in real time.

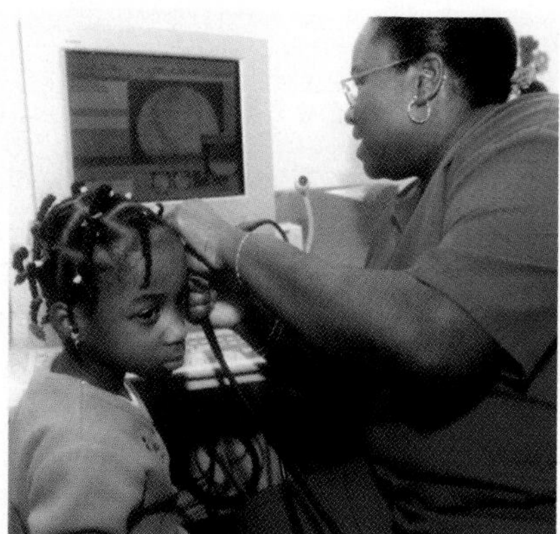

REMOTE DIAGNOSIS
At remote locations, such as the New York childcare center shown here, trained employees provide physicians with the real-time data (sent via the Internet) they need for diagnosis.

TELESURGERY
Using voice or computer commands, surgeons can now perform operations via the Internet; a robotic system uses the surgeon's commands to operate on the patient.

FIGURE 7-8
Examples of telemedicine applications.

Telemedicine

Telemedicine is the use of communications technology to provide medical information and services. In addition to the remote medical monitoring systems already discussed, some physicians offer additional telemedicine services, such as e-mail consultations and Web-based appointment scheduling. Other possibilities include using videoconferencing to communicate with other physicians or with hospitalized patients; to perform remote diagnosis of patients (in which local healthcare workers at rural locations, childcare facilities, and other locations with telemedicine equipment use video cameras, electronic stethoscopes, and other tools to send images and vital statistics of a patient to a physician located at a medical facility); and to perform *telesurgery* (see Figure 7-8).

Telesurgery is a form of *robot-assisted surgery*, in which a robot controlled by a physician operates on the patient. Robot-assisted surgery systems typically use cameras to give the human surgeon an extremely close view of the surgical area. In addition, these systems are typically more precise and make smaller incisions than human surgeons. This allows for less invasive surgery (for example, not having to crack through the rib cage to access the heart), resulting in less pain for the patient, a faster recovery time, and fewer potential complications.

Some robot-assisted surgery takes place with the doctor, patient, and robotic device in the same operating room; with telesurgery, at least one of the surgeons performs the operation by controlling the robot remotely, such as over the Internet. In general, telemedicine has enormous potential for providing quality care to individuals who live in rural or underdeveloped areas and who do not have access to sufficient medical care. Telemedicine will also be necessary for future long-term space explorations—such as a trip to Mars and back that may take three years or more—since astronauts will undoubtedly need medical care while on the journey.

>**Telemedicine.** The use of communications technology to provide medical information and services. >**Telesurgery.** A form of robot-assisted surgery in which the doctor is in a different physical location from the patient and controls the robot remotely over the Internet or another communications medium.

TYPES OF NETWORKS

Networks can be identified by their *topology*, *architecture*, and size. These topics are described in the next few sections.

Network Topologies

Computer networks vary in physical arrangement or *topology*. Four of the most common topologies are *star*, *bus*, *ring*, and *mesh* (see Figure 7-9).

Star Networks

The **star network**—the oldest topology for computer networks—typically consists of a central device (usually a *hub*, *switch*, or *router*, all of which are discussed later in this chapter) to which all the computers and other devices in the network connect, forming a star shape. The central device contains multiple ports that are used to connect the various network devices (such as a server, PCs, and a printer); all network transmissions are sent through the central device. Star networks are common in traditional mainframe environments, as well as in small office and home networks.

Bus Networks

A **bus network** has no central hub. Instead, it consists of a central cable to which all network devices are attached. For example, the bus network illustrated in Figure 7-9 contains three PCs and a printer attached to a single bus line. In a bus network, all data is transmitted down the bus line from one device to another, and only one device can transmit at a time.

Ring Networks

A less common alternative to the star and bus topologies is the **ring network**. Like a bus network, ring networks do not have a central hub, but the computers and other network devices are connected in a ring formation from one device to the next, without the use of a central cable (see the third illustration in Figure 7-9). In a ring network, data travels from one device to another around the ring in one direction only.

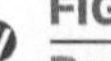

FIGURE 7-9

Basic network topologies. Common topologies are star, bus, ring, and mesh.

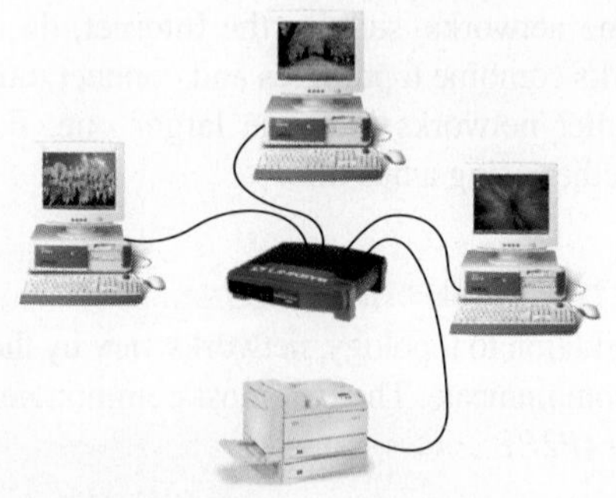

STAR NETWORK
Uses a central hub to connect each device directly to the network.

BUS NETWORK
Uses a single central cable to connect each device in a linear fashion.

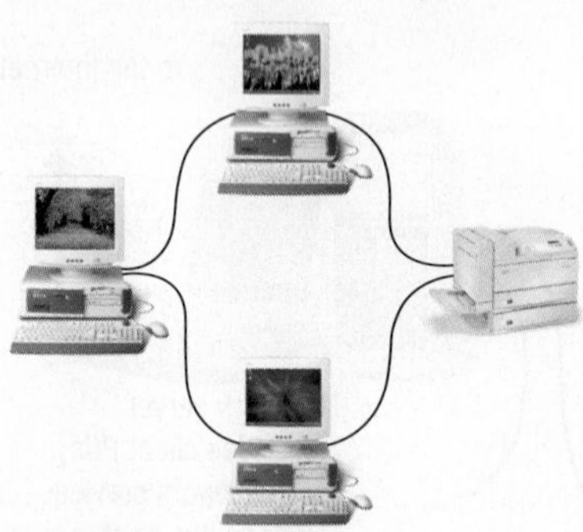

RING NETWORK
Connects computers and other devices one to the next in a loop; there is no central hub or cable.

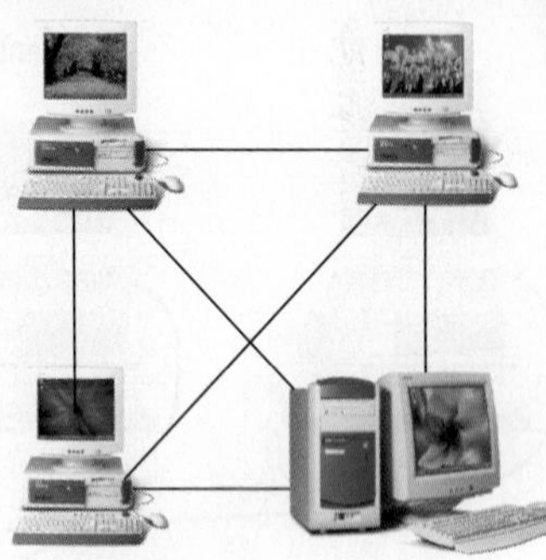

MESH NETWORK
Each computer or device is connected to all other devices.

>**Star network.** A network that uses a host device connected directly to several other devices. >**Bus network.** A network consisting of a central cable to which all network devices are attached. >**Ring network.** A network that connects devices in a closed loop.

Mesh Networks

In a **mesh network**—also called an *ad hoc network*—there are a number of different connections between the devices on the network so that messages can take any of several possible paths from source to destination, instead of having to follow one specific path, as in star, bus, and ring networks. With a *full mesh topology* (such as the one shown in Figure 7-9), each device on the network has a connection to every other device on the network. With a *partial mesh topology*, some devices are connected to all the others, but some are connected only to those other nodes with which they exchange the most data.

Mesh networks are most often used with wireless networks, such as to extend *Wi-Fi networks* or to allow emergency workers within a single agency—such as a city fire department, the highway patrol, or the U.S. Coast Guard—to communicate with workers from other agencies during an emergency, even if they use different radio systems. Wireless networks are discussed in more detail shortly.

Combination Topologies

Some networks, such as the Internet, do not conform to a standard topology. Some networks combine topologies and connect multiple smaller networks, in effect turning several smaller networks into one larger one. For example, two star networks may be joined together using a bus line.

Network Architectures

In addition to topology, networks vary by their *architecture*; that is, the way they are designed to communicate. The two most common network architectures are *client-server* and *peer-to-peer* (*P2P*).

Client-Server Networks

Client-server networks include both *clients* (PCs and other devices on the network that request and utilize network resources) and *servers* (computers that are dedicated to processing client requests). There are a number of different tasks that a server can perform. For example, a *network server* manages network traffic, a *file server* manages shared files, a *print server* handles printing-related activities, and a *mail server* and *Web server* are dedicated to managing e-mail and Web page requests, respectively. Not all networks require all of these server functions, and a single server can perform more than one function. For instance, there is only one server in the network illustrated in Figure 7-10, and it is capable of performing all server tasks for that network.

Network servers are typically powerful computers with lots of memory and a very large hard drive. They can be high-end PCs, midrange servers, or mainframe computers. Regardless of the type of server used, retrieving files from a server

FIGURE 7-10
Client-server networks. With this type of network, client PCs communicate through one or more servers, which provide access to e-mail, the Internet, programs and files stored on the network, network printers, and other network resources.

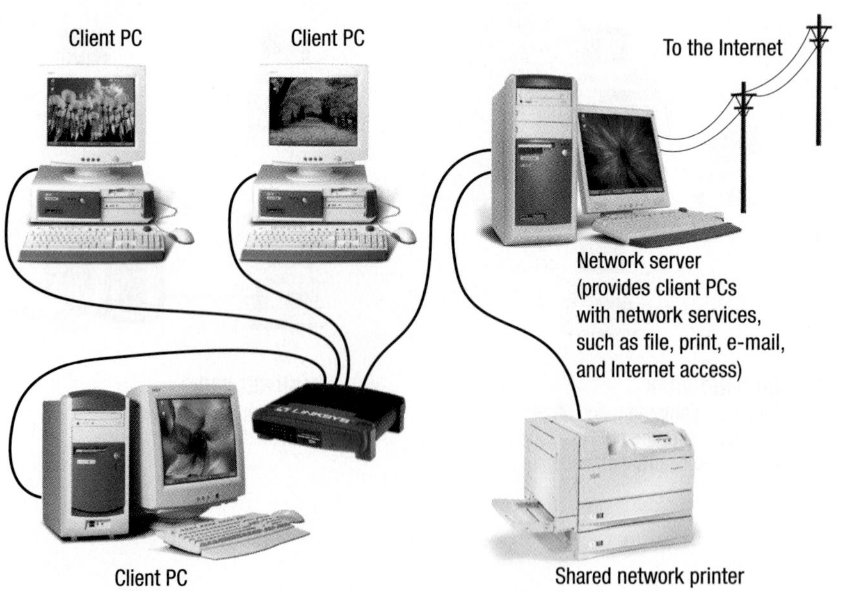

>**Mesh network.** A network in which there are multiple connections between the devices on the network so that messages can take any of several possible paths.

is called *downloading*; transferring data from a client PC to a server is referred to as *uploading*.

Peer-to-Peer Networks

With a *peer-to-peer (P2P) network*, a central server is not used (see Figure 7-11). Instead, all the computers on the network work at the same level, and users have direct access to the other computers and the peripherals attached to the network. For instance, users can access files stored on a peer computer's hard drive and print using a peer computer's printer, provided those devices have been designated as shared devices. Peer-to-peer networks are less expensive and less complicated to implement than client-server networks since there are no dedicated servers, but they may not have the same performance as client-server networks under heavy use. Peer-to-peer capabilities are built into many personal operating systems for small office or home networks.

P2P HOME NETWORK
(PCs connect and communicate via network cabling and other networking hardware.)

INTERNET P2P NETWORK
(PCs connect and communicate via the Internet.)

FIGURE 7-11
Peer-to-peer networks. With this type of network, PCs communicate directly with one another, without going through a central server.

Another type of peer-to-peer networking—sometimes called *Internet peer-to-peer (P2P) computing*—is performed via the Internet. Instead of placing content on a Web server for others to view via the Internet, content is exchanged over the Internet directly with the other users of the peer-to-peer network. For instance, one user can copy a file from another user's hard drive to his or her own PC via their Internet connections. Internet P2P networking is commonly used for exchanging music files with others over the Internet—an illegal act if the music is copyright-protected and the exchange is unauthorized, although legal Internet P2P networks exist, as discussed more in Chapter 9. Copyright law, ethics, and other topics related to peer-to-peer file exchanges are covered in Chapter 16.

NET

LANs, WANs, and Other Types of Networks

One additional way networks are classified is by their size, which specifies how large an area the network services and what users the network is designed to service. Some of the most common types of networks are listed next.

Local Area Networks (LANs)

A **local area network** (**LAN**) is a network that covers a relatively small geographical area, such as a home, office building, or school. The devices (sometimes called *nodes*) on the network can be connected with either wired or wireless communications media. The network shown in Figure 7-10 is an example of a LAN.

Wide Area Networks (WANs)

A **wide area network** (**WAN**) is a network that covers a large geographical area. Typically, a WAN consists of two or more LANs, which could be relatively close to one another (such as in the same city) or far apart. The Internet, by this definition, is the world's largest WAN. WANs may be publicly accessible, like the Internet, or may be privately owned and operated.

>**Local area network (LAN).** A network that connects devices located in a small geographical area, such as within a building. >**Wide area network (WAN).** A network that connects devices located in a large geographical area.

Metropolitan Area Networks (MANs)

A *metropolitan area network* (*MAN*) is a network designed for a metropolitan area, typically a city or county. MANs fall between LANs and WANs on the size continuum and typically consist of multiple LANs. Most MANs are owned and operated by a city or by a network provider who sells access to the MAN to others in that location. Increasingly, wireless MANs are being created to provide free or low-cost Internet access to area residents. According to one estimate, more than 50 cities in the United States have or are in the process of implementing a city-wide wireless network.

FIGURE 7-12
E-clothing. The jacket shown here has compartments to connect the devices in a personal area network (PAN) to each other, as well as to the built-in rechargeable battery pack.

Personal Area Networks (PANs)

A *personal area network* (*PAN*) is a network of personal devices for one individual, such as his or her portable PC, cell phone, and portable printer. The devices in a PAN must be physically located close together and are connected to share data, hardware, and/or an Internet connection. PANs can be either wired or wireless. To facilitate a wired PAN, some *e-clothing* products exist, such as the jacket shown in Figure 7-12 that contains pockets and compartments designed for cell phones, handheld PCs, portable digital music players, and other common devices. In addition to conveniently storing the devices, many e-garments include built-in channels through the lining of the garment to connect the devices easily and without visible wires. The e-jacket in Figure 7-12 even contains built-in solar panels and a corresponding battery pack that can be used to power the devices. In addition to offering convenient hands-free operation, e-garments also allow frequent travelers to speed up the process of going through airport security by allowing them to just remove the e-garment (typically a jacket or vest) to put it through the x-ray machine, instead of having to removing each device separately from the pockets.

Wireless PANs have the convenience of no wires to manage and the ability to use devices (such as a portable printer carried in a briefcase) whenever they are needed without having to physically connect them first. They have the added benefit of enabling a collection of devices to communicate automatically and wirelessly with each other (such as to synchronize portable devices with a desktop PC as soon as the individual returns home or to the office), whenever the devices get within a certain physical distance of each other, even though they are not physically connected.

Intranets and Extranets

An **intranet** is a private network, such as a company LAN, set up by an organization for use by its employees. Intranets are set up like the Internet, with data posted to Web pages that are accessed with a Web browser, so little or no employee training is required, and intranet content can be accessed using a variety of computer types. Intranets today are used for many purposes, such as making company publications available to employees, disseminating forms, and enabling employees to communicate and work together on projects (see Figure 7-13).

>**Intranet.** A private network that is set up similar to the Internet and is accessed via a Web browser.

An intranet that is at least partially accessible to authorized outsiders is called an **extranet**. Extranets are usually accessed via the Internet, and can be used to provide customers and business partners with access to the data they need. Access to intranets and extranets is typically restricted to employees and other authorized users, similar to company networks.

USES FOR INTRANETS

Facilitating internal e-mail.
Providing access to company contact information, procedure manuals, and other frequently updated documents.
Posting and submitting employee forms.
Posting internal job listings.
Providing electronic catalogs for ordering supplies.
Facilitating collaborative computing.
Scheduling meetings and appointments.
Posting financial statements and other types of corporate information.
Maintaining shared calendars, project timelines, and other project documents.
Providing access to company databases and order systems.

FIGURE 7-13
Uses for intranets.

Virtual Private Networks (VPNs)

A **virtual private network** (**VPN**) is a private, secure path across a public communications network (usually the Internet) that is set up to allow authorized users private, secure access to the company network. For instance, a VPN could allow a traveling employee, business partner, or employee located at a satellite office to connect securely to the company network via the Internet. VPN connections can be temporary or permanent. In either case, the connection between the sender and receiver acts as if it were completely private, even though it takes place over a public network. A process called *tunneling* is used to carry the data over the Internet; special *encryption* technology is used to protect the data, so it cannot be understood if it is intercepted during transit (encryption is explained in Chapter 9). Essentially, VPNs allow an organization to provide secure, remote access to the company network without the cost of extending the physical network.

HOW DOES DATA TRAVEL OVER A NETWORK?

Data transmitted over a network has specific characteristics, and it can travel over a network in various ways. Network devices communicate either through a *wired connection*—via physical cables—or by a *wireless connection*—typically through radio signals. These topics are discussed in the next few sections.

Data Transmission Characteristics

There are a number of characteristics related to data transmission, such as whether the data will be sent in *analog* or *digital* format; the amount of data that can be sent at one time; and the type, direction, and timing used with the transmission.

Analog vs. Digital

One of the most fundamental distinctions in data communications is the difference between analog and digital transmissions. The regular phone system, established many years ago to handle voice traffic, is designed for *analog* signals, which represent data by *continuous* waves over a certain frequency range. Some wireless networks—such as those using *Wi-Fi* or *Bluetooth* technology—as well as some cable TV broadcasts, also use analog signals. Virtually all computing equipment, in contrast, transmit *digital* signals. Some mobile phone networks, television broadcasts (such as HDTV), and cable TV broadcasts are now digital, as well. Digital signals represent data in two *discrete* states: 0s and 1s. Whenever data moves from a digital medium to an analog medium (such as from a computer to a telephone line), an interface (such as a *modem*, discussed shortly) is needed.

Bandwidth

Bandwidth (also called *throughput*) refers to the amount of data that can be transmitted over a communications medium at one time. Text data requires the least amount of bandwidth; video data requires the most. Just as a wide fire hose permits more water to pass

>**Extranet.** An intranet that is at least partially accessible to authorized outsiders. >**Virtual private network (VPN).** A group of secure paths over the Internet that provide authorized users a secure means of accessing a private network via the Internet. >**Bandwidth.** The amount of data that can be transmitted over a communications medium at one time; higher bandwidth media deliver data faster than lower bandwidth media.

01000001

SERIAL TRANSMISSION
All the bits in one byte follow one another over a single path.

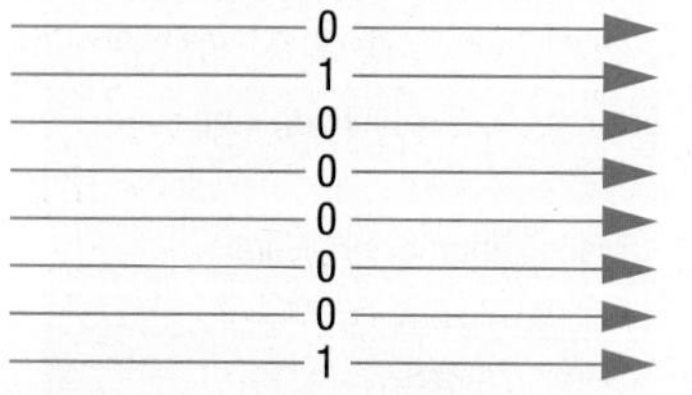

PARALLEL TRANSMISSION
The eight bits in each byte are transmitted over separate paths at the same time.

FIGURE 7-14
Serial vs. parallel transmission.

through it per unit of time than a narrow garden hose, a medium with a high bandwidth allows more data to pass through it per unit of time than a medium with a small bandwidth. Bandwidth is usually measured in the number of bits transferred per second, either in *bits per second* (*bps*), *Kbps* (thousands of bits per second), or *Mbps* (millions of bits per second). A medium with a higher bandwidth will deliver data faster than a medium with a lower bandwidth.

Serial vs. Parallel Transmission

Within a computer or over a transmission media, data can travel using *serial transmission* or *parallel transmission*. With **serial transmission**, data is sent one *bit* at a time, one after the other along a single path (see Figure 7-14). If **parallel transmission** is used, the message is sent at least one *byte* at one time with each bit in the byte taking a separate path (refer again to Figure 7-14). While parallel transmission is frequently used within computer components (such as for buses) and for some short-distance applications (such as connecting a printer to a computer, for instance), communications media typically use serial transmission.

Transmission Timing

When data is sent using serial transmission, a technique must be used to separate the bits into groups so that all the bits in one byte can be identified and retrieved together. Three ways of timing serial transmissions are *synchronous*, *asynchronous*, and *isochronous* (see Figure 7-15). Although with all three methods the bits are sent one at a time, the methods vary with how the bits are organized for transfer.

FIGURE 7-15
Transmission timing.
Most network transmissions use synchronous transmission.

- *Synchronous transmission*—data is organized into groups or blocks of a set number of bits, which are transferred at regular, specified intervals. In other words, the transmissions are synchronized and both devices know when to expect data to be sent and

SYNCHRONOUS TRANSMISSION
Data is sent in blocks and the blocks are timed so that the receiving device knows that it will be getting them at regular intervals.

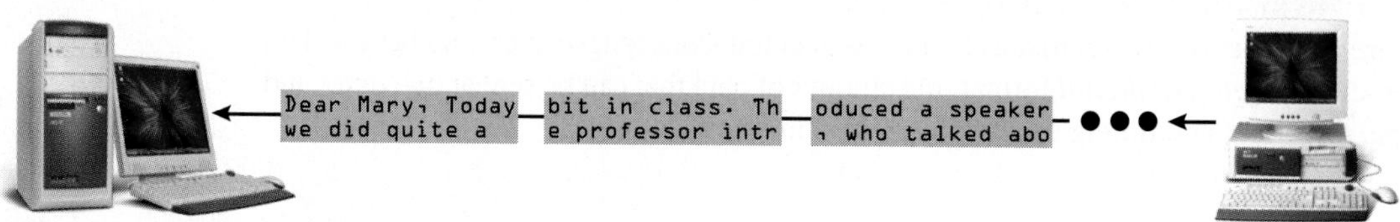

ASYNCHRONOUS TRANSMISSION
Data is sent one character at a time, along with a start and stop bit.

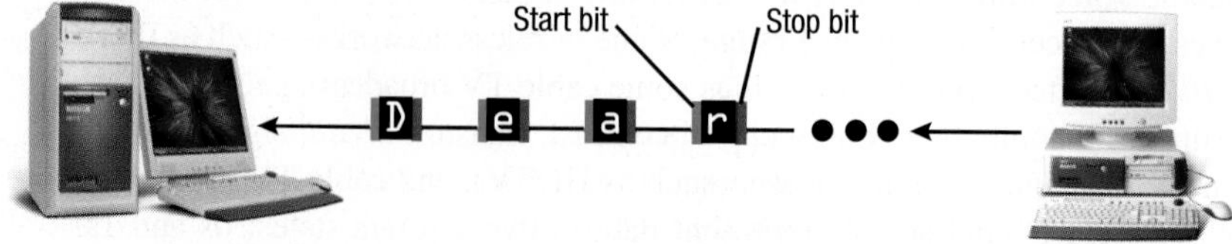

ISOCHRONOUS TRANSMISSION
The entire transmission is sent together after requesting and being assigned the bandwidth necessary for all the data to arrive at the correct time.

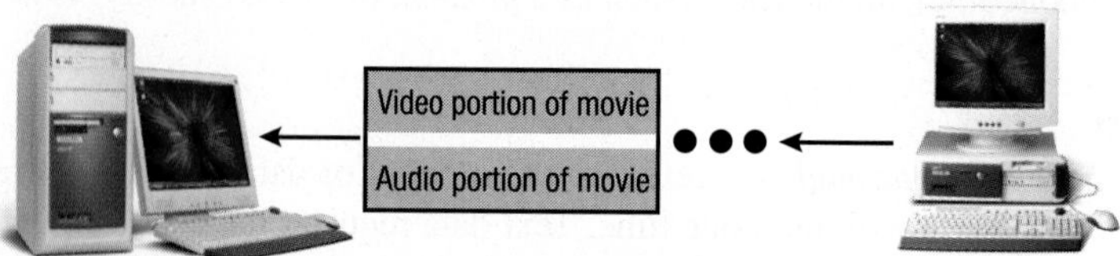

>**Serial transmission.** Data transmission in which the bits in a byte travel down the same path one after the other. >**Parallel transmission.** Data transmission in which bytes of data are transmitted at one time, with the bits in each byte taking a separate path.

when it should arrive. Most communications within a computer are synchronous, as are most network transmissions.

- *Asynchronous transmission*—data is sent when it is ready to be sent, without being synchronized. To identify the bits that belong in each byte, a *start bit* and *stop bit* are used at the beginning and end of the byte, respectively, which makes it less efficient than synchronous transmission. Asynchronous transmission is commonly used for communications between computers and peripheral devices.
- *Isochronous transmission*—data is sent at the same time as other, related, data. For example, when sending multimedia data, the audio data must be received in time to be played with the video data. With isochronous transmission, the entire necessary bandwidth is reserved for that transmission, and no other device can transmit until the transmission is completed, to ensure that the data arrive within the required time period.

Transmission Directions

Another distinction between types of transmissions is the direction in which transmitted data moves (see Figure 7-16).

- *Simplex transmission*—allows data to travel in a single direction only, such as a doorbell. Simplex transmission is relatively uncommon in computer communications since most devices that are usually one-directional, such as a printer, can still transmit error messages and other data back to the PC.
- *Half-duplex transmission*—allows messages to move in either direction, but only in one direction at a time, such as a walkie-talkie in which only one person can talk at a time. Some network transmissions are half-duplex.
- *Full-duplex transmission*—allows data to move in both directions at the same time, like a standard telephone line. Full-duplexing is ideal for hardware devices that need to pass large amounts of data between each other. Many network and most Internet connections are full-duplex.

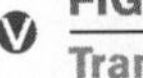

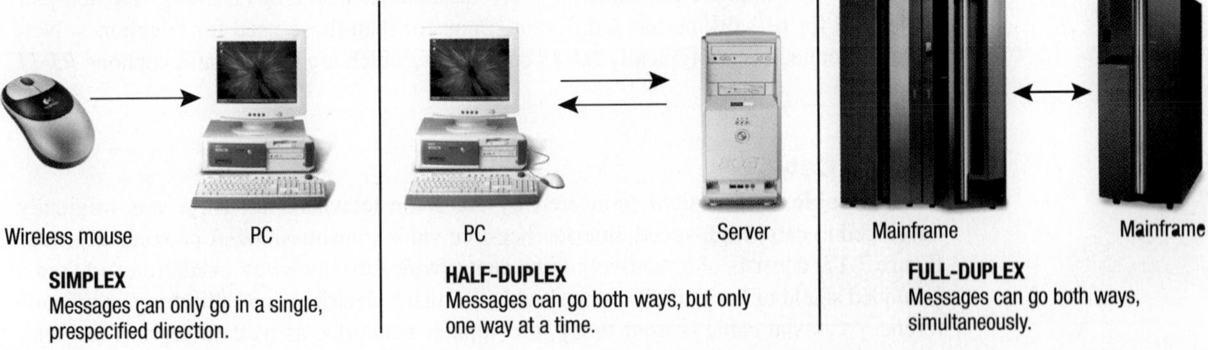
Wireless mouse
PC
SIMPLEX
Messages can only go in a single, prespecified direction.
PC
Server
HALF-DUPLEX
Messages can go both ways, but only one way at a time.
Mainframe
Mainframe
FULL-DUPLEX
Messages can go both ways, simultaneously.

FIGURE 7-16
Transmission directions. Transmissions can be simplex (one direction only), half-duplex (one direction at a time), or full-duplex (both directions at one time).

NET

Wired vs. Wireless Connections

With a **wired network** connection, the PC is physically cabled to the network. Wired networks are very common in schools, businesses, and government facilities; they are also found in homes. In general, wired computer networks are less expensive than *wireless*

>**Wired network.** A network in which computers and other devices are connected to the network via physical cables.

networks and are faster. They tend to be easier to secure and are the most efficient way of moving large amounts of data, particularly video and other types of multimedia data, at high speeds. However, they are much more difficult to install in existing structures than *wireless networks*.

Wireless networks typically use radio waves to send data through the air instead of over a physical cable. Consequently, they allow easy connections when physical wiring is impractical or inconvenient (such as inside an existing home or outdoors), as well as give users much more freedom regarding where they can use their PCs. With a wireless network connection, for example, you can surf the Web on your notebook PC from anywhere in your house; access the Internet while traveling just by being close to a public wireless access point in a restaurant, park, or airport; and create a home network without having to run wires between the rooms of your house. Wireless networks are rapidly becoming more popular in both homes and businesses; wireless hotspots are also commonly available in public locations (such as coffee houses, businesses, airports, hotels, and libraries) to allow network access while users are on the road. It is estimated that there were approximately 20,000 public wireless hotspots in the United States at the end of 2004—that number is expected to climb to 150,000 by 2007.

Wired Network Transmission Media

The most common types of wired transmission media are *twisted-pair*, *coaxial*, and *fiber-optic cable*.

Twisted-Pair Cable

Twisted-pair cable (made up of pairs of thin strands of insulated wire twisted together, as illustrated in Figure 7-17) is the least expensive type of networking cable and has been in use the longest. It is the same type of cabling that is found inside the walls of most homes for telephone communications. It is also commonly used for LANs. Twisted-pair cable is rated by category. *Category 3* twisted-pair cabling is regular telephone cable; higher speed cabling—such as *Category 5* and *Category 6*—is frequently used for home or business networks. Twisted-pair wire is twisted together to reduce interference and improve performance. To further improve performance it can be *shielded* with a metal lining. Twisted-pair cable used for networking has a different connector than those used for telephones. Networking connectors are typically *RJ-45* connectors, which are larger than telephone *RJ-11* connectors.

Coaxial Cable

Coaxial cable, the medium pioneered by the cable television industry, was originally developed to carry high-speed, interference-free video transmissions. A coaxial cable (see Figure 7-17) consists of a relatively thick center wire surrounded by insulation and then a grounded shield of braided wire (the shield minimizes electrical and radio frequency interference). Coaxial cable is used today in computer networks, as well as in short-run telephone transmissions outside of the home and for cable television delivery. Although more expensive than twisted-pair cabling, it is much less susceptible to interference and can carry more data more quickly.

>**Wireless network.** A network in which computers and other devices are connected to the network without physical cables; data is typically sent via radio waves. >**Twisted-pair cable.** A communications medium consisting of wire strands twisted in sets of two and bound into a cable. >**Coaxial cable.** A communications medium consisting of a center wire inside a grounded, cylindrical shield, capable of sending data at high speeds.

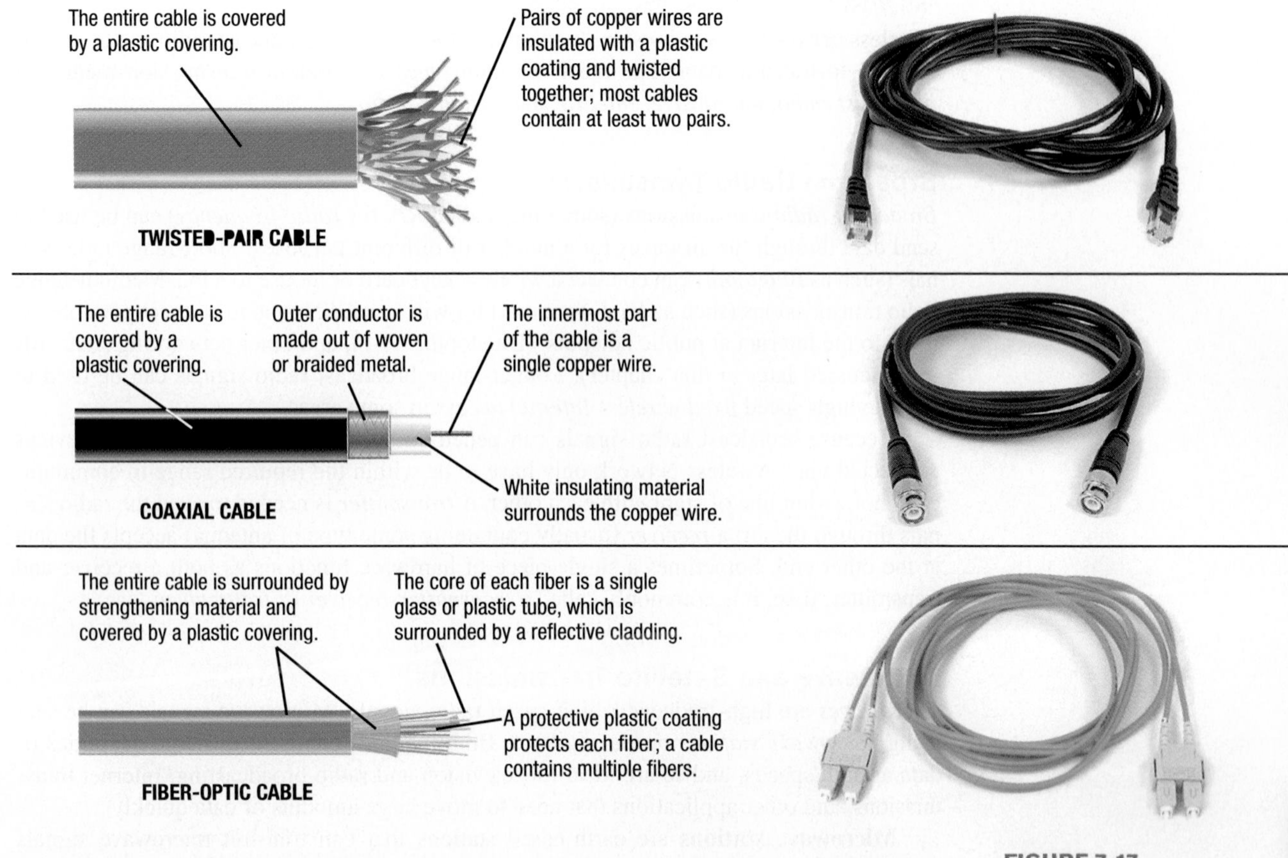
The entire cable is covered by a plastic covering.
Pairs of copper wires are insulated with a plastic coating and twisted together; most cables contain at least two pairs.
TWISTED-PAIR CABLE
The entire cable is covered by a plastic covering.
Outer conductor is made out of woven or braided metal.
The innermost part of the cable is a single copper wire.
White insulating material surrounds the copper wire.
COAXIAL CABLE
The entire cable is surrounded by strengthening material and covered by a plastic covering.
The core of each fiber is a single glass or plastic tube, which is surrounded by a reflective cladding.
A protective plastic coating protects each fiber; a cable contains multiple fibers.
FIBER-OPTIC CABLE

FIGURE 7-17
Wired network transmission media.

Fiber-Optic Cable

Fiber-optic cable is the newest and fastest wired transmission medium. It uses clear glass or plastic fiber strands, each about the thickness of a human hair, to transfer data represented by light pulses (refer again to Figure 7-17). The light pulses are sent through the cable by a laser device at speeds of billions or even trillions of bits per second. Each hair-like fiber has the capacity to carry data for several television stations or thousands of two-way voice conversations. Typically, multiple fibers—sometimes several hundred fibers—are wrapped inside a single fiber-optic cable. Fiber-optic connectors are less standardized than for other types of wired media, so it is important to use cables with the connectors that match the hardware with which the cable will be used. Common connectors include *SC* and *ST*; the SC connector is shown in Figure 7-17.

Fiber-optic cable is commonly used for the high-speed backbone lines of a network, such as to connect networks in separate buildings or for Internet infrastructure. It is also used for telephone backbone lines. The biggest advantage of fiber optic cabling is speed. For example, while it may take a few seconds to transmit a single page of Webster's dictionary over conventional wire cabling, an entire 15-volume set of the *Encyclopedia Britannica* could be transmitted over fiber-optic cable in just a fraction of a second. Another advantage is that data can be transmitted digitally, instead of as analog signals like twisted-pair, coaxial cable, and most wireless media. The main disadvantage of fiber-optic cabling is the initial expense of both the cable and the installation.

>**Fiber-optic cable.** A communications medium that utilizes hundreds of hair-thin, transparent fibers over which lasers transmit data as light.

Wireless Network Transmission Media

Wireless networks use *radio signals*, similar to those used to broadcast radio and television content, to transmit data. The most common types of wireless transmission media are *broadcast radio*, *microwave*, *satellite*, and *cellular radio*.

Broadcast Radio Transmissions

Broadcast radio transmissions (sometimes called *RF*, for *radio frequency*) can be used to send data through the airwaves for a number of different purposes. Short-range radio signals (such as *Bluetooth*) can connect a wireless keyboard or mouse to a PC. Medium-range radio transmissions (such as *Wi-Fi*) are used for wireless LANs and to connect portable PC users to the Internet at public hotspots. (Bluetooth, Wi-Fi, and other networking standards are discussed later in this chapter). Longer-range broadcast radio signals can be used to provide high-speed *fixed wireless Internet access* in some areas.

Because broadcast radio signals can penetrate buildings and other objects, devices connected via a wireless network only have to be within the required range to communicate, not within line of sight with each other. A *transmitter* is needed to send the radio signals through the air; a *receiver* (usually containing some type of antenna) accepts the data at the other end. Sometimes a single piece of hardware functions as both a receiver and transmitter; if so, it is commonly called a *transmitter-receiver* or *transceiver*.

Microwave and Satellite Transmissions

Microwaves are high-frequency, high-speed radio signals. Microwave signals can be sent using *microwave stations* or via *satellites*. Both methods can transmit large quantities of data at high speeds, and so are ideal for television and radio broadcasting, Internet transmissions, and other applications that need to move large amounts of data quickly.

Microwave stations are earth-based stations that can transmit microwave signals directly to each other over distances of up to about 30 miles. Unlike broadcast radio, microwave transmission is line of sight, which means that the microwaves must travel in a straight line from one station to another without encountering any obstacles. To avoid buildings, mountains, and the curvature of the earth obstructing the signal, microwave stations are usually placed on tall buildings, towers, and mountaintops. Microwave stations typically contain both a disc-shaped *microwave antenna* and a transceiver. When one station receives a transmission from another, it amplifies it and passes it on to the next station. Microwave stations can also exchange data transmissions with satellites. Microwave stations designed specifically to communicate with satellites, such as for satellite TV and Internet services, are typically called *satellite dishes*. Satellite dishes are usually installed permanently where they are needed, but can also be mounted on trucks, boats, and other types of transportation devices when portable transmission capabilities are necessary or desirable, such as on military or recreational vehicles.

Communications satellites are space-based devices placed into orbit around the earth to receive and transmit microwave signals to and from earth (see the satellite Internet example in Figure 7-18). Originally used primarily to facilitate microwave transmission when microwave stations were either not economically viable (such as over large, sparsely populated areas) or physically impractical (such as over large bodies of water), satellites can now send and receive transmissions to and from a variety of other devices, such as personal satellite dishes used for television and Internet transmissions, GPS receivers, satellite radio receivers, and satellite phones.

>**Microwave station.** An earth-based device that sends and receives high-frequency, high-speed radio signals. >**Communications satellite.** An earth-orbiting device that relays communications signals over long distances.

4. The ISP's satellite dish receives the data and transfers it to the Internet.

The Internet

5. Data travels over the Internet as usual. Information requested from the Internet takes a reverse route back to the individual.

3. An orbiting satellite receives the data and beams it down to the ISP's satellite dish.

2. Data is sent up to a satellite from the individual's satellite dish.

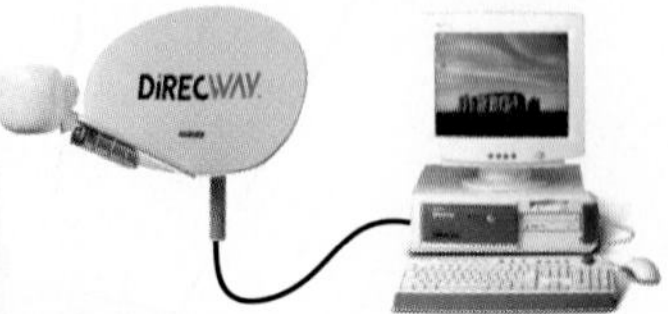

1. Data is sent from the individual's PC to the satellite dish.

FIGURE 7-18
How satellite Internet works.

Traditional satellites maintain a *geosynchronous* (also called *geostationary*) orbit, 22,300 miles above the earth. Geosynchronous satellites travel at a speed and direction that keeps pace with the earth's rotation, so they appear to remain stationary over a given spot on the globe. Geosynchronous satellites are so far above the surface of the earth that it takes only two of them to blanket the entire planet. Although geosynchronous satellites are excellent for transmitting data, they are so far away that there is a slight delay while the signals travel from the earth, to the satellite, and back to the earth again. This delay—less than a half-second—is very small for the distance involved and does not really interfere with data communications, but it does make geosynchronous satellite transmissions less practical for voice, gaming, and other real-time communications.

Low earth orbit (*LEO*) satellite systems were developed so that telephone communications systems could avoid the delay problem. LEO satellites typically are located about 500 miles above the earth and use between 50 and 60 satellites to cover the earth. LEO satellites are cheaper to build, and, because of their lower orbits, they provide faster message transmission than traditional satellites. *Medium earth orbit* (*MEO*) systems using satellites located about 6,400 miles above the earth are currently being developed for both telephone and Internet service. GPS satellites, which are about 12,000 miles above the earth, are considered MEO satellites, as well.

Cellular Radio Transmissions

Cellular radio is a form of broadcast radio designed for use with cellular telephones. Cellular transmissions take place via *cellular towers*—tall metal poles with antennas on top to receive and transmit cellular radio signals. Cellular service areas are divided into honeycomb-shaped zones called *cells*, each usually measuring between 2 and 10 miles across and containing one cellular tower (see Figure 7-19). When a cell phone user begins to make a call, it is picked up by the cell tower in the cell in which the caller is located. The cell tower then forwards the call to its designated cellular company switching office, and it travels to the recipient via his or her telephone service provider. When a cell phone user moves out of the current cell into a new cell, the call is handed off from the cell tower in the current cell to the cell tower in the cell the user is entering, usually without the user realizing the call has been transferred. To allow multiple conversations to take place at the same time over a single cellular network, different transmission frequencies are used. To avoid interference, towers in adjacent cells always transmit on different frequencies.

Cellular phone use has become incredibly popular for both business and personal use—around 779 million phones were sold worldwide in 2005, according to the research

FURTHER EXPLORATION

For links to further information about wired and wireless communications media, go to www.course.com/uc11/ch07

>**Cellular radio.** A form of broadcast radio that broadcasts using antennas located inside honeycomb-shaped cells.

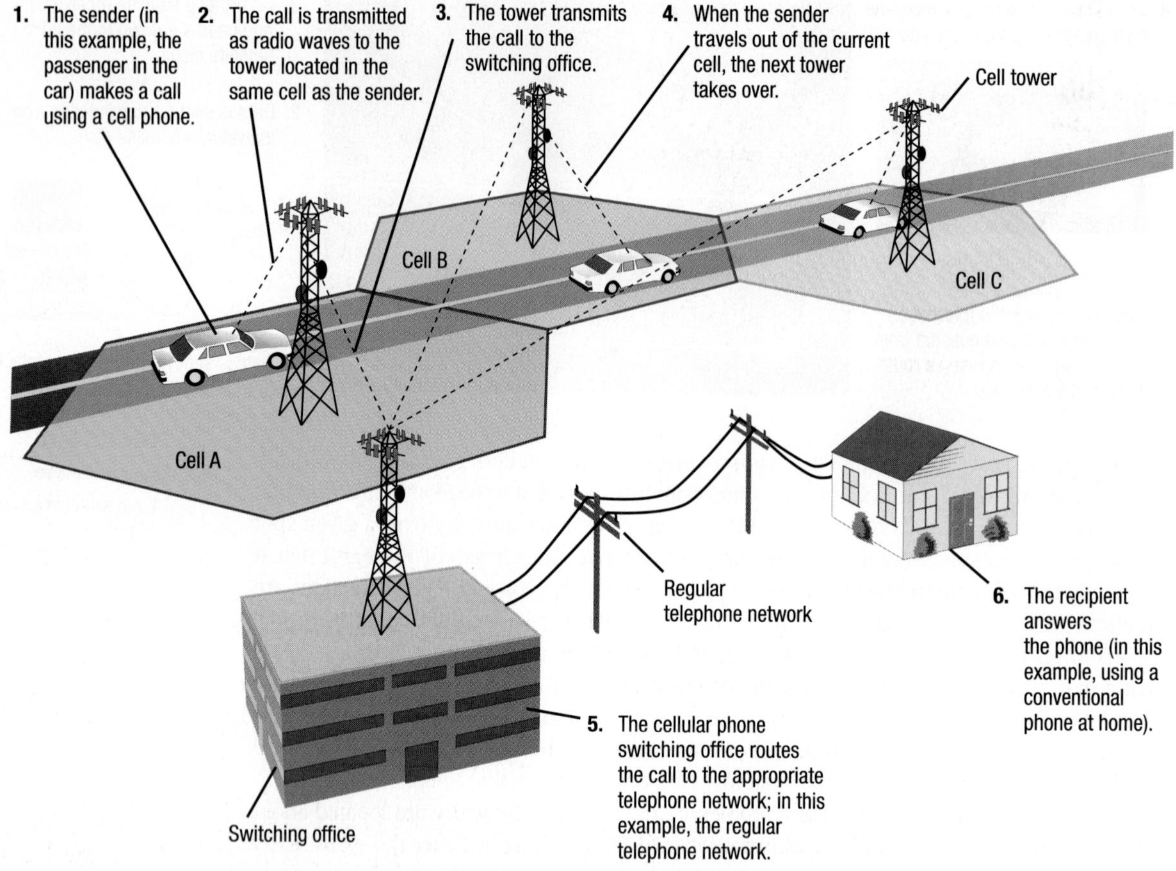

1. The sender (in this example, the passenger in the car) makes a call using a cell phone.
2. The call is transmitted as radio waves to the tower located in the same cell as the sender.
3. The tower transmits the call to the switching office.
4. When the sender travels out of the current cell, the next tower takes over.
Cell tower
Cell A
Cell B
Cell C
Regular telephone network
6. The recipient answers the phone (in this example, using a conventional phone at home).
5. The cellular phone switching office routes the call to the appropriate telephone network; in this example, the regular telephone network.
Switching office

FIGURE 7-19
How cellular transmissions work. Cell phones send and receive calls via cellular radio towers covering a limited geographical area. As the cell phone user moves, the call is transferred from cell tower to cell tower.

group Gartner. That number is expected to exceed 1 billion by 2007, when it is estimated that 2.6 billion people worldwide will actively use a cell phone. Today's cell phones are usually *second-generation (2G)* or *third-generation (3G)* phones. The original *first-generation* phones were analog and designed for voice data only. Newer cell phones, starting with 2G, are digital, support both data and voice, and are faster (2G has a maximum speed of 14.4 Kbps, and 3G phones are designed to transfer data at rates up to 128 Kbps while driving in a car, 384 Kbps in a pedestrian environment, and 2 Mbps in a fixed setup). *Fourth-generation (4G)* cellular services, which are expected to move data at 100 Mbps or more, might arrive as soon as 2006.

COMMUNICATIONS PROTOCOLS

A *communications protocol* is an agreed-upon standard for transmitting data between two devices on a network. Protocols specify how devices physically connect to a network, how data is packaged for transmission, how receiving devices acknowledge signals from sending devices (a process called *handshaking*), how errors are handled, and so forth. Just as people need a common language to communicate effectively, machines need a common set of rules—communications protocols—for this purpose. Two of the most common protocols used to transfer data over a network are *Ethernet* (for wired networks) and *Wi-Fi* (for wireless networks). Other possibilities are *Token Ring* (for wired networks); *Bluetooth* and *Ultra Wideband* (for short-range wireless connections); *TCP/IP* and *WAP* (for Internet communications); *Phoneline* and *Powerline* (for home networks); and the emerging *WiMAX*, *Mobile-Fi*, and *xMax* standards.

Ethernet

Ethernet is one of the most widely used wired networking protocols. It is typically used with LANs that have a bus or star topology and use twisted-pair or coaxial cables. The original Ethernet protocol (called *10Base-T*) was developed in the mid-1970s and supports transmission rates of 10 Mbps. The most common Ethernet standard for LANs today is *Fast Ethernet* (*100Base-T*), which supports data transfer rates of up to 100 Mbps. *Gigabit Ethernet* (*1000Base-T*) is even faster at 1,000 Mbps (1 Gbps) and is most often used for data-intensive business LANs or WANs. The emerging *10-Gigabit Ethernet* standard supports data transfer rates of 10 Gbps.

When transmitting data, an Ethernet network uses a set of procedures collectively called *CSMA/CD*, which stands for *Carrier Sense Multiple Access* and *Collision Detection* (see Figure 7-20). *Carrier sense* means that when a computer on the network is ready to send a message, it first "listens" for other messages on the line. If it senses no messages, it sends one. *Multiple access* means that two computers might try to send a message at exactly the same time, so a *collision* may occur. *Collision detection* means that just after a computer transmits a message, it listens to see if the message collided with a message from another computer (collisions are not noticeable to the user). When a collision takes place,

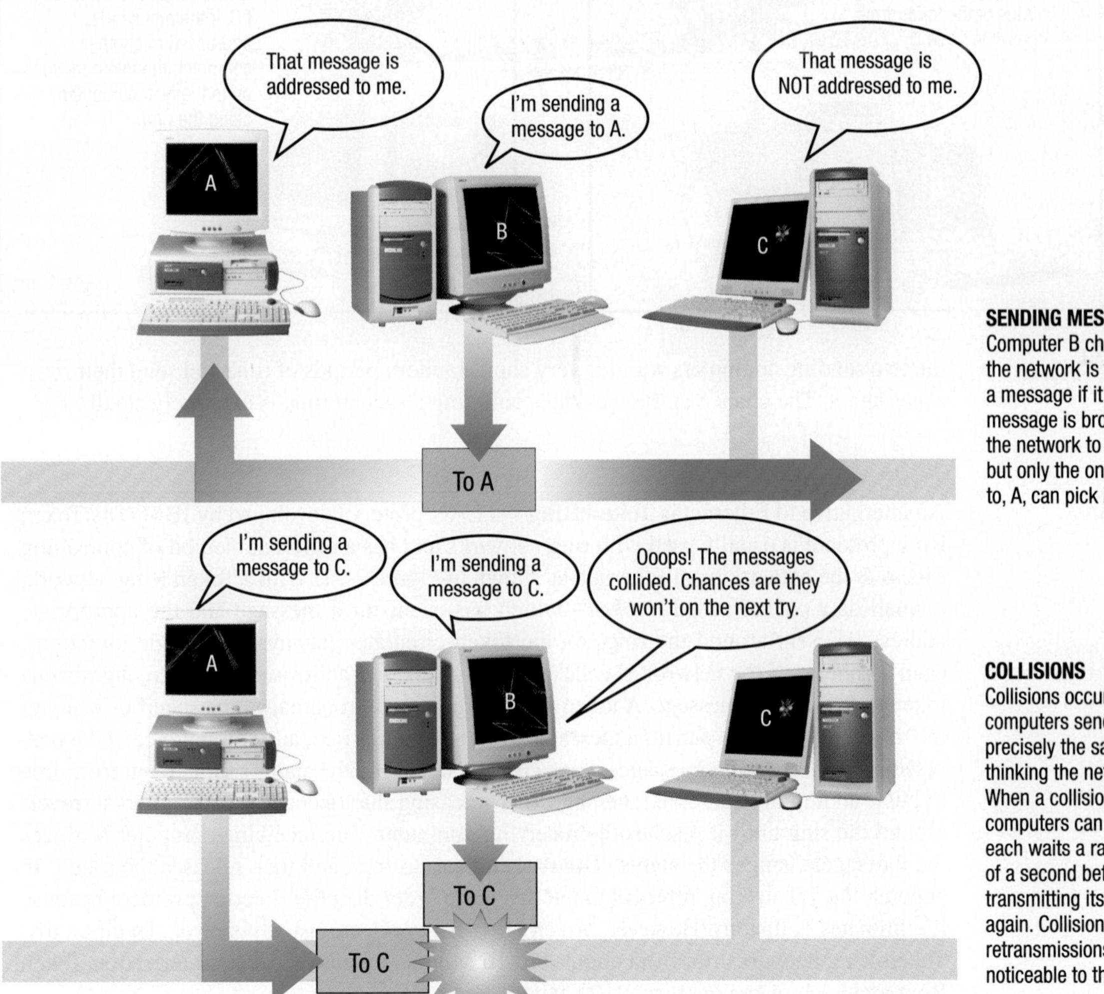

FIGURE 7-20
How Ethernet networks work.

SENDING MESSAGES
Computer B checks to see if the network is free and sends a message if it thinks it is. The message is broadcast across the network to all computers, but only the one it is addressed to, A, can pick it up.

COLLISIONS
Collisions occur when two computers send messages at precisely the same time, both thinking the network is free. When a collision occurs, the computers can sense it, and each waits a random fraction of a second before transmitting its message again. Collisions and retransmissions are not noticeable to the user.

NET

>**Ethernet.** A widely used communications protocol for a LAN.

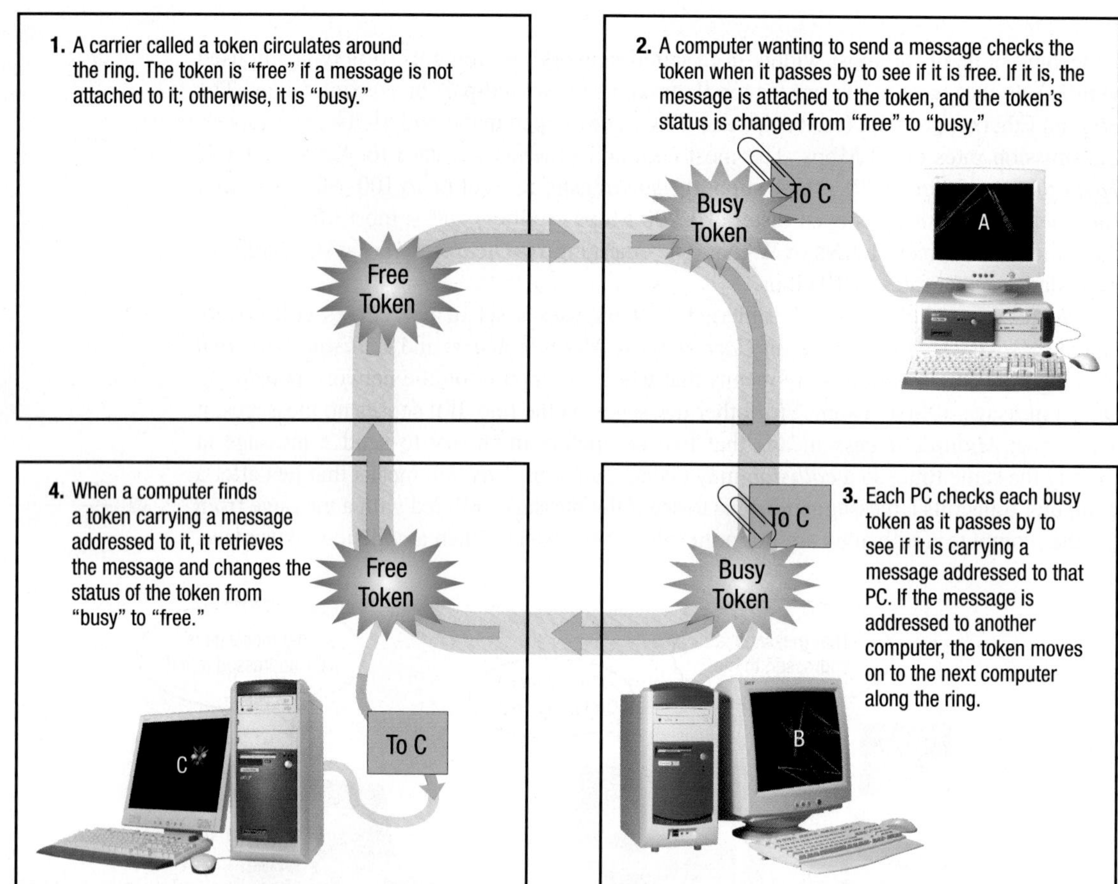

1. A carrier called a token circulates around the ring. The token is "free" if a message is not attached to it; otherwise, it is "busy."
2. A computer wanting to send a message checks the token when it passes by to see if it is free. If it is, the message is attached to the token, and the token's status is changed from "free" to "busy."
3. Each PC checks each busy token as it passes by to see if it is carrying a message addressed to that PC. If the message is addressed to another computer, the token moves on to the next computer along the ring.
4. When a computer finds a token carrying a message addressed to it, it retrieves the message and changes the status of the token from "busy" to "free."
Free Token
Busy Token
To C
A
Busy Token
To C
B
Free Token
To C
C

FIGURE 7-21

How Token Ring networks work. Token Ring networks use token passing to control access.

the two sending computers wait for very short, random periods of time and send their messages again. The chance of the messages colliding a second time is extremely small.

Token Ring

An alternative to Ethernet is **Token Ring**—a LAN protocol developed by IBM. The Token Ring protocol is usually used with ring networks and has a different method of controlling access to the network from Ethernet, as shown in Figure 7-21. With a Token Ring network, a small data packet called a *token*—which has room for a message and the appropriate address—is sent around the ring. As the token circulates (always in a single direction), each computer on the network checks to see if the token is addressed to it; if so, it grabs the token to retrieve the message. A token also contains a control area, which specifies whether the token is free or if it carries a message. When a token is free, any computer can take possession of it to attach a message. It does this by changing the status of the token from free to busy, adding the addressed message, and releasing the token. The message then travels around the ring until it reaches the receiving computer. The receiving computer retrieves the message, changes the status of the token back to free, and then releases the token. In general, the Token Ring protocol maintains more order than the Ethernet protocol because it eliminates collisions. However, Token Ring networks are usually slower. Traditionally, Token Ring networks run from about 4 to 16 Mbps. The newer, second-generation Token Ring architecture can operate at 100 Mbps.

>**Token Ring.** A communications protocol that uses token passing to control the transmission of messages.

Wi-Fi (802.11)

Developed in the late 1990s, **Wi-Fi** (for *wireless fidelity*) is a family of wireless networking standards. Wi-Fi (also known as **802.11** for its official standard number issued by *IEEE*, a nonprofit organization involved with setting standards for computers and communications technology) is the current standard for wireless networks in the home or office, as well as for connecting wirelessly to the Internet via a public hotspot—a geographic area covered by a Wi-Fi *wireless access point*. Wi-Fi can be used to create an entirely wireless network, as well as to add wireless capabilities to an existing wired Ethernet network. For instance, a homeowner may wish to use Wi-Fi to connect a notebook computer to an existing wired home network so the notebook computer can be used anywhere in the house or yard, or a business may wish to add wireless capabilities to the company network to provide Internet and network access in meeting rooms, lobbies, cafeterias, and other common areas. Colleges typically have hotspots on campus to enable students to wirelessly connect to the campus network (see Figure 7-22), and public Wi-Fi hotspots are also becoming increasingly common. Although you cannot get continuous coverage while on the go with Wi-Fi (such as you can with Internet service through a cellular provider, for instance), Wi-Fi is a fast alternative for users who need Internet access while close to an accessible hotspot. Some public hotspots can be accessed for free; others charge by the minute or hour. Numerous cities—such as Spokane and Philadelphia—have set up large wireless networks to provide free or low-cost wireless Internet access for that community. A series of connected hotspots may provide wider, more comprehensive Wi-Fi coverage in the future—such setups are in the experimentation stage.

COLLEGE HOTSPOT
This hotspot is located in the student union in a college in England.

LIBRARY HOTSPOT
This hotspot is located at the New York City Public Library.

FIGURE 7-22
Wireless hotspots.
Wireless hotspots are commonly found on college campuses, public libraries, and other public locations.

Wi-Fi is designed for medium-range data transfers—in theory, no more than 300 feet away indoors or 1,000 feet outdoors, although the maximum distances achieved in real situations are often much less. Factors that affect performance include the distance from the access point, the number of solid objects (such as walls) between the access point and the PC, and possible interference from cordless phones, baby monitors, and other devices that also operate on the same radio frequency (usually 2.4 GHz).

There are a number of different versions of the 802.11 standard; some are new standards, others are improvements to the existing standards. The three most common 802.11 standards are listed in Figure 7-23, along with an emerging standard expected to be finalized in 2007. The *802.11g* standard is the norm today, although it will likely be replaced with one of the improved emerging standards—such as *802.11n*, once it becomes available.

FIGURE 7-23
Wi-Fi standards.

WI-FI STANDARD	DESCRIPTION
802.11b	The original Wi-Fi standard; supports data transfer rates of 11 Mbps.
802.11a (also called *Wi-Fi5*)	About five times faster (up to 54 Mbps) than 802.11b, but it is more expensive and uses a different radio frequency (5 GHz) than 802.11b (2.4 GHz), making the two standards incompatible.
802.11g	The current Wi-Fi standard; supports data transfer rates of 54 Mbps, but it uses the same 2.4 GHz frequency as 802.11b, so their products are compatible.
802.11n	A Wi-Fi standard currently in development that is expected to increase Wi-Fi speeds to more than 100 Mbps; currently uses MIMO technology and is sometimes called *Fast Wi-Fi*.

>**Wi-Fi (802.11).** A widely used communications protocol for wireless networks.

NET

One new application for Wi-Fi is *Voice over Wi-Fi*, which allows users to make telephone calls via a Wi-Fi network. At the present time Voice over Wi-Fi is used mainly by employees who work at large facilities covered by Wi-Fi networks, such as schools, hospitals, and corporate headquarters. As Wi-Fi networks become larger, however, Voice over Wi-Fi could become a viable alternative to conventional or wireless telephone service. Other Wi-Fi applications under development include the *Wi-Fi Positioning System*, which is an alternative to GPS, and large *municipal Wi-Fi networks* (sometimes called *Wi-Fi clouds*), which are very large Wi-Fi hotspots that are designed to provide Internet access to a particular area. For instance, the wireless network being created in the city of Philadelphia, Pennsylvania will cover all 135 square miles of Philadelphia—when completed, this network will be the world's largest Wi-Fi network. To accomplish these large hotspots, *mesh* technology is typically used; mesh and other additional wireless technologies are discussed next.

Mesh Networks, WiMAX, Mobile-Fi, and xMax

A number of wireless networking technologies are currently in development, designed to be used in conjunction with Wi-Fi or instead of Wi-Fi to extend the range of wireless networks. Some of the most promising are discussed next.

Mesh Networks

The phenomenal growth in the number of wireless networks and the use of wireless devices in recent years has created the need to connect these devices and networks. For instance, an individual using Wi-Fi access inside a Starbucks coffeehouse is not able to continue that connection when he or she leaves that immediate area. Instead, the individual needs to locate another hotspot at his or her next location. And, while emergency workers within a single agency—such as a city fire department, the highway patrol, or the U.S. Coast Guard—can communicate with other workers within their agency, they often cannot communicate with other workers from other agencies because they use different radio systems. These problems can be solved by an emerging wireless networking standard known as *wireless mesh*.

FURTHER EXPLORATION

For links to further information about wireless networking protocols, go to www.course.com/uc11/ch07

Developed in the military, wireless mesh networks use a mesh topology, so messages can take any of several possible paths from source to destination. The most common use of mesh technology today is to create MANs. For instance, the city of Medford, Oregon, created Oregon's first wireless mesh network in 2004. This 24-square mile network was implemented to provide high-speed data communications to city workers, including those at law enforcement, fire, rescue, public works, and building inspection agencies. Other mesh MANs are used to provide wireless Internet access to residents in a particular geographic area.

WiMAX

Another emerging wireless standard is **WiMAX** (also known as *802.16*). WiMAX is a series of standards designed to provide wireless Internet access at speeds up to 70 Mbps over a distance of up to 30 miles. In addition to speed and distance, WiMAX does not require line of site and works in areas containing buildings and trees. Similar to Wi-Fi, WiMAX is designed for fixed hotspot locations, but the hotspots are significantly larger. In fact, one of the leaders in WiMAX—Intel—expects it to eventually replace Wi-Fi. A version of WiMAX being developed for mobile use is called *mobile WiMAX* or *802.16e* and is

>**WiMAX.** An emerging wireless networking standard that is faster and has a greater range than Wi-Fi.

expected to be available by the end of 2006. Products for the original WiMAX standards were released at the end of 2005; mobile WiMAX products and services are expected to be available in the United States sometime in 2006.

Mobile-Fi

Mobile-Fi, also known as *802.20* and *Mobile Broadband Wireless Access* (*MBWA*), is another standard currently in development for providing high-speed mobile Internet access. Mobile-Fi is designed to be used while in cars or while traveling in other vehicles, such as trains, which are moving at up to 155 miles per hour. Currently a competitor of WiMAX, Mobile-Fi is expected to be compatible with WiMAX. Some experts predict that WiMAX will be used to create large hotspots to provide access to stationary users and users moving around within a limited geographic area, while Mobile-Fi will be used for broader coverage and in high-speed mobile situations, such as to provide Internet access for individuals who commute to work via train. Mobile-Fi products are expected to be available sometime in 2006.

TIP

WiMAX and Mobile-Fi are two of the technologies that mobile carriers are investigating as possible options for delivering *4G* mobile phone services.

xMax

An additional possibility for longer range wireless connections is *xMax*—a technology recently developed by a company called *xG*. xMax is designed to transfer data over the unused portions of radio channels currently used for pagers and TV signals. Because xMax uses very low frequencies, it can transmit over longer distances than other wireless technologies. Consequently, less hardware is required to cover a specific geographic location, making it more feasible for providing wireless Internet to rural areas. Prototype xMax networks are currently being built in Florida.

Bluetooth and Ultra Wideband (UWB)

Bluetooth is another wireless standard that uses radio technology, but it is designed for very short-range (less than 10 meters, approximately 33 feet) communications. It is most appropriate for communications between computers or mobile devices and peripheral devices, such as to connect a wireless keyboard or mouse to a desktop PC, to send print jobs wirelessly from a portable PC to a portable printer, or to connect a smart phone to an earpiece (see Figure 7-24). Since Bluetooth devices automatically recognize each other when they get within transmission range, handheld PCs, desktop PCs, and mobile devices can always be networked wirelessly when they are within range. For instance, Bluetooth can be used to automatically synchronize a handheld PC with a desktop PC on entering the home or office. In addition, some industry experts predict that all major household appliances will be Bluetooth-enabled in the future, resulting in an automatic, always connected, smart home.

FIGURE 7-24

Bluetooth. Bluetooth is designed for short-range wireless communications between PCs or mobile devices and other hardware.

The notebook PC and printer form a piconet when they are within range to communicate with each other.

The desktop PC, keyboard, and mouse form a piconet to communicate with each other.

The headset and cell phone form a piconet when they are within range to communicate with each other.

NET

>**Bluetooth.** A communications standard for very short-range wireless connections; the devices are automatically connected once they get within the allowable range.

Bluetooth works using radio waves in the frequency band of 2.4 GHz, the same as Wi-Fi, and supports data transfer rates of up to 3 Mbps. Once two Bluetooth-enabled devices come within range of each other, their software identifies each other (using their unique identification numbers) and establishes a link. Because there may be many Bluetooth devices within range, up to 10 individual Bluetooth networks (called *piconets*) can be in place within the same physical area at one time (see Figure 7-24). Each piconet can connect up to eight devices, for a maximum of 80 devices within any 10-meter radius. To facilitate this, Bluetooth divides its allocated radio spectrum into multiple channels of 1 MHz each. Each Bluetooth device can use the entire range of frequencies, jumping randomly (in unison with the other devices in that piconet) on a regular basis to minimize interference between piconets, as well as from other devices (such as garage-door openers, Wi-Fi networks, and some cordless phones and baby monitors) that use the same frequencies. Since Bluetooth transmitters change frequencies 1,600 times every second automatically, it is unlikely that any two transmitting devices will be on the same frequencies at the same time. For control, one device in each piconet acts as the *master* device and continually emits requests for other devices to join the network. Any device wishing to network with the master device answers with its identification number and becomes a *slave* device in that piconet.

Another short-range wireless technology used to connect devices is *Ultra Wideband* (*UWB*). UWB was originally developed for the military in the 1960s to locate tanks, enemies, and other objects hidden behind walls or in foliage, but it is now beginning to be used to wirelessly network consumer multimedia devices. UWB can be used to wirelessly deliver multimedia content—such as video, music, and photos—stored on a computer or DVR to other devices that are within range (about 100 feet away or less). The speed of UWB at the present time depends on the distance between the devices being used, but at 100 Mbps at 10 meters (about 33 feet) or 480 Mbps at 2 meters (about 6.5 feet), UWB is significantly faster than Bluetooth and has a greater range. The UWB standard is still evolving and some predict a speed of 1 Gbps by 2007. One of the most recent developments related to UWB is the announcement that new Bluetooth standards may use UWB to speed up connections between Bluetooth devices for transferring larger quantities of data, such as to transfer music or video files from a PC to a mobile phone. Another development is the proposed *wireless USB* standard. Backed by Intel and based on UWB, wireless USB is designed to connect peripheral devices, similar to Bluetooth, and will transfer data at up to 480 Mbps. It is expected that wireless USB will be aimed at PC use, while Bluetooth will continue to be prominent for use with portable PCs and mobile devices.

TCP/IP and Wireless Application Protocol (WAP)

TCP/IP is the protocol used for transferring data over the Internet. It actually consists of two protocols: *Transmission Control Protocol* (*TCP*) and *Internet Protocol* (*IP*). TCP/IP uses a technique called *packet switching* to transmit data over the Internet. With packet switching, messages are separated into small units called *packets*. Packets contain information about the sender and the receiver, the actual data being sent, and information about how to reassemble the packets in order to reconstruct the original message. Packets travel along the network separately, based on their final destination, network traffic, and other network conditions. When the packets reach their destination, they are reassembled in the proper order (see Figure 7-25).

TIP

A related protocol—*Voice over IP (VoIP)*—used to make telephone calls over the Internet using Internet Protocol is discussed in Chapter 8.

>**TCP/IP.** A communications protocol that uses packet switching to facilitate the transmission of messages; the protocol used with the Internet.

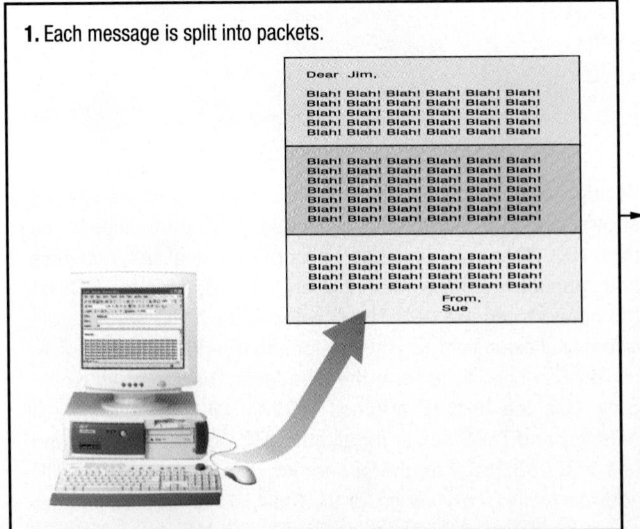

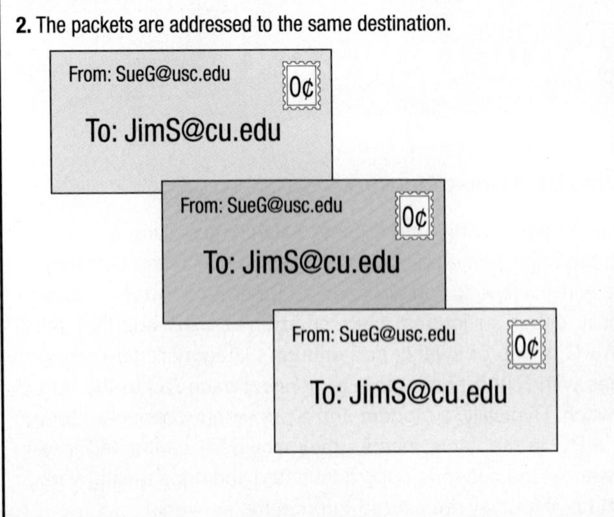

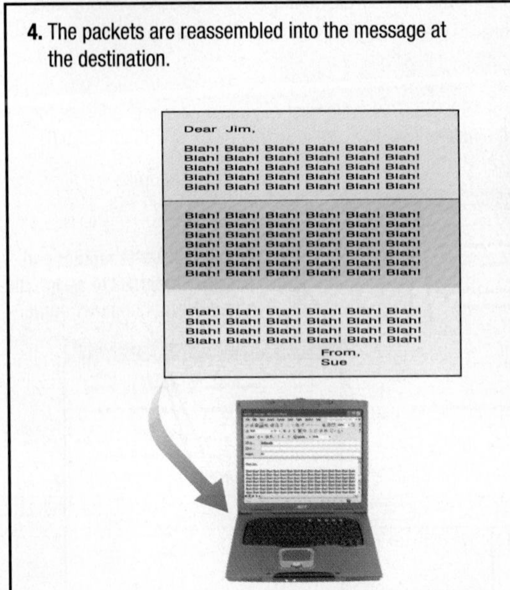

4. The packets are reassembled into the message at the destination.
1. Each message is split into packets.
Dear Jim,
From, Sue

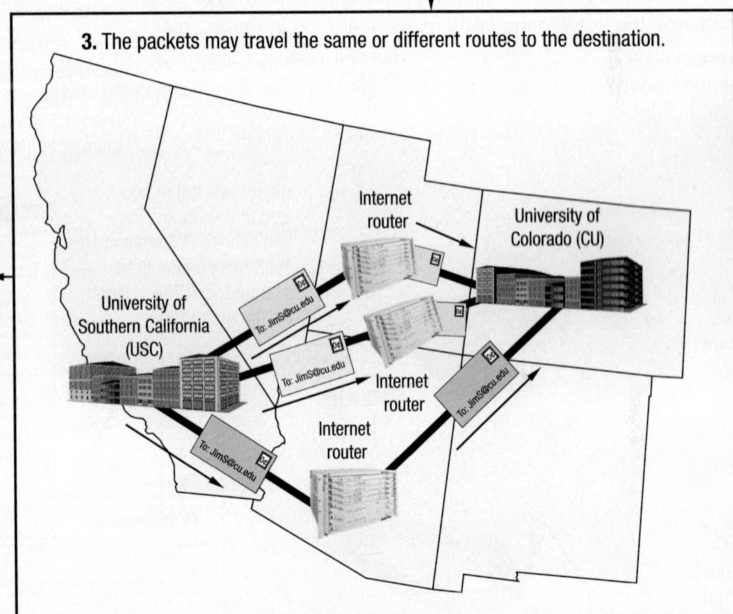

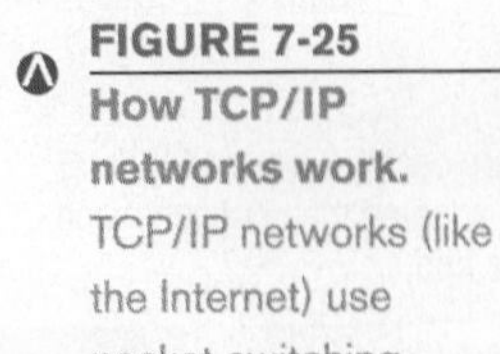

3. The packets may travel the same or different routes to the destination.
Internet router
University of Colorado (CU)

Internet router
Internet router

FIGURE 7-25
How TCP/IP networks work.
TCP/IP networks (like the Internet) use packet switching.

Support for TCP/IP is built into many operating systems, and IP addresses are commonly used in conjunction with other protocols, such as Ethernet, to identify computers on a LAN. In recent years, packet switching has also begun to be used by telephone companies to provide faster, cheaper transmissions over telephone lines. For a look at how IP addresses are used when setting up an Ethernet home network with Windows PCs, see the How it Works box.

Wireless Application Protocol (**WAP**) is a standard for delivering content to mobile devices, smart phones, pagers, and other wireless communications devices using a cellular telephone network. The content that can be delivered using WAP includes both Web page content and e-mail. To display Web content, a WAP-enabled browser—sometimes called a *microbrowser*—needs to be installed on the device.

>**Wireless Application Protocol (WAP).** A standard for delivering content, such as Web pages, to mobile devices.

NET

HOW IT WORKS

Setting Up a Home Network

The first step in setting up a home network is making sure you have the appropriate hardware and that it is installed correctly. For a wired network, you will need an Ethernet network adapter (usually either an internal card or external USB adapter) for each PC, a hub or switch, and enough Category 5 networking cables with RJ-45 connectors to connect each PC to the hub or switch. (Typically, a modem and a printer are connected to a single PC in the same manner they would be connected to a PC without the network; once connected and once the network is set up, then they are shared through the network.)

Next, you can run the Windows Networking Wizard, or you can change the networking settings manually (as in the accompanying illustration). In either case, you will need to assign a common network name, a unique computer name, and a unique IP address to each PC. The *host* PC connected to the Internet should use an IP address of 192.168.0.1 (IP addresses in the form 192.168.xxx.xxx are reserved for private local area networks and cannot be used as Internet IP addresses); the other PCs on the network can use 192.168.0.xxx, with each PC having a different final extension. You can assign the IP addresses manually, or you can choose to have the IP address assigned automatically. Use the host IP address (192.168.0.1) as the default *gateway* and *DNS server* for all other PCs on the network and use 255.255.255.0 as the *subnet mask*; also use the host IP address as the *proxy server* for the browsers on all other PCs to share the Internet connection. Finally, use Windows Explorer and the *Printers* option in the Control Panel to share drives, folders, and printers as needed, and you are good to go!

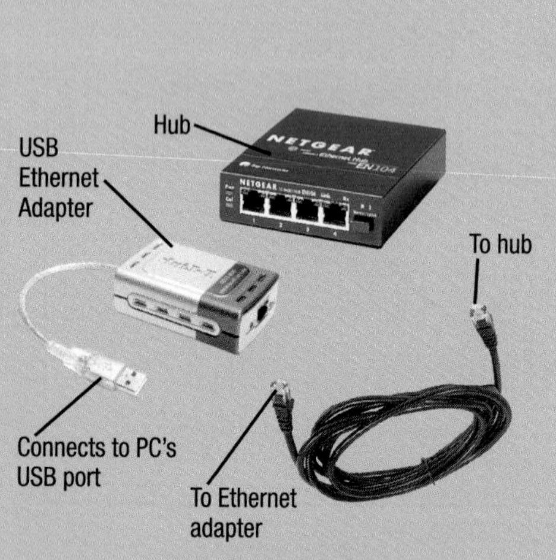

1. Make sure each PC has an Ethernet network adapter, then connect each PC to the hub.

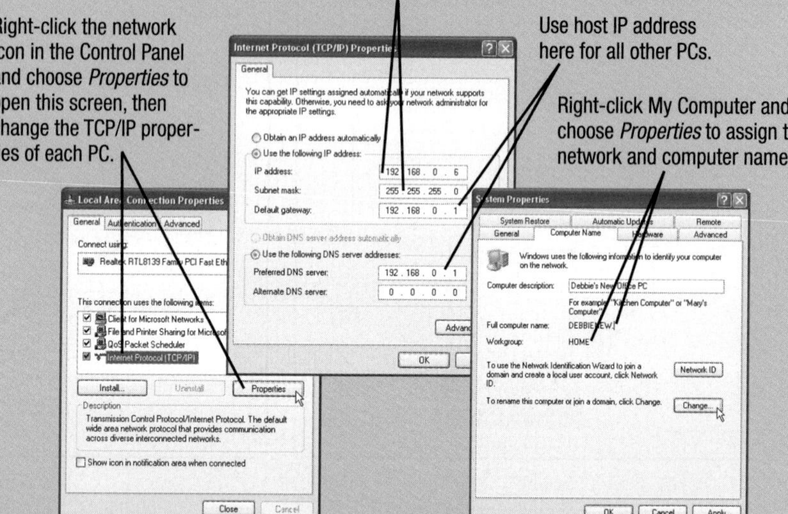

Use an IP address of 192.168.0.1 for the host PC; use a unique IP address for each other PC on the network. All PCs use a Subnet mask of 255.255.255.0.
Right-click the network icon in the Control Panel and choose *Properties* to open this screen, then change the TCP/IP properties of each PC.
Use host IP address here for all other PCs.
Right-click My Computer and choose *Properties* to assign the network and computer name.

2. Assign an appropriate network name, computer name, and IP address to all PCs on the network. Use the host IP address as the default gateway and DNS server for all other PCs on the network.

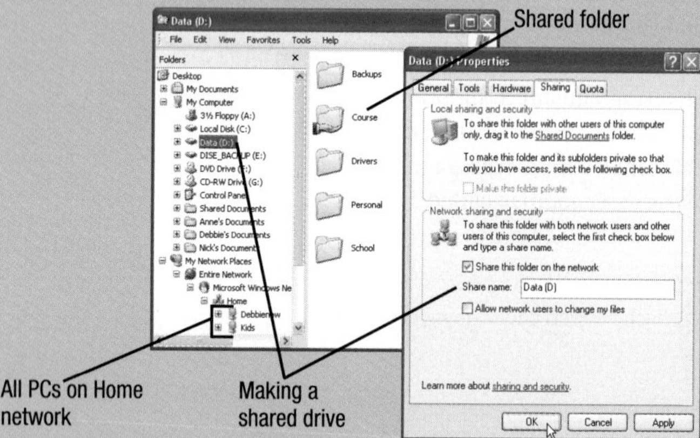

4. Share files, folders, and printers by right-clicking them and choosing the *Sharing* option.

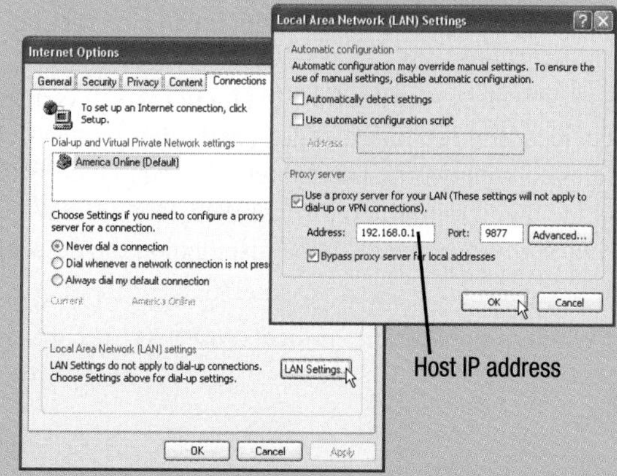

3. Change the settings of each PC's browser to use the host IP address as the proxy server.

Phoneline and Powerline Networks

The *Phoneline* (more officially called the *Home Phoneline Networking Association* or *Home PNA*) standard allows computers to be networked through ordinary phone wiring and phone jacks, without interfering with voice telephone calls. At its original speeds of 1 Mbps and then 10 Mbps, Phoneline has not been especially fast, but it is geared toward setting up quick and easy home networks, provided that phone jacks already exist at the necessary locations. The newest version of this standard—*HomePNA 3.0*—supports speeds up to 128 Mbps.

The *Powerline* standard allows PCs to be networked over existing power lines using conventional electrical outlets. Similar to Phoneline networks, Powerline networks are quick and easy to set up. In addition, they have the advantage that houses usually have more power outlets than phone outlets. Although relatively slow at roughly 10 Mbps (but a speed increase to 85 Mbps is expected in the near future), the Powerline standard also has great potential for countries in which phone jacks are not as prevalent as they are in the United States. While the original Powerline standard is designed for home computer networks, the upcoming second-generation Powerline standard—named *HomePlug AV*—is designed to network home entertainment devices at speeds of up to 200 Mbps. HomePlug AV will enable a variety of home entertainment devices (such as televisions, DVD players, cable boxes, stereo systems, and DVRs) to connect to each other and to the Internet for access to movies, music, and other forms of digital entertainment.

NETWORKING HARDWARE

Typically, there are a number of pieces of hardware necessary to create a computer network, to connect multiple networks together, or to connect a computer or network to the Internet. Some of the most common types of networking hardware are discussed next.

Network Adapters

A **network adapter**, also called a **network interface card** (**NIC**) when it is in the form of an expansion card, is used to connect a PC to a network. A network adapter connects the PC physically to the network in order to send outgoing data from the PC to the network and to retrieve all incoming data sent via the network to the PC. The type of network adapter used depends on the type of network and communications media being used. For instance, to connect a PC to an Ethernet network using twisted-pair cabling, an Ethernet network adapter with an RJ-45 connector would be used. To connect a PC to a Wi-Fi network, a Wi-Fi network adapter would be used, but no cable is needed since it is a wireless connection. To connect to a Phoneline or Powerline network, a Phoneline or Powerline adapter, respectively, would be required.

In addition, the type of device being used and the available expansion slots and ports need to be considered. For example, network adapters for desktop PCs typically come in either PCI or USB format, and adapters for portable PCs usually connect via USB or a PC Card slot. The version of the networking protocol being used may also affect the type of networking hardware used. For instance, Ethernet hardware is rated for a particular speed. While networking hardware is backward compatible (so an adapter compatible with both the 10 and 100 Mbps standards could be used with either type of network), using a 100 Mbps adapter with a 10 Mbps network would only allow connection speeds of up to 10 Mbps. Some examples of network adapters are shown in Figure 7-26. Increasingly, computers and mobile devices are coming with networking capabilities built in, either via a network adapter or directly integrated into the device.

>**Network adapter.** A network interface, such as an expansion card or external network adapter. >**Network interface card (NIC).** An expansion card through which a computer can connect to a network.

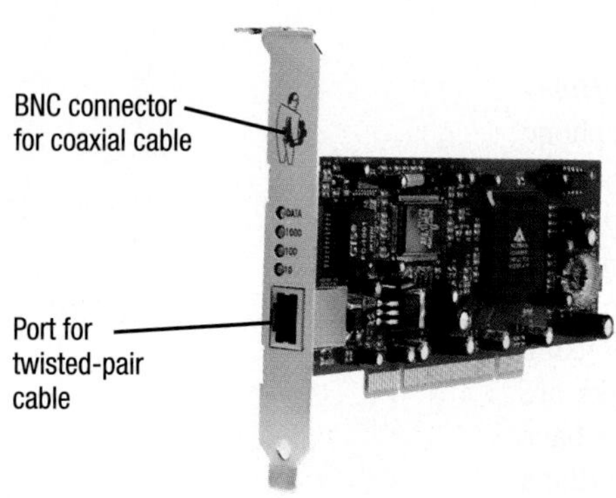

PCI ETHERNET ADAPTER FOR DESKTOP PC

USB BLUETOOTH ADAPTER FOR DESKTOP OR NOTEBOOK PC

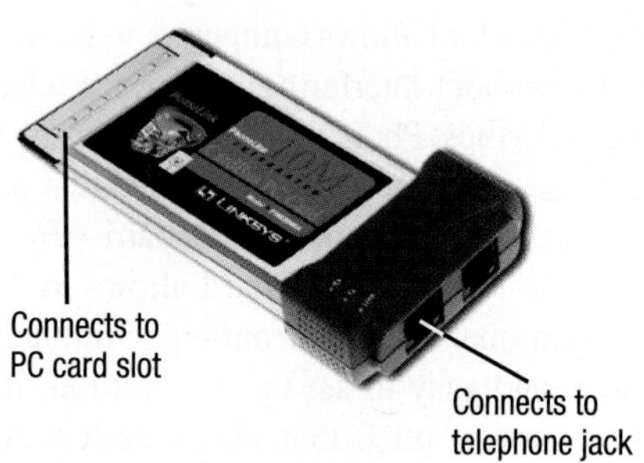

PHONELINE ADAPTER FOR NOTEBOOK PC

USB ETHERNET ADAPTER FOR DESKTOP OR NOTEBOOK PC

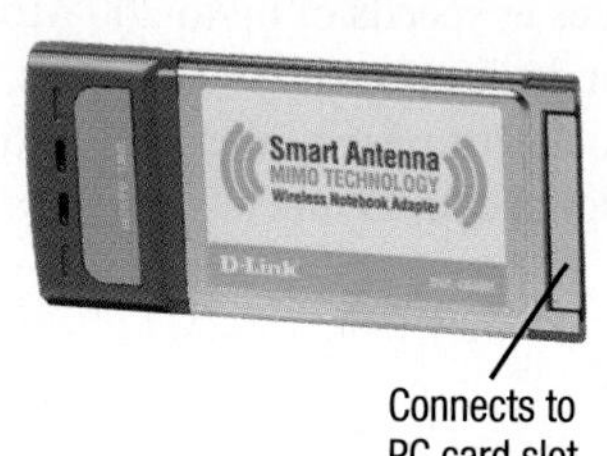

WI-FI ADAPTER FOR NOTEBOOK PC

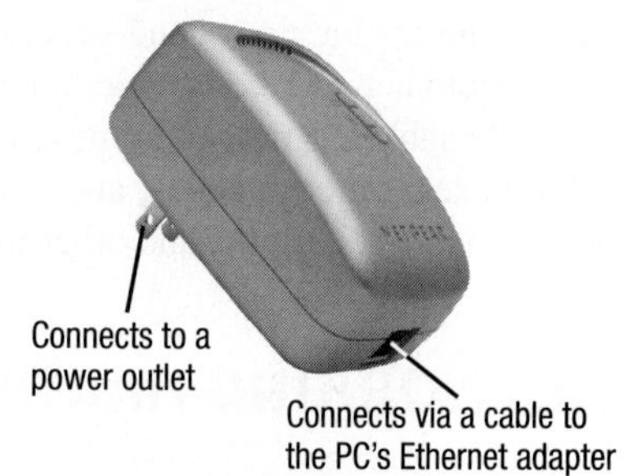

POWERLINE ETHERNET BRIDGE FOR DESKTOP OR NOTEBOOK PC

FIGURE 7-26
Network adapters. Network adapters are available in a variety of configurations.

Some wireless network adapters today conform to a new antenna technology called *MIMO* (for *multiple in, multiple out*), developed to speed up wireless networks or to extend their range. MIMO uses multiple smart antennas to transmit data directly to client devices, instead of transmitting in all directions like older Wi-Fi products. Consequently, data is transmitted faster and further. Network adapters that support the use of MIMO (such as the Wi-Fi adapter for a notebook PC shown in Figure 7-26) are now available. The current version of the emerging 802.11g *Fast Wi-Fi* standard uses MIMO technology.

Modems

Modem is the term used for a device that connects a computer to the Internet. The name comes from the terms *modulation* and *demodulation*. Modulation refers to converting digital signals (such as those from a PC) to analog form so they can be transmitted over analog media (such as conventional telephone lines). Demodulation refers to the translation from analog form back to digital form. There are a number of different types of modems today, each matching a particular type of Internet connection (such as *conventional dial-up*, *cable*, and *DSL*). Although not all of these types of connections require conversion between analog and digital form, the collection of devices used to connect a PC to the Internet are collectively referred to as "modems." Modems are available in a variety of formats—such as PCI, PC card, or external devices that connect via a USB or Ethernet connection (see Figure 7-27)—although not all types of modems may be available in all formats. Some common types of modems are discussed next; the types of Internet services that utilize these modems are discussed in more detail in Chapter 8.

>**Modem.** A communications device that enables digital computers to communicate over analog media, such as connecting to the Internet via telephone lines.

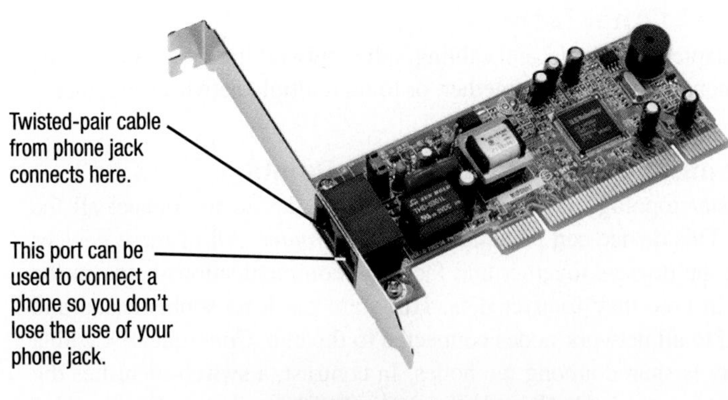

Twisted-pair cable from phone jack connects here.
This port can be used to connect a phone so you don't lose the use of your phone jack.

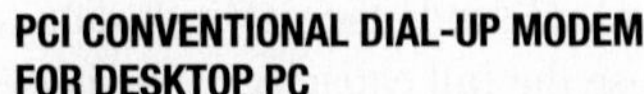
PCI CONVENTIONAL DIAL-UP MODEM FOR DESKTOP PC

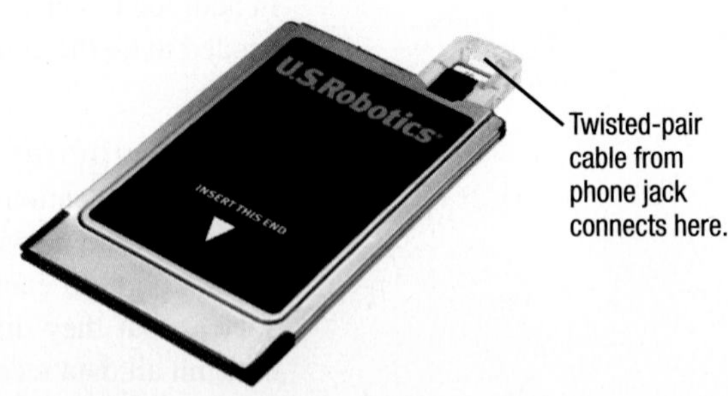

PC CARD CONVENTIONAL DIAL-UP MODEM FOR NOTEBOOK PC

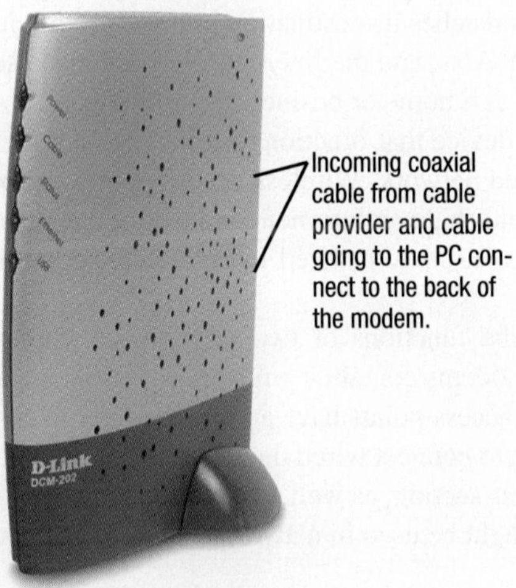

Incoming coaxial cable from cable provider and cable going to the PC connect to the back of the modem.

CABLE MODEM

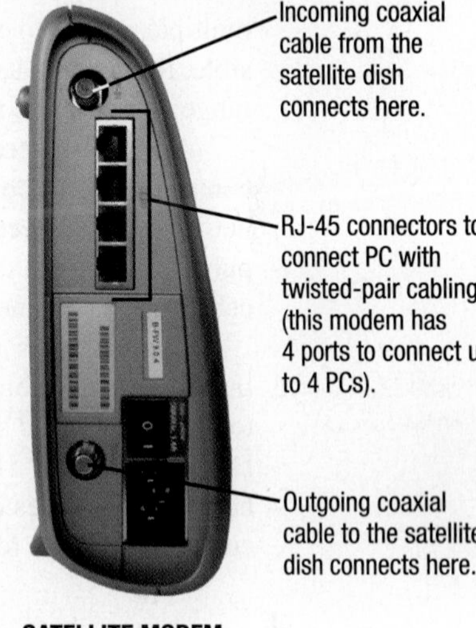

SATELLITE MODEM

FIGURE 7-27
Modems.

- *Conventional dial-up modems*—used to transmit and receive data via regular telephone lines and telephone jacks. The maximum speed for a conventional dial-up modem is 56 Kbps.
- *ISDN* (*integrated services digital network*) *modems*—used to transmit and receive data via ordinary telephone lines, similar to conventional dial-up, but by combining (*multiplexing*) signals, ISDN can transmit data faster than a conventional dial-up modem—up to 128 Kbps. To use an ISDN modem, the computer to which you are connecting (such as the one located at your ISP) must support ISDN service.
- *DSL* (*digital subscriber line*) *modems*—used to transmit and receive data over standard telephone lines and use a technology that does not tie up your telephone line, so you can use the Internet and make voice calls at the same time; data transmission is faster than via conventional or ISDN modems. DSL can only be used within three miles of a telephone switching station, and the speed degrades as the distance gets closer and closer to the three-mile limit. Consequently, DSL service is not available in all areas.
- *Cable modems*—used to connect a PC to cable Internet service, similar to the way cable boxes are used to obtain cable-TV service. Cable transmissions are similar in speed to DSL—around 1.5 Mbps.
- *Satellite modems*—used to transmit and receive data via a personal satellite dish. Satellite transmissions are a little slower than both DSL and cable transmissions, but they have the advantage of being able to be used in rural areas.

TIP

On a small network, such as a home network, if one PC has a modem and is set up to access the Internet, all PCs on the network can be set up to share that Internet connection without needing additional modems—they connect to the Internet via the network.

NET

Hubs, Switches, and Other Networking Hardware

In addition to network adapters, modems, and cabling, other networking hardware is often needed to tie the components of a network together, or to tie multiple networks together.

Hubs, Switches, Routers, and Wireless Access Points

As already mentioned, star topology networks need a central device to connect all the devices on the network. This device can be a *hub*, *switch*, or *router*. All of these devices contain ports to connect the devices together and facilitate communications between the devices, but they differ in how they transfer data. **Hubs** are the least sophisticated and transmit all data received to all network nodes connected to the hub. Consequently, with a hub, the network capacity is shared among the nodes. In contrast, a **switch** identifies the device for which the data is intended and sends the network data to that node only. This allows each node on the network to use the full capacity of the network. **Routers** are even smarter—they pass data on to the intended recipient only, but they can plan a path through multiple routers to ensure the data reaches its destination in the most efficient manner possible. Routers are used in LANs, WANs, and the Internet. They are also used to extend the range of a wireless network, such as a home or business Wi-Fi network.

A **wireless access point** is a device that functions similarly to a hub, but it is used to connect wireless devices to a wired network. Wireless access points can be used in home networks to connect the devices and share an Internet connection; they can also be used at public hotspots to connect wireless users to a wired Internet connection, such as DSL or cable Internet connections.

Some devices may contain the functions of two or more networking devices. For instance, some cable or satellite modems contain a built-in router to connect multiple PCs to the modem, and some wireless access points have a built-in router to connect a cable or DSL modem plus a built-in switch to connect wired devices to the network. An example of how all the devices discussed in this section, as well as the other networking hardware discussed in the next few sections, might be used in networks is shown in Figure 7-28.

Gateways and Bridges

When one network needs to connect to another network, a gateway or bridge is used.

- A *gateway* is a device that connects two *dissimilar* networks, such as two networks using different networking communications protocols.
- A *bridge* is a device that connects two networks based on *similar* technology—such as a LAN in one city and a similar LAN in another. Bridges can also be used to partition one large LAN into two smaller ones.

Repeaters

Repeaters are devices that amplify signals along a network. They are necessary whenever signals have to travel farther than would otherwise be possible over the networking medium being used.

Multiplexers and Concentrators

High-speed communications lines are expensive and almost always have far greater capacity than a single device can use. Because of this, signals from multiple devices are often combined and sent together to share a single communications medium. A *multiplexer* combines

>**Hub.** A device that is a central location where data arrives and is then transferred in one or more directions. >**Switch.** A device on a network to which data is sent so it can be forwarded to the appropriate network node. >**Router.** A device on a network that sends data via the most efficient route to travel to a specific location. >**Wireless access point.** A device used to connect wireless devices to a wired network.

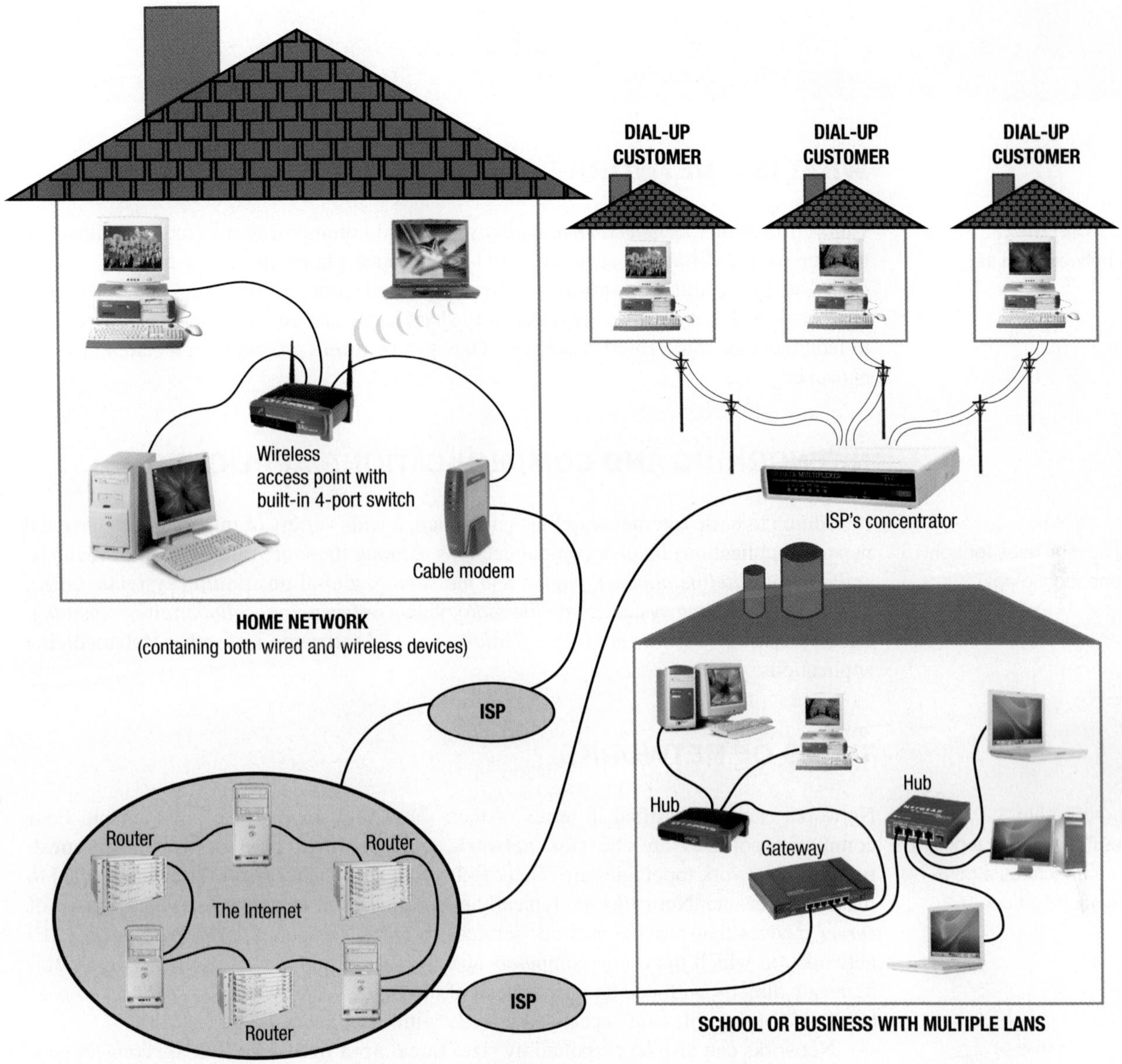

FIGURE 7-28
Networking hardware. As shown in this example, many different types of hardware are needed to connect networking devices.

the transmissions from several different devices and sends them as one message. With *Frequency Division Multiplexing* (*FDM*), each signal is assigned a different frequency over which to travel; with *Wave Division Multiplexing* (*WDM*), each signal is assigned a different wavelength (WDM can be used with fiber-optic cables only). With any type of multiplexing, when the combined signal reaches its destination, the individual messages are separated from one another. Multiplexing is frequently used with fiber-optic cables and other high-capacity media to increase data throughput. For instance, if eight signals are multiplexed together and sent over each fiber in a fiber-optic cable, the throughput of the cable is increased by a factor of eight. Using more wavelengths, such as in *Dense WDM* (*DWDM*), even more data can be transmitted at one time.

A *concentrator* is a type of multiplexer that combines multiple messages and sends them via a single transmission medium in such a way that all the individual messages are simultaneously active, instead of being sent as a single combined message. For example, ISPs often use concentrators to combine the signals from their conventional dial-up modem customers to be sent over faster communications connections to their Internet destinations.

SUMMARY

WHAT IS A NETWORK?

Chapter Objective 1: Define a network and its purpose.

Communications, or *telecommunications*, refers to communications from one device to another over a distance—such as over long-distance phone lines, via privately owned cables, or by satellite. A **computer network** is a collection of computers and other hardware devices that are connected together to share hardware, software, and data, as well as to facilitate electronic communications. One area of recent growth is in the area of *home networks*.

NETWORKING AND COMMUNICATIONS APPLICATIONS

Chapter Objective 2: Describe several uses for communications technology.

In addition to basic Internet searching and e-mail, a wide variety of important business and personal applications involve communications. Among these are **mobile phones** (namely, *cellular* and *satellite phones*), *paging* and *messaging*, **global positioning systems (GPS)**, electronic monitoring systems, *satellite radio*, **videoconferencing**, *collaborative computing*, **telecommuting**, *digital data distribution*, and **telesurgery** and other **telemedicine** applications.

TYPES OF NETWORKS

Chapter Objective 3: Understand the various topologies and architectures a computer network might use.

Networks can be classified in terms of their *topologies*, or physical arrangement. Four common topologies are the **star network**, **bus network**, **ring network**, and **mesh network**. Network topologies are often combined when smaller networks are connected to make a larger one. Networks are typically either *client-server* networks, which consist of *server* devices that provide network services to *client* computers, or *peer-to-peer* (*P2P*) networks, in which the users' computers and the shared peripherals in the network communicate directly with one another instead of through a server. With *Internet peer to peer (P2P) computing*, files are exchanged directly with other peers via the Internet.

Chapter Objective 4: Explain the difference between a LAN, a WAN, and a PAN, and between an intranet, an extranet, and a VPN.

Networks can also be classified by size. **Local area networks (LANs)** connect geographically close devices, such as within a single building. **Wide area networks (WANs)** span relatively wide geographical areas. Other possibilities include *metropolitan area networks* (*MANs*) that provide Internet access to cities; *personal area networks* (*PANs*) that connect the devices immediately around an individual; **intranets** (private networks that implement the infrastructure and standards of the Internet and World Wide Web); **extranets** (intranets that are accessible to authorized outsiders); and **virtual private networks (VPNs)** used to transfer private information over a public communications system.

HOW DOES DATA TRAVEL OVER A NETWORK?

Chapter Objective 5: Understand characteristics about data and how it travels over a network.

Data that travels over a network can be *analog*—that is, sent as continuous waves. Computer hardware, however, are *digital* devices that handle data coded into 0s and 1s. Data transmissions can be characterized by their **bandwidth** (the amount of data that can be transferred over the medium at one time), whether they use **serial transmission** or **parallel transmission**, whether they transmit in *simplex*, *half-duplex*, *or full-duplex* directions, and how the transmissions are timed (namely, *synchronous*, *asynchronous*, or *isochronous transmission*).

Computer networks can be **wired networks** or **wireless networks**, depending on the type of transmission media used. Wired transmission media include **twisted-pair**, **coaxial**, and **fiber-optic cable**. Wireless networks typically send messages through the air in the form of *radio signals*. Wireless networks typically use *broadcast radio*, **microwave stations**, or **communications satellites** (which send and receive data to and from microwave stations and satellites), or **cellular radio** (which sends and receives data via cell towers located within designated areas or *cells*) technology. Wired networks are found in businesses and some homes. Wireless networks are becoming more common in businesses and homes because they do not require physical wiring and they allow the user more mobility. Wireless networks are also commonly used in public locations to provide a wireless connection to a public wireless access point, designed to provide Internet access to the general public.

Chapter Objective 6:
Name specific types of wired and wireless transmission media and explain how they transmit data.

COMMUNICATIONS PROTOCOLS

A *communications protocol* is a collection of procedures to establish, maintain, and terminate transmissions between devices. Because devices transmit data in so many ways, they collectively employ scores of different protocols. Four of the most commonly used networking protocols are **Ethernet**, **Token Ring**, **Wi-Fi (802.11)**, and **TCP/IP**. Wi-Fi is designed for medium-range wireless transmissions, and there are various versions of the standard; the most common today is *802.11g*. Other emerging wireless standards are *wireless mesh* (used to connect wireless devices and networks, as well as to extend the range of wireless networks), **WiMAX** (an emerging wireless standard with a larger range than Wi-Fi), *Mobile-Fi* (a version of WiMAX designed for use while on the go), and *xMax* (which utilizes the unused portions of radio channels used for pagers and TV signals). Wireless networks typically use the 802.11 (Wi-Fi) protocol. For short-range applications (such as wirelessly connecting a keyboard to a PC), **Bluetooth** can be used. *Ultra Wideband* (*UWB*) is a newer standard that can connect devices faster and with a longer range than Bluetooth. **Wireless Application Protocol (WAP)** is a standard for delivering content, such as Web pages, to mobile devices. For home networks, the *Phoneline* or *Powerline* standards may be used instead.

Chapter Objective 7:
Identify different protocols that can be used to connect the devices on a network.

NETWORKING HARDWARE

Computer networks require a variety of hardware. PCs usually connect to a network through either a **network adapter**—called a **network interface card** (**NIC**) when it is in the form of an expansion card—or a **modem**, which converts signals between digital and analog mode as needed. The type of adapter or modem used depends on the type of connection and computer to be used. Possible modems include *conventional dial-up*, *ISDN* (*integrated services digital network*), *DSL* (*digital subscriber line*), *cable*, and *satellite modems*. A **hub** is a device on a network that provides a central location where data arrives and then is transferred on. **Switches** and **routers** can also be used to pass network messages along to their destinations. A **wireless access point** is used to connect wireless devices to a network. Devices on two dissimilar networks can communicate with each other if the networks are connected by a *gateway*. Devices on two similar networks can communicate with each other if they are connected by a *bridge*. *Repeaters*, *multiplexers*, and *concentrators* are most commonly used with larger networks.

Chapter Objective 8:
List several types of networking hardware and explain the purpose of each.

REVIEW ACTIVITIES

KEY TERM MATCHING

Instructions: Match each key term on the left with the definition on the right that best describes it.

a. bandwidth

b. Bluetooth

c. computer network

d. Ethernet

e. global positioning system (GPS)

f. local area network (LAN)

g. mesh network

h. network interface card (NIC)

i. TCP/IP

j. WiMAX

1. ______ A collection of computers and other hardware devices that are connected together to share hardware, software, and data, as well as to communicate electronically with one another.

2. ______ A communications standard for very short-range wireless connections; the devices are automatically connected once they get within the allowable range.

3. ______ A network in which there are multiple connections between the devices on the network so that messages can take any of several possible paths.

4. ______ A network that connects devices located in a small geographical area, such as within a building.

5. ______ An emerging wireless networking standard that is faster and has a greater range than Wi-Fi.

6. ______ An expansion card through which a computer can connect to a network.

7. ______ A system that uses satellites and a receiver to determine the exact geographic location of the receiver.

8. ______ A widely used communications protocol for a LAN.

9. ______ The amount of data that can be transmitted over a communications medium at one time.

10. ______ The communications protocol that uses packet switching to facilitate the transmission of messages; the protocol used with the Internet.

SELF-QUIZ

Instructions: Circle **T** if the statement is true, **F** if the statement is false, or write the best answer in the space provided. **Answers to the self-quiz are located in the References and Resources Guide at the end of the book.**

1. T F GPS systems are used only by the government.

2. T F With serial transmissions, each bit of data is sent individually.

3. T F The Internet is an example of a LAN.

4. T F The type of cable used inside most homes for telephone service is twisted-pair wire.

5. T F A router is a type of modem.

6. Using communications technology to work from home is called ______.

7. With a(n) ______ network topology, all devices are connected in a line to a central cable.

8. A(n) ______ orbits the earth to send and receive high-frequency, high-speed radio signals.

9. A(n) ______ is a network that transfers private information securely over the Internet or other public network.

10. Match each description to its communications application, and write the corresponding number in the blank to the left of the description.

a. ______ To diagnose a patient from a distance.
b. ______ To conduct a meeting between people located at the corporate headquarters in Los Angeles and a Miami-based clothing designer to decide which pieces to include in the final summer swimsuit line.
c. ______ To work from New York when you live in California.
d. ______ To drive across the country listening to continuous music.
e. ______ To receive telephone calls while you are out shopping.
f. ______ To determine your physical location while hiking in the mountains.

1. Satellite radio **3.** GPS **5.** Telemedicine
2. Telecommuting **4.** Videoconferencing **6.** Cellular phone

EXERCISES

1. Answer the following questions about the network to the right.

   a. What topology does the network use? ______
   b. How many nodes are connected to the network? ______
   c. Is this a wired or wireless network? ______
   d. Does this network use a hub? ______

2. For each modem, indicate whether or not it allows for data transmission over ordinary telephone lines.

Type of Modem	Transmits Over Telephone Lines?
a. Cable modem	______
b. Conventional dial-up modem	______
c. DSL modem	______
d. ISDN modem	______
e. Satellite modem	______

3. If you need to download a 350 KB file and have a 56 Kbps conventional dial-up modem, how long should it take to download the file? What real-world conditions might affect this download time?

4. What communications protocol does the Internet use?

5. Explain the difference between Wi-Fi and Bluetooth, including what purposes each protocol is designed for.

DISCUSSION QUESTION

With so many wireless devices available today, interference is happening much more often than in the past. For instance, unlicensed walkie-talkies used on the set of the *Law & Order* television show interfered with real police radios, military radios now using the same frequency as some garage door openers are opening and closing nearby garage doors, and British air traffic control transmissions have been interrupted by transmissions from nearby baby monitors. Although the Federal Communications Commission (FCC) regulates the airwaves in the United States, there are some radio frequencies—such as the popular 2.4 GHz band used by cordless phones and most versions of Wi-Fi—that are unregulated. If commonly used devices interfere with each other, whose fault is it? The individual for buying multiple products that use the same radio frequency? The manufacturers for not developing safeguards for their products to ensure the products switch channels if one is in use? The government for allowing unregulated airwaves? Regulating all airwaves would solve the problem, but then products that normally use unregulated airwaves (Wi-Fi networks, cordless phones, two-way radios, baby monitors, and so forth) would likely not be developed or would be significantly more expensive. In addition, since these products have already found acceptance and wide-spread use among the general public, there would probably be an uproar over such regulation. Is there a solution to this problem? With an increasing number of products going wireless, the problem is likely to get worse before it gets better. Who, if anyone, should be responsible for fixing this problem?

PROJECTS

HOT TOPICS

1. **WiMAX vs. Wi-Fi** As discussed in the chapter, WiMAX and Wi-Fi are both wireless networking standards.

   For this project, research WiMAX and Wi-Fi to determine their current status and the differences between the two standards. Are they designed for the same or different purposes? Explain. Are they both being used today? If not, when are they expected to become available? Do you think the standards will coexist in the future, or will one eventually replace the other? At the conclusion of your research, prepare a one-page summary of your findings and submit it to your instructor.

SHORT ANSWER/ RESEARCH

2. **E-Clothing** As computing and communications devices continue to grow smaller and be carried by many individuals at all times, clothing manufacturers have begun to adapt by creating shorts, pants, jackets, vests, and more with pockets and compartments for cell phones, handheld PCs, portable digital music players, ear buds, and so forth.

   For this project, research e-clothing and identify at least two products that are commercially available. Summarize each product, listing all of the capabilities of the garment, what devices the garment is designed for, and what market the product is designed for. Do any of the products contain features to facilitate a PAN? Be sure to include where the product can be purchased and the suggested retail price. Would you buy either of these garments? Why or why not? Do you think the e-clothing trend will continue to grow, or is it a passing fad? Submit your findings and opinion to your instructor in the format of a one-page paper.

3. **Unwired** As discussed in the chapter, home networks—particularly wireless home networks—are becoming very common today.

   For this project, suppose that you have a home desktop computer and are planning to buy a notebook PC to use at home, as well as on the go. You would like to network the two PCs wirelessly. Determine the hardware you will need to accomplish this. Create a labeled sketch of the network and a list of the hardware you would need to acquire. Next, research the approximate cost of the hardware to determine the overall cost of the network. Does the cost seem reasonable? Would you want to network your home PCs in this manner? If you wanted to also use a printer with both PCs, would you need any additional hardware? At the conclusion of your research, prepare a one-page summary of your findings and submit it to your instructor, along with your sketch and list of hardware.

HANDS ON

4. **Network Topology** As discussed in the chapter, a network's topology refers to the shape in which the computers are connected to the network.

   For this project, investigate a computer lab you have access to on your campus. Draw a sketch of the lab to indicate how the computers are connected, what type of cabling is being used, and what other hardware is included on the network. Indicate the network's topology, as well as whether it is a client-server network or a peer-to-peer network. Finally, log on to a computer in the lab and determine the network resources (such as network hard drives and printers) available to you. At the conclusion of this task, prepare a one-page summary of its findings to submit to your instructor along with the network diagram.

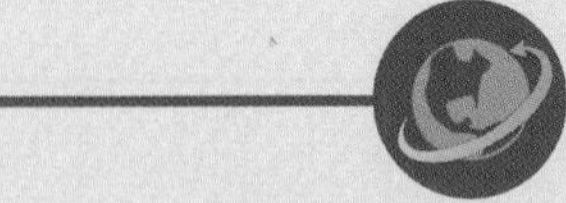

5. **Geocaching** Geocaching is a GPS application that is essentially a form of high-tech hide and seek—someone hides a water-tight container filled with a "treasure" (usually toys or cheap collectors' goodies) and posts the location of the cache (in GPS coordinates) on a geocaching Web site. Other individuals use their GPS equipment to find the cache and then sign a log (if one is included in the cache), take an item from the cache, and put another object into the cache as a replacement. Many caches are stored in scenic locations that individuals and organizations would like others to experience.

   For this project, by searching online or visiting a geocaching Web site, such as geocaching.com, find out how to geocache, including what GPS equipment you would need and any "rules" or courtesies common among geocachers regarding listing or finding a cache, appropriate items for including in a cache, and so forth. Next, use the site to find information about a cache currently hidden close to your city and determine what you would need to do in order to find it. At the conclusion of your research, prepare a one-page summary of your findings and submit it to your instructor.

WRITING ABOUT COMPUTERS

6. **Internet P2P** As discussed in the chapter, peer-to-peer (P2P) networking involves sharing files and other resources directly with other computers, without going through a network server. It is often used for small home networks, as well as via the Internet. Internet P2P computing has been used in the past to illegally exchange copyrighted materials, such as music and movie files. However, it also has legitimate applications.

   For this project, research P2P computing and identify two legal and ethical uses of Internet P2P networking. What are the advantages over using a client-server network for these applications? Are there any disadvantages? How, if at all, should Internet P2P networks be regulated? What if a P2P network set up for legitimate use is used for illegal purposes—should the organization or person who set up the P2P network be responsible? Why or why not? Do you think P2P network use will continue to grow? Would you want to use a P2P network? Submit this project to your instructor in the form of a short paper, not more than two pages in length.

NET

PRESENTATION/ DEMONSTRATION

7. **Wired Home Network** If you have two or more computers at home and want to share files, an Internet connection, or a printer, you will need to set up a home network. Although a wireless network is an option, wired networks still exist and new options for wired networks are emerging.

   For this project, suppose that you want to set up a wired home network. Create a scenario (real or fictitious) that describes the number of PCs and other devices involved, where each item is located, and the tasks for which the network will be used. Select a wired networking option (such as Ethernet, Powerline, or Phoneline) and determine the steps and equipment necessary to implement that network for your scenario. Be sure to include the cost of the necessary hardware and how the network would be physically installed. Share your findings (including a diagram of your proposed network) with your class in the form of a presentation. The presentation should not exceed 10 minutes and should make use of one or more presentation aids, such as the chalkboard, handouts, overhead transparencies, or a computer-based slide presentation (your instructor may provide additional requirements). You may also be asked to submit a summary of the presentation to your instructor.

GROUP DISCUSSION

8. **Regulating Broadband** The year 2005 had a number of interesting rulings and proposed legislation regarding broadband Internet. Two examples are the decision by the Federal Communications Commission (FCC) to free telephone companies from the requirement of sharing their broadband lines with rival ISPs and the ruling by the Supreme Court that freed cable companies from similar requirements. These decisions are expected to impact a number of ISPs who relied on these communications media to provide Internet access—typically DSL Internet access—to their customers. An additional example is the proposed legislation by U.S. House of Representatives member Pete Sessions to prohibit cities from providing any Wi-Fi service that is "substantially similar" to services provided by private companies—essentially banning the free or low-cost Wi-Fi Internet access many cities are currently offering or are planning to offer to their citizens. How much government interference and regulation is needed in the communications industry? If numerous small ISPs are driven out of business by the FCC and U.S. Supreme Court decisions, what impact will that have on ISP selection, services, and price? Does the federal government have the right to ban cities or states from providing Internet access to its residents? Why or why not?

   For this project, form an opinion of the appropriate level of governance needed in the communications industry and be prepared to discuss your position (in class, via an online class discussion group, or in a class chat room, depending on your instructor's directions). You may also be asked to write a short paper expressing your opinion.

WEB ACTIVITIES

The *Understanding Computers* Web site located at **www.course.com/uc11** features many resources to help reinforce your understanding of the chapter content and help you prepare for exams. Your instructor may also assign specific activities to be completed that will count toward your final grade in the course.

Instructions: Go to **www.course.com/uc11/ch07** to work the following online activities.

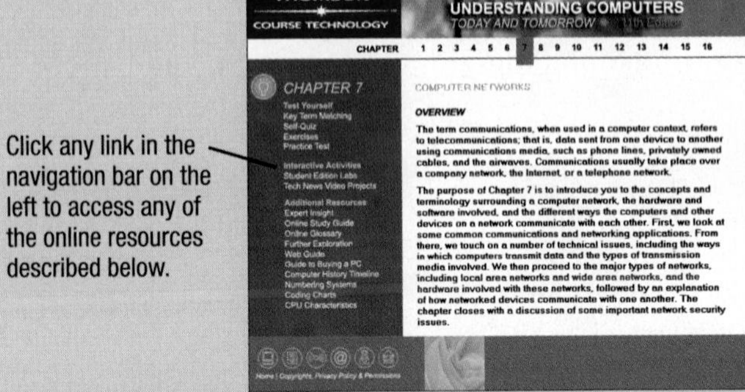

Click any link in the navigation bar on the left to access any of the online resources described below.

INTERACTIVE ACTIVITIES

1. **Crossword Puzzle** Practice your knowledge of the key terms in Chapter 7 by completing the interactive Crossword Puzzle.
2. **Tech News Video Project** Watch the **"Witness Vehicle Protection System"** video clip that features a vehicle protection system that uses GPS and other communications technology to locate your car, unlock the doors, and perform other tasks at your request. After watching the video online, complete the corresponding project.
3. **Student Edition Labs** Reinforce the concepts you have learned in this chapter by working through the **Networking Basics** and **Wireless Networking** interactive labs.

NET

TEST YOURSELF

1. **Key Term Matching** Test your knowledge of selected chapter key terms by matching the terms with their definitions.
2. **Self-Quiz** Test your retention of chapter concepts by taking the Self-Quiz.
3. **Exercises** Work these short exercises to review the concepts and terms covered in the chapter.
4. **Practice Test** Test how ready you are for an upcoming exam by completing the online Practice Test.

STUDY TOOLS/ ADDITIONAL RESOURCES

The Understanding Computers Web site has a wide range of additional resources, including an **Online Study Guide** (containing study tips, a chapter outline with room to add your own notes, and a chapter checklist of the activities to complete when the chapter is covered in class and when you are preparing for a test) and an **Online Glossary** for each chapter; **Further Exploration** links; a **Web Guide**, a **Guide to Buying a PC**, and a **Computer History Timeline**; more information about **Numbering Systems**, **Coding Charts**, and **CPU Characteristics**; and much, much more!

The Internet and World Wide Web

OUTLINE

LEARNING OBJECTIVES

After completing this chapter, you will be able to:

1. Discuss how the Internet evolved and what it is like today.
2. Identify the various types of individuals, companies, and organizations involved in the Internet community and explain their purposes.
3. Describe device and connection options for connecting to the Internet, as well as some considerations to keep in mind when selecting an ISP.
4. Understand how to effectively search for information on the Internet and how to properly cite Internet resources.
5. List several useful things that can be done using the Internet, in addition to basic Web browsing and e-mail.
6. Discuss censorship and privacy, and how they are related to Internet use.
7. Describe the possible format, structure, and use of the Internet in the future.

OVERVIEW

It is hard to believe that before 1990 few people outside the computer industry and academia had ever heard of the Internet, and even fewer had used it. Why? Because the hardware, software, and communications tools needed to unleash the power of the Internet as we know it today were not available then. In fact, it is only in the last few years that technology has evolved enough to allow multimedia applications—such as downloading music and movies, playing interactive games, and viewing animated presentations—to become an everyday activity. What a difference a few years can make. Today, the Internet and the World Wide Web are household words, and in many ways they have redefined how people think about computers and communications.

Despite the popularity of the Internet, however, many users cannot answer some important basic questions about it. What makes up the Internet? Is it the same thing as the World Wide Web? How did the Internet begin, and where is it heading? What types of tools are available to help people make the optimal use of the Internet? How can the Internet be used to find specific information? This chapter addresses these types of questions.

Chapter 8 begins with a discussion of the evolution of the Internet, from the late 1960s to the present, followed by a look at the many individuals, companies, and organizations that make up the Internet community. Next, the chapter covers the different options for connecting to the Internet, including the types of Internet access devices, Internet connections, and ISPs available today. Then, it is on to one of the most important Internet skills you should acquire—efficient Internet searching. To help you appreciate the wide spectrum of resources and activities available through the Internet, we also take a brief look at some of the most common applications available via the Internet. The final sections of the chapter discuss a few of the important societal issues that apply to Internet use and take a look at the Internet's future. ■

EVOLUTION OF THE INTERNET

The **Internet** is a worldwide collection of separate, but interconnected, networks that are accessed daily by millions of people to obtain information, disseminate information, or communicate with others. Just as the shipping industry has simplified transportation by providing standard containers for carrying all sorts of merchandise via air, rail, highway, and sea, the Internet furnishes a standard way of sending messages and information across virtually any type of computer platform and transmission media. While *Internet* has become a household word only during the past decade, it has actually operated in one form or another for much longer than that.

>**Internet.** The largest and most well-known computer network, linking millions of computers all over the world.

From ARPANET to Internet2

The roots of the Internet began with an experimental project called *ARPANET*. The Internet we know today is the result of the evolution of ARPANET and the creation of the *World Wide Web*.

ARPANET

ARPANET was created in 1969 by the U.S. Department of Defense's *Advanced Research Projects Agency* (*ARPA*). One objective of the ARPANET project was to create a computer network that would allow researchers located in different places to communicate with each other. Another objective was to build a computer network capable of sending or receiving data over a variety of paths to ensure that network communications could continue even if part of the network was destroyed, such as in a nuclear attack or by a natural disaster.

Initially, ARPANET connected four supercomputers. As it grew during its first few years, ARPANET enabled researchers at a few dozen academic institutions to communicate with each other and with government agencies on topics of mutual interest. However, with the highly controversial Vietnam War in full swing, ARPANET's e-mail facility began to handle not only legitimate research discussions but also heated debates about United States involvement in Southeast Asia. As students were granted access to ARPANET, other unintended uses—such as playing computer games—also began.

As the experiment grew during the next decade, hundreds of college and university networks were connected to ARPANET. These local area networks consisted of a mixture of DOS-based and Windows-based computers, Apple Macintosh computers, and UNIX workstations. Over the years, *protocols* (standard procedures) were developed for tying this mix of computers and networks together, for transferring data over the network, and for ensuring that data was transferred intact. Other networks soon connected to ARPANET, and this *internet*—or network of networks—eventually evolved into the present day Internet.

The Internet infrastructure today can be used for a variety of purposes, such as exchanging e-mail and instant messages; participating in discussion groups, chat sessions, and videoconferences; downloading software and music; purchasing goods and services; accessing computers remotely; and transferring files between Internet users. One of the most widely used Internet resources is the *World Wide Web*.

The World Wide Web

In its early years, the Internet was used primarily by the government, scientists, and educational institutions. Despite its popularity in academia and with government researchers, the Internet went virtually unnoticed by the general public and the business community for over two decades because it required a computer, and it was hard to use (see the left image in Figure 8-1). As always, however, technology improved and new applications quickly followed. First, communications hardware improved, and then computers gained speed and better graphics capabilities. Then, in 1989, a researcher named Tim Berners-Lee proposed the idea of the **World Wide Web** while working at *CERN* (a physics laboratory in Europe). He envisioned the World Wide Web as a way to organize information in the form of pages linked together through selectable text or images (today's hyperlinks) on the screen. Although the introduction of Web pages did not replace other Internet resources (such as e-mail and collections of downloadable files), it became a popular way for researchers to provide written information to others.

>**ARPANET.** The predecessor of the Internet, named after the Advanced Research Projects Agency (ARPA), which sponsored its development.
>**World Wide Web.** The collection of Web pages available through the Internet.

Things really got rolling with the arrival of the graphical user interface. In 1993, a group of professors and students at the University of Illinois *National Center for Supercomputing Applications* (*NCSA*) released *Mosaic*, the first graphically based Web browser. Mosaic used a graphical user interface and allowed Web pages to include graphical images in addition to text. Soon after, use of the World Wide Web began to increase dramatically because the graphical interface and graphical Web pages made using the World Wide Web both easier and more fun than in the past. Today's Web pages are a true multimedia experience. They can contain text, graphics, animation, sound, video, and three-dimensional virtual reality objects (refer to the right image in Figure 8-1).

EARLY 1990s
Even at the beginning of the 1990s, using the Internet for most people meant learning how to work with a cryptic sequence of commands. Virtually all information was text-based.

TODAY
Today's Web pages organize much of the Internet's content into easy-to-read pages that can contain text graphics, animation, and more. Instead of typing cryptic commands to access information, users click hyperlinks.

FIGURE 8-1
Using the Internet: Back in the "old days" versus now.

Although the Web is only part of the Internet, it is by far one of the most popular and one of the fastest-growing parts. As interest in the Internet snowballed, companies began looking for ways to make it more accessible to customers, to make the user interface more functional, and to make more services available over it. Today, most companies regard their use of the Internet and World Wide Web as an indispensable competitive business tool, and many individuals view the Internet as a vital research and communications medium.

One remarkable characteristic of both the Internet and World Wide Web is that they are not owned by any person or business, and no single person, business, or organization is in charge. Web pages are developed by individuals and organizations and hosted on Web servers owned by an individual; a school, business, or other organization; or a service provider. PCs and other devices used to access the Internet typically belong to individuals, organizations, or public facilities. Each network connected to the Internet is owned and managed individually by that network's administrator, and the main communications media used as the *Internet backbone* are typically owned by telecommunications companies, such as telephone and cable companies. As a whole, the Internet has no owner or network administrator. The closest the Internet has to a governing body is the variety of organizations—such as the *Internet Society* (*ISOC*), *Internet Corporation For Assigned Names and Numbers* (*ICANN*), and the *World Wide Web Consortium* (*W3C*)—committed to overseeing it. These organizations are involved with such issues as establishing the protocols used on the Internet, making recommendations for changes, and encouraging cooperation between and coordinating communications among the networks connected to the Internet.

Internet2

The next significant improvements to the Internet infrastructure might be a result of *Internet2*, a consortium of over 200 universities working together with industry and the government. Internet2 was created to develop and implement advanced Internet applications and technologies, which may lead to improvements for tomorrow's Internet. One of the primary goals of the Internet2 project is to ensure that new network services and applications are quickly applied to the broader Internet community, not just to the Internet2 participants. It is important to realize that Internet2 does not refer to a new physical Internet that will eventually replace the Internet—it is simply a research and development project geared to developing technology to ensure that the Internet in the future can handle tomorrow's applications.

A complementary project is the *Next Generation Internet* (*NGI*). While Internet2 is university sponsored, NGI is a federal government-sponsored, multi-agency research and development program working to develop advanced networking technologies and revolutionary applications that require advanced networking capabilities. Internet2 is working in cooperation with the NGI project, as well as forming partnerships with similar projects in other countries, to ensure a cohesive and interoperable advanced networking infrastructure for the Internet of the future.

The Internet Community Today

The Internet community today consists of individuals, businesses, and a variety of organizations located throughout the world. Virtually anyone with a computer that has communications capabilities can be part of the Internet, either as a user or as a supplier of information or services. Most members of the Internet community fall into one or more of the following groups.

Users

Users are people who use the Internet for activities, such as to look up a telephone number, browse through an online catalog, make an online purchase, download a music file, or send an e-mail message. According to Nielsen/NetRatings, about two-thirds of the population of the United States are Internet users, using the Internet at work, schools, libraries, or homes. Free Internet access at libraries, schools, and other public locations, as well as the availability of low-cost PCs and Internet access in many areas today, has helped Internet use begin to approach the popularity and widespread use of phones and TVs.

FURTHER EXPLORATION

For links to further information about types of Internet access and ISPs, go to www.course.com/uc11/ch08

Internet Service Providers

Internet service providers (ISPs)—often called *service providers* or *access providers*—are businesses or other organizations that provide Internet access to others, typically for a fee. As shown in Figure 8-2, a variety of communications and media companies—such as conventional and wireless telephone companies, as well as cable and satellite TV providers—offer Internet service over their respective media. In addition, a variety of other ISPs provide services over existing communications media. Some, such as America Online and EarthLink, provide service nationwide; others provide service to a more limited geographical area. In either case, ISPs are an onramp to the Internet, providing their subscribers with access to the World Wide Web, e-mail, and other Internet resources. In addition to Internet access, some ISPs provide proprietary online services available only to their subscribers. These ISPs are sometimes referred to as *online service providers*. A later section of this chapter covers ISPs in more detail, including factors to consider when selecting an ISP.

FIGURE 8-2
ISPs today include telephone, cable, and satellite companies, in addition to regional and national ISPs.

TELEPHONE COMPANIES

CABLE AND SATELLITE COMPANIES

REGIONAL AND NATIONAL ISPS

>**Internet service provider (ISP).** A business or other organization that provides Internet access to others, typically for a fee.

Internet Content Providers

Internet content providers supply the information that is available through the Internet. Internet content providers can be commercial businesses, nonprofit organizations, educational institutions, individuals, and more. Some examples of content providers are listed next.

- A photographer who posts samples of her best work on a Web page.
- A political action group that sponsors an online forum for discussions about topics that interest its members.
- An individual who publishes his opinion on various subjects to an online journal or *blog*.
- A software company that creates a Web site to provide product information and software downloads.
- A national newspaper that maintains an online site to provide up-to-the-minute news, feature stories, and video clips.
- A television network that develops a site for its newest reality TV show, including statistics, photographs, and live video feeds.
- A music publisher that creates a site to provide song demos and to sell downloads of its artists' songs and albums.
- A film student who releases her original short movie to be viewed on the Web.

Application Service Providers and Web Services

Application service providers (ASPs) are companies that manage and distribute software-based services to customers over the Internet. Instead of providing access to the Internet like ISPs do, ASPs provide access to software applications via the Internet. In essence, ASPs rent software access to companies or individuals—typically, customers pay a monthly or yearly fee to use the applications. One advantage to using an ASP over buying software outright is less up-front money, which means small businesses might be able to afford the same state-of-the-art applications that larger companies use. Another advantage is that using ASP software may result in a reduction of staffing needs for computer support for the company utilizing the ASP service, since the software is not installed on user PCs. In addition, all users see the most up-to-date software each time they use the application, and free or low-cost technical support and training may be available from the ASP. Leasing applications in this manner also gives customers the flexibility of trying a different application whenever desired (assuming a trial or short-term contract is available), without potentially wasting money purchasing software that might not fit the company's needs. Common ASP applications are office suites, collaboration and communications software, accounting programs, and e-commerce software. Some industry experts—such as the CEOs of Sun Microsystems and Microsoft—predict that within a relatively short period of time, software purchasing as we know it today will not exist. Instead, they believe software will be delivered as a service, and the option to purchase software outright might not exist.

One type of self-contained business application designed to work over the Internet or a company network is a **Web service**. Web services are programs written to strict specifications so that they can work together with other Web services and be used with many different computer systems. Unlike most other applications, Web services themselves do not

NET

>**Internet content provider.** A person or an organization that provides Internet content. >**Application service provider (ASP).** A company that manages and distributes software-based services over the Internet. >**Web service.** A self-contained business application that operates over the Internet.

have a user interface—they are simply a standardized way of allowing different applications and computers to share data and processes via a network. However, a Web service can be added to a Web page or an application program to provide specific functionality to end users. For example, Web services can be used to facilitate communications between suppliers and customers, to provide a service via a Web site that was otherwise not feasible (such as the inclusion of mapping information on a Web site or Web application using Microsoft's MapPoint .NET Web service), or to add functionality to the end user via the Internet (such as a proposed Web service for Microsoft Office users that allows them to print to any Kinko's locations from their program's File menu). A company that provides Web services is sometimes referred to as a *Web services provider*.

Infrastructure Companies

Infrastructure companies are the enterprises that own or operate the paths or "roadways" along which Internet data travels. Examples of infrastructure companies include telephone, satellite, and cable companies.

Hardware and Software Companies

There is a wide variety of hardware and software companies that make and distribute the products used with the Internet and Internet activities. For example, companies that create or sell the software used in conjunction with the Internet (such as Web browsers, e-mail programs, *e-commerce* and *multimedia* software, and Web development tools) fall into this category. So, too, do the companies that make the hardware (modems, cables, routers, servers, PCs, and smart phones, for instance) that are used in conjunction with the Internet.

The Government and Other Organizations

Many other organizations influence the Internet and its uses. Governments have among the most visible impact; their laws can limit both the information made available via Web servers located in a particular country, as well as access to the Internet for individuals residing in that country. For example, in France it is illegal to sell items or post online content related to racist groups or activities and China has imposed tight controls on what information is published on China Web servers and the information its citizens have access to. In the United States, anything illegal offline (illicit drugs, child pornography, and so forth) is illegal online. In addition, rulings—such as the 1968 *Carterfone Decision* (that allowed companies other than AT&T to utilize the AT&T infrastructure), the 1996 *Telecommunications Act* (that deregulated the entire communications industry so that telephone companies, cable-TV and satellite operators, and firms in other segments of the industry were free to enter each other's markets), and the recent ruling by the U.S. Supreme Court that cable companies will not have to share their infrastructure with competing Internet service providers—have had a large impact on the communications industry in general. The ability of the government to block potential mergers between communications companies and to break apart companies based on antitrust law to prevent new monopolies also impacts the Internet and communications industry.

Key Internet organizations are responsible for many aspects of the Internet. For example, the Internet Society (ISOC) provides leadership in addressing issues that confront the future of the Internet and oversees the groups responsible for Internet infrastructure standards, such as which protocols can be used and how Internet addresses are constructed. ICANN (Internet Corporation for Assigned Names and Numbers) is charged with such responsibilities as IP address allocation and domain name management. The World Wide Web Consortium (W3C) is a group of over 450 organizations dedicated to developing new protocols and specifications to promote the evolution of the Web and to ensure its interoperability. In addition, many colleges and universities support Internet research and manage blocks of the Internet's resources.

Myths About the Internet

Because the Internet is so unique in the history of the world—and its content and applications keep evolving—several widespread myths about it have surfaced.

Myth 1: The Internet Is Free

This myth stems from the fact that there has traditionally been no cost associated with online content—such as news and product information—or e-mail exchange, other than what the Internet users pay their ISPs for Internet access. And many people—such as students, employees, and consumers who opt for free Internet service or use free access available at public libraries or other public locations—pay nothing for Internet access. Yet it should also be obvious that someone, somewhere, has to pay to keep the Internet up and running.

Businesses, schools, public libraries, and most home users pay Internet service providers flat monthly fees to connect to the Internet; businesses, schools, libraries, and other larger organizations might also have to lease high-capacity communications lines (such as from a telephone company) to support their high level of Internet traffic. ISPs, phone companies, cable companies, and other organizations who own part of the Internet infrastructure pay to keep their respective physical parts of the Internet running smoothly. ISPs also pay software and hardware companies for the resources they need to support their subscribers. Eventually, most of these costs are passed along to end users through ISP fees. Usually, ISPs that offer free Internet access obtain funds by selling onscreen ads (either ads displayed within the browser interface whenever Web pages or e-mail messages are being viewed or *pop-up* ads that display in new browser windows) or by selling personal or demographic data obtained from subscribers.

Another reason that this is a myth is the growing trend of subscription or per-use fees to access resources—such as journal or newspaper articles, music, and games—via the Internet. Typically, these fees are relatively small, and many companies are working on ways to make the processing of small fees (sometimes called *micropayments*) practical, such as charging a few cents to read each online article and then including all user's micropayments on his or her telephone or credit card bill. In lieu of a mandatory fee, some sites request donations for use of the site (see Figure 8-3). Many experts expect the use of fee-based Internet content to continue to grow at a rapid pace.

FIGURE 8-3
Fee-based Web content. Both required fees and requested donations for accessing Web content are becoming common.

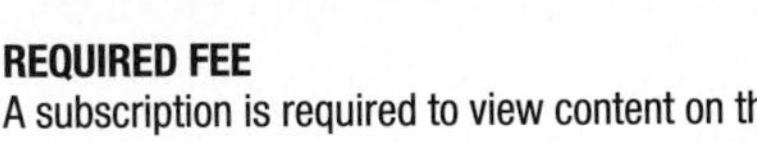

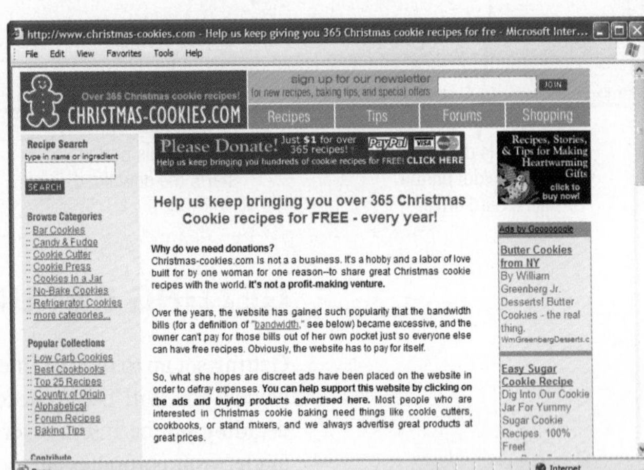

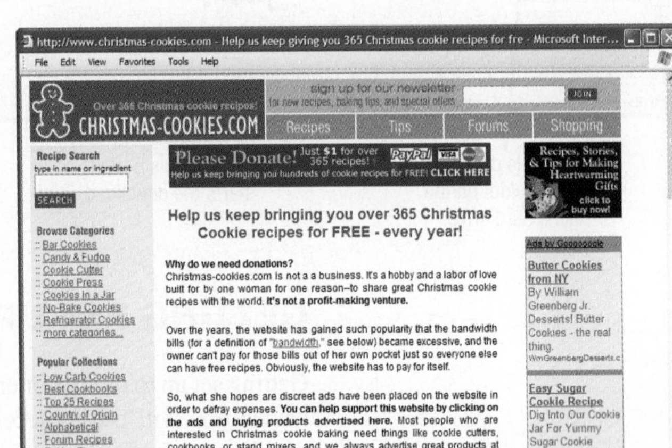

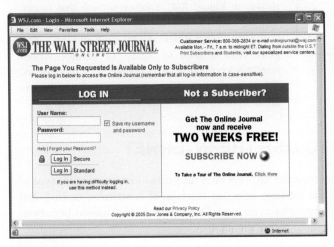

REQUIRED FEE
A subscription is required to view content on this site.

REQUESTED DONATION
A donation is requested for using this site.

Myth 2: Someone Controls the Internet

The popularity of conspiracy theories in past years has contributed to the spread of this myth. In fact, as already discussed, no single group or organization controls the Internet. Governments in each country have the power to regulate the content and use of the Internet within their borders, as allowed by their laws. However, legislators often face serious obstacles getting legislation passed into law—let alone getting it enforced. Making governmental control even harder is the "bombproof" design of the Internet itself. If a government tries to block access to or from a specific country, for example, users can establish links between the two countries through a third country.

FIGURE 8-4

FTP. An FTP program, such as the one shown here, can be used to upload or download files to or from an FTP server.

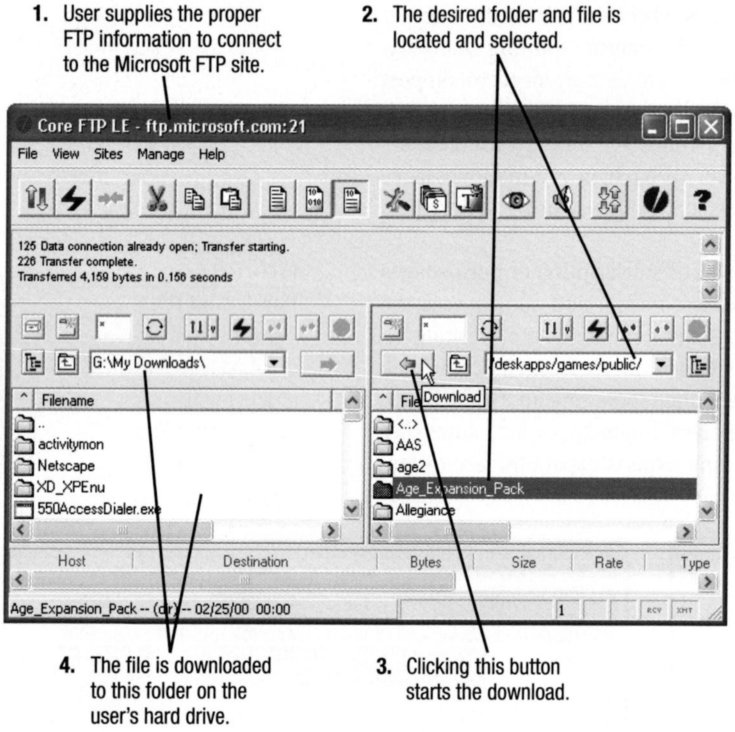

1. User supplies the proper FTP information to connect to the Microsoft FTP site.
2. The desired folder and file is located and selected.
3. Clicking this button starts the download.
4. The file is downloaded to this folder on the user's hard drive.

Myth 3: The Internet and World Wide Web Are Identical

Since you can now use a Web browser to access most of the Internet's resources, many people think the Internet and the Web are the same thing. Although in everyday use many people use the terms *Internet* and *Web* interchangeably, they are not the same thing. Technically, the Internet is the physical network, and the Web is the collection of Web pages accessible over the Internet. The majority of Internet activities today take place via Web pages, but there are Internet resources other than the Web. For instance, *FTP* (*File Transfer Protocol*) is a protocol different from the HTTP protocol used to view Web pages. FTP is a common means of uploading files to or downloading files from an *FTP server*—a server set up by a business specifically to host files others might need to access. FTP access can be open to anyone (such as to allow the general public to download software updates or trial programs) or can be password protected (such as to allow only authorized employees or partners access to company files). While FTP can be performed via a Web browser (by using the *ftp://* protocol indicator instead of *http://* followed by the name of the FTP server), it is more often performed using a stand-alone FTP program, such as the one shown in Figure 8-4. Another service that is performed over the Internet but does not use a Web browser is *Telnet*. Telnet is a *terminal emulation* program that is used to access or control servers remotely via the Internet or another TCP/IP network. Telnet is often used in colleges and universities to allow students access to the campus network.

GETTING SET UP TO USE THE INTERNET

Getting set up to use the Internet typically involves three decisions—determining the type of device you will use to access the Internet, selecting the type of connection desired, and deciding on the Internet service provider to be used. Once these determinations have been made, your computer can be set up to access the Internet.

Type of Device

The Internet today can be accessed by a variety of devices. The type of device used depends on a combination of factors, such as the devices available to you, if you need access just at home or while on the go, and what types of Internet content you want to access. Some possible devices are shown in Figure 8-5 and discussed next.

Desktop, Notebook, or Tablet PCs

Most users who have access to a desktop (see Figure 8-5), notebook, or tablet PC at home, work, or school will use it to access the Internet. One advantage of using PCs for Internet access is that they have large screens and can be connected to high-speed Internet connections. They also can be used with virtually any content that can be contained on or accessed from a Web page, such as graphics, animation, music files, games, and video clips. A final advantage is that they usually have a large hard drive and are connected to a printer so Web pages, e-mail messages, and downloaded files can be easily saved and/or printed.

DESKTOP, NOTEBOOK, OR TABLET PC

Internet Appliances

Internet appliances—devices that are designed specifically for accessing the Internet—are most often used in homes that do not have a PC. Also known as *information appliances*, *Internet tablets*, and *Web pads*, these devices are typically very easy to use and can access Web pages, e-mail, or both. Usually, Web page graphics can be displayed, although all multimedia content might not necessarily be accessible. Disadvantages of Internet appliances include little or no local storage space for saving e-mails or downloads (often everything must be stored online), possibly not being able to connect the device to a printer, and not being able to use the device for tasks other than Internet activities. In addition, many of these devices work only with a single specified provider, such as America Online, MSN, or a proprietary service designed just for that type of Internet appliance. Some Internet appliances are designed to be located in a kitchen or other central location (see Figure 8-5); others take the form of a set-top box located on or near a living room TV and can manage television viewing and recording, in addition to Internet access.

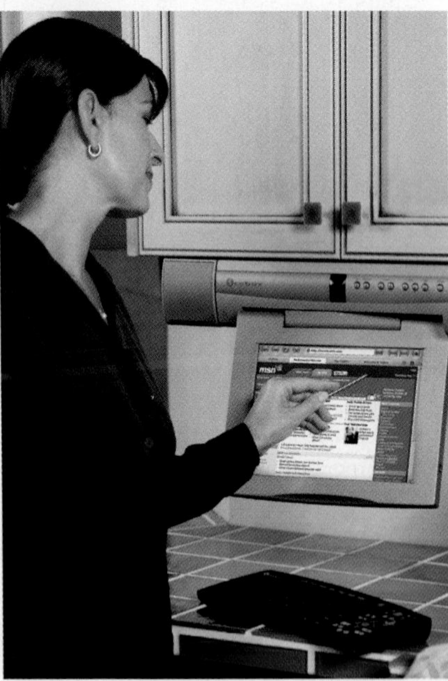

INTERNET APPLIANCE

Mobile Devices

Mobile Web use—or *wireless Web*, as it is frequently called—is one of the fastest growing uses of the Internet today. Handheld PCs and mobile phones increasingly have built-in Internet connectivity and can be used to view Web page content, exchange e-mail and instant messages, and download music and other online content. Some devices, such as the handheld PC shown in Figure 8-5, include a keyboard for easier data entry; others utilize pen input instead.

HANDHELD PC OR SMART PHONE

FIGURE 8-5
A variety of devices can be used to access the Internet.

Type of Connection and Internet Access

In order to use the Internet, your computer needs to be connected to it. Typically, this occurs by connecting your PC to another computer (usually belonging to an ISP, your school, or your employer) that is connected continually to the Internet. As discussed in Chapter 7, there are a variety of wired and wireless ways to connect to another computer. Some Internet connections are *dial-up connections*, meaning your PC dials up and connects to your ISP's computer only when needed. Other Internet connections are *direct* or *always-on connections*, meaning your computer is connected to your ISP whenever your computer is on. Direct Internet connections are typically *broadband* connections; that is, connections that allow more than one signal to be transferred over the transmission medium at one time. Therefore, direct Internet connections are much faster than dial-up connections. In theory, they can be up to 100 times as fast as a dial-up connection, but actual speeds at the present time are closer to 25 to 50 times as fast. This discrepancy is due to outside factors, such as the speed of the device being used, the condition of the transmission media being used, and the amount of traffic currently using the same transmission medium and Web server.

NET

TYPE OF INTERNET CONNECTION	DIAL-UP?	ALWAYS ON?	AVAILABILITY	APPROXIMATE MAXIMUM SPEED *	APPROXIMATE MONTHLY PRICE
Conventional dial-up	Yes	No	Anywhere there is telephone service	56K	Free – $20
Cable	No	Yes	Virtually anywhere cable TV service is available	1.5–3.0 Mbps	$40
DSL	No	Yes	Within 3 miles of a switching station that supports DSL	1.5–3.0 Mbps	$25
Satellite	No	Yes	Anywhere there is a clear view to the southern sky and a satellite dish can be mounted	500 Kbps–1 Mbps	$65 **
Fixed wireless	No	Yes	Mainly urban areas where service is available	500 Kbps–1.5 Mbps	$35
Mobile wireless	No	Yes	Anywhere cellular phone service is available	14.4 Kbps–2 Mbps	Varies greatly

* Many connections have slower upload speeds.

** Also requires expensive hardware, such as a satellite dish or transceiver.

FIGURE 8-6
Internet connection options.

Although dial-up Internet is still common, home broadband use is growing rapidly. More than half of all home Internet connections are now broadband connections, and that percentage is expected to climb to 75% by 2010. Types of Internet connections are discussed next, and the most common types of Internet connections used by individuals are summarized in Figure 8-6.

Dial-Up Connections

Dial-up connections usually work over standard telephone lines. To connect to the Internet, your computer dials its modem and connects to a modem attached to a computer belonging to your ISP. While you are connected to your ISP, your PC can access Internet resources. To end your Internet session, you disconnect from your ISP. One advantage of a dial-up connection is security. Since you are not continually connected to the Internet, it is much less likely that anyone (such as a *hacker*) will gain access to your computer via the Internet, either to access the data located on your PC or, more commonly, to use your computer in some type of illegal or unethical manner.

One disadvantage of using a dial-up connection is the inconvenience of having to instruct your PC to dial up your ISP every time you want to check your e-mail or view a Web page. Also, your telephone line will be tied up while you are accessing the Internet, unless you use a second phone line or an Internet call-waiting or call-forwarding service to notify you about incoming telephone calls while you are connected to the Internet. These services are generally set up to allow the person to leave a short message; some systems give you a short window of time to disconnect from the Internet and pick up the telephone call, if desired. Newer dial-up modems help to facilitate some type of call-waiting service, as well. The two most common forms of dial-up Internet service are *conventional dial-up* and *ISDN*.

TIP

Before using a dial-up access number to connect to the Internet, verify that it is a local telephone number; if it is not, you will incur long-distance charges.

>**Dial-up connection.** A type of Internet connection in which the PC or other device must dial up and connect to a service provider's computer via telephone lines before being connected to the Internet.

Conventional Dial-Up

Conventional (*standard*) **dial-up Internet access** uses a conventional dial-up modem connected to a standard telephone jack with regular twisted-pair telephone cabling. Conventional dial-up Internet service is commonly used with home PCs and Internet appliances; it can also be used with notebook PCs or other portable devices, provided the device has a conventional dial-up modem. Conventional dial-up Internet access ranges from free to about $20 per month. Advantages include inexpensive hardware, ease of setup and use, and widespread availability. The primary disadvantage, in addition to the disadvantages pertaining to all types of dial-up connections discussed in the previous paragraph, is slow connection speed.

Conventional dial-up connects to the Internet at a maximum of 56 Kbps, although some ISPs offer what they call *high-speed dial-up access*. Although the connection speed is still a maximum of 56 Kbps, high-speed dial-up uses *caching*—saving Web page content on your PC—so the pages that you view often can load faster. Users who visit pages that change frequently or need the pages to load completely from the Web server each time they are viewed (such as pages containing news, stock quotes, and other timely information) may not see much of an increase in speed over conventional dial-up Internet.

ISDN

ISDN (*integrated services digital network*) **Internet access** also transfers data over ordinary telephone lines, but it is faster than conventional dial-up. It typically uses two phone lines to transfer data up to 128 Kbps—over twice as fast as conventional dial-up service—and the telephone calls and the Internet can be used at the same time, although Internet speeds might decline during telephone calls. Fairly pricey for the speed at about $60 per month, ISDN requires a special ISDN modem and is used primarily by businesses.

Direct Connections

Unlike dial-up connections that connect to your ISP only when you need to access the Internet, **direct** (*always-on*) **connections** keep you continually connected to your provider and, therefore, continually connected to the Internet. With a direct connection, Internet access requires only opening a Web browser program, such as Internet Explorer, Netscape Navigator, or Firefox. Direct Internet connections are commonly used in homes and offices. In addition, they are often available at hotels, libraries, and other public locations for use by individuals. Users can connect to direct Internet connections via either wired or wireless media.

Because direct connections keep your computer connected to the Internet at all times (as long as your PC is powered up), it is important to protect your computer from unauthorized access or hackers. Consequently, all home and office PCs with a direct Internet connection should use a *firewall* program. Firewall programs block access to a PC from outside computers and enable each user to specify which programs on his or her PC are allowed to have access to the Internet. Firewalls and other network and Internet security precautions are discussed in more detail in Chapter 9.

The most significant characteristics of the most common types of direct Internet connections are discussed next. Other alternatives—such as the emerging *broadband over power lines* (*BPL*) standard discussed in Chapter 7, which allows people to connect to the Internet through their power outlets—will likely be more available in the future.

T1 Lines

T1 lines are high-speed (about 1.5Mbps) dedicated lines that schools and large businesses often lease from the telephone company or an Internet service provider to provide a fast,

NET

>**Conventional dial-up Internet access.** Dial-up Internet access via a conventional dial-up modem and standard telephone lines. >**ISDN Internet access.** Dial-up Internet access that is faster than conventional dial-up, but still uses standard telephone lines. >**Direct connection.** An always-on type of Internet connection in which the PC or other device is continually connected to the Internet. >**T1 line.** Fast, direct Internet access via a leased high-speed dedicated line.

direct connection to the Internet for the PCs on their networks. Very large businesses might choose to lease a faster *T3 line* (which transmits data at speeds of up to about 30 Mbps), but these are more commonly used for Internet backbone connections and connections from ISPs to the Internet.

Cable

Cable Internet access is the most widely used type of home broadband connection, with over 50% of the home broadband market. Cable connections are very fast and are available wherever cable TV access is available, provided the local cable provider supports Internet access. Consequently, cable Internet is not widely available in rural areas. Cable Internet service requires a cable modem and costs about $40 per month just for Internet access; cable TV is optional and requires an additional fee.

DSL

As mentioned in Chapter 7, **DSL** (*Digital Subscriber Line*) **Internet access** provides fast transmissions over telephone lines and uses a technology that does not tie up your telephone line. DSL requires a DSL modem and is available only to users who are relatively close (within three miles) to a telephone switching station and who have telephone lines capable of handling DSL. The speed of the connection degrades as the distance between the modem and the switching station gets closer and closer to the three-mile limit, so DSL is typically used in more urban areas. Despite these limitations, DSL Internet access is growing rapidly and has captured over 40% off the home broadband market. Typical monthly fees are around $25 for basic service; some providers offer a premium, faster service for a higher monthly fee.

Satellite

Satellite Internet access is typically a little slower and more expensive than cable or DSL access, but it is often the only broadband option for rural areas. In addition to a satellite modem, it requires a *transceiver* satellite dish mounted outside the home or building to receive and transmit data to and from the satellites being used. Installation requires an unobstructed view of the southern sky (to have a clear line of sight between the transceiver and appropriate satellite), and performance might degrade or stop altogether during very heavy rain or snowstorms. Typical cost is about $65 per month.

Fixed Wireless

Fixed wireless Internet access is similar to satellite Internet in that it requires a modem and sometimes an outside-mounted transceiver, but it uses radio transmission towers instead of satellites. Fixed wireless has traditionally been available only in large metropolitan areas, although a new option is emerging that uses existing cell phone towers to transmit fixed wireless signals, which allows the service to extend to more rural areas. Cost for service is about $35 per month.

Mobile Wireless

Mobile wireless (sometimes called *wireless Web*) **Internet access** is most commonly used with handheld PCs, smart phones, and other mobile devices to keep them connected to the Internet, even as you carry them from place to place. These devices are connected typically through a wireless network and wireless provider using a wireless modem or built-in Internet connectivity. The speed of mobile wireless depends on the standard being used. Common *second-generation (2G) wireless standards* include *GSM* (*Global System for Mobile Communications*) and *CDMA* (*Code Division Multiple Access*), which support speeds up to 14.4 Kbps. *Third-generation (3G) wireless standards*, such as *GPRS* (*general packet radio service*), *3GSM*, and *UMTO* (*Universal Mobile Telecommunications System*) support

---

>**Cable Internet access.** Fast, direct Internet access via cable TV lines. >**DSL Internet access.** Fast, direct Internet access via standard telephone lines. >**Satellite Internet access.** Fast, direct Internet access via the airwaves using a satellite dish and satellite modem. >**Fixed wireless Internet access.** Fast, direct Internet access available in large metropolitan areas via the airwaves and a radio transceiver. >**Mobile wireless Internet access.** Internet access via a wireless communications network, such as the ones used with cellular phones.

faster speeds—from 128 Kbps while traveling in a car to up to 2 Mbps in a fixed setting. There have also been improvements to increase the speed of 2G services, such as *EDGE* (*Enhanced Data Rates for Global Evolution*) and *EV-DO* (*Evolution Data Optimized*)—3G technologies being used by some providers to allow consumers to send and receive data at least three times faster than usual. Costs for mobile wireless Internet access vary widely, with some packages including unlimited Internet, some charging by the number of minutes of Internet use, and some charging by the amount of data transferred. A typical cost for unlimited mobile wireless Internet is about $65 per month.

COFFEEHOUSES
Typically fee-based.

HOTELS
Often free for guests.

PUBLIC AREAS
Usually free for residents and visitors, such as at this location in Rome.

CORPORATE MEETING ROOMS
Usually free for employees and visitors.

FIGURE 8-7
Hotspots. Hotspots are used to wirelessly connect to the Internet via the Internet connection belonging to a business, city, school, or other organization.

Hotspots

Both free and fee-based wireless Internet are becoming available at *public hotspots*—public locations with a direct Internet connection that allow users to wirelessly connect to that Internet connection. Examples include the Internet service available at many Starbucks coffee houses and a number of McDonald's restaurants; wireless access points at hotels, airports, and other locations frequented by business travelers; and free hotspots located in the vicinity of some larger metropolitan area libraries, subway stations, parks, and other public locations (see Figure 8-7). Many businesses are also setting up hotspots within the corporate headquarters for use by employees in their offices, as well as employees and guests in conference rooms, waiting rooms, lunchrooms, and other onsite locations. Users typically connect to hotspots via a Wi-Fi connection, although other options—such as the faster WiMAX, discussed in Chapter 7—might soon be an option for some locations.

Selecting an ISP and Setting Up Your PC

Once the type of Internet access to be used is determined, the final steps to getting connected to the Internet are selecting an ISP and setting up your system.

Selecting an ISP

The type of device used (such as a desktop PC or handheld PC), the type of Internet connection and service desired (such as conventional dial-up or cable), and your geographical location will likely limit your ISP choices. The pricing and services available through any two ISPs might differ somewhat. For example, some ISPs simply provide you with an onramp to the Internet; others might include additional content or services, such as instant messaging, music management, Web site hosting, personal online photo galleries, Web site filtering, spam filtering, virus protection, and a personalized starting page. The questions listed in Figure 8-8 can help you understand the factors you need to consider when choosing an ISP.

NET

AREA	QUESTIONS TO ASK
Services	Can I use the browser of my choice?
	Does the e-mail service support attachments, spam filtering, and multiple mailboxes?
	How many e-mail addresses can I have?
	What is the size limit on incoming and outgoing e-mail messages and attachments?
	Do I have a choice between conventional and Web-based e-mail?
	Is there dial-up service that I can use when I'm away from home (for both dial-up and broadband connections)?
	Are there any special member features or benefits?
	Is space available for posting a personal Web site or personal photos?
Speed	How fast are the maximum and usual downstream (ISP to my PC) speeds?
	How fast are the maximum and usual upstream (my PC to ISP) speeds?
	How much does the service slow down under adverse conditions, such as high traffic or poor weather?
	If it's a dial-up connection, how often should I expect to get a busy signal? (A customer-to-modem ratio of about 10:1 or less is optimal.)
Support	Is 24/7 telephone technical support available?
	Is any technical support available through a Web site, such as e-mail support or an online knowledge base?
	What is the response time to answer my phone calls or e-mails when I have a problem?
	Is there ever a charge for technical support?
Cost	What is the monthly cost for the service? Is it lower if I prepay a few months in advance?
	If it's a dial-up connection, is there a local access telephone number to avoid long-distance charges?
	Are there services that can be added or deleted (such as number of e-mail addresses or Web page hosting) to increase or decrease the monthly cost?
	Is there a set-up fee? If so, can it be waived with a 6-month or 12-month agreement?
	What is the cost of any additional hardware needed, such as modem or transceiver? Can the fee be waived with a long-term service agreement?
	Are there any other services (conventional or wireless telephone service, or cable or satellite TV, for instance) available from this provider that I have or want and that can be combined with Internet access for a lower total cost?

FIGURE 8-8
Choosing an ISP.
Some questions to ask before making your final selection.

Setting Up Your PC

The specific steps for setting up your PC to use your new Internet connection depend on the type of device, the type of connection, and the ISP you have chosen to use. Once the necessary hardware (your modem and any additional hardware, such as a satellite transceiver or set-top box) has been acquired and is in place, you will usually need to run installation software to set up your system to use the ISP you selected. Typically, the installation process includes downloading and installing any additional required software, setting up your telephone dialing software (for some conventional dial-up connections only), and walking through selecting a username (used to log on to some Internet connections and for your e-mail address), an access telephone number (for dial-up connections), and a payment method. Some ISPs provide the installation program on CD; the installation programs for several common ISPs are also preinstalled on many new PCs. In either case, you need to start the installation program, and then just follow the onscreen instructions to complete the setup process. If you already have an Internet connection and are looking for a new ISP, the necessary installation program can typically be downloaded to your PC from the ISP's Web site and then run on your PC to begin the setup process. If your ISP does not have an installation program, follow its instructions to set up your Web browser and telephone-dialing software (if needed).

Selected screens of the installation process with one provider (America Online) are shown in Figure 8-9; the same general steps occur with most ISP installation programs, although they might occur in a different order.

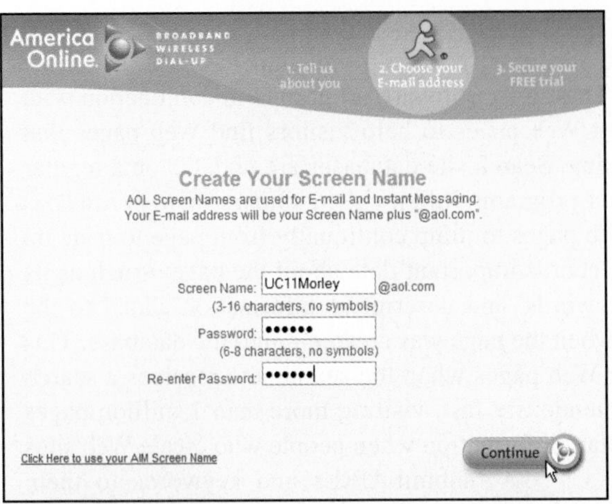

STEP 1: SELECT A SCREEN NAME
The screen name (username) and password you select is typically used for logging on to the Internet, as well as for e-mail.

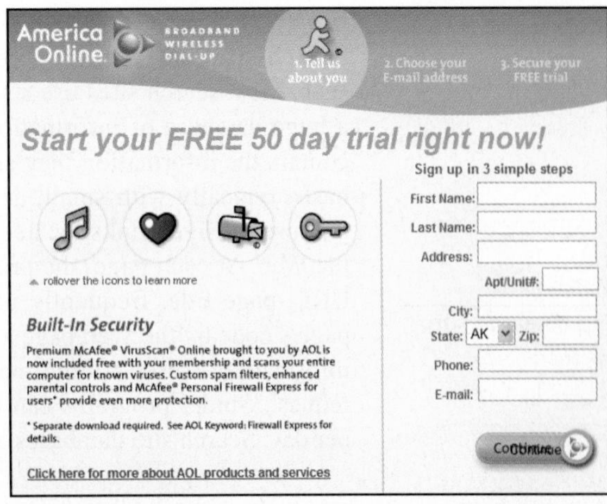

STEP 2: PROVIDE CONTACT AND BILLING INFORMATION
The setup process includes specifying your contact and billing information.

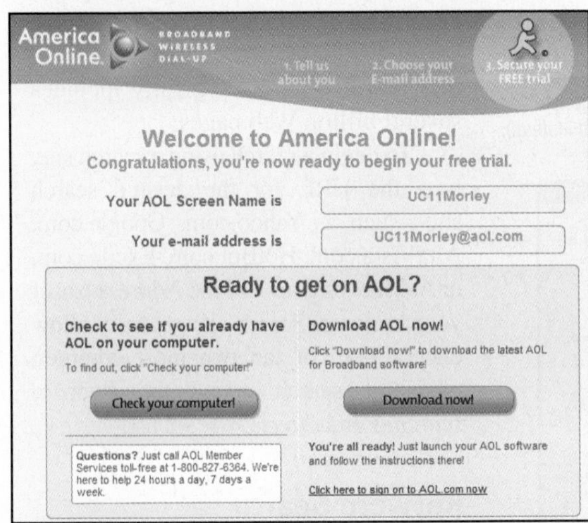

STEP 3: DOWNLOAD SOFTWARE AND SELECT AN ACCESS NUMBER
The necessary software will be downloaded. For dial-up connections, you will then need to select at least one local telephone number for your PC to dial to access the Internet.

STEP 4: LOG ON AND START SURFING
After the browser software is downloaded and installed, you can log on to your new service (with your assigned username and password) and start surfing the Web!

FIGURE 8-9
Setting up a PC for Internet access.
Most ISPs have an installation program that walks new subscribers through the setup process.

SEARCHING THE INTERNET

Most people who use the Internet turn to it to find specific information. For instance, you might want to find out the lowest price of the latest Tom Cruise DVD, the flights available from Los Angeles to New York on a particular day, a recipe for clam chowder, the weather forecast for the upcoming weekend, the text of Martin Luther King's "I Had a Dream" speech, or a map of hiking trails in the Grand Tetons. The Internet provides access to a vast amount of interesting and useful information, but that information is useless if you cannot find it when you need it. Consequently, one of the most important skills an Internet user can acquire today is how to successfully search for and locate information on the Internet. Basic Internet searching was introduced in Chapter 1, but understanding the various types of search sites available and how they work, as well as some key searching strategies, can help you save time by performing more successful Internet searches. These topics are discussed next.

Search Sites

Search sites are Web sites designed specifically to help you find information on the Web. Most search sites use a **search engine**—a software program—in conjunction with a huge database of information about Web pages to help visitors find Web pages that contain the information they are seeking. Search site databases are updated on a regular basis, typically with small, automated programs (often called *spiders* or *webcrawlers*) that use the hyperlinks located on Web pages to jump continually from page to page on the Web. At each page, the program records important data about the page—such as its URL, page title, frequently used keywords, and descriptive information added to the page's code by the Web page author when the page was created—into the database. This information is used to find matching Web pages when the search site receives a search request. Spider programs can be tremendously fast, visiting more than 1 million pages per day. Search site databases also obtain information when people who create Web sites submit URLs and keywords to them through an option on the search site, as discussed more in Chapter 11. Some search sites also use human editors to manually classify the Web pages according to content. The size of the search database varies with each particular search site, but typically includes several billion Web pages.

To begin a search using a search site, type the URL for the desired search site—such as Yahoo.com, Google.com, AltaVista.com, HotBot.com, Excite.com, or AskJeeves.com—in the Address bar of your browser. Search sites usually allow one or both of the two most common types of search operations: *keyword searches* and *directory searches*.

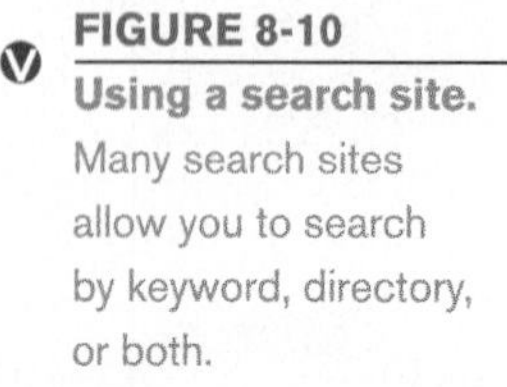

FIGURE 8-10
Using a search site. Many search sites allow you to search by keyword, directory, or both.

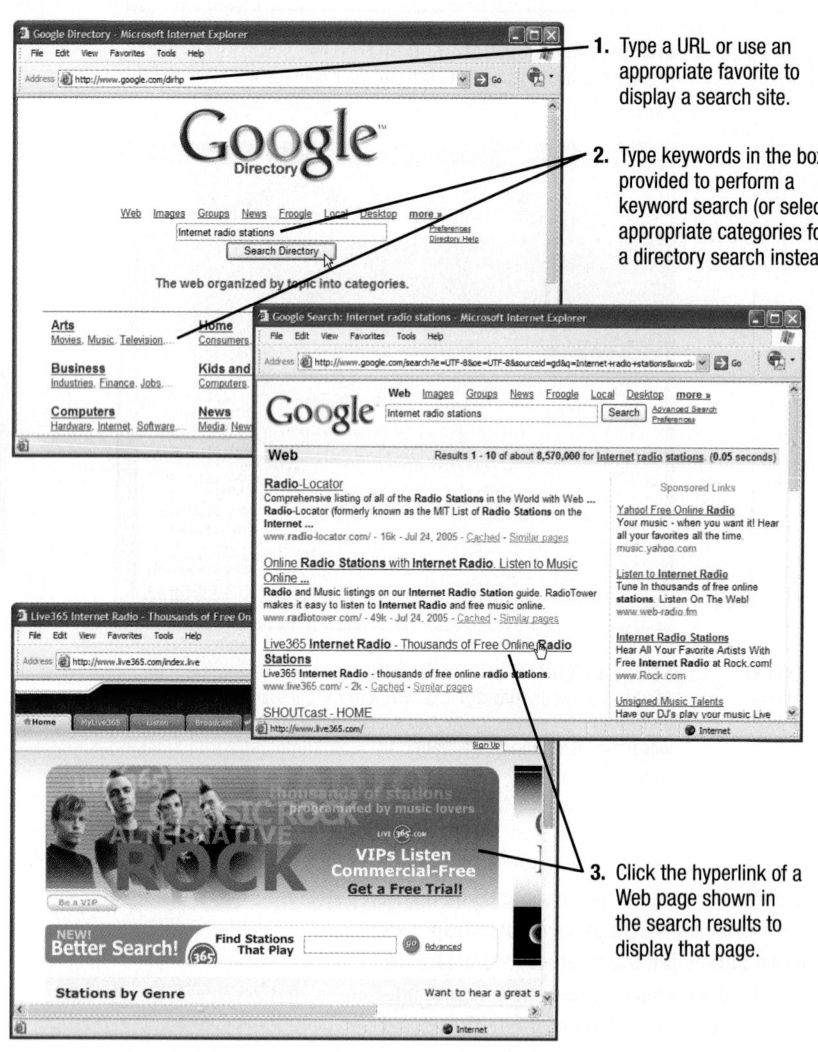
1. Type a URL or use an appropriate favorite to display a search site.
2. Type keywords in the box provided to perform a keyword search (or select appropriate categories for a directory search instead).
3. Click the hyperlink of a Web page shown in the search results to display that page.
Google Directory
Internet radio stations
Search Directory
The web organized by topic into categories.
Google
Search
Radio-Locator
Online Radio Stations with Internet Radio. Listen to Music Online ...
Live365 Internet Radio - Thousands of Free Online Radio Stations
SHOUTcast - HOME
VIPs Listen Commercial-Free
Get a Free Trial!
Better Search!
Find Stations That Play
Stations by Genre

Keyword Search

To perform a **keyword search**, enter appropriate **keywords** (one or more key terms) describing what you are looking for in the search box and press Enter. The site's search engine then uses those keywords to return a list of matching pages (called *hits*) that can be viewed by clicking the hyperlinks (see Figure 8-10). Search sites differ in how close a match between the specified search criteria and a Web page has to be before a link to that page is displayed, so the number of hits from one search site to another may vary.

>**Search site.** A Web site designed to help users search for Web pages that match specified keywords or selected categories. >**Search engine.** A software program used by a search site to retrieve matching Web pages from a search database. >**Keyword search.** A type of Internet search in which keywords are typed in a search box to locate information on the Internet. >**Keyword.** A word typed in a search box on a search site to locate information on the Internet.

To reduce the number of hits displayed, good search strategies (discussed shortly) can be used. Sites also differ regarding the order in which the hits are displayed. Some sites list the most popular sites (usually judged by the number of Web pages that link to it); others list Web pages belonging to organizations that pay a fee to receive a higher rank (typically called *sponsored links*) first.

The keyword search is the most commonly used search type. As shown in Figure 8-11, a keyword search option can be found on many different types of sites. Keyword searches can be found on *metasearch sites* (sites that search multiple search sites and consolidate the results) and *natural language search sites* (sites that are designed to be used with search criteria in full sentence form, instead of just keywords), in addition to conventional search sites. In addition, many Web sites include keyword search capabilities to allow visitors to find information located on the site, such as products in an online catalog.

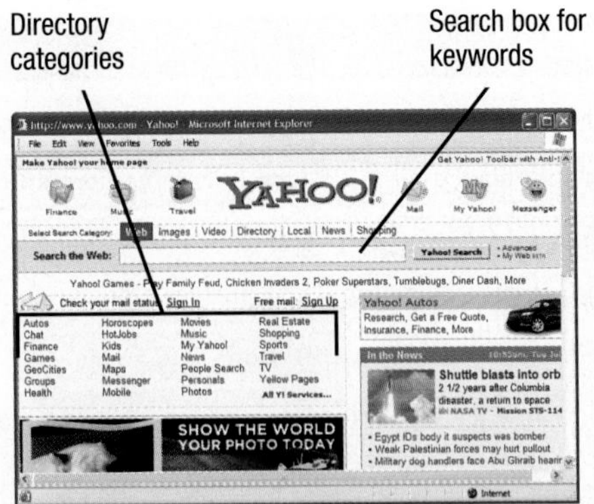

CONVENTIONAL SEARCH SITE
Allows users to search by both keyword and directory.

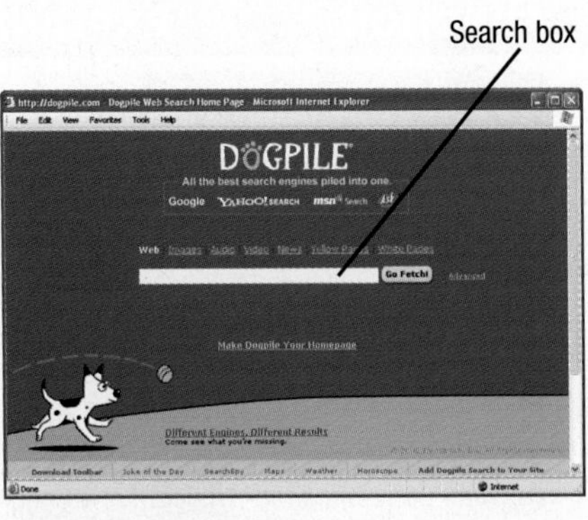

METASEARCH SITE
Allows users to search by keyword and displays hits from several different search sites.

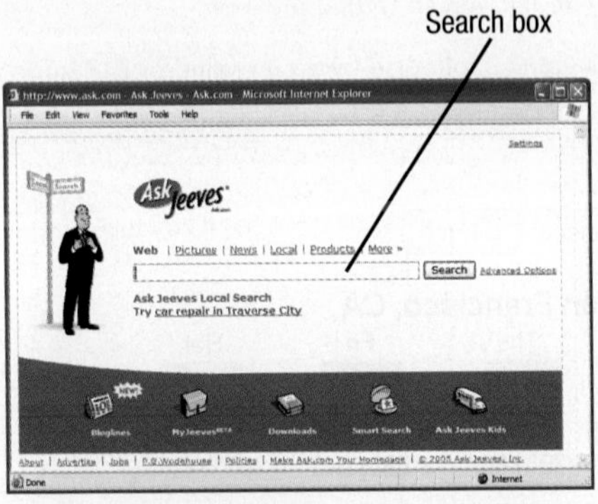

NATURAL LANGUAGE SITE
Allows users to search by using natural language sentences.

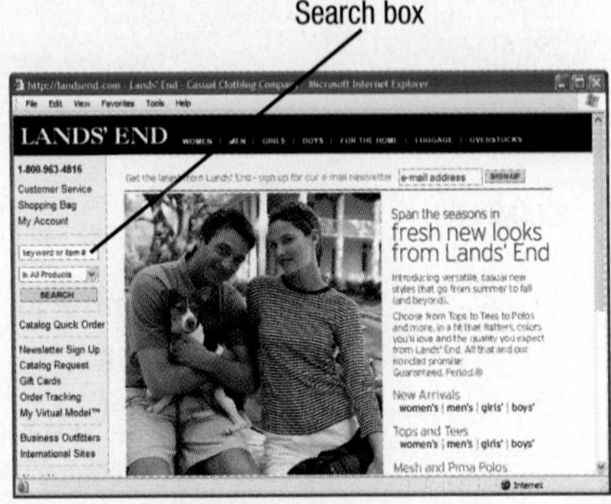

E-COMMERCE WEB SITE
Allows users to search the Web site to find products and product information.

FIGURE 8-11
Types of searches.
There are many types of searches available through search sites, and many regular Web pages have search capabilities built in.

NET

Directory Search

A **directory search** uses a list of categories displayed on the screen (refer again to Figure 8-11). Directories are usually a good choice if you want information about a particular category but do not have a very specific subject in mind. A directory also uses a database, but one that is typically screened by a human editor, so it is much smaller, although often more accurate. For example, a spider program might classify a Web page about computer chips under the keyword "chips" together with information about potato chips, but a human editor would not categorize those two "chips" concepts together. One of the largest directories—the *Open Directory Project*, located at dmoz.org—has classified over 5 million Web pages using around 70,000 volunteer editors.

To use a directory located on a search site, click the category that best matches what you are looking for. A list of more specific subcategories for the main category that you selected is then displayed, along with a list of matching Web pages. To reach more specific subcategories and matching Web pages, keep selecting categories. Whenever the name of an appropriate Web page appears in the list of matching Web pages, click its hyperlink to display that page.

>**Directory search.** A type of Internet search in which categories are selected to locate information on the Internet.

FUNCTION	EXPLANATION
Calculator	Enter a mathematical expression or a specific conversion to see the result.
Currency converter	Enter an amount and desired currency type to see the corresponding value.
Dictionary	Enter the term "define" followed by a term to view definitions from online sources.
Flight information	Enter an airline and flight number to see status information on that flight.
Number search	Enter a tracking number, area code, UPC code, etc. to view the associated information.
Phonebook	Enter a name and either a city name, area code, or ZIP code to look up that person's address and phone number.
Reverse phonebook	Enter a telephone number to look up the person or business associated with that number.
Site search	Enter the term "site" followed by keywords to search only that site.
Stock quotes	Enter one or more ticker symbols to retrieve stock quotes.
Street maps	Enter an address to find a map to that location.
Weather	Enter the term "weather" followed by a city name or ZIP code to view the weather for that location.
Yellow pages	Enter a type of business and city name or ZIP code to view businesses in that local area.

EXAMPLES:

weather san francisco Search

Weather for **San Francisco, CA**

75°F
Clear
Wind: N at 7 mph
Humidity: 53%

Thu 78° | 50°
Fri 66° | 54°
Sat 63° | 52°

10 miles in feet Search

10 miles = 52 800 feet

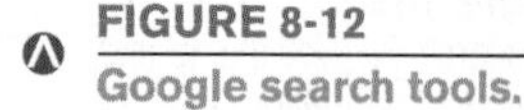

FIGURE 8-12
Google search tools.

Search Site Tools

Many search sites contain a variety of tools that can be used to search for specific types of information, For instance, some search sites include options for searching for items other than Web pages, such as music files, image files, newsgroups, news articles—even files on your computer. Others allow you to search for maps of locations, search for people or telephone numbers, and other helpful features. Google is one of the most versatile search sites at the present time and is continually adding new search options. Some examples of search tools that can be performed using the Google search box are listed in Figure 8-12.

Search Strategies

There are a variety of strategies that can be employed to help whittle down a list of hits to a more manageable number (some searches can return millions of Web pages). Some search strategies can be employed regardless of the search site being used; others are available only on certain sites. Some of the most useful search strategies are discussed next.

Using Phrases

One of the most straightforward ways to improve the quality of the hits returned is to use *phrase searching*—essentially typing more than one keyword in a keyword search. Most search engines automatically return the hits that include all the keywords typed first, followed by the hits matching most of the keywords, continuing down to the hits that fit only one of the keywords. To force this type of sorting, virtually all search engines allow you to use some type of character—often quotation marks—to indicate that you want to search for all the keywords. Because search options vary from site to site, it is best to look for a search tips link on the search site you are using; the search tips should explain the options available for that particular site. Examples of the results from using various search phrases at different sites to find Web pages about hand signals used with dogs are listed in Figure 8-13.

TIP

When searching, be efficient—if an appropriate Web page is not included among the first page or two of hits, redo the search using more specific criteria or a different search strategy.

GUIDELINE	EXPLANATION
Evaluate the source.	Information from the company or organization in question is generally more reliable than information found on an individual's Web site. Government and educational institutions are usually good sources for historical or research data. If you clicked a link on a Web page to open a document, double-check the URL to make sure you still know what organization the page is from–it may be located on a completely different Web site than the page from which it was accessed.
Evaluate the author.	Does the author have the appropriate qualifications for the information in question? Does he or she have a bias, or is the information supposed to be objective?
Check the timeliness of the information.	Web page content may be updated regularly or posted once and forgotten. Always look for the publication date on online newspaper and magazine articles; check for a "last updated" date on pages containing other types of information you'd like to use.
Verify the information.	When you will be using Web-based information in a report, paper, Web page, or other document in which accuracy is important, try to locate the same information from other reputable Web sources to verify the accuracy of the information you plan to use.

FIGURE 8-15

Evaluating search results. Before using information obtained from a Web page, use the following criteria to evaluate its accuracy and appropriateness.

Citing Internet Resources

According to the online version of the Merriam-Webster dictionary, the term *plagiarize* means "to steal and pass off the ideas or words of another as one's own" or to "use another's production without crediting the source." To avoid plagiarizing Web page content, you need to credit Web pages sources—as well as any other Internet resources—when you use them in papers, on Web pages, or in other documents.

The guidelines for citing Web page content are similar to those for written material. Some guidelines for crediting some Internet-based resources are listed next, based on the guidelines obtained from the American Psychological Association Web site. Figure 8-16 shows some citation examples. If in doubt when preparing a research paper, check with your instructor as to the style manual he or she prefers you to follow and refer to that guide for direction.

- *Web page article (journal, magazine, etc.).* List the author, date of publication, article title, and periodical information, similar to a print source, and then add a "Retrieved" statement and date with the appropriate URL of the Web page used.
- *Web page content (not an article).* List the author (if there is one), date of publication (if available; if not, use *n.d.* for "no date"), and Web page title, followed by a "Retrieved" statement and date with the appropriate URL of the Web page used.
- *E-mail correspondence.* List the sender's name followed by a "personal communication" statement and the date received next to the reference in the text. This reference is not included in the references section.

FIGURE 8-16

Citing Web sources. It is important to properly credit your Web sources. These examples follow the American Psychological Association (APA) citation guidelines.

NET

TYPE OF RESOURCE	CITATION EXAMPLE
Web page article (magazine)	Naughton, Keith. (2003, September 29). Chrysler Shifts Gears. *Newsweek.* Retrieved March 13, 2006 from http://www.msnbc.com/news/969677.asp?0dm=s118k.
Web page article (journal)	Mion, L. (2003, May 31). Care Provision for Older Adults: Who Will Provide? *Online Journal of Issues in Nursing*, 8 no. 2. Retrieved March 1, 2006, from http://www.nursingworld.org/ojin/topic21/tpc21_3.htm.
Web page article (not appearing in a periodical)	Sullivan, Bob (2003, September 26). New Arrest in Internet Attacks case. MSNBC. Retrieved February 11, 2006, from http://msnbc.com/news/972467.asp?0dm=C14OT.
Web page content (not an article)	*Biography of Ronald Reagan.* (n.d). Retrieved March 5, 2006 from http://www.whitehouse.gov/history/presidents/rr40.html.
E-mail (cited in text, not reference list)	L.A. Chafez (personal communication, March 28, 2006).

BEYOND BROWSING AND E-MAIL

In addition to basic browsing, searching for specific information, and e-mail, there are a host of other activities that can take place via the Internet. Some of the most common additional Web-based applications are discussed next.

Discussion Groups, Instant Messaging, and Other Types of Online Communications

Many types of online communications methods exist. For example, e-mail and *instant messaging* (*IM*) are extremely popular today, *Voice over IP* (*VoIP*) is emerging, and specialty types of electronic correspondence—such as *electronic invitations* and *electronic greeting cards*—can be sent via *e-vite* or electronic greeting card Web sites. E-mail was discussed in Chapter 1. Some of the most common other types of online communications are discussed next.

Discussion Groups

Discussion groups (also called *message boards*, *newsgroups*, or *online forums*) facilitate written discussions between people on specific subjects, such as TV shows, computers, movies, gardening, music, photography, hobbies, and politics. When a participant posts a message, it is displayed for anyone accessing the message board to read and respond to. Messages are usually organized by topics (called *threads*). Participants can post new messages in response to an existing message and stay within that thread, or they can post discussion group messages that start brand new threads. Many discussion groups can be accessed with just a Web browser, as in Figure 8-17; others require a *newsreader* (a special program for handling newsgroup messages that is often incorporated into e-mail programs). Participants in discussion groups do not have to be online at the same time because messages can be posted and responded to at each participant's convenience.

FIGURE 8-17
Types of online communications.

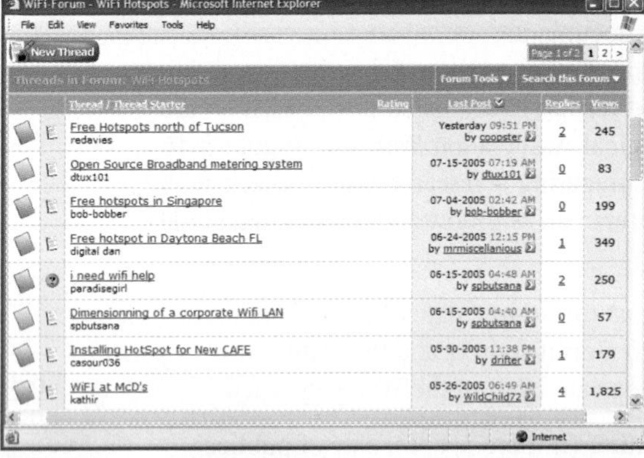

DISCUSSION GROUPS
Allow individuals to carry on written discussions with a variety of people on a specific topic; since messages remain on the site once they are posted, users don't need to be online at the same time to participate.

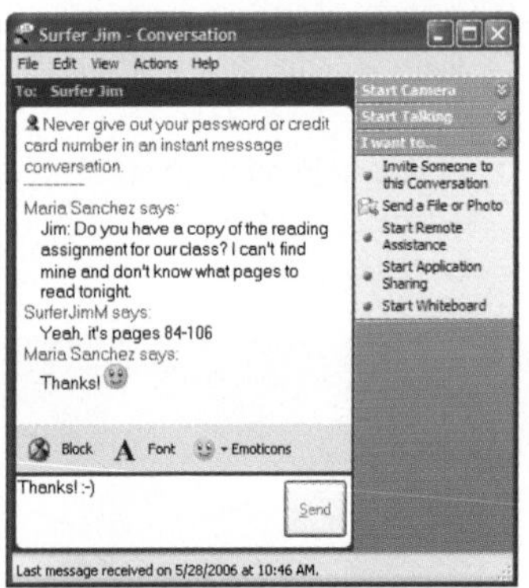

INSTANT MESSAGING
Enables real-time written conversations with friends and other "buddies" who are online at the same time.

VIDEOCONFERENCING
Allows multiple individuals to talk with and see each other during a real-time online meeting. Used both by individuals and businesses.

Chat Rooms

A **chat room** is an Internet service that allows multiple users to *chat* (exchange *real-time* typed messages). Unlike e-mail and discussion groups, chat rooms require participants to be online at the same time. Like discussion groups, chat rooms are typically set up for specific topics. While most chat rooms are open to anyone, an individual can set up a private chat room that is reserved only for users (typically family, friends, or coworkers) who know the proper password.

>**Discussion group.** A type of Internet communications that enables individuals to post messages on a particular topic for others to read and respond to. >**Chat room.** A type of Internet communications that allows multiple users to exchange written messages in real time.

Instant Messaging (IM)

Instant messaging (**IM**) is a form of private chat that allows you to exchange real-time messages easily with people on your *buddy list*—a list of individuals (such as family, friends, and business associates) that you specify. Popular instant messaging services include *AOL Instant Messenger*, *MSN Messenger*, *Windows Messenger*, and *Yahoo! Messenger*. Because there is no single IM standard at the present time, you and your buddies must use the same (or compatible) instant messaging systems in order to exchange instant messages. Whenever one of your buddies is online (that is, connected to the Internet and signed in to the IM program), you can send a short message to that person and it immediately appears on his or her computer (see Figure 8-17). In addition to sending typed messages, IM programs typically include other options, such as sending a photo or file, starting a voice or video conversation, playing an online game, and viewing news headlines or weather forecasts. Originally a popular communications method among friends, IM has also become a valuable business tool. IM frequently takes place on mobile phones, in addition to being used on desktop PCs. According to a late 2004 report by the Pew Internet and American Life Project, about 30% of IM users report using IM at least as much as they use e-mail—a surprising new shift—and use of IM on mobile devices has doubled in the past year, according to AOL.

Videoconferencing

Videoconferencing (also called *teleconferencing* or *Web conferencing*) refers to the use of computers, video cameras, microphones, and other communications technologies to conduct face-to-face meetings among people in different locations over the Internet. Small videoconferences can take place using the participants' PCs, as in Figure 8-17; large group videoconferences might require a more sophisticated setup, such as a dedicated videoconferencing room set up with video cameras, large monitors, microphones, and other hardware. Most videoconferences are two-way, with all users sending and receiving video. Some uses for one-way Internet videoconferencing include locating PC cameras in child-care centers and schools to allow parents to watch live video of their children throughout the day, and setting up surveillance PC cameras in homes and offices to check for intruders and other problems when the location is unoccupied. Videoconferencing can also take place today via smart phones and other mobile devices.

NET

Voice over Internet Protocol (VoIP)

Internet telephony is the original industry term for the process of placing telephone calls over the Internet. In its early stages, Internet telephony took place either from your PC to the recipient's PC (using the PC's speakers and microphones instead of a telephone) or from your PC to the recipient's telephone, depending on the setup. Some free Internet telephony is still available for PC-to-PC phone calls—such as those supported by some IM programs and the popular Skype service, purchased in 2005 by eBay—but the newest Internet telephony applications today involve placing telephone-to-telephone calls over the Internet—called **Voice over Internet Protocol** (**VoIP**). With VoIP, telephone calls are routed over the Internet to and from the user's regular telephone, via his or her Internet connection. VoIP is one of the fastest growing communications applications today and is currently available from a number of telephone, cable, and VoIP companies. *Voice over Wi-Fi*—making telephone calls via a Wi-Fi network—is an emerging related option. For a look at how VoIP works, see the How it Works box.

>**Instant messaging (IM).** A form of private chat set up to allow users to easily and quickly exchange real-time typed messages with the individuals they specify. >**Videoconferencing.** The use of computers, video cameras, microphones, and other communications technologies to conduct face-to-face meetings over the Internet. >**Voice over Internet Protocol (VoIP).** The process of placing telephone calls via the Internet.

HOW IT WORKS

Voice over IP (VoIP)

Voice over Internet Protocol (VoIP) is a technology that allows you to make voice telephone calls using an Internet connection instead of a regular telephone line. A conventional phone call uses *circuit switching*, in which a connection (or *circuit*) is made between the two parties, and that connection is kept open for the duration of the call, but VoIP uses *packet switching*, like the Internet, in which data is divided into small pieces (called *packets*), and each piece is sent independently of each other piece. Because of this, VoIP is much more efficient than the conventional telephone system.

VoIP services are currently available from a number of Internet telephone companies (such as Packet8, Net2Phone, Vonage, and WebPhone), as well as from mainstream communications companies (such as AT&T, Verizon, Comcast, and Time Warner Cable). In fact, the most growth in the VoIP area lately has been from cable companies, which are packaging low-cost VoIP phone service with television and Internet services. VoIP services work via a broadband Internet connection—typically cable, DSL, or a T1 line.

Some VoIP services are designed so that subscribers make calls using a computer microphone and speakers, but most use a standard phone plugged into an adapter box that is connected to a broadband modem, as shown in the accompanying illustration. In either case, you can usually call any telephone number, but the price typically varies from free (for calling a person from your computer to his or her computer, or for calling a person who subscribes to the same VoIP service) to about four cents per minute for domestic calls. Increasingly, VoIP services offer unlimited local and long-distance calls for as little as $20 per month. One of the biggest disadvantages of VoIP at the present time is that it does not function during a power outage or if your Internet connection goes down. In addition, calls to 911 might not be identified with your home address, depending on your VoIP service and how it was set up. To solve this problem, the FCC has ruled that all VoIP phone companies must provide *enhanced 911 (e911)* service by the end of 2005. With e911, consumers must supply their home address to their VoIP provider, and emergency calls are routed directly to a switchboard in the subscriber's area to relay to emergency services.

Although it might take some time to happen, it is likely that circuit-switching telephone networks will eventually be replaced with packet-switching technology. Close to 3 million consumers in the United States used VoIP in 2005, and the Probe Group estimates that 27% of phone users worldwide will use VoIP by 2008.

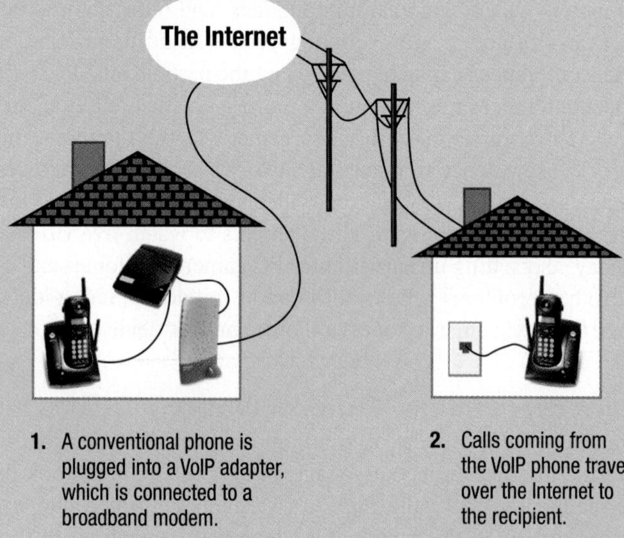

1. A conventional phone is plugged into a VoIP adapter, which is connected to a broadband modem.

2. Calls coming from the VoIP phone travel over the Internet to the recipient.

Online Shopping and Investing

Online shopping and *online investing* are examples of *e-commerce*—online financial transactions. It is very common today for individuals and businesses to order products, buy and sell stock, pay bills, and manage their financial accounts online. In fact, online sales in the United States for 2004 alone were nearly $100 billion, and Forrester research predicts that online sales will reach approximately $331 billion (about 13% of all retail sales) by 2010.

Since *online fraud*, *credit card fraud*, and *identity theft* (a situation in which someone gains enough personal information to pose as another person) are growing problems, it is important to be cautious when participating in online financial activities. To protect yourself, use a credit card whenever possible when purchasing goods or services online so that any fraudulent activities can be disputed, but be sure to enter your credit card number only on a secure Web page. To identify a secure Web page, look for a locked padlock or a complete—unbroken—key at the bottom of your Web browser screen, a URL that begins with *https* instead of *http*, or some other indication that a *secure Web server* is being used.

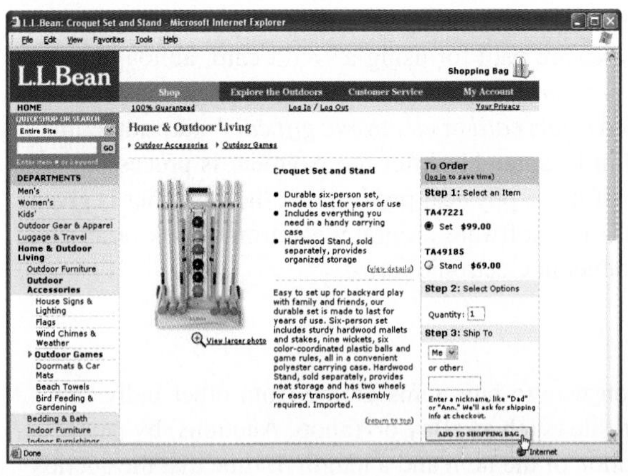

ONLINE SHOPPING
Allows you to purchase goods and services online. As items are selected, they are moved to an online shopping cart or bag.

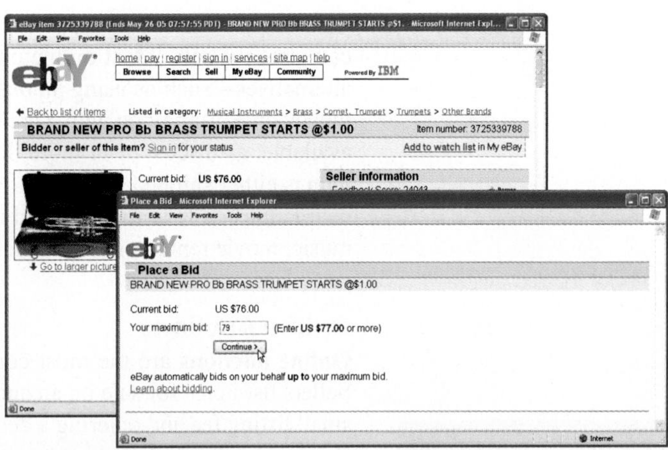

ONLINE AUCTION
Allows you to bid on goods for sale by other individuals; the highest bidder purchases the item.

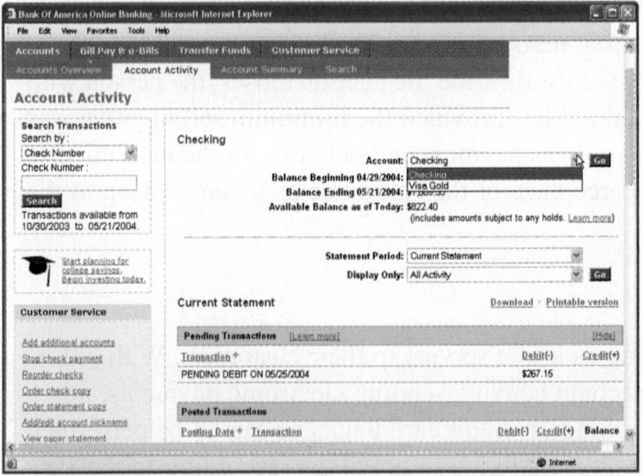

ONLINE BANKING
Allows you to check your account balances, make electronic payments, view your transaction history, and more.

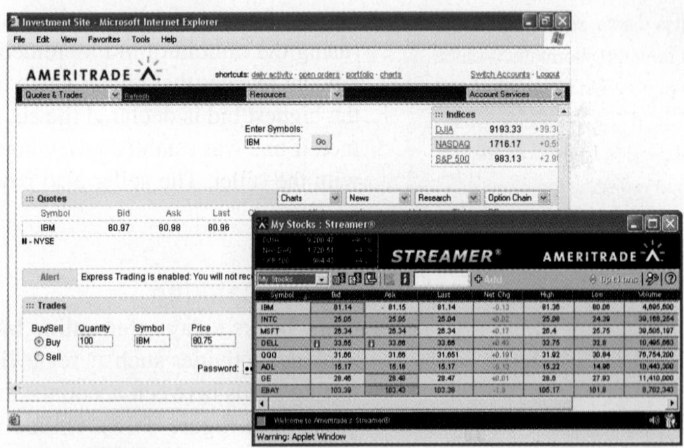

ONLINE INVESTING
Allows you to buy and sell stocks, view your portfolio, get real-time quotes, and more.

NET

FIGURE 8-18
Common e-commerce activities.

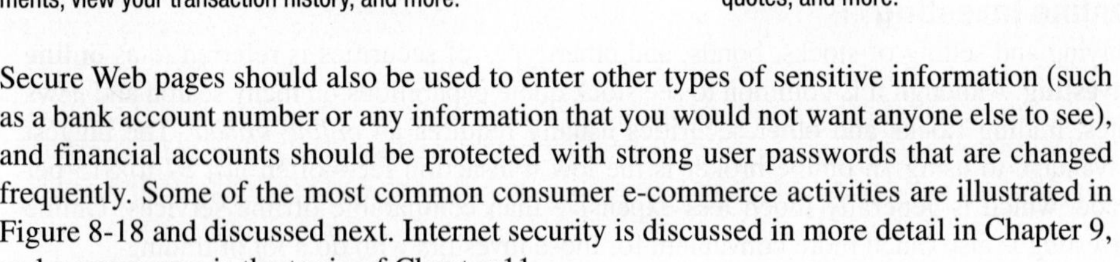
Secure Web pages should also be used to enter other types of sensitive information (such as a bank account number or any information that you would not want anyone else to see), and financial accounts should be protected with strong user passwords that are changed frequently. Some of the most common consumer e-commerce activities are illustrated in Figure 8-18 and discussed next. Internet security is discussed in more detail in Chapter 9, and e-commerce is the topic of Chapter 11.

Online Shopping

With **online shopping**, products can be purchased directly from large companies—such as L.L. Bean, Dell Computer, Wal-Mart, Amazon.com, and Macy's—via their Web sites (see Figure 8-18), as well as from a large number of small retailers. Typically, shoppers locate the items they would like to purchase by searching an online retailer site or browsing through the company online catalog, and then adding the items to their online *shopping carts* or *shopping bags*. When shoppers finish shopping, they follow the checkout

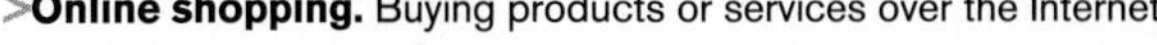
>**Online shopping.** Buying products or services over the Internet.

procedures—including supplying the necessary billing and shipping information—to complete the sale. Most online purchases are paid for using a credit card, although other alternatives—such as using an *online payment account* like *PayPal*, sending in a check or money order, or paying with a preloaded *smart card* or *electronic gift card*—are sometimes available, as discussed in more detail in Chapter 11. After the payment is processed, the item is either shipped to the customer (if it is a physical product), or the customer is given instructions on how to download it (if it is a software program, electronic book or article, music, movie rental, or some other product in electronic form).

Online Auctions

Online auctions are the most common way to buy items online from other individuals. Sellers list items for sale on an auction site (such as eBay or Yahoo! Auctions) by paying a small listing fee and entering a description of the item and a length of time that the auction should run. They can specify a starting bid amount (that bidders see), as well as a minimum selling price (that bidders do not see) that must be met in order for there to be a winning bidder. Individuals can enter bids on auction items (see Figure 8-18) until the end of the auction. For convenience, most auction sites allow bidders to enter a maximum bid amount for a particular auction, and the auction site will automatically bid for that person (using the minimum bid increment for that item) whenever the bidder is outbid, until the amount reaches that bidder's maximum bid. At the time the auction closes, the person with the highest bid is declared the successful bidder (provided the minimum selling price was met, if one was established), who then arranges payment and delivery for the item directly with the seller. The seller also pays a percentage of the sale price as a commission to the auction site.

TIP

The data on Web pages—such as on an online auction page—is typically not updated automatically once it is displayed on your screen. To get updated information—such as the current bid for an auction and auction time remaining—use your browser's Refresh or Reload button to redisplay the page.

Online Banking

Many banks today offer **online banking** as a free service to their customers. With online banking, activities such as reviewing account activity, sending electronic payments, transferring funds between accounts, and looking up credit card balances can all be performed online (see Figure 8-18). Online banking is continually growing—according to the Pew Internet & American Life Project, more than 50 million U.S. adults now bank online.

Online Investing

Buying and selling of stocks, bonds, and other types of securities is referred to as **online investing**. Although it is common to see stock quote capabilities on many search and news sites, trading stocks and other securities usually requires an *online broker*. The biggest advantage to using an online broker is the low transaction fee—often just $7 to $15 per trade, which is generally much less expensive than comparable offline services. Online investing is also much more convenient for those investors who do a lot of trading.

Once an online brokerage account is set up, you can order stock sales and purchases just as you would with an offline broker. Usually the history of your orders can be viewed online, and open orders can be cancelled before they are executed. Many brokerage and financial sites also have convenient access to a variety of performance histories, corporate news, and other useful information for investors. In addition, most online brokers allow you to set up an *online portfolio* that displays the status of the stocks you specify. On some Web sites, stock price data is delayed 20 minutes; on other sites, real-time quotes

>**Online auction.** An online activity for which bids are placed on items, and the highest bidder purchases the item. >**Online banking.** Performing banking activities over the Internet. >**Online investing.** Buying and selling stocks or other types of investments over the Internet.

are available. It is important to realize that Web page data—such as stock price data—is current at the time it is retrieved via a Web page, but it will not be updated (and you will not see current quotes, for instance) until you reload the Web page using your browser's Refresh or Reload toolbar button. An exception to this rule is if the Web page is set up to refresh the content automatically for you on a regular basis. For example, the portfolio shown in Figure 8-18 uses a *Java applet*—a small program built into a Web page—to redisplay updated data continuously.

Online Entertainment

There are an ever-growing number of ways to use the Web for entertainment purposes, such as listening to music, watching videos, and playing online games (see Figure 8-19). Some applications can be accessed with virtually any type of Internet connection; others are only practical with a broadband connection.

Online Music

Online music is perhaps one of the hottest Web-based entertainment activities today. Some of the most widely used possibilities are listening to online radio broadcasts and downloading music singles and albums. Online radio is broadcast from *online radio stations*, also called *Internet radio stations*. To listen to an Internet radio station, you open the radio station's Web page in your browser and click an appropriate hyperlink (see Figure 8-19). A *media player program* usually automatically opens, and you begin to hear the broadcast. Many common media players (such as *Windows Media Player* and *RealOne Player*) are available free of charge and include tools to help you not only listen to radio stations but also organize both your online and offline music.

A number of *online music stores*, such as the iTunes Music Store, RealPlayer Music Store, Napster, Yahoo! Music, and Wal-Mart Music Downloads (see Figure 8-19), are now available to legally download music singles and albums in digital format. Sales of digital music are growing rapidly. The iTunes Music Store exceeded 500 million downloads in mid-2005, and the worldwide online music market is expected to reach $1 billion in sales in 2005, according to the research firm In-Stat. Some online music stores are stand-alone services; others are integrated into a media player program so that songs can be purchased, played, organized, and transferred to a CD or portable music player all from the same program. Still other online music services—such as Real's Rhapsody subscription service—are designed for unlimited access to an enormous collection of online music that can be listened to on demand for a set fee (typically about $10 per month). Music services for cell phones are also available. Consumers are currently spending billions of dollars on ringtones, and cell phones capable of downloading and storing hundreds of songs became available in late 2005. In fact, many expect the cell phone to eventually replace the MP3 player and market research firm Strategy Analytics expects mobile music to be a $9 billion business by 2010.

To avoid copyright violations, all legal downloaded music is available either as free downloads (sometimes found on sites featuring new artists, for example) or for purchase (typically 99 cents per song, part of which is used for royalties owed to the artist or record company for the download). Once downloaded, music files can be played from your PC's hard drive using a media player program installed on your PC. Provided the download agreement did not preclude it, music files can also be copied to a CD to create a custom music CD or transferred to a portable digital music player, such as an iPod.

NET

>**Online music.** Music played or obtained via the Internet.

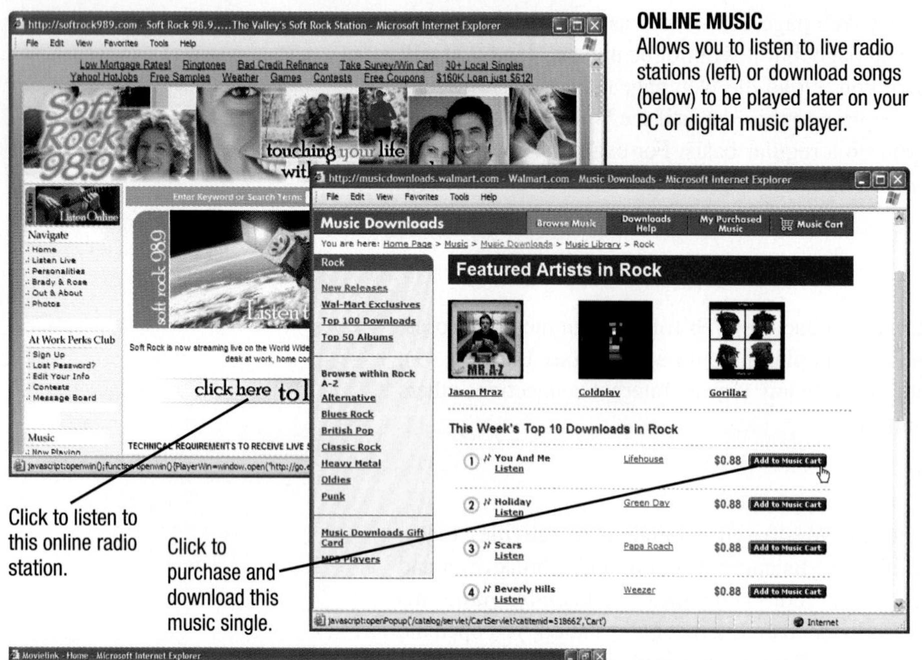

ONLINE MUSIC
Allows you to listen to live radio stations (left) or download songs (below) to be played later on your PC or digital music player.

Click to listen to this online radio station.

Click to purchase and download this music single.

VIDEO-ON-DEMAND
Allows you to download and watch feature films and other fee-based video content.

Click a movie to download it.

In this game, an *avatar* represents each player; each avatar's movement and speech are controlled by its player.

ONLINE GAMING
Allows you to play games online either alone or with other players, as in this example.

FIGURE 8-19
Common online entertainment activities.

Online TV, Videos, and Video-On-Demand

Additional online entertainment applications include television shows, movies, and video clips. It is common to find news clips, movie trailers, music videos, taped interviews, and similar short, pre-recorded videos on Web sites today. Live online TV is fairly limited at the present time, although there are some Web sites that provide live video feeds, such as the interactive Web sites that accompany television shows like *Big Brother*. *Interactive TV (iTV)*—which allows users to perform interactive activities (such as participating in games, ordering merchandise, voting, or looking up related trivia) during a television broadcast—is an emerging option, particularly for cable or satellite TV subscribers. One of the most promising new applications is **video-on-demand (VOD)**.

With VOD, individuals order movies and television shows over the Internet, which are then typically sent via the Internet to their PCs or digital video recorders (DVRs). With VOD, a portion of the movie usually downloads first, and then the movie can be played while the rest of it finishes downloading. This type of delivery—called *streaming media*—is commonly used with both audio and video distributed over the Internet to reduce the time needed to begin to hear or view the selection. One example of a video-on-demand service available today is Movielink (shown in Figure 8-19), which offers downloads of full-length feature films.

>**Video-on-demand (VOD).** The process of downloading movies and televisions shows, on demand, via the Internet.

Downloadable movies are typically "pay-per-view" movies that can only be viewed during a limited time, such as 24 hours after activation; at the end of that time, the downloaded file becomes unusable. For convenience, many VOD services allow users to download pay-per-view downloadable movies up to a month ahead of time, but once the movie has started to play, it only works for a 24-hour period. To watch the movie again after that point requires an additional fee, although the movie does not have to be downloaded again, unless it was deleted from the user's hard drive. Typical fees for video-on-demand movies are comparable with conventional video rental services—about $3 to $5 each—but they provide end users the convenience of not having to leave their houses to pick up or return the movies, and end users get movies faster than services that rent DVDs via regular mail.

In addition to being used with home computers and televisions, VOD is also available for cell phones and other types of mobile devices, as discussed in the Chapter 1 Trend box. For example, in late 2005 Apple introduced an iPod capable of playing video and downloading video and TV shows. Episodes of hit TV shows like *Desperate Housewives* and *Lost* can be downloaded to the iPod the day after they air on television for about $1.99 each.

Online Gaming

Online gaming refers to games played over the Internet. Many sites—especially children's Web sites—include games for visitors to play. There are also sites whose sole purpose is hosting games that can be played online. Some of the games, such as Solitaire, are designed to be played alone. Online *multiplayer* games, such as Hearts, Doom EverQuest, Final Fantasy XI, and City of Heroes (see Figure 8-19), can be played online against other online gamers. Online multiplayer games are especially popular in countries, such as South Korea, that have high levels of both high-speed Internet installations and Internet use in general. As of mid-2004, nearly 80% of the homes in South Korea had broadband Internet access, and one South Korean online gaming network estimates it has about 40 million subscribers for its most popular online game, with an average of 500,000 people playing it at any given time.

Online gaming is also associated quite often with *Internet addiction*—the inability to stop using the Internet or to prevent extensive use of the Internet from interfering with other aspects of one's life. Internet addiction is a growing concern and is discussed in more detail in Chapter 16.

E-Books

E-books—electronic versions of books sometimes also called *online books*—are plentiful. From the entire works of Shakespeare to new best sellers, thousands of books can be read online or downloaded. There are online libraries that host online books (many in HTML format so they can be displayed using a Web browser), and there are online bookstores where e-books can be purchased and downloaded. E-books are most commonly viewed using a handheld PC, but they can be viewed on a variety of other devices, including desktop PCs and special devices designed for reading e-books. Depending on the format, one of several free e-book reader programs (such as *Microsoft Reader*, *Adobe Reader*, or *Palm Reader*) can be used to view e-books.

E-books are also becoming available for checkout via county libraries (see Figure 8-20). After checkout, the books are downloaded to the patron's PC or mobile device and can only be read until the book's

FIGURE 8-20
Library e-books.
E-books, that typically only function for a specified check-out time period, can now be downloaded from some public libraries.

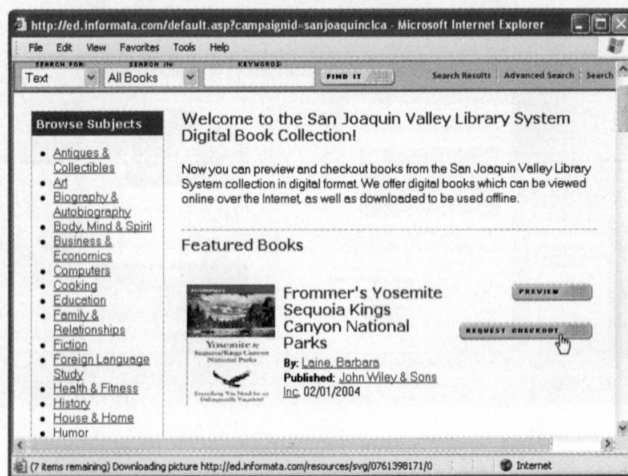

>**Online gaming.** Playing games over the Internet. >**E-book.** A book obtained in electronic format.

due date. The e-books are usually in PDF format and are checked out using the patron's library card number and a PIN number obtained from the local library. When the checkout period expires, the e-book becomes unreadable, and the user simply deletes it from his or her PC. Like books checked out from the local library, there is a limit to the number of copies of each e-book that can be checked out at one time—once the due date is reached, the book is considered "returned," and it becomes available to be digitally checked out by another patron. Unlike conventional library books, e-books never incur overdue charges.

Peer-to-Peer File Sharing

One of the earliest widespread applications of **peer-to-peer (P2P) file sharing**—sharing resources directly between users via the Internet—was *Napster*, a P2P music sharing service in place several years ago. Instead of storing music files on the Napster server to facilitate the file sharing, files downloaded using the Napster service were downloaded from one Napster user's PC to another Napster user's PC—from one peer to another. Napster and other P2P sites in place at that time did not have any technology in place to ensure that files were not being shared illegally. As a result, a flood of lawsuits from the music industry eventually shut down Napster and other P2P sites that were being used to exchange copyright-protected content illegally.

FURTHER EXPLORATION

For links to further information about the Napster controversy and other related peer-to-peer file sharing issues, go to www.course.com/uc11/ch08

Today, peer-to-peer file sharing is still available over the Internet—some legal, and some not. In 2005, the U.S. Supreme Court ruled against one P2P services provider (*Grokster*) and said that companies with the active intent of encouraging copyright infringement should be held liable for their customers' illegal actions. One of the first P2P file sharing services set up to allow legal content distribution between members is Peer Impact, launched in 2005. Peer Impact technology allows music and other digital content to be purchased and shared legally, with artists and record labels being paid appropriately for all music shared via the site. In fact, the Peer Impact service encourages legal file sharing because members who help sell and redistribute authorized content to others earn money for their participation (see Figure 8-21). Other companies have been working to develop technology to allow legal P2P file sharing, but Peer Impact has a distinct head start—by early 2005, all four of the major recording companies agreed to sell their music via the Peer Impact service.

FIGURE 8-21
Legal P2P file sharing. The Peer Impact P2P service shown here reimburses artists and record labels for downloads and also pays participants for facilitating downloads.

With the availability of legal ways to obtain digital content—such as online music stores and legal P2P services, some experts predict that, eventually, these legal alternatives will become the norm for consumers looking for music to use on their PCs, portable music players, home stereos, car stereos, cell phones, and any other device used to play music. But for a look at how illegal file sharing can affect college students in the meantime, see the Technology and You box.

Online News and Research

There is an abundance of news and research information available through the Internet. The following sections discuss a few of these resources. For a look at an alternate way businesses and individuals can keep others up to date—RSS feeds—see the Inside the Industry box.

>**Peer-to-peer (P2P) file sharing.** The process of sharing resources directly between users via the Internet.

INSIDE THE INDUSTRY

RSS Feeds

Really Simple Syndication (*RSS*) is an XML-based format, originally developed by Netscape, which is designed for sharing headlines and other content published to a Web site. A Web site sets up an *RSS feed*—a stream of regularly updated information from the Web site—and then visitors can use an *RSS reader* (usually a stand-alone program, although it might also be built into a Web browser) to retrieve the RSS feed information on a regular basis. Typically, users *subscribe* (add a feed to their RSS readers) to an RSS feed by using a link on a Web page, as shown in the accompanying figure.

Many different types of Web sites today offer RSS feeds, but some of the most common RSS feeds are for national, sports, finance, technical, or entertainment news. As shown in the accompanying figure, many RSS readers—called *RSS aggregators*—can be used to display RSS feeds from multiple Web sites. Clicking the name of a feed displayed within the RSS reader interface usually displays the headlines for that feed somewhere on the screen, and then clicking a headline retrieves that article from the corresponding Web site. Typically, RSS readers are set up to refresh the headlines for all feeds on a regular basis—such as every three hours—but most can be customized to retrieve the headlines more or less frequently.

To help individuals find RSS feeds that match their interests, there are lists of RSS feeds and RSS feed search sites available on the Internet. There are also subscription-based RSS services that provide individuals access to RSS feeds without requiring the individual to manually locate and add each RSS feed to his or her RSS reader. With this type of service, the subscriber selects topics of interest, and then the RSS service provides links to related RSS feeds. These RSS services provide easy access to a large number of RSS feeds—one services claims it has RSS feeds from more than 200,000 Web sites—and cost about $5 to $25 per month, depending on the number of topics and other services selected. Personalized *portal* pages, such as the My Yahoo! Web page available through Yahoo!, are also beginning to incorporate RSS feeds into their members' personalized pages.

There are several versions of RSS (the most widely used is *RSS 2.0*), as well as competing formats—such as the *ATOM* format designed as a universal publishing standard for blogs. Fortunately, most RSS readers today are compatible with most or all of the possible news feed formats. And since virtually all of the feed formats are *XML* (*Extensible Markup Language*)*-based*, they are flexible, so the data contained in a news feed can be delivered to a wide variety of devices. For example, in addition to PC-based RSS readers, RSS feeds today can be delivered to cell phones and other mobile devices. Some companies are even replacing e-mail with RSS for employee and customer notifications—for instance, one Web site uses RSS to alert subscribers to new coupons, and another uses RSS to notify subscribers of new computer virus threats. In the future, expect to see RSS feeds delivered to televisions—perhaps even to watches, refrigerators, and other display devices of the future.

1. Web sites include links to RSS feeds, typically identified with an XML or RSS button. Visitors right-click the link to copy the RSS feed URL.

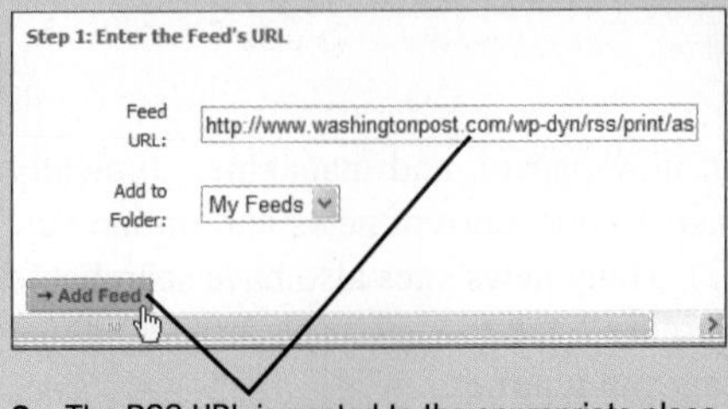

2. The RSS URL is pasted to the appropriate place in the RSS reader program in order to add the RSS feed to the individual's available RSS feeds.

Click to add another feed.

Articles in the selected RSS feed are listed here.

All current RSS feeds.

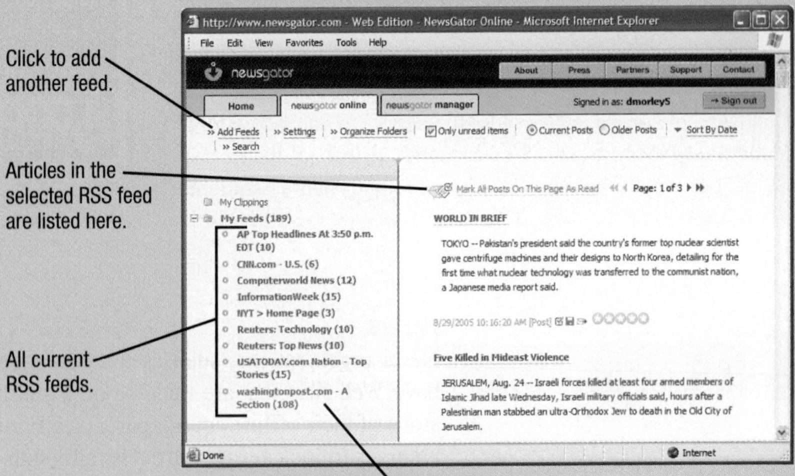

3. The RSS feed is then available in the RSS reader.

TECHNOLOGY AND YOU

P2P Legal Implications for College Students

Since Napster, many individuals—often high school and college students—have been illegally exchanging copyrighted music files via P2P networks. Although Napster and other file sharing services that facilitated the illegal exchange of copyrighted music and movies were eventually shut down, P2P file sharing continues. Since September 2003, recording companies have filed more than 9,000 lawsuits against individuals illegally exchanging music files via P2P services. The most recent focus by the Recording Industry Association of America (RIAA) is on college students. In mid-2005, the RIAA filed more than 400 copyright infringement lawsuits targeted at college students at 18 college campuses who downloaded copyrighted music files for free. The students named in this round of lawsuits were using high-speed networking technologies created in conjunction with the Internet2 project, designed to develop technologies for the next-generation Internet. According to the RIAA, the file sharing was "an emerging epidemic of music theft" and an illegitimate use of Internet2 technology.

Copyright infringement fines are steep—up to $150,000 per instance. In addition to personal liability for students, high amounts of P2P file exchanges also impact colleges—both by making the college vulnerable to industry lawsuits and by slowing down network performance. One solution offered by Dell and the new legal Napster is using Dell servers located on campus to store the entire Napster collection and then legally distributing that music to students for a small fee. Since downloads only need to be transmitted over the college network and not the Internet, student downloads of music files via the Napster service and its local cache of music will have minimal impact on a college's network bandwidth. At most colleges using the Dell/Napster service, a flat fee for the service is passed on to all students–typically around $3 per month instead of the normal $9.95 per month that Napster charges—and then all students have unlimited access to the Napster collection (see the accompanying screen shot of the Napster service).

Despite these efforts, the risk of prosecution, and the risk of accidentally downloading *spyware* (a software program installed without the user's knowledge that secretly gathers information about the user and transmits it through his or her Internet connection, as discussed later in this chapter), a computer virus, or a corrupted file when downloading a file from another person's PC, illegal file sharing continues. For instance, the number of songs downloaded illegally from P2P services in March 2005 totaled nearly 275 million, more than 10 times the number of songs downloaded legally, according to The NPD Group. However, as more peer-to-peer users understand the risks, legal implications, and ethical implications involved with illegal P2P file sharing, they will likely consider it worth their while to pay the roughly $1 per song for music downloads from a legitimate site instead of obtaining the song illegally. And with consumers beginning to want quality, efficiency, and safety, in addition to value, legal digital media distribution is expected to eventually become the norm.

News

News organizations, such as television networks, newspapers, and magazines, typically have Web sites that are updated on a continual basis to post current news and online versions of their offline counterparts (see Figure 8-22). Many news sites also have searchable archives to look for past articles, although some require a fee to view back articles. There are also news radio programs that are broadcast over the Internet.

Product, Corporate, and Government Information

The Web is a very useful tool for locating product and corporate information. Before buying an item online (or in a conventional *brick-and-mortar store*, for that matter), many people research product options online. Manufacturer and retailer Web sites, such as the one in Figure 8-22, often include product specifications, instruction manuals, and other useful information. For investors, a variety of corporate information is available online, both from the corporation directly and from sites, such as Hoover's Online, which contain free company summaries as well as fee-based in-depth corporate information.

Government information is also widely available on the Internet. Most state and federal agencies have Web sites to provide information to citizens, such as government publications, archived documents, forms, and legislative bills. You can also perform tasks, such as downloading tax forms and filing your tax returns online; many cities, counties, and states allow you to pay your car registration, register to vote, view property tax information, or update your driver's license online, as well.

NEWS
News organizations typically update their sites several times per day to provide access to the most current news and information.

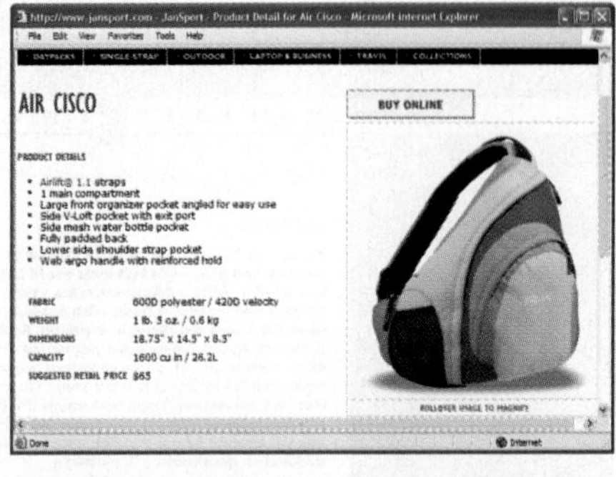

PRODUCT INFORMATION
Businesses use Web sites to provide specifications, instruction manuals, and other types of product information.

GOVERNMENT INFORMATION
Government (local, state, and federal) Web sites provide a variety of information. Some, like this county site, also provide a variety of e-services.

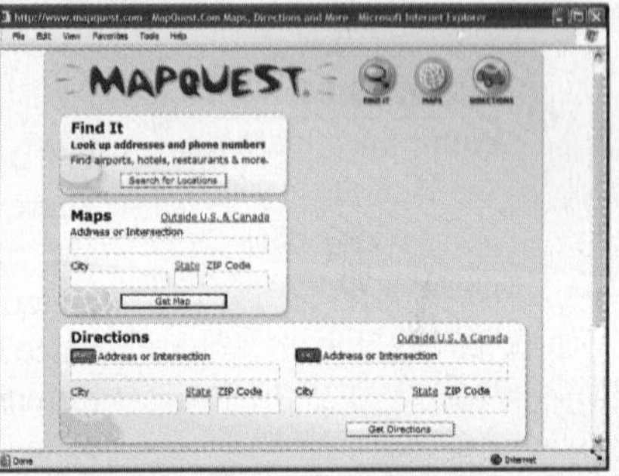

REFERENCE TOOLS
Reference Web sites, such as this site that allows you to generate map and driving directions, provide access to specific types of useful information.

FIGURE 8-22
News and research. Up-to-the minute news, reference tools, product information, and more abound on the Web.

Reference Sites and Portals

There are a number of *reference sites* on the Web, such as those used to generate maps, check the weather forecast, or provide access to encyclopedias, dictionaries, ZIP code directories, and telephone directories. To find an appropriate reference site, type the information you are seeking (such as *ZIP code lookup* or *topographical map*) as keywords in a search site. Some reference sites, such as the MapQuest site shown in Figure 8-22, allow you to send data (such as maps and driving directions) from the Web site to your mobile phone. Additional mobile reference tools are available through some wireless providers.

Portal Web pages are Web pages designed to be selected as a browser's home page and visited on a regular basis. Portal pages typically include reference tools, search capabilities, and other useful content; they also usually allow users to customize the page to display the news of their choice, such as sports, technology, weather, and national or local news. Once the portal page is customized, each time the user visits the portal page, the specified information will be displayed. Popular portals include Yahoo!, AltaVista, MSN, AOL, and Bolt.

>**Portal.** A Web site designed to be designated as a browser home page; typically can be customized to display personalized content.

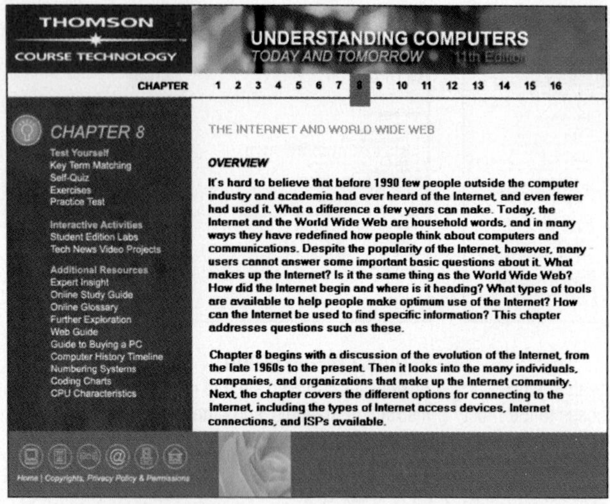

THOMSON
COURSE TECHNOLOGY
UNDERSTANDING COMPUTERS
TODAY AND TOMORROW
CHAPTER 1 2 3 4 5 6 7 8 9 10 11 12 13 14 15 16
CHAPTER 8
Test Yourself
Key Term Matching
Self-Quiz
Exercises
Practice Test
Interactive Activities
Student Edition Labs
Tech News Video Projects
Additional Resources
Expert Insight
Online Study Guide
Online Glossary
Further Exploration
Web Guide
Guide to Buying a PC
Computer History Timeline
Numbering Systems
Coding Charts
CPU Characteristics
THE INTERNET AND WORLD WIDE WEB
OVERVIEW
It's hard to believe that before 1990 few people outside the computer industry and academia had ever heard of the Internet, and even fewer had used it. What a difference a few years can make. Today, the Internet and the World Wide Web are household words, and in many ways they have redefined how people think about computers and communications. Despite the popularity of the Internet, however, many users cannot answer some important basic questions about it. What makes up the Internet? Is it the same thing as the World Wide Web? How did the Internet begin and where is it heading? What types of tools are available to help people make optimum use of the Internet? How can the Internet be used to find specific information? This chapter addresses questions such as these.
Chapter 8 begins with a discussion of the evolution of the Internet, from the late 1960s to the present. Then it looks into the many individuals, companies, and organizations that make up the Internet community. Next, the chapter covers the different options for connecting to the Internet, including the types of Internet access devices, Internet connections, and ISPs available.
Home | Copyrights, Privacy Policy & Permissions

FIGURE 8-23

Web-based learning. The Web site that supplements this book provides Web-based learning opportunities that include online quizzes and other activities, useful Web links, interesting video clips, and more.

Online Education and Writing

Online education—using the Internet to facilitate learning—is a rapidly growing Internet application. The Internet can be used to deliver part or all of any educational class or program, such as through *Web-based training* (*WBT*) and *distance learning*; it can also be used to supplement or support traditional education, such as with *online testing* and *online writing*. In addition, many high school and college courses use Web content—such as online syllabi, schedules, chat rooms, discussion boards, study guides, and tutorials—as required or suggested supplements. For example, the Web site that supplements this book contains an online study guide, online quizzes, online hands-on labs, Web links, and other resources for students taking a course that uses this textbook (see Figure 8-23). The next few sections take a look at some of the most widely used online education applications.

Web-Based Training and Distance Learning

There are more opportunities for online learning today than ever before. Both businesses and schools are utilizing **Web-based training** (**WBT**) for employee training or course materials, and millions of people take classes via **distance learning** each year. With distance learning, students take classes from a location, such as from home or work, which is different from the one where the delivery of instruction takes place. Distance learning (also called *online learning* and *e-learning*) is available through many high schools, colleges, and universities; it is also used for corporate education and training. Distance learning can be used for training employees in just one task or new skill, as well as for an entire college course or degree program. It can enable high school students living in rural areas to take advanced courses not offered at their local schools; young athletes can use distance learning to fit school around their training regimens. Typically the majority of distance learning coursework is completed over the Internet via class Web pages, discussion groups, chat rooms, and e-mail, although schools might require some in-person contact, such as sessions for orientation and testing. Distance learning classes often utilize Web-based training components.

Web-based training and distance learning are typically experienced individually and at the user's own pace. Online content for Web-based training components is frequently customized for each individual user, according to his or her mastery of the material already completed. Online content and activities (such as exercises, exams, and animations) are accessed in real time, just as other Web pages are. Some advantages of Web-based training and distance learning include the following:

- *Self-paced instruction.* Students can usually work at their own pace and at their convenience, at any time of the day or night.
- *Flexible location.* Students do not need to live close to any particular facility to take part in the educational program because Web-based training can be accessed from home, while traveling, or basically anywhere the student has access to a computer with an Internet connection.

>**Web-based training (WBT).** Instruction delivered on an individual basis via the World Wide Web. >**Distance learning.** A learning environment in which the student is physically located away from the instructor and other students; commonly, instruction and communications take place via the Internet.

- *Up-to-date material.* Since all instructional material is hosted on a Web server, it can be updated whenever necessary simply by updating the content on the Web site. Once content is updated, all users will see the newest version of the instructional material the next time they access the Web site.
- *Immediate feedback and customized content.* Web-based training components can be set up to provide immediate feedback from online activities by displaying supplemental material for any problem areas that are identified based on the user's responses. It can also require mastery of material before the student is allowed to move on to the next test or assignment, and it can jump students to more advanced topics as appropriate. This flexibility can result in highly customized content, based on a student's progress and abilities.

While the advantages of Web-based training and distance learning are numerous, potential disadvantages are a concern and include the following:

- *Technology requirements and problems.* In order to participate in Web-based training or distance learning, users must have access to a computer and the Internet. Slow PCs or Internet connections can be frustrating for students as they try to download materials or participate in online discussions. Technological problems—such as a computer crashing or Web server inaccessibility during a test day—can create significant problems for students and instructors.
- *Anonymity.* Because students are in remote locations, it can be difficult to ensure that the student registered for the class is the actual student participating in online discussions and online exams. Some instructors choose to require face-to-face exams at either the school or an authorized testing center in the student's geographical area; newer authentication technology, such as smart cards, fingerprint scanners, and digital signatures, might help to overcome this problem in the future.
- *Lack of face-to-face contact.* Many educators view the interactive exchange of ideas as a very important part of the educational experience. Although interactivity can take place online via chat rooms and discussion groups, the lack of face-to-face contact, which allows students to see, ask questions of, or have discussions with other students and their instructor in person, is cited as a disadvantage by some educators.

NET

Online Testing

In both distance learning and traditional classes, *online testing*—which allows students to take quizzes or tests via the Internet—is a growing trend. Both objective tests (such as those containing multiple choice or true/false questions) and performance-based exams (such as those given in computer classes to test student mastery of software applications) can be administered and taken online. Typically online tests are automatically graded, freeing up instructor time for other activities, as well as providing fast feedback to the students.

Online Writing

Online writing applications used in an educational context today include *blogs*, *wikis*, and *e-portfolios* (*electronic portfolios*). Students might also publish original written material online via personal Web pages. Blogs and wikis are often used for personal and professional commentary, in addition to being used for educational purposes.

A **blog**—also called a *Web log*—is a Web page that contains short, frequently updated entries in chronological order. Basically, a blog is an online personal journal accessible to the

>**Blog.** A Web page that contains short, frequently updated entries in chronological order, typically by just one individual; also called a Web log.

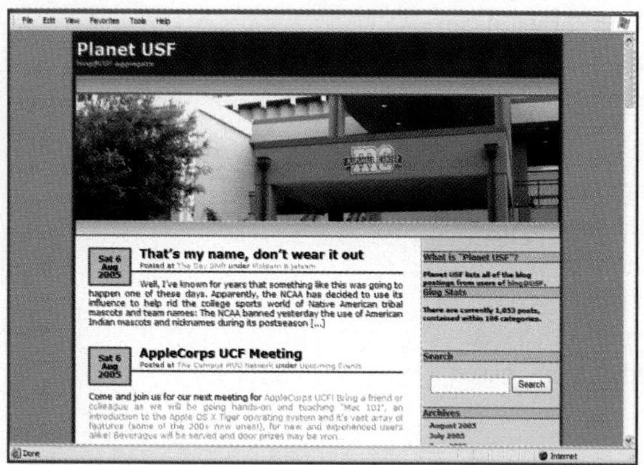

BLOGS
Blogs can be accessed individually or via a blog aggregator. For example, this blog aggregator displays blog entries from all blogs at the University of South Florida.

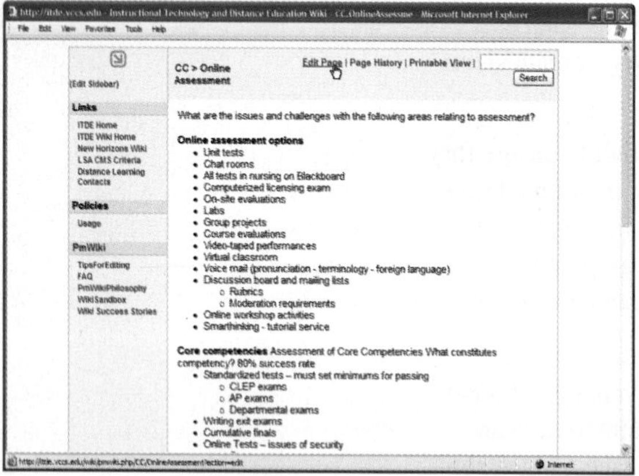

WIKIS
This faculty wiki provides information about distance learning classes at one community college district; the *Edit Page* option at the top of the page is used to edit the page content.

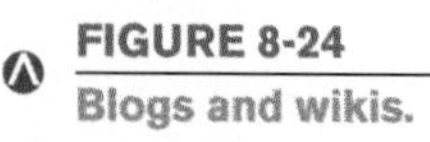

FIGURE 8-24
Blogs and wikis.

public and is typically updated by one individual. Blogs can be used to post personal commentary, research updates, comments on college classes, and more. Blogs can also be set up to have multiple authors, such as a group of employees collaborating on a project or all the students in a particular writing class. *Blog aggregators* collect entries from a variety of blogs—such as all student blogs for a particular university—and post them in a single location (see Figure 8-24). In addition to being published on a school, business, or personal Web site, blogs can also be published to a blogging site, such as Blogger.com. Blogs are usually updated frequently, and entries can be posted via e-mail and mobile devices, in addition to a PC, and entries can contain text, photos, and voice updates stored as MP3 files. For a look at an activity related to blogging—*podcasting*—see the Trend box.

With their increased use and audiences, bloggers and the *blogosphere* (the complete collection of blogs on the Internet) are beginning to have increasing influence on businesses and politicians today. Some popular bloggers have huge audiences, so the impact of blogging is more influential than in the past. As a result of the increasing influence of blogs, there are news services available that monitor blogs—some watch around 100,000 blogs each day—and relay any new blog articles that mention specified company names, brands, people, competitors, or other selected criteria to the subscriber. These services are designed to help businesses and other organizations identify interest in competitor's products or services, potential problems with an existing product or service, and new issues related to their products that they might not be aware of.

Wikis are related to blogs but have a different purpose. From the Hawaiian phrase *wiki wiki* meaning *quick*, a wiki is a way of creating and editing collaborative Web pages quickly and easily. Similar to a blog, the content on a Wiki page can be edited and republished to the Web just by pressing a Save or Submit button, but whereas a blog contribution is added to the existing content (and does not modify the previous blog content), the entire wiki page can be edited to create a new updated page. In a nutshell, blogs are designed for primarily one-way running communications, while wikis are intended to be modified by others. In an educational setting, wikis can be used to create and access a shared workspace easily, such as one used by students or faculty who are collaborating on a group or class project (see Figure 8-24). They can also be used to create and publish Web pages for class projects or presentations easily. To protect the content of a wiki from sabotage, editing privileges can be password protected. One of the largest wikis is *Wikipedia*, a free online encyclopedia that contains over 1.5 million entries in 76 languages. Visitors can read, as well as update, entries.

An **e-portfolio**, also called an *electronic portfolio* or *Webfolio*, is a collection of an individual's work accessible through a Web site. Today's e-portfolios are typically linked to a collection of student-related information, such as résumés, papers, projects, and other original works. Some e-portfolios are used for a single course; others are designed to be used and updated throughout a student's educational career, culminating in a comprehensive collection of information that can be used as a job-hunting tool.

TIP

There are numerous online blog search engines and directories—such as BlogStreet.com—to help you find blogs that meet your interests.

>**Wiki.** A collaborative Web page that is designed to be edited and republished by a variety of individuals. >**E-portfolio.** A collection of an individual's work accessible through a Web site.

TREND

Podcasting

Podcasting is a method of publishing audio broadcasts via the Internet. Podcasts are created by recording audio (typically MP3) files and then making those files available for users to download. The term "podcast" is derived from the iPod digital music player (the first widely used device for playing digital audio files), although podcasts today can be listened to using a desktop or handheld PC, in addition to an iPod or other type of portable digital media player (see the accompanying photograph). With a PC, podcasts can be downloaded manually, or they can be downloaded automatically after subscribing to a particular podcast using *podcatching software*, similar to the way RSS feeds are subscribed to using an RSS reader or aggregator. Downloaded podcasts can be transferred to a digital music player when desired.

Podcasting enables individuals to create self-published, inexpensive Internet radio broadcasts, such as talk shows, to express their opinions on particular subjects, or as a means to share original poems, songs, or short stories with interested individuals. Originally created and distributed by individuals, podcasts are now also being created and distributed by businesses. Some commercial radio stations are making portions of their broadcasts available via podcast, and a growing number of new sites–including ABC News and ESPN–have podcasts. In fact, some view podcasts as the new and improved radio since it is an easy way to listen to your favorite radio broadcasts on your own schedule. The next step? Video podcasting is emerging to deliver both audio and video files.

CENSORSHIP AND PRIVACY ISSUES

There are many important societal issues related to the Internet. One—network and Internet security—will be covered in Chapter 9. Two other important issues—*censorship* and *privacy*—are discussed next, in the context of Internet use. Other societal issues and how they relate to computer use in general are discussed in further detail in Chapters 15 and 16.

Censorship

The First Amendment to the U.S. Constitution guarantees a citizen's right to free speech. This protection allows people to say or show things to others without fear of arrest. People must observe some limits to free speech, of course, such as the prohibition of obscenity over the public airwaves and of child pornography.

But how does the right to free speech relate to alleged patently offensive or indecent materials available over the Internet, where they might be observed by children and the public at large? There have been some attempts at Internet content regulation—what some would view as *censorship*—in recent years, but the courts have had difficulty defining what is "patently offensive" and "indecent" as well as finding a fair balance between protection and censorship. For example, the *Communications Decency Act* was signed into law in 1996 and made it a criminal offense to distribute patently indecent or offensive material online. Although intended to protect children from being exposed to inappropriate Web content, the Supreme Court, in 1997, declared this law unconstitutional on the basis of free speech. The *Children's Online Privacy Protection Act of 1998*, which regulates how Web sites can collect information from minors and provides tax incentives for Web sites and ISPs that protect minors from accessing materials deemed harmful to them, is one example of legislation that has held up under scrutiny.

Internet filtering—blocking access to particular Web pages or types of Web pages—can be used on home computers (for instance, by individuals to protect themselves from material they would view as offensive or by parents to protect their children from material they feel is inappropriate for them). It is also commonly used by employers to keep non-work-related material out of the workplace, by some ISPs and search sites to block access to potentially objectionable materials, and by many schools and libraries. Available through both browser settings (see Figure 8-25) and stand-alone programs, Internet filtering typically restricts access to Web pages that contain specified keywords or that exceed a rating for potentially offensive categories, such as language, nudity, sex, or violence. One limitation with this procedure, however, is that the descriptions of the site and how these categories apply to its content are provided voluntarily by the content provider, not by an independent rating organization. Typically, a password is required to change the filter settings to prevent them from being changed by an unauthorized individual, such as a child or an employee.

An ongoing debate has been whether or not public computers should use Internet filtering. Filtering advocates want to protect children at public locations (such as libraries and schools) from accessing adult material. Individuals and organizations against Internet filtering at libraries and schools believe that filtering violates the patrons' First Amendment rights to free speech. The *Child Internet Protection Act* (*CIPA*) that went into effect in 2001 required public libraries and schools to use Internet filtering to block Internet access to certain materials in order to receive public funds. Although intended to protect children, it was fought strenuously by free speech advocacy groups and some library associations and was ruled unconstitutional by a federal court in 2002. In a 6 to 3 ruling in 2003, however, the Supreme Court reversed the lower court decision and ruled that the law was constitutional because the need for libraries to prevent minors from accessing obscene materials outweighs the free speech rights of library patrons and Web site publishers.

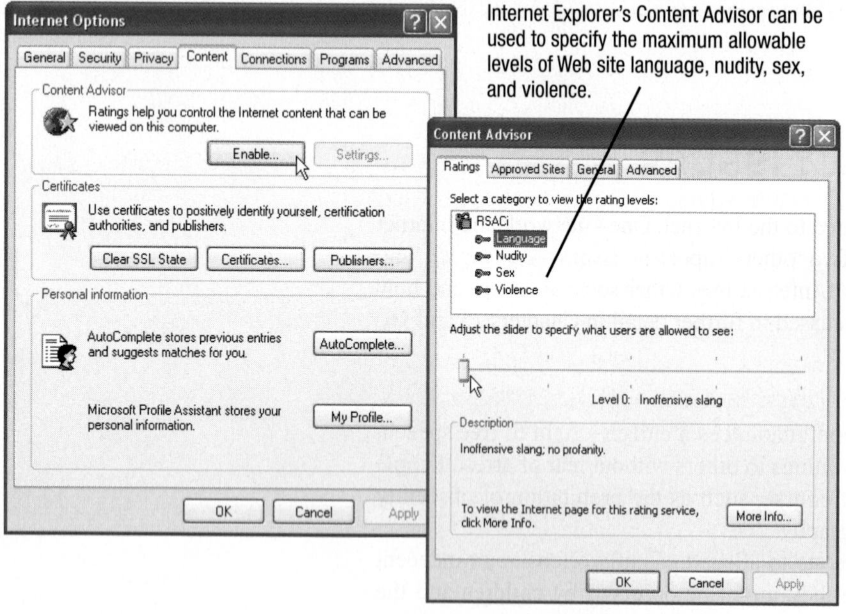

FIGURE 8-25
Internet filtering. Browser settings can be changed to deny access to Web pages with objectionable content.

>Internet filtering. Using a software program or browser option to block access to particular Web pages or types of Web pages.

Web Browsing Privacy

Privacy, as it relates to the Internet, encompasses what information about individuals is available, how it is used, and by whom. As more and more transactions and daily activities are being performed online, there is the potential for vast amounts of private information to be collected and distributed without the individual's knowledge or permission. Therefore, it is understandable that public concern regarding privacy and the Internet is on the rise.

One area of concern for many individuals who browse the Web on a regular basis is maintaining the privacy of where they go and what they do at Web sites. You might wonder: Does anyone keep track of which Web sites I visit, what hyperlinks I click on, how long I stay on a Web site, and what things I download and buy? What about the information I provide to a Web site? Can I specify who gets to see it? The answer to each of these questions is "yes" to some extent, but it depends on the specific Web sites visited, the settings on your PC, and what other precautions you have taken to protect your privacy. Although privacy will be discussed in more detail in Chapter 15, a few issues that are of special concern to Internet users regarding Web browsing privacy and e-mail privacy are discussed in the next few sections.

Cookies

Many Web pages today use **cookies**—small text files that are stored on your hard drive by a Web server, typically the one associated with the Web page being viewed—to identify return visitors and their preferences. While some individuals view all cookies as a potentially dangerous invasion of privacy, the use of cookies can provide some benefits to consumers. For example, as shown in Figure 8-26, cookies can enable a Web site to remember preferences for customized Web site content (such as displaying your local weather and your horoscope on your portal page), as well as to retrieve a shopping cart containing items selected during a previous session. Some Web sites use cookies to keep track of which pages on their Web sites each person has visited, in order to recommend products on return visits that match that person's interests.

Cookies are relatively safe from a privacy standpoint. Web sites can read only their own cookie files; they cannot read other cookie files on your PC or any other data on your computer, for that matter. A cookie file might, however, record the pages viewed on the site associated with the cookie, the amount of time spent on pages with similar content, the person's geographic location (which can be determined by his or her PC's IP address, as well as by demographic data supplied while visiting the site), and other factors used to target third-party advertisements. For instance, if you spend a lot of time checking airline prices on a travel site, you might start seeing ads for hotels, rental cars, airfare, and other travel-oriented goods and services displayed on the pages of your travel site—and many of the ads will be from third-party organizations with which the site has an advertising relationship.

The information stored in a cookie file typically includes the name of the cookie, its expiration date, the domain that the cookie belongs to, and either selected personal information that you have entered while visiting the Web site or an ID number assigned by the Web site that allows the Web site's server to retrieve your information from its database. Such a database can contain two types of information: *personally identifiable information* (*PII*) and *non-personally identifiable information* (*Non-PII*). Personally identifiable data is connected with a specific user's identity—such as his or her name, address, and credit card number provided to the site—and is typically given during the process of ordering goods or services. Non-personally identifiable information is anonymous data—such as which product pages were viewed or which advertisements located on the site were clicked—that is not directly associated with the visitor's name or another personally identifiable characteristic.

NET

>**Cookie.** A small file stored on a user's hard drive by a Web server; commonly used to identify personal preferences and settings for that user.

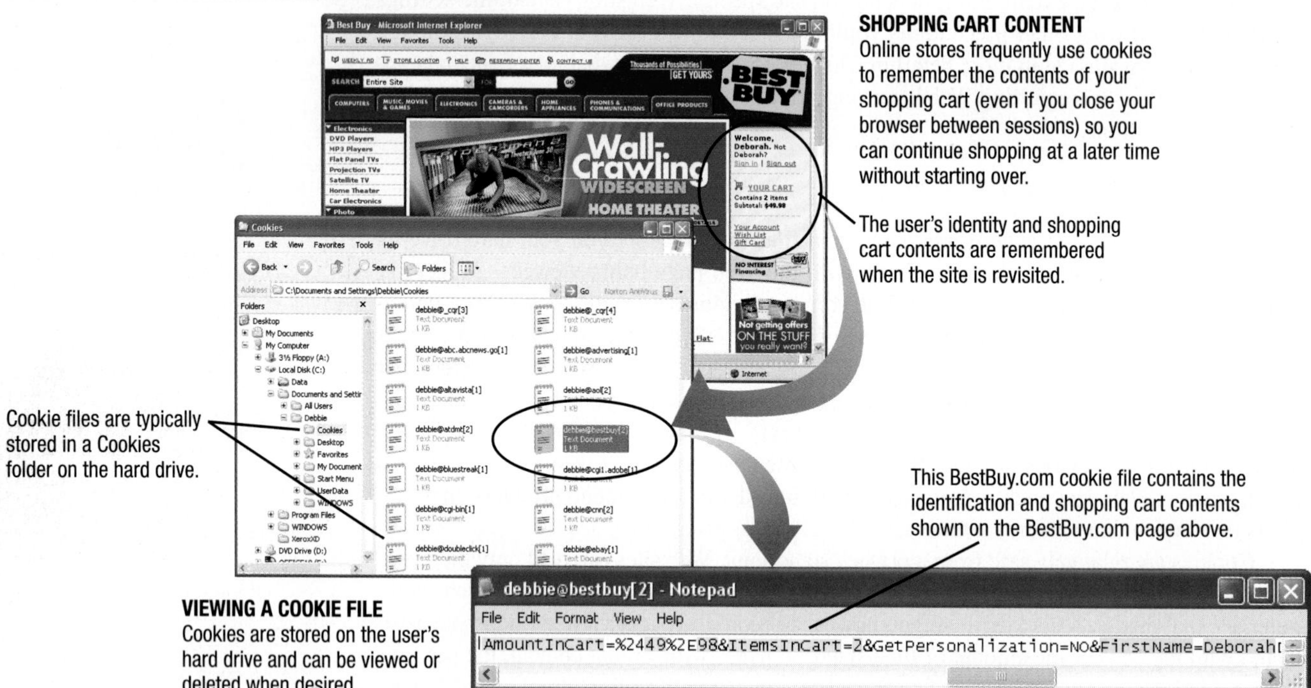

CUSTOMIZED CONTENT
Many Web sites use cookies to keep track of display preferences, such as the customized news, weather, stock quote, and TV listing information shown here for a Yahoo! user.
SHOPPING CART CONTENT
Online stores frequently use cookies to remember the contents of your shopping cart (even if you close your browser between sessions) so you can continue shopping at a later time without starting over.
The user's identity and shopping cart contents are remembered when the site is revisited.
Cookie files are typically stored in a Cookies folder on the hard drive.
This BestBuy.com cookie file contains the identification and shopping cart contents shown on the BestBuy.com page above.
VIEWING A COOKIE FILE
Cookies are stored on the user's hard drive and can be viewed or deleted when desired.
debbie@bestbuy[2] - Notepad
AmountInCart=%2449%2E98&ItemsInCart=2&GetPersonalization=NO&FirstName=Deborah

FIGURE 8-26
Cookies. Web site cookies are commonly used to remember customized settings and to facilitate online shopping.

Cookies are typically stored in a Cookies folder on each user's hard drive and can be looked at, if desired—although sometimes deciphering the information contained in a cookie file is difficult. The bottom part of Figure 8-26 shows the content of the cookie file generated by shopping at the BestBuy.com site. Notice that the cookie file contains information about both the shopping cart contents and the signed-in user.

Browser privacy settings can be changed to specify which type of cookies (if any) are allowed to be used, such as permitting the use of regular cookies, but not *third-party cookies* (cookies placed by companies, such as advertising firms who have placed ads on that page) or cookies using personally identifiable information (see Figure 8-27). Turning off cookies entirely might make some features—such as a shopping cart—on some Web sites inoperable. The *Medium High* privacy option in Internet Explorer is a widely used setting since it allows the use of regular cookies but blocks third-party cookies that use personally identifiable information without explicit permission. Both Internet Explorer and Netscape Navigator users who want more control over their cookies can choose to accept or decline cookies as they are encountered. Although this option interrupts your Web surfing frequently, it is interesting to see the cookies generated from each individual Web site. For example, the two cookie prompts shown in the bottom of Figure 8-27 were generated while visiting the BestBuy.com Web site. Although the first cookie request came from the BestBuy.com Web site directly, the second was a third-party cookie from Atlas DMT, an online marketing company. Another alternative for controlling cookies is to delete the cookie files stored on your hard drive periodically, either by using an option available through your Web browser or by finding the Cookie folder located on your hard drive and deleting its contents using your file management program.

Although many individuals are slowly becoming more comfortable with the use of cookies, increased use of targeted ads based on e-mail or Web site activities might raise consumer objections, similar to the outrage evoked by the *DoubleClick* fiasco several years ago. DoubleClick, an Internet advertising firm, began the practice of trying to track an individual's Web activity by using multiple cookies. Because DoubleClick had banner ads on literally thousands of different Web sites, that company was in the unique position of being able to place many cookies on a single user's hard drive—one for each site the user visited that contained a DoubleClick ad. DoubleClick then used all of the DoubleClick cookies located on that user's hard drive to get an idea of his or her overall Web activity. Although the data collected was not associated with the person's actual identity, DoubleClick subsequently bought a catalog marketing company and announced plans to merge Web-activity data collected in the future with the consumer data in the newly acquired marketing company database, in order to track customers' Web activity using their identities—and then to sell the information to others. A flood of privacy lawsuits were filed, such as the one by the privacy watchdog group *EPIC* (the *Electronic Privacy Information Center*), which eventually led DoubleClick to agree, in 2002, to obtain permission from consumers before combining any personally identifiable data with Web-surfing history.

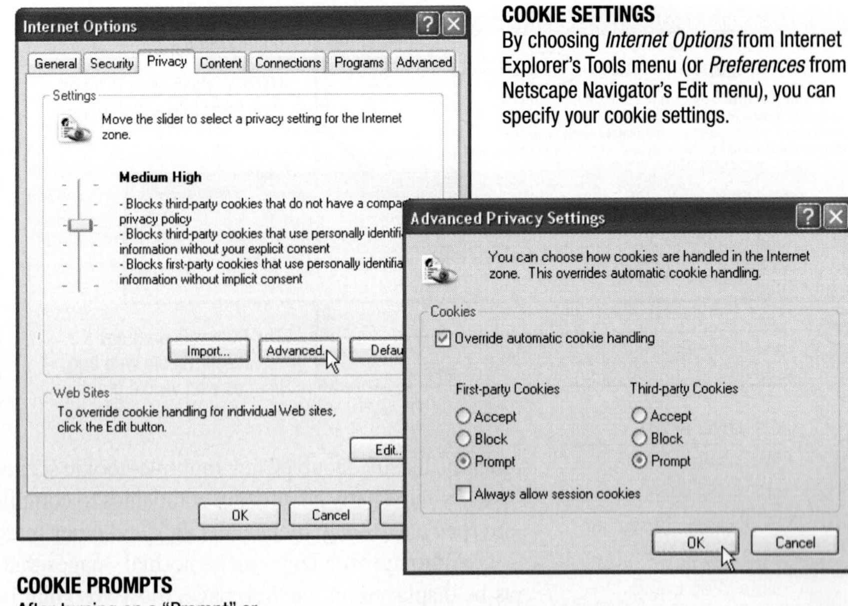

COOKIE SETTINGS
By choosing *Internet Options* from Internet Explorer's Tools menu (or *Preferences* from Netscape Navigator's Edit menu), you can specify your cookie settings.

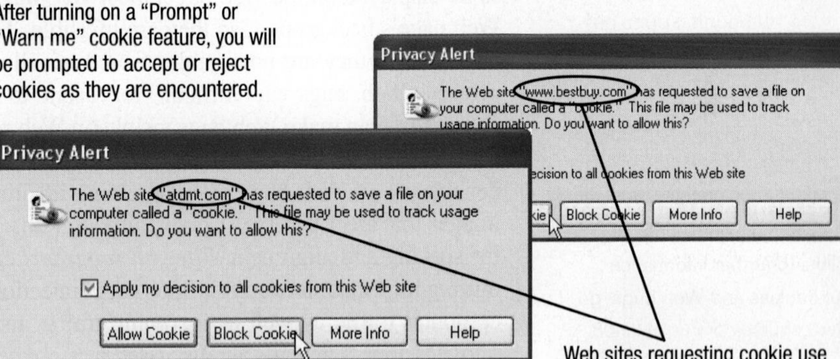

COOKIE PROMPTS
After turning on a "Prompt" or "Warn me" cookie feature, you will be prompted to accept or reject cookies as they are encountered.

FIGURE 8-27
Browser cookie management. The desired cookies settings can be specified in the browser settings.

In response to the DoubleClick controversy, the advertising industry formed the *Network Advertising Initiative* (*NAI*) and is hoping that voluntary compliance to online marketing standards can be used in lieu of legislation. The NAI works in conjunction with the Federal Trade Commission (FTC) to develop privacy standards for NAI members, which include DoubleClick and several other large Internet advertising companies. These standards detail under what conditions non-personally identifiable information can be merged with personally identifiable information, as well as require that consumers be given the choice to opt out from data collection entirely. However, as consumer concerns about Web privacy continue to grow, legislation is becoming more likely. In late 2003, the European Union adopted privacy regulations on electronic communications, including a ban on all commercial e-mail unless a recipient has asked for it, and set strict rules for the use of cookies. In the United States, there were several bills introduced in Congress in 2005 that addressed the use of personally identifiable information collection on Web sites, and a law in California that went into effect in mid-2004 sets requirements for all Web sites collecting personally identifiable information from California residents.

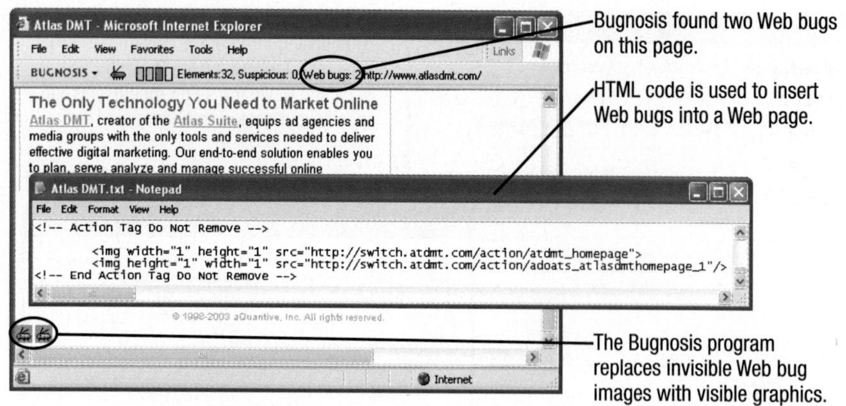

FIGURE 8-28
Web bugs. Some software, such as the Bugnosis program, is available to detect possible Web bugs, although it does not stop their functionality.

Web Bugs

A **Web bug** is usually a very small (often 1 pixel by 1 pixel) image on a Web page that transmits data about a Web page visitor back to the Web page's server. Web bugs are commonly used to gather usage statistics about a Web site, such as the number of visitors to the site, the most visited pages on the site, the time of each visit, and the Web browser used. Web bugs can also be used to retrieve and relay data stored in a cookie file, if the Web bug and cookie are both from the same Web site or advertising company. Consequently, like the DoubleClick multiple-cookie scenario previously discussed, Web bugs can be used by third-party advertising companies to compile data about individuals. In fact, Web bugs are used extensively by DoubleClick and other Internet advertising companies.

Although Web bugs can be normal images that are set up to transfer information, as well as be displayed on the Web page, most Web bug images are tiny and match the color of the Web page's background, so they are invisible. This is perhaps the biggest objection to Web bugs—since they are not visible, users typically are not aware of this potential invasion of privacy. Web bugs are difficult for users to identify, but special programs—such as *Bugnosis*—can make Web bugs visible on Web pages as you surf the Web (see Figure 8-28). Cookie management software can prevent the use of cookies by Web bugs, and some can hinder the use of Web bugs by suppressing all images of a specified dimension, such as all images that are 1 pixel by 1 pixel, although this also suppresses small invisible images used for spacing and alignment. *Firewall programs* can protect against *spyware* programs transmitting information over your Internet connection, since firewalls typically control outgoing computer traffic as well as incoming traffic and will notify the user of any unauthorized transmissions. Firewalls are discussed in more detail in Chapter 9.

FURTHER EXPLORATION

For links to further information about cookies and Web bugs, go to www.course.com/uc11/ch08

Spyware and Adware

Spyware is the term used for any software program that is installed without the user's knowledge and that secretly gathers information about the user and transmits it through his or her Internet connection—typically, to advertisers. Just as with cookies and Web bugs, the information gathered by the spyware software is usually not associated with a person's identity. Instead, it is typically used to provide advertisers with information to be used for marketing purposes, such as to help select advertisements to display on each person's PC. Like Web bugs, people are not normally aware when spyware is being used. Instead of being embedded into a Web page like a Web bug, however, spyware programs are installed—without the user's knowledge—on the user's computer. Spyware programs are usually installed secretly at the same time another program is installed, such as a program downloaded from a Web site or a P2P service. Spyware can also be used by unscrupulous individuals to retrieve personal data stored on your PC and is discussed in more detail in Chapter 9.

A related type of software is *adware*—free or low-cost software that is supported by onscreen advertising. Many free programs that can be downloaded from the Internet, such as the free version of the *NetZero* e-mail program, include some type of adware, which results in onscreen advertising. The difference between spyware and adware is that adware

>**Web bug.** A very small (usually invisible) image on a Web page that transmits data about the Web page visitor to a Web server.

typically does not gather information and relay it to others via the Internet (although it can), and it is not installed without the user's consent. Adware might, however, be installed without the user's direct knowledge, since many users do not read licensing agreements before clicking OK to install a new program. When this occurs with a program that contains adware, the adware components are installed without the user's direct knowledge.

Both spyware and adware can be annoying and use up valuable system resources. In addition, privacy advocates object to spyware because it secretly collects and transmits data about individuals to others, and it can bog down a user's Internet connection without the user's knowledge.

E-Mail Privacy

Many people mistakenly believe that the e-mail they send and receive is private and will never be read by anyone other than the intended recipient. Since it is transmitted over public media, however, only *encrypted* (electronically scrambled) e-mail can be transmitted safely, as discussed in Chapter 9. Although unlikely to happen to your personal e-mail, *nonencrypted* e-mail can be intercepted and read by someone else. Consequently, from a privacy standpoint, a nonencrypted e-mail message should be viewed more like a postcard than a letter (see Figure 8-29).

It is also important to realize that your employer and your ISP have access to the e-mail you send through those organizations, such as to scan incoming e-mail for spam filtering and virus protection, as well as for employee monitoring purposes. Businesses and ISPs typically also *archive* (keep copies of) e-mail messages that travel through their servers and are required to comply with subpoenas from law enforcement agencies for archived e-mail messages.

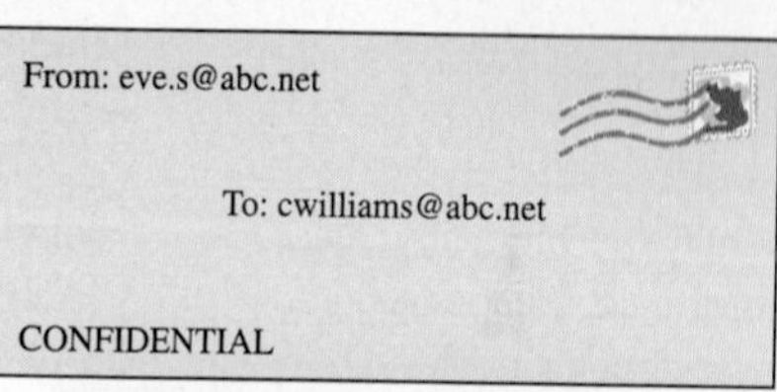

Chris,
The meeting is Monday at 2 pm. Please bring all related personnel files detailing the anticipated firing of Joe D.
Eve
To: cwilliams@abc.net
From: eve.s@abc.net
REGULAR (NONENCRYPTED E-MAIL) = POSTCARD
From: eve.s@abc.net
To: cwilliams@abc.net
CONFIDENTIAL
ENCRYPTED E-MAIL = SEALED LETTER

FIGURE 8-29
You cannot assume e-mail messages are private, unless they are encrypted.

THE FUTURE OF THE INTERNET

The Internet has changed a great deal since its inception. From only four supercomputers, it has evolved into a vast network connecting virtually every type of computer. The use of the Internet has changed dramatically, as well. As the structure of the Internet evolves and improves, it can support new types of activities. New types of applications also drive the technological improvements necessary to support them.

The exact composition of the Internet of the future is anyone's guess. It will likely be a very high-speed optical network with virtually unlimited bandwidth. It will be accessed by the PC of the day, which will probably be much smaller and less obtrusive than the standard PC today—possibly built directly into desks, refrigerators, and other objects, or carried around on your body or as some type of portable device. The primary interface will likely be the voice, and most network connections will be wireless.

Chances are the Internet will continue to be used for an ever-growing number of day-to-day activities, such as shopping, making voice or video phone calls, controlling home appliances, ordering and downloading TV shows or movies, ordering groceries, paying bills, and telecommuting. It will also continue to be widely used for business purposes, and high bandwidth connections will allow a much higher level of real-time video communications, resulting in even more use of telecommuting, videoconferencing, and home-based offices. A universal payment system for micropayments is likely to facilitate paying small fees for Web content. Ideally, all of an individual's micropayments will be combined into a single monthly bill.

This is an exciting time for the Internet. It is already firmly embedded in our society, and it will be exciting to see what becomes of all the breathtaking new applications and technological improvements on the horizon and how the Internet will continue to evolve.

SUMMARY

EVOLUTION OF THE INTERNET

Chapter Objective 1: Discuss how the Internet evolved and what it is like today.

The origins of the **Internet**—a worldwide collection of interconnected networks that is accessed by millions of people daily—date back to the late 1960s. At its start and throughout its early years, the Internet was called **ARPANET**. It was not until the development of graphical user interfaces and the **World Wide Web** that public interest in the Internet began to soar. Most companies have Web sites today and consider the Web to be an indispensable business tool. While the Web is a very important and widely used Internet resource, it is not the only one. Over the years *protocols* have been developed to download files, send e-mail messages, and other tasks, in addition to using Web pages. Today, the term *Internet* has become a household word and, in many ways, has redefined how people think about computers and communications. The next significant improvement to the Internet infrastructure may be the result of projects such as *Internet2* and *Next Generation Internet (NGI)*.

Chapter Objective 2: Identify the various types of individuals, companies, and organizations involved in the Internet community and explain their purposes.

The Internet community is made up of individual *users*; companies, such as **Internet service providers (ISPs)**, **Internet content providers**, **application service providers (ASPs)**, *infrastructure companies*, and a variety of software and hardware companies; the government; and other organizations. Virtually anyone with a computer with communications capability can be part of the Internet, either as a user or supplier of information or services. **Web services** are self-contained business functions that operate over the Internet.

Because the Internet is so unique in the history of the world—and it remains a relatively new phenomenon—several widespread myths about it have surfaced. Three such myths are that the Internet is free, that it is controlled by some central body, and that it is synonymous with the World Wide Web.

GETTING SET UP TO USE THE INTERNET

Chapter Objective 3: Describe device and connection options for connecting to the Internet, as well as some considerations to keep in mind when selecting an ISP.

When preparing to become connected to the Internet, you need to decide which type of device (PC, *Internet appliance*, or mobile device) to use, which type of connection—**dial-up connection** (**conventional dial-up** or **ISDN Internet access**) or **direct connection** (through a **T1 line**, **cable**, **DSL**, **satellite**, **fixed wireless**, or **mobile wireless Internet access**, or via a *hotspot*)—to use, and which specific Internet service provider to use. Once all these decisions are made, you can acquire the proper hardware and software and set up your system for Internet access.

SEARCHING THE INTERNET

Chapter Objective 4: Understand how to effectively search for information on the Internet and how to properly cite Internet resources.

Search sites—Web sites that enable users to search for and find information on the Internet—typically locate pages using a **keyword search** (in which the user specifies **keywords** for the desired information) or a **directory search** (in which the user selects categories corresponding to the desired information). Both types of searches use a *search database* that contains information about pages on the Web and a **search engine** to retrieve the list of matching Web pages from the database. Search site databases are generally maintained by automated *spider* programs; directory databases are typically maintained by human editors. *Metasearch engines* use multiple search engines, some search sites are *natural language* sites, and many search sites use a combination of search options.

There are a variety of search strategies that can be used, including typing phrases instead of single keywords; using *Boolean operators*; trying the search at multiple search sites; and using *synonyms*, *variant word forms*, *wildcards*, and *field searches*. Once a list of links to Web pages matching the search criteria is displayed, the hits need to be evaluated for their relevancy. If the information found on a Web page is used in a paper, report, or other original document, the source should be credited appropriately.

BEYOND BROWSING AND E-MAIL

The Internet can be used for many different types of activities besides basic Web browsing and e-mail exchange. Other common types of online communications tools include **discussion groups** (where people post messages on a particular topic for others to read and respond to), **chat rooms** (online locations where multiple users can carry on real-time typed conversations), **instant messaging (IM)** (a form of private chat in which messages are sent in real time to online "buddies"), **videoconferencing** (real-time meetings taking place online using video cameras and microphones for participants to see and hear each other), and **Voice over Internet Protocol (VoIP)**, which refers to making voice telephone calls over the Internet.

Chapter Objective 5: List several useful things that can be done using the Internet, in addition to basic Web browsing and e-mail.

Common Web activities for individuals include a variety of consumer *e-commerce* activities, such as **online shopping**, **online auctions**, **online banking**, and **online investing**. When performing any type of financial transaction over the Internet, it is very important to use only *secure* Web pages.

Online entertainment applications include downloading *MP3* files and other types of **online music**, *interactive TV* and **video-on-demand (VOD)**, **online gaming**, and **e-books**. **Peer-to-peer (P2P) file sharing** is also commonly used to exchange entertainment media. A wide variety of news, reference, government, product, and corporate information is available via the Web as well. News, reference, and search tools are commonly found on **portal** Web pages. **Web-based training (WBT)**, **distance learning**, *online testing*, **blogs**, **wikis**, and **e-portfolios** are commonly used *online education* applications.

CENSORSHIP AND PRIVACY ISSUES

Among the most important societal issues relating to the Internet are censorship and *privacy*. Web content is not censored as a whole, but **Internet filtering** can be used by parents, employers, educators, and anyone wishing to prevent access to sites they deem objectionable on computers for which they have control. *Privacy* is a big concern for individuals, particularly as it relates to their Web activity. **Cookies** are typically used by Web sites to save customized settings for that site and can also be used for advertising purposes. Other items of possible concern are **Web bugs** and *spyware*. Unless an e-mail message is *encrypted*, it should not be assumed to be completely private.

Chapter Objective 6: Discuss censorship and privacy, and how they are related to Internet use.

THE FUTURE OF THE INTERNET

The Internet has evolved remarkably over the past few decades and will, no doubt, evolve in new ways that most people cannot even dream of. The future Internet will likely be high-speed and accessed by wireless devices and appliances. Multimedia applications, such as real-time video communications and TV on demand, will likely be a reality in the near future.

Chapter Objective 7: Describe the possible format, structure, and use of the Internet in the future.

REVIEW ACTIVITIES

KEY TERM MATCHING

Instructions: Match each key term on the left with the definition on the right that best describes it.

a. cookie

b. dial-up connection

c. direct connection

d. distance learning

e. Internet

f. keyword

g. search engine

h. video-on-demand (VOD)

i. Web bug

j. World Wide Web

1. ______ A learning environment in which the student is physically located away from the instructor and other students; commonly, instruction and communications take place via the Internet.

2. ______ An always-on type of Internet connection in which the PC or other device is continually connected to the Internet.

3. ______ A small file stored on a user's hard drive by a Web server; commonly used to identify personal preferences and settings for that user.

4. ______ A software program used by a search site to retrieve matching Web pages from a search database.

5. ______ A type of Internet connection in which the PC or other device must dial up and connect to a service provider's computer via telephone lines before being connected to the Internet.

6. ______ A very small (usually invisible) image on a Web page that transmits data about the Web page visitor to a Web server.

7. ______ A word typed in a search box on a search site to locate information on the Internet.

8. ______ The collection of Web pages available through the Internet.

9. ______ The largest and most well-known computer network, linking millions of computers all over the world.

10. ______ The process of downloading movies and televisions shows, on demand, via the Internet.

SELF-QUIZ

Instructions: Circle **T** if the statement is true, **F** if the statement is false, or write the best answer in the space provided. **Answers to the self-quiz are located in the References and Resources Guide at the end of the book.**

1. T F When the Internet was first developed, it was called Mosaic.

2. T F On the Internet, an *access provider* and a *content provider* are essentially the same thing.

3. T F With a direct connection, you need only open your browser to start your Internet session.

4. T F A locked padlock on the browser's status bar indicates that the Web page currently being viewed is secure.

5. T F With peer-to-peer (P2P) file sharing, individuals upload files to a central server, and then others can download them from that server.

6. ______ is a type of always-on broadband Internet service that transmits data over standard telephone lines.

7. With a(n) ______ search, keywords are typed into the search box; with a(n) ______ search, users select categories to find matching Web pages.

8. ______ is a form of private chat set up to allow users to easily and quickly exchange real-time typed messages with the individuals they specify.

9. With a(n) ______, people bid on products over the Internet, and the highest bidder purchases the item.

10. Match each Internet application with its possible situation and write the corresponding number in the blank to the left of each situation.

a. ________ To communicate with a friend in a different state.
b. ________ To rent a movie without leaving your home.
c. ________ To pay only as much as you specify for an item purchased through the Internet.
d. ________ To pay a bill without writing a check.
e. ________ To post your original papers, résumé, and other original materials created for school classes.
f. ________ To find Web pages containing information about growing your own Bonsai trees.

1. Online banking
2. E-mail
3. Online auction
4. Internet searching
5. Video-on-demand (VOD)
6. E-portfolio

EXERCISES

1. Match each type of Internet access with its description and write the corresponding number in the blank to the left of each description.

a. ________ A fast type of Internet access via standard phone lines; does not tie up your phone.
b. ________ The most widely used type of home broadband connection; does not use standard phone lines.
c. ________ Accesses the Internet via standard phone lines and ties up your phone; the maximum speed is 56 Kbps.
d. ________ Accesses the Internet wirelessly via a handheld PC or mobile device.
e. ________ Requires a transceiver and a clear view of the southern sky.
f. ________ Accesses the Internet via standard phone lines and does not tie up your phone; the maximum speed is 128 Kbps.

1. Conventional dial-up
2. ISDN
3. DSL
4. Cable
5. Satellite
6. Mobile wireless

2. What would each of the following searches look for?

a. hot AND dogs ________________________________
b. snorkel* ________________________________
c. text:"Internet privacy" domain:gov ________________________________

3. List three different sets of keywords that could be used to search for information on how to maintain a trumpet.

4. Explain the difference between a blog, a wiki, and a podcast.

5. List one advantage and one disadvantage of the use of Web site cookies.

DISCUSSION QUESTION

Although slow to embrace new technology, courtrooms today are becoming high-tech. For example, videoconferencing systems that allow defendants and witnesses to participate in proceedings from remote locations are becoming more common. Allowing defendants to participate via teleconferencing from the jail facility saves travel time and expense, as well as eliminates any risk of flight. Remote testimony from witnesses can save both time and money. But could having defendants and witnesses participate remotely affect the jury's perspective? If the videoconference takes place via the Internet, can it be assured that proceedings are confidential? Do you think the benefits of these systems outweigh any potential disadvantages? Can you think of other "virtual" courtroom applications or tools that might be a reality in the future? Do you think they should become a reality?

PROJECTS

HOT TOPICS

1. **Blogs** Short for *Web log*, a *blog* is a Web page that serves as a publicly accessible personal journal for an individual. Blogs have been around for several years but could not be implemented on a wide scale because creating and publishing Web pages was fairly complicated; today, *blog tools* make it much simpler to update a blog on a regular basis (many blogs are updated daily). Consequently, there has been a tremendous increase in the use of blogs for personal expression, as well as for work-related collaborations and in writing classes.

   For this project, investigate blogs. By searching a news site (such as MSNBC.com or CNN.com) or by using a search site (such as Google.com), find at least two blogs and review them. What types of information is the user sharing? Why do you think he or she prefers to put this information on the Web instead of in a private written journal? Did the blogs you found belong to a private individual, a well-known person, or an individual representing an organization? Would you want to have your own blog? Why or why not? Do you think blog use will continue to grow? Why or why not? At the conclusion of your research, prepare a one-page summary of your findings and submit it to your instructor.

SHORT ANSWER/ RESEARCH

2. **Auction Pirates** Pirated software being sold via online auctions is reaching epidemic proportions. One estimate by the Software and Information Industry Association was that over 90% of all software sold through online auctions is pirated. Pirated movies are prevalent as well, often available over the Internet before they are released on DVD—sometimes even before they are released worldwide in the theater.

   For this project, consider the following scenario: While on an online auction site, you run across what looks like a great deal on a DVD movie that was just in the movie theater a few months ago. You win the item and, after receiving and cashing your personal check, the seller ships your DVD. When it arrives, the return address is in Thailand, and the text on the cover of the DVD is not English, so you realize that you have bought an Asian import DVD. When you contact the seller, he says that he buys his DVDs in the store in his country, so they cannot be bootleg copies. Next, research the legality of selling DVDs in the United States that are produced in other countries. If a DVD is available for retail sale in a foreign country, does that mean it can be bought there by an individual and then brought into the United States or imported for resale? Is there any way to check whether or not a DVD bought via an online auction is legitimate? Finally, consider the scenario explained above again and determine how this problem might have been avoided in the first place, and what (if anything) could be done after the fact, if you were not happy with your purchase. At the conclusion of your research, submit your findings and opinions to your instructor in the form of a short paper, no more than two pages in length.

3. **Online Travel Planning** Planning and booking travel arrangements online is a very popular Internet activity today. There are a number of sites that claim to give discount rates on airplane tickets, hotel rooms, rental cars, and more. Some sites also offer information about weather, places of interest, and more to help you plan your vacation.

   For this project, review two popular travel sites, such as Expedia.com and Travelocity.com, to see what services they offer and how easy, or difficult, it is to locate the information needed to plan and book a vacation via those sites. Select a destination and use the search facility located on one of the travel sites to obtain a quote for a particular flight on a particular day. Next, go to the Web site for the airline of the flight you were just quoted and use the site to obtain a quote for the same flight. Is there a difference in price or flight availability? Could you make a reservation online through both sites? Would you feel comfortable booking a vacation yourself online, or are there other services that a travel agent could provide that you feel would be beneficial? Do you think these sites are most appropriate for making business travel plans or vacation plans, or are they suited to either? At the conclusion of your research, prepare a one-page summary of your findings and submit it to your instructor.

HANDS ON

4. **Wi-Fi Hotspots** As discussed in the chapter, there are an increasing number of public locations offering Wi-Fi hotspots available for public use.

   For this project, find at least one location in your local area that offers public Wi-Fi access (possibilities include your public library; retail locations such as McDonald's, Starbucks, and Borders; and hotspots set up by parks and other public locations). Once you have identified a public hotspot, either visit the location or call the provider on the phone to find out the following information.

   a. Is there a fee to use the hotspot? If so, do you have to subscribe on a regular basis, or can you pay only when you want to use the hotspot? Where and how is payment made?

   b. Do you need any special software to access the hotspot? Do you need to be assigned a username or WEP (Wired Equivalent Privacy), WPA (Wi-Fi Protected Access), or WPA 2 key before you can use the service?

   At the conclusion of your research, submit your findings to your instructor in the form of a short summary.

5. **Web Searching** As discussed in the chapter, search sites can be used to find Web pages containing specific information, and there are strategies that can be used to make Web searching an efficient and useful experience.

   For this project, perform the following search tasks, answering the questions or printing the information as instructed below. After you have completed all four tasks, submit your results and printouts to your instructor. (Note: Some of the answers will vary from student to student.)

   a. Go to the Google search site located at www.google.com and Search for *rules*. How many pages were found? What is the name of the first page in the list of hits?

   b. Next, search for *backgammon rules*. How many pages were found? Click on the first page and look for a picture of how a backgammon board is initially set up. When you find one, print the page. If you cannot find one on that site, select different pages in the list of hits or perform another search (such as an image search) until you find the proper illustration, and then print the page.

   c. Perform a new search by clicking the link at the top of the Google page to go to the Advanced Search option. Use the form fields to perform a search for pages that contain all the words *hiking trails Sierra*, do not contain the word *horse*, and have the domain *.gov*. After the list of Web pages matching your search criteria is displayed, record the actual search phrase that is now listed in the search box along with the name and URL of the first page displayed in the list of hits.

   d. Use Google to search for a Web site that includes a telephone directory. Go to that site and supply the necessary information to search for yourself in the telephone directory. (If you are not currently listed in the phone book, search for a family member or friend that you know has a listed number.) Print the page displaying the requested information.

   At the conclusion of this task, submit your answers and printed pages to your instructor.

RITING ABOUT OMPUTERS

6. **Online Job Hunting** There are a number of Web sites dedicated to online career planning, posting and reviewing résumés and job announcements, listing average salary information for various positions, and other useful job-hunting tools.

For this project, visit at least two career-oriented Web sites (such as Monster.com or CareerBuilder.com) and review the types of information and services available from the perspective of both a job seeker and an employer. Are there fees for any of the services? If you post a résumé, is it available for anyone to see, or are there restrictions on access? When it comes time for you to look for a new job, would you want to use one of these sites? Are the sites useful from an employer's perspective? List any advantages and disadvantages you can think of for using one of these sites to find a new job. Submit your findings and opinions to your instructor in the form of a short paper, not more than two pages in length.

PRESENTATION/ DEMONSTRATION

7. **Free and Low-Cost Internet** There are several free and low-cost ($5 to $10 per month) ISPs. For example, Juno and NetZero (www.juno.com or www.netzero.net) offer users 10 hours of free dial-up access per month, and 550Access.com offers unlimited dial-up service for $5.50 per month.

For this project, research Juno or NetZero plus one other free or low-cost ISP and investigate their services. Do any of these offer unlimited Internet access for free? Is there still a 10-hour limit with Juno/NetZero? If so, what happens if you go over that limit? Are there any tradeoffs for using these free or low-cost ISPs? If you were looking for a dial-up provider, would you consider using either of your selected ISPs? Why or why not? Would these services be useful for other applications, such as for business travelers or for back up service for broadband subscribers? Share your findings and opinions with the class in the form of a short presentation. The presentation should not exceed 10 minutes and should make use of one or more presentation aids, such as the chalkboard, handouts, overhead transparencies, or a computer-based slide presentation (your instructor may provide additional requirements). You may also be asked to submit a summary of the presentation to your instructor.

GROUP DISCUSSION

8. **Rural Broadband** Citizens who live in rural areas typically have less access to broadband Internet than those in more highly populated areas. Maryland's Speaker of the House Casper R. Taylor views this as the real digital divide. Without broadband, he believes that "our kids are not going to have the advantage of urbanized society going into the future if we're disconnected from the rest of the world...If we don't accomplish this, we are clearly creating a second-class society." There are differing opinions regarding the importance of broadband Internet and whose responsibility it is to provide it. If a region has only 56K dial-up service, does that really put it at a disadvantage? Is the digital divide more about separating those who have access to technology, such as the Internet, and those who do not, or is it about the quality of that technology? What about the government's role—should it provide the necessary infrastructure to ensure an appropriate level of Internet access to all U.S. citizens? If not, how will the digital divide within the United States be eliminated? Will it ever be eliminated?

For this project, form an opinion of the necessity of broadband Internet and the role of the government (if any) in providing broadband Internet access to its citizens and be prepared to discuss your position (in class, via an online class discussion group, or in a class chat room, depending on your instructor's directions). You may also be asked to write a short paper expressing your opinion.

WEB ACTIVITIES

The *Understanding Computers* Web site located at **www.course.com/uc11** features many resources to help reinforce your understanding of the chapter content and help you prepare for exams. Your instructor may also assign specific activities to be completed that will count toward your final grade in the course.

Instructions: Go to **www.course.com/uc11/ch08** to work the following online activities.

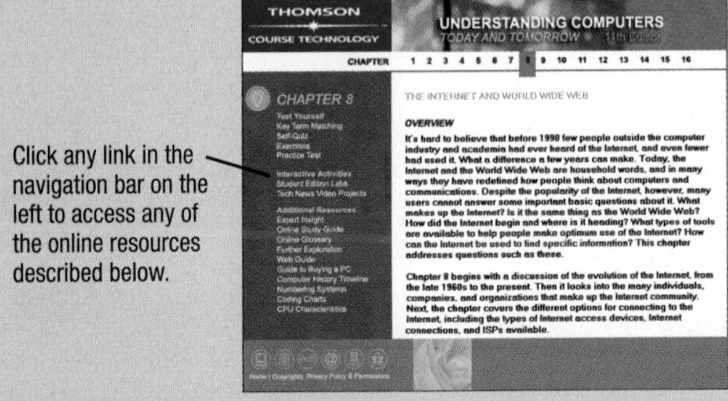
Click any link in the navigation bar on the left to access any of the online resources described below.
THOMSON
COURSE TECHNOLOGY
UNDERSTANDING COMPUTERS
TODAY AND TOMORROW
CHAPTER 8
THE INTERNET AND WORLD WIDE WEB
OVERVIEW

INTERACTIVE ACTIVITIES

1. **Crossword Puzzle** Practice your knowledge of the key terms in Chapter 8 by completing the interactive Crossword Puzzle.
2. **Tech News Video Project** Watch the **"Free Wi-Fi Blankets San Francisco"** video clip that takes a look at the "Bay Area Wireless Network"—a network of Wi-Fi access points that provides free Internet access to the surrounding areas. After watching the video online, complete the corresponding project.
3. **Student Edition Labs** Reinforce the concepts you have learned in this chapter by working through the interactive **Connecting to the Internet** and **Getting the Most Out of the Internet** labs.

Student Edition Labs

TEST YOURSELF

1. **Key Term Matching** Test your knowledge of selected chapter key terms by matching the terms with their definitions.
2. **Self-Quiz** Test your retention of chapter concepts by taking the Self-Quiz.
3. **Exercises** Work these short exercises to review the concepts and terms covered in the chapter.
4. **Practice Test** Test how ready you are for an upcoming exam by completing the online Practice Test.

STUDY TOOLS/ ADDITIONAL RESOURCES

The Understanding Computers Web site has a wide range of additional resources, including an **Online Study Guide** (containing study tips, a chapter outline with room to add your own notes, and a chapter checklist of the activities to complete when the chapter is covered in class and when you are preparing for a test) and an **Online Glossary** for each chapter; **Further Exploration** links; a **Web Guide**, a **Guide to Buying a PC**, and a **Computer History Timeline**; more information about **Numbering Systems**, **Coding Charts**, and **CPU Characteristics**; and much, much more!

CHAPTER 9 Network and Internet Security

OUTLINE

LEARNING OBJECTIVES

After completing this chapter, you will be able to:

1. Explain why computer users should be concerned about network and Internet security.
2. List several examples of unauthorized access, unauthorized use, and computer sabotage.
3. Explain what risks access control systems, firewalls, antivirus software, and encryption protect against.
4. Discuss online theft, identity theft, Internet scams, spoofing, phishing, and other types of dot cons.
5. Detail steps an individual can take to protect against online theft, identity theft, Internet scams, spoofing, phishing, and other types of dot cons.
6. Identify personal safety risks associated with Internet use.
7. List steps individuals can take when using the Internet to safeguard their personal safety.
8. Name several laws related to network and Internet security

OVERVIEW

The increased use of networks and the Internet helps users finish many tasks quickly and efficiently and adds convenience to many people's lives. However, there is a downside, as well. As more and more personal and business data is stored on computer networks, the risks and consequences of unauthorized computer access, theft, fraud, and other types of computer crime increase; so do the chances of data loss due to crime or employee misconduct. Some online activities can even put your personal safety at risk, if you are not careful.

This chapter looks at a variety of security concerns stemming from the use of computer networks in our society, including topics such as unauthorized access and use, computer viruses and other types of sabotage, and online theft and fraud. Safeguards for each of these concerns are also covered, with an explanation of precautions that can be taken to reduce the risk of experiencing problems related to these security concerns. Personal safety issues related to the Internet are also discussed, and the chapter closes with a look at legislation related to network and Internet security. ■

WHY BE CONCERNED ABOUT NETWORK AND INTERNET SECURITY?

From a *computer virus* making your PC function abnormally, to a *hacker* using your personal information to make fraudulent purchases, to someone harassing you online in a discussion group, a variety of security concerns related to computer networks and the Internet abound. Many Internet security concerns today can be categorized as **computer crimes**. Computer crime—sometimes referred to as *cybercrime*—includes any illegal act involving a computer. Many computer crimes involve breaking through the security of a network; others include theft of financial assets or information. Still other computer crimes involve manipulating data, such as grades, for personal advantage. Increasingly, computer crimes involve acts of sabotage, such as releasing a computer virus or shutting down a Web server. Regardless of its form, computer crime is an important security concern today.

All computer users should be aware of the security concerns surrounding computer network and Internet use, including the risks and the associated consequences, and they should take appropriate precautions. In some cases, such as when a *spyware program* changes your browser's home page, the consequence may be just an annoyance. In other cases, such as when someone steals your identity and purchases items using your name or credit card number, the consequences are much more serious. The most common types of security concerns related to network and Internet use, along with some precautions users can take to reduce the risks associated with these concerns, are discussed throughout the remainder of this chapter.

>**Computer crime.** Any illegal act involving a computer.

UNAUTHORIZED ACCESS, UNAUTHORIZED USE, AND COMPUTER SABOTAGE

Unauthorized access occurs whenever an individual gains access to a computer, network, file, or other resource without permission. **Unauthorized use** involves using a computer resource for unauthorized activities. Unauthorized use can occur even if the user is authorized to access that computer or network but is not authorized for that particular activity. For instance, while a student may be authorized to access the Internet via a campus computer lab, some use—such as viewing pornography—may be deemed off-limits. If so, viewing that content from a school computer would be considered unauthorized use. For employees of some companies, checking personal e-mail at work might be classified as unauthorized use.

Unauthorized access and many types of unauthorized use are criminal offenses in the United States and other countries and can be committed by both *insiders* (people who work for the company against which the crime occurred) and *outsiders* (people who do not work for that company). In fact, according to the 2005 "Computer Crime and Security Survey" performed by the Computer Security Institute and the FBI, insiders commit computer crimes about as often as outsiders, although companies may be reluctant to press charges against employees fearing bad publicity and loss of public confidence. Whether or not a specific act constitutes unauthorized use or is illegal depends on the circumstances, as well as the specific company or institution involved. To explain acceptable computer use to their employees, students, or other users, many organizations and educational institutions publish guidelines for behavior. These rules are frequently called *codes of conduct* (see Figure 9-1). Codes of conduct typically address prohibited activities, such as installing personal software on the network, violating copyright laws, causing harm to the PC and network, and snooping in other people's files.

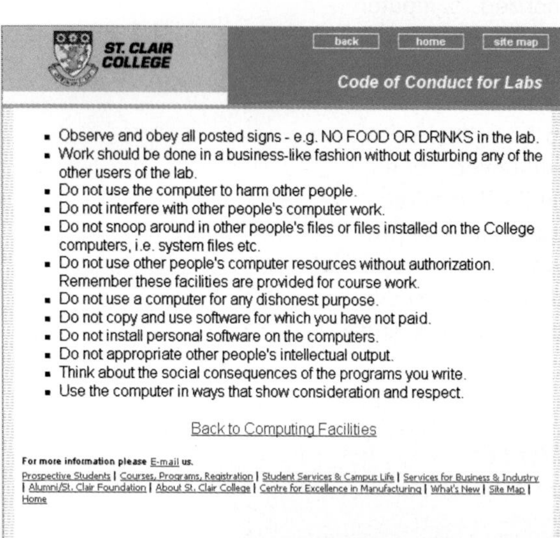

COLLEGE CODE OF CONDUCT
This code, posted on the campus Web site, notifies students of allowable and off-limit actions regarding campus computer lab use.

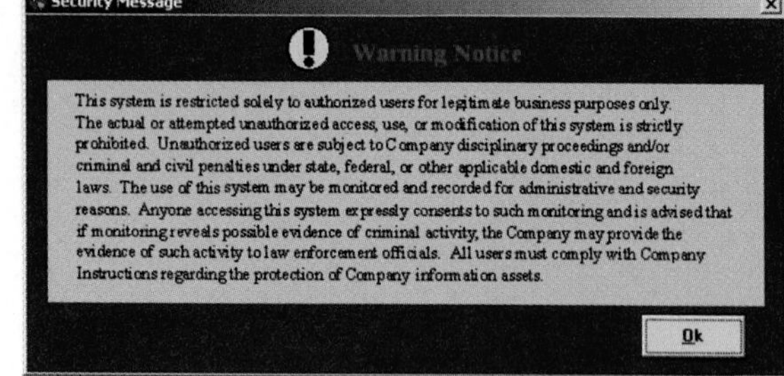

BUSINESS CODE OF CONDUCT
This code, displayed whenever an employee logs on to the company network, notifies employees that the network can be used for legitimate business purposes only.

FIGURE 9-1
Sample codes of conduct.

Hacking

Hacking refers to the act of breaking into another computer system. The person doing the hacking is called a *hacker*. By definition, hacking involves unauthorized access and is illegal. An exception is authorized hacking, such as *professional hacking* that takes place at the request of an organization to test the security of its system (these individuals are sometimes referred to as *white hat hackers* to differentiate them from *black hat hackers* who break the law) and hacking into computers set up (usually by hacker organizations) specifically to enable hackers to practice their skills legally. Unless authorized, hacking in the United

>**Unauthorized access.** Gaining access to a computer, network, file, or other resource without permission. >**Unauthorized use.** Using a computer resource for unapproved activities. >**Hacking.** Using a computer to break into another computer system.

States and many other countries is a crime and is becoming more vigorously prosecuted. The 2001 *USA Patriot Act* expands the government's authority to prosecute hacking activities and increases the penalties for unauthorized hacks.

Often, the motivation for hacking is to steal information, sabotage a computer system, or perform some other type of illegal act. The recent rash of security breaches of credit card numbers and cardholder information shows that the theft of data is a growing trend. For instance, about 40 million credit card numbers were stolen from the third-party credit card payment processor CardSystems Solutions in 2005—the largest reported data breach to date. Another growing trend is to hack into a PC and "hijack" it for use in an illegal or unethical act, such as generating spam or hosting pornographic Web sites.

Sometimes hackers break into a system just to prove their computer expertise, to expand their knowledge, or to bring attention to a social cause. One example is the collection of attacks in 2002 by two hackers calling themselves the *Deceptive Duo*. These two individuals broke into secured databases (including an airlines database containing flight schedules and passenger manifests, a bank database, and a NASA employee database) and published selected information to Web pages belonging to a variety of government agencies to prove that the databases had been accessed. In their explanation regarding the motivation for the attack, the Deceptive Duo claimed that they hacked into the secure systems in the interest of national security, to bring attention to these systems' vulnerabilities. Both pleaded guilty and were sentenced in 2005—one to four months in prison and three years of probation; the other to two years of probation. They also had to pay restitution—a total of just over $100,000. Regardless of the motivation, unauthorized hacking is illegal.

In addition to the threat toward individuals and businesses, hacking is considered a very serious threat to our nation's security. With the increased number of computers and systems online and with the abilities of hackers continually improving, some experts believe the risk of *cyberterrorism*—in which terrorists launch attacks via the Internet—has increased significantly. In response to this possibility, U.S. White House technology adviser Richard Clarke announced in early 2002 that the United States "reserves the right to respond in any way appropriate" to Internet warfare, including military action against cyberterrorists, and the government released the report "The National Strategy to Secure Cyberspace" in 2003. Current concerns include attacks against the computers controlling such vital systems as the nation's power grids, banks, and water filtration facilities, as well as computers related to national defense. And attacks on Defense Department computers have been steadily increasing. There were almost 75,000 incidents recorded in 2004—almost twice as many as in 2002. The United States continues to show its commitment to protecting government systems against cyberattacks—the budget in 2006 alone for the National Cyber Security Division (NCSD) of the Department of Homeland Security (DHS) is over $70 million.

The general public tends to use the term *hacker* to refer to any type of computer break-in regardless of what activities take place after the security breach. However, many hackers differentiate between types of hacking, and they prefer the term *cracker* when referring to individuals who break into systems to be destructive or for material gain.

Wi-Fi Hacking

While in the past hacking took place primarily via telephone lines or the Internet, it is common today for hackers to also gain access to a computer via a wireless—such as a Wi-Fi (802.11)—network. It is easier to hack into a wireless network than a wired network because it is possible to gain access just by being within about 300 feet of a wireless access point, unless the access point is sufficiently protected. For instance, in 2004 two men allegedly hacked into the Wi-Fi network belonging to a Lowe's Home Improvement store in Michigan and stole several customer credit card numbers. The men were charged with violating the *Computer Fraud and Abuse Act*—the main federal law regarding computer crime—and one has been sentenced to nine years in federal prison.

Although security features are built into Wi-Fi hardware, they are typically not turned on by default. As a result, many wireless networks belonging to businesses and individuals—some estimates put the number as high as 70% of all Wi-Fi networks—are left unsecured. This leaves the transmissions sent by individuals, the company, and customers (such as individuals using a hotspot's Wi-Fi service or hotel guests using the hotel's complementary Wi-Fi Internet access) open to interception. Improvements to the Wi-Fi standards are expected to provide increased security capabilities in the future; one significant improvement recommended by some security experts would be if hardware manufacturers begin enabling security features on Wi-Fi hardware by default so users would have to act to disable the features, instead of the other way around. Despite these potential improvements in the future, however, individuals and businesses with wireless networks should realize that wireless networks are inherently less secure than wired networks since data travels through the air instead of through a physical transmission medium, and they should be especially vigilant in protecting access to those networks.

War Driving

Accessing someone else's Wi-Fi network to gain free access to the Internet is called **war driving**. A form of "bandwidth stealing," war driving is usually accomplished by driving around neighborhoods in a car with a portable computer and appropriate software looking for an unsecured Wi-Fi network to "borrow." While many view war driving as a fun activity, it is a security risk as well as an ethically—if not a legally—questionable act. Possible consequences to the owner of a Wi-Fi network as a result of increased use by outsiders include a slower response time, the introduction of computer viruses (either intentionally or unintentionally), and unauthorized access to the data located on PCs connected to that network. It is also possible that use of an Internet connection by multiple users violates the legitimate user's agreement with his or her ISP and may result in the cancellation of the Internet service. While products are available to help mobile users locate Wi-Fi networks (see Figure 9-2) and some mapping programs (such as *Yahoo! Maps*) have an option to display Wi-Fi hotspot locations on any map, these services are intended to help individuals locate authorized hotspots.

Advocates of war driving state that, unless individuals or businesses protect their access points, they are welcoming others to use them. Critics compare that logic to the case of an unlocked front door—you cannot legally enter a home just because the front door is

FIGURE 9-2
Locating accessible Wi-Fi networks.

WI-FI FINDERS
Indicate the strength of Wi-Fi networks within range.

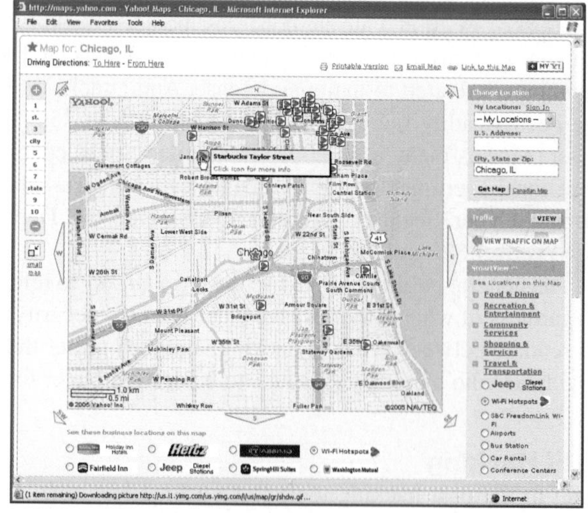

YAHOO! MAPS WI-FI HOTSPOT OPTION
Displays information about public hotspots in the mapped area currently displayed.

>**War driving.** Driving around an area with a Wi-Fi-enabled computer or mobile device to find a Wi-Fi network to access and use without authorization.

unlocked. Although some wireless network owners do leave their access points unsecured on purpose and some communities are creating a collection of wireless access points to provide wireless Internet access to everyone in that community, it is difficult—if not impossible—to tell if an unsecured access point was left that way intentionally or if it is just a private network that has not yet been properly protected (see Figure 9-3). Some feel the ethical distinction of using an unsecured wireless network is determined by the amount of use, believing that it is acceptable to borrow someone's Internet connection to do a quick e-mail check, but that continually using a neighbor's Internet connection to avoid paying for your own is crossing over the line. Others feel that allowing outsiders to share an Internet connection is acceptable use, as long as the owner does not charge the outsider for that access. Still others believe that an Internet connection is intended for use only by the subscriber and that sharing it with others is unfair to the ISP. This issue is beginning to be addressed by the courts, and some answers regarding the legality of war driving and Internet connection sharing will likely be forthcoming in the near future. However, the ethical questions surrounding this issue may take longer to resolve.

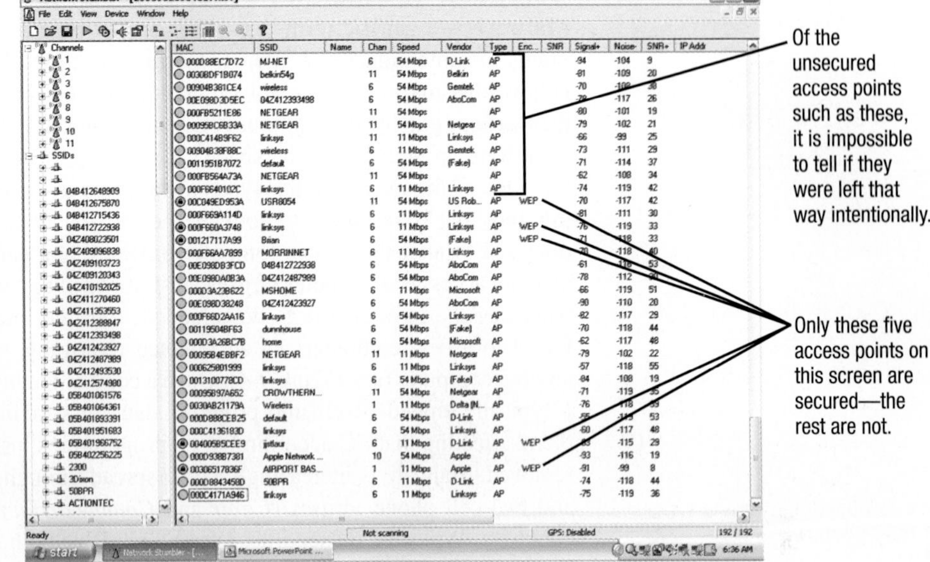
Network Stumbler - [20050323054527.ns1]
Of the unsecured access points such as these, it is impossible to tell if they were left that way intentionally.
Only these five access points on this screen are secured—the rest are not.

FIGURE 9-3
War driving. On a 20 mile war drive in Massachusetts in 2005, 240 wireless access points were detected and over 77% were unprotected.

NET

Interception of Communications

To gain access to data stored on a particular computer, some criminals attempt to hack directly into that computer—sometimes in person, but more often via the Internet. It is also possible, however, to gain unauthorized access to data, files, e-mail messages, and other content as they are being sent over the Internet. And the increased use of wireless networks and the increased use of wireless connections to transmit data via cell phones, handheld PCs, and other portable devices have opened up new opportunities for data interception. Once intercepted, the content can be read, altered, or otherwise used for unintended purposes. Although it is unlikely that anyone would be interested in intercepting personal e-mail sent to friends and relatives, proprietary corporate information and sensitive personal information (such as credit card, bank account, or brokerage account information) is at risk if it is sent over the Internet—or over a wireless home or corporate network—unsecured.

Computer Sabotage

Computer sabotage—acts of malicious destruction to a computer or computer resource—is another common type of computer crime today. Computer sabotage can take several forms, including launching a *computer virus* or a *denial of service attack*, altering the content of a Web site, or changing data or programs located on a computer. Computer sabotage is illegal in the United States, and acts of sabotage are estimated to cost individuals and organizations billions of dollars per year, primarily for labor costs related to virus removal or other necessary actions, lost productivity, and lost sales.

>**Computer sabotage.** An act of malicious destruction to a computer or computer resource.

Computer Viruses and Other Types of Malware

Malware is a generic term that refers to any type of malicious software. Malware programs are intentionally written to perform destructive acts, although some researchers believe that many young malware creators do not realize the potential consequences of their actions and the huge amount of destruction and expense that can result from releasing a malware program into cyberspace.

One of the most familiar types of malware is the **computer virus**—a small software program that is installed without the permission or knowledge of the computer user, is designed to alter the way a computer operates, and can replicate itself to infect any new media it accesses. Computer viruses are embedded into program or data files and are spread whenever the infected file is downloaded from the Internet or another network, is transferred to a new computer via an infected removable storage medium, or is e-mailed to another computer (see Figure 9-4). Once a copy of the infected file reaches a new computer, it typically embeds itself into program, data, or system files on the new PC and remains there, affecting that PC according to its programmed instructions, until it is discovered and removed. Malware is increasingly being spread through files attached to instant messages, and two cell phone viruses (*Cabir* and *Commwarrior*) have hit mobile phones in many countries. Typically, these viruses spread via Bluetooth connections or text messages. The mobile virus *Sybos/Cardtrap* that was introduced in late 2005 is reportedly the first cell phone virus that tries to move beyond cell phones. It masquerades as pirated software for mobile phones and copies itself to the phone's flash memory card so that any PC into which that flash memory card is later inserted will become infected. According to IBM, more malware directed to cell phones and devices—such as cars—that contain embedded computers is expected in the near future, as those devices continue to incorporate more computer software components and, consequently, become more vulnerable to malware.

FURTHER EXPLORATION

For links to further information about computer viruses and virus detection, go to www.course.com/uc11/ch09

Most malware is designed to harm the computers they are transmitted to—for example, by damaging programs, deleting files, erasing the entire hard drive, or slowing down performance of the PC. This damage can take place immediately after infection, or it can begin when a particular condition is met. A computer virus that activates when it detects a certain condition, such as when a particular keystroke is pressed or an employee's name is deleted from an employee file, is called a *logic bomb*. A logic bomb whose trigger is a particular date or time is called a *time bomb*. In addition to destructive computer viruses, there are so-called "benign" viruses that are not designed to do any permanent damage, but instead they make their presence known by displaying a text or video message, or by playing a musical or audio message. Even though benign viruses may not cause any lasting harm (although some do unintentional damage because of programming errors), they are annoying, can require enormous amounts of time to get rid of, and can disrupt communications for the organizations involved.

Instead of being used to disable computers, malware is increasingly being used to gain access to individuals' PCs—usually to steal identity information, passwords, corporate secrets, and other sensitive data. For instance, many experts believe that the *Sobig* virus released in mid-2003 was created by spammers as a way of gaining access to people's PCs in order to hijack them for spam distribution.

Computer viruses are very expensive because of the labor costs associated with removing the virus and correcting any resulting damage, as well as the cost of lost productivity of employees. In the 2005 "Computer Crime and Security Survey," computer viruses were listed as the most expensive type of computer crime, and a 2005 InfoWorld study revealed that nearly 50% of the respondents cited the increased sophistication of malware as the most serious security challenge their companies will face in the next year.

>**Malware.** Any type of malicious software. >**Computer virus.** A software program installed without the user's knowledge and designed to alter the way a computer operates or to cause harm to the computer system.

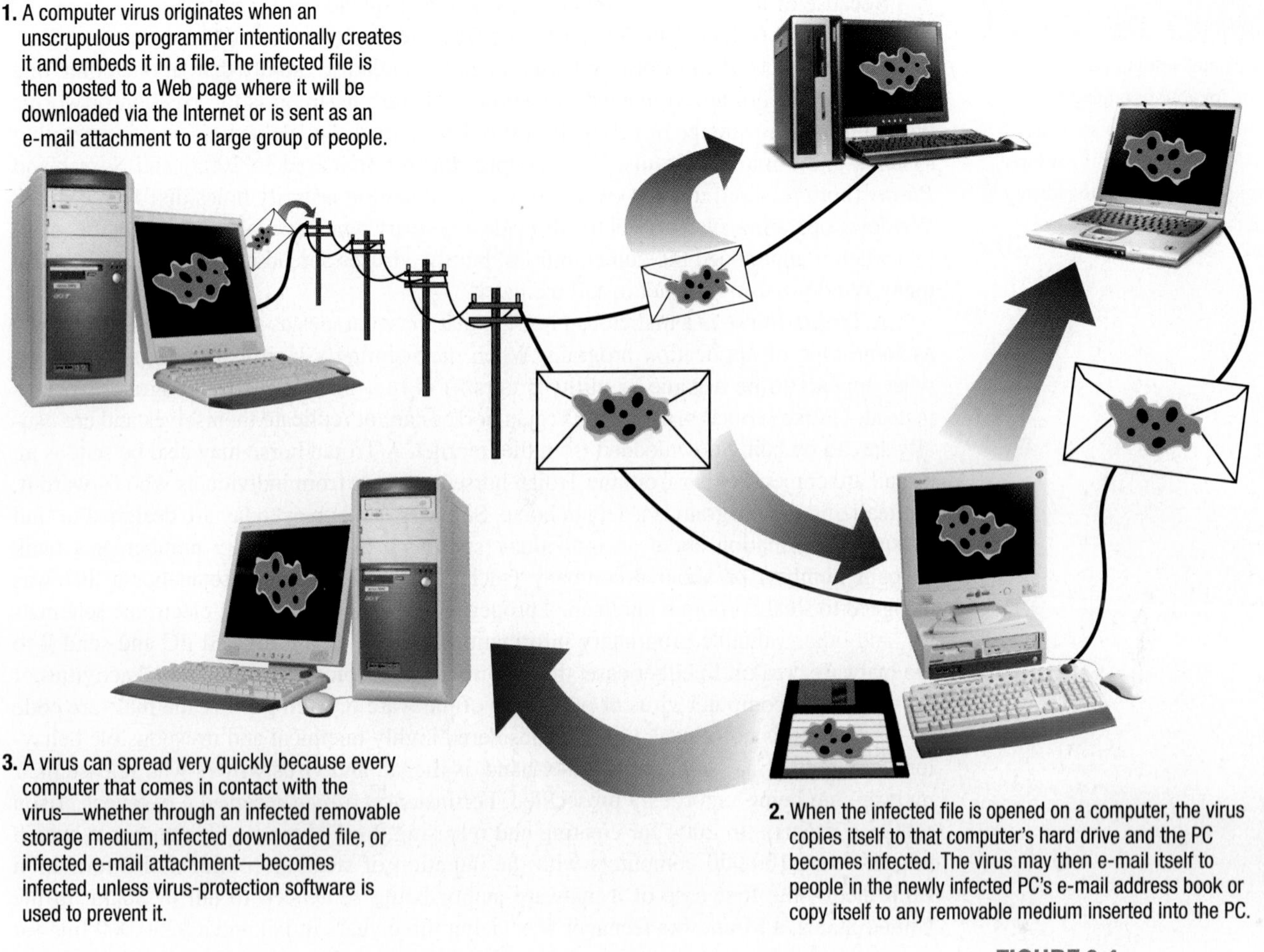

1. A computer virus originates when an unscrupulous programmer intentionally creates it and embeds it in a file. The infected file is then posted to a Web page where it will be downloaded via the Internet or is sent as an e-mail attachment to a large group of people.
2. When the infected file is opened on a computer, the virus copies itself to that computer's hard drive and the PC becomes infected. The virus may then e-mail itself to people in the newly infected PC's e-mail address book or copy itself to any removable medium inserted into the PC.
3. A virus can spread very quickly because every computer that comes in contact with the virus—whether through an infected removable storage medium, infected downloaded file, or infected e-mail attachment—becomes infected, unless virus-protection software is used to prevent it.

FIGURE 9-4
How a computer virus or other type of malicious software might spread.

Although there are other types of malware in addition to computer viruses, it is common practice for all types of malware to be generically referred to as "viruses," even though some may not technically be true computer viruses. Two other common forms of malware are *computer worms* and *Trojan horses*.

Like a computer virus, a **computer worm** is a malicious program designed to cause damage. Unlike a computer virus, however, a computer worm does not infect other computer files to replicate itself; instead, it spreads by creating copies of itself and sending those copies to other computers via a network. Often, the worm is sent as an e-mail attachment to other computers. After the infected e-mail attachment is opened by an individual, the worm inflicts its damage, and then automatically sends copies of itself to other computers via the Internet or a private network, typically using addresses in the e-mail address book located on the newly infected PC. When those e-mail messages and their attachments are opened, those new computers become infected and the cycle continues. Some newer worms do not require any action by the users (such as opening an e-mail attachment) to infect their PCs. Instead, the worm scans the Internet looking for computers that are vulnerable to that particular worm and sends a copy of itself to those PCs to infect them. Other worms just require the user to view the e-mail message, in order to infect the PC.

>**Computer worm.** A malicious program designed to spread rapidly to a large number of computers by sending copies of itself to other computers.

TIP

Always install update security patches for your operating system and e-mail program as soon as they become available; if you have the option to update automatically, select that option.

Because of its distribution method, a worm can spread very rapidly. For instance, the *Slammer* worm (released in 2003) reached 90% of the Internet within 10 minutes of its release, and the *Mydoom* worm (released in 2004) spread so rapidly that, at one point, one out of every 10 e-mails contained the worm. A disturbing trend is the creation of worms written to take advantage of newly discovered *security holes* (vulnerabilities) in operating systems and e-mail programs. For example, *Blaster* (released in 2003) and *Sasser* and *Plexus* (both released in 2004) were all written to exploit security holes discovered in the Windows operating system. Microsoft made a *security patch* available to correct the problem when it announced the vulnerabilities, but the viruses spread rapidly anyway because many Windows users did not install the patch.

A **Trojan horse** is a malicious program that masquerades as something else—usually as some type of application program. When the seemingly legitimate program (such as what appears to be a game or utility program) is run, the destructive program executes instead. Unlike viruses and worms, Trojan horses cannot replicate themselves and are usually spread by being downloaded from the Internet. A Trojan horse may also be sent as an e-mail attachment, either from the Trojan horse author or from individuals who forward it, not realizing the program is a Trojan horse. Some Trojan horses today are designed to find sensitive information about an individual (such as a Social Security number or a bank account number) or about a company (such as the 2005 *Myfip* Trojan horse that was designed to steal corporate intellectual property—mechanical designs, electronic schematics, and other valuable proprietary information) located on an infected PC and send it to the malware creator. In either case, this information is typically used in illegal activities.

Writing a computer virus or other type of malware or even posting the malware code on the Internet is not illegal, but it is considered highly unethical and irresponsible behavior. Distributing malware, on the other hand, is illegal, and virus writers who release their malware are being vigorously prosecuted. For instance, a man received a two-year prison sentence in Spain in 2004 for creating and releasing the *Cabronator* Trojan horse, which infected over 100,000 computers with the intention of stealing confidential information from them—the first case of a malware author being sentenced to jail in Spain. In the United States, a Minnesota teenager was facing three years in jail and a $250,000 fine for creating and unleashing a variant of the *MSBlaster* worm that infected nearly 50,000 computers and caused over a million dollars worth of damage, according to federal investigators. In 2005, the teenager pled guilty to the crime and was sentenced to 18 months in prison and 225 hours of community service.

Denial of Service Attacks

A **denial of service (DoS) attack** is an act of sabotage that attempts to flood a network server or Web server with so many requests for action that it shuts down or simply cannot handle legitimate requests any longer, causing legitimate users to be denied service. For example, a hacker might set up one or more computers to continually *ping* a server (contact it with a request to send a responding ping back) with a false return address or to continually request nonexistent information. If enough useless traffic is generated, the server has no resources left to deal with legitimate requests (see Figure 9-5).

During the past few years, many leading Web sites have been the victims of DoS attacks. Most of these attacks utilized multiple computers (which is referred to as a *distributed denial of service attack* or *DDoS attack*). To perform DDoS attacks, hackers have begun more frequently to access and take control of unprotected PCs with direct Internet connections (such as those located in schools, businesses, or homes) to use in DDoS attacks. These computers (referred to as *zombies*) participate in the attacks without

>**Trojan horse.** A malicious program that masquerades as something else. >**Denial of service (DoS) attack.** An act of sabotage that attempts to flood a network server or a Web server with so much activity that it is unable to function.

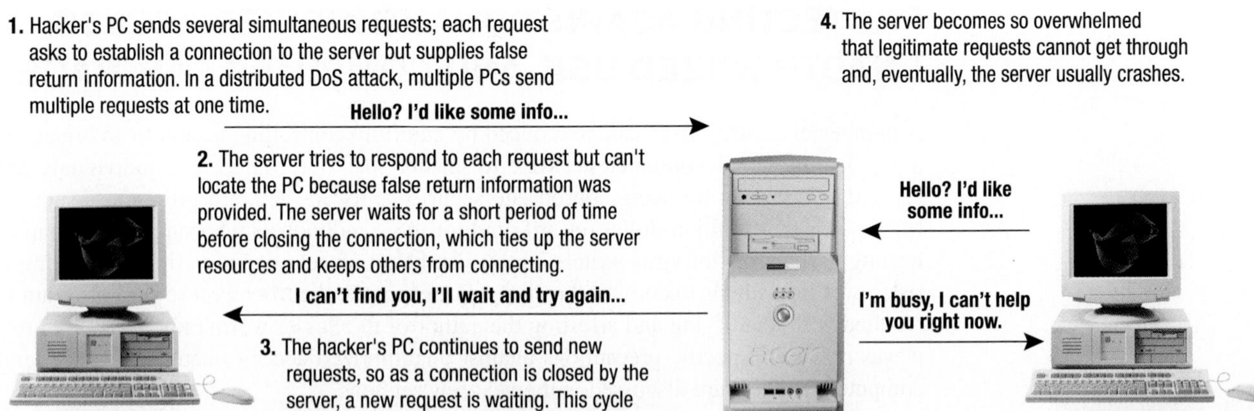

1. Hacker's PC sends several simultaneous requests; each request asks to establish a connection to the server but supplies false return information. In a distributed DoS attack, multiple PCs send multiple requests at one time.
Hello? I'd like some info...
2. The server tries to respond to each request but can't locate the PC because false return information was provided. The server waits for a short period of time before closing the connection, which ties up the server resources and keeps others from connecting.
I can't find you, I'll wait and try again...
3. The hacker's PC continues to send new requests, so as a connection is closed by the server, a new request is waiting. This cycle continues, which ties up the server indefinitely.
Hello? I'd like some info...
4. The server becomes so overwhelmed that legitimate requests cannot get through and, eventually, the server usually crashes.
Hello? I'd like some info...
I'm busy, I can't help you right now.
HACKER'S PC
WEB SERVER
LEGITIMATE PC

FIGURE 9-5
How a denial of service (DoS) attack might work.

the owners' knowledge. Because home PCs tend to be less protected than school and business PCs, hackers are increasingly targeting home PCs for use as zombie PCs. According to Symantec, up to 2 million computers worldwide are infected with software allowing them to be controlled remotely by a hacker, typically for a DDoS attack or to deliver spam or *phishing* e-mails (phishing is discussed shortly). Another trend is to use malware to launch a DoS attack. For example, the Mydoom worm was programmed to use infected computers as zombies to unleash a DDoS attack on Web sites belonging to Microsoft, the Recording Industry Association of America (RIAA), and SCO Group (a Utah company embroiled in an intellectual property battle regarding the use of Linux). Denial of service attacks can be very costly in terms of business lost (such as when an e-commerce site is shut down), as well as the time and expense required to bring the site back online.

Data or Program Alteration

Another type of computer sabotage occurs when a hacker breaches a computer system in order to delete data, change data, modify programs, or otherwise alter the data and programs located there. For example, students have been caught changing grades in their schools' databases, and disgruntled or former employees have performed vengeful acts, including altering programs so they work incorrectly, deleting customer records or other critical data, or randomly changing data in a company's database. Like other forms of computer sabotage, data and program alteration is illegal.

Web site defacement—defacing or otherwise changing Web sites without permission (see Figure 9-6)—is a type of data alteration that has become more common over the past few years. A form of *cybervandalism*, Web site defacement has become a widely used method for hackers who want to draw attention to themselves or to a specific cause. U.S. Web sites modified by hackers in the last few years include those belonging to the Library of Congress, the FBI, the *New York Times*, CNN, the secretary of defense, Sandia National Laboratories, NASA Jet Propulsion Laboratories, and Stanford University.

FIGURE 9-6
Cybervandalism. Some Web site defacements are politically motivated; many are done just for notoriety.

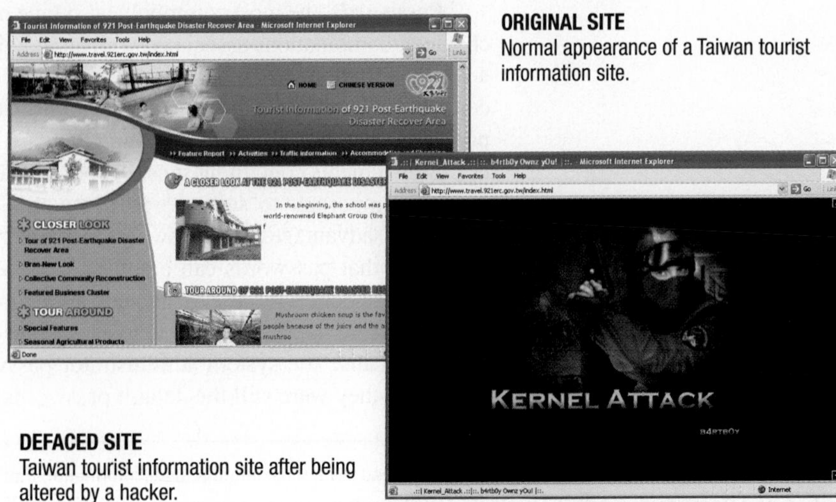

ORIGINAL SITE
Normal appearance of a Taiwan tourist information site.

DEFACED SITE
Taiwan tourist information site after being altered by a hacker.

PROTECTING AGAINST UNAUTHORIZED ACCESS, UNAUTHORIZED USE, AND COMPUTER SABOTAGE

A number of security risks can be reduced by carefully controlling access to an organization's facilities and computer network to ensure that only authorized individuals are granted access, and by using appropriate security software. Reward programs—such as Microsoft's multimillion-dollar reward fund for those individuals who supply information leading to the arrest of virus writers—may also help reduce computer crime by making it riskier for individuals to commit the crime. For example, the Microsoft reward program is credited with identifying and arresting the author of the Sasser worm only one week after it was released. Specific precautions against unauthorized access, unauthorized use, and computer sabotage are discussed in the next few sections.

Access Control Systems

Access control systems are used to control access to facilities, computer networks, and other assets. *Identification systems* can be used to verify that the person trying to access the facility or system is listed as an authorized user, and *authentication systems* can be used to determine whether or not the person attempting access is actually who he or she claims to be. Controlling access to company databases is critical today, considering the vast amount of personal data contained there. And the recent security breaches reveal that many of today's companies need to improve their access systems. Improvements in this area—such as the new *Payment Card Industry (PCI)* security standards imposed by major credit card companies on all companies that store, process, or transmit credit cardholder data—are expected to help. The PCI standards include restricting physical access to cardholder data, using a *firewall*, changing default passwords, *encrypting* cardholder data transmissions (encryption and firewalls are discussed shortly), and other security precautions.

The three most common types of access systems are discussed next, followed by a discussion of additional considerations for controlling access to wireless networks.

Possessed Knowledge Access Systems

A **possessed knowledge access system** is an identification system that requires the individual requesting access to provide information that only the authorized user is supposed to know. *Passwords*, *usernames* (typically a variation of the person's first and/or last names), and *PINs* (*personal identification numbers*, such as those used with ATM cards) fall into this category.

Passwords, the most commonly used type of possessed knowledge, are secret words or character combinations associated with an individual. They can be used to restrict access to a facility or, more commonly, to a network or other computing resource. For example, a company or institution might require an authorized user to use one password to access a corporate or school computer system, and then use a different password to access drives, folders, or documents containing sensitive or confidential information on that same network.

It is important to select good passwords and change them frequently. One of the biggest disadvantages of password-only systems is that passwords can be forgotten; another is that passwords can be guessed or deciphered by a hacker's PC easily if good password selection strategies are not applied. For example, it was discovered that the Deceptive Duo hackers were able to access the databases from which they retrieved information because the system administrator passwords for those databases had never been changed—they were still the default passwords (the ones assigned to the programs during

---

>**Possessed knowledge access system.** An access control system that uses information that only an individual should know to identify that individual. >**Password.** A secret combination of characters used to gain access to a computer, computer network, or other resource.

PASSWORD STRATEGIES

Make the password at least eight characters, if allowed by the application. A four- or five-character password can be cracked by a computer program in less than one minute. A ten-character password, in contrast, has about 3,700 trillion possible character permutations and could take a regular computer decades to crack.
Choose an unusual sequence of characters to create a password that will not be in a dictionary–for instance, mix numbers and special characters with abbreviations or unusual words you will remember. The password should be one that you can remember, yet one that does not conform to a pattern a computer can readily figure out.
To help you remember strong passwords used to protect sensitive data, consider using a *passphrase* that you can remember and using corresponding letters and symbols (such as the first letter of each word) for your password. For instance, the passphrase "My son John is five years older than my daughter Abby" could help you remember the strong password "Msji5yotMd@".
Do not use your name, your kids' or pets' names, your address, your birthdate, or other public information as your password.
Do not keep a written copy of the password in your desk or taped to your monitor. If you need to write down your password, create a password-protected file on your PC to contain all your passwords.
Use a different password for your highly sensitive activities (such as online banking or stock trading) than for Web sites that remember your settings or profile (such as online news, auction, shopping, or bookstore sites). Computers storing passwords used on nonsensitive Web sites are usually easier to break into than those storing passwords used on high-security sites, and if a hacker determines your password on a low-security site, he or she can use it on your accounts containing sensitive data if you use the same password on those accounts.
Change your passwords frequently.

manufacturing) and so were commonly known. As illustrated by this example, any individual possessing the proper password will be granted access to the system because the system recognizes the password, regardless of whether or not the person using the password is the authorized user.

The best passwords are *strong passwords*—at least eight characters long; use a combination of letters, numbers, and symbols; and do not form words found in the dictionary or that match the username. Some additional strategies for selecting secure passwords are listed in Figure 9-7. Passwords, usernames, and PINs are often used in conjunction with each other, as well as with *possessed object access systems* and *biometric access systems*, to add another level of security—called *two-factor authentication.*

FIGURE 9-7
Strategies for creating secure passwords.

FIGURE 9-8
Possessed objects, such as the magnetic card being used here, protect against unauthorized access.

NET

Possessed Object Access Systems

Possessed object access systems use physical objects for identification purposes and are frequently used to access facilities and computer systems. Common types of possessed objects are smart cards, encoded badges, and magnetic cards that are similar to credit cards (see Figure 9-8) and that are swiped through or placed close to a reader to be read. Increasingly, *USB security tokens* or *e-tokens*—flash memory drives that are inserted into a PC to grant access to a network, supply Web site passwords, and provide other security features—are being used. For a closer look at how e-tokens are being used to secure computers at one college campus, see the Technology and You box.

One disadvantage of using possessed objects is that the object can be lost or, like passwords, used by an unauthorized individual. This latter disadvantage can be overcome by requiring the user to supply a password or be authenticated by a fingerprint or other type of *biometric* data in order to use the possessed object. For example, some smart card readers and some USB security keys contain *fingerprint readers* used to authenticate that the person using the possessed object is the authorized individual. This type of two-factor authentication is much more secure than security procedures involving only one factor.

>**Possessed object access system.** An access control system that uses physical objects that an individual has in his or her possession to identify that individual.

Biometric Access Systems

Biometrics is the study of identifying individuals using measurable biological characteristics. **Biometric access systems** identify users by a particular unique biological characteristic (such as a fingerprint, hand, face, or *iris*—the colored portion of the eye), although a personal trait (such as a voice or signature) can be used in some systems. Because the means of access (usually a part of the body) cannot be lost or forgotten and because it cannot be transferred to another individual or used by anyone other than the authorized individual, biometric access systems can perform both identification and authentication.

Biometric access systems use *biometric readers* (such as *fingerprint, hand geometry, face*, and *iris readers*) in conjunction with software and a database to match the supplied biometric data with the biometric data previously stored in the database to identify and authenticate an individual. To speed up the process, many access systems require users to identify themselves first (such as with a username, PIN number, magnetic card, or smart card), and then the system uses the identifying information to verify that the supplied biometric data matches that person. In general, biometric access systems are very accurate. According to IrisScan, an industry leader in iris-recognition technology, the odds of two different irises being declared a match are 1 in 10^{78}—even identical twins (who have the same DNA structure) have different fingerprints and irises. Systems based on biological characteristics (such as a person's iris, hand geometry, face, or fingerprint) tend to be more accurate than those based on a personal trait (such as an individual's voice or a written signature) because biological traits do not change, unlike physical traits that might change (such as an individual's voice, which might be affected by a cold, or a written signature, which might be affected by a broken wrist). Some examples of the most commonly used types of biometric devices are shown in Figure 9-9, along with their primary advantages and disadvantages.

FINGERPRINT READER
Typically used to protect access to office PCs, to replace Web site passwords on home PCs, to pay for products or services, and to access resources such as Welfare benefits.

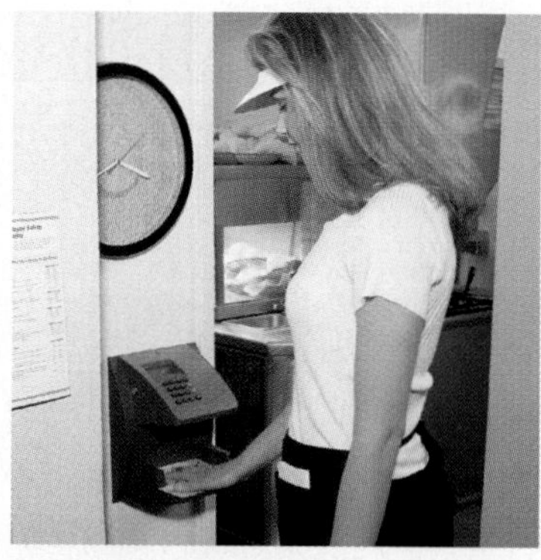

HAND GEOMETRY READER
Typically used to control access to facilities (such as government offices, prisons, and military facilities) and to punch in and out of work.

FACE READER
Typically used to control access to highly secure areas, as well as to identify individuals for law enforcement purposes.

IRIS SCANNER
Typically used to control access to highly secure areas, such as nuclear facilities and prisons; beginning to be used to authenticate users of ATMs and other banking facilities, as shown here.

TYPE OF READER	ADVANTAGES	DISADVANTAGES
Fingerprint	Easy to use; inexpensive.	Sometimes harder to read on older individuals; usually requires contact with scanner; possible negative social image.
Hand	Easy to use.	Usually requires contact with scanner; fairly expensive.
Face	Requires no direct contact with user; can be used without the person's cooperation.	Lighting, disguised appearance, and other factors may affect results; fairly expensive.
Iris	Requires no direct contact with user; easy to use.	Lighting may affect results; expensive.

FIGURE 9-9
Types of biometric devices.

>**Biometric access system.** An access control system that uses one unique physical characteristic of an individual (such as a fingerprint, face, or voice) to authenticate that individual.

TECHNOLOGY AND YOU

E-Tokens on Campus

E-tokens have arrived on campus at Dartmouth College in New Hampshire. Instead of just usernames and passwords, sensitive data and applications on the campus network are beginning to be protected by e-tokens—special USB keys that are used to authenticate individuals for network access. The e-tokens contain a digital certificate associated with the individual using the e-token. In addition to being used to identify the individual for access to network resources, the e-token can be used to digitally sign e-mail and other electronic documents and to encrypt documents and data.

To use the e-token (shown in the accompanying photograph), the individual first connects it to his or her PC (via a USB port), and then the individual supplies his or her password. The appropriate applications are then "unlocked" and available to that individual. The two levels of authentication (the actual key and the student's password) provide a more secure way to verify users to network applications than the traditional username/password approach. At Dartmouth, the e-tokens are currently used to gain access to information on the Dartmouth intranet (such as student grades, administrative files, and personal data), as well to education programs, such as Blackboard.

In addition to the conventional academic applications, the Dartmouth computer network is also beginning to host other resources available to students, such as television and telephone service. The goal is to create a ubiquitous campus network that provides both wired and wireless access to network resources anywhere on the entire campus.

Biometric access systems offer a great deal of convenience. Consequently, they are increasingly being used to grant access to secure facilities (such as corporate headquarters and prisons), log users on to computer systems and secure Web sites (by using an external reader or one built into the PC), punch employees in and out of work, and confirm consumers' identities at ATM machines and check-cashing services. Biometric readers are also increasingly being built into notebook PCs, handheld computers, and other devices to protect against unauthorized use and to authenticate online purchases and other financial transactions. Emerging biometric devices identify individuals based on their skin, the veins in their hands, or a combination of biometric features (such as skin, face, and fingerprint)—called *fusion biometrics*.

TIP

Cuts or other changes to a finger may prevent access via a fingerprint reader. To avoid this problem, be sure to enroll more than one finger, if possible, whenever you are being set up in a system that uses a fingerprint reader. Many systems allow the user to enter images for more than one finger and any of the registered fingers may be used for access.

Wireless Network Access Considerations

As already discussed, wireless networks—such as those accessed via a Wi-Fi connection—are less secure, in general, than wired networks. There are Wi-Fi security procedures, however, that can be used to protect against unauthorized use of a wireless network and to encrypt data sent over the network so that it is unreadable if intercepted. The original Wi-Fi security standard—*WEP* (*Wired Equivalent Privacy*)—is in the process of being replaced with the more secure *WPA* (*Wi-Fi Protected Access*) and the even more secure *802.11i* (also known as *WPA2*) standard. However, Wi-Fi security features only work if they are enabled. Most Wi-Fi hardware today is shipped with the security features switched off, and many Wi-Fi home network users never enable them, leaving those networks unsecured. To protect against unauthorized access, Wi-Fi network owners should secure their networks by enabling *encryption*, hiding their networks by not broadcasting the network names, and changing the default network administrator passwords. Once the *key* (essentially a password) is assigned to the network, users who want to connect to that network would need to supply the network identifying information and the appropriate key (see Figure 9-10).

FIGURE 9-10
Wi-Fi security. Wi-Fi networks should be secured to prevent unauthorized access, such as by using WPA keys as shown here.

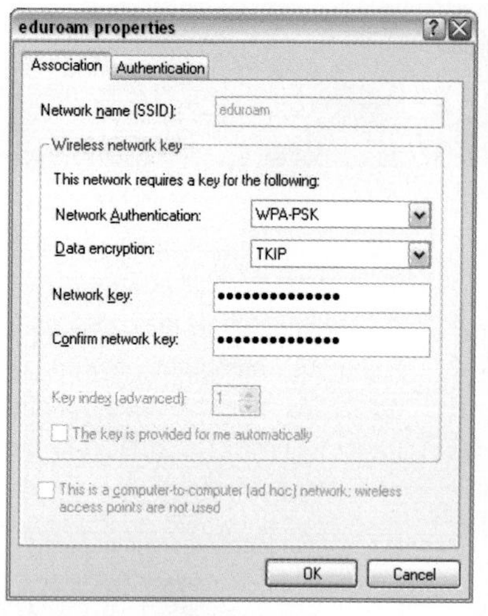

SECURITY SETTINGS
Owners of wireless networks should enable encryption and assign keys to be used by authorized individuals.

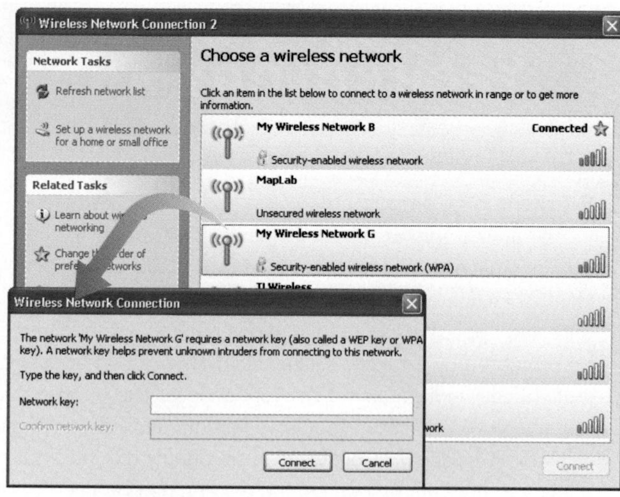

ACCESSING THE NETWORK
To access the network, the appropriate key must be supplied.

Firewalls and Antivirus Software

A **firewall** is a security system that provides a protective boundary between a computer or network and the outside world in order to protect against unauthorized access. *Personal firewalls* are typically software-based systems that are geared toward protecting home PCs from hackers attempting to access those computers through their Internet connections. Hackers who gain access to home PCs can access the information on them (such as passwords stored on the hard drive), as well as use those computers in denial of service attacks and other illegal activities. Consequently, all PCs with direct Internet connections (such as DSL, cable, or satellite Internet access) should use a firewall (PCs using dial-up Internet access are relatively safe from hackers). Firewalls designed to protect business networks may be software-based, hardware-based, or a combination of the two. They can typically be used both to prevent network access by hackers and other outsiders, and to control employee Internet access.

FIGURE 9-11
A personal firewall program.

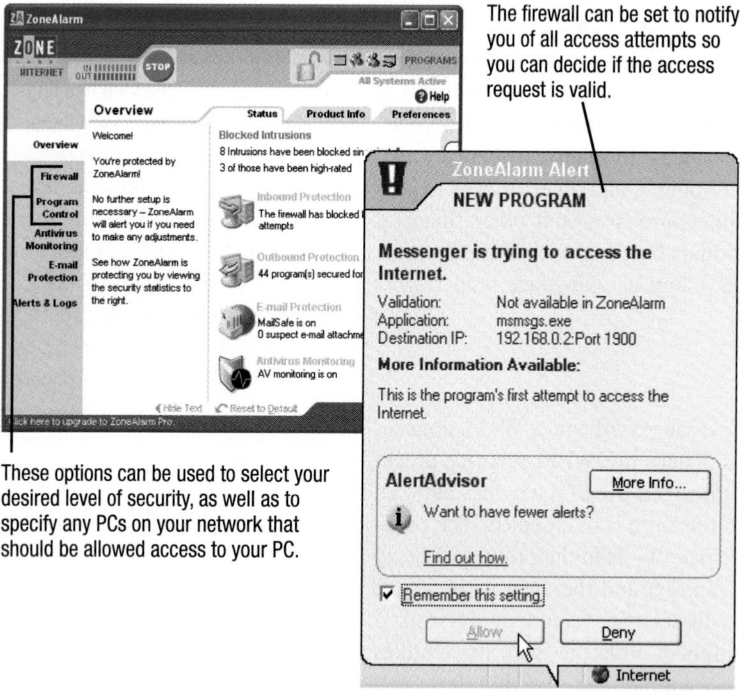

The firewall can be set to notify you of all access attempts so you can decide if the access request is valid.

These options can be used to select your desired level of security, as well as to specify any PCs on your network that should be allowed access to your PC.

Firewalls work by closing down all external *communications port addresses*—the electronic connections that allow a PC to communicate with other computers—to unauthorized computers and programs for both incoming and outgoing activities. While business firewalls are set up by the network administrator and those settings cannot typically be changed by end users, personal firewalls will usually notify the user when an application program on the PC is trying to access the Internet or another computer on a home network is trying to access the firewall-protected PC. At that point, the user may either grant or deny access (see Figure 9-11). In addition to protecting your

>**Firewall.** A collection of hardware and/or software intended to protect a computer or computer network from unauthorized access.

PC from outside access, firewall programs also protect against inside attacks from computer viruses and other malicious programs that may have slipped through your virus protection. If communications port addresses are not blocked by a firewall, malware programs can open the ports and send data from your PC to a hacker at the hacker's request.

To protect against becoming infected with a computer virus or other type of malware, all PCs in both homes and offices should have **antivirus software** installed. To be effective, antivirus software should be set up to run continuously whenever the computer is on to check incoming e-mail messages, instant messages, and downloaded files; it should also be set up to run a complete scan of the entire PC on a regular basis, such as once per week. Antivirus software can protect your PC against getting a virus since it deletes or quarantines any suspicious e-mail attachments or downloaded files on their way in to your PC, and it can detect and remove any viruses or worms that may find their way onto your PC (see Figure 9-12). If a known virus or worm is found, the program will remove it and try to repair any damage it caused.

New viruses and other types of malware are released all the time (according to McAfee Security, a manufacturer of antivirus and security software, there were over 100,000 known viruses in late 2005, with new viruses and other types of malware being introduced at a rate of about 500 per month), so it is vital to keep your antivirus program up to date. Antivirus programs are usually set up to automatically download new virus definitions from its associated Web site on a regular basis—an important precaution. Most

TIP

To ensure you have the latest security updates for your operating system, enable *automatic updates* for your operating system. Windows users should also run the Windows Update program manually at least once per month.

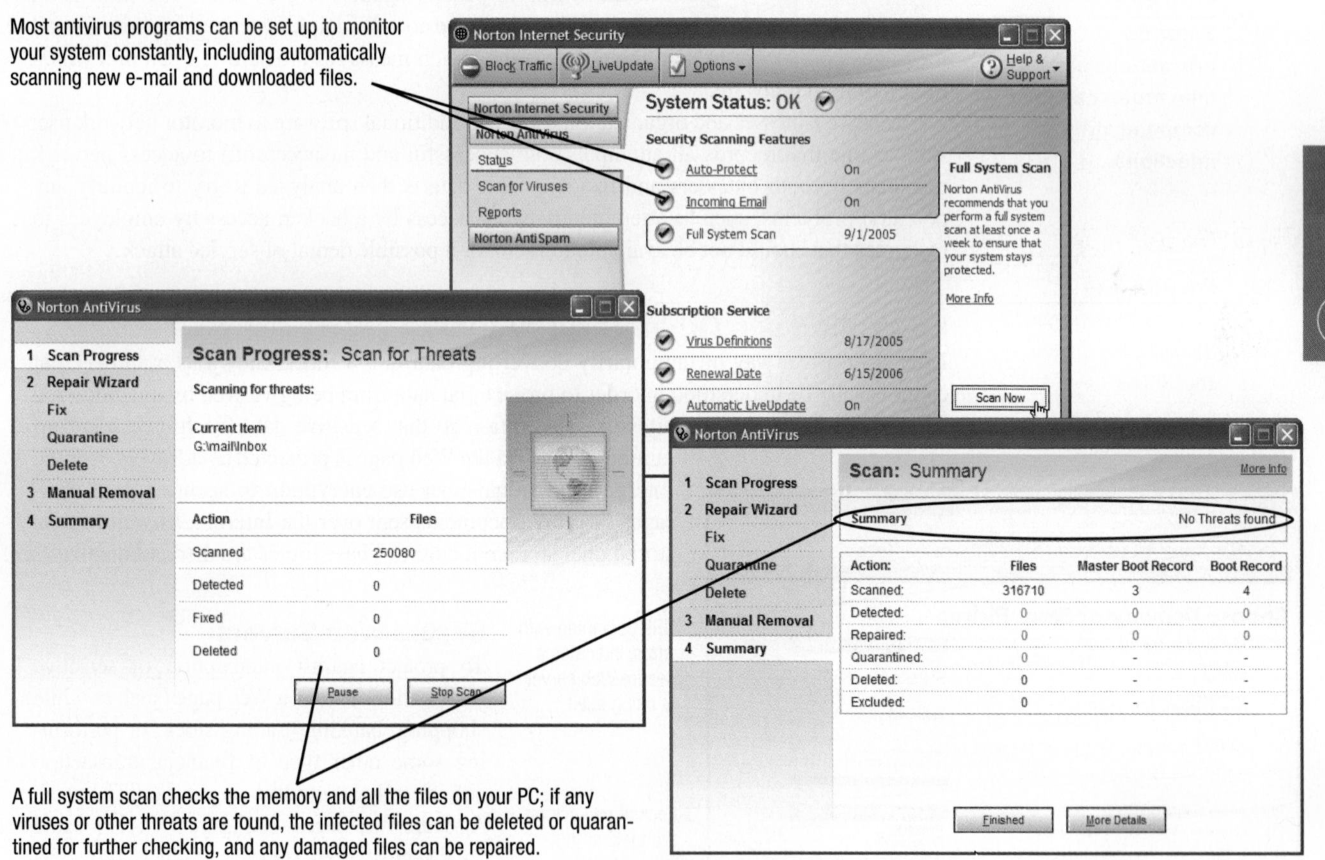

FIGURE 9-12
Antivirus software. Antivirus programs, such as this one, are used to detect and remove malware infections.

NET

>**Antivirus software.** Software used to detect and eliminate computer viruses and other types of malware.

VIRUS PREVENTION STRATEGIES

Use antivirus software to check incoming e-mail messages and files, and download updated virus definitions on a regular basis.

Limit the sharing of disks and other removable storage media with others.

Only download files from reputable sites.

Only open e-mail attachments that come from people you know and that do not have an executable file extension (such as *.exe*, *.com*, *.bat*, or *.vbs*); double-check with the sender before opening a seemingly legitimate executable attachment.

Keep the preview window of your e-mail program closed so you will not view messages until you determine that they are safe to view.

Regularly download and install the latest security patches available for your operating sytem, browser, and e-mail program.

Avoid downloading files from P2P sites.

FIGURE 9-13
Sensible precautions can help protect against computer virus infections.

antivirus programs come with a year of access to free updates; users should purchase additional years after that to continue to be protected. Schools and businesses should also ensure that students and employees connecting to the campus or company network with personal PCs are using up-to-date antivirus software so they will not inadvertently infect the network with malware. Some colleges now require new students to go through a quarantine process, in which students are not granted access to the network until they go through a security process that checks their PCs for security threats, updates their operating systems, and installs antivirus software. Some additional virus-prevention strategies are listed in Figure 9-13.

Some antivirus programs also scan for other threats in addition to malware, such as *spyware* and possible *phishing* e-mails (discussed shortly). Many also include a firewall and other security components. In addition to using installed antivirus software, your ISP may offer antivirus protection. Typically, ISP antivirus software scans all incoming e-mail messages at the mail server level to filter out messages containing a virus. If a message containing a virus is detected, typically it is deleted and the recipient is notified that the message contained a virus and was deleted. Another type of program in the works to protect against viruses sent via e-mail is an *e-mail authentication system*—a system designed to tell recipients exactly where e-mail messages come from to help them determine which messages are safe to open and which might contain malware.

Many businesses and organizations also use additional software to monitor network use, such as one that records all attempts (both successful and unsuccessful) to access network resources by both outsiders and insiders. This data is then analyzed to try to identify any potential problems, such as attempted network access by a hacker, access by employees to resources that should not be available to them, or a possible denial of service attack.

Encryption and Other Security Tools

Encryption is a way of temporarily converting data into a form, known as a *cipher*, that cannot easily be understood in order to protect that data from being viewed by unauthorized people. For instance, Web sites use encryption so that sensitive data (such as credit card numbers) sent via the Web page is protected as it travels over the Internet. Individuals can use encryption to secure e-mail messages or other documents sent over the Internet, as well as data stored on a storage medium. These topics are discussed next.

FIGURE 9-14
Secure Web pages. Sensitive information should only be submitted via secure Web pages.

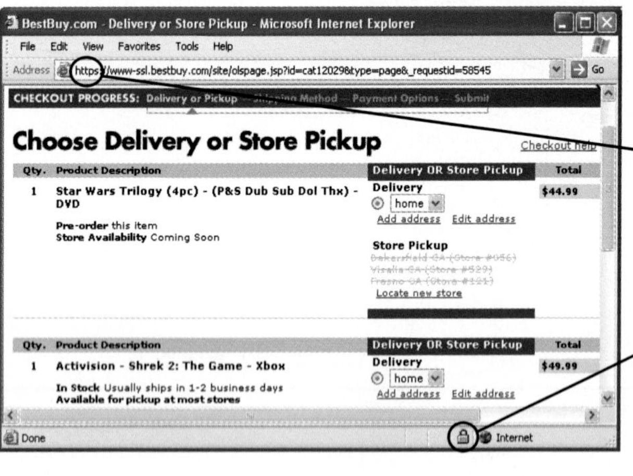

Secure Web Servers

To protect against interception of sensitive information sent via a Web page (such as while shopping, banking, trading stock, or performing some other type of financial transaction online), only *secure Web pages* should be used. A secure Web page (see Figure 9-14) is located on a **secure Web server**, which is protected against unauthorized access and encrypts data

>**Encryption.** A method of scrambling e-mail or files to make them unreadable if they are intercepted by an unauthorized user. >**Secure Web server.** A Web server that uses encryption to protect information transmitted via the Web pages stored on that server.

going to and coming from the server. To indicate a secure Web page, most Web browsers display a locked padlock or a solid (unbroken) key on the status bar at the bottom of the browser window. The most common security protocol used with secure Web pages is *Secure Sockets Layer* (*SSL*). The URL for Web pages using SSL begin with *https:* instead of *http:*.

E-Mail and File Encryption

Although it may not seem likely that the e-mail messages and files you send and receive via the Internet might be intercepted and read by someone else, it is a possibility if they are not secured. To secure e-mail messages or other documents sent over the Internet, encryption techniques are used. An encrypted document is essentially scrambled and as such is unreadable until it is *decrypted*—or unscrambled—correctly. Files, e-mail messages, and instant messages can be encrypted before they are sent over the Internet; individual files can also be encrypted before they are stored on a hard drive so they will be unreadable if opened by an unauthorized person. Encryption is often implemented using a third-party encryption program, such as *Pretty Good Privacy* (*PGP*). How the data is encrypted depends on the *encryption algorithm*—such as *Blowfish* or *Advanced Encryption Standard* (*AES*)—being used. There are also special USB flash memory drives that are designed to encrypt the files on a PC—to access the decrypted versions of those files, the flash memory drive must be inserted in the PC's USB port. *Automatic encryption* (which automatically encrypts all data written to the drive) is beginning to be built into hard drives used in portable PCs so the data will be unreadable if the PC is stolen.

The two most common types of encryption are *private key encryption* and *public key encryption*. **Private key encryption**, also called *symmetric key encryption*, uses a single secret key to both encrypt and decrypt the file or message. It is often used to encrypt files stored on an individual's PC, since the individual who selects the private key is likely the only one who will need to access those files. Private key encryption can also be used to securely send files to others, provided both the sender and recipient agree on the private key (essentially a secret password) that will be used to access the file. For a look at how private key encryption works, see the How it Works box.

Public key encryption, also called *asymmetric key encryption*, utilizes two encryption keys to encrypt and decrypt documents. Specifically, public key encryption uses a pair of keys (a public key and a private key) that has been assigned to a particular individual—each key is a very long number that is mathematically related to the other key. An individual's *public key* is not secret and is available for anyone to use, but a *private key* is used only by the individual to whom it was assigned. Documents or messages encrypted with a public key can only be decrypted with the matching private key.

Public/private key pairs are either generated by the encryption program being used or are obtained through a *Certificate Authority*, such as VeriSign or Thawte (Certificate Authorities are discussed in more detail in a later section). Key pairs obtained from a Certificate Authority need to be installed in your browser, e-mail program, and any third-party encryption program before they can be used, although often this is done automatically for you if your key pairs are downloaded from the Internet. Obtaining a business public/private key pair usually requires a fee, but free key pairs are available for personal use through some Certificate Authorities. Some encryption programs (such as PGP) are also available without charge for personal use.

NET

>**Private key encryption.** A type of encryption that uses a single key to encrypt and decrypt the file or message. >**Public key encryption.** A type of encryption that uses key pairs to encrypt and decrypt the file or message.

HOW IT WORKS

Private Key Encryption

Stand-alone private key encryption programs can be used to encrypt individual files or an entire hard drive. Private key encryption is also incorporated into a variety of programs–such as Microsoft Office, the WinZip file compression program, and Adobe Acrobat (the program used to create PDF files)–to encrypt documents created in those programs so that they can be stored in an encrypted form on a storage medium. As shown in the accompanying illustration of encrypting a Microsoft Word document, once the file is encrypted, the password assigned to that file must be entered to open the original file or any copies of the file, such as those sent via e-mail. A separate password can be issued if you want to control who is able to modify the file; otherwise, anyone with the password to open the file can modify it. To send a privately encrypted file to another individual, the sender uses the agreed-upon private key to encrypt the file, and the recipient uses that same key to decrypt and open the file.

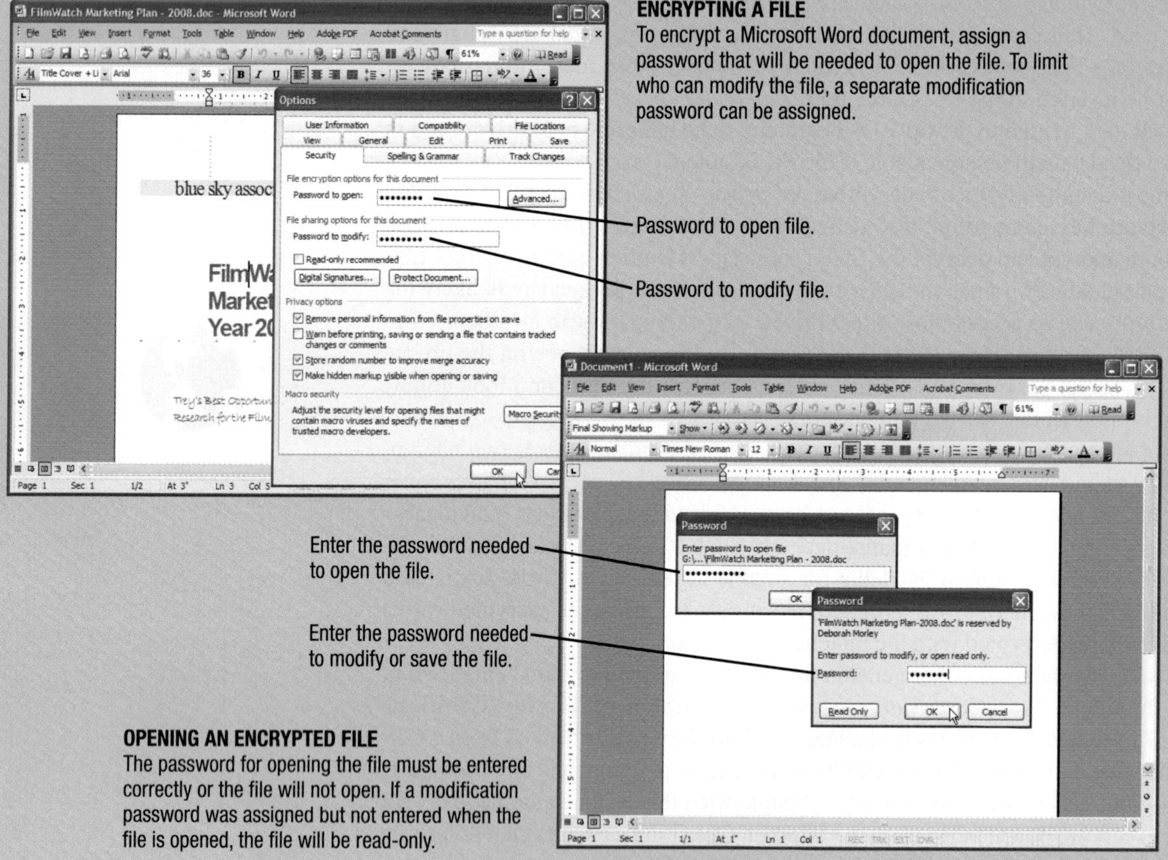

ENCRYPTING A FILE
To encrypt a Microsoft Word document, assign a password that will be needed to open the file. To limit who can modify the file, a separate modification password can be assigned.
Password to open file.
Password to modify file.
Enter the password needed to open the file.
Enter the password needed to modify or save the file.
OPENING AN ENCRYPTED FILE
The password for opening the file must be entered correctly or the file will not open. If a modification password was assigned but not entered when the file is opened, the file will be read-only.

To send someone an encrypted message using public key encryption, you need his or her public key. If that person has previously sent you his or her public key (such as via an e-mail message), it was likely stored by your e-mail program in your address book or by your encryption program in a special *key ring* feature used by that program. In either case, that public key is available whenever you want to send that person an encrypted document. If you do not already have the public key belonging to the individual to whom you wish to send an encrypted message, you will need to request it from that individual or find it in a *public keyserver*—a database of public keys available through a Web site. Once the recipient's public key has been used to encrypt the file and the message is sent, the recipient uses his or her private key to decrypt the file (see Figure 9-15).

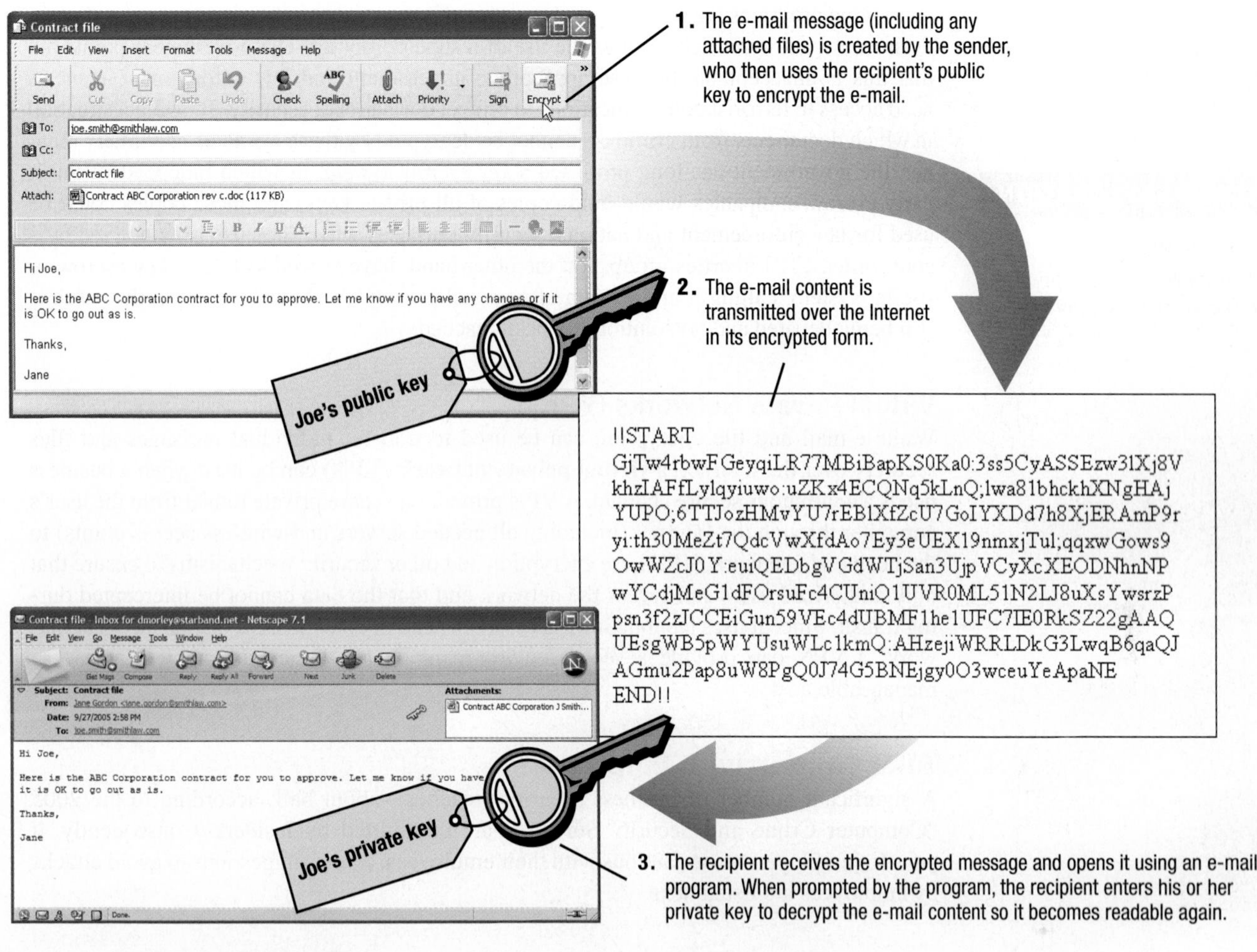
Contract file
File Edit View Insert Format Tools Message Help
Send Cut Copy Paste Undo Check Spelling Attach Priority Sign Encrypt
To: joe.smith@smithlaw.com
Cc:
Subject: Contract file
Attach: Contract ABC Corporation rev c.doc (117 KB)
Hi Joe,
Here is the ABC Corporation contract for you to approve. Let me know if you have any changes or if it is OK to go out as is.
Thanks,
Jane
Joe's public key
1. The e-mail message (including any attached files) is created by the sender, who then uses the recipient's public key to encrypt the e-mail.
2. The e-mail content is transmitted over the Internet in its encrypted form.
!!START
GjTw4rbwFGeyqiLR77MBiBapKS0Ka0:3ss5CyASSEzw31Xj8V
khzIAFfLylqyiuwo:uZKx4ECQNq5kLnQ;lwa81bhckhXNgHAj
YUPO;6TTJozHMvYU7rEB1XfZcU7GoIYXDd7h8XjERAmP9r
yi:th30MeZt7QdcVwXfdAo7Ey3eUEX19nmxjTul;qqxwGows9
OwWZcJ0Y:euiQEDbgVGdWTjSan3UjpVCyXcXEODNhnNP
wYCdjMeG1dFOrsuFc4CUniQ1UVR0ML51N2LJ8uXsYwsrzP
psn3f2zJCCEiGun59VEc4dUBMF1he1UFC7IE0RkSZ22gAAQ
UEsgWB5pWYUsuWLc1kmQ:AHzejiWRRLDkG3LwqB6qaQJ
AGmu2Pap8uW8PgQ0J74G5BNEjgy0O3wceuYeApaNE
END!!
Contract file - Inbox for dmorley@starband.net - Netscape 7.1
Subject: Contract file
Attachments:
Contract ABC Corporation J Smith...
Hi Joe,
Here is the ABC Corporation contract for you to approve. Let me know if you have it is OK to go out as is.
Thanks,
Jane
Joe's private key
3. The recipient receives the encrypted message and opens it using an e-mail program. When prompted by the program, the recipient enters his or her private key to decrypt the e-mail content so it becomes readable again.

FIGURE 9-15
Using public key encryption to secure an e-mail message.

To avoid the need to obtain the recipient's public key before sending that person an encrypted e-mail, *Web-based encrypted e-mail* can be used. Web-based encrypted e-mail works similarly to regular Web-based e-mail (in which e-mail is composed and viewed on a Web page belonging to the Web-based e-mail service), but Web-based encrypted e-mail systems use secure Web servers to host the Web pages that are used to compose and read e-mail messages. With some Web-based encrypted e-mail systems, the recipient is notified via his or her regular e-mail address that an encrypted e-mail message is waiting, and, using the link included in the e-mail message, the recipient can view the message on a secure Web page. With this type of system, often only the sender is required to have an account through the Web-based encrypted e-mail service. Other Web-based encrypted e-mail systems—such as the popular free *HushMail* service—require both the sender and recipient to have accounts through that system. Since all e-mail sent through the service is automatically encrypted, users just log on to the HushMail Web page and provide their password when requested in order to decrypt and view any encrypted e-mail messages sent to their HushMail e-mail addresses.

There are various strengths of encryption available; the stronger the encryption, the more difficult it is to crack. Older 40-bit encryption (which can only use keys that are 40 bits or 5 characters long) is considered *weak encryption*. Stronger encryption is available today—such as *strong 128-bit encryption* (which uses 16-character keys) and *military-strength 2,048-bit encryption* (which uses 256-character keys)—although not without some objections from law enforcement agencies and the government. According to the government, terrorists routinely use encryption methods to communicate. Current commercial

NET

encryption programs are so strong that cracking them can take government agencies days or even weeks and typically requires the use of a supercomputer. The government points out that this is unacceptable because appropriate government and law enforcement agencies need access to terrorist communications to protect our national security. To avoid a situation in which documents from criminals cannot be decrypted by these agencies in a timely manner, the government has long proposed a *key escrow system*, in which independent third-party escrow companies would hold copies of all private keys, and those copies could be used for law enforcement and national security purposes when such use is authorized by a court order. Civil liberties groups, on the other hand, have vowed to fight a key escrow or similar system, calling it an invasion of personal privacy. At the present time, this issue is still being debated and no solution has been reached.

FURTHER EXPLORATION

For links to further information about encryption, go to www.course.com/uc11/ch09

Virtual Private Networks (VPNs)

While e-mail and file encryption can be used to transfer individual messages and files securely over the Internet, a **virtual private network** (**VPN**) can be used when a business needs a continuous secure channel. A VPN provides a secure private tunnel from the user's computer through the Internet (including all needed servers and wireless access points) to the business's network. VPNs use encryption and other security mechanisms to ensure that only authorized users can access the network and that the data cannot be intercepted during transit. Since it uses a public infrastructure instead of an expensive private physical network, a VPN can provide a secure environment over a large geographical area at a manageable cost.

Take Caution with Employees

A significant number of business security breaches—about half, according to the 2005 "Computer Crime and Security Survey"—are committed by insiders. Consequently, it pays for employers to be cautious with their employees. Some suggestions to avoid attacks by employees are listed next.

Screen Potential New Hires Carefully

Employers should carefully investigate the background of all potential employees. Some people falsify résumés to get jobs. Others may have criminal records or currently be charged with a crime. One embarrassing mistake made by Rutgers University was to hire David Smith, the author of the *Melissa* virus, as a computer technician when he was out on bail following the arrest for that crime.

Watch for Disgruntled Employees and Ex-Employees

The type of employee who is most likely to commit a computer crime is one who has recently been terminated or passed over for a promotion, or one who has some reason to want to "get even" with the organization. Limiting access for each employee to only the resources needed for his or her job and monitoring any attempts to access off-limits resources can help prevent some types of sabotage. According to a 2005 "Insider Threat Study" by the U.S. Secret Service National Threat Assessment Center (NTAC) and the Software Engineering Institute's Computer Emergency Response Team (CERT), 57% of the insiders who sabotaged their companies were perceived as disgruntled employees and, in 92% of the cases, an event or series of events (such as a dispute with another employee or a demotion) triggered the incident. In the majority (nearly 60%) of the cases,

---

>**Virtual private network (VPN).** A secure path over the Internet that provides authorized users a secure means of accessing a private network via the Internet.

the sabotage took place after the employee left the company and about half of the ex-employees had been fired. Consequently, it is vital that whenever an employee leaves the company for any reason, all access to the system (username, password, e-mail address, and so forth) should be removed immediately—for employees with high levels of system access, simultaneously removing access while the employee is being terminated is even better. Waiting even a few minutes can be too late, since just-fired employees have been known to barricade themselves in their office immediately after being terminated in order to change passwords, sabotage records, and perform other malicious acts. Some wait slightly longer, such as one salesman at a New York staffing company who allegedly accessed the company computer system the evening after being fired and deleted all the e-mail belonging to his boss. He was charged in federal court with one count of unauthorized access to a computer and intentionally causing more than $5,000 in damage. He faces a maximum sentence of 10 years in prison and a fine of $250,000.

Develop Policies and Controls

All companies should develop policies and controls regarding security matters. Employees should be educated about the seriousness and consequences of computer crime, and they should be taught what to do when they suspect a computer crime. Policies such as shredding sensitive documents that are no longer needed, limiting employee access to only needed parts of the network, immediately removing access for any employee who leaves the company, and separating employee functions as much as possible are all wise precautions. Employees should also be instructed about proper computer and e-mail usage policies—such as whether or not downloading and installing software on company PCs is allowed and how to avoid opening attachments containing malware—to avoid accidentally creating a security problem.

Ask Business Partners to Review their Security

In this networked economy, many organizations provide some access to internal resources for business partners. If those companies are lax with their security measures, attacks from business partners' employees are possible. Consequently, businesses should make sure that their business partners maintain adequate security policies and controls. Regulations—such as the *Sarbanes-Oxley Act of 2002*—increasingly require businesses to ensure that adequate controls are in place to preserve the integrity of financial reports. This includes outside companies—such as business partners and *outsourcing companies* (outside vendors for specific business tasks, as discussed in Chapter 12)—if they have access to sensitive corporate data,

NET

ONLINE THEFT, FRAUD, AND OTHER DOT CONS

A booming area of computer crime involves online fraud, theft, scams, and related activities collectively referred to as **dot cons**. The Internet Crime Complaint Center (a joint venture of the FBI and the National White Collar Crime Center, formerly called Internet Fraud Complaint Center) received around 100,000 reports of fraudulent activities taking place over the Internet in 2004. Common types of dot cons include theft of data, information, and other resources; *identity theft*; *online auction fraud*; and *Internet offer scams*, *spoofing*, and *phishing*.

>**Dot con.** A fraud or scam carried out through the Internet.

Theft of Data, Information, and Other Resources

Data theft or *information theft*—the theft of data or information usually located on a computer—can be committed by stealing an actual PC (as discussed in more detail in Chapter 15); it can also take place over the Internet or a network after a hacker gains unauthorized access to a computer system. Common types of stolen data and information include customer data and proprietary corporate information. Stolen customer data, such as credit card numbers and Social Security numbers, can be used to commit *credit card fraud*, *identity theft*, and other crimes. Recently, there have been numerous examples of personal data stolen via computers, in addition to CardSystems credit card number theft mentioned earlier in this chapter. For instance, 1.4 million credit card numbers were stolen from a DSW Shoe Warehouse database; data about 100,000 alumni, graduate students, and past applicants was compromised when a laptop containing that data was stolen from a U.C. Berkeley office; and around 300,000 records in University of Southern California's online application database were exposed when that database was hacked.

Money is another resource that can be stolen via a computer. Company insiders sometimes steal money by altering company programs to transfer small amounts of money—for example, a few cents' worth of bank account interest—from a very large number of transactions to an account controlled by the thief. This type of crime is sometimes called *salami shaving*. Victims of salami-shaving schemes generally are unaware that their funds have been accessed because the amount taken from each individual is trivial. Another example of monetary theft using computers involves hackers electronically transferring money illegally from online bank accounts, traditional bank accounts, credit card accounts, or accounts at online payment services, such as PayPal. The largest case of Internet fraud to date that has resulted in a conviction involves a California man who stole over $37 million from about 900,000 credit card owners. He signed them up, without their knowledge, for access to his fee-based Web site. He was sentenced in 2004 to more than 11 years in prison and ordered to pay full restitution to his victims.

Identity Theft

Identity theft occurs when someone obtains enough information about a person (such as name, date of birth, Social Security number, address, phone number, and credit card numbers) to be able to masquerade as that person for a variety of activities—usually to buy products or services in that person's name (see Figure 9-16). Typically, identity theft begins with obtaining a person's name and Social Security number, often from a credit application, rental application, or similar form. Once the thief finds that individual's home address (either from the same form or by using a telephone book or an Internet search), he or she usually has enough information to order a copy of the individual's birth certificate over the phone, to obtain a "replacement" driver's license, and to open credit or bank accounts in the victim's name. Assuming the thief requests a change of address for these new accounts after they are opened, it may take quite some time—often until a company or collections agency contacts the victim about overdue bills—for the victim to become aware that his or her identity has been stolen. Although identity theft often takes place via a computer today, information used in identity theft can be gathered from trash dumpsters, mailboxes, and other locations. It can also be obtained by *skimming* (stealing credit card or debit card numbers by attaching a special storage device to ATM machines or credit card readers) or via *social engineering* (pretending to be a bank officer, potential employer, or other trusted individual in order to get the potential victim to offer personal information). In 1998, the federal government passed the *Identity Theft and Assumption Deterrence Act*, which made identity theft a federal crime.

>**Identity theft.** Using someone else's identity to purchase goods or services, obtain new credit cards or bank loans, or otherwise illegally masquerade as that individual.

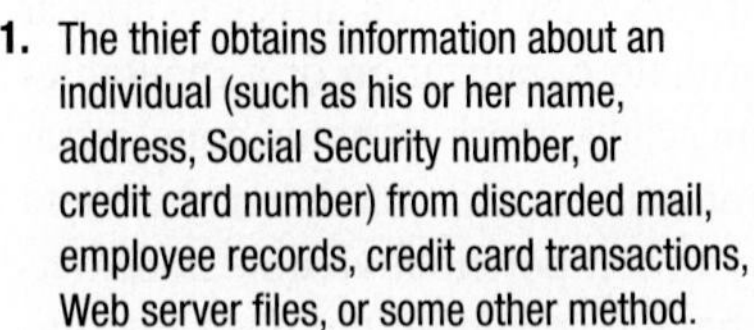

1. The thief obtains information about an individual (such as his or her name, address, Social Security number, or credit card number) from discarded mail, employee records, credit card transactions, Web server files, or some other method.
2. The thief uses the information to make online purchases, open new credit card accounts, sign up for a service, buy or rent property, and more—all in the victim's name. Often, the thief changes the address on the account to delay the victim's discovery of the theft.
3. The victim eventually finds out, usually by being denied credit or by being contacted about overdue bills generated by the thief. Although victims can file reports and complaints, cancel accounts, and dispute unauthorized charges, clearing their names after identity theft is time-consuming and can be very difficult and frustrating.

FIGURE 9-16
How identity theft works.

Unfortunately, identity theft is on the rise—it has topped the list of complaints received by the Federal Trade Commission (FTC) for the past five years and represents about 40% of all complaints filed in 2004. Several studies estimate the number of identity theft victims in the United States per year to be close to 10 million individuals, and it is estimated that identity theft cost businesses and consumers more than $52 billion in 2004. The largest identity theft case in U.S. history to date came to light in late 2002 when federal investigators charged three men with running an identity theft ring—based on information obtained from stolen consumer credit reports—that impacted more than 30,000 consumers and cost nearly $3 million in losses.

Identity theft can be extremely distressing for victims, can take years to straighten out, and can be very expensive. According to the Identity Theft Resource Center, identity theft victims spend an average of 600 hours and $1,400 trying to clear their names. Some victims, such as Michelle Brown, believe that they will always be dealing with their "alter reality" to some extent. For a year and a half, an identity thief used Brown's identity to obtain over $50,000 in goods and services, to rent properties—even to engage in drug trafficking. Although the culprit was arrested and convicted eventually for other criminal acts, she continued to use Brown's identity and was even booked into jail using Brown's stolen identity. As a final insult after the culprit was in prison, the real Michelle Brown was detained by U.S. customs agents when returning from a trip to Mexico because of the criminal record of the identity thief. Brown states that she has not traveled out of the country since, fearing an arrest or some other serious problem resulting from the theft of her identity, and estimates she has spent over 500 hours trying to correct all the problems related to the identity theft.

Online Auction Fraud

Online auction fraud (sometimes called *Internet auction fraud*)—which occurs when a buyer pays for merchandise that is never delivered, or it is delivered but is not as represented—is an increasing risk for online auction bidders. According to the Internet Crime Complaint Center, online auction fraud accounted for about 71% of all reported Internet fraud cases in 2004.

>**Online auction fraud.** When an item purchased through an online auction is never delivered after payment, or the item is not as specified by the seller.

Like other types of fraud, online auction fraud is illegal, but these criminals are often difficult to stop, as well as to identify and prosecute. As is the case in many types of Internet cons, prosecution is difficult because multiple jurisdictions are usually involved. In addition, some online auction fraud victims pay by personal check or money order and know very little about the seller's identity. Although most online auction sites have policies that suspend sellers with a certain number of complaints lodged against them, it is very easy for those sellers to come back using a new e-mail address and identity.

Internet Scams, Spoofing, and Phishing

Internet offer scams include a wide range of scams offered through Web sites or unsolicited e-mails. The anonymity of the Internet makes it very easy for con artists to appear to be almost anyone they want to be, including a charitable organization or a reputable-looking business. Common types of scams include loan scams, work-at-home cons, pyramid schemes, bogus credit card offers and prize promotions, and fraudulent business opportunities and franchises. These offers typically try to sell potential victims nonexistent services or worthless information, or they try to convince potential victims to voluntarily supply their credit card details and other personal information, which are then used for fraudulent purposes.

Some scams involve **spoofing**—making it appear that an e-mail or a Web site originates from somewhere other than its actual source. For instance, con artists create **phishing** (pronounced "fishing") e-mails that appear to be generated by America Online, eBay, PayPal, Citibank, or another well-known organization. They send these e-mails to a wide group of individuals stating that the individual's credit card or account information needs to be updated and requesting that the recipient of the e-mail click the link provided in the e-mail in order to keep the account active (see Figure 9-17). The link actually goes to a Web site belonging to the con artist, although the Web site is usually set up to look as if it belongs to the legitimate organization—an act called *Web site spoofing*.

FIGURE 9-17

Phishing. Phishing schemes use legitimate-looking e-mails to trick users into providing private information.

To accomplish this, the con artist typically uses a copy of the legitimate Web page (sometimes the spoofed Web site even contains live links to selected Web pages of the legitimate site) and a secure connection between the victim and the con artist's server (so the unbroken key or locked padlock on the status bar appears as normal). The con artist can also use JavaScript commands to overwrite the URLs displayed on the browser's status bar and Address bar so that the displayed URLs match the URLs of the legitimate site, which makes a spoofed Web site even more difficult to identify. Because the site looks and responds like the legitimate site, victims often supply the requested information and carry out any additional activities in a seemingly normal fashion, allowing the con artist access to all information—such as account numbers, credit card numbers, and passwords—provided by the victim via the spoofed Web page. To make matters even worse, some phishing e-mail messages now contain a Trojan horse program. After just viewing the phishing e-mail message, the Trojan horse program redirects specific URLs that the user subsequently types (such as the URL for the bank that the phishing e-mail was spoofing) so the

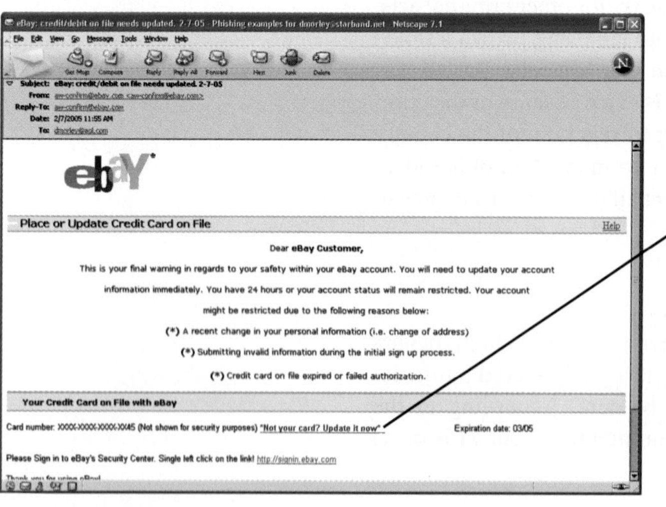

This e-mail looks legitimate, but the link goes to a fraudulent Web page that is set up to look like the legitimate Web site and that requests personal information from the potential victim for fraudulent purposes.

>**Spoofing.** Making it appear that an e-mail or a Web site originates from somewhere other than where it really does; typically used with dot cons.
>**Phishing.** The use of spoofed e-mail messages to gain credit card numbers and other personal data to be used for fraudulent purposes.

TREND

Pharming

As if phishing is not bad enough, now there is *pharming*. Similar to phishing, pharming is used to obtain personal information (such as credit card numbers, account numbers, and passwords) to be used in fraudulent activities, but the technique is a little different, and it is directed at large groups of people at one time, instead of individuals. With pharming, the criminal hacks into a *DNS server*—the computer that translates URLs it receives into the appropriate IP addresses used to display the Web page corresponding to that URL—in order to reroute traffic intended for a commonly used Web site to a phony, usually look-alike, Web site set up by the pharmer. Although pharming can take place at one of the 13 root DNS servers for the Internet, the hacking more often takes place at a company DNS server used to route Web page requests to the appropriate company server. For instance, a company may have several different Web servers set up to process requests received via its Web page URLs, and the company DNS server routes individual requests to an available Web server via that Web server's IP address. After hacking into a DNS server, the pharmer assigns bogus IP addresses to a particular URL (called *DNS poisoning*) so that Web page requests made via that legitimate URL are routed (via the company's poisoned DNS server) to a phony Web site located on the pharmer's Web server. So, even though a user types the proper URL for a Web site in his or her browser, the phony site is displayed instead. Since the phony sites are set up to look like the legitimate sites, the user typically does not notice any difference, and any information sent to the pharmer's server is captured. To avoid suspicion, some pharming sites capture the user's account name and password as it is entered the first time on the phony site, and then display a password error message. The phony site then sends the user back to the legitimate site where he or she is able to log on to the legitimate site, thinking he or she must have just mistyped the password the first time. But, by then, the pharmer has already captured the victim's username and password and can use that information to gain access to the victim's account.

Pharming is much more difficult to recognize than phishing, since it does not require the user to click a hyperlink in an unsolicited e-mail message and the browser and Web pages respond in a legitimate manner to user requests. The best defense against pharming is for businesses to use strong security with their DNS servers, upgrade their DNS server software as needed, and use secure Web servers so that *digital certificates* can be used to verify the site is legitimate. If the name on the digital certificate ever does not match the IP address being used, a warning message will appear (see the accompanying illustration). When this occurs, users should not proceed with the transaction.

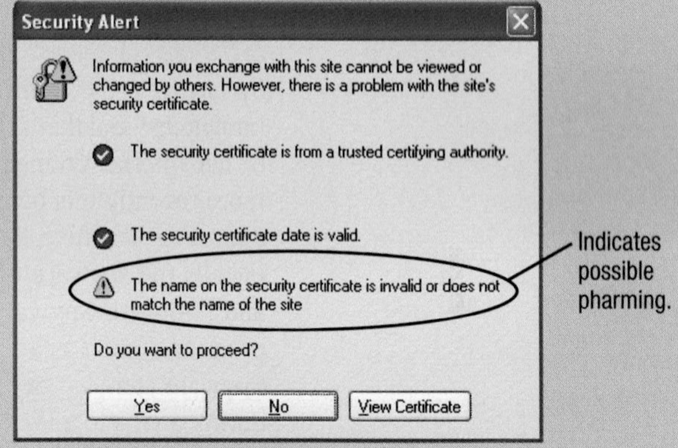

If a message such as this occurs when accessing a secure Web page, it is safer not to proceed.

spoofed site is displayed instead of the legitimate site. Phishing is also now used in conjunction with *spyware*, discussed shortly.

Phishing is growing rapidly. It is estimated that over half of all Americans have received a phishing e-mail and, according to the research firm Gartner, about 1.2 million U.S. consumers suffered phishing-related losses between May 2004 and May 2005, for a total loss of over $900 million. Federal legislation—such as the *Anti-Phishing Act of 2005* that would allow prison time of up to five years and fines of up to $250,000 for people who design fake Web sites for the purposes of stealing money or credit card numbers—has been introduced, but none had passed at the time of this writing, For a look at a new activity related to phishing—*pharming*—see the Trend box.

One ongoing Internet scam is the Nigerian letter fraud scheme, in which an e-mail message appearing to come from the Nigerian government promises the potential victim a share of a substantial amount of money, in exchange for the use of the victim's bank account to supposedly facilitate a wire transfer (but the account is emptied instead) and/or up-front cash to pay for nonexistent fees (that is kept by the con artist with nothing given in return). The theme of these scams (sometimes called *419 scams* after the number of the relevant section of Nigerian criminal law code) sometimes changes to fit current events like the war in Iraq or the Katrina hurricane, but the scams always involve a so-called fortune that is inaccessible to the con artist and individuals lose money when they pay fees or provide bank account information in hopes of sharing in the wealth. Another common scheme involves con artists who solicit donations after disasters and other tragic events, but who keep the donations instead of giving them to any charitable organization. For instance, right after Hurricane Katrina hit the United States in August 2005, a number of fraudulent Web sites appeared that were designed to take advantage of people's sympathy for the hurricane victims by soliciting donations meant for Katrina victims, but these donations were diverted into private accounts instead. In fact, more than 2,500 Katrina- or storm-related domain names were registered—over 450 with the word "Katrina" in them—right after the hurricane. Although some were sites set up to really help victims or solicit legitimate donations, the FBI reports that over 60% of the 2000 sites it has reviewed that claim to offer aid to Katrina victims are registered to people outside the United States and so are likely to be fraudulent.

Another common scam involves setting up a pornographic site that requires a valid credit card, supposedly to prove that the visitor is of the required age (such as over 18), but which is then used for credit card fraud. A new type of scam involves posting fake job listings on job search sites to elicit personal information—such as Social Security numbers—from job seekers. An even more recent twist is to hire individuals through online job sites for seemingly legitimate positions involving money handling (such as bookkeeping or accounting positions), but then use those individuals—often without their knowledge—as legitimate-looking go-betweens to facilitate Internet auction scams and other monetary scams.

Spyware

Spyware is the term used for any software program that is installed without the user's knowledge and that secretly gathers information about the user and transmits it through his or her Internet connection. Traditionally, this information was directed to advertisers, but more recently it is being used in conjunction with phishing schemes to transmit passwords and other sensitive data to the phisher. Typically, clicking a link in the phishing e-mail installs the spyware on the victim's computer, and it will remain there until it is detected and removed. Spyware programs can also be installed secretly at the same time another program—such as a program downloaded from a Web site or a P2P service—is installed. Spyware can also be installed via an instant message, or it can be installed automatically during a visit to a Web site (sometimes called a *drive-by download* because the installation requires no action on the part of the Web site visitor other than visiting the site), if the user's browser security settings do not prevent the installation.

Unfortunately, spyware use is on the rise. A 2004 study by AOL and the National Cyber Security Alliance found that more than 80% of all Internet users have spyware programs installed on their computers, and a 2004 study of two million computers performed by EarthLink and Webroot Software found an average of 26.5 spyware programs installed on each PC. And, according to a 2005 Pew Internet & American Life Project study, nine out of ten Internet users say they have adjusted their online behavior, such as no longer visiting particular Web sites or no longer downloading software, for fear of being infected with spyware. In addition to the potential security risk associated with spyware, these programs can also affect the performance of a PC, such as slowing it down or causing it to work improperly. In 2004, computer manufacturer Dell reported that more than 12% of all technical support calls in its consumer hardware division were due to spyware, and Microsoft claims that half of all computer malfunctions reported by its customers are

>**Spyware.** A software program installed without the user's knowledge that secretly collects information and sends it to an outside party via the user's Internet connection.

caused by spyware. And the problem will likely become worse before it gets any better. Some spyware programs—sometimes referred to as *stealthware*—are getting more aggressive, such as delivering ads regardless of the activity you are doing on your PC, changing your browser home page or otherwise resetting your browser settings (referred to as *browser hijacking*), and performing other annoying actions. The worst spyware programs rewrite your computer's main instructions—such as the *Windows Registry*—to change your browser settings back to the hijacked settings each time you reboot your PC, undoing any changes you may have made to your browser settings.

PROTECTING AGAINST ONLINE THEFT, FRAUD, AND OTHER DOT CONS

Businesses and consumers can both help to prevent some types of online theft—businesses by using good security measures to protect the data stored on their computers, and consumers by only sending sensitive information via secure servers. Various other techniques (as discussed next) can help protect against identity theft, online auction fraud, and other types of dot cons. With any of these cons, it is important to act quickly if you think you have been a victim—work with your local law enforcement agency, credit card companies, and the three major consumer credit bureaus (*Equifax*, *Experian*, and *TransUnion*) to close any accessed or fraudulent accounts, place fraud alerts on your credit report, and take other actions to prevent additional fraudulent activity while the fraud is being investigated.

Arrests and prosecutions by law enforcement agencies may also help cut down on cybercrimes. One successful investigation—called *Operation Web Snare*—has led to the arrests and convictions of over 100 people to date for online theft, online fraud, computer intrusions, and other computer crimes. This cooperative investigation among numerous U.S. attorneys and law enforcement agencies, including the FBI, Secret Service, Postal Inspection Service, and Federal Trade Commission, began in mid-2004 and uncovered more than 870,000 victims with losses topping over $210 million.

NET

Protecting Against Identity Theft

In a nutshell, the best protection against identity theft is to protect your identifying information. Do not give out personal information—especially your Social Security number or mother's maiden name—unless it is absolutely necessary and, before revealing any personal information to a new organization, find out how it will be used and if it will be shared with other organizations. Also, never give out sensitive personal information to anyone who requests it over the phone or by e-mail. Most businesses that need bank account information, passwords, or credit card numbers already have all the information they need and will not call or e-mail a request for more information. If additional information is needed, it will almost always be requested in writing. To prevent someone from using the preapproved credit card offers and other documents containing personal information that frequently arrive in the mail, be sure to tear them up or shred them before throwing them in the trash. To prevent theft of outgoing mail containing sensitive information, do not place it in your mailbox—mail it at the post office or in a USPS drop box.

FURTHER EXPLORATION

For links to further information about how to prevent identity theft and online auction fraud, as well as how to deal with it if it occurs, go to www.course.com/uc11/ch09

To catch instances of credit card fraud or identity theft early, it is a good idea to keep a close eye on your credit card bills and credit history. Make sure your bills come in every month (some thieves will change your mailing address to delay detection), and read credit card statements carefully to look for unauthorized charges. Be sure to follow up on any calls you get from creditors, instead of assuming it is just a mistake. Most security experts also recommend ordering a full credit history on yourself a few times a year to check for accounts listed in your name that you did not open and any other problems. The *Fair and Accurate Credit Transactions Act* (*FACTA*), enacted in December 2003, enables all Americans to get up to three free credit reports per year upon request. For a look at how to get a free credit report online, see the Inside the Industry box. Other legislation related to identity theft—such as one proposed bill that would require businesses to encrypt sensitive data and another that

INSIDE THE INDUSTRY

Getting a Free Online Credit Report

One of the best ways to check for identity theft is to keep a close eye on your credit reports. These reports, such as the ones available through the consumer credit bureaus Equifax, Experian, and TransUnion, contain information about inquiries related to new accounts requested in your name, as well as any delinquent balances or other negative reports. The Fair and Accurate Credit Transactions Act (FACTA), enacted in December 2003, enables all Americans to get a free copy of their credit report, upon request, each year from the three major consumer credit bureaus. Ideally, you will request one every four months to regularly monitor your credit.

One of the easiest ways to get a copy of your credit report is using a Web site, such as the AnnualCreditReport.com site shown in the accompanying illustration. You will first typically be asked your state and then asked to supply identifying information, such as your name, date of birth, and Social Security number. After verifying that the information displayed is your correct information, you will need to correctly answer one or more questions about your credit that only you should know the answer to. After verification, you will be provided with a link to view your report online. Notice that all screens in the process are displayed using a secure Web page.

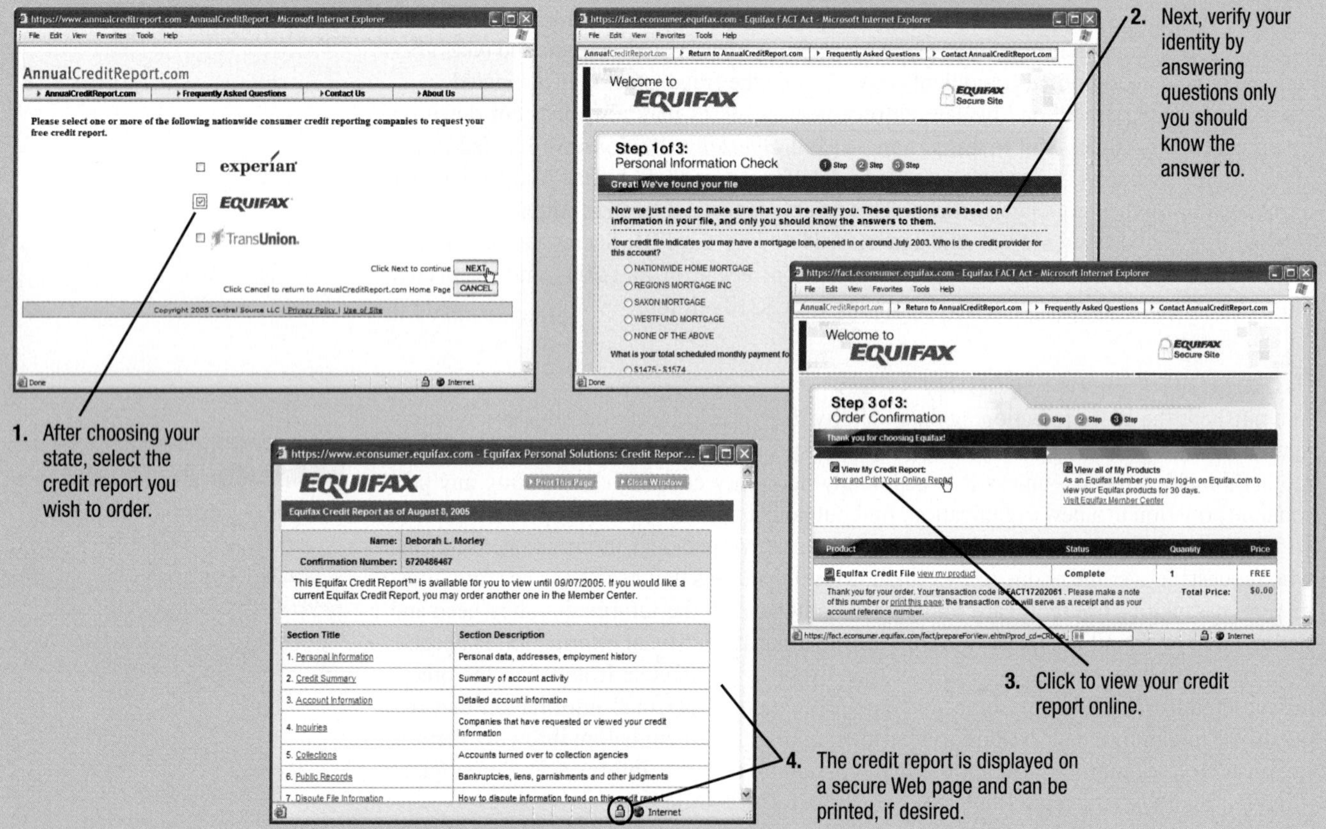

would prohibit businesses from requesting Social Security numbers if another type of identifier could be used instead—is under consideration. Some homeowner's and rental policies include coverage for financial losses resulting from identity theft; stand-alone identity theft insurance is also available.

1. After choosing your state, select the credit report you wish to order.
2. Next, verify your identity by answering questions only you should know the answer to.
3. Click to view your credit report online.
4. The credit report is displayed on a secure Web page and can be printed, if desired.

One emerging possibility for protecting against identity theft is a move by some companies—such as financial institutions and America Online—to offer token-based security systems to protect against unauthorized use of online accounts. Similar to the USB security tokens available to provide access to private networks, these e-tokens are assigned to an individual and used to authenticate that individual when logging on to an account on the Internet. Instead of being physically connected to the PC, the tokens are battery powered and display a different six-digit code every 60 seconds. In order to log on to the financial institution's Web site or an individual's AOL account, the customer must enter his or her username and password, as well as the code displayed on the token (see Figure 9-18). A secure database contains information linking the customer's account to his or her token, as well as the codes generated by the token device.

While two-factor authentication systems such as these are common in other countries, and a few U.S. companies are using two-factor authentication systems to authenticate employees, two-factor authentication systems are not widely used in the United States. But it is expected that more two-factor authentication systems will be introduced in the near future. In fact, one of the recommendations in an FDIC study on identity theft released in 2005 was replacing existing password-based single-factor customer authentication systems with two-factor authentication.

FIGURE 9-18
Token-based authentication. In order to log on to his AOL account, this customer must enter the six-digit code displayed on the token, in addition to his username and password.

Protecting Against Other Dot Cons

The key to protecting against Internet offer scams and other dot cons is common sense. Be extremely cautious of any unsolicited e-mail messages you receive and realize that if an offer sounds too good to be true, it probably is. When dealing with individuals online through auctions and other person-to-person activities, it makes sense to be cautious. Before bidding on an auction item, check out the feedback rating of the seller to see comments written by other auction sellers and buyers (see Figure 9-19). Whenever possible, pay for auctions and other online purchases using a credit card or an online payment service (such as PayPal) that accepts credit card payments so you can dispute the transaction through your credit card company, if needed. Some auction sites offer free buyer protection against

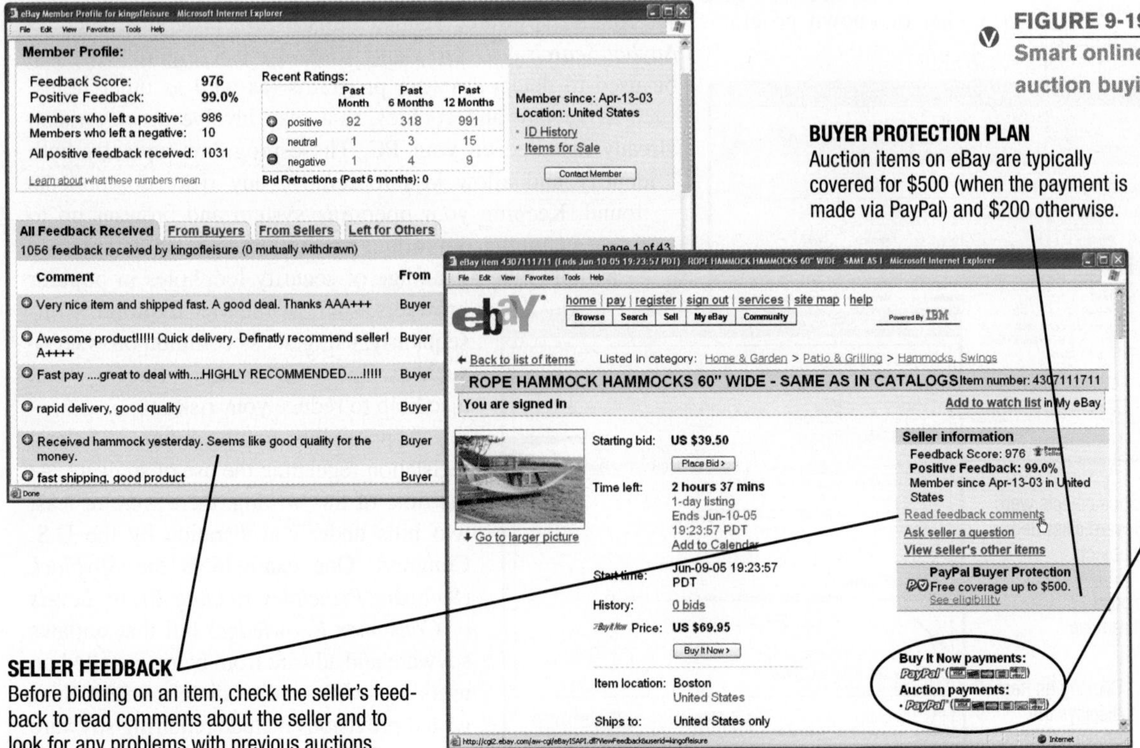

FIGURE 9-19
Smart online auction buying.

undelivered items or auction items that are significantly different from their description provided in the auction information. For instance, eBay offers buyer protection for up to $500 for all items paid for by PayPal and up to $200 for items paid for with other methods. Additional coverage can be purchased, if desired. For expensive items, consider using an *escrow service*, which allows you to ensure that the merchandise is as specified before your payment is released to the seller.

To avoid spoofing and phishing schemes, never respond to e-mail requests for updated credit card information. Some tips for identifying phishing e-mails are shown in Figure 9-20. If you think an e-mail may be legitimate—if, for instance, the credit card you used to automatically pay for your Internet connection or other ongoing service is about to expire—type the URL for the site in your browser to load the legitimate site before updating your account information. *Never* click a link in an e-mail message to update your information. And make sure your operating system and browser are up to date. For instance, Microsoft has released a patch to prevent the installation of the phishing Trojan horse program that redirects URLs, but the patch has to be installed for it to work. Finally, watch your credit card and telephone bills for any erroneous or fraudulent charges.

A PHISHING E-MAIL OFTEN . . .
Tries to scare you into responding by sounding urgent, including a warning that your account will be cancelled if you do not respond, or telling you that you have been a victim of fraud.
Asks you to provide personal information, such as your bank account number, an account password, credit card number, PIN number, mother's maiden name, or Social Security number.
Contains links that do not go where the link text says it will go (point to a hyperlink in the e-mail address to view the URL for that link).
Uses legitimate logos from the company the phisher is posing as.
Does not include a personalized greeting.
Appears to be text or text and images but is actually a single image; it has been created that way to avoid being caught in a *spam filter* (a program that sorts e-mail based on legitimate e-mail and suspected spam) since spam filters cannot read text that is part of an image in an e-mail message.
Contains spelling or grammatical errors.

FIGURE 9-20
Tips for spotting phishing e-mail messages.

Protecting Against Spyware

To prevent spyware from being installed on your computer, you can check Web sites that list known spyware programs before downloading a program to see if the program is on a list of known programs that contain spyware. Special *antispyware* programs, such as *Spybot Search & Destroy* and *Ad-Aware* (see Figure 9-21) can be used to detect spyware programs (as well as other items, such as adware and cookies, that may involve privacy risks) already installed on your PC. These programs typically both identify and allow you to remove any risky components found. Keeping your operating system and browser up to date is another important precaution since some spyware authors take advantage of security loopholes in popular browsers, such as Internet Explorer. Consequently, using a less common browser—such as Opera or Mozilla's Firefox—can also help to reduce your risk.

A possibility for the future is federal legislation regulating the use of spyware. At the time of this writing, there were at least two bills under consideration by the U.S. Congress. One example is the *Spyblock* (*Software Principles Yielding Better Levels of Consumer Knowledge*) bill that outlaws spyware and adware from being installed on users' PCs without their direct consent. Suggested provisions include requiring spyware

FIGURE 9-21
Spyware checkers.
Spyware removal programs can be used to detect and remove spyware programs.

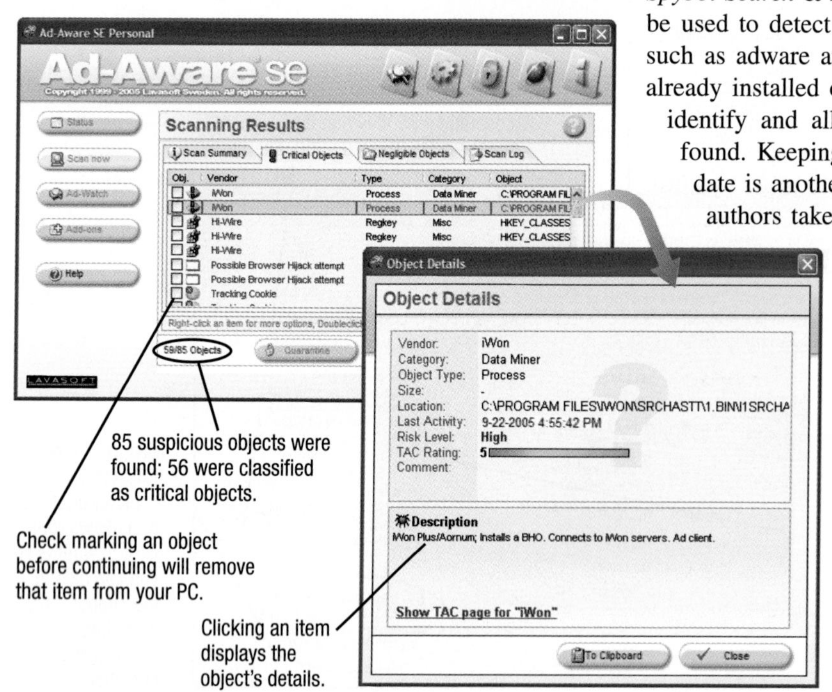

Ad-Aware SE Personal
Ad-Aware se
Scanning Results
Object Details
Vendor: iWon
Category: Data Miner
Object Type: Process
Risk Level: High
Description
Show TAC page for "iWon"
85 suspicious objects were found; 56 were classified as critical objects.
Check marking an object before continuing will remove that item from your PC.
Clicking an item displays the object's details.

makers to disclose the presence and function of their software more clearly to users (possibly by requiring the users to specifically indicate that they have read and agree with the licensing terms in order for the software to be installed), prohibiting the use of browser hijacking, requiring an uninstall option to be installed along with the program, and giving the FTC responsibility to oversee these new requirements. Successful spyware prosecution may also be a deterrent. For instance, one company was ordered to pay $7.5 million in 2005 for bundling hidden spyware in programs given away for free after it was ruled that the company broke New York state laws prohibiting false advertising and deceptive business practices.

Using Digital Signatures and Digital Certificates

While encryption is used to ensure that a document cannot be intercepted or altered during transmission, the purpose of *digital signatures* and *digital certificates* is to authenticate and guarantee the identity of a person or Web site.

Digital signatures are used to verify the identity of the sender of a document. Digital signatures typically use public key encryption, but the sender's *private* key is used to sign the document instead of his or her public key. The private key and the document being signed are used to generate the actual digital signature (a unique digital code); consequently, the signature is different with each signed document. When a digitally signed document is received, the recipient's PC uses the sender's *public* key to verify the digital signature. Since the document is signed with the sender's private key (that only the sender should know) and the digital signature will be deemed invalid if even one character of the document is changed after it is signed, digital signatures guarantee that the document was sent by a specific individual and that it was not tampered with during transit. Often the digital signature indicator appears as a statement at the bottom of the e-mail or a button that can be clicked to see the identity of the verified sender, as shown in Figure 9-22. Digital signatures can be applied to both encrypted and nonencrypted files and messages.

Since the passing of *The Federal Electronic Signatures in Global and National Commerce Act*, which then-President Clinton signed in 2000 with a digital signature, electronic signatures are as legally binding as handwritten signatures for e-commerce transactions. Designed to facilitate consumer transactions, this law enables people and

FURTHER EXPLORATION

For links to further information about digital signatures and digital certificates, go to www.course.com/uc11/ch09

NET

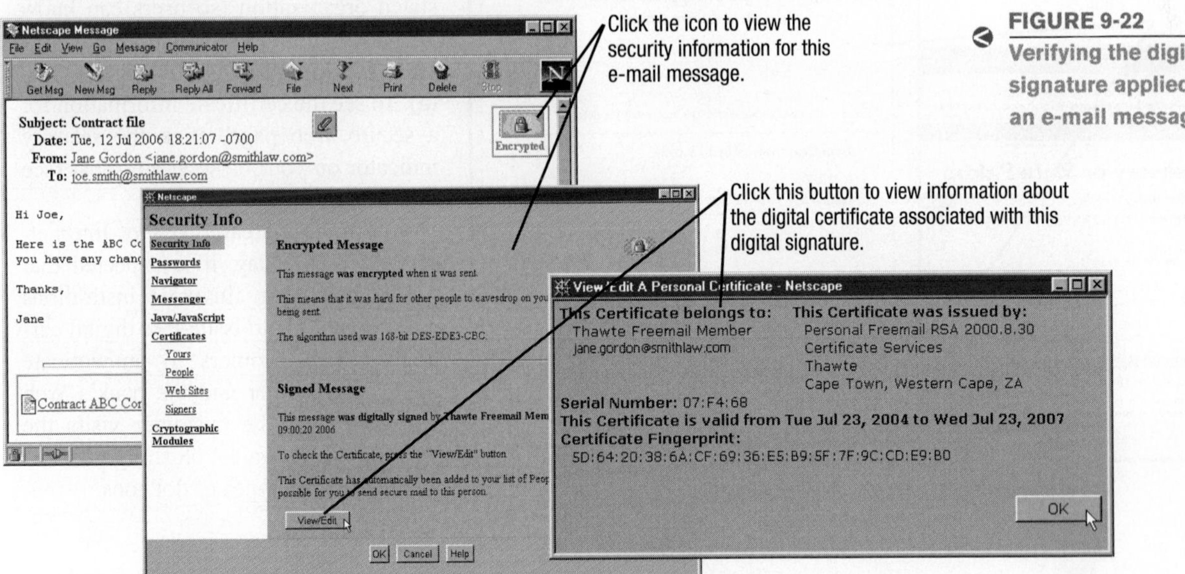

FIGURE 9-22
Verifying the digital signature applied to an e-mail message.

>**Digital signature.** A unique digital code that can be attached to an e-mail message or document to verify the identity of the sender and guarantee the message or file has not been changed since it was signed.

businesses to buy insurance, get a mortgage, open a brokerage account, or finalize other transactions that require a signed authorization, without waiting for physical documents to be mailed back and forth. Although not widely used by individuals, digital signatures are increasingly being used by businesses and the government and are expected to become extremely important as contracts and other legal documents begin to be exchanged more commonly over the Internet. For instance, in 2005, the U.S. Department of Health and Human Services began using digital signatures to approve official correspondence and regulations, and the U.S. Defense Department has already issued more than 5 million smart cards with digital signature capabilities. Experts predict that most federal civilian agencies will begin using digital signatures by 2007. Digital signatures are also used in the *e-mail authentication* systems currently in development by several companies. These systems use digital signatures to authenticate e-mail messages sent from companies, in order to better detect phishing schemes.

In order to add a digital signature to an e-mail message or file, usually a **digital certificate** is needed. Digital certificates are obtained from a *Certificate Authority* and typically contain the name of the person, organization, or Web site being certified along with a certificate serial number, an expiration date, and a pair of keys (one public, one private) that can be used with both digital signatures and encryption. The Certificate Authority guarantees that individuals or organizations granted digital certificates are, in fact, who they claim to be, usually only after verifying their identity with a financial institution or through some other authentication procedure. Certificates issued to businesses and individuals are typically installed in their browser, e-mail program, and any third-party encryption program so that the certificate information is available for use whenever a file or e-mail message needs to be digitally signed or encrypted. Some application programs—such as Microsoft Word—include the option to add a digital signature to documents created in that program, using your digital certificate.

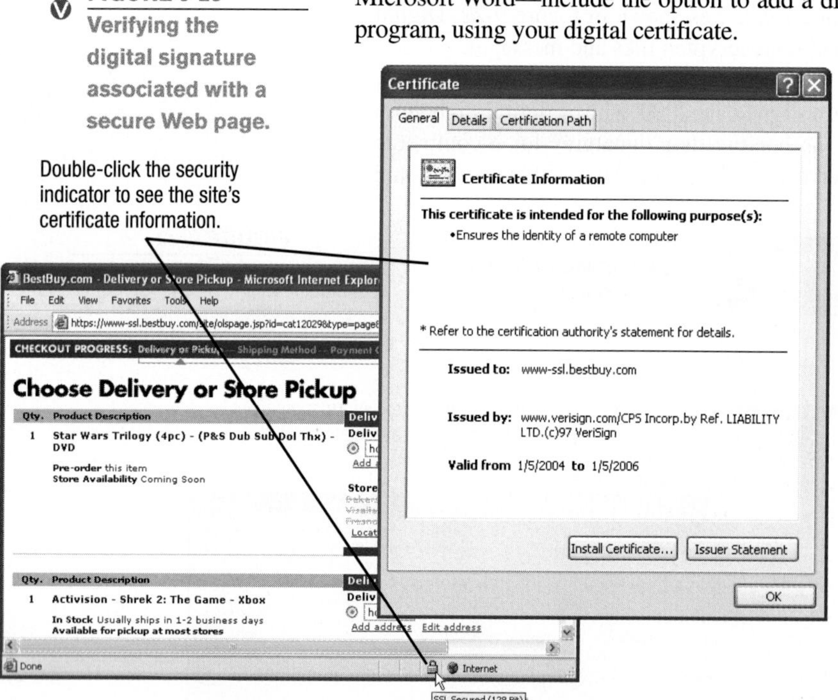

FIGURE 9-23
Verifying the digital signature associated with a secure Web page.

In addition to being used to sign and encrypt files and e-mail messages, digital certificates are also used with secure Web sites to guarantee that the Web site is secure and actually belongs to the stated organization (so users can know for sure who their credit card number or other sensitive data is really being sent to). To see the certificate information for a secure Web page, click the security indicator on your browser's taskbar (see Figure 9-23).

With the increased risk of Internet-related fraud today, it is expected that banks and other financial institutions may soon begin to issue free digital certificates to customers to authenticate both the customer and the bank's Web site each time the customer visits the site, to protect against phishing, identity theft, and other types of dot cons.

>**Digital certificate.** A group of electronic data, such as encryption key pairs and a digital signature, that can be used to verify the identity of a person or organization.

PERSONAL SAFETY ISSUES

Cybercrime can be expensive (as in the case of theft and fraud) and a huge inconvenience (as in the case of identity theft). In addition, it can be physically dangerous. Although most of us may not ordinarily view using the Internet as a potentially dangerous activity, cases of physical harm due to Internet activity do happen. For example, children and teenagers have become the victims of pedophiles who arranged face-to-face meetings by using information gathered via e-mail, discussion groups, or chat rooms. There are also a growing number of *e-bullying* incidents, in which children are getting threatened by classmates via e-mail, Web site posts, or text messages. Adults have fallen for unscrupulous or dangerous individuals who misrepresented themselves online; they have also been victims of *cyberstalking*. In addition, the availability of personal information online has made it more difficult for individuals to hide from people who may want to do them harm, such as abused women trying to hide from their abusive husbands.

Cyberstalking

Cyberstalking can be defined as repeated threats or harassing behavior via e-mail or another Internet communications method. Cyberstalkers often find their victims online—for instance, someone in a chat room who makes a comment or has a screen name that the cyberstalker does not like. There have also been reported cases of employers being stalked online by ex-employees who were fired or otherwise left their position under adverse conditions. Cyberstalking often begins with online harassment, such as sending harassing or threatening e-mail messages or unwanted files to the victim, posting inappropriate messages in chat rooms about the victim or as the victim, signing the victim up for pornographic or otherwise offensive e-mail newsletters, and publicizing the victim's home address and telephone number. Although there is no one exact definition of cyberstalking, the generally accepted definition covers any harassing online activity that would cause a reasonable person to experience fear or some sense of dread or threat. There are as yet no specific federal laws against cyberstalking, but all states have made it illegal, and some federal laws do apply if the online actions include computer fraud or another type of crime, suggest a threat of personal injury, or involve sending obscene e-mail messages.

It has been estimated that about 500,000 people stalk someone online each year. Most cyberstalkers are not caught, however, due in part to the anonymity of the Internet, which assists cyberstalkers in concealing their true identities. Cyberstalking can lead to offline stalking and possibly physical harm—in at least one case, it led to the death of the victim.

Online Pornography

There is a variety of controversial and potentially objectionable material on the Internet. Many parents are concerned about the vast amount of pornography available online. Although there have been attempts to ban this type of material from the Internet, they have not been successful. For example, the *Communications Decency Act*, signed into law in 1996—which made it a criminal offense to distribute patently indecent or offensive material online—was ruled unconstitutional in 1997 by the U.S. Supreme Court. However, like its printed counterpart, online pornography involving minors is illegal. Because of the strong link they believe exists between child pornography and child molestation, many experts are very concerned about the amount of child pornography that can be found and distributed via the Internet. They also believe that the Internet makes it easier for sexual predators to act out, such as by striking up "friendships" with children in chat rooms and convincing them to

>**Cyberstalking.** Repeated threats or harassing behavior via e-mail or another Internet communications method.

meet them in real life. And this can have devastating consequences, as it did for a 13-year-old girl from Connecticut who was strangled to death in 2002 by a 25-year-old man she met in an online chat room, who allegedly confessed to the crime. Although he maintains that the strangling was accidental, the man was sentenced in late 2003 to a total of 40 years in prison for state and federal charges relating to the incident.

PROTECTING AGAINST CYBERSTALKING AND OTHER PERSONAL SAFETY CONCERNS

There is no surefire way to protect against cyberstalking and other online dangers completely, but some common-sense precautions can reduce the chance of becoming involved in serious personal safety problems due to online activities.

Safety Tips for Adults

It is wise to be cautious and discreet in chat rooms, discussion groups, and other online locations where individuals communicate with strangers. To protect yourself against cyberstalking and other types of online harassment, use gender-neutral, nonprovocative identifying names, such as *jsmith*, instead of *janesmith* or *iamcute*. Do not reveal personal information—such as your real name, address, or telephone number—to people you meet in a chat room. Although they may feel like new friends, they are strangers and you have no idea who they really are or what they are like in real life. In addition, do not respond to any insults or other harassing comments you may receive online. You may also wish to request that your personal information be removed from online directories—especially those associated with your e-mail address or other online identifier.

TIP

Search for yourself using search sites and online telephone books to see what personal information is available about you on the Internet.

Safety Tips for Children

Most experts agree that the best way to protect children from online dangers is to stay in close touch with them as they explore the Internet. To be able to check up on their online activities quickly, it is a good idea to have children—including teenagers—use a PC in a family room or other public location, instead of their bedroom, and they should be told which activities are allowed, which types of Web sites are off-limits, and why. In addition, it should be made clear that they are never to reveal personal information about themselves online without a parent's permission. They should also be instructed to tell a parent (or teacher if at school) if an individual ever requests personal information or a personal meeting via an e-mail message, a chat room, an instant message, or other communications medium.

NETWORK AND INTERNET SECURITY LEGISLATION

Although new legislation is passed periodically to address new types of computer crimes, it is difficult for the legal system to keep pace with the rate at which technology changes. In addition, there are both domestic and international jurisdictional issues because many computer crimes affect businesses and individuals located in geographic areas other than the one in which the computer criminal is located, and hackers can make it appear that activity is coming from a different location than it really is. Nevertheless, computer crime legislation continues to be proposed and computer crimes are being prosecuted. In 2005, for instance, a disgruntled Philadelphia Phillies fan charged with 79 counts of computer fraud and identity theft was sentenced to four years in prison. He was found guilty of hacking into individuals' personal computers and using those computer to send hundreds of spam e-mails (using spoofed return addresses so they look liked they came from sports writers for various newspapers) complaining about the

Phillies. Other recent examples include the conviction of a man on 120 counts of unauthorized access of a protected computer, during which he hacked into a marketing database and gained access to over 1 billion consumer records; the sentencing of a former graduate student to 8 months in prison for hacking into computers at several major companies and installing Trojan horse software to capture usernames and passwords in order to gain unauthorized access to other computers; and the conviction and sentencing (to 5 months in prison, 3 years probation, and $60,000 in restitution) of a man charged with 12 counts of wire fraud and seven counts of mail fraud in connection with an eBay Internet auction scam in which he sold items that were never delivered to buyers.

A list of selected federal laws concerning network and Internet security is shown in Figure 9-24. As shown in this figure, the main piece of legislation regarding computers crime—the *Computer Fraud and Abuse Act*—has been regularly amended to better define its scope and to clarify its intent. The law currently outlaws unauthorized access to data stored in federal government computers and federally regulated financial institutions. It also outlaws the deliberate implantation of computer viruses in those computers. The *USA Patriot Act* (*USAPA*), implemented in 2001, grants federal authorities expanded surveillance and intelligence-gathering powers, such as broadening their ability to obtain the real identity of Internet users and to intercept Internet communications. The *Homeland Security Act of 2002* includes a number of provisions that deal with cyberterrorism and powers for obtaining information from computer and ISP sources, such as protecting ISPs against suits from customers for revealing private information to law enforcement agencies, and a variety of acts (such as the Sarbanes-Oxley Act of 2002 and the *Health Insurance Portability and Accountability Act* or *HIPPA*) require increased security for computer networks to project information stored on network servers. The most recent federal computer crime law at the time of this writing was the *Identity Theft Penalty Enhancement Act*, signed into law in mid-2004, which adds extra years to prison sentences for criminals who use identity theft (including the use of stolen credit card numbers) to commit other crimes, including credit card fraud and terrorism. Additional legislation regarding spyware, phishing, and identity theft is under consideration and may become law in the future.

FIGURE 9-24
Computer network and Internet security legislation.

DATE	LAW AND DESCRIPTION
2004	**Identity Theft Penalty Enhancement Act** Adds extra years to prison sentences for criminals who use identity theft (including the use of stolen credit card numbers) to commit other crimes, including credit card fraud and terrorism.
2003	**Fair and Accurate Credit Transactions Act (FACTA)** Amends the Fair Credit Reporting Act (FCRA) to require, among other things, that the three nationwide consumer reporting agencies (Equifax, Experian, and TransUnion) provide to consumers, upon request, a free copy of their credit report once every 12 months.
2003	**PROTECT Act** Includes provisions to prohibit virtual child pornography.
2003	**Heath Insurance Portability and Accountability Act (HIPAA)** Includes a Security Rule that sets minimum security standards to protect health information stored electronically.
2002	**Homeland Security Act** Includes provisions to combat cyberterrorism, including protecting ISPs against lawsuits from customers for revealing private information to law enforcement agencies.
2002	**Sarbanes-Oxley Act** Requires archiving a variety of electronic records and protecting the integrity of corporate financial data.
2001	**USA Patriot Act (USAPA)** Grants federal authorities expanded surveillance and intelligence-gathering powers, such as broadening the ability of federal agents to obtain the real identity of Internet users, intercept e-mail and other types of Internet communications, follow online activity of suspects, expand their wiretapping authority, and more.
1998	**Identity Theft and Assumption Deterrence Act of 1998** Makes it a federal crime to knowingly use someone else's means of identification, such as name, Social Security number, or credit card, to commit any unlawful activity.
1997	**No Electronic Theft (NET) Act** Expands computer piracy laws to include distribution of copyrighted materials over the Internet.
1996	**National Information Infrastructure Protection Act** Amends the Computer Fraud and Abuse Act of 1984 to punish information theft crossing state lines and crack down on network trespassing.
1994	**Computer Abuse Amendments Act** Amends the Computer Fraud and Abuse Act of 1984 to include computer viruses and other harmful code.
1986	**Computer Fraud and Abuse Act of 1986** Amends the 1984 law to include federally regulated financial institutions.
1984	**Computer Fraud and Abuse Act of 1984** Makes it a crime to break into computers owned by the federal government.

SUMMARY

WHY BE CONCERNED ABOUT NETWORK AND INTERNET SECURITY?

Chapter Objective 1: Explain why computer users should be concerned about network and Internet security.

There are a number of important security concerns related to computers and the Internet. Many of these are **computer crimes**. Because computers and networks are so widespread, there is unprecedented opportunity for criminals and other individuals to commit acts that are not in the public interest. All computer users should be aware of the risks of using networks and the Internet so they can take appropriate precautions.

UNAUTHORIZED ACCESS, UNAUTHORIZED USE, AND COMPUTER SABOTAGE

Chapter Objective 2: List several examples of unauthorized access, unauthorized use, and computer sabotage.

Two important risks related to computer networks and the Internet are **unauthorized access** and **unauthorized use**. **Hacking** is the term used for using a computer to break into a computer system. Hacking can take place via the Internet or via a wireless network. **War driving** is the act of looking for unsecured Wi-Fi networks to access without authorization. Data can also be intercepted as it is transmitted over the Internet or a wireless network.

Common types of **computer sabotage** include **malware** (**computer viruses**, **computer worms**, **Trojan horses**, and other programs designed to cause harm to computer systems), **denial of service (DoS) attacks** (attempts to shut down a network or Web server by flooding it with more requests than it can handle), data and program alteration, and *cybervandalism*.

PROTECTING AGAINST UNAUTHORIZED ACCESS, UNAUTHORIZED USE, AND COMPUTER SABOTAGE

Chapter Objective 3: Explain what risks access control systems, firewalls, antivirus software, and encryption protect against.

There are many options for protecting a network against unauthorized access and use. For instance, *access control systems* include **possessed knowledge access systems** that use **passwords** or other types of possessed knowledge; **possessed object access systems** that use physical objects, such as badges and cards; and **biometric access systems** that identify users by a particular unique biological characteristic, such as a fingerprint, hand, face, or iris. To be effective, passwords should be *strong passwords*; *two-factor authentication systems* that use multiple control factors are more effective than single-factor systems.

To protect wireless networks, security features should be enabled. **Firewalls** protect networks and individual computers against unauthorized access; **antivirus software** protects against getting malware, as well as removing it should it ever be installed on your PC. Firewalls and antivirus software can also help prevent against some other types of sabotage, such as your computer being used in a denial of service attack. Keeping your operating system, Web browser, and e-mail programs up to date, such as by installing security patches as soon as they become available, is another good precaution.

Sensitive transactions should be performed only on **secure Web servers**; sensitive files and e-mails should be secured with **encryption** techniques, such as **public key encryption** (in which a private key and matching public key are used) or **private key encryption** (in which only a private key is used). *Web-based encryption* is also available. The strength of an encryption method is measured by the length of its keys, such as *weak* (40-bit) *encryption*, *strong 128-bit*, and *military-strength 2,048-bit encryption* that is very difficult to crack. A **virtual private network (VPN)** can be used to provide a secure remote connection to a company network. Employers should take appropriate precautions to reduce the change of an attack by a current or former employee.

ONLINE THEFT, FRAUD, AND OTHER DOT CONS

There are a variety of types of theft, fraud, and scams related to the Internet—collectively referred to as **dot cons**—that all Internet users should be aware of. Data, information, or money can be stolen from individuals and businesses. Sometimes this occurs in conjunction with **identity theft**, in which an individual poses as another individual. **Online auction fraud**, *Internet offer scams*, **spoofing**, and **phishing** are other common possibilities. **Spyware** programs can also be used to gather sensitive information about individuals, as well as to deliver ads and other possibly annoying content to Internet users.

Chapter Objective 4:
Discuss online theft, identity theft, Internet scams, spoofing, phishing, and other types of dot cons.

PROTECTING AGAINST ONLINE THEFT, FRAUD, AND OTHER DOT CONS

To protect against identity theft, individuals should guard their personal information carefully. To check for identity theft, watch your bills and credit history. When interacting with other individuals online or buying from an online auction, it is wise to be conservative and use a credit card whenever possible. To avoid other types of dot cons, be very wary of responding to unsolicited offers and e-mails, and steer clear of offers that seem too good to be true. Never click a link in an e-mail message to update your personal information. To verify the sender of a document, **digital signatures** can be used. Digital signatures are obtained as part of a **digital certificate** acquired through a *Certification Authority* (*CA*) after the applicant's identity is verified. Digital certificates can also be used to verify the identity of secure Web pages, and the keys included in the certificate can be used for sending encrypted files to others. *Antispyware* programs can help detect and remove spyware installed on your PC.

Chapter Objective 5:
Detail steps an individual can take to protect against online theft, identity theft, Internet scams, spoofing, phishing, and other types of dot cons.

PERSONAL SAFETY ISSUES

There are also personal safety risks for both adults and children stemming from Internet use. **Cyberstalking**—online harassment that frightens or threatens the victim—is more common in recent years, even though most states have passed laws against it. *E-bullying* is a growing risk for children, as is the potential exposure to online pornography and other materials inappropriate for children.

Chapter Objective 6:
Identify personal safety risks associated with Internet use.

PROTECTING AGAINST CYBERSTALKING AND OTHER PERSONAL SAFETY CONCERNS

To protect their personal safety, adults and children should be cautious in online communications. They should be wary of revealing any personal information or meeting online acquaintances in person. To protect children, parents should keep a close watch on their children's online activities, and they should never reveal personal information to others online without a parent's consent.

Chapter Objective 7:
List steps individuals can take when using the Internet to safeguard their personal safety.

NETWORK AND INTERNET SECURITY LEGISLATION

Although the rapid growth of the Internet and jurisdictional issues have contributed to the lack of network and Internet security legislation, some important pieces of legislation are in place, such as the *USA Patriot Act*, *Identity Theft and Assumption Act*, and *Computer Fraud and Abuse Act*.

Chapter Objective 8:
Name several laws related to network and Internet security.

REVIEW ACTIVITIES

KEY TERM MATCHING

Instructions: Match each key term on the left with the definition on the right that best describes it.

a. computer virus

b. denial of service (DoS) attack

c. dot con

d. encryption

e. firewall

f. hacking

g. identity theft

h. password

i. spoofing

j. spyware

1. ______ A collection of hardware and/or software intended to protect a computer or computer network from unauthorized access.

2. ______ A fraud or scam carried out through the Internet.

3. ______ A method of scrambling e-mail or files to make them unreadable if they are intercepted by an unauthorized user.

4. ______ A secret combination of characters used to gain access to a computer, computer network, or other resource.

5. ______ A software program installed without the user's knowledge that secretly collects information and sends it to an outside party via the user's Internet connection.

6. ______ A software program installed without the user's knowledge and designed to alter the way a computer operates or to cause harm to the computer system.

7. ______ An act of sabotage that attempts to flood a network server or a Web server with so much activity that it is unable to function.

8. ______ Making it appear that an e-mail or a Web site originates from somewhere other than where it really does; typically used with dot cons.

9. ______ Using a computer to break into another computer system.

10. ______ Using someone else's identity to purchase goods or services, obtain new credit cards or bank loans, or otherwise illegally masquerade as that individual.

SELF-QUIZ

Instructions: Circle **T** if the statement is true, **F** if the statement is false, or write the best answer in the space provided. **Answers to the self-quiz are located in the References and Resources Guide at the end of the book.**

1. **T F** A computer virus can only be transferred to another computer via a storage medium.
2. **T F** An access system that uses a fingerprint reader is a biometric access system.
3. **T F** Spyware is a malicious program that masquerades as something else.
4. **T F** Secure Web servers use encryption.
5. **T F** Cyberstalking is the use of spoofed e-mail messages to gain credit card numbers and other personal data to be used for fraudulent purposes.
6. A person who drives around looking for a Wi-Fi network to access is said to be ______.
7. A(n) ______ device uses some type of unique physical characteristic of a person to identify or grant access to individuals.
8. A(n) ______ protects a computer or network from unauthorized access by closing down external communications port addresses to unauthorized programs or requests.
9. With ______ encryption, two keys are used—one to encrypt the file or e-mail message and one to decrypt it.

10. Match each type of computer crime with its description and write the corresponding number in the blank to the left of each description.

   a. ______ A person working for the Motor Vehicle Division deletes a friend's speeding ticket from a database.
   b. ______ An individual attaches a file to an e-mail message that will automatically send itself to the first 10 people on the recipient's e-mail address book when the file is opened.
   c. ______ An individual does not like someone's comment in a chat room and begins to send that individual harassing e-mail messages.
   d. ______ An individual sells the same item to 10 individuals via an online auction site.
   e. ______ A person creates an e-mail message that looks like it belongs to a legitimate company but contains a link to the individual's Web site instead, and sends the e-mail message to numerous individuals.
   f. ______ A person accesses a computer belonging to the IRS without authorization.

   1. Online auction fraud
   2. Hacking
   3. Computer sabotage
   4. Data or program alteration
   5. Phishing
   6. Cyberstalking

EXERCISES

1. Write the appropriate letter in the blank to the left of each term to indicate whether it is related to unauthorized access (U), computer sabotage (C), online theft or fraud (O), or personal safety (P).

   a. ______ Cyberstalking
   b. ______ Phishing
   c. ______ Cybervandalism
   d. ______ Time bomb
   e. ______ War driving
   f. ______ Denial of service (DoS) attack
   g. ______ Malware
   h. ______ Spoofing
   i. ______ Hacking

2. Is the password *john1* a good password? Why or why not? If not, suggest a better password.

3. Supply the missing words to complete the following statements.

   a. With an encrypted e-mail message, the recipient's ______ key is used to encrypt the message, and the recipient's ______ key is used to decrypt the message.
   b. With a digital signature, the sender's ______ key is used to sign the document, and the sender's ______ key is used to validate the signature.

4. To secure files on your PC so they are unreadable to a hacker who might gain access to your PC, what type of encryption (public key or private key) would be the most appropriate. Explain.

5. List two precautions that individuals can take when purchasing items via an online auction to avoid loss due to online auction fraud.

NET

DISCUSSION QUESTION

According to security experts, new variants of several worms released in mid-2004 and 2005 contain more than just the virus code—they contain messages taunting other virus writers and code to remove competing malware from the PCs they infect. For instance, the Netsky worm includes code to remove the Mydoom and Bagle worms from PCs that the Netsky worm infects, and the latest variant of the Bozori worm removes competing worms, like Zotob, from the PCs it infects. The goal seems to be not only to gain control of an increasing number of infected machines—a type of "bot war" to build the biggest network of infected zombie PCs—but also to one-up rivals. Some virus writers may just want to obtain notoriety, but another more alarming possibility is that an increasing percentage of virus writers are interested in gaining control of PCs for monetary gain—such as through identity theft and other fraudulent activities. And the increased use of spam to spread viruses just makes the entire situation worse. If this trend continues, do you think it will affect how hackers and other computer criminals will be viewed? Will they become cult heroes or be viewed as dangerous criminals? Will continuing to increase prosecution of these individuals help or hurt the situation?

PROJECTS

HOT TOPICS

1. **Top Ten Dot Cons** As discussed in the chapter, dot cons are a rapidly growing area for thieves and con artists. In addition to the regular cons that have been around for years, new types of cons—such as Web site spoofing—appear on a regular basis.

   For this project, type the search phrase "FTC top ten dot cons" into the search box of your favorite search site to locate the Federal Trade Commission (FTC) Top Ten Dot Cons Web page. Review the listed cons to determine how many are computer-related. Choose one computer-related dot con and read the information available through the site to figure out how it works and determine what actions a consumer can take to avoid falling prey to this type of dot con. At the conclusion of your research, prepare a one-page summary of your findings and submit it to your instructor.

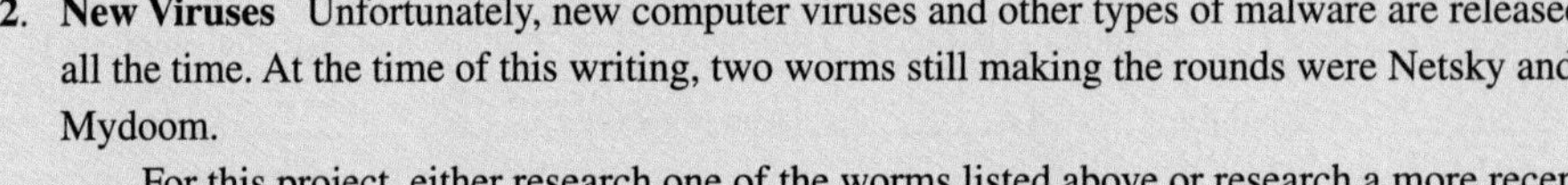

SHORT ANSWER/ RESEARCH

2. **New Viruses** Unfortunately, new computer viruses and other types of malware are released all the time. At the time of this writing, two worms still making the rounds were Netsky and Mydoom.

   For this project, either research one of the worms listed above or research a more recent example of malware (most security companies, such as Symantec and McAfee, list the most recent security threats on their Web sites) and answer the following questions: When was it introduced? What did it do? How was it spread? How many computers were affected? Is there an estimated cost associated with it? Is it still in existence? At the conclusion of your research, prepare a one-page summary of your findings and submit it to your instructor.

3. **Digital Certificates** When you want the capability to both digitally sign and encrypt e-mail messages, a digital certificate is typically your best bet. Although some digital certificates require a fee, free personal certificates are available.

   For this project, locate a Certificate Authority (CA) that provides free digital certificates for personal use. Determine the minimum amount of information needed to obtain one and, if you have Internet access at home, sign up for a free certificate using that process on your home PC. When the digital certificate is sent to you on your home PC, install it for use with your e-mail program, and then send yourself an e-mail that is signed or encrypted. Retrieve the e-mail to make sure it came through in one piece and to see what it looks like on the recipient's end. Does this CA offer a more secure certificate after further authentication? If you were able to send and receive an encrypted e-mail, how easy was the process? Would you want to use it to secure or sign sensitive e-mails in the future? At the conclusion of your research, submit your findings and opinions to your instructor in the form of a short paper, no more than two pages in length.

HANDS ON

4. **Virus Check** There are several Web sites that include a free virus check, as well as other types of diagnostic software.

   For this project, go to the home page for a company that makes antivirus software (such as Symantec at www.symantec.com or McAfee at mcafee.com) and choose the option to run a free virus check (sometimes called a security check). NOTE: The programs may require temporarily downloading a small program or ActiveX component. If you are unable to perform this task on a school PC, ask your instructor for alternate instructions. If the check takes more than 10 minutes and there is an option to limit the check to a particular drive and folder, redo the check just scanning part of the hard drive (such as the My Documents folder) to save time. After the virus scan is completed, print the page displaying the result. Did the program find any viruses or other security threats? At the conclusion of this task, submit your printout with any additional comments about your experience to your instructor.

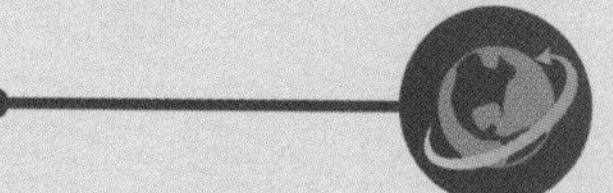

5. **Virus Hoaxes** In addition to the valid reports about new viruses found in the news and on antivirus software Web sites, reports of viruses that turn out to be hoaxes abound on the Internet. In addition to being an annoyance, virus hoaxes waste time and computing resources. In addition, they may eventually lead some users to routinely ignore all virus warning messages, leaving them vulnerable to a genuine, destructive virus.

   For this project, visit at least two Web sites that identify virus hoaxes, such as the Symantec and McAfee antivirus software Web sites and the government Hoaxbusters site, currently found at hoaxbusters.ciac.org. Explore the sites to find information about recent virus hoaxes, as well as general guidelines for identifying virus hoaxes and other types of online hoaxes. At the end of this task, prepare a one-page summary of your findings to submit to your instructor.

WRITING ABOUT COMPUTERS

6. **Hacktivism** *Hacktivism* can be defined as the act of hacking into a computer system for a politically or socially motivated purpose. The individual who performs an act of hacktivism is said to be a *hacktivist*. While some view hacktivists no differently than they view other hackers, hacktivists contend that they break into systems in order to bring attention to political or social causes. Two recent examples of hacktivism include the Web defacements in 2002 by two individuals calling themselves the "Deceptive Duo" and the Web defacements following the death of a Chinese airman when his jet fighter collided with a U.S. surveillance plane in 2001.

   For this project, research one of the two examples of hacktivism mentioned above (or a more recent hacktivism example). Were the hackers identified or found guilty of a crime? What seemed to be the motivation behind the hacks? Form an opinion about hacktivism in general, such as whether or not this is a valid method of bringing attention to specific causes, and whether or not hacktivists should be treated any differently when caught than other types of hackers are treated. Submit this project to your instructor in the form of a short paper, not more than two pages in length.

NET

PRESENTATION/ DEMONSTRATION

7. **Online Rip-Off** Imagine this: You have just been ripped of by an unscrupulous online vendor, and you want to know what you can do about it. The situation surrounding the rip-off was not uncommon. You were surfing the Web about two weeks ago and found this great e-book for sale at one-third the price that you have seen for sale elsewhere, and you decided to use your credit card to purchase it over the Internet. When it was delivered today, the package contained a cardboard version of the e-book consisting of a scrolled piece of paper with two thumb wheels and a cheap pen. You start to panic and one of your friends reminds you of a few organizations that may come to your aid. These organizations are the Internet Fraud Complaint Center, Fraud.org, and the Federal Trade Commission (FTC), as well as your credit card company.

   For this project, consider this scenario and determine what each of these organizations might be able to do to help. In addition, draft a few general guidelines to follow when purchasing products over the Web and give some suggestions for how this rip-off could have been avoided in the first place. Share your findings with the class in the form of a short presentation. The presentation should not exceed 10 minutes and should make use of one or more presentation aids, such as the chalkboard, handouts, overhead transparencies, or a computer-based slide presentation (your instructor may provide additional requirements). You may also be asked to submit a summary of the presentation to your instructor.

GROUP DISCUSSION

8. **Homeless Hacker** Hackers who try to gain access to business and government computers and networks are a growing problem. Some hackers do it for monetary gain; others supposedly to bring attention to system vulnerabilities or other, purportedly more noble, purposes. One example of a business and government network hacker is Adrian Lamo, a young freelance security consultant who regularly tries to hack into computer systems without authorization, looking for their security holes. If hackers like Lamo continue to use real networks and Web servers to practice and improve their hacking skills, what are the implications? Will it expose the data located on those networks to greater danger, or will it result in tightened security and, ultimately, a more secure system? Lamo says that, while he is an intruder, he is guided by a sense of curiosity, and he is helping corporations and consumers understand the limits of Internet security. Should these hackers be treated differently than hackers who break into systems to steal data or other resources? Are there varying degrees of criminal hacking, or is a hack just a hack, regardless of the motivation? Lamo has begun publicizing his successful hacks through the media, instead of contacting the company directly. Does that make his motives more questionable? In 2004, Lamo was indicited and pled guilty to breaking into a database at the New York Times containing employee records for op-ed columnists. He was sentenced to serve two years probation and pay $65,000 in restitution. Does his arrest change your opinion at all about so-called "harmless hacking"?

   For this project, form an opinion of the impact of hackers breaching the security of business and government computers and networks and be prepared to discuss your position (in class, via an online class discussion group, or in a class chat room, depending on your instructor's directions). You may also be asked to write a short paper expressing your opinion.

WEB ACTIVITIES

The *Understanding Computers* Web site located at **www.course.com/uc11** features many resources to help reinforce your understanding of the chapter content and help you prepare for exams. Your instructor may also assign specific activities to be completed that will count toward your final grade in the course.

Instructions: Go to **www.course.com/uc11/ch09** to work the following online activities.

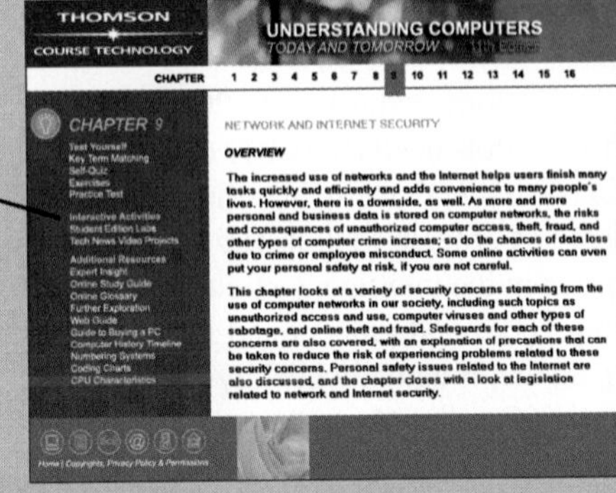

Click any link in the navigation bar on the left to access any of the online resources described below.

INTERACTIVE ACTIVITIES

1. **Crossword Puzzle** Practice your knowledge of the key terms in Chapter 9 by completing the interactive Crossword Puzzle.
2. **Tech News Video Project** Watch the **"Understanding Spoofing"** video clip that takes a look at how spoofing and personal firewalls work. After watching the video online, complete the corresponding project.
3. **Student Edition Labs** Reinforce the concepts you have learned in this chapter by working through the interactive **Keeping Your Computer Virus Free** lab.

Student Edition Labs

NET

TEST YOURSELF

1. **Key Term Matching** Test your knowledge of selected chapter key terms by matching the terms with their definitions.
2. **Self-Quiz** Test your retention of chapter concepts by taking the Self-Quiz.
3. **Exercises** Work these short exercises to review the concepts and terms covered in the chapter.
4. **Practice Test** Test how ready you are for an upcoming exam by completing the online Practice Test.

STUDY TOOLS/ ADDITIONAL RESOURCES

The Understanding Computers Web site has a wide range of additional resources, including an **Online Study Guide** (containing study tips, a chapter outline with room to add your own notes, and a chapter checklist of the activities to complete when the chapter is covered in class and when you are preparing for a test) and an **Online Glossary** for each chapter; **Further Exploration** links; a **Web Guide**, a **Guide to Buying a PC**, and a **Computer History Timeline**; more information about **Numbering Systems**, **Coding Charts**, and **CPU Characteristics**; and much, much more!

EXPERT INSIGHT ON . . .
Networks and the Internet

A conversation with **JEFF BARDIN**
Chief Information Security Officer, The Hanover Insurance Group

My Background . . .

I've been working in the Information Technology industry for 20 years. As the Dotcoms started to implode, I saw the need for greater security controls in all the newly created software, hardware, and associated systems and applications. I began more in-depth study into the area, tested for and received several security certifications, and attended classes at Carnegie Mellon University's Software Engineering Institute. My military background and experience in the intelligence field (I held Top Secret clearances while working for the U.S. government breaking codes and ciphers and performing Arabic language translations) provided a necessary level of paranoia that is actually healthy when working in a security position.

As the CISO of The Hanover Insurance Group today, some of my main responsibilities surround developing cost effective information security programs; overseeing the establishment, implementation, and adherence to policies, guidelines, and procedures related to the protection of mission critical assets; conducting risk assessments; interfacing with third-party auditors and state examiners; ensuring proper security controls are in place; managing the security operations team providing perimeter and internal security, including incident handling, investigative support, and forensics activities.

"In a short 20 years we have taken technology that filled two rooms and put the same power into the palm of your hand."

It's Important to Know . . .

Basic networking principles. This ensures a strong foundation upon which to build. Regardless of the industry, establishing a strong educational base is key to understanding additional, more complex concepts.

The possible threats to your devices and information. If you do not understand the threats targeting your network and computing infrastructure, it can be very difficult to determine what types of protection strategies to employ. To secure yourself against the enemy, you have to first know who your enemy is and what tools the enemy has in his arsenal.

Safeguards that can reduce risk. Safeguards reduce risk, but they don't usually eliminate risk completely. Risk left over after the safeguard is applied (residual risk) may be acceptable as long as the risk is kept to a level that fits the sensitivity of the data and criticality of the system. In the risk management model, every risk is analyzed and controlled to an acceptable level by applying safeguards, or countermeasures, to the risk. Once a risk is reduced to an acceptable level, it must be monitored and re-evaluated throughout the systems development lifecycle so that the risk does not rise to an unacceptable level. If it does, new safeguards are selected and applied. The cycle of assessing and managing risk is continuous.

Jeff Bardin is currently the Chief Information Security Officer for The Hanover Insurance Group. He has served in the United States Air Force and the United States Army National Guard, and has worked at the National Security Agency. Jeff is an active security consultant and the author of several articles on information security and IT governance. He has also taught several classes on information security.

We are an "always on" culture where any activity at any time can be filmed, photographed, recorded, and reported. The privacy concerns are huge. The benefits are just as great.

How I Use this Technology . . .

I have often performed war driving to provide examples of the ratio of secured vs. unsecured wireless access points. At home, I have a LAN extended by wireless that is also extended further with high gain, omni-directional antennas. Multiple laptops and desktop computers connect to this 'secure' network as well as a wireless printer. Wireless storage is available as well.

What the Future Holds . . .

The security marketplace is still evolving and immature in several areas. Regulations will only continue to tighten security and privacy. The millions of individual exposures of personally identifiable information we have seen reported (and I stress reported) lately are speeding the regulatory and legislative cycles.

More and more cities will offer wireless access. Commerce will continue to take a larger share of the shopping pie. Biometrics and identity management functions will continue to merge and become the norm. Credit cards will change in form and merge with your cell phone. Television and the Internet will continue their merger as the ability to push this content over wireless channels continues. From health-care diagnosis devices to legal testimony, the Internet will become an essential part of every home, and new homes will be built for the "always on," "always available," "always accessible" world we demand.

The technology has and will continue to have a significant impact on our daily lives. We have become a culture of near real-time communications over various protocols and methods. In a short 20 years we have taken technology that filled two rooms and put the same power into the palm of your hand. We are an "always on" culture where any activity at any time can be filmed, photographed, recorded, and reported. The privacy concerns are huge. The benefits are just as great. In another 20 years, working from home should be expected in several career fields as we look to cut fuel consumption, cease wasted travel time, and squeeze more productivity out of the most productive workforce in the world.

NET

My Advice to Students . . .

Never marry yourself to any one technology because you will die with it through commoditization and obsolescence. Don't be a technology bigot. To prepare for the future, continue to take traditional computer science courses, but also strongly consider a Master's degree that focuses on business management, international organizational management, and technology management. Learning to manage a diverse workforce without borders is critical for success.

Discussion Question

Jeff Bardin views the security and privacy controls in place today as still immature, with room for improvement. Think about the systems that contain personal data about you. How would you feel if those systems were breached and your information was stolen? Does your viewpoint change if the information was monetary (such as credit card information) versus private information (such as grades or health information)? What security precautions, if any, do you think should be imposed by laws? Are organizations that hold your personal data morally responsible for going beyond the minimum requirements? What types of security measures would you implement to protect these systems? Be prepared to discuss your position (in class, via an online class discussion group, or in a class chat room, depending on your instructor's directions). You may also be asked to write a short paper expressing your opinion.

>For more information on network and Internet security, visit www.scmagazine.com, csrc.nist.gov, www.uscert.gov, www.cisecurity.org, www.isc2.org, www.cert.org, and www.ists.dartmouth.edu.

REFERENCES AND RESOURCES GUIDE

INTRODUCTION

When working on a PC, you often need to look up information related to computers. For instance, you may need to find out when the IBM PC was first invented, you may want tips about what to consider when buying a PC, or you may want to learn how to send an e-mail message. To help you with the tasks just mentioned and more, this References and Resources Guide brings together in one convenient location a collection of computer-related references and resources. Some of the resources are located in this handy section; these resources plus additional resources (such as information on numbering systems, characteristics of past and current CPUs, and URLs for useful Web resources) are located on the Web site that accompanies this textbook, which is located at www.course.com/uc11.

OUTLINE

COMPUTER HISTORY TIMELINE

The earliest recorded calculating device, the abacus, is believed to have been invented by the Babylonians sometime between 500 B.C. and 100 B.C. It and similar types of counting boards were used solely for counting.

500 B.C.

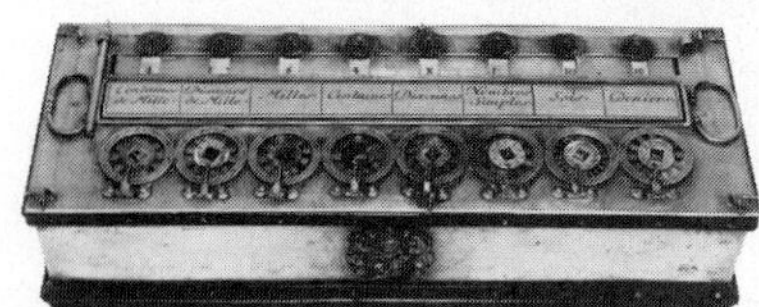

Blaise Pascal invented the first mechanical calculator, called the Pascaline Arithmetic Machine. It had the capacity for eight digits and could add and subtract.

1642

Dr. John V. Atanasoff and Clifford Berry designed and built ABC (for Atanasoff-Berry Computer), the world's first electronic computer.

1937

Precomputers and Early Computers

1621

The slide rule, a precursor to the electronic calculator, was invented. Used primarily to perform multiplication, division, square roots, and the calculation of logarithms, its wide-spread use continued until the 1970's.

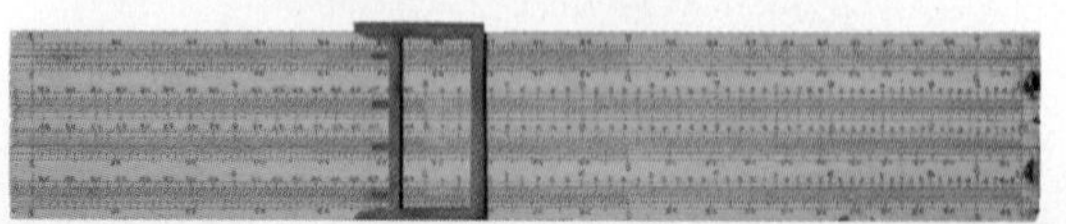

1804

French silk weaver Joseph-Marie Jacquard built a loom that read holes punched on a series of small sheets of hardwood to control the pattern weaved. This automated machine introduced the use of punch cards and showed that they could be used to convey a series of instructions.

1944

The Mark I, considered to be the first digital computer, was introduced by IBM. It was developed in cooperation with Harvard University, was more than 50 feet long, weighed almost five tons, and used electromechanical relays to solve addition problems in less than a second; multiplication and division took about six and twelve seconds, respectively.

Precomputers and Early Computers (before approximately 1945)

Most precomputers and early computers were mechanical machines that worked with gears and levers. Electromechanical devices (using both electricity and gears and levers) were developed toward the end of this era.

First Generation (approximately 1946–1957)

Powered by vacuum tubes, these computers were faster than electromechanical machines, but they were large and bulky, generated excessive heat, and had to be physically wired and reset to run programs. Input was primarily on punch cards; output was on punch cards or paper. Machine and assembly languages were used to program these computers.

UNIX was developed at AT&T's Bell Laboratories; Advanced Micro Devices (AMD) was formed; and ARPANET (the predecessor of today's Internet) was established.

REF

The UNIVAC 1, the first computer to be mass produced for general use, was introduced by Remington Rand. In 1952, it was used to analyze votes in the U.S. presidential election and correctly predicted that Dwight D. Eisenhower would be the victor only 45 minutes after the polls closed, though the results were not aired immediately because they weren't trusted.

The COBOL programming language was developed by a committee headed by Dr. Grace Hopper.

The first floppy disk (8 inches in diameter) was introduced.

IBM unbundled some of its hardware and software and began selling them separately, allowing other software companies to emerge.

1951 **1960** **1967** **1969**

First Generation | Second Generation | Third Generation

1947 **1957** **1964** **1968**

The FORTRAN programming language was introduced.

Robert Noyce and Gordon Moore founded the Intel Corporation.

John Bardeen, Walter Brattain, and William Shockley invented the transistor, which had the same capabilities as a vacuum tube but was faster, broke less often, used less power, and created less heat. They won a Nobel Prize for their invention in 1956 and computers began to be built with transistors shortly afterwards.

The IBM System/360 computer was introduced. Unlike previous computers, System/360 contained a full line of compatible computers, making upgrading easier.

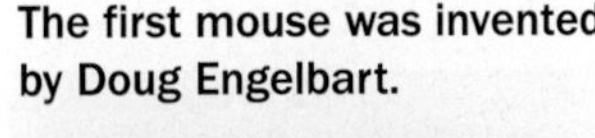

The first mouse was invented by Doug Engelbart.

Second Generation (approximately 1958–1963)

Second-generation computers used transistors instead of vacuum tubes. They allowed the computer to be physically smaller, more powerful, more reliable, and faster than before. Input was primarily on punch cards and magnetic tape; output was on punch cards and paper; and magnetic tape and disks were used for storage. High-level programming languages were used with these computers.

Third Generation (approximately 1964–1970)

The third generation of computers evolved when integrated circuits (IC)—computer chips—began being used instead of conventional transistors. Computers became even smaller and more reliable. Keyboards and monitors were introduced for input and output; magnetic disks were used for storage. The emergence of the operating system meant that operators no longer had to manually reset relays and wiring.

1971

The first microprocessor, the Intel 4004, was designed by Ted Hoff. The single processor contained 2,250 transistors and could execute 60,000 operations per second.

1975

Bill Gates and Paul Allen wrote a version of BASIC for the Altair, the first computer programming language designed for a personal computer. Bill Gates dropped out of Harvard to form Microsoft with Paul Allen.

Hailed as the first "personal computer," the Altair—allegedly named for a destination of the Starship Enterprise from a Star Trek TV episode—began to be sold as a kit for $395. Within months, tens of thousands were ordered.

1979

Software Arts Inc.'s Visi-Calc, the first electronic spreadsheet and business program for PCs, was released. This program is seen as one of the reasons PCs first became widely accepted in the business world.

Fourth Generation

1972

The C programming language was developed by Dennis Ritchie at Bell Labs.

Seymor Cray, called the "father of supercomputing," founded Cray Research, which would go on to build some of the fastest computers in the world.

1976

Steve Wozniak and Steve Jobs founded Apple computer and released the Apple I (a single-board computer), followed by the Apple II (a complete PC that became an instant success in 1977). They originally ran the company out of Job's garage.

1980

Sony Electronics introduced the 3.5-inch floppy disk and drive.

Seagate Technologies announced the first Winchester 5.25-inch hard disk drive, revolutionizing PC storage.

IBM chose Microsoft to develop the operating system for its upcoming PC. That operating system was PC-DOS.

Fourth Generation (approximately 1971–present)

The fourth generation of computers began with large-scale integration (LSI), which resulted in chips that could contain thousands of transistors. Very large-scale integration (VLSI) resulted in the microprocessor and the resulting microcomputers. The keyboard and mouse are predominant input devices, though many other types of input devices are now available; monitors and printers provide output; storage is obtained with magnetic disks, optical discs, and memory chips.

REF

1981

IBM introduced the IBM PC. This DOS-based PC used a 4.77 MHz 8088 CPU with 64 KB of RAM and quickly became the standard for business PCs.

1982

Intel introduced the 80286 CPU.

TIME magazine named the computer its "Machine of the Year" for 1982, emphasizing the importance the computer had already reached in our society at that time.

1983

Compaq Corporation released the first IBM-compatible PC that ran the same software as the IBM PC, marking the beginning of the huge PC-compatible industry.

1984

The first version of Microsoft Windows, a graphical enviro-ment, was released.

The Apple Macintosh debuted. It featured a simple, graphical user interface, used an 8 MHz, 32-bit Motorola 68000 CPU, and had a built-in 9-inch black and white screen.

1985

The first general-interest CD-ROM product (*Grolier's Electronic Encyclopedia*) was released, and computer and electronics companies worked together to develop a universal CD-ROM standard.

Intel introduced the Intel386 CPU.

Quantum Computer Services was founded; this company became AOL.

1986

Microsoft was listed on the New York Stock Exchange and began to sell shares to the public; Bill Gates became one of the world's youngest billionaires.

Apple's Steve Jobs founded Pixar.

1989

Tim Berners-Lee of CERN created the World Wide Web.

Intel introduced the Intel486 chip, the world's first million transistor CPU.

1993

Marc Andreessen and James H. Clark founded Netscape Communications and released Netscape Navigator, a graphical Web browser based on the Mosaic browser Andreessen had created the previous year.

Intel introduced the Pentium CPU.

1994

Linus Torvalds created Linux, which launched the open source revolution. The penguin logo/mascot soon followed.

1997

The first DVD players used for playing movies stored on DVD discs were sold.

After winning 2 of 6 games in their first contest in 1996, the IBM computer Deep Blue beat chess master Garry Kasparov in a chess match.

The Intel Pentium II was introduced.

1999

Shawn Fanning, 19, wrote the software to drive his Napster P2P service and began the debate about P2P filesharing and online music.

Palm released the Palm VII, its first handheld PC with wireless Internet access.

The Intel Pentium III CPU was introduced.

1995

Windows 95 was released and sold more than one million copies in four days.

Both eBay and Amazon.com were founded.

Sun Microsystems released Java, which is still one of the most popular Web programming languages.

1998

Microsoft shipped Windows 98.

Apple released the iMac, a modernized version of the Macintosh computer. Its futuristic design helped to make this computer immensely popular.

2000

Intel introduced its Pentium 4 CPU chip. A popular advertising campaign, launched in 2001, featured the Blue Man Group.

The first USB flash memory drives were released.

E-commerce skyrocketed, but unprofitable dot-com companies began going out of business at a record pace.

Microsoft released the Windows 2000 Professional Server business operating systems and Windows ME for home users.

People are registered trademarks of Nokia Corporation.; **Figure 5-21**, Courtesy of Symantec; **How box**, Copyright 1991-2005 WinZip International LLC. WinZip® is a registered trademark of WinZip International LLC. WinZip is available from http://www.winzip.com. WinZip screen images reproduced with permission of WinZip International LLC.; **Figure 5-24**, Copyright 1991-2005 WinZip International LLC. WinZip(R) is a registered trademark of WinZip International LLC. WinZip is available from http://www.winzip.com. WinZip screen images reproduced with permission of WinZip International LLC.; **Trend box**, Courtesy Google.

Chapter 6

Figure 6-1a, Adobe product screen shot(s) reprinted with permission from Adobe Systems Incorporated.; **Inside box**, Courtesy OpenOffice.org; **Figure 6-3a**, Courtesy of Symantec; **Trend box**, Courtesy Protocall Technologies Incorporated; **Figure 6-4**, Courtesy of onProject, Inc. www.onproject.com; **Figure 6-5a**, Courtesy Microsoft Corporation; **Figure 6-5b**, Box shot reprinted with permission of Corel Corporation; **Figure 6-5c**, Courtesy of IBM Corporation; **Figure 6-5d**, Courtesy of Sun Microsystems; **Figure 6-6ad**, Courtesy DataViz, Inc.; **Figure 6-6b**, Image provided by palmOne, Inc.; **Figure 6-6cef**, Courtesy Microsoft Corporation; **Figure 6-20h**, © Fujitsu Siemens Computers; **Figure 6-23b**, Adobe product screen shot(s) reprinted with permission from Adobe Systems Incorporated.; **6-23c**, Courtesy Nero AG / Nero Inc.; **Figure 6-24**, Courtesy of Madison Media Software, Inc. and Sony Media Sound Forge 8 is/are [a] trademark/registered trademarks of Madison Media Software, Inc. All rights reserved.; **Figure 6-25**, Courtesy Sonic Solutions; **Figure 6-26**, Copyright © 1995-2002 RealNetworks, Inc. All rights reserved. RealNetworks, Real.com, RealAudio, RealVideo, RealSystem, RealPlayer, RealJukebox and RealMedia are trademarks or registered trademarks of RealNetworks, Inc.; Photo by Joanne Savio; **How box**, Courtesy Sonic Solutions; **Figure 6-27a**, Quark, QuarkXPress and other Quark, Inc. trademarks are the property of Quark, Inc. and all applicatable affiliated companies. Portions © 2000 Quark, Inc. All rights reserved.; **Figure 6-27b**, © 2005 Riverdeep Interactive Learning Limited, and its licensors www.riverdeep.net; **Figure 6-27c**, Courtesty of Sage Software SB, Inc. The Peachtree Logo is a registered trademark of Sage Software SB, Inc.; **Figure 6-27d**, Courtesy of Punch! Software, LLC. www.punchsoftware.com; **Figure 6-27e**, Courtesy Microsoft Corporation; **Figure 6-27f**, Courtesy FranklinCovey; **You box**, Courtesy Agilix Labs; **Expert Insight**, Courtesy Novell, Inc.

Chapter 7

Figure 7-2a, Courtesy Alcatel; **Figure 7-2b**, Photo courtesy of Globalstar LLC.; **Trend box a**, Courtesy Talking Street www.talkingstreet.com; **Trend box b**, Courtesy Office of Parking and Transportation, California State University, Fresno; **Figure 7-3**, Courtesy CommtechWireless; **Figure 7-4**, Courtesy Magellan Consumer Products; **Figure 7-5ab**, Courtesy Health Hero Network; **Figure 7-5c**, Courtesy of ViewSonic Corporation; **Figure 7-5d**, Courtesy of Panasonic; **Figure 7-6ac**, Courtesy XM Satellite Radio; **Figure 7-6b**, Courtesy SIRIUS Satellite Radio; **Figure 7-7a**, Courtesy SightSpeed www.sightspeed.com; **Figure 7-7b**, Courtesy of Motorola; **Inside box**, Courtesy Dust Networks; **Trend box a**, Courtesy Sling Media, Inc.; **Trend box b**, © Fujitsu Siemens Computers; **Figure 7-8a**, Courtesy InTouch Health, Inc.; **Figure 7-8b**, Courtesy, University of Rochester; **Figure 7-8c**, Photo made available by St. Joseph's Healthcare Hamilton; **Figure 7-9a**, Courtesy Acer America; **Figure 7-9b**, Courtesy of Linksys; Courtesy of IBM Corporation; **Figure 7-10a**, Courtesy Acer America; **Figure 7-10b**, Courtesy of Linksys; **Figure 7-10c**, Courtesy of IBM Corporation; **Figure 7-11a**, Courtesy Acer America; **Figure 7-11b**, Courtesy of Linksys; **Figure 7-11c**, Courtesy of IBM Corporation; **Figure 7-12**, Courtesy of SCOTTeVEST, www.scottevest.com; **Figure 7-15**, Courtesy Acer America; **Figure 7-16a**, Courtesy of Logitech; **Figure 7-16b**, Courtesy Acer America; **Figure 7-16c**, Courtesy of IBM Corporation; **Figure 7-17a**, Courtesy of Black Box Corporation; **Figure 7-17b**, Courtesy of Belkin Corporation; **Figure 7-18ac**, Photo(s) courtesy of Hughes Network Systems, LLC.; **Figure 7-18b**, Courtesy Alcatel; **Figure 7-18d**, Courtesy Acer America; **Figure 7-20**, Courtesy Acer America; **Figure 7-21**, Courtesy Acer America; **Figure 7-22a**, Photograph: Courtesy of the Information Services Publications and Marketing Team, University of Nottingham.; **Figure 7-22b**, Courtesy of Intel Corporation; **Figure 7-24**, Courtesy Bluetooth SIG; **Figure 7-25a**, Courtesy Acer America; **Figure 7-25b**, Courtesy Juniper Networks; **How box a**, Courtesy D-Link Systems; **How box b**, Courtesy NETGEAR; **How box c**, Courtesy of Belkin Corporation; **Figure 7-26af**, Courtesy NETGEAR; **Figure 7-26bc**, Courtesy of Linksys; **Figure 7-26de**, Courtesy D-Link Systems; **Figure 7-27ab**, Courtesy US Robotics; **Figure 7-27c**, Courtesy D-Link Systems; **Figure 7-27d**, Courtesy Spacenet Inc.; **Figure 7-28a**, Courtesy Acer America; **Figure 7-28b**, Courtesy D-Link Systems; **Figure 7-28c**, Courtesy Data Comm for Business Inc.; **Figure 7-28d**, Courtesy of Linksys; **Figure 7-28e**, Courtesy NETGEAR; **Figure 7-28f**, Courtesy Apple Computer, Inc.

Chapter 8

Figure 8-1a, Courtesy of ViewSonic Corporation; **Figure 8-1b**, CBS and the CBS Eye are registered trademarks of CBS Broadcasting Inc. The Survivor: Guatemala - The Maya Empire Logo is a registered trademark of Survivor Productions, LC. CBS.COM website contents © CBS Broadcasting Inc. Used by permission.; **Figure 8-2a**, Courtesy Sprint; **Figure 8-2b**, Courtesy Road Runner; **Figure 8-2c**, Courtesy EarthLink; **Figure 8-2d**, America Online, AOL and the Running Man icon are registered trademarks of America Online, Inc. The AOL Triangle logo is a trademark of America Online, Inc. AOL content © 2005 by America Online, Inc. The America Online content, name, icons and trademarks are used with permission; **Figure 8-2e**, Courtesy Cingular Wireless;; **Figure 8-2f**, Courtesy Spacenet Inc.; **Figure 8-2g**, Courtesy Pacific LightNet; **Figure 8-2h**, Courtesy Clearwire; **Figure 8-4**, Courtesy CoreFTP.com; **Figure 8-5a**, Courtesy Acer America; **Figure 8-5b**, Courtesy of Salton, Inc.; **Figure 8-5c**, Courtesy Danger, Inc.; **Figure 8-7ab**, Photo provided courtesy of the Wi-Fi Alliance; **Figure 8-7c**, Courtesy of Siemens AG/Siemens press picture; **Figure 8-7d**, Courtesy Bluetooth SIG; **Figure 8-9**, America Online, AOL and the Running Man icon are registered trademarks of America Online, Inc. The AOL Triangle logo is a trademark of America Online, Inc. AOL content © 2005 by America Online, Inc. The America Online content, name, icons and trademarks are used with permission; **Figure 8-10ab**, Courtesy Google; **Figure 8-11a**, Courtesy Yahoo!; **Figure 8-11b**, © 2006 InfoSpace, Inc. All rights reserved. Reprinted with permission of InfoSpace, Inc.; **Figure 8-11c**, Courtesy Ask Jeeves, Inc.; **Figure 8-12b**, Courtesy Google; **Figure 8-17c**, Courtesy SightSpeed www.sightspeed.com; **How box a**, Courtesy Vonage; **How box b**, Courtesy D-Link Systems; **Figure 8-18b**, These materials have been reproduced with the permission of eBay Inc. COPYRIGHT © EBAY INC. ALL RIGHTS RESERVED.; **Figure 8-19a**, Used by Permission of Clear Channel Radio.; **Figure 8-19b**, © 2000-2005, Wal-Mart.com USA, LLC and Wal-Mart Stores, Inc.; **Figure 8-19c**, © 2005 Movielink, LLC. All rights reserved. Paycheck © MMIII by PARAMOUNT PICTURES CORPORATION AND DREAMWORKS LLC. All rights reserved. Cruel Intentions 3 © 2004 Sony Pictures Television International. All rights reserved. Along Came Polly © 2004 Universal Studios. All rights reserved. Mystic River © 2003 Warner Bros. Entertainment Inc. All rights reserved. Osama © 2004 United Artists Films Inc. All rights reserved. Scary Movie 3 © 2003 Miramax Film Corp. All rights reserved. The Cooler © 2003 Cooler Productions, LLC. All rights reserved.; **Figure 8-19d**, Courtesy of IGN.com; **Figure 8-21**, Courtesy of Wurld Media, Inc.; **You box**, Napster logo and marks reprinted with the permission of Napster, LLC.; **Figure 8-22d**, The MapQuest.com logo is a registered trademark of MapQuest, Inc. MapQuest.com content © 2005 MapQuest, Inc. Used with permission.; **Trend box**, Courtesy of Edupodder; **Figure 8-26a**, Courtesy Yahoo!; **Figure 8-28**, Courtesy Bugnosis.org.

Chapter 9

Figure 9-1b, Courtesy Lance Fischer; **Figure 9-2a**, Courtesy Kensington Technology Group, www.kensington.com; **Figure 9-2b**, Courtesy Yahoo! Maps; **Figure 9-3**, Courtesy Jeff Bardin; **Figure 9-4**, Courtesy Acer America; **Figure 9-5**, Courtesy Acer America; **Figure 9-8**, Courtesy The CBORD Group, Inc.; **Figure 9-9ac**, Courtesy of Identix Inc. Minnetonka, MN, USA; **Figure 9-9b**, Courtesy of IR Recognition Systems, and Ingersoll-Rand Business; **Figure 9-9d**, Courtesy Diebold, Incorporated; **You box**, Joseph Mehling, Dartmouth College; **Figure 9-10a**, Courtesy of SURFnet; **Figure 9-11**, Copyright ©1999-2005 Zone Labs. All rights reserved.; **Figure 9-12**, Courtesy of Symantec; **Figure 9-15**, Netscape and the "N" logo are registered trademarks of Netscape Communications Corporation. Netscape content © 2005 Netscape. Used with permission.; **Trend box**, Courtesy of pharming.org and learnsecurity.com; **Inside box**, Courtesy Equifax; **Figure 9-18**, Courtesy RSA Security; **Figure 9-19**, These materials have been reproduced with the permission of eBay Inc. COPYRIGHT © EBAY INC. ALL RIGHTS RESERVED.; **Figure 9-21**, Courtesy Lavasoft AB; **Figure 9-22**, Netscape and the "N" logo are registered trademarks of Netscape Communications Corporation. Netscape content © 2005 Netscape. Used with permission.; **Expert Insight**, Courtesy Jeff Bardin.

References and Resources Guide

Computer History Timeline: 1, 2, 5, 6, 9, 12, 19, Courtesy of IBM Archives; **3**, Courtesy Iowa State University; **4**, Courtesy Jim Bready; **7**, Courtesy Unisys Corporation ; **8**, Courtesy U.S. Navy; **10, 37**, Courtesy Texas Instruments; **11**, Courtesy of Bootstrap Institute/Alliance; **13, 22, 28, 32, 34**, Courtesy of Intel Corporation; **14, 15, 36**, Courtesy Microsoft Corporation; **16**, Courtesy Dan Bricklin; **17**, Courtesy Cray Inc.; **18, 23**, Courtesy Apple Computer, Inc.; **20, 39**, Courtesy, Hewlett-Packard Company; **21**, Fabian Bachrach, courtesy W3C; **24**, Netscape and the "N" logo are registered trademarks of Netscape Communications Corporation. Netscape content © 2005 Netscape. Used with permission. **25**, Courtesy Larry Ewing lewing@isc.tamu.edu and The GIMP; **26**, Courtesy of Panasonic; **27, 43**, Image provided by palmOne, Inc.; **29**, Courtesy Microsoft Museum; **30**, [eBay Mark] is a trademark of eBay Inc.; **31**, Java and the Java Coffee Cup logo are trademarks or registered trademarks of Sun Microsystems, Inc.; **33**, Courtesy Kingston Technology Company Inc.; **35, 41**, Microsoft, Windows and the Windows logo are either registered trademarks or trademarks of Microsoft Corporation in the United States and/or other countries.; **38**, Courtesy GoTV Networks; **40**, © 2003, 2005 Advanced Micro Devices, Inc., Reprinted with permission. AMD, the AMD logo, AMD Athlon, and combinations thereof are trademarks of Advanced Micro Devices, Inc.; **42**, Courtesy Oakley; **R-7a**, Netscape and the "N" logo are registered trademarks of Netscape Communications Corporation. Netscape content © 2005 Netscape. Used with permission.

CREDITS

Throughout the modules: Screen shots of Microsoft Access®, Excel®, Paint®, PowerPoint®, Publisher®, Visual Basic®, Word®, and Windows® reprinted with permission from Microsoft Corporation. Copyright © Microsoft Explorer® reprinted with permission from Microsoft Corporation.

Chapter 1

Figure 1-1a, Photo courtesy of Nokia. Copyright © 2005 Nokia. All rights reserved. Nokia and Nokia Connecting People are registered trademarks of Nokia Corporation.; **Figure 1-1b**, Courtesy Alcatel; **Figure 1-2a**, Courtesy of Microsoft Corporation; **Figure 1-2b**, © Flying Colours Ltd/Getty Images; **Figure 1-2c**, © Fujitsu Siemens Computers; **Figure 1-2d**, Courtesy TMIO, Inc.; **Figure 1-3a**, Courtesy of Microsoft Corporation; **Figure 1-3b**, Courtesy Infocus Corporation; **Figure 1-3c**, Courtesy U.S. Marines; **You box,** Courtesy Stanford University Medical Center; **Figure 1-4a**, Courtesy of Siemens AG/Siemens press picture; **Figure 1-4b**, Courtesy of Symbol Technologies, Inc.; **Figure 1-4c**, Courtesy Xybernaut Corporation; **Figure 1-5ab**, Courtesy Deutsche Lufthansa AG; **Figure 1-5c**, Courtesy of Garmin Ltd. or its subsidiaries; **Figure 1-5d**, Courtesy of Siemens AG/Siemens press picture; **Figure 1-7ace**, Courtesy IBM Corporate Archives; **Figure 1-7b**, Courtesy U.S. Army; **Figure 1-7d**, Courtesy, Hewlett-Packard Company; **Figure 1-8a**, Courtesy of Gateway, Inc.; **Figure 1-8b**, Courtesy, Hewlett-Packard Company; **Figure 1-8c**, Courtesy of Logitech; **Figure 1-8d**, Courtesy SanDisk Corporation; **Figure 1-12c**, Courtesy of Microsoft Corporation/photo by Joanne Savio; **Figure 1-12e**, Courtesy RedLobster.com; **Figure 1-13a**, Photo courtesy of Nokia. Copyright © 2005 Nokia. All rights reserved. Nokia and Nokia Connecting People are registered trademarks of Nokia Corporation.; **Figure 1-13b**, Courtesy of Suunto; **Trend box**, Courtesy GoTV Networks; **Figure 1-14a**, Courtesy Acer America; **Figure 1-14b**, Courtesy of Lenovo; **Figure 1-14c**, Photo or screen shot(s) reprinted with permission from MPC Computers, LLC; **Figure 1-15a**, Courtesy Acer America; **Figure 1-15b**, Courtesy of Motion Computing®; **Figure 1-15cde**, Courtesy of ViewSonic Corporation; **Inside box a**, Courtesy of CrazyModders.be; **Inside box b**, Courtesy of Kurt Villcheck website: TrickedOutPC.net; **Inside box c**, Courtesy Tulip; **Inside box d**, Courtesy VoodooPC; **Figure 1-16a**, Courtesy of Research In Motion (RIM); **Figure 1-16b**, Courtesy OQO; **Figure 1-17a**, Courtesy of Symbol Technologies, Inc.; **Figure 1-17b**, Courtesy OQO; **Figure 1-18a**, © Fujitsu Siemens Computers; **Figure 1-18b**, Courtesy DataWind, Inc.; **Figure 1-18c**, MSN TV Set Top Box from Microsoft; **How box bd1**, Courtesy Acer America; **How box d2**, Courtesy of Symantec; **How box e**, Courtesy Kensington Technology Group, www.kensington.com; **Figure 1-19a**, Courtesy Sutter Gould Medical Foundation; **Figure 1-19b**, © Fujitsu Siemens Computers; **Figure 1-20**, © Corbis; **Figure 1-21**, LLNL photo; **Figure 1-22a**, Courtesy of Gateway, Inc.; **Figure 1-22bcd**, Courtesy Acer America; **Figure 1-22e**, Courtesy of IBM Corporation; **Figure 1-25a**, Courtesy Acer America; **Figure 1-25b**, ARTHUR Web site © 2005 WGBH; underlying ARTHUR TM/© Marc Brown.; **Figure 1-27**, BHG.com screen shot courtesy of Meredith Corporation; **Figure 1-28**, Courtesy Google; **Figure 1-29**, Courtesy Acer America; **Figure 1-30**, Courtesy of Symantec; **Expert Insight**, Photo courtesy of Nokia. Copyright © 2005 Nokia. All rights reserved. Nokia and Nokia Connecting People are registered trademarks of Nokia Corporation.

Chapter 2

Figure 2-7ac, Courtesy of Intel Corporation; **Figure 2-7b**, © 2003, 2005 Advanced Micro Devices, Inc., Reprinted with permission. AMD, the AMD logo, AMD Athlon, and combinations thereof are trademarks of Advanced Micro Devices, Inc.; **You box**, Courtesy adidas-Salomon AG; **Figure 2-9**, Courtesy Kingston Technology; **Figure 2-11**, © 2005 Spansion, LLC, Reprinted with permission. **Figure 2-12a**, Courtesy NETGEAR; **Figure 2-13a**, Courtesy of Intel Corporation; **Figure 2-13b**, Courtesy MSI.; **Figure 2-14a**, Courtesy Acer America; **Figure 2-14b**, Courtesy of Belkin Corporation; **Figure 2-15**, © Fujitsu Siemens Computers; **Figure 2-16**, Courtesy of Linksys; **Figure 2-17**, © Fujitsu Siemens Computers; **Figure 2-18**, Image provided by palmOne, Inc.; **Inside box**, Courtesy of Intel Corporation; **Trend box**, Courtesy TAEUS International Corporation; **Figure 2-21b**, Courtesy SimpleTech, Inc.; **Figure 2-24**, Courtesy Epson America Inc.; **Figure 2-26a**, Courtesy of Intel Corporation; **Figure 2-26b**, Courtesy Kingston Technology; **Figure 2-27**, Image reproduced by permission of IBM Research, Almaden Research Center. Unauthorized use not permitted.; **Exercise 5a**, Courtesy NETGEAR; **Exercise 5d**, Courtesy SimpleTech, Inc.

Chapter 3

Figure 3-1, © Fujitsu Siemens Computers; **Figure 3-7**, Courtesy of Seagate Technology LLC; **Inside box**, Courtesy of DriveSavers, Inc. www.drivesavers.com; **Figure 3-10a**, Courtesy SimpleTech, Inc.; **Figure 3-10b**, Courtesy of Intel Corporation; **Figure 3-10c**, Courtesy of Seagate Technology LLC; **Figure 3-11a**, Copyright © Iomega Corporation. All Rights Reserved. Iomega, the stylized "i" logo and all product images are property of Iomega Corporation in the United States and/or other countries. Zip and REV are registered trademarks of Iomega Corporation in the United States and/or other countries.; **Figure 3-11b**, Courtesy XIMETA, Inc.; **Figure 3-11c**, Courtesy of Seagate Technology LLC; **Figure 3-11d**, Courtesy of Toshiba Storage Device Division, a Division of Toshiba America Information Systems, Inc.; **Figure 3-12**, Copyright © Iomega Corporation. All Rights Reserved. Iomega, the stylized "i" logo and all product images are property of Iomega Corporation in the United States and/or other countries. Zip and REV are registered trademarks of Iomega Corporation in the United States and/or other countries.; **Figure 3-14**, Courtesy CD Digital Card www.cddigitalcard.com; **How box**, Courtesy RosArt Multimedia, Inc.; **Figure 3-15a**, Courtesy Memorex Products, Inc.; **Figure 3-15bc**, Courtesy of Maxell Corporation of America; **Figure 3-15d**, Courtesy of Sony Electronics Inc.; **Trend box**, Courtesy Imation Corp.; **Figure 3-16a**, Courtesy of Sony Electronics Inc.; **Figure 3-16bf**, Courtesy SanDisk Corporation; **Figure 3-16d**, Courtesy SimpleTech, Inc.; **Figure 3-16e**, Image provided by palmOne, Inc.; **Figure 3-17acd**, Courtesy SanDisk Corporation; **Figure 3-17b**, Courtesy of Lexar Media, Inc.; **Figure 3-17e**, Courtesy of Sony Electronics Inc.; **Figure 3-18ab**, Copyright © Iomega Corporation. All Rights Reserved. Iomega, the stylized "i" logo and all product images are property of Iomega Corporation in the United States and/or other countries. Zip and REV are registered trademarks of Iomega Corporation in the United States and/or other countries.; **Figure 3-18c**, Courtesy RememberUs.co.uk; **Figure 3-19a**, Courtesy Fotki, Inc. Fotki.com; **Figure 3-19b**, Courtesy Xdrive, Inc.; **You box**, Courtesy Pikeville College; **Figure 3-20a**, Courtesy of Siemens AG/Siemens press picture; **Figure 3-21**, Courtesy InPhase Technologies; **Figure 3-22**, Courtesy 3PARdata, Inc.; **Exercise 2b**, Courtesy of Seagate Technology LLC; **Exercise 2cd**, Courtesy SanDisk Corporation; **Exercise 2e**, Courtesy of Siemens AG/Siemens press picture; **Exercise 2f**, Courtesy of Maxell Corporation of America.

Chapter 4

Figure 4-1, Courtesy of Logitech; **Figure 4-2a**, Courtesy of Sierra Wireless; **Figure 4-2b**, Courtesy Digit Wireless; **Figure 4-2c**, Courtesy of Logitech; **Figure 4-3a**, Courtesy Optorite Inc.; **Figure 4-3b**, Courtesy Acer America; **Trend box**, Courtesy Virtual Devices; **Figure 4-4a**, Courtesy of Symbol Technologies, Inc.; **Figure 4-4b**, Courtesy of Microsoft Corporation; **Figure 4-4c**, Courtesy of Salton, Inc.; **Figure 4-5b**, Courtesy Active Ink Software; **Figure 4-6a**, Courtesy of C Technologies AB/Anoto Group AB (publ); **Figure 4-6b**, Courtesy Wacom Technology Co; **Figure 4-6c**, Courtesy of Hand Held Products, Inc.; **Figure 4-7a**, Courtesy Deutsche Lufthansa AG; **Figure 4-7b**, Courtesy PC America; **Figure 4-8ab**, Courtesy of Logitech; **Figure 4-8cd**, © Fujitsu Siemens Computers; **Figure 4-9**, Courtesy of Symbol Technologies, Inc.; **Figure 4-10a**, Courtesy, Hewlett-Packard Company; **Figure 4-10b**, Courtesy of C Technologies AB/Anoto Group AB (publ); **Figure 4-10c**, Courtesy of Visioneer, Inc.; **You box**, Courtesy INTELLIFIT; **Figure 4-11abd**, Courtesy of Symbol Technologies, Inc.; **Figure 4-11c**, Courtesy of Hand Held Products, Inc.; **Figure 4-12a**, Courtesy of Intermec Technologies Corporation; **Figure 4-12b**, Courtesy of Symbol Technologies, Inc.; **Figure 4-13**, Courtesy Chatsworth Data Corporation; **Figure 4-14**, Courtesy of Sierra Pacific; **Figure 4-15a**, Courtesy of NCR Corporation; **Figure 4-16a**, Courtesy of IR Recognition Systems, and Ingersoll-Rand Business; **Figure 4-16b**, © Fujitsu Siemens Computers; **Figure 4-17ac**, Courtesy of Sony Electronics Inc.; **Figure 4-17b**, Courtesy SanDisk Corporation; **Figure 4-17d**, Photo courtesy of Nokia. Copyright © 2005 Nokia. All rights reserved. Nokia and Nokia Connecting People are registered trademarks of Nokia Corporation.; **Inside box adefg**, Courtesy of Intermec Technologies Corporation; **Inside box bc**, Courtesy Texas Instruments; **Inside box hi**, Courtesy of NCR Corporation; **Figure 4-18a**, Courtesy of Sony Electronics Inc.; **Figure 4-18b**, Courtesy Apple Computer, Inc.; **Figure 4-19a**, Courtesy David Shopper/ScanSoft; **Figure 4-19b**, Courtesy Acer America; **Figure 4-20**, Courtesy Creative Labs; **Figure 4-21a**, © Fujitsu Siemens Computers; **Figure 4-21b**, Courtesy of Research In Motion (RIM); **Figure 4-21c**, Courtesy Alcatel; **Figure 4-21d**, Courtesy Creative Labs; **Figure 4-21e**, Courtesy Ceiva Logic, Inc.; **Figure 4-21f**, Courtesy of Garmin Ltd. or its subsidiaries; **Figure 4-22**, Courtesy Acer America; **Figure 4-23**, Courtesy of ViewSonic Corporation; **Inside box**, Courtesy Gyricon LLC; **Figure 4-24**, Courtesy Acer America; **Figure 4-25**, Copyright ATI Technologies Inc. 2006; **Figure 4-26a**, Courtesy PureDepth, Ltd; **Figure 4-26b**, Image courtesy of Actuality Systems, Inc. Bedford, MA USA (copyright 2004, David Shopper); **Figure 4-26c**, Courtesy of Eyeneo SAS; **Figure 4-27a**, Courtesy Acer America; **Figure 4-27b**, Courtesy Creative Labs; **Figure 4-27c**, Courtesy Samsung; **Figure 4-28a**, Courtesy of Sony Electronics Inc.; **Figure 4-29**, Courtesy of Universal Display Corporation; **Figure 4-30**, Courtesy of ViewSonic Corporation; **Figure 4-31a**, Courtesy Printek, Inc.; **Figure 4-32bc**, Courtesy, Hewlett-Packard Company; **Figure 4-33b**, Courtesy, Hewlett-Packard Company; **Figure 4-34a**, Courtesy Epson America Inc.; **Figure 4-34b**, Courtesy of Intermec Technologies Corporation; **Figure 4-34c**, Courtesy of Symbol Technologies, Inc.; **Figure 4-34d**, Courtesy, Hewlett-Packard Company; **Figure 4-35**, Courtesy of Altec Lansing; **Expert Insight**, Courtesy, Hewlett-Packard Company.

Chapter 5

Figure 5-1a, Courtesy Bluetooth SIG; **Figure 5-8a**, Courtesy of Seagate Technology LLC; **Figure 5-8b**, Courtesy SimpleTech, Inc.; **Inside box**, Courtesy Jellyvision www.jellyvision.com; **Figure 5-11ac**, Courtesy of Microsoft Corporation; **Figure 5-11bd**, Courtesy Apple Computer, Inc.; **Figure 5-12abc**, Courtesy Acer America; **Figure 5-12d**, Courtesy of IBM Corporation; **Figure 5-14**, Courtesy of Microsoft Corporation; **Figure 5-15**, Courtesy of Microsoft Corporation; **Figure 5-16**, Courtesy of Microsoft Corporation; **Figure 5-17**, Courtesy Apple Computer, Inc.; **Figure 5-18**, Courtesy Novell, Inc.; **You box**, Courtesy, Volvo Cars of North America, LLC; **Figure 5-19a**, Courtesy of Motorola; **Figure 5-19b**, Courtesy Creative Labs; **Figure 5-20a**, Image provided by palmOne, Inc.; **Figure 5-20bc**, Photo courtesy of Nokia. Copyright © 2005 Nokia. All rights reserved. Nokia and Nokia Connecting

2001

Intel's first 64-bit CPU, the Itanium, was introduced.

Microsoft released its XP line of products, including Windows XP and Office XP.

2003

Digital camera sales in the United States exceeded 14 million, surpassing film camera sales for the first time.

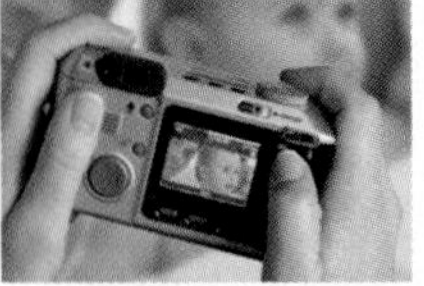

Microsoft shipped the Office 2003 editions of its Microsoft Office System.

AMD released the 64-bit Opteron server microprocessor and the Athlon 64, the first 64-bit CPU designed for desktop PC use.

2004

The Internet and wireless networks enabled people to work and communicate with others wherever they go.

Spyware became a major problem; some studies indicated that over 80% of computers had spyware installed.

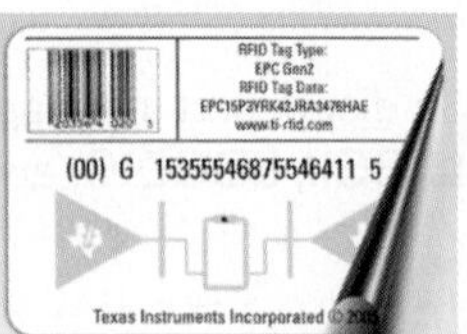

Wal-Mart and other major retailers announced requirements for suppliers to begin using RFID tags on shipments.

2005

Portable media players, such as the iPod, were common; digital music capabilities were built into a growing number of objects and devices, such as the OAKLEY THUMP sunglasses shown here.

Intel and AMD both released their first dual-core CPUs.

Phishing and identity theft became household words as an increasing number of individuals fell victim to these Internet scams.

The capabilities of mobile devices continued to grow; Palm's LifeDrive comes with a 4 GB hard drive and built-in Wi-Fi and Bluetooth support.

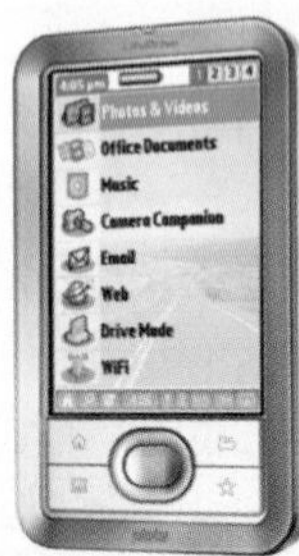

2006

Broadband Internet access approached the norm and improvements to wireless networking (such as WiMAX) continued to be developed.

Use of the Internet for online shopping, as well as downloads of music, movies, games, and television shows continued to grow.

Delivery of TV shows and other media to cell phones became more common.

CODING CHARTS

As discussed in Chapter 2 of this text, coding systems for text-based data include ASCII, EBCDIC, and Unicode. ■

ASCII and EBCDIC

Figure R-1 provides a chart listing the ASCII and EBCDIC representations (in binary) for most of the symbols found on a typical keyboard.

FIGURE R-1
ASCII and EBCDIC binary codes for typical keyboard symbols.

SYMBOL	ASCII	EBCDIC
A	0100 0001	1100 0001
B	0100 0010	1100 0010
C	0100 0011	1100 0011
D	0100 0100	1100 0100
E	0100 0101	1100 0101
F	0100 0110	1100 0110
G	0100 0111	1100 0111
H	0100 1000	1100 1000
I	0100 1001	1100 1001
J	0100 1010	1101 0001
K	0100 1011	1101 0010
L	0100 1100	1101 0011
M	0100 1101	1101 0100
N	0100 1110	1101 0101
O	0100 1111	1101 0110
P	0101 0000	1101 0111
Q	0101 0001	1101 1000
R	0101 0010	1101 1001
S	0101 0011	1110 0010
T	0101 0100	1110 0011
U	0101 0101	1110 0100
V	0101 0110	1110 0101
W	0101 0111	1110 0110
X	0101 1000	1110 0111
Y	0101 1001	1110 1000
Z	0101 1010	1110 1001
a	0110 0001	1000 0001
b	0110 0010	1000 0010
c	0110 0011	1000 0011
d	0110 0100	1000 0100

SYMBOL	ASCII	EBCDIC
e	0110 0101	1000 0101
f	0110 0110	1000 0110
g	0110 0111	1000 0111
h	0110 1000	1000 1000
i	0110 1001	1000 1001
j	0110 1010	1001 0001
k	0110 1011	1001 0010
l	0110 1100	1001 0011
m	0110 1101	1001 0100
n	0110 1110	1001 0101
o	0110 1111	1001 0110
p	0111 0000	1001 0111
q	0111 0001	1001 1000
r	0111 0010	1001 1001
s	0111 0011	1010 0010
t	0111 0100	1010 0011
u	0111 0101	1010 0100
v	0111 0110	1010 0101
w	0111 0111	1010 0110
x	0111 1000	1010 0111
y	0111 1001	1010 1000
z	0111 1010	1010 1001
0	0011 0000	1111 0000
1	0011 0001	1111 0001
2	0011 0010	1111 0010
3	0011 0011	1111 0011
4	0011 0100	1111 0100
5	0011 0101	1111 0101
6	0011 0110	1111 0110
7	0011 0111	1111 0111

SYMBOL	ASCII	EBCDIC
8	0011 1000	1111 1000
9	0011 1001	1111 1001
(	0010 1000	0100 1101
)	0010 1001	0101 1101
/	0010 1111	0110 0001
-	0010 1101	0110 0000
*	0010 1010	0101 1100
+	0010 1011	0100 1110
,	0010 1100	0110 1011
.	0010 1110	0100 1011
:	0011 1010	0111 1010
;	0011 1011	0101 1110
&	0010 0110	0101 0000
\	0101 1100	1110 0000
$	0010 0100	0101 1011
%	0010 0101	0110 1100
=	0011 1101	0111 1110
>	0011 1110	0110 1110
<	0011 1100	0100 1100
!	0010 0001	0101 1010
|	0111 1100	0110 1010
?	0011 1111	0110 1111
@	0100 0000	0111 1100
_	0101 1111	0110 1101
`	0110 0000	1011 1001
{	0111 1011	1100 0000
}	0111 1101	1101 0000
~	0111 1110	1010 0001
[	0101 1011	0100 1010
]	0101 1101	0101 1010

Unicode

When consistent worldwide representation is needed, Unicode is typically used. Unicode can be used to represent every written language, as well as a variety of other symbols. Unicode codes are typically listed in hexadecimal notation—a sampling of Unicode is shown in Figure R-2.

The capability to display characters and other symbols using Unicode coding is incorporated into many programs. For instance, when the Symbol dialog box is opened using the Insert menu in Microsoft Office Word, the Unicode representation (as well as the corresponding ASCII code in either decimal or hexadecimal representation) can be viewed (see Figure R-3). Some programs allow you to enter a Unicode symbol using its Unicode hexadecimal value. For instance, in Microsoft Office programs you can use the Alt+X command when the insertion point is just to the right of a Unicode hex value to convert that hex value into the corresponding symbol. For example, the keystrokes

2264Alt+X

result in the symbol corresponding to the Unicode code 2264 (the less than or equal sign ≤) being inserted into the document; entering 27B2 and then pressing Alt+X inserts the symbol shown in the Word screen in Figure R-3.

A 0041	N 004E	a 0061	n 006E	0 0030	{ 007B	* 002A	■ 25A0	অ 0985
B 0042	O 004F	b 0062	o 006F	1 0031	| 007C	+ 002B	□ 25A1	গ 0997
C 0043	P 0050	c 0063	p 0070	2 0032	} 007D	, 002C	▲ 25B2	ে 09C7
D 0044	Q 0051	d 0064	q 0071	3 0033	~ 007E	- 002D	℅ 2105	৶ 09F6
E 0045	R 0052	e 0065	r 0072	4 0034	! 0021	. 002E	℞ 211E	څ 0685
F 0046	S 0053	f 0066	s 0073	5 0035	" 0022	/ 002F	⅓ 2153	ڴ 06B4
G 0047	T 0054	g 0067	t 0074	6 0036	# 0023	₤ 20A4	⅔ 2154	ڪ 06AA
H 0048	U 0055	h 0068	u 0075	7 0037	$ 0024	∑ 2211	♕ 2655	α 03B1
I 0049	V 0056	i 0069	v 0076	8 0038	% 0025	∅ 2205	☂ 2602	β 03B2
J 004A	W 0057	j 006A	w 0077	9 0039	& 0026	√ 221A	❐ 2750	Δ 0394
K 004B	X 0058	k 006B	x 0078	[005B	' 0027	∞ 221E	❂ 2742	φ 03A6
L 004C	Y 0059	l 006C	y 0079	\ 005C	(0028	≤ 2264	➲ 27B2	Ω 03A9
M 004D	Z 005A	m 006D	z 007A	] 005D	) 0029	≥ 2265	♥ 2665	Ϋ 03AB

FIGURE R-2
Selected Unicode codes.

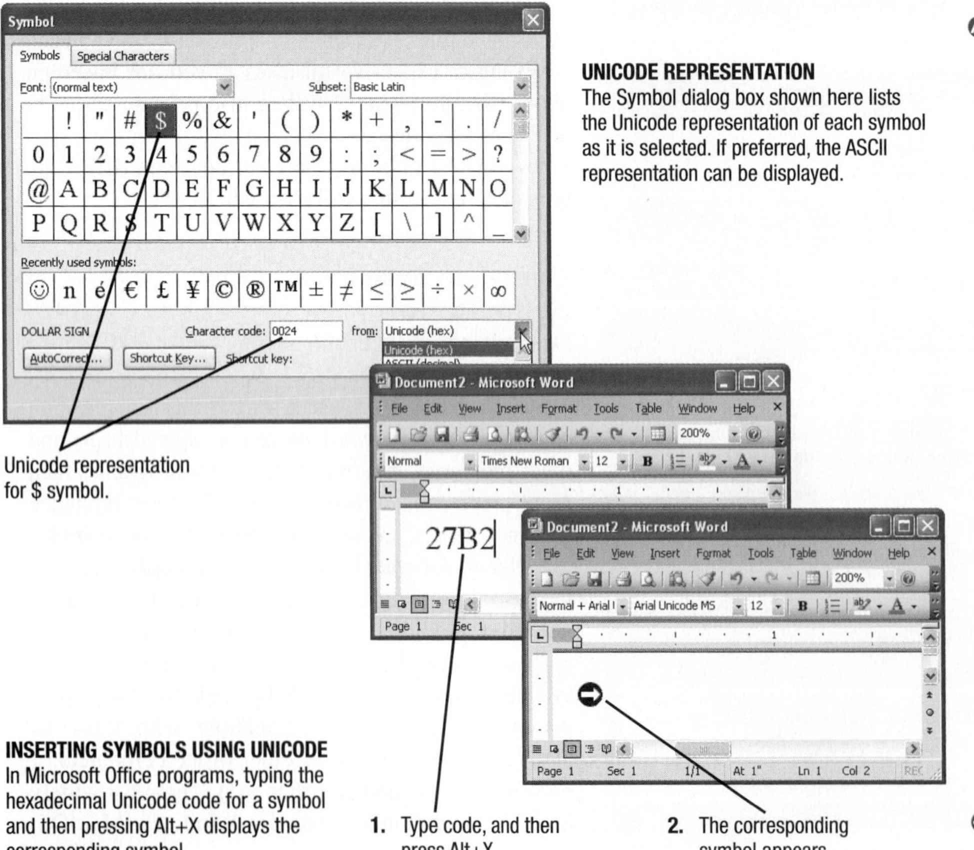

UNICODE REPRESENTATION
The Symbol dialog box shown here lists the Unicode representation of each symbol as it is selected. If preferred, the ASCII representation can be displayed.

INSERTING SYMBOLS USING UNICODE
In Microsoft Office programs, typing the hexadecimal Unicode code for a symbol and then pressing Alt+X displays the corresponding symbol.

1. Type code, and then press Alt+X.
2. The corresponding symbol appears.

FIGURE R-3
Using Unicode.

GUIDE TO BUYING A PC

Before buying a new PC, it is important to give some thought to what your needs are, including what software programs you wish to run, any other computers with which you need to be compatible, how you might want to connect to the Internet, and whether or not portability is important. This section of the References and Resources Guide explores topics related to buying and upgrading a PC. ■

Analyzing Needs

When referring to a computer system, a need refers to a functional requirement that the computer system must be able to meet. For example, at a video rental store, a computer system must be able to enter barcodes automatically from videos or DVDs being checked in and out, identify customers with overdue movies, manage movie inventories, and do routine accounting operations. Requiring portability is another example of a need. For example, if you need to take your computer with you as you travel or work out of the office, you will need a portable computer instead of a desktop computer.

Selecting a PC for home or business use must begin with the all-important question "What do I want the system to do?" Once you have determined what tasks the system will be used for, you can choose among the software and hardware alternatives available. Making a list of your needs in areas discussed in the next few sections can help you get a picture of what type of system you are shopping for. If you are not really sure what you want a system to do, you should think twice about buying one yet—you can easily make expensive mistakes if you are uncertain about what you want a system to do. Some common decision categories are discussed next; Figure R-4 provides a list of questions that can help you define the type of computer that will meet your needs.

FIGURE R-4
Questions to consider when getting ready to buy a PC.

POSSIBLE QUESTIONS
What tasks will I be using the computer for (writing papers, accessing the Internet, graphic design, composing music, playing games, etc.)?
Do I prefer a Mac or a PC-compatible? Are there any other computers I need my documents and storage media to be compatible with?
How fast do I need the system to be?
Do I need portability? If so, do I need the features of a conventional PC (notebook or tablet) or can I use a handheld PC?
What size and type of screen do I need?
What removable storage media will I need to use in the PC (such as standard floppy disks, CDs, DVDs, flash memory cards, or a USB flash memory drive)?
Do I need to be able to connect the PC to the Internet? If so, what type of Internet access will I be using (such as conventional dial-up, ISDN, DSL, cable, satellite, or wireless)?
Do I need to be able to connect the PC to a network? If so, is it a wired or wireless network and what type of network interface card is needed to connect to that network?
What additional hardware do I need (scanner, printer, or digital camera, for example)?
When do I need the computer?
Do I want to pay extra for a better warranty (such as a longer time period or on-site service)?

Operating Systems and Application Software

Determining what functions you want the system to perform will help you decide which application software is needed. Most users start with an application suite containing a word processor, spreadsheet, and other programs. In addition, specialty programs, such as tax preparation, drawing, home publishing, reference software, games, and more may be needed or desired.

Not all software is available for all operating systems. Consequently, if a specific piece of software is needed, that choice may determine which operating system you need to use. In addition, your operating system decision may already be made for you if your documents need to be compatible with those of another computer (such as other office computers or between a home and an office PC). The most widely used PC operating systems are Windows, Mac OS, and Linux.

Platforms and Configuration Options

If your operating system has already been determined, that is a good start in deciding the overall platform you will be looking for—most users will choose between the IBM-compatible and Apple Macintosh platform. IBM and compatible PCs usually run either Windows or Linux; Apple computers almost always use Mac OS.

Configuration decisions initially involve determining the size of the machine desired. For nonportable systems, you have the choice between tower, desktop, or all-in-one configurations; in addition, the monitor size and type (CRT or flat-screen) needs to be determined. Portable, fully functioning PCs can be notebook or tablet PCs. For tablet PCs, you need to decide if you will require keyboard use on a regular basis; if so, a convertible tablet PC would be the best choice. If a powerful, fully functioning PC is not required, you may decide to go with a more portable option, such as a handheld PC.

You should also consider any other specifications that are important to you, such as the size of the hard drive, type of other storage device needed, amount of memory required, and so forth. As discussed in the next section, these decisions often require reconciling the features you want with the amount of money you are willing to spend.

Power vs. Budget Requirements

As part of the needs analysis, you should look closely at your need for a powerful system versus your budgetary constraints. Most users do not need a state-of-the-art system. Those who do should expect to pay more than the average user. A PC that was top of the line six months or a year ago is usually reasonably priced and more than adequate for most users' needs. Individuals who just want a PC for basic tasks, such as using the Internet and word processing, can likely get by with an inexpensive PC designed for home use.

When determining your requirements, be sure to identify the features and functions that are absolutely essential for your primary PC tasks (such as a large hard drive and lots of memory for multimedia applications, a fast video card for gaming, a fast Internet connection, and so forth). After you have the minimum configuration determined, you can add optional or desirable components, as your budget allows.

Listing Alternatives

After you consider your needs and the questions mentioned in Figure R-4, you should have a pretty good idea of the hardware and software you will need. You will also know what purchasing options are available to you, depending on your time frame (while some retail stores have systems that can be purchased and brought home the same day, special orders or some systems purchased over the Internet may take a few weeks to arrive). The next step is to get enough information from possible vendors to compare and contrast a few alternative systems that satisfy your stated needs. Most often, these vendors are local stores (such as computer stores, warehouse clubs, and electronic stores) and/or online stores (such as manufacturer Web sites and e-tailers). To compare prices and specifications for possible computer systems, find at least three systems that meet or exceed your needs by looking through newspaper advertisements, configuring systems online via manufacturer and e-tailer Web sites, or calling or visiting local stores. A comparison sheet listing your criteria and the systems you are considering, such as the one in Figure R-5, can help you summarize your options. Although it is sometimes very difficult to compare the prices of systems since they typically have somewhat different configurations, you can assign an approximate dollar value to each extra feature a system has (such as $100 for an included printer or $50 for a larger hard drive). Be sure to also include any sales tax and shipping charges when you compare the prices of each total system.

If your budget is limited, you will have to balance the system you need with extra features you may want. But do not skimp on memory or hard drive space because sufficient memory can help your programs to run faster and with fewer problems and hard drive space is consumed quickly. Often for just a few extra dollars, you can get additional memory, a faster CPU, or a larger hard drive—significantly cheaper than trying to upgrade any of those features later. A good rule of thumb is to try to buy a little more computer than you

COMPONENT	EXAMPLE OF DESIRED SPECIFICATIONS	SYSTEM #1 VENDOR:	SYSTEM #2 VENDOR:	SYSTEM #3 VENDOR:
Operating System	Windows XP			
Manufacturer	HP or Dell			
Style	Tower			
CPU	AMD 2.4 GHz or higher			
RAM	512 MB or higher			
Hard drive	200 GB or higher			
Removable storage	8-in-1 flash memory card reader			
Optical drive	DVD-RW			
Monitor	Flat-panel 17-inch			
Video card and video RAM	Prefer dedicated video RAM			
Keyboard	Prefer speaker control keys			
Mouse	Optical with scroll wheel			
Sound card/speakers	Want subwoofer			
Modem	Cable			
Network card	Wi-Fi (802.11g)			
Printer	Ink-jet if get deal on price with complete system			
Scanner	Don't need			
Included software	Microsoft Office or Works			
Warranty	3 years min. (1 year onsite if not a local store)			
Other features	2 front USB ports minimum			
Price				
Tax				
Shipping				
TOTAL COST				

FIGURE R-5
Comparing PC alternatives. A checklist such as this one can help to organize your desired criteria and evaluate possible systems.

think you need. On the other hand, do not buy a top-of-the-line system, unless you fall into the power user category and really need it. Generally, the second or third system down from the top of the line is a very good system for a much more reasonable price. Some guidelines for minimum requirements for desktop PCs for most home users are as follows:

- 3 GHz Pentium 4 (or equivalent) CPU (generally, any CPU currently being sold today is fast enough for most users).
- 512 MB or more of memory (RAM).
- 160 GB or more hard drive space.
- Recordable or rewritable CD or DVD drive.
- Conventional dial-up modem plus a special modem, if needed, for an alternative type of Internet access.
- Sound card and external speakers.
- At least 2 USB ports.

System Troubleshooting and Upgrading

After your new system has been purchased and is up and running (refer to the Chapter 1 How it Works box for a review of how to set up a new PC), chances are at some point you will need to do some troubleshooting and upgrading.

Troubleshooting

Troubleshooting refers to actions taken to diagnose or solve a problem. Unfortunately, many problems are unique to specific types of hardware and software, so no simple troubleshooting remedy works all of the time. Nonetheless, the following simple steps and guidelines can help you to identify and correct a number of common problems.

- Try again. A number of procedures work when you try a second time. You may have pressed the wrong keys the first time, not pressed the keys hard enough, or have a special function activated (such as the ones activated by pressing the Caps Lock, Num Lock, or Insert key on the keyboard). If you have accidentally activated such a function, pressing the key again should turn the function off and correct the problem.
- Check to see that all the equipment is plugged in and turned on and that no cables are detached or loose.
- Reboot the system. Many software problems are corrected after the computer is restarted and the program is opened again. Some operating systems—such as Windows—will also try to reconfigure devices identified as having a problem when the system is restarted, as well as give you the option of temporarily disabling certain devices if your system crashed, to help you determine the device that is causing the problem. If for some reason the system does not boot at all, use your system startup disc (most systems either come with one or suggest you make one using a system option).
- Update your operating system and scan for viruses and spyware. A known bug or a virus or spyware program installed on your PC might be causing the problem and so installing the needed patch or removing the offending virus or spyware program might correct the problem.
- Recall exactly what happened between the time the system was operating properly and the time you began to encounter problems. For example, perhaps you installed a new piece of hardware or software during your last session, and it is affecting the way your current application works. If you can think of a recent change, try to undo it and see if that corrects the problem. Windows users can also try to use the System Restore option to roll their PC's settings back to a prior configuration.
- Be observant. If you heard a strange noise the last time you used your PC, it might be important. Even though solving the problem may be beyond your capabilities, the information may help the person who will assist you in figuring out the problem.
- Check the *documentation* that came with the system. Many products come with a hard-copy manual that includes a troubleshooting checklist; software programs usually have an online help feature that can help you solve many problems.
- Use diagnostic software. *Diagnostic utility programs* (discussed in Chapter 5) can be used to test your system to see if parts of it are malfunctioning or if it is just not performing well, for some reason. Sometimes when new hardware or software is installed, it creates a conflict with other hardware or software. Also, hard drives can get fragmented with use over time and may need to be defragmented; temporary Internet files need to be periodically deleted.

You should weigh the time that it takes to solve a problem yourself against the cost of outside help. It is not a personal failure to give up if the problem is more than you can handle. It is simply an admission that your time is valuable and that you are wise enough

to know when to call in a professional for assistance. Options for technical assistance include:

- *Manufacturer*. Many manufacturers have toll-free phone numbers, fax numbers, e-mail addresses, and support information on their Web sites for users with technical assistance questions. If your system is still under warranty, you should contact the manufacturer before trying any other technical support options. Your PC manufacturer may also have recent software patches or updated drivers available via its Web site. These items are almost always available free of charge.
- *Third-party support*. If your system is out of warranty, you can get help from a third-party firm, such as a local computer repair company or a company that will provide assistance via the phone or Web. Typically you are charged by the minute or hour (with a minimum fee often assessed) for assistance acquired via a third party.
- *User support*. You can also get suggestions from other users via online discussion groups. To find an appropriate group, check the manufacturer's Web site to see if it has a link to a discussion group for the product in question, or locate an appropriate group from a third-party technical support Web site. The message you post might be read by literally hundreds of other users, and there is a good possibility that someone out there has encountered and solved the problem you are now wrestling with. While you may get the answer you are seeking without paying a dime, do not be surprised if you have to wait for a few days or more to have your plea for help read by the right person.

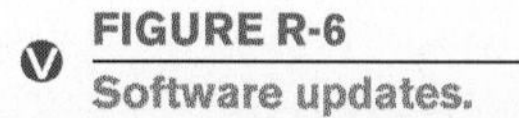

FIGURE R-6
Software updates.

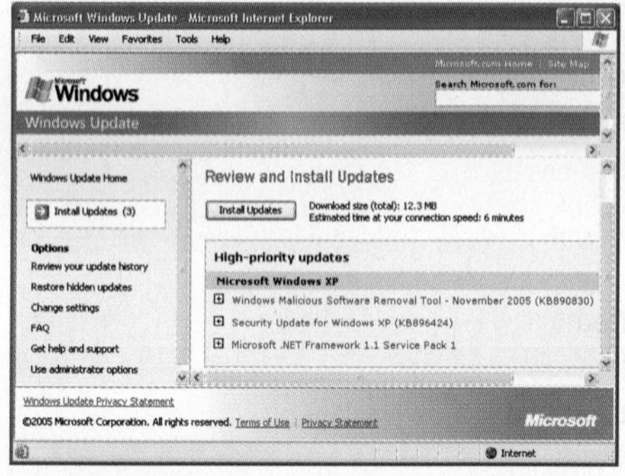

WINDOWS UPDATE
The Windows Update feature can be used to regularly locate and install patches and other updates for Windows and Internet Explorer.

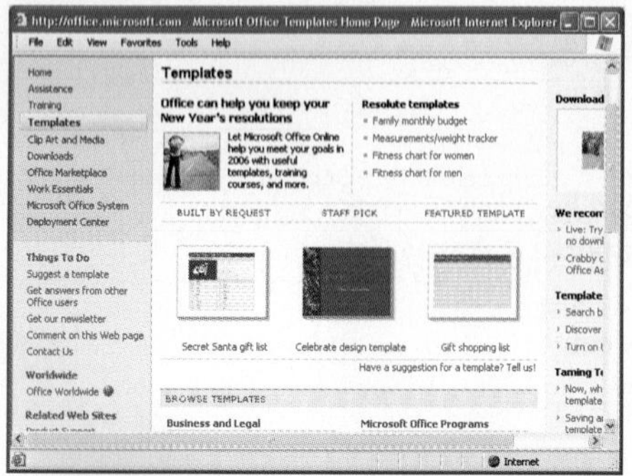

SOFTWARE WEB SITES
Support Web sites for specific software programs (such as the one for Microsoft Office shown here) can be used to locate free templates, clip art, and other resources to be used with that program.

Upgrading

Hardware and software generally need to be upgraded over time. *Upgrading* a computer system means buying new hardware or software components that extend the life of your current system. The question you must ask when considering an upgrade is the same one that you would ask when considering costly repairs to a car: Should I spend this money on my current system or start fresh and buy a completely new system? For example, it is usually not cost-effective to upgrade a computer that is more than three years old, since some new PCs today sell for $300 or less.

Upgrading Hardware

Some common hardware upgrades include adding more RAM or an additional storage device to a system, installing a different type of modem or additional memory, adding an expansion card to provide a new functionality, and adding new peripheral devices, such as a scanner or color printer.

Upgrading Software

Many PC software vendors enhance their products in some major way every year or two, prompting users to upgrade. Each upgrade—called a *version*—is assigned a number, such as 1.0, 2.0, 3.0, and so on. The higher the number, the more recent and more powerful the software is. Minor versions, called *releases*, typically increase their numbers in increments of 0.1—such as 1.1, 1.2, and 1.3—or .01. For example, release 3.11 might follow release 3.1, and release 7.1 might follow 7.0. Releases are usually issued in response to bugs or shortcomings in the version and are often free.

When a free update is available for a program that you use, or when a patch to fix a known problem becomes available, typically these are downloaded via the software publisher's Web site (see Figure R-6). Many software publishers also offer free templates, clip art, and other downloaded resources via their Web sites-one example is shown in Figure R-6. Full software upgrades are more often purchased in physical form and they generally cost less than buying the full version. Before upgrading to a new version, be sure to weigh the benefits against its costs. Unless the new version has a feature that you require, it may not be necessary to upgrade to that version.

E-MAIL FUNDAMENTALS

As discussed in Chapter 1, an e-mail program (such as Netscape Mail, Microsoft Outlook Express, Microsoft Outlook, or a proprietary mail program used by your ISP) is used to send conventional (non-Web-based) e-mail. You first need to set up the e-mail program with your name, e-mail address, incoming mail server, and outgoing mail server information and then you can begin to send and receive e-mail. This section of the References and Resources Guide includes the basic steps involved with sending, receiving, and managing e-mail. ■

Sending E-Mail

To send an e-mail message, first open your e-mail program and select the appropriate option to start a new message. Type one or more e-mail addresses in the To: box, enter an appropriate subject line, and then type the message in the appropriate area (see Figure R-7). Send the message using the Send toolbar button. To make it easier to send e-mails to people you contact frequently, you can add their names, nicknames, and their e-mail addresses to your e-mail program's *address book* (you can typically right-click on a sender's e-mail address to get an option to add that individual to your address book). When you begin to type a name or nickname in a To: box for which you have a related address book entry, the e-mail program will then fill in the appropriate e-mail address automatically.

Receiving E-Mail

In order to receive a new e-mail message, it must be retrieved from your ISP. To retrieve new e-mail messages waiting for you at your ISP's mail server, open your e-mail program. If your e-mail program does not then check for new messages, click the appropriate toolbar button, such as Get Msg or Send/Recv (refer to the bottom screens in Figure R-7). For convenience, you can typically select an option to have your e-mail program check for new messages on a regular basis; if you have a direct Internet connection, you can leave your e-mail program open at all times to have all new e-mail messages retrieved automatically. To read a specific e-mail message, click it; double-clicking an e-mail message typically opens the message in a new window for easier reading.

All new e-mail messages are usually placed in your *Inbox* folder. Once an e-mail message is displayed, it can be printed, replied to, forwarded to someone else, filed into a different folder, or deleted using your e-mail program's toolbar buttons.

Managing E-Mail

When you send e-mail, copies of the messages that you send are typically stored in a folder named Sent, Sent Items, Sent Messages, or something similar so that you can read them or resend them, if necessary. These messages remain there, and your retrieved e-mail messages remain in your Inbox folder, until you delete them or move them into a different folder (you can create new folders in most e-mail programs, as needed). Once an e-mail message is deleted, it is usually moved into a special folder for deleted items (called Trash, Deleted Items, Trash Can, or something similar). Messages in a deleted items folder typically remain there until you permanently delete them by selecting the appropriate option (such as *Empty Trash* from Netscape Mail's File menu or *Empty 'Deleted Items' Folder* from Outlook Express' Edit menu). Deleting unneeded messages frees up space on your hard drive.

FIGURE R-7
Sending and receiving e-mail.

SENDING E-MAIL
This example uses Netscape Mail.

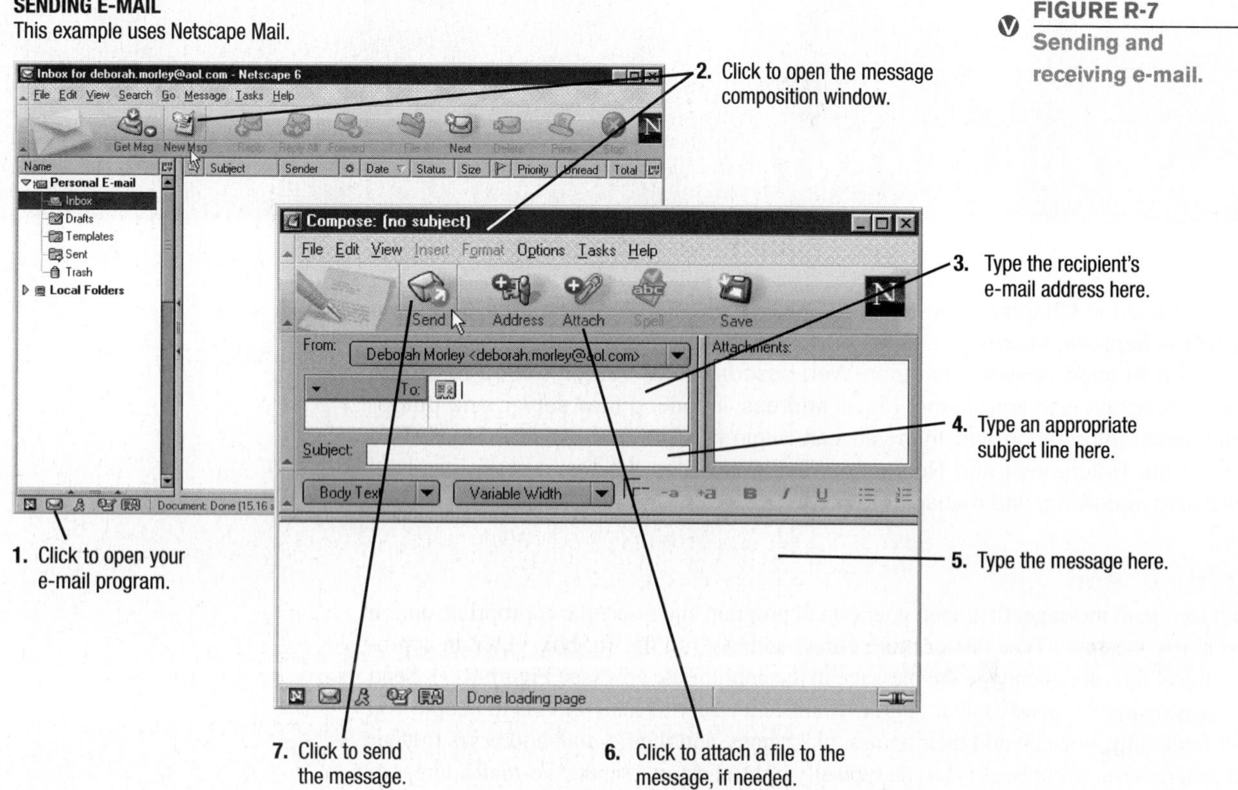

1. Click to open your e-mail program.
2. Click to open the message composition window.
3. Type the recipient's e-mail address here.
4. Type an appropriate subject line here.
5. Type the message here.
6. Click to attach a file to the message, if needed.
7. Click to send the message.

RECEIVING E-MAIL
This example uses Outlook Express.

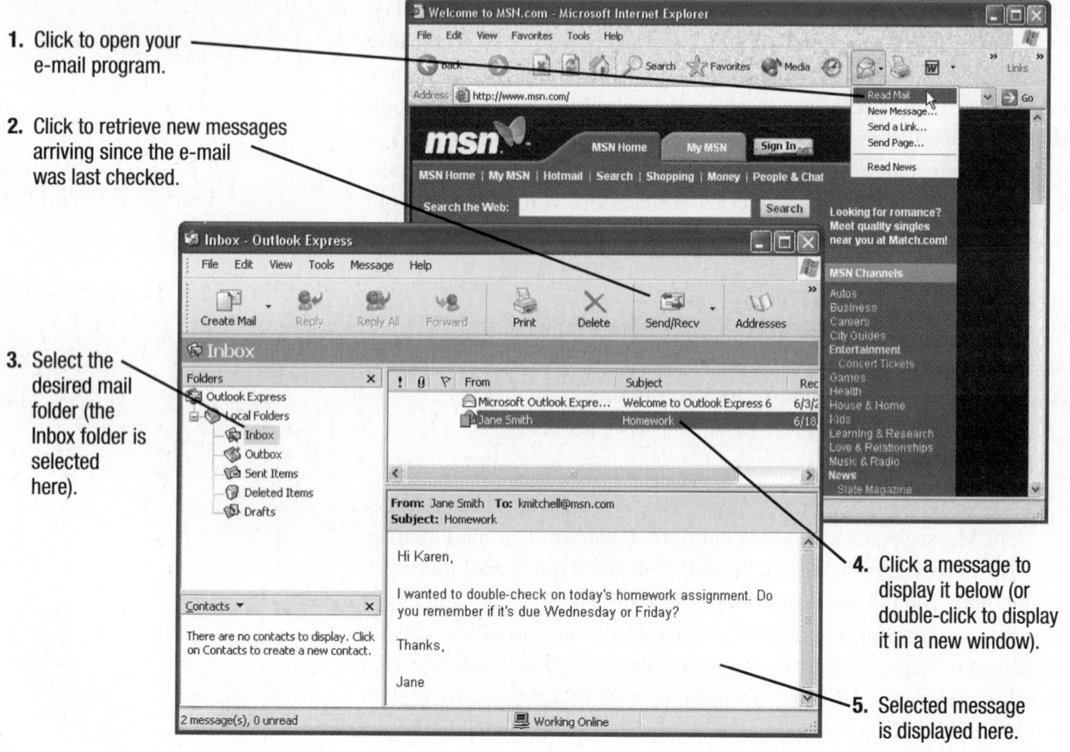

1. Click to open your e-mail program.
2. Click to retrieve new messages arriving since the e-mail was last checked.
3. Select the desired mail folder (the Inbox folder is selected here).
4. Click a message to display it below (or double-click to display it in a new window).
5. Selected message is displayed here.

ANSWERS TO SELF-QUIZ

Chapter 1

1. T **2.** F **3.** F **4.** F **5.** T **6.** Input **7.** tablet **8.** hyperlinks **9.** electronic mail or e-mail **10. a.** 4 **b.** 2 **c.** 1 **d.** 3

Chapter 2

1. T **2.** F **3.** T **4.** T **5.** F **6.** 13 **7.** random access memory or RAM **8.** port **9.** pipelining **10. a.** 6 **b.** 2 **c.** 4 **d.** 9 **e.** 7 **f.** 1 **g.** 8 **h.** 5 **i.** 3

Chapter 3

1. F **2.** T **3.** F **4.** F **5.** T **6.** volatile **7.** 4.7 GB **8.** smart card **9.** flash memory **10. a.** 2 **b.** 3 **c.** 1

Chapter 4

1. F **2.** F **3.** T **4.** T **5.** F **6.** handwriting recognition **7.** scanner, optical scanner, flatbed scanner, or handheld scanner **8.** pixel **9.** flat-panel or LCD; cathode-ray tube or CRT **10. a.** 4 **b.** 3 **c.** 6 **d.** 2 **e.** 5 **f.** 1

Chapter 5

1. T **2.** F **3.** F **4.** F **5.** T **6.** operating system; utility **7.** Linux **8.** file compression **9.** back up **10. a.** 3 **b.** 6 **c.** 1 **d.** 2 **e.** 5 **f.** 4

Chapter 6

1. T **2.** T **3.** F **4.** F **5.** T **6.** open source **7.** insertion point **8.** function **9.** table **10. a.** 4 **b.** 3 **c.** 5 **d.** 2 **e.** 1

Chapter 7

1. F **2.** T **3.** F **4.** T **5.** F **6.** telecommuting **7.** bus **8.** satellite **9.** virtual private network or VPN **10. a.** 5 **b.** 4 **c.** 2 **d.** 1 **e.** 6 **f.** 3

Chapter 8

1. F **2.** F **3.** T **4.** T **5.** F **6.** Digital Subscriber Line or DSL **7.** keyword; directory **8.** instant messaging or IM **9.** online auction **10. a.** 2 **b.** 5 **c.** 3 **d.** 1 **e.** 6 **f.** 4

Chapter 9

1. F **2.** T **3.** F **4.** T **5.** F **6.** war driving **7.** biometric **8.** firewall **9.** public key or asymmetric key **10. a.** 4 **b.** 3 **c.** 6 **d.** 1 **e.** 5 **f.** 2

GLOSSARY/INDEX

E

F

J

K

L

Q

R

T

W

X

Y

Z